PSYCHOLOGY
AN INTRODUCTION

PSYCHOLOGY
AN INTRODUCTION

JEROME KAGAN

Harvard University

ERNEST HAVEMANN

Harcourt, Brace & World, Inc.
New York   Chicago   San Francisco   Atlanta

Acknowledgments and copyrights for illustrations begin on page 643.

© 1968 by Harcourt, Brace & World, Inc.

ISBN: 0-15-572601-3

Library of Congress Catalog Card Number: 68-11245

PRINTED IN THE UNITED STATES OF AMERICA

PREFACE

Psychology: An Introduction represents an attempt to provide a new kind of textbook to meet the vastly changed conditions that many of today's instructors and students face in the introductory course. We planned it from the beginning as a brief text: sixteen chapters of reasonable length. At the same time, we aimed for thorough coverage of all the topics that have been traditionally considered essential to a broad basic understanding of psychology.

The book is especially intended for courses that must be completed within a single quarter or semester, or where more time is available but the instructor wishes to assign extensive outside readings or to concentrate intensively on some particular aspects of psychology. The book takes full account of the fact that many students in the introductory course will have no further exposure to psychology and are interested chiefly in the application of its principles to their life situations, while others will go on to further study and must have a sound scientific foundation for their advanced courses. Our aims have been 1) to write an introductory textbook that, though brief, still offers a complete and contemporary summary of the facts and principles essential to an understanding of psychology, and 2) to present materials of interest to all types of students and to do so clearly and simply, without becoming simplistic or compromising any of the fundamental issues of the behavioral sciences.

The textbook represents a collaboration between an academic psychologist and a professional writer. The academic psychologist provided the same kind of substantive coverage that he would offer students in his own introductory course. The professional writer endeavored to present this scope of coverage in the sixteen-chapter limit through rigorous economy in organization and exposition. Perhaps we can best describe our roles by stating that one of us has been primarily concerned with comprehensiveness of content, the other with comprehensibility of style.

There is an early and heavy emphasis in the book on learning; Chapters 2, 3, and 4 are devoted to this topic. This emphasis reflects the belief that the acquisition of habits and changes in behavior and cognitive processes are perhaps the core problems in psychology today. It also provides a useful framework for the topics that follow. Students seem to grasp the essential content of the introductory course much better when the principles of learning are presented as a unifying theme to help explain and therefore link such otherwise disparate topics as perception, problem solving, emotions, motives, frustration and conflict, development, and social behavior.

We have included full coverage of the biological correlates of behavior, discussed in Chapter 7 (The Genes, Glands, and Nervous System) and Chapter 8 (The Senses). Instructors who prefer to omit these topics will find that their students can skip the two chapters without jeopardizing their progress in the rest of the book. In the discussion of statistics (Chapter 13, Measurement), instructors have an additional option. The first half of Chapter 13, which explains the important implications that descriptive and inferential statistics hold for the behavioral sciences, does so in general terms and without reference to the mathematics. The arithmetical computations have been reserved for the second half of the chapter and may be included or omitted as the instructor sees fit.

One problem that we faced in our attempt to produce a brief book was the profusion of journal articles and experimental reports now available, but we have resisted the temptation to become encyclopedic. Under each topic we have endeavored to present the contemporary empirical work that most clearly explains the principles and theories to the beginning student, without redundancy or confusion of detail. Where an older experiment offers the most concise explanation, however, we have not hesitated to use it. Our aim throughout has been to keep in mind the needs of the student while preserving the integrity of the science.

JEROME KAGAN
ERNEST HAVEMANN

ACKNOWLEDGMENTS

The authors are greatly indebted to the following psychologists, who read portions of the manuscript during its preparation and made many valuable comments and suggestions: Irving Alexander, Duke University; Robert C. Carson, Duke University; Lane K. Conn, Jr., Harvard University; Stephen Cool, University of Texas, School of Biomedical Sciences; William N. Dember, University of Cincinnati; Charles G. Gross, Harvard University; Norman Guttman, Duke University; Gerald L. Hershey, Fullerton Junior College; Stewart H. Hulse, The Johns Hopkins University; Janellen Huttenlocher, Teachers College, Columbia University; Robert B. McCall, University of North Carolina; Stanley Milgram, City University of New York; Edward J. Murray, University of Miami; Gregory K. Sims, The College of San Mateo; Karl E. Weick, University of Minnesota.

The authors also wish to express thanks to Ruth Havemann, Joan Hays, Gayle Henkin, Caroline Mechem, Henriette Salek, Doris Simpson, and Richard Stein for their help in the preparation of the book.

CONTENTS

PART **3**
INTERPRETIVE BEHAVIOR

PART 4
THE PHYSICAL BASIS OF BEHAVIOR

PART 5
THE MOTIVES AND FEELINGS THAT UNDERLIE BEHAVIOR

PART 6
PERSONALITY

PART **7**
INDIVIDUAL DIFFERENCES

PART **8**
THE CHILD, THE ADULT,
AND SOCIETY

PSYCHOLOGY
AN INTRODUCTION

PART 1

WHAT IS PSYCHOLOGY?

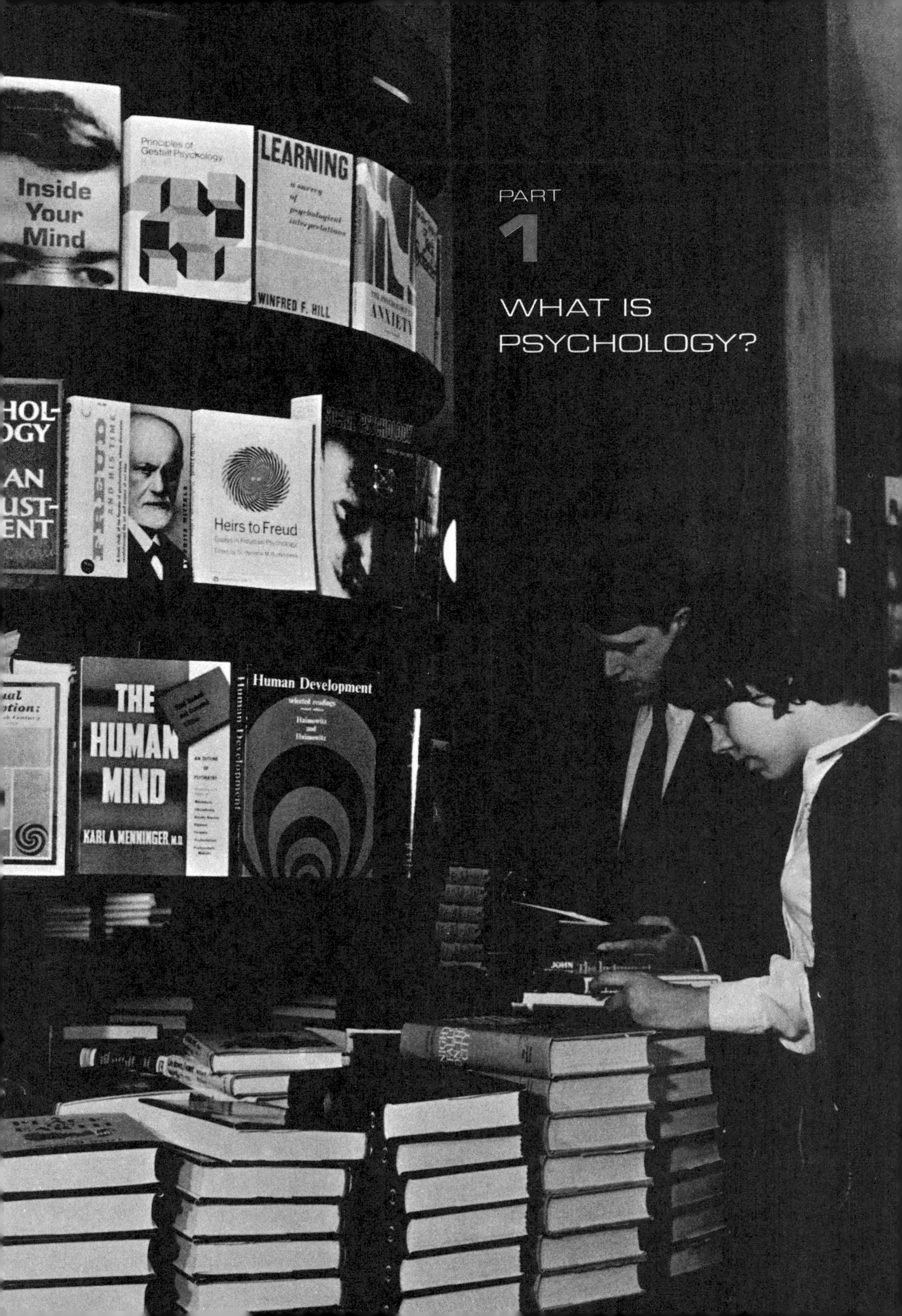

Psychology is a relatively new science that deals with age-old questions. Its subject matter is something that has interested and puzzled mankind since the beginning of history—namely, the way human beings and other living creatures behave and the reasons for their behavior.

Because the subject matter is so old and the methods so new, psychology is still widely misunderstood. An introductory textbook must begin, therefore, with a discussion of what the science is and what it is not.

Chapter 1, "The Scope and Goals of Psychology," suggests the wide range of activities covered by the term *behavior* and the methods used by psychology in its attempt to understand why the living organism behaves as it does. The chapter includes a brief section on the history of the science and its founders. It also describes how the findings of psychology have been applied to the practical problems of everyday life and have helped people get along better in school, jobs, and human relations.

A DEFINITION OF PSYCHOLOGY

Psychology and Behavior
The Variety of Human Behavior
Drives, Motor Skills, and Problem Solving
Motivated Behavior
Emotional Behavior
Anxiety and Defenses
The Goals of Psychology
Predicting, Understanding, and Theory

THE HISTORY OF PSYCHOLOGY

Wilhelm Wundt and His Laboratory
Francis Galton and Measurement
William James's "Science of Mental Life"
John Watson, Behaviorist
Modern Psychology

HOW PSYCHOLOGY STUDIES BEHAVIOR

The Experiment
Naturalistic Observation
Tests
Interviews
Questionnaires

APPLICATIONS OF PSYCHOLOGY

Psychology in the School
Vocational Guidance
Psychology in Industry
Public Opinion Surveys
Clinical Psychology

CHAPTER

1

THE SCOPE
AND GOALS
OF PSYCHOLOGY

Although the science of psychology is only about a hundred years old, the word *psychology* has become one of the most popular in the English language. People often say they "use psychology" to get a job or a raise or to talk parents into a larger allowance. They talk about striking at the "psychological moment." When a friend starts behaving strangely, they say he has a "psychological problem." To judge by the number of times the word is used in everyday conversation, one might suppose that everybody who speaks English knows exactly what it means.

Yet, in actual fact, psychology is extremely difficult to define. Moreover, the science of psychology is quite different from what most people believe it to be, and often its findings are contrary to what people have generally taken for granted about human nature. Many businessmen, for example, pride themselves on being "good psychologists" who can size up another man just by looking at him, can judge the other man's feelings by studying his facial expressions, and can certainly decide whether to hire him on the basis of a personal interview. Scientific investigation has proved that this is not easy at all. If you and your friends try to match the faces to the professions of the people in FIGURE 1.1, you will probably find that none of you have much success. You will probably have the same trouble guessing the emotions that are being expressed in FIGURE 1.2.

By the time a student arrives at college he has usually been tested and retested in numerous ways—for intelligence, mechanical skill, mathematical ability, and various kinds of vocational aptitude. He has also seen many other tests in newspapers and magazines; he has been invited to score himself as an introvert or an extrovert, an optimist or a pessimist, a good marriage prospect or a bad one. Thus many students think of psychology as being first of all the source for tests of all kinds of human traits and abilities. This is partly true, for tests have been devised that are good predictors of school grades, musical performance, and ability to work efficiently as an accountant or an electronics engineer or a hospital nurse. But testing is only one small part of psychology. And many of the tests seen in news-

A

B

C

D

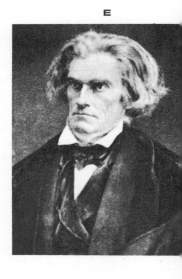

E

FIGURE 1.1

Can You Judge a Person by Appearance?
All these people figured prominently in
the news some years ago. They were a
famous inventor, novelist, murderer,
United States vice president, British
prime minister, composer, labor leader,
and millionaire. After trying to match
the photos with these terms, turn to
page 8 for the correct answers.

F

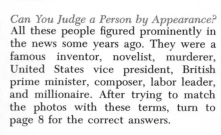

G

H

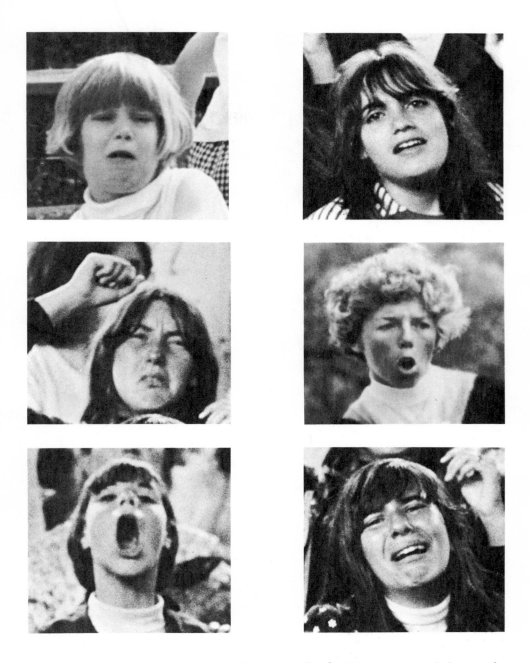

What Emotions Do These Faces Show?   These are unposed photographs of people expressing emotions. Of all the human emotions—such as joy, rage, fear, anger, grief, contentment—which are they? After you have made your guesses, check them against FIGURE 1.2a on page 8.

FIGURE 1.2

The Answer to the Emotional Faces
The woman is a golfer urging a putt to fall. The little girl is a somewhat dubious softball player. The four teenagers are responding—each in her own way—to a performance by the Beatles.

FIGURE 1.2a

papers and magazines have no scientific value at all; they are merely parlor games. A psychologist would want to know a lot more than can be revealed by a few true-false questions before he would attempt to assess your personality or try to predict how you might succeed at such a complicated human relationship as marriage.

The people shown in FIGURE 1.1 are: **A**, British Prime Minister Lloyd George; **B**, novelist Willa Cather; **C**, millionaire John D. Rockefeller; **D**, labor leader John L. Lewis; **E**, Vice President John C. Calhoun; **F**, inventor Henry Ford; **G**, composer Claude Debussy; and **H**, convicted murderer Ruth Snyder.

8

Some students are so surprised by the content of an
introductory psychology textbook that they have a
difficult time getting the "feel" of the subject; they keep looking for what
they had expected to find and fail to appreciate what is actually there. If
you approach the subject with an open mind and are prepared to enjoy
being surprised, you will have a much easier and more rewarding time.

As the poet Alexander Pope wrote, "The proper study of mankind is
man"—and one way to start trying to define psychology would be as the
science that studies man. But this is only a partial definition. To seek a
better one, let us start with some of the actual subject matter—some of the
experiments and observations that have accumulated over the years. Out of
all the thousands of such items that can be found in libraries, the following
have been chosen partly at random, partly in an attempt to suggest the wide
scope of the science. Note that many of them involve animals. Because many
experiments can be performed with animals that would be impossible or
unethical with human beings, psychology is concerned with "animal nature"
as well as human nature.

1. A child will usually learn faster if he is rewarded for his successes
rather than punished for his failures and if he is rewarded every other time
he succeeds rather than every time. A student trying to memorize a poem
or a speech is likely to do better in six study periods of three minutes each
than in one study period of eighteen minutes. These are some of the experimental findings on the subject of learning, which is treated in Chapters
2, 3, and 4.

2. Our senses often play tricks on us, as is demonstrated in FIGURE 1.3.
The photograph seems to show three men of very different size. Actually,
they are about the same size, but the man at left is twice as far from the
camera as the man at right—a fact concealed by trick construction of the
room. This is a deliberately produced optical illusion, but, as will be seen in
Chapter 5, even our everyday perception of the world around us depends
on many factors besides the simple evidence provided by our senses.

3. In the course of brain operations performed under local anesthetic it
has been found that a mild electrical current applied to one part of the
brain may cause the patient to see colors and patterns. When the current is
applied elsewhere on the brain, the patient may hear sounds. Sometimes the
current brings back vivid and detailed memories of something the patient
thought he had long since forgotten; he seems to be actually listening to a
piece of music heard long ago or to a telephone conversation that he once
took part in, almost as if a tape recording of it were being played (1).°

° The numbers in parentheses, which will be found throughout the book, are keyed to references
and source materials (concerning both text and illustrations) that are listed at the end of
the volume.

FIGURE 1.3

Fooling the Human Eye The man at the left seems to be unusually small, the man in the center of average size, the man at right a giant. Actually the three men are about the same in size, but they are standing in a room built to create an optical illusion. The distance from floor to ceiling is much higher at the left than at the right, and the man at the left is standing about twice as far from the camera as the man at the right.

FIGURE 1.4

"Fighting" a Bull by Radio

A wild bull charges Dr. José M. R. Delgado of the Yale University School of Medicine, who is armed only with a cape and a radio transmitter.

Dr. Delgado presses a button on the transmitter and the bull stops short, raising clouds of dust. The radio transmitter sends a mild current to electrodes that have been carefully planted in particular spots in the bull's brain.

One of the most dramatic demonstrations of what electrical stimulation of the brain can do is shown in FIGURE 1.4. What these observations and experiments mean will be discussed in detail in Chapter 7.

4. In one experiment, volunteer subjects were kept in bed as shown in FIGURE 1.5. In a similar experiment, they were fitted with a sort of diver's helmet and suspended in water held at skin temperature (3). The subjects saw nothing but a dim light or no light at all and heard nothing more than a steady low hum; they smelled and tasted nothing, and their sense of touch was masked as much as possible. In other words, all activity of their senses—the subject of Chapter 8 of this book—was held to almost zero. Rather quickly, it was discovered, many of them found themselves unable to think logically. Their memories became disorganized. Sometimes they felt strangely happy, and at other times they felt anxious or even panicky. Some of them began to develop symptoms that are often associated with severe mental disturbance; for example, they "saw" imaginary sights and "heard" imaginary sounds.

5. In the experiment shown in FIGURE 1.6, it was the "executive" monkey, the one in control of the key shutting off the shock, that got the ulcer. The other monkey, which had no control at all over the shock, did not get an

FIGURE 1.5

An Experiment in Blocking off the Senses This man is taking part in an experiment designed to show what happens when activity of the human senses is reduced as nearly as possible to zero. The eyeshade permits him to see nothing but a dim haze. The arm casts mask the sense of touch in his hands. The room is sound-proofed, and he hears nothing but the constant soft hum of a fan. For what happens to him under these conditions, see the text. (The wires shown at the top of the photo were used to record brain waves.) (2)

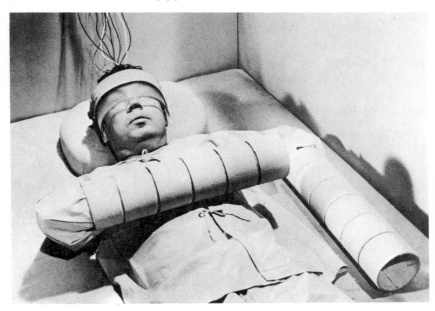

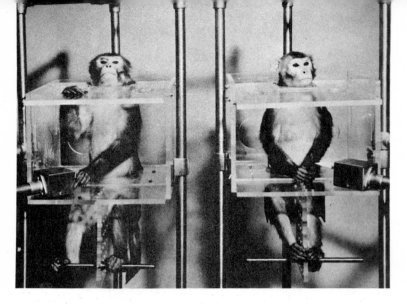

FIGURE 1.6

Which Monkey Gets the Ulcer? The two monkeys sit in identical cages. Every twenty seconds both see a red warning light. Immediately thereafter, both receive an electrical shock on the feet—unless the monkey at left presses the lever on the box in his cage. To avoid the shock altogether, the monkey at left must press the lever every twenty seconds. The monkey at right soon learns that the key on his box has no effect and afterward ignores it. The first time the experiment was tried, at the Walter Reed Army Institute of Research, the monkeys were kept in the cages for six hours, then given a six-hour rest. After about three weeks of this, one of the monkeys died, apparently of a stomach ulcer. To find out which monkey it was, see the text.

ulcer (4). The reason will be clarified when stress is discussed in Chapter 7 and anxiety in Chapter 10.

6. Children from small families generally score better on intelligence tests than do children from large families but for a reason you may not suspect until you have come to the discussion of testing of intelligence and personality in Chapter 14.

7. A girl of only moderate intelligence, not particularly attractive physically and not very good at expressing herself, may strike other people as exuding such an air of quiet ability and self-confidence that they consider her a born leader and seek her advice—while another girl of greater intelligence and better appearance may seem so unsure and apologetic that people ignore her. These reactions by other people may lead the first girl to consider herself far superior to the second girl, and the second girl to consider herself far inferior to the first. This is one of the complex ways in which a person's attitude about himself is influenced by other human beings, as will be discussed in Chapter 16.

Psychology and Behavior

Why do all these seemingly unrelated matters deserve our attention? The answer is that all of them have one important thing in common. In every case, a living organism is behaving; it is doing something; it is acting or reacting. And the best possible definition of psychology is: *Psychology is the science that systematically studies and attempts to explain observable behavior and its relationship to the unseen mental processes that go on inside the organism and to external events in the environment.*

The Variety of Human Behavior

To show what a wide range of subject matter this definition covers, let us examine how a college woman might have started this day, from the time she woke up until the time she arrived at her first class.

She wakens quickly at the sound of the alarm, turns off the clock, and turns on the light in her bedroom. Looking out a window for signs of the weather, she notes that the sky is cloudy. For further information she turns on the radio. But she has just missed the weather report; so she calls her mother. As it happens, her mother has not heard a report either; she therefore dials the telephone number of a friend who is always up early. The friend says there is only a 25 percent chance of rain, and she decides to ignore it.

She puts on a shower cap and turns the water to a comfortable temperature. Dressing after her shower, she gets a run in one stocking; so she rummages through a dresser drawer until she finds another pair of the right color. In another drawer she finds a scarf to match her blouse and sweater.

By the time she has finished breakfast she finds that rain is falling; so she quickly changes into a dress that water will not damage and goes to the closet for an umbrella. As she starts her automobile she sees that the gasoline is low and makes a note to stop at a filling station. Backing out of the driveway, she waits for two school children who are walking by, then for a mail truck. She stops for a traffic light, turns into the street she usually takes to school, finds it blocked off for repairs, and proceeds to an alternate route. The lot in which she usually parks is filled; so she goes to a different one. Since she does not know the quickest route to her classroom from this lot, she asks a girl who is also getting out of a car. The directions are complicated —turn left after a block, then right, then cut across a corner of the campus— but she has no trouble following them and is in her usual seat when the class starts.

And so the day begins. It is still very early in the morning of a more or less typical day in the life of a more or less typical student. Yet what a remarkable amount of activity has already occurred!

In this age of electronic computers it has become fashionable to admire the speed and precision of the computer and, conversely, to take a somewhat disparaging view of human capabilities. The computer can add and multiply faster than any human being; it can guide spaceships to the moon and to Mars. Why then should we not concede that the human being is a poor rival to the computer and rapidly becoming obsolete? Why should we bother studying the psychology of a human machine that is so overshadowed by the electronic machine?

The young woman, waking and going to school, gives us the answer. She demonstrates that the electronic machine, for all its brilliant accomplishments, does not as yet hold a candle to the skill and versatility of the human machine.

Note all the very complicated "inputs" that our human machine has received in the course of the early morning: the sounds of the alarm clock, the radio, the telephone, and the verbal instructions on how to walk to the classroom; the sight of the sky, the traffic and traffic signals, and the blocked roadway. Note all the "data processing" she has done: making the decisions on what to wear, to change clothes, to take an alternate route to the campus, to park in an alternate lot. And note how many complicated actions she took: bathing, dressing, eating, driving a car, asking directions, walking to the classroom. The human organism is still the most remarkable "machine" ever created. The more one studies it, the more one is forced to marvel at its intricate workings.

Drives, Motor Skills, and Problem Solving

The young woman's behavior on this early morning falls into several categories that will be taken up in detail later in the book. Her sleeping is a response to an inborn *biological drive* that demands satisfaction. All of us have to satisfy this drive; we cannot help it. We sleep because our bodies and brains are built in such a way that we have to sleep. (There is a "sleep system," deep in the lower part of the brain, that controls the drive from birth; the newborn baby wakes up when hungry or in pain, then goes back to sleep.) But our adult sleeping habits are also partly the result of that important psychological process called *learning*, and they are geared to the fact that the day has twenty-four hours. Most of us learn to sleep for eight hours and stay awake for sixteen hours, although it would be possible to learn to sleep for nine hours and stay awake eighteen.

The reason the young woman ate breakfast and drank milk and coffee as part of it was to satisfy two other biological drives, hunger and thirst. Her movements while showering, dressing, and driving her automobile were *motor skills*, originally learned with some difficulty but now performed with a minimum of conscious effort. The first unusual aspect of the automobile trip—the blocked roadway—immediately made the young woman fully conscious of what she was doing. Her decision to take an alternate road was an example of *problem solving* (the subject of Chapter 6); it may seem like routine behavior, but actually it required some complicated associations between what she saw and her past learning. In everyday language, we would merely say the young woman "remembered" that there was another road to the campus and "just naturally" took it. But human memory is itself a remarkable and baffling phenomenon. We know that the computer stores its "memories" of facts and figures on strips of magnetic tape or on magnetic discs. We do not know where the human brain stores its memories or how it manages to pull out the appropriate one—in this case, the fact that there was an alternate road.

If we follow the young woman into the classroom, we see no behavior except her movements as she writes notes of her professor's lecture. But another kind of behavior is going on inside her. She listens to the professor's words, relates them to her past experience and past learning, selects what she believes to be the most important ideas, and uses words of her own to record the gist of these ideas in her notebook. *Thinking,* though impossible to see and difficult to study, is another form of human activity that psychology explores.

Motivated Behavior

Even if the things mentioned up to now were the only forms of human behavior, we would have a rich field of study. But there is a good deal more still to come, as can be seen if we compare the young woman with one of the young men in her class.

Let us say that this young man exhibited much the same kind of behavior on this early morning. He, too, woke to an alarm clock, dressed according to the weather, ate breakfast, drove to a parking lot, and walked to the class. He sits there now taking notes just as the young woman is doing. He is the same age. He comes from much the same kind of family and went to the very same high school. On their College Boards they made about the same scores (see FIGURE 1.7).

There the resemblance ends. She is content to get C's in her courses. He studies hard and usually makes A's. Her special ambition is to become a wife and a mother. His ambition is to be rich and famous. She likes to spend her spare time reading or in the quiet company of a few close friends. He spends his spare time in extracurricular activities and hopes to become the president of several campus organizations; he has many acquaintances but few close friends. She likes to seek advice. He shuns advice. If she is criticized, she tends to become flustered and to apologize. If he is criticized, he strikes back. She seldom says an unkind word about anyone. He is frequently sarcastic and insulting.

These two young people have the same biological drives. They have many of the same motor skills. They have an approximately equal capacity for problem solving and thinking. What, then, makes them so different?

Two Students—Alike Yet Different In age, background, and College Board scores, these two students are very much alike; in their present behavior in college, they are very different. Why? For a possible answer, see the text.

FIGURE 1.7

Miss A.	BACKGROUND	Mr. B.
18	AGE	18
Excellent	HEALTH	Excellent
None	PHYSICAL DEFECTS	None
Physician	FATHER	Physician
Ex-teacher	MOTHER	Ex-teacher
San Pedro H.S.	HIGH SCHOOL	San Pedro H.S.
	COLLEGE BOARD SCORES	
521	VERBAL	519
542	MATH	545
	RECORD IN COLLEGE	
C's	GRADES	A's
None	EXTRACURRICULAR ACTIVITIES	Many
Few, but close	FRIENDS	Many
Yes	SEEKS ADVICE?	No
Apologetic	USUAL RESPONSE TO CRITICISM	Angry

One reason human behavior varies so much is that it springs from a variety of *motives*. We are born with certain kinds of physical capacities and a certain kind of nervous system, which in themselves demand a certain kind of fulfillment. Just as a mole is born to burrow in the ground and a bird is born to fly, a human being is born to exercise his body and his own unique ability for thinking and problem solving. In addition, we learn from our childhood experiences, our parents, and our friends to seek certain specific goals in life. Our desires to attain all these objectives are called our motives.

Those of us who have grown up in the United States have many motives in common. Almost all of us want to show that we are competent to fill some kind of role in society, whether as housewife, businessman, sportsman, or scholar. We all seek acceptance, love, and some kind of social status, and to a greater or lesser extent we seek power and money. But, in each of us, these motives come in a different sort of mixture. The young woman, for example, is most strongly motivated to obtain love and acceptance. The young man is most strongly motivated to prove his competence and to obtain power and money.

Our motives also have different sources. The young woman may want love and acceptance because she admires and hopes to imitate her mother, a woman of kindly and winning manners. The young man may want power and money because he loves and hopes to imitate an aggressive and successful father. Or he may want them because he feels hostile toward an unsuccessful father and hopes to prove that he is the better man of the two. Chapter 9 will discuss the subject of motives in detail.

Emotional Behavior

Let us make another comparison between the two students. In the class this morning the professor hands back some papers he has graded. Both the young woman and the young man made C-plus. The young woman is pleased. The young man is angry, although he is not sure whether he is angry at the professor or at himself. If we could give him a physical examination at this moment, we would find that his pulse rate has jumped; his blood pressure is higher; his breathing is faster; his muscles are tense. The young woman very seldom gets angry, but the young man gets angry often. In fact he has a stomach ulcer, just like the executive monkey in FIGURE 1.6, and his doctor tells him that the ulcer is caused by the fact that he gets too tense and emotional about his ambitions and his failures.

All of us know from experience what an *emotion* is; we know what it means to be pleased, angry, or afraid. One way in which all of us differ is in what it takes to arouse these emotions in us, how strong the emotions are, and how well we control them. Emotions are the subject of Chapter 10.

Anxiety and Defenses

Every human being does a good deal of what is commonly called worrying. We worry about all kinds of things—getting hurt, getting sick, failing an examination, running out of money, antagonizing our friends, losing the regard of someone we love.

A more scientific word for worry is *anxiety,* which can best be defined as a vague unpleasant feeling—a premonition that something bad may be about to happen. In complicated ways that will be discussed in Chapter 11, all of us acquire many forms of anxiety as we grow up. Perhaps the first time we feel anxiety is when we are babies and discover what a painful experience it is to have our mothers walk out of the room and leave us alone. Later, we acquire anxieties over the physical harm that might result from an automobile or airplane accident, over possible rejection by our parents or friends, over the fact that we may fail in a situation where we want very badly to succeed, and over many other matters.

All of us differ in sources and intensities of anxiety. The reason our woman student is flustered by criticism may be anxiety over showing anger or hostility, which would violate the image she has of herself as a kindly and well-mannered person like her mother. The young man, on the other hand, may suffer anxiety when criticized because he is afraid that he will not fight back as hard as he feels an aggressive and successful person should.

Anxiety is a highly unpleasant state, and to relieve it we all develop what are called *defenses*. One defense used by the young man is to throw himself into hard work, both studying and extracurricular activities, and to accumulate tokens of success such as good grades and official positions in campus organizations. Defenses take many different forms and vary greatly from person to person, thus helping to account for the wide variations in human behavior. In some cases the defenses that a person adopts fail to work and he suffers mental or emotional disturbances, discussed in Chapter 11 under *abnormal psychology*.

The Goals of Psychology

The scope of psychology is wide; the subject matter of the science covers all the *overt* or observable behavior that organisms exhibit and also the *covert* or hidden processes that go on inside the organism and often affect overt behavior. *The goals of psychology*, it can be added, *are to understand and to predict behavior.*

This urge to understand and to predict is common to all sciences. The chemist wants to understand the chemical properties of hydrogen and oxygen and to predict what will happen when they come together. The astronomer wants to understand the movements of the planets and stars and to predict celestial events such as eclipses. The physicist wants to understand the nature of matter and energy and to predict what will happen when matter is converted into energy, as in an atomic explosion.

Will we ever be able to predict exactly how each organism will behave in any given situation? Probably not. Exact prediction seems to be impossible even for inanimate objects. Tear a little scrap of paper, hold it high in the air, and let it drop to the floor. A physicist who watched you do this might thoroughly understand the law of gravity and all there is to know about air flow, yet he would not be able to predict *the exact spot* on the floor where the scrap of paper will land.

We may never be able to understand behavior completely or to predict it exactly—particularly not on the individual basis that would be of greatest interest to most of us. Our aim is to advance as close to the goal as possible.

Predicting, Understanding, and Theory

The difference between predicting and understanding is somewhat difficult to grasp and deserves further explanation.

It is often possible to predict events without understanding them. In the field of human behavior, let us say we have observed that Professor X, when smoking, rubs the bowl of his pipe against his cheek every few minutes. Even though we have no idea why he does this, we can successfully predict that shortly after he lights his next pipe he will rub the bowl against his cheek. Even in cases where events are actually *mis*understood, prediction is sometimes possible. The Greek mathematician Ptolemy misunderstood the nature of the astronomical universe; he believed that the sun and the stars revolved around the earth. Yet he correctly predicted many eclipses.

Successful prediction, therefore, does not always imply understanding. But understanding does imply prediction. If we have an adequate understanding, we can put together a *theory*, or statement of general principles, that not only explains events observed in the past but also tells us what will happen under a given set of circumstances in the future. Albert Einstein, for example, acquired an understanding of the relation between matter and energy that he expressed in a theory ($E = mc^2$) that successfully predicted what would happen in an atomic explosion long before anyone knew how to create such an explosion.

Thus the fact that the goals of psychology are to understand and predict behavior can be stated another way. The goal, as in every science, is to create satisfactory theories—in this case, statements of general principle that provide a plausible explanation for the phenomena of behavior and mental life observed in the past and that, if sufficiently accurate, will be borne out by future phenomena. It is because we have some fairly powerful theories of learning, derived from the evidence of the past, that we can predict that most children will learn faster when rewarded for successes than when punished for failures.

Mankind's efforts to understand and to predict human behavior go back, presumably, to the very origins of the

THE HISTORY OF PSYCHOLOGY

human race. We can assume, from what is known about some of the primitive tribes that exist today in isolation from modern civilization, that men have always been mystified by their dreams. A man goes to sleep and in his dreams seems to travel. He goes fishing on a distant river; he goes hunting on a distant plain; he meets his friends; he even meets and converses with people who are long since dead. When he wakes up, anyone can tell him that his body has not moved at all from his bed. What could be more natural than to suppose that the human body is also inhabited by a human soul, which can leave and reenter the body at will and survives after death?

The ancient Greek philosophers were also fascinated by this apparent division of human existence into body and soul. And they speculated endlessly on the nature of the human mind, which they conceived to be a part of the soul, or perhaps the same thing. This was the age in which the science of mathematics was reaching great heights, and the Greek philosophers marveled that the human mind could create the world of mathematics—a world, though purely imaginary and theoretical, that was much more logical and "pure" than the real world of sleeping and eating and physical illness and death.

As for attempts to predict behavior, the Greeks had their oracles, notably the Delphic Oracle, who were supposed to bring them messages from the gods. Presumably all civilizations, and even the generations that preceded civilization, have had soothsayers, witch doctors, and wise men to whom they looked for guidance about the future. We still have them today, even in our modern scientific America. Almost every city has its fortune tellers, and the newspapers print columns in which astrologers predict what will happen today to people born under the sign of Taurus or of Pisces (see FIGURE 1.8).

What distinguishes psychology from previous attempts to understand and predict human behavior is that it refuses to regard man as the creature of totally unproved forces such as the influence of the stars. Nor does it seek divine revelations. It is not content to describe man as some past philosopher, however brilliant, may have imagined man to be. It is not content to accept the adages of previous generations, no matter how commonsensical those adages may seem to be. (Many of the adages, as a matter of fact, are mutually contradictory. Is it true that "a bird in the hand is worth two in the bush," or do we do better to believe "nothing ventured, nothing gained"?)

Instead, the science of psychology is *empirical*—that is, it is based on controlled experiments and on observations made with the greatest possible precision and objectivity. This is the quality it shares with other natural sciences such as physics and chemistry; this, indeed, is what makes it a science.

Wilhelm Wundt and His Laboratory

Like other sciences, psychology evolved slowly and was the result of many contributions by many men. The philosophers of the seventeenth and eighteenth centuries helped create the realistically inquiring attitude of mind that made the science possible. The physiologists of the nineteenth century did their part by making numerous discoveries about the human nervous system and the human brain. The year in which all these factors came together and psychology emerged as a science in its own right is

Some Nonscientific Attempts to Predict Human Behavior For people who want it, there is a plentiful supply of predictions about what is going to happen in the future—including astrological advice, fortune telling systems, phrenologists who "read" the bumps of the head, newspaper horoscopes, and even a Japanese bird that picks out envelopes containing predictions.

FIGURE 1.8

usually put at 1879, when Wilhelm Wundt established the first psychology laboratory at Germany's University of Leipzig.

Wilhelm Wundt was a solemn, hard-working, and tireless man who devoted himself to scholarship from the time he was a boy until he died at the age of eighty-eight. A preacher's son, he first became a physician, but, instead of practicing medicine, he taught as a professor of physiology. He soon lost interest in the physical aspects of human behavior, for he was much more concerned with consciousness. His laboratory was the first place in the world where a serious and organized attempt was made to analyze and explain human consciousness.

Wundt was the University of Leipzig's most popular lecturer; no classroom there was big enough to hold all the students who wanted to listen. And his laboratory attracted scholars from all over the world, including a number from the United States, who absorbed the notion of experimental psychology and returned to their homelands to introduce the work to others.

Compared with some of the experiments discussed at the beginning of this chapter, Wundt's work may seem rather unexciting. For example, he was interested in the human reaction to the sounds of a metronome, and he and his students spent hours in the laboratory listening to the click of a metronome set at low speeds and high speeds, sometimes sounding only a few clicks at a time, sometimes sounding many. As they listened, they tried to analyze their conscious experiences. Wundt decided that listening to some kinds of clicks was more pleasant than listening to others. He noticed that he had a feeling of slight tension before each click and a feeling of relief afterward. He also concluded that a rapid series of beats made him conscious of excitement and that a slow series made him relaxed. Wundt and his students listened to the same kinds of clicks, then carefully reported their conscious experiences and compared notes. They may not have produced powerful laws about behavior, but they did establish a systematic method of study.

Francis Galton and Measurement

Wilhelm Wundt and his followers were interested mostly in discovering in what ways human beings are alike—in particular, whether they had the same kinds of conscious experiences in response to the same kinds of events such as the clicks of a metronome. To this day, the sameness of human behavior is one of our chief interests; we still seek laws governing the kinds of behavior that all people have in common.

Another of our modern interests, however, is the study of *individual differences,* a phrase you will find used time and again in this book and in any future psychology courses you may take. We try to learn, for example, why the young woman discussed earlier in this chapter is so different from the

FIGURE 1.9   *Two Pioneers of Psychology*   Wilhelm Wundt (*left*), a German, was the founder of modern psychology. Francis Galton (*right*) was the first of the important British psychologists.

young man in her class. No two human beings, not even identical twins, are exactly alike; they do not look alike, their bodies are different, and their behavior is different. We want to know why and how they got this way.

In this area the pioneer was Francis Galton, an Englishman whose most important work was done in the 1880's, shortly after Wilhelm Wundt's laboratory first opened its doors. By coincidence, Galton was also a physician by early training, but there the resemblance to Wundt ends—proof that even two of the founding fathers of the same science can display enormous individual differences.

As can be seen in FIGURE 1.9, the two men were quite unlike in physical appearance. And where Wundt was solemn and studious, Galton was quick and restless. Before he began concentrating on the work that made him famous in psychology, he was at various times an inventor, world traveler, geographer, and meteorologist.

Galton began his psychological studies because of an interest in heredity. He made a study that showed that men who had achieved unusual success in life had sired a greater number of successful sons than less eminent fathers. He also discovered that, when a tall man married a tall woman, their children were usually taller than average. This seemed to him to be another proof of the importance of heredity, although he was baffled by

23

the fact that the children, though taller than average, were usually not so tall as the parents. From these studies and observations he moved on to attempt measurements of human size, strength, and abilities. He invented devices to test people's hearing, sense of smell, color vision, and ability to judge weights and used them on thousands of people. At one time he set up his equipment at an International Health Exhibition in London. So great was popular interest in the emerging science of psychology that people actually paid an entrance fee to visit his laboratory and contribute their measurements to his growing array of statistics.

No matter what Galton measured, he always found wide individual differences. Galton established the principle that all human traits vary over a wide range from small to large, weak to strong, slow to fast; this is true of height, weight, physical strength, and various kinds of abilities, including, as we now know, the ability to learn, which is commonly called intelligence. There can be no further doubt, after Galton's discoveries, that the men who drew up the Declaration of Independence were only partly right when they wrote, "All men are created equal." Men may be equal in the eyes of God or at the bar of justice, but in other respects they are not identical.

William James's "Science of Mental Life"

The most prominent of the early American psychologists was William James, whose photograph appears in FIGURE 1.10. James was another man who studied medicine but never practiced. Like Galton, he possessed many talents and had a difficult time finding his true vocation. At one time he wanted to be an artist, then a chemist, and once he joined a zoological expedition to Brazil. In his late twenties he suffered a severe mental breakdown and went through a long period of depression in which he seriously thought of committing suicide. But he recovered—largely, he believed, through what he called "an achievement of the will"—and went on to become a Harvard professor and a prolific writer on psychology and philosophy.

James firmly believed in experimentation, and there is some evidence that he established a laboratory of sorts at Harvard even before the more famous Wundt laboratory opened in Leipzig. But James himself never conducted any experiments; he was much more interested in observing the workings of his own mind and the behavior of other people in real-life situations. He had no doubt about the proper definition of psychology; a textbook he wrote began with the words, "Psychology is the science of mental life." The distinguishing feature of mental life, he felt, was that human beings constantly seek certain end results and must constantly choose among various means of achieving them. The study of the long-term and short-term goals men seek and the actions they take or abandon in pursuing these goals was the core of James's work. In one passage he wrote:

FIGURE **1.10**   *Two Influential American Psychologists*   William James (*left*) was the first of the important American psychologists. John Watson (*right*) was for many years the most influential.

I would . . . if I could, be both handsome and fat and well-dressed, and a great athlete, and make a million a year, be a wit, a *bon-vivant*, and a lady-killer, as well as a philosopher; a philanthropist, statesman, warrior, and African explorer, as well as a "tone-poet" and saint. But the thing is simply impossible. The millionaire's work would run counter to the saint's; the *bon-vivant* and the philanthropist would trip each other up; the philosopher and the lady-killer could not well keep house in the same tenement of clay. Such different characters may conceivably at the outset of life be possible to a man. But to make any of them actual, the rest must more or less be suppressed. . . . This is as strong an example as there is of . . . selective industry of the mind. (5)

James contributed some valuable observations on specific aspects of human experience such as habits, emotions, religious feelings, and mental disturbances. But mostly he was interested in the broad pattern of human strivings—the cradle-to-grave progress of human beings as thinking organisms who adopt certain goals and ambitions, including spiritual ones, and struggle by various means to attain the goals or become reconciled to failure.

John Watson, Behaviorist

Was William James perhaps more a philosopher than a scientist? One American who thought so was John Watson (FIGURE 1.10), who in 1913 founded the movement known as *behaviorism*. He declared that "mental life" was something that cannot be seen or measured and thus cannot be studied scientifically. Instead of trying to examine any such vague thing as "mental life" or consciousness, he concluded, psychologists should concentrate on overt behavior—the kind of actions that are plainly visible.

Watson was inclined to doubt that there was any such thing as a human mind. He conceded that human beings had thoughts, but he believed that these were simply a form of talking to oneself, by making tiny movements of the vocal cords that science would eventually be able to measure. He also conceded that people have what they call feelings, but he believed that these were some kind of glandular activity.

There was no room in Watson's theories for anything like William James's "achievement of the will." He believed that everything we do is automatically predetermined by our past experiences; to him all human behavior was a series of *conditioned reflexes*, a type of response to outward events that will be discussed in detail in Chapter 2. He once said that he could take any dozen babies at birth and, by training them in various ways, turn them into anything he wished—doctor, lawyer, beggar, or thief.

Watson's theories burst upon the world at a time when many psychologists were dissatisfied with the progress of their science. The attempts to examine man's consciousness—his "mental life," to use the James terminology—had not been very fruitful; there was some question whether looking inward into the human mind was really scientific at all. The notion that it is better to examine and measure overt behavior than to try to study the invisible mind was very appealing, and for many years Watson was the most influential of American psychologists.

Modern Psychology

There is no doubt that Watson and his followers did a great deal to advance psychology. They emphasized that a science must be empirical and based insofar as possible on controlled experiments and measurements of behavior and that too much *introspection*, or inward examination of a "mental life" that nobody but its possessor can see in operation, can lead to chaos. But for many years behaviorism put psychology into a straitjacket. There is a good deal more to life and behavior than a series of conditioned reflexes following one after another in a pattern over which we have no control. Human beings are by no means pieces of machinery that automatically perform in a certain way every time a certain button is pushed. We do make choices, as William James pointed out. We have complicated thoughts, feelings, emotions, and attitudes that cannot possibly be explained by a simple pushbutton theory.

All these aspects of "mental life," once ruled out of bounds by the behaviorists, have now been drawn back into the field of study. It appears likely that psychology in the second half of the twentieth century is entering upon its richest and most rewarding period—in which it will manage to combine all the best features of Wundt's introspective experiments, Galton's interest in individual differences and statistical measurements, James's concern with man's will and spiritual aspirations, and Watson's warning that science must be kept empirical.

Because human behavior takes such a wide variety of forms, psychology has had to adopt a number of different ways of trying to study it and is constantly seeking new ways. Among the most prominent methods of study now in use are the following.

HOW PSYCHOLOGY STUDIES BEHAVIOR

The Experiment

Many of the seven examples of our subject matter mentioned earlier utilized the study method known as the *experiment*. Applying an electrical current to a part of the brain of a human being or of a wild bull is an experiment. The experimenter applies the current and then observes what happens. If each time he applies the current to the same spot the subject's arm moves, and if this happens not just with one person but with many, then the experimenter is justified in concluding that this part of the brain must have some connection with arm movement.

Our knowledge that it is easier to memorize a poem in six three-minute study periods than in one period of eighteen minutes comes from an experiment of a different kind. The experimenter took two groups of people and asked them to study the same poem—one group for six short periods of time, the other group for a single long period. Then he compared the results by seeing how much of the poem they remembered. Note that an experiment of this kind must be conducted with extreme care. It would be of no scientific value to try the experiment with only two people, because one person might be much better at memorizing poems than the other. The experimenter must test a number of people, divided into two carefully matched groups. In each group he must have an equal number of males and females, an equal number of people of various ages and school experience, and an equal number of people who have scored high, low, or average on intelligence tests. In addition he would want both groups to study under the same conditions of illumination, noise level in the room, and time of day. He would want to test them in exactly the same way and after the same length of time. Otherwise he could never be sure whether the results of his experiment were caused by the different methods of study or by something else.

In almost every human situation there are many *variables*—that is, conditions that are subject to change. Any of these variables, by changing, can in turn change the kind of behavior that results. Since the investigator wants to know the effect of only one variable—in this case, the number and length of the study periods—he makes every effort to hold all the other variables constant. When one group then shows a much better performance than the other, the experimenter can be confident that a series of short study periods is more efficient than a single long study period for learning a poem—at least that particular poem. He would have to repeat the experiment with other poems and indeed with many other matched groups before deciding that he had discovered a viable law of learning.

The experiment is the most powerful tool of science. It can be repeated at another time and another place, ruling out the possibility that the results were accidental. It can be repeated by a different experimenter, ruling out the possibility that the results obtained by the first experimenter were influenced by his own personality or his own preconceptions of what would happen. When facts have been established by the experimental method and verified time and again by other experimenters, we have great faith in their validity.

Naturalistic Observation

In many cases experiments are impossible; this is true not only in psychology but in other sciences as well. Astronomy, for example, cannot manipulate the planets and the stars; it can only watch their behavior—but always with extreme care and precision and with an open and unprejudiced mind.

In psychology, similarly, some of our most valuable knowledge of the behavior of infants and how they develop has come from observers who actually went into the homes where babies were growing up. Or sometimes babies have been brought into nurseries where they could be watched in contact with other children, often by observers looking through a one-way mirror so that they could see the children without themselves being seen, as shown in FIGURE 1.11. This is the study method known as *naturalistic observation*.

Unlike the experimenter, the investigator who is using the method of naturalistic observation does not manipulate the situation and cannot control all the variables. Indeed he tries to remain unseen, as behind the one-way mirror, or at least as inconspicuous as possible, lest his very presence affect the behavior that he is trying to study. This method has been especially useful in adding to our knowledge not only of children but also of animals and the people of primitive societies.

In a sense all human beings constantly use the technique of observation; everybody observes the behavior of other people and draws some conclusions

FIGURE 1.11

A Hidden Observer Studies Child Behavior Unseen behind a one-way mirror, an investigator uses the method of naturalistic observation to study a child at play. From the outside the panel looks like a sheet of clear glass. From the inside it looks like a mirror.

from this behavior. If we note that a woman student dislikes speaking up in a classroom and blushes easily in social situations, we conclude that she is shy, and we treat her accordingly. (We may try to put her at her ease, or, if we feel so inclined, we may enjoy embarrassing her and making her squirm.) Scientific observations are much more rigorously disciplined than those ordinarily made in everyday life. The observer sticks to the facts. He tries to describe behavior objectively and exactly, and he is loath to jump to conclusions about the motives behind it.

Tests

The pioneer work done by Francis Galton on tests of human abilities has already been mentioned. Since Galton's time, many more tests have been devised, measuring not only abilities but feelings, motives, attitudes, and opinions; and the tests have been tried on enough persons to determine exactly what they measure and how well. As will be seen in Chapter 14, a carefully designed test—which itself has been tested by repeated use and by analysis of the results—is a valuable tool for exploring human behavior and especially for comparing one human being with another.

FIGURE 1.12

An Interviewer at Work Alfred Kinsey is shown here conducting one of the many interviews that he and his staff made while gathering material for *Sexual Behavior in the Human Female.*

Interviews

One of the best-known studies using the interview method was the work of Alfred Kinsey, who became interested in human sexual behavior when some of his students at Indiana University asked him for sexual advice. When he went to the university library for information, he found many books of opinion about sexual behavior but almost none that cast any light on what kind of sexual experiences men and women actually had in real life or how often. So Kinsey determined to find out, and the only possible way seemed to be to interview as many men and women as he could and ask them about their sexual feelings and experiences from childhood until the present time, as he is shown doing in FIGURE 1.12. The result was his well-known reports on male and female sexual behavior.

Questionnaires

Closely related to the interview is the *questionnaire,* which is especially useful in gathering information quickly from large numbers of people. A questionnaire is a set of written questions that can easily be answered, usually by putting a checkmark in the appropriate place. In order to obtain accurate results, a questionnaire must be carefully worded. For example, an investigator interested in crime might want to know whether the inmates of a state penitentiary had fathers who tended to be very lenient or very strict.

But if he simply asked, "Was your father very lenient toward you?" he might not get accurate answers. For one thing, many convicts would not know the meaning of the word *lenient*. For another, many people tend to answer *yes* to any question just to be agreeable. So he would probably put the question like this:

When you did something that your father did not like, did he
- □ always spank you?
- □ sometimes spank you?
- □ bawl you out?

- □ tell you you were a bad boy and let it go at that?
- □ laugh and forget it?

Interviews and questionnaires are sometimes challenged by critics who think that the people who are asked the questions may not tell the truth. Kinsey's work, for example, has been attacked on the ground that nobody would be likely to be honest about his sexual behavior. But an investigator who is experienced in interviewing or in making up questionnaires and checking them against the facts that he can obtain in other ways knows how to recognize people who are not telling the truth or who are exaggerating. Interviews and questionnaires do not always reveal the complete truth, but, when carefully planned and executed, they can be extremely useful.

To summarize this section on the methods of psychological investigation, it should be pointed out again that human behavior is considerably more complex than the behavior of even the most remarkable computer ever invented. It is certainly much harder to study than is the behavior of two chemicals in a test tube or gas in a pressure chamber. Moreover, human beings cannot be manipulated the way the chemist can manipulate chemicals. If we want to find out whether overly lenient or overly harsh treatment by parents inclines a child toward being a criminal, we cannot deliberately overindulge a thousand selected children and subject another thousand to brutal discipline. We have to study human behavior as best we can, by any method that seems scientifically promising.

APPLICATIONS OF PSYCHOLOGY

All our modern sciences were founded by men whose chief motive was simply to satisfy their own curiosity about the mysteries of the universe. The first physicists were curious about the nature of physical energy, the first chemists about the nature of matter. These pioneers sought knowledge for the sake of knowledge; they were interested in *pure science;* they did not know or especially care whether their discoveries would ever serve any useful purpose.

Yet the discoveries of the pure scientists have of course been put to practical use, and in our modern world we are surrounded on all sides by *applied science.* The physicist's knowledge of electricity has been put to use in lighting and air-conditioning our homes. The automobile is also a product of applied physics, as are radios, television sets, and spaceships. Applied chemistry has purified our city water supplies, relieved our headaches, and given us plastic toothbrush handles and nylon stockings.

Psychology, too, is a pure science that has already had many practical applications, even though it is much younger than physics or chemistry. In today's world, many psychologists are busy studying the pure science; they are interested solely in increasing our knowledge of human behavior. Many other psychologists, however, are engaged in the practice of applied science and are using the knowledge we now have in many practical ways. This work has changed our world more than most people realize.

Psychology in the School

In the world of education, psychology's best-known contribution has been the standardized test, such as the intelligence tests that most elementary school pupils take, the Iowa achievement tests that compare their progress year by year with other pupils throughout the nation, and the College Boards that predict their success or failure in college with accuracy.

Before these tests were developed, educators had no really efficient way of judging students or measuring their progress. In the second grade, for example, one boy might have been doing what appeared to be outstanding work; it would have been only natural for his teachers and parents to develop high expectations for him. Two other boys might have been failing consistently to get their work done, and both of them might have been considered to need the same kind of discipline to bring them into line. Nowadays, however, intelligence tests might very well show that the first boy has somewhat less than average learning ability and for some reason— probably strong motivation—is performing far above his normal level. The second boy might prove to be much below average and unable to keep up with his school work even though trying his very best. The third boy might be a near-genius who simply cannot get interested in second-grade work. Armed with this knowledge, school and parents can take far more realistic action than in the past.

In the days before standardized tests a school board and a school principal could only guess whether their teachers were doing a superior, average, or poor job. Now the Iowa tests and others provide a good yardstick for measuring the performance of schools as well as of students. It used to be difficult for college admissions boards to judge whether an all-A student at one high school would have made A's, B's, or C's at another and possibly more difficult school. Now the College Boards provide a further and more objective measure of probable success in college.

Psychological studies also have had a more general effect on the philosophy of education. At one time, for example, every student was required to study Latin and ancient Greek—not because he was ever expected to use the languages for profit or for pleasure but because educators firmly believed that these two languages somehow exercised, trained, and disciplined the mind. Once you had learned Latin and Greek, the theory went, you would then be able to learn anything else much more quickly and efficiently. Like so many old beliefs about human behavior, this was largely incorrect. Modern investigations have shown that studying Latin and Greek has little effect on learning ability, except insofar as any kind of study can help the student acquire good work habits and a good attitude toward learning.

Many of the principles of learning that will be discussed in Part 2 of this book can be applied to schoolwork; they are useful in making studying easier and more productive. Some colleges, indeed, have a special course in the applied psychology of learning designed to help students do better in their classes. And many courses have been constructed, many textbooks written, and many educational films produced with the principles of learning in mind.

Vocational Guidance

A few generations ago, the spectacle of a man or woman trying to succeed at a totally unsuitable job was so common that there was a popular phrase for such a person: he was called "a square peg in a round hole." The phrase is heard much less frequently today—partly because of *vocational guidance*, which means helping a person select the right lifetime occupation.

An intelligence test is in itself a rough guide to the proper occupation. It has been established, for example, that almost all accountants score in the upper quarter on intelligence tests (6). A person scoring below the upper quarter, therefore, would not be advised to try to take up accounting. On the other hand there are many jobs, particularly those involving monotonous detail work, in which the ability to score well on an intelligence test is a severe handicap.

In addition to intelligence tests we now have numerous other specialized tests of physical strength and dexterity and of the skills required in many different jobs ranging all the way from clerical work to electronics engineering, as shown in FIGURE 1.13. Anyone who is undecided about a career can take these tests and discover what kinds of jobs he seems best able to perform.

To obtain the greatest possible satisfaction from a job, a person not only must have the ability to do the job well but also must be interested in the work. Therefore, tests have been developed to measure a person's likes and dislikes on a wide range of matters such as reading, recreation, and social life, and these tests have been given to large numbers of accountants, bankers, dentists, engineers, lawyers, librarians, and so on. A person attempting to choose a career can take these tests and compare his own likes and dislikes with those of people in various occupations. If he discovers that his own tastes and preferences are very much unlike those of most bankers and very much like those of most life-insurance salesmen, he has a valuable clue to the kind of work he would probably enjoy.

Psychology in Industry

In the business world, new developments in testing have been used to help select employees, and findings about learning have been used to help train employees. Many previously unsuspected facts have been discovered about worker fatigue, working hours, rest periods, and employee morale.

In the past, many businessmen thought that the most efficient work week was the longest number of hours that they could persuade the workers to stay on the job. It was not very many years ago that manual workers in some industries worked twelve hours a day seven days a week, and office workers often worked twelve hours a day six days a week. The fact of the matter, it has now been found, is that nobody can work efficiently on such schedules. Almost all workers, in all kinds of jobs, take a brief period early in the morning to warm up to the job; as soon as they have done so, they are at their peak of efficiency. After a few hours of work their efficiency begins to fall off rapidly and continues steadily downward for the rest of the day, except sometimes for a brief spurt right after lunch. By the end of the day most workers are accomplishing very little; either they are not producing anything to speak of or they are making a great many mistakes in their work. In many jobs, it has been found, a worker will actually accomplish more in an eight-hour day than in a ten-hour day. A work week of around thirty-five to forty hours is the most efficient. In cases of emergency a worker will produce more in a week of around fifty hours but not nearly so much more as the increase in time spent on the job would indicate. Anything over about fifty-five hours is sheer waste (7).

Rest periods, which were frowned on by the old-fashioned businessman, have proved to increase production rather than hamper it. Men who do hard physical work profit most dramatically from rest periods; they accomplish more in the course of the day if they take frequent rests—as much as ten minutes every hour—than if they try to stay constantly at the job. But even office workers who expend very little physical energy do better if they have regularly scheduled rest periods such as coffee breaks. The proper planning of rest periods, in accordance with the nature of the job, has helped many businessmen achieve two goals—both higher production and happier workers.

FIGURE **1.13**

Some Vocational Guidance Tests The young man is taking a test for skill at using tools, the young woman a test of manual dexterity.

The old-fashioned businessman thought that his employees were interested solely in the size of their pay checks, but we now know that pay is by no means the most important factor in employee morale (8). What seems to matter most of all are the warmth or coldness of the worker's relations with his immediate boss—his foreman or department head—and the amount of respect that each displays toward the other. The attempt to teach supervisors how best to work with their employees has become a part of the industrial psychologist's job.

The fact that the morale of women workers in particular depends on many factors the old-fashioned boss would never have thought important was established in an experiment started at the Western Electric Company in 1927. This began as a study of illumination; the company merely wanted to know what kind of lighting would result in the most production in rooms where young women were assembling telephone apparatus. It was soon discovered that production went up when the lighting was increased, but it also went up when the lighting was decreased. It even went up when an electrician pretended to change all the bulbs in a room but put the same ones back. Company officials were baffled and spent the next five years trying to find the explanation.

The company tried giving the girls rest periods, and production went up again. It changed their working hours and production went up. It shortened their work week, and production went up again. Then the company took away the rest periods and went back to the old schedule of hours. Common sense said that now production would go down, but instead it went still higher. The only possible conclusion was that the young women in the plant were responding to the attention being paid them, not to the specific form that the attention took from day to day. The changes convinced them that the company was interested in them; this made them feel important and they worked harder. Their morale made more difference to their production than any mere physical changes in their working conditions (9).

Another development in industrial psychology has been *human engineering*—the design of equipment and machinery to fit the actual size, strength, and capabilities of the human beings who will use it. The table telephone, for example, was modified after measuring the faces of thousands of people and after experiments in which handsets of various weights were tried. The newest phone, shown with two of its predecessors in FIGURE 1.14, has a handset that is lighter in weight than the one on older sets and shorter in distance from ear to mouth. The dial has been replaced by pushbuttons, which are faster and easier to use, and the mouthpiece is set at a different angle, found to suit the maximum number of people.

The armed services have been among the biggest users of human engineering, which has helped them design more efficient instruments for airplanes and submarines, as well as vehicles that are less tiring to operate. An experiment by the Air Force some years ago opened up another new area in which psychological methods have been found of great value. The specifications and blueprints for a new type of radar equipment were given to a psychologist, who was asked to work out an estimate of how many men, with what kind of skills, would be needed to operate it. In truth the equipment was already in use, but the psychologist was not told this. Although he had nothing but the plans to work from, his estimate almost exactly matched the numbers and kinds of workers the Air Force had discovered in actual practice were needed to keep the equipment operating. Since then the Air Force has assigned a number of psychologists to work out personnel lists and training programs for new equipment that will not be ready until some time in the future.

FIGURE 1.14

How Human Engineering Changed the Telephone   On the basis of tests with actual users, the old-fashioned telephone was redesigned with a handset of different size and shape and with numbers outside instead of inside the holes, then most recently into a pushbutton arrangement that is even easier to use.

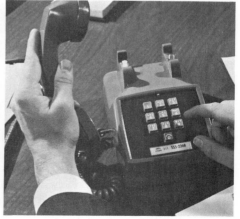

Public Opinion Surveys

The Gallup Poll is one well-known example of the application of psychological techniques to the examination of public opinion; it is noteworthy because it has had a good record of success in a field where previous polls, not based on scientific principles, were often embarrassing failures. In the 1920's and 1930's, for example, a magazine called *Literary Digest* made surveys of voter sentiment; in 1936 it made the unfortunate and financially ruinous mistake of predicting that Alfred Landon would be elected over Franklin Roosevelt, when in fact Landon carried only two states. The reason for the mistake was that *Literary Digest* chose the people whose opinions it asked by picking names at random from telephone books and lists of automobile owners. In 1936 telephones and automobiles were far less common than now, and most of them were owned by people with above-average incomes. The wealthy, telephone-owning class did vote for Landon, but it was far outnumbered by Roosevelt votes from less wealthy Americans.

The Gallup Poll and the other new public opinion surveys like it do a careful job of sampling. They first determine how many Americans live in big cities, how many in small cities, how many on farms; how many are Catholics, Protestants, and Jews; how many fall into various income brackets from the lowest to the highest; how many have gone to high school and how many to college. Then they select a group of people that is representative of the entire population. Since about one American out of four is a Catholic, for example, they make sure that one person out of four in the sample group is a Catholic.

Besides predicting election results with improved accuracy the polls have provided valuable insights into what Americans are thinking about such matters as foreign affairs, Supreme Court decisions, labor disputes, and farm policies. Businessmen have also used opinion surveys to advantage, as in testing the popularity of television shows and the reaction to various types of sales, advertising, and public relations campaigns. Some advertising slogans have been found so ineffective that only one or two people in a hundred recognized them, while other slogans were recognized by as many as seventy people in a hundred.

Clinical Psychology

The largest of all fields of applied psychology is *clinical psychology*—the diagnosis and treatment of behavior problems. More than a third of all psychologists specialize in this field, performing a wide variety of important services for individuals, families, schools, business firms, and communities.

Many problems call for the clinical psychologist's diagnosis. For example, a preschool child may be listless, uninterested in his surroundings, and slow to learn such skills as talking, eating from a plate, and dressing himself. The reason may be that he is mentally retarded, that is, simply lacking in intelligence, or that he is suffering from the rather common form of mental disturbance known as schizophrenia. An older child may be unable to learn to read; in this case the cause may again be mental retardation, or it may be a special form of brain damage or simply a lack of motivation. A child suffering from asthma may have a physical allergy that causes his condition, or he may be reacting with physical symptoms to such psychological factors as overprotection by his mother. In all these cases a careful diagnosis, often made with the help of psychological tests described in Chapter 14, is the first step in dealing with the problem.

Many clinical psychologists work in the schools, where they not only attempt to diagnose the cause of pupils' problems but also work closely with teachers and families in an attempt to change the conditions that have helped create the problems. Others work in industry, where it has been found that many employees fail at the job not because of lack of skill but because of bad personal relations with their fellow workers or bosses and where a large percentage of absenteeism and accidents has also been traced to personality difficulties.

In the treatment of behavior disorders clinical psychology uses the method called *psychotherapy,* which generally takes the form of getting the patient to talk about his fears and conflicts and perhaps, with the psychologist's help, to see them in a new and more constructive light. In general, clinical psychologists believe that mental and emotional disorders that have no obvious physical basis are the result of an unfortunate form of learning; it is the patient's prior experiences, the attitudes he has learned toward them, and the emotions they now arouse that account for his present troubles. Psychotherapy, to most clinical psychologists, consists in helping the patient to understand the source and nature of his problems and to relearn better ways of coping with his life situation. Many clinical psychologists practice *group therapy,* which is the treatment of a number of people at the same time. Group therapy is less expensive than individual therapy, and in many cases it appears to be more effective. Many other clinical psychologists specialize in helping communities eliminate the social conditions that seem to cause or to aggravate personality difficulties.

In addition to diagnosing and treating mental problems, clinical psychologists are constantly conducting new research into the origins, symptoms, and possible cures of these problems. In the long run this research may prove to be psychology's greatest practical contribution to human happiness. We are still only a few hundred years removed from the time when the mentally ill were treated by boring holes in their skulls to let the evil spirits out. The whole subject of mental disturbance, despite recent progress, is still shrouded in mystery and uncertainty. The clinical psychologist does the best he can with the knowledge now at his command, but he is all too painfully aware that much more knowledge is needed. The search for this knowledge is one of our most stimulating challenges.

SUMMARY

1. Psychology is best defined as the science that systematically studies and attempts to explain observable (overt) behavior and its relationship to the unseen (covert) mental processes that go on inside the organism and to external events in the environment.

2. The subject matter of psychology includes motor skills and motor behavior, thinking, problem solving, and the effects of learning, biological drives, motives, emotions, anxiety, and defenses against anxiety.

3. The goals of psychology are to understand and to predict behavior.

4. Psychology began as a science when Wilhelm Wundt opened the first psychology laboratory in 1879.

5. Other important early psychologists were Francis Galton, who was interested in measuring individual differences; William James, who believed psychology to be "the science of mental life"; and John Watson, the founder of behaviorism.

6. The science of psychology is empirical, which means that it is based on studies made with the utmost possible precision and objectivity.

7. Methods used to study behavior include experiments, naturalistic observation, tests, interviews, and questionnaires.

8. Although psychology is a pure science, interested in knowledge for the sake of knowledge, many of its findings have had a practical application in modern life. Examples of applied psychology include:
   a. The use in schools of standardized tests and the principles of learning.
   b. Vocational guidance based on measurement of learning ability and specific skills and interests.
   c. The use by industry of studies of the effect of fatigue, working hours, and employee morale; and the development of human engineering, which is the design of equipment and machinery to fit the physical characteristics and capabilities of the people who use it.
   d. Public opinion surveys such as the Gallup Poll.
   e. Clinical psychology, which is the diagnosis and treatment of behavior problems and disorders.

Boring, E. G. *History of experimental psychology*, 2nd ed. New York: Appleton-Century-Crofts, 1950.

Coopersmith, S. *Frontiers of psychological research*. San Francisco: W. H. Freeman, 1964.

Hall, C. S. and Lindzey, G. *Theories of personality*. New York: Wiley, 1957.

Herrnstein, R. J. and Boring, E. G., eds. *A source book in the history of psychology*. Cambridge, Mass.: Harvard University Press, 1965.

Lindzey, G. and Hall, C. S., eds. *Theories of personality: primary sources and research*. New York: Wiley, 1965.

Murphy, G. *Historical introduction to modern psychology*, rev. ed. New York: Harcourt, Brace & World, 1949.

Postman, L., ed. *Psychology in the making: histories of selected research problems*. New York: Knopf, 1962.

Scott, W. A. and Wertheimer, M. *Introduction to psychological research*. New York: Wiley, 1962.

Underwood, B. J. *Psychological research*. New York: Appleton-Century-Crofts, 1957.

Watson, R. I. *The great psychologists: from Aristotle to Freud*. Philadelphia: Lippincott, 1963.

Wolman, B. B. *Contemporary theories and systems in psychology*. New York: Harper & Row, 1960.

HOW BEHAVIOR
IS LEARNED

Part 1 described some of the responses to biological drives and some of the motor skills, thinking, and problem solving that constituted a young woman's behavior on a typical morning. It also described some of the many striking ways in which her behavior differed from the behavior of a young man in her college class, largely because of differences in their motives, emotions, anxieties, and defenses.

All these matters, from biological drives to psychological defenses, are important fields of study, and later in the book you will find further and more complete discussions of what has been discovered about them.

The key problem of psychology, however, is this:

At birth, the young woman was incapable of all this varied behavior. She did possess the biological drives of hunger and thirst, but all she could do about them was cry and make sucking movements with her lips. Her motor behavior was limited to some rather simple and uncoordinated movements of the muscles of her arms, legs, and body. She was incapable of thinking or problem solving. She had no motives or emotions, at least not in the sense that adults have them.

How did the young woman become capable of the many kinds of behavior that she now exhibits?

How did the young man, who also started as a helpless baby, become capable of the kind of behavior *he* exhibits today—and why is his behavior so different from the young woman's behavior?

The answer is that the young woman and the young man *learned.*

Almost all the behavior we exhibit as adults has been learned. Thus learning is a central concern of psychology and a logical place to start studying the science. This second part of the book, therefore, contains three chapters on various aspects of the learning process.

THE "NATURE VERSUS NURTURE" ARGUMENT

THE REFLEX

Types of Reflex Responses
The Reflex Mechanism

THE CONDITIONED REFLEX

Reinforcement in Classical Conditioning
Extinction and Spontaneous Recovery
Stimulus Generalization and Stimulus Discrimination
Conditioned Reflexes in Life Situations
Conditioning and Emotions
Conditioned Reflexes and Illness

OPERANT BEHAVIOR

OPERANT CONDITIONING

Operant Extinction, Recovery, Generalization, and Discrimination
The Shaping of Operants
Reinforcement as the Key to Learning
    Delay of Reinforcement; Schedule of Reinforcement; Kinds of Reinforce-
        ment;
    Secondary Reinforcement; Operant Escape and Avoidance; Is Reinforce-
        ment Essential?; Reinforcement and Attention

THE UNITS THAT ARE LEARNED

Learning Without Overt Action
Learning by Imitation
The Learning "Connection"
Kinds of Mediational Units
    Sets and Perceptual Expectations; Words and Language; Concepts;
    Motives and Standards; Emotions; Attitudes

CHAPTER

THE PRINCIPLES
OF LEARNING

Two baby robins, pecking their way out of the eggs, are destined to lead much the same kind of lives; both of them will exhibit much the same kind of behavior from birth to death. Two human babies, lying in adjoining cribs in a hospital, are not set in any such pattern. They will behave very differently as children and still more differently as adults.

Much of the behavior of birds, insects, and fish is regulated by *instincts*, which are elaborate inborn patterns of activity, occurring automatically and without prior learning. The robin, even if it never sees another robin build a nest, will instinctively build the round and shallow nest characteristic of the species. The vireo will instinctively build a hanging nest and the penguin a nest of stones. The spider will weave its characteristic web. The salmon will migrate from its birthplace in a river to the depths of the ocean, then will return to the shallows of the river to spawn.

This is not true of human behavior. If there are any human instincts, they play an insignificant part in our behavior, and some psychologists believe that there are no human instincts at all. Certainly most of the popular talk about human instincts is in error. People often say that human beings have an "instinctive fear" of snakes, but this is incorrect. A child who has not learned to fear snakes may eagerly try to play with one, just as he might play with a puppy. People also talk of an "acquisitive instinct," as if all human beings liked to accumulate money and possessions. But there are many societies in which human beings never learn to show interest in acquiring property.

THE "NATURE VERSUS NURTURE" ARGUMENT

The plasticity of human behavior—the fact that it can be molded in ways that the more rigid and predetermined behavior of lower organisms cannot be molded—has always impressed observant men and has been the center of one of the important philosophic arguments of history, the "nature versus nurture" argument. The argument revolves around this question: To how great an extent is human behavior determined by factors present at birth, and to what extent is it molded through experience and learning? Sometimes the question is put another way: To what extent does human behavior depend on heredity and to what extent on environment (which is the sum total of all the influences exerted by family and society)?

John Locke, the seventeenth-century philosopher, popularized the idea that the mind of the human baby is what has been called a *tabula rasa,* a "blank tablet" on which anything can be written through experience and learning. This idea greatly influenced other philosophers who helped create the intellectual climate in which psychology was born as a science, and it was also attractive to many of the early psychologists. Note that it is a very optimistic idea. If the mind of the human baby is indeed a "blank tablet," then human history has unlimited possibilities. All the evils that have plagued humanity—jealousy, emotional conflicts, crime, even war—are not inevitable but are the result of the wrong kind of learning. By discovering the principles of learning we can point the way toward a brighter future for mankind.

Many thinkers of the past, however, rejected the idea of the *tabula rasa.* They argued that every human being was born, if not with instincts that would unfold as detailed patterns of behavior, at least with strong predispositions toward certain kinds of behavior. They believed that one baby inherited the tendency to be happy, another to be melancholy; one baby was born to be a leader, another to be a timid follower, another to be a troublemaker or even a criminal. Carried far enough, this becomes a rather fatalistic view of human behavior, containing little hope for any improvement. If the future of the human being is laid down at birth to any substantial degree, then there is not much point in parents' attempting to find better ways of bringing up their children or in the schools' attempting to find better ways of educating them.

The argument between these two very different points of view still continues, and there are influential thinkers on both sides. Most psychologists lean toward the *tabula rasa* or "blank tablet" idea, though with important reservations. Obviously nature sets certain limits on human behavior. All human babies are more or less alike at birth; all of them, whether born to a savage mother in some remote jungle or to a college-educated mother in Denver, have much the same kind of bones, muscles, sense organs, nervous systems, and glands. It is unlikely that any human being will ever learn to run 100 yards in less than eight seconds, and it is certainly impossible for any human being to learn to fly like a bird or to live underwater like a fish (although we have learned to build mechanical devices that enable us to imitate these feats).

We know now that many of the individual differences that interested Sir Francis Galton—traits ranging from potential size to potential learning ability—are present at birth, controlled by the pattern of genes inherited from one's ancestors. Everybody's life is shaped to some extent by the particular physical, glandular, and nervous equipment that he inherits. But our inborn equipment appears to set only the limits and the broad tendencies of behavior, leaving room for a wide range of possibilities. The human baby, newborn and lying helpless in his crib, will not lead his life—at least not to any appreciable degree—as the slave to any instincts laid down at his birth. One of the great contrasts between instinctive behavior and learned behavior is illustrated in FIGURE 2.1. No human baby is predestined to build a certain kind of house, or court his mate in any specific way, or travel to a certain part of the world to live his maturing years and then return to his birthplace to sire his children.

By and large and within our inherited limitations, we human beings become what we are through the process of learning. One man learns to become an Adolf Hitler. Another man, not very different at birth, learns to become a benefactor of humanity. One woman learns to become a notorious poisoner of six husbands. Another woman, not much different at birth, learns to become an outstanding schoolteacher and later the successful mother of happy children.

Let us examine the elements of learning, starting with the simplest of them and proceeding to the more complex and noting, as we go, how each of the elements forms the firm foundation for the next.

THE REFLEX

All human babies exhibit the same form of behavior in response to certain events. If you brush a baby's lips, he makes a sucking motion. If you stroke a baby's cheek at the left side of his mouth, he turns his head to the left. If you stroke the right cheek, he turns his head to the right. If you tickle the sole of his foot, he lifts and spreads his toes. If you clap your hands and make a loud noise, he raises his arms and legs. When an object is placed in the palm of his hand, he closes his fingers around it.

These actions are called *reflexes*. They are automatic reactions to something that happens to the organism. They come naturally. They are not learned. They take place without any conscious effort. Like the instincts of lower organisms, they are inborn. But they are not elaborate processes such as the building of the robin's nest or the migration of the salmon. Instead they are merely one particular action or group of actions—usually an action that protects the organism from damage or harm or that in some way helps the organism adjust to changes in the environment.

If you touch a hot piece of metal, for example, you immediately pull your hand away. This is a reflex action. You do not have to stop and think.

FIGURE 2.1   *Instinctive Versus Learned Home Building*   The top row of photographs shows how various birds always build the kind of nest distinctive for the species: from left, the vireo, penguin, and robin. Below are some of the many kinds of houses human beings have learned to build: jungle hut, Eskimo igloo, and modern apartment building.

As a matter of fact, you seem to pull your hand away before you actually become aware that the metal is hot. The reflex action protects you from being burned.

If you walk into a dark room, the pupils of your eyes automatically grow larger. If a bright light strikes your eyes, the pupils automatically and very quickly grow smaller. These are reflex actions that help your eyes adjust to the condition of the environment—that is to say, to the amount of light that is present.

Types of Reflex Responses

Reflexes can involve any part of the body. Sometimes they are movements of the *striped muscles*—the muscles over which we ordinarily have conscious control, such as the muscles of our arms, hands, legs, and feet. Such is the reflex that pulls our hands or feet away from something painful like a hot piece of metal. Sometimes they are movements of *smooth muscles,* such as the muscles of the pupil of the eye, over which we do not have any conscious control. Our internal organs, which have smooth muscles, often respond by reflex action; vomiting, for example, is a reflex action that can be triggered by pressures or chemical changes in the alimentary canal. Reflexes also take the form of *glandular activity;* for example, if we put food in our mouths, the glands of the mouth immediately begin to produce saliva.

One of the most complicated and interesting of the human reflexes is the *startle pattern*, which occurs in response to sudden and unexpected events and occurs in every person in much the same way. If someone fired a gun close behind you at this moment, your first reaction would be substantially as shown in FIGURE 2.2. Your head would move forward and the muscles of your neck would stand out. Your arms and legs would tense. Your mouth might open, almost like the mouth of an animal baring its teeth. At the same time, some unseen responses would take place inside your body. It is likely that your heart would beat faster; the level of sugar in your blood would rise; and blood would flow away from the digestive organs and out toward the striped muscles. You would probably have a feeling of fear.

All this would happen automatically and very quickly—so quickly that you might not even be aware of the muscular movements. In the next instant you would probably take some kind of conscious action. You might laugh in relief to learn that the gunshot was a joke. Or, if the shot had been fired by a robber, you might run after him or away from him. Afterward you would probably remember this conscious action and not the reflex that preceded it. But photographic studies of many people have shown that the first reaction to being startled is this almost instantaneous reflex, which usually involves the muscles of the neck, arms, legs, eyelids, and lips (2).

FIGURE **2.2**

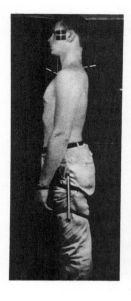

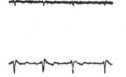
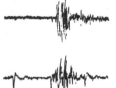

The Startle Pattern   The young man, standing comfortably, is startled by the slamming of a door. Note the many reflex movements resulting in a forward thrust of the head, shoulders, and arms, and a tensing of the legs. The tracings, from electrodes attached to two sets of neck muscles, show the burst of muscular activity. (1)

The entire reflex, both external and internal, is of such a nature that it prepares the organism to fight back against attack.

The Reflex Mechanism

What causes a reflex? How does a reflex operate? A full answer to these questions will have to wait until Chapter 7, which discusses the human nervous system and the internal glandular system that helps control such activities as rate of heartbeat and level of blood sugar. (One of the problems of studying psychology is that, no matter where you start to discuss human behavior, you run into complications that cannot be fully understood until you have also discussed all the other aspects of behavior.) For now, let us state merely that reflexes depend on what might be called the "wiring" inside us.

The human organism can be roughly compared to a house that is wired in a certain way for electricity. If you press a button inside the front door, the outside entrance light goes on. You can press other buttons that will turn on the garage light, the television set, a fan, or an air conditioner. The "wiring" of the human organism—which is of course the network of nerves through our bodies—is so constructed that the touch of hot metal makes our fingers draw away; a beam of light makes our pupils grow smaller, and so on. The "wiring" that produces the knee jerk that everyone has experienced at one time or another in the doctor's office is shown in FIGURE 2.3.

The reflex starts with a *stimulus,* which can be defined as any form of energy capable of exciting the nervous system. In the case of the knee jerk, the stimulus is the mechanical energy exerted by the doctor's rubber hammer. The stimulus sets off nervous impulses, which then travel a built-in pattern. The result is a *response,* which can be defined as any kind of behavior that results from a stimulus. In this case, the response is the contraction of a muscle in the thigh, causing the lower part of the leg to jerk upward.

As can be seen in FIGURE 2.3, the reflex of the knee jerk operates independently of the brain. The "wiring" is such that nervous impulses set off by the stimulus travel to a spot in the spinal cord, where they in turn set off nervous impulses that travel to the thigh muscle. This is characteristic of reflexes. The "wiring" is simple and direct. The reflex takes place automatically, without any thinking.

A human being, however, is not so simple as a building. When you push a button in the house, the light to which it is wired goes on every time. But the stimulus that produces a human reflex response on one occasion will not necessarily produce it every time. If you are determined not to move your leg when the doctor strikes your knee with his hammer, the response will not occur. Your salivary glands will not respond to food when you are already stuffed from a large meal. The baby who ordinarily responds to a

FIGURE 2.3

Nerve Pathways for the Knee Jerk   The doctor's hammer excites nerves that run from the tendon below the knee to the spinal cord. Impulses traveling over these nerves in turn excite nerves that run from the spinal cord to the muscle of the thigh. The result is to make the muscle contract, causing the quick upward movement of the lower leg known as the knee jerk.

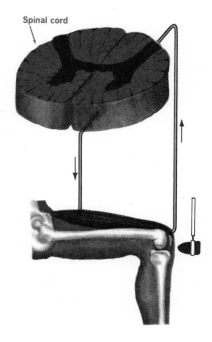

Spinal cord

loud noise by reflex movements of his arms and legs—the infant's equivalent of the startle pattern—will not respond if he is expecting the sound. Thus behavior that is going on in other parts of our bodies—particularly activity in the higher part of the brain—has an effect on our reflex responses.

Reflexes, though not themselves learned, can also be modified by learning—a fact that constitutes the second element of learning.

THE CONDITIONED REFLEX   Perhaps the best-known single experiment in the history of psychology was performed in the early years of this century by the Russian scientist Ivan Pavlov, a man whose name and work will certainly survive as long as the science itself. The laboratory arrangement for Pavlov's experiment is shown in FIGURE 2.4. Pavlov began the

Pavlov's Dog   The dog is strapped into a harness in which it has grown used to standing. A tube attached to the dog's salivary gland collects any saliva secreted by the gland, and the number of drops from the tube is recorded on a revolving drum outside the chamber. A laboratory attendant can watch the dog through a one-way mirror and can deliver food to the dog's feed pan by remote control. Thus there is nothing in the chamber to distract the dog's attention except the food, when it is delivered, and any other stimulus that the attendant wishes to present, such as the sound of a metronome. For the discoveries Pavlov made with this apparatus, see the text. (3)   FIGURE **2.4**

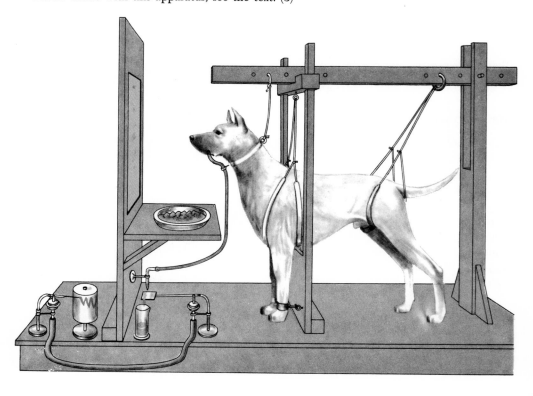

experiment by making a sound, such as the beat of a metronome, that the dog could hear. The dog made a few restless movements, but no saliva flowed from the glands of its mouth. This was what Pavlov had expected. The stimulus for reflex action of the salivary glands is the presence of food in the mouth—not the sound of a metronome. As far as the salivary reflex is concerned, sound is a neutral stimulus that has no effect one way or the other. When food was delivered and the dog took it into its mouth, saliva of course flowed in quantity.

Now Pavlov set about trying to connect the neutral stimulus of the sound with the reflex action of the salivary glands. While the metronome was clicking he delivered food to the dog, setting off the salivary reflex. After a time he did the same thing again—sounded the metronome and delivered food. After he had done this many times, he tried something new. He sounded the metronome but did not deliver any food. Saliva flowed anyway. The sound alone was now a sufficient stimulus to set off the salivary reflex (4).

The response of the glands to the sound is called a *conditioned reflex*. The dog had been conditioned, through a very simple form of learning, to associate the sound with the presence of food in its mouth and to salivate when it heard the sound. In this form of learning, which is called *classical conditioning*, the food is the *unconditioned stimulus*—the stimulus that naturally and automatically produces the salivary reflex, without any learning. The sound is the *conditioned stimulus*, which is neutral at the start but eventually produces a similar response. The reflex action of the salivary glands when food is placed in the dog's mouth is the *unconditioned reflex*, the one that is naturally built into the animal's "wiring" and takes place automatically, without any kind of learning. The response of the glands to the sound is the *conditioned reflex*, resulting from some kind of change in the "wiring" that is caused by pairing the conditioned stimulus with the unconditioned stimulus.

Reinforcement in Classical Conditioning

Once Pavlov had established the conditioned salivary reflex, he was interested in learning how long and under what circumstances it would persist. When he merely sounded the metronome without ever again presenting food, he found that in a very short time the flow of saliva in response to the sound began to decrease, and soon it stopped altogether, as shown in FIGURE 2.5. But if he occasionally followed the sound with food—not every time but sometimes—the conditioned reflex could be made to continue indefinitely. Since pairing the food with the sound not only established the conditioned reflex but also strengthened it and kept it alive, Pavlov called this process *reinforcement*.

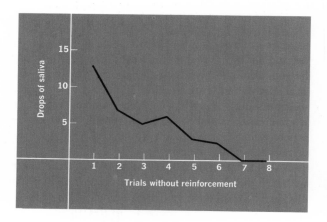

Extinction This graph shows what happened to Pavlov's dog when the conditioned stimulus of sound was no longer reinforced by the unconditioned stimulus of food. The conditioned salivary reflex, very strong at first, gradually grew weaker. By the seventh time the metronome was sounded the conditioned reflex had disappeared. Extinction of the reflex was complete.

FIGURE 2.5

Extinction and Spontaneous Recovery

Pavlov's experiments demonstrated many of the rules and provided much of the terminology of learning. The process through which the conditioned reflex (or any other learned behavior) tends to disappear if reinforcement is withdrawn is called *extinction*. But Pavlov also discovered that even after extinction the conditioned reflex tends to operate again after a rest. This phenomenon is called *spontaneous recovery*.

Pavlov found that he could just as easily condition the dog's salivary reflex to the sound of a bell or to a flash of light as to the metronome. Subsequent experimenters have shown that apparently almost any kind of reflex can be conditioned and that almost any kind of previously neutral stimulus can be used as the conditioned stimulus. If the conditioned reflex is reinforced by occasional pairings of the conditioned stimulus and the unconditioned stimulus, it continues to operate. If not, it undergoes extinction.

Stimulus Generalization and Stimulus Discrimination

Another important fact about learning demonstrated in the Pavlov experiments was this: once the dog had been conditioned to salivate to the sound of a bell, it would also salivate to the sound of a different bell or of a buzzer. If the sound was very similar to that of the original bell, the dog salivated in quantity. As the sound became more and more different from the original bell, the amount of salivation decreased, and sometimes no salivation occurred at all.

This phenomenon is called *stimulus generalization*—which means that once the organism has learned to associate a stimulus with a certain kind of behavior, it tends to display this behavior toward similar stimuli.

54

After Pavlov had established the principle of stimulus generalization in the dog, he went on to demonstrate its counterpart, which is called *stimulus discrimination*. He continued to reinforce salivation to the bell by presenting food. But, when a different bell or a buzzer was sounded, no reinforcement was presented. Soon the dog learned to salivate only to the sound of the original bell, not to the other sounds; the animal had learned to discriminate between the stimulus of the bell and the other stimuli. If the experiment is carried far enough, it can be shown that a dog is capable of quite delicate stimulus discrimination; it can learn to respond to the tone of middle C, yet not to respond to tones that are only a little higher or a little lower.

Conditioned Reflexes in Life Situations

The conditioned reflex is far more than just a strange phenomenon that can be made to happen in a specially constructed laboratory. As a matter of fact, Pavlov began his laboratory experiments because he had already noticed something about dogs that aroused his curiosity. In studying the digestive system of dogs he had noticed that their saliva and other digestive juices began to flow not only when they actually had food in their mouths but also when they merely saw the food—or even the man who usually fed them. In other words, the salivary reflex of the dogs had already been conditioned to the stimulus provided by the sight of food or of the man who was the customary source of food. In his laboratory experiments Pavlov showed how this kind of conditioning takes place.

Nor is classical conditioning something that happens only to animals. Many kinds of human reflexes have also been conditioned to many kinds of stimuli. For example, the sound of the first note of Beethoven's Fifth Symphony has no effect on the human eyelid. A puff of air directed at the eye, however, produces a reflex action in which the eyelid blinks shut. If you sit in a laboratory long enough while an experimenter sounds the musical note and then quickly directs a puff of air toward your eye, eventually the first note of the symphony will produce the reflex of blinking.

Conditioning and Emotions

Some far-reaching effects of classical conditioning among human beings were discovered by John Watson, who was mentioned in Chapter 1 as the founder of behaviorism. One study that Watson helped conduct is known as the "Albert experiment"—referring to the first name of the eleven-month-old boy who was the subject. A child, as has been noted, automatically responds to an unexpected loud noise with the infant's equivalent of the startle pattern and shows signs of fear. Watson was interested in learning whether this reflex response could be conditioned to other stimuli. He therefore showed Albert a rat. Displaying no signs whatever of fear, Albert tried to play with the rat. Then the rat was shown again, and a loud noise was sounded. As illustrated in FIGURE 2.6, Albert showed signs of fear and shrank back. After this was repeated several times, Albert showed signs of fear whenever he saw the rat, even when the noise was not sounded. The unconditioned reflexes associated with the emotion of fear, set off automatically by the unconditioned stimulus of a loud noise, had now been conditioned to respond to the conditioned stimulus of the rat. In fact Albert, in accordance with the law of stimulus generalization, now showed signs of fear when he saw anything that was furry like a rat, including a rabbit or a man with a beard.

Something very similar to the Albert experiment often happens to children in real-life situations. For example, another unconditioned stimulus that automatically sets off the reflexes associated with fear is the sensation of falling. Now suppose that a dog—even a dog that the child has previously known and liked—suddenly jumps on him and knocks him down. In the future the child will probably show signs of fear at the very sight of the

FIGURE 2.6   *Conditioning the Fear Reflex*   The unconditioned baby reaches eagerly toward a rat (A). Then a loud noise is presented at the same time as the rat (B). After this conditioning, the baby fears the rat (C) and even a man whose beard resembles the furry animal (D). (5)

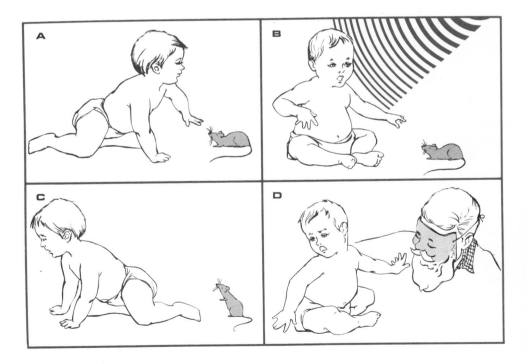

dog, which after one single pairing has become a conditioned stimulus setting off a conditioned reflex.

Conditioned Reflexes and Illness

Some recent experiments in classical conditioning have raised the possibility that the conditioned reflex may be a direct source of psychosomatic illnesses—that is, illnesses in which the physical symptoms seem to have mental and emotional causes. (Some examples of psychosomatic illnesses might be abdominal pains, fainting spells, ulcers, and asthma.) In one experiment, rats were dosed with the drug insulin, which caused a rapid drop in the level of blood sugar and put them into a state of shock. The unconditioned stimulus of insulin was paired with a bright flash of light and of course with the slight pain of the hypodermic needle used to inject the insulin. After a number of pairings the light flash and needle without the insulin put the animals into shock; these had become a conditioned stimulus that was now sufficient to produce the conditioned reflex of a drop in blood sugar and the resulting state of shock (6).

If a bodily reaction as dramatic as the state of shock can be conditioned to a previously neutral stimulus, then presumably many other bodily reflexes can also be conditioned, and perhaps many psychosomatic pains and disorders are simply the result of unfortunate pairings of reflexes and some kind of external events, such as job difficulties or social stresses. Some recent reports by Russian scientists raise the further possibility that the conditioned stimulus may sometimes come from inside the body rather than from the outside. These scientists say that they have managed to condition the salivary reflex of a dog to pressure on the intestinal wall (7)—which would indicate that the organism can learn to respond to one kind of bodily change with other kinds of changes that would otherwise be inexplicable.

John Watson, impressed by the many ways in which classical conditioning can be shown to modify behavior, decided that the conditioned reflex was the basic unit of behavior. Depending on how a person's reflexes had been conditioned, he believed, a given stimulus would always produce the same response—almost as automatically as the unconditioned stimulus of food produces the unconditioned reflex of salivation.

Certainly the reflex and the conditioned reflex constitute one of the important ways in which behavior is modified by learning. And the laws that Pavlov discovered by studying classical conditioning—the principles of reinforcement, extinction, spontaneous recovery, stimulus generalization, and stimulus discrimination—are keys that have unlocked some of the mysteries of learning.

But the reflex, as later investigators have emphasized, is not the only kind of behavior. There is another kind that is perhaps even more important.

The reflex is respondent behavior, a response to a specific stimulus. Another kind of activity in which human beings and other organisms engage is quite different and is known as *operant behavior*.

Operant is an important word, essential to any understanding of how behavior is learned. As a start toward defining it, let us think again about the behavior of the young woman described in Chapter 1.

She wakes, showers, dresses, eats, drives to a parking lot, walks to class, takes notes, feels pleased when she gets her grade. How much of this behavior is reflex action—either unconditioned or conditioned—and how much is something else?

Waking to the sound of the alarm is perhaps a reflex. The flow of saliva and other digestive juices while eating is a reflex. But certainly taking a shower and dressing are not reflex actions, because the "wiring" for human reflexes was established before we had showers or the kind of clothing we wear today. Nor can driving an automobile, walking to a classroom, or taking notes in a class be considered reflexes.

None of these actions is an automatic or even a learned response to some outside stimulus such as a flash of light or a sound. There are undoubtedly stimuli, but they come from the inside, not the outside. The actions seem to be spontaneous. The young woman herself puts them in motion. Instead of having something in the outside environment produce a response, we have here the opposite; the young woman acts on her environment. She "operates" on the world around her, so to speak, and often changes it. Hence the phrase *operant behavior*.

An important example of operant behavior is human speech. There is no outside stimulus that would automatically make anybody say the word *milk*. Even if there were such a stimulus, it would not elicit the same response from all human beings, for where Americans say *milk* Spaniards say *leche* and the French say *lait*. How then do human beings learn to say the word *milk* and all the other thousands of words they use in everyday conversation?

A start toward the answer is provided by the next element of learning.

The simplest and most direct explanation of how operant behavior is modified through learning was provided by the American psychologist B. F. Skinner, who in the 1930's invented the device shown in FIGURE 2.7. The rat was placed in the box and began, as might have been expected, a series of random movements. It sniffed at its new cage, stood up to get a better look, scratched itself, washed itself, moved around, and touched various parts of the cage with its paws.

FIGURE 2.7

The Skinner Box With this simple but ingenious invention, a box in which pressing the bar automatically releases a pellet of food or a drop of water, B. F. Skinner demonstrated many of the rules of operant behavior. For what happens to the rat placed in the box, see the text.

Eventually it pressed the bar, and a pellet of food dropped into the dish. The rat did not even notice the food but continued its random movements as before. Eventually it pressed the bar again, and another pellet dropped. At last it noticed the food, discovered that pressing the bar produced another pellet, and began pressing the bar as fast as it could eat one pellet and get back to the bar (8).

The process by which the rat learned to press the bar to obtain food is called *operant conditioning*. In its random movements the rat "operated" on the box in various ways. One particular kind of operant behavior, pressing the bar, had a satisfying result; it produced food. Using the same language that is applied to classical conditioning, we say that the presentation of the food constituted a reinforcement of the bar-pressing behavior. The law of operant conditioning is that operant behavior that is reinforced tends to be repeated, while operant behavior that is not reinforced takes place only at random intervals or is abandoned.

Operant Extinction, Recovery, Generalization, and Discrimination

Operant conditioning follows the same laws that Pavlov discovered for classical conditioning. If reinforcement is withdrawn, the conditioned operant behavior goes through the process of extinction; if we stop rewarding the rat with food when it presses the bar, it eventually stops pressing it. After a rest period away from the Skinner box, however, it will again start pressing the bar, demonstrating that conditioned operant behavior, like the conditioned reflex, obeys the law of spontaneous recovery.

The manner in which operant conditioning follows the laws of stimulus generalization and stimulus discrimination has been best shown in experiments with pigeons placed in a variation of the Skinner box. Once a pigeon

59

has learned to obtain food by pecking at a white button, it will also peck at a red or green button. But, if only the operant behavior toward the white button is reinforced, the pigeon will quickly learn to discriminate among the three stimuli, pecking at the white button and ignoring the red and green.

The Shaping of Operants

Operant conditioning begins with what is called *random* behavior—purposeless actions such as the movements of a baby in his crib or the babbling sounds that are eventually refined into human speech. A particular form of random behavior is reinforced and becomes a *conditioned operant*—a form of behavior with which the organism operates on its environment *to obtain a desired result*.

In the Skinner box the situation is simple. Pressing the bar is random behavior through which the rat more or less stumbles upon the secret of obtaining food. The manner in which animals and human beings learn to perform more complicated actions through operant conditioning involves the principle known as *shaping*, which can best be explained by describing another experiment performed with a somewhat different kind of Skinner box. In this case a pigeon was the subject, and an attempt was made to condition the pigeon to peck at a black dot inside a white circle on one wall of the box, as shown in FIGURE 2.8. To a pigeon, this action is quite unnatural. Left to its own devices, the pigeon might never have stumbled upon the action. But its operant behavior was shaped into the desired form step by step.

Making its random movements, the pigeon moved about and eventually faced the white circle. This behavior was reinforced by the presentation of food. When the pigeon again faced the circle, reinforcement was repeated.

FIGURE 2.8   *Shaping A Pigeon's Behavior*   At first the pigeon merely looks about the box at random (A). When it faces the circle (B), it receives the reinforcing stimulus of food in the tray below (C). The next time the pigeon approaches the circle (D), it is again rewarded with food. Later the

A   B   C

The next time this happened, however, reinforcement was withheld. Not until the pigeon happened to take a step toward the circle while facing it was the behavior reinforced. Later reinforcement was withheld until the pigeon pecked at the white circle, and finally it was withheld until the pigeon pecked at the black dot. Thus the pigeon was led to the end result. A simple free operant—facing by chance toward the white circle—was "shaped" into a conditioned operant that for a pigeon is extremely complicated and difficult.

Anyone who tries to teach a dog to carry a newspaper from the front door to its master is engaged in the process of shaping. You start with the fact that the dog sometimes grasps objects in its mouth and shape this one rather simple form of operant behavior into a much more complicated process. As shown in FIGURE 2.9, modern animal trainers achieve some striking results with shaping; they have taught bears to ride bicycles and raccoons to play basketball. People who watch trained animals sometimes feel sorry for them, imagining that they must have been subjected to brutal punishment to force them to learn their stunts. But the fact is that most modern animal training is done with shaping, based on the principle of operant conditioning and with food as the reinforcing stimulus. The animals' only discomfort lies in the fact that they have to be kept hungry during the training and at the time of their performance, so that the food will actually serve as a reinforcing stimulus.

Reinforcement as the Key to Learning

As was mentioned earlier, the basic law of operant conditioning is that behavior that is reinforced tends to be repeated, while behavior that is not reinforced takes place only at random intervals or is abandoned. Thus rein-

pigeon is not rewarded until it approaches closer to the circle (E), and still later it is not rewarded until it pecks at the circle (F). The next step, not illustrated here, will be to withhold reward until the pigeon pecks at the small black dot inside the circle.

D **E** **F**

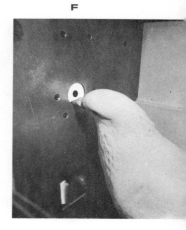

FIGURE 2.9   *Some Results of Shaping*   Among the accomplishments of animal trainers, using the technique of shaping and the reward of food, are a bear that rides a bicycle, porpoises that leap high in the air in perfect formation, a cat that can turn on a lamp, and a raccoon that plays basketball.

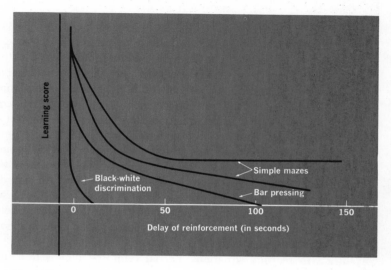

FIGURE 2.10   *The Effect of Delayed Reinforcement* The curves show the results of four different experiments in learning by rats, in which the food used as a reinforcing stimulus was presented immediately to some of the animals, after a delay of from several seconds to two minutes or more to the others. In all four experiments even a small delay of reinforcement was found to greatly reduce the amount of learning that took place. (9; summarizing data, 10, 11, 12, 13)

forcement is the key to operant conditioning. The amount of learning that takes place depends in large part upon the kind of reinforcement that is provided and the timing of the reinforcement.

DELAY OF REINFORCEMENT The simplest aspect of reinforcement has to do with the length of time that elapses between the operant act and the presentation of the reinforcing stimulus. The sooner the reinforcing stimulus is provided, the greater is its effect. As is illustrated in FIGURE 2.10, even very short delays in reinforcement have been found to greatly reduce or to eliminate learning in the operant conditioning of animals.

This principle has many implications. If you want to teach a dog a trick, you must reward it immediately after its successful attempts, not two hours later. In school, it would be much better if each new accomplishment could be rewarded immediately with a good grade or the teacher's approval. One reason some students do not improve in their ability to master a subject is that there is usually such a long delay between learning and the grade it produces on the next examination or at the end of the school term.

SCHEDULE OF REINFORCEMENT Another important principle of reinforcement can be demonstrated by placing two rats in Skinner boxes and rewarding them on different schedules. One rat receives a food pellet every time it presses the bar. The other rat receives food every fourth time. The second rat is thus on a schedule of what is called *partial reinforcement* or *intermittent reinforcement*—receiving a reward not every time but only sometimes. Which kind of reinforcement is more effective, constant or partial?

One way to answer this question is to stop giving the two rats any reinforcement at all and observe how long it takes before they stop pressing the bar. When this is done, it is found that extinction is much faster for the animal that was on a schedule of constant reinforcement than for the animal that was on a schedule of partial reinforcement. An experiment of this type, using mazes rather than a Skinner box, gave the results illustrated in FIGURE 2.11—a convincing demonstration that operant behavior conditioned by partial reinforcement persists longer than behavior conditioned by constant reinforcement.

In real-life situations, partial reinforcement is the rule rather than the exception. The rat that has learned to seek food in certain ways will not succeed every time. The human baby who has learned to say "milk" will not get milk every time, but only on occasions when his mother is present

FIGURE 2.11   *Partial Versus Constant Reinforcement*   In this experiment in maze running by rats, some of the animals were on a schedule of constant reinforcement (100 percent). Others received partial reinforcement—after 30, 50, or 80 percent of their successful trials. Once they had learned to run the maze quickly, they were given twenty trials without any reinforcement at all. Note that the process of extinction during these twenty trials was fastest for the animals that had received constant reinforcement and that the animals on a 30 percent schedule of partial reinforcement resisted extinction the most. (14)

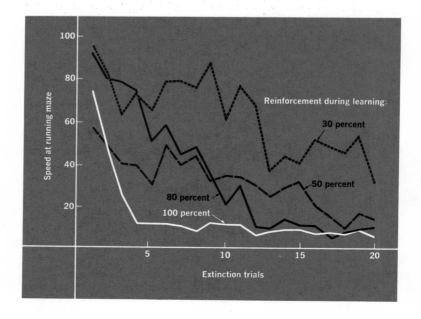

and perhaps not always even then. The boy who swings the baseball bat does not get a home run every time. In adult life, the persistence of behavior learned through partial reinforcement helps explain why a woman who once won a consolation prize in a slogan contest will keep entering contests for years without further reward and why a man who once won a daily double at the race track keeps trying despite a long succession of losing days. As golfers say, all it takes is one good drive or one long putt to keep a person coming back for more.

As another experiment by Skinner has shown, partial reinforcement may also account for a good deal of behavior that does not make much sense. In this experiment a pigeon was placed in the Skinner box, which was now arranged so that food was presented on an arbitrary time schedule. When the moment decided on in advance by the experimenter arrived, the food was presented, regardless of what the pigeon was doing at the time. Under these circumstances the pigeon learned some very foolish things. One pigeon learned to peck at its tail feathers, another to swing around in a sort of circle. One pigeon learned to hop sideways and did so 10,000 times before it at last gave up.

In human terms, we can say that the pigeons had acquired superstitions: they "believed" that certain behavior would get them food when in reality the behavior had nothing to do with the food. Because behavior learned through partial reinforcement tends to persist so long, they continued to practice their superstitions for a long time. Human superstitions probably have the same kind of origin. One widely held superstition may have been started by a small boy who fell into a mud puddle and remembered that a black cat had just crossed his path and another by a little girl who found a gold piece in the road just after she had seen a clover with one too many leaves.

The strength of partial reinforcement also accounts for the persistence of behavior that did once serve a purpose but no longer does so. Children, surrounded by adults who are so much bigger and more powerful than they, sometimes manage to get their own way through temper tantrums or through shouting and often continue this kind of behavior in their own adulthoods, when it is unnecessary and inappropriate. Some children succeed at times in avoiding punishment by assuming a very humble and apologetic attitude and, even when they have become adults, continue to behave as if other people were older and stronger than they. Partial reinforcement is one reason old habits, even bad ones, are often so hard to break.

KINDS OF REINFORCEMENT   In the operant conditioning of animals, reinforcement is a simple matter. As long as the animal is hungry, food always serves as an effective reinforcing stimulus. To a thirsty animal, water is a good reinforcing stimulus. In the case of human beings, however, it is often

FIGURE 2.12

Learning with a Teaching Machine An elementary school class studies with the help of teaching machines. With this type of machine the student who has correctly answered a question turns the knob to the next step in the instruction.

difficult to say what will serve as a reinforcing stimulus. The woman student whose behavior has been followed has seldom been hungry or thirsty for any long period of time. The many kinds of operant conditioning that have taken place in her life were hardly reinforced with a pellet of food or a drop of water.

As a generalization, it can be said that anything the organism finds rewarding can serve as a reinforcing stimulus. But what is a rewarding event? What are the rewards that have reinforced the young woman's behavior or the behavior of any other human being?

This is not an easy question to answer, for what is a reward to one person is not necessarily a reward to another. Take, for example, the teaching machine shown in FIGURE 2.12, which has come into wide use in recent years. When using a teaching machine, the student studies a subject in a series of brief steps. At the end of each step a question is presented to the student; he writes in the answer, and the machine immediately tells him if he was right. The assumption behind the teaching machine is that getting the right answer is in itself a reinforcing stimulus for the student and will lead him to go on and learn additional right answers as additional reinforcements. Many students do learn quickly with the teaching machine. But other students do not. To them, getting the right answer is apparently not a sufficent reward.

We could not say what particular rewards have served as reinforcing stimuli for the woman student without knowing a great deal about her. Her reinforcements—as is true of all human beings—could have been provided by almost anything. A child's behavior can be reinforced by food, candy, a parent's smile, a teacher's kindly tone of voice, or the envy his playmates show when he is trying to climb a high fence. The behavior of adult human beings is reinforced by the favorable regard of their husbands or wives, by the respect of their friends and neighbors, and by money or by getting one's name in the newspaper.

Many of the reinforcing stimuli for human beings, as a matter of fact, come from inside ourselves. The young woman may have gone through all the complicated shaping of operant behavior necessary for many of her skills with no more reinforcement than was provided by the feeling of self-satisfaction generated by each successful performance of a new step in the process. People practice new techniques of golf for hours at a time with no more reinforcement than is afforded by the pleasure of executing a good shot or watching a long putt roll into the hole. And people donate money anonymously to charities with no more reinforcement than is provided by the inner glow of doing a good deed.

The only completely accurate definition is this: *A reinforcing event is anything that strengthens and induces repetitions of the behavior that preceded it.* This is hardly more than saying that a reinforcing stimulus is anything that provides reinforcement. But even though the formal definition must be unsatisfactory, a good deal is known about the various kinds of reinforcing events.

SECONDARY REINFORCEMENT   Much of the variety in human reinforcement stems from a fact that can be demonstrated in another kind of experiment with a rat and the Skinner box. In this experiment, before being put into the box, the rat is kept in an ordinary cage and is fed food one pellet at a time. Each time it gets a pellet of food a buzzer sounds. This situation, you will note, is much like the Pavlov experiment in conditioning the salivary reflex to a conditioned stimulus. But in this case we are not interested in whether the rat will begin to salivate to the sound of the buzzer alone. We are interested only in what will happen when it is put into the Skinner box, which is now rearranged so that pressing the bar does not release a pellet of food but instead sounds a buzzer.

What happens is that, as before, the rat makes his random free operant movements, eventually presses the bar, and hears the buzzer. And now it turns out that the buzzer serves as a very effective reinforcing stimulus. The rat is quickly conditioned to press the bar by the reward of hearing the buzzer.

Food, for the rat and indeed for any hungry organism, is a *primary reinforcing stimulus,* something that is in itself rewarding to the organism. The buzzer is a *secondary reinforcing stimulus,* something that has become rewarding through association with a primary reinforcement.

FIGURE **2.13**

Secondary Reinforcement of a Chimpanzee
The chimpanzee has been operantly conditioned by the secondary reinforcement of a poker chip, which he now drops into a vending machine to obtain the primary reinforcement of food.

Many experiments have been performed in which animals have been operantly conditioned through secondary reinforcement. Chimpanzees, for example, have been conditioned not only with primary reinforcement provided by food but also with secondary reinforcement provided by poker chips that they can put into a sort of vending machine that delivers food when a chip is dropped into a slot, as shown in FIGURE 2.13.

The human parallel, of course, is that for a child jelly beans may provide strong reinforcement, and money, at the beginning, no reinforcement at all. But, since money can buy jelly beans, it becomes a secondary reinforcing stimulus through association.

Many of the things that human beings consider rewards seem to acquire their reinforcement value in this way. For example, it may well be that to the infant the primary reinforcing stimuli of food and fondling become associated with the sight of his mother, the person who gives him these things, who therefore becomes a secondary reinforcing stimulus. The sight of the mother then becomes associated with the sound of her voice, and the sound of her voice becomes associated with the particular words she uses. The mere fact that she is present somewhere on the premises becomes associated with the physical surroundings of the home—and at this point just being home or returning home from a strange place can provide reinforcement. In later years the home can become associated with the community, and the community with certain standards of good citizenship for which the community seems to stand. All these are called *higher order reinforcements,* meaning that they are even further removed from primary reinforcement than is secondary reinforcement.

The possible chain of reinforcements, leading one to another, is almost endless. One higher order stimulus that has helped condition our young woman to take her morning shower and to dress as she does and to take her notes and pass her courses may very well be some notion of community approval going all the way back, through a complex series of associations, to the original primary reinforcements of food and care supplied by her mother.

OPERANT ESCAPE AND AVOIDANCE   Among the things that the organism can find rewarding and that can thus provide reinforcement for operant conditioning is the escape from an unpleasant situation. Again we are indebted to the Skinner box for the simplest and most convincing demonstration.

This time let us arrange the box so that the rat is standing on an electric grill. When current flows through the grill, it produces a mild but thoroughly unpleasant shock. We place the rat in the box and turn on the current. The rat makes its random movements—now much more rapidly because of its discomfort—and happens to press the bar. The result, instead of a food pellet, is an end to the shock. Under these circumstances the rat soon learns to press the bar to escape from the shock.

Avoidance of as well as escape from an unpleasant situation can provide reinforcement, as was demonstrated in an experiment in which a dog was placed in a box that had two compartments, separated by a hurdle. A light was turned on, and ten seconds later an electric shock was administered. By jumping over the hurdle into the other compartment, the dog could get away from the shock. After a few trials the animal learned to avoid the shock by leaping the hurdle when the light went on. This conditioned operant behavior was remarkably resistant to extinction. Even though the dog never again felt a shock, it would continue day after day to leap into the other compartment when the light went on (15).

A great deal of human behavior represents some form of operant escape or avoidance. For example, a young child finds the presence of a stranger in the home distasteful and seeks to escape. He makes a series of random movements and eventually hides his head in his mother's lap, thus shutting out the sight and sound of the stranger. Having once found hiding from an unpleasant situation to be successful, he may be inclined to withdraw from all unpleasant situations and turn into the kind of adult who stays away from social functions and remains as inconspicuous as possible at the most inconspicuous possible kind of job.

Defenses against anxiety are a common form of operant escape or avoidance. When the woman student is made anxious by criticism, it was noted, she becomes apologetic. This apologetic behavior is perhaps a conditioned operant that in some way served as a successful defense against anxiety in the past.

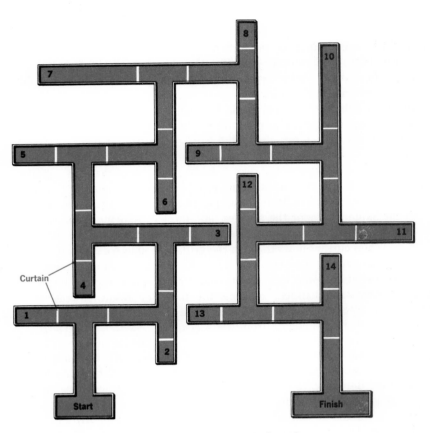

A Maze Used in Learning Experiments   This is the maze used in the
experiment described in the text, in which some animals received the
reinforcement of food at the end of the correct pathway and others did
not. Learning in a maze is measured by the ability to follow the path
from start to finish with a minimum of waste motion going into the
fourteen blind alleys. Each time the animal goes into a blind alley, it
is counted as an error. (16)

FIGURE **2.14**

IS REINFORCEMENT ESSENTIAL?   Adding to the complications of defining
reinforcement is the possibility that, despite everything that has been said
about its importance, learning may take place without it. In the laboratory
this question has been raised by the following experiment.

Three groups of rats were placed in a maze, the kind of learning device
shown in FIGURE 2.14. Group 1 always found food at the end of the maze.
For this group the reinforcing stimulus was obvious. The operant behavior
to which the rats were conditioned was running a direct route from the
start of the maze to the finish. Their progress in learning was measured by
counting the number of errors they made by going into blind alleys. As

might be expected, group 1 did better every day. In the original experiment of this type, the group 1 rats made about ten errors the first day but only about four errors on the tenth day.

Group 2 never found food at the end of the maze. These rats were simply placed in the maze and permitted to move around in any way they chose for a given period of time. Group 3 was treated the same way as group 2 for the first ten days. On the eleventh day, however, and on every day thereafter, food was placed at the end of the maze. The results of the experiment are shown in FIGURE 2.15. Even in just wandering around the maze, without reinforcement, the group 3 rats apparently had learned a great deal about the correct path. As soon as reinforcement was provided, they began to demonstrate their knowledge.

The kind of learning that the group 3 rats did on the first ten days is called *latent learning*—that is, learning that takes place but lies latent, not being put into overt performance until reinforcement is provided. It is also called *incidental learning,* meaning that it takes place casually, almost as if by accident. The rats received no apparent reinforcement, but they learned anyway.

In another experiment, a light was flashed in view of a dog. At the same time a buzzer was sounded. Except for this pairing of the two different stimuli, nothing happened. The dog made no response. Neither of the stimuli was attached to any kind of reflex or operant behavior. After 200 pairings, however, this part of the experiment ended and a new phase began. Now,

Maze Learning With and Without Reinforcement   The graph shows the progress at learning the maze in FIGURE 2.14 made by three groups of rats under different conditions of reinforcement. For the meaning of these results, see the text. (16)

FIGURE **2.15**

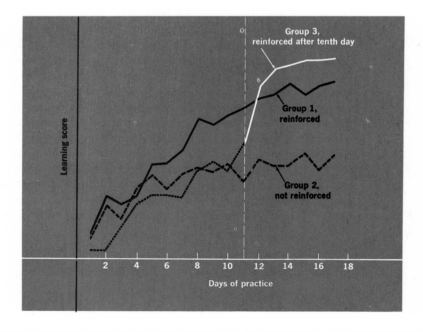

when the light flashed, the dog received an electric shock on one paw—which served as an unconditioned stimulus for the unconditioned reflex of pulling the paw away. As the principles of classical conditioning would predict, the dog soon was conditioned to pull its paw away when the light was flashed, regardless of whether or not it felt a shock. Next, the light was omitted but the buzzer was sounded. Again the dog pulled away. Apparently the mere pairing of the two stimuli, the light and the buzzer, had led to some kind of association between them (17), so that they were interchangeable as conditioned stimuli for pulling away from the shock.

In everyday human affairs there are many examples of latent or incidental learning. A friend takes you on an automobile ride to the nearby city of Smithville. You have no intention of ever returning to Smithville. You make no effort to learn the route. Still, if the occasion ever arises when you yourself have to drive to Smithville, you find that you remember the way, at least to some extent. Wandering through the downtown district of the city in which you live, you pass a shop that has pipes and smoking tobacco in the window. As a nonsmoker, you take no interest in the shop. Later, when you decide to become a pipe smoker, you find that you remember the location of the shop.

REINFORCEMENT AND ATTENTION   The problem of reinforcement, as the preceding discussion indicates, has always been a puzzle. At one time it was generally believed that all primary reinforcing stimuli were satisfactions of the biological drives, notably hunger and thirst. To the hungry rat, food provides reinforcement; so does sugar water that substitutes for his usual food; so does water sweetened with saccharine, which tastes like sugar water. The idea of secondary and higher order reinforcement readily accounts for the fact that saccharine water can become a reward to the rat.

There also seems to be a possibility, however, that saccharine water serves as a reinforcing stimulus because of the sheer pleasure—unrelated to biological drives—of tasting something sweet. There is evidence, indeed, that there may be some kind of "pleasure center," deep in the brain, that plays a prominent role in reinforcement. In one experiment, an electrode was planted in this part of a rat's brain. The rat was then put in a Skinner box, hooked up so that pressure on the bar sent a mild electrical stimulus through the electrode. The rat was operantly conditioned to press the bar through the reinforcement provided by this kind of brain stimulation. Indeed, when given a choice, a hungry rat sometimes preferred the brain stimulation to food (18).

One recent line of speculation is based on the observation that the stimuli that are called reinforcements generally seem to have an effect on the *attention* of the organism. For example, in Pavlov's classical conditioning experiment, the food that serves as the unconditioned stimulus for the salivary reflex appears to attract the dog's attention to the general situation. It makes him sit up and take notice, so to speak; it tunes him in to what is also occurring at the time or has just occurred, such as the sound of the metronome. In operant conditioning in the Skinner box, the arrival of the food pellet may similarly operate to attract attention. The idea that attention may be closely related to reinforcement in human learning fits in neatly with something that the history of mankind seems to show: that human beings are lively and curious animals who constantly exhibit a keen interest in their world and their fellows.

The basic building blocks of behavior have now been described: 1) the simple and unlearned reflex, built into the organism's "wiring"; 2) the way the unconditioned reflex can be modified and turned into a conditioned reflex; 3) operant behavior; and 4) the wide range of behavior learned through operant conditioning. Now the question must be asked: When we learn, *what* do we learn?

THE UNITS THAT ARE LEARNED

At first thought, this seems like a simple question with an obvious answer. You may be inclined to say: "That's easy; we learn to *do* something." Pavlov's dog learns to salivate to the sound of a metronome; the rat in the Skinner box learns to press the bar to get food; the woman student learns to cook breakfast and drive an automobile. This answer is correct as far as it goes, but it does not explain the entire learning process.

To demonstrate why this is true, let us begin with another experiment in simple conditioning. Suppose that we put a dog in a harness like Pavlov's, arranged so that one hind paw rests on a metal plate. We pass an electric current through the plate, and the dog responds by pulling its paw away. Now we dose the dog's leg with curare. This is a well-known drug used by South American Indians on the darts they shoot through blow guns. Curare paralyzes the nerves that cause muscle movement; in sufficient dosage it kills the victim by immobilizing his heart and the muscles of his lungs. With a smaller dose, we can prevent any movement of the dog's leg without killing the animal.

While the dog's leg is immobilized, we pair a high-pitched sound with a shock and present a low-pitched sound without administering a shock. The dog hears the tones and sometimes feels the shock but *cannot pull its paw away*. It makes no movement in response to either the shock or the high-pitched sound. Nothing has happened, so far as we can see. Under these circumstances, does any conditioning take place? Does the dog learn that the high-pitched tone is associated with shock?

If we go on the theory that learning is always a matter of doing something, we would have to say no. But, when we let the curare wear off and then sound the tones, we are in for a surprise. When the dog hears the high tone it pulls its paw away; when it hears the low tone it does not. The behavior of pulling the paw away has been conditioned to the high tone even though the action was never taken during the conditioning process (19).

The experiment is an indication that even in the simplest form of conditioning the actual physical response is not always essential to learning. What the dog has learned is not the overt action but some kind of invisible and rather mysterious connection between the unconditioned stimulus of the shock and the conditioned stimulus of the tone.

Learning Without Overt Action

For a demonstration of how human beings often learn without any kind of overt action, you can try your own experiment, using a word such as *syzygy*. This is an unusual word, seldom heard by the average person. It is pronounced siz-i-jee, with the *siz* as in *scissors*, the *i* as in *it*, and the *jee* as in *jeep*; it means "a joining together." As your experiment, say to a friend: "Don't say anything. Just listen. The word is *syzygy*. Don't say anything." Then change the subject. A half hour later, ask your friend: "What word did I say a while ago?" Almost surely, he will answer correctly, "Syzygy."

Even though he had never heard the word before and took no overt action when you first said the word to him, he managed to learn it. Again, as in the case of the dog with the paralyzed paw, some kind of connection was set up inside him. It was this connection, not an overt response, that was learned.

Much human learning takes place in this way. A small child learns the meaning of words long before he learns to speak them; he can point to his nose or his mouth while still unable to say either of those words. An older child watches a moving picture or a television program and several days later, at play, acts out one of the scenes. An adult watches a plumber repair a leaky faucet, does nothing at the time, but weeks later can fix the faucet himself. All of us, if we keep an observant eye on our behavior, will find ourselves doing things that we saw one of our parents do years ago. We did not repeat our parents' behavior at the time; we took no overt action at all; but some sort of lasting connection was formed inside us, and we act that way now.

Learning by Imitation

The acquisition of skills and habits by watching another person is called *learning by imitation* or, as some psychologists prefer, *learning through modeling*. It is a complex and high-level form of learning that is characteristic of the human organism, although it is displayed to a lesser extent by some animals as well.

Although we learn speech in part through operant conditioning, as has been pointed out, we learn more of it by imitation: we pronounce words as our parents did, and we copy their sentence structure and grammar. We learn to write by imitating the strokes the teacher makes on the blackboard. We copy the movements of more experienced baseball players, knitters, and painters.

Much of our social behavior is learned by imitation. Note, for example, the behavior of the children in FIGURE 2.16, which illustrates one of the best known of all experiments in this area (20). These children are displaying aggressive responses that they did not learn through classical conditioning or through operant conditioning but by watching a moving picture of an adult behaving that way.

Learning by imitation occupies an important place in the study of psy-

FIGURE2.16

Imitation of Aggression Why are the boy and girl above acting so aggressively toward the toy? And why does their aggressive behavior take such a remarkably similar form? The answer is that they were imitating the behavior of a model—the woman to the right, who had behaved in exactly this fashion in a movie they had watched.

chology, especially in such fields as development, personality, and social behavior. For obviously we learn a great many things by imitation, and the question then becomes: Whom do we imitate, and why? Clinical psychologists who work in schools and communities are well aware that the delinquent underachiever is imitating the conduct of one kind of model and the well-behaved and ambitious student the conduct of quite a different model.

The Learning "Connection"

All learning depends upon association. Some kind of connection has to be formed. What is the nature of this connection? Presumably it is some kind of change in the nervous system and especially the brain, which is an enormously complicated switchboard of nerve fibers. As will be seen in Chapter 7, certain tiny but probably significant chemical changes seem to take place in or between nerve fibers when learning occurs. But little is known about the actual physical nature of learning connections. We have to be content to describe the way in which they operate and wait for future investigations to tell us exactly how and why.

One word that is often used to describe the learning connection is *engram*—a rather vague word that means some kind of lasting trace or impression formed in living protoplasm by a stimulus. Or the connection can be called an association or a bond. The important thing is that there is a relationship between an external stimulus and some kind of central unit in the brain, to which various names have been applied. One increasingly popular term is *mediational unit*—a term derived from the fact that the learning connections, whatever their exact nature may be, act as intermediaries between environment and behavior. An event in the world, a stimulus, excites the nervous system. Somehow the result is to set up a mediational unit, a go-between, which becomes a more or less permanent part of the organism. At any time, immediately or in the future, the mediational unit can go to work and produce behavior. The chain of events is *stimulus* to *mediational unit* to *behavior*.

Kinds of Mediational Units

One kind of mediational unit is called an *image*, which is the recollection of a sensory experience. You can close your eyes and "see" the face of someone you know well or the front of the house you lived in for many years. You can "hear" a song you know well. You can imagine the taste of a hamburger, the smell of onions, or the feel of a pinprick.

Another type of mediational unit is called a *symbol.* The most common example is language. All words are symbols. *Food* is a symbol for the things we eat. *Water* is a symbol for the combination of hydrogen and oxygen that falls as rain or flows through the pipes of our houses. *Page* is a symbol for this piece of printed paper that you are reading, and *book* is a symbol for the collected volume of pages.

There are many other kinds of symbols. The skull and crossbones on a medicine bottle is a symbol for poison. The cross is a symbol of the church. A big automobile or a mink coat is a symbol of success and wealth. Mathematics is a collection of symbols. To find out how many apples there will be in each group if ninety-nine apples are divided into three parts, we do not have to find ninety-nine apples and make three piles. We can get the answer by using numbers as a symbol for apples.

Even animals, which do not use words or mathematics, seem to learn symbols, as was demonstrated many years ago in the experiment illustrated in FIGURE 2.17. The experiment showed that animals still went to the right

FIGURE **2.17**   *The Delayed Reaction Experiment*   An animal is operantly conditioned to go to whichever of three doorways is lighted, because food is always found behind the lighted doorway but not behind the other two. After the animal has been conditioned, it is restrained behind a wire barrier. The light is flashed briefly, then turned off. After a delay of several seconds or several minutes the barrier is removed. The question is whether the animal will still go to the right doorway. For the answer, see the text. (21)

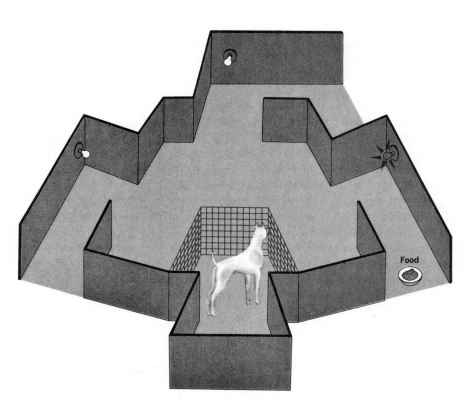

doorway even after a delay, although the amount of delay that they could withstand varied greatly. In the original experiment the most delay possible for a rat was ten seconds, for a cat eighteen seconds, and for a dog three minutes (21). To avoid the possibility that the animals merely poised themselves physically to move toward the right doorway as soon as the barrier was removed, they were turned around while behind the barrier. Thus the experiment seemed to indicate that they had learned some kind of symbol that enabled them to go to the doorway as soon as they had the opportunity.

In commonsensical terms, we might say that the animals in this experiment *remembered* which of the three doorways was the right one. Memory is indeed the everyday term that people use for mediational units. But *memory* is a very inexact word. For example, can we call the rat's ability to go to the right doorway a matter of memory when it persists for only ten seconds at the most? Can we be sure that a rat or a cat or a dog really has such a thing as a memory? In the case of human learning, what about such matters as higher order reinforcements? Our woman student may behave as she does to gain community approval, a reinforcement that goes back, through a complex series of associations, to the original primary reinforcing stimulus of food provided by her mother. She is not conscious of these associations and certainly could not remember how they were formed. How then can we say that the reinforcement effect of community approval represents a memory?

Mediational unit is a term that gets around these difficulties (and also satisfies both the psychologists who still lean toward John Watson's more or less mechanical view of human behavior and the psychologists who lean toward the William James emphasis on mental life). The definition of the term must be somewhat long-winded: *A mediational unit is some sort of more or less permanent change inside the organism. It is a connection established through learning between a stimulus, on the one hand, and, on the other hand, other units or acts; it serves as an intermediary between the stimulus and immediate or future behavior.*

With this definition in mind, let us now examine some of the various categories of learning—the kinds of units that are learned.

SETS AND PERCEPTUAL EXPECTATIONS   Let us imagine that someone has created ten different crossword puzzles, all of which have been proved through testing to be of exactly equal difficulty. If you start solving these puzzles, you will find that you do better on the tenth one than on the first one. This is not because the tenth puzzle is any easier—as can be shown by having someone else solve the ten puzzles in reverse order—but because you have acquired the mediational unit known as a set. You are set to solve puzzles. In a sense, you have learned to learn.

Sets usually are a help in behavior. Study habits, for example, are a form of set. The more you study, if you do so with any kind of efficiency, the better you get at studying. A lawyer is better in the courtroom on his tenth appearance than on his first. An architect does a better job of designing his tenth house than his first one.

But sets also can hinder behavior, as happens in a light-hearted experiment invented many years ago. Spell the word *MacPherson* for a friend and ask him to pronounce it. Next spell *MacTavish, MacPhail,* and *MacDonald.* Then spell *machinery.* Often your friend will pronounce it "MacHinery," because he is set to react with the *Mac* sound. (The role of sets will be discussed in detail in Chapter 4, "Efficiency in Learning.")

One particular kind of set that plays an important role in the branch of psychology called perception deserves special mention. Very few of the world's sights and sounds really surprise an adult human being. We know what a steak or an apple is going to taste like before we bite in. We know in advance that a tweed jacket will feel rough to the touch, that velvet will feel smooth, and that snow will feel cold and wet. We are set for metal to be hard, a whistle to sound shrill. These sets are called *perceptual expectations.* The stimuli that excite our sense organs have resulted in certain kinds of awareness, called perceptions, in the past, and we fully expect them to do the same thing again. Our perceptual expectations are so strong, indeed, that they often influence and distort what we see or hear. (This will be discussed in detail in Chapter 5, "Perception.")

WORDS AND LANGUAGE   Of all the mediational units involved in human behavior, the words with which we label all the aspects of our environment are perhaps the most important. We can act as readily to the sound of the word *fire* as to the actual sight or feel of fire and to the word *food* as to the sight of food. No other organism behaves in this manner. Although some of the lower animals seem to communicate with each other in a primitive way, with certain sounds standing for the presence of danger or of food, human beings are the only organisms that have been capable of developing an elaborate language system. (This is one of the topics of Chapter 6, "Language, Thinking, and Problem Solving.")

CONCEPTS   Using words helps us arrive at another useful mediational unit called the *concept,* which is the grouping together of objects or events that have certain features in common. The word *shirt* is a concept that includes many things, ranging from a bright-colored, short-sleeved sports shirt to the fancy kind of white shirt worn with formal tails; what all these have in common is that they are worn by men over the upper part of the body. *Men's wear* is a concept that includes not only shirts but also trousers, jackets, suits, and neckties worn by men. *Clothing* is a concept that includes not only the things worn by men but also those worn by women and children.

Animals seem to be able to form some kinds of concepts. Rats, for example, can learn to distinguish triangles from other kinds of geometrical figures; they will learn that food is always found behind a three-sided figure, regardless of what kind of triangle it happens to be. But for animals this kind of learning is slow and laborious. With the help of words, human beings form concepts easily and use them to advantage in the mental process called thinking. (This is also discussed in Chapter 6.)

MOTIVES AND STANDARDS   The effect of motivation has already been discussed as one reason the behavior of the woman student differed so much from the behavior of the young man in her class. Like other mediational units, *motives* are acquired through learning and affect behavior in many ways. Closely related to motives are *standards*, which are the rules we set for our own behavior. All of us acquire certain standards of honesty, generosity, bravery, dignity, and masculinity or femininity. Some of us have high standards; we demand a great deal of ourselves. Others have lower standards; we are satisfied with less. But, for all of us, standards have a considerable influence, because we feel good when we live up to our standards and bad when we do not. (Chapter 9, "Motives")

EMOTIONS   In the human baby, stimuli that automatically set off the internal reflexes associated with crying and unpleasant feelings include a sudden loud noise (or some other intense and unexpected change in stimulus level, such as a bright light) and the sensation of falling. The internal reflexes associated with smiling, babbling, and feelings of pleasure seem to be set off in the baby by sensations of physical comfort, such as being well-fed, dry, and warm.

Through learning, these internal reflexes that seem close to emotions become attached to stimuli that would not have caused any emotional response at all in the baby—for example, to the sight of a rival, a teacher, a boss, someone we love, a newspaper headline, the thought of an approaching examination. Moreover, the emotional feelings that result from the internal bodily changes are themselves the product of learning. The emotions of the human adult are complex mediational units that are aroused by a combination of internal sensations and the environment of the moment and that are perceived as feelings of fear, anger, joy, grief, and so on. (Chapter 10, "Emotions")

All emotions have a profound effect upon behavior, especially the emotion of *anxiety*. Some psychologists, in fact, believe that much of human behavior—including work, hobbies, social life, and relationships inside the family—is largely an attempt to relieve anxiety. (Chapter 11, "Frustration and Conflict")

ATTITUDES   All of us, as we grow from infancy to adulthood, acquire many mediational units called *attitudes*—that is, well-defined and emotionally tinged ways in which we tend to regard such things as capitalism, communism, other nations, political parties, the other people in our communities, the police, the church, children, men as opposed to women, and women as opposed to men.

Some of our attitudes take the interesting and sometimes dangerous form of *prejudices*, which means that they are fixed and unyielding and likely to persist even in the face of strong factual evidence that they are incorrect. Attitudes and prejudices are of special significance in influencing our behavior toward other people and as members of the society in which we live. (Chapter 16, "Social Psychology")

These, then, are some of the categories of learning—the mediational units we acquire through experience, in accordance with the principles of learning that have been described in this chapter. As future chapters of this book will show, the basic subject matter of psychology is 1) how we learn these units, 2) how they function and interact, and 3) the kinds of behavior that result.

SUMMARY

1. Much of the behavior of lower organisms represents the operation of *instincts,* which are inborn patterns of activity. Most human behavior, however, is learned.
2. One basic element in learning is the *reflex,* an unlearned and inborn *response* to a *stimulus* (which is defined as any form of energy capable of exciting the nervous system).
3. Through learning, a reflex can become attached to a stimulus that did not originally cause the reflex. This process, first demonstrated when Pavlov "taught" a dog to respond to a sound with the salivary reflex originally caused by the presence of food in the mouth, is called *classical conditioning.*
4. In classical conditioning the stimulus that naturally causes the reflex is called the *unconditioned stimulus.* The previously neutral stimulus to which the reflex becomes attached is called the *conditioned stimulus.* The original reflex is called the *unconditioned reflex,* and the response to the conditioned stimulus is called the *conditioned reflex.*
5. The pairing of the unconditioned stimulus and the conditioned stimulus is called *reinforcement.* When reinforcement is withdrawn, the condi-

tioned reflex tends to disappear—a process called *extinction*. After a rest period, however, it tends to reappear—a process called *spontaneous recovery*.

6. When a reflex has been conditioned to one stimulus, it is also likely to be aroused by similar stimuli—a process called *stimulus generalization*. Through further training, however, the organism can learn to respond to a particular conditioned stimulus but not to other stimuli even when they are very similar—a process called *stimulus discrimination*.

7. Another basic element in learning is *operant behavior*, such as the random, purposeless actions of a rat in its cage or a human baby in its crib.

8. Through learning, operant behavior can become attached to a specific stimulus. This process is called *operant conditioning*. The learned behavior is called a *conditioned operant*, meaning a type of behavior with which the organism "operates" on its environment to obtain a desired result.

9. The learning of complicated tasks through operant conditioning is called *shaping*, a process by which complicated actions are built up from simpler ones.

10. In operant conditioning, *reinforcement* can be provided by a wide variety of things; it typically acts to induce the organism to repeat his behavior. In animal learning, food is generally used as the reinforcing stimulus. For human beings, the reinforcing stimulus can be anything from a piece of candy to one's own feelings of satisfaction at learning each new step in a complex shaping of operant behavior.

11. *Partial reinforcement* takes place when conditioned operant behavior is rewarded on only some occasions, not all occasions. Behavior learned through partial reinforcement, which is common in real-life situations, tends to be especially persistent.

12. *Secondary reinforcements* and *higher order reinforcements* are provided by stimuli that have acquired their reinforcement value through association with primary reinforcing stimuli. An example, starting with the primary reinforcement that food and fondling constitute for a hungry baby, is the secondary reinforcement that the mother's presence becomes through association with food and care, and the higher order reinforcements in which the sight of the mother becomes associated with the sound of her voice and later with particular words that she uses.

13. *Operant escape* and *avoidance* are behavior, learned through operant conditioning, through which the organism seeks to escape or avoid an unpleasant stimulus such as an electric shock or criticism or rejection by other persons.

14. *Learning by imitation* (also called *learning through modeling*) is a complex and characteristically human form of learning in which the behavior of another person (the model) is copied.

15. What is usually learned is a *mediational unit*—that is, a connection that serves to join a new stimulus with innate or previously learned behavior or other units. A mediational unit (which can also be called an engram, association, or bond) presumably involves some kind of change inside the organism, but the nature of the change is not very well understood.

16. Among the mediational units we learn are:

Sets (Chapter 4, "Efficiency in Learning") and *perceptual expectations* (Chapter 5, "Perception")

Words and *language* (Chapter 6, "Language, Thinking, and Problem Solving")

Concepts (also discussed in Chapter 6)

Motives and *standards* (Chapter 9, "Motives")

Emotions (Chapter 10, "Emotions"), including *anxiety* (Chapter 11, "Frustration and Conflict")

Attitudes (Chapter 16, "Social Psychology")

RECOMMENDED READING

Birney, R. C. and Teevan, R. C., eds. *Reinforcement*. Princeton, N.J.: Van Nostrand, 1961.

Deese, J. E. and Hulse, S. *The psychology of learning*, 3rd ed. New York: McGraw-Hill, 1967.

Hall, J. F. *The psychology of learning*. Philadelphia: Lippincott, 1966.

Hilgard, E. R. and Bower, G. H. *Theories of learning*, 3rd ed. New York: Appleton-Century-Crofts, 1966.

Kimble, G. A. *Hilgard and Marquis' conditioning and learning*, 2nd ed. New York: Appleton-Century-Crofts, 1961.

Pavlov, I. P. *Conditioned reflexes: an investigation of the physiological activity of the cerebral cortex*. London: Oxford University Press, 1927 [reprinted by Dover, New York, 1960].

Skinner, B. F. *The behavior of organisms*. New York: Appleton-Century-Crofts, 1938.

LEARNING CURVES

The Learning Curve of Decreasing Returns
The Learning Plateau
Other Learning Curves

CURVES OF FORGETTING

HOW LEARNING AND FORGETTING ARE MEASURED

Learning and Performance
    Motive for Performance; Absence of Conflicting Behavior and Performance
The Three Measuring Rods
    Recall; Recognition; Relearning
Redintegration: A Special Kind of Remembering

ONE-TRIAL LEARNING

THE REQUIREMENTS FOR LEARNING

The Distinctive Stimulus
    Complex Learning Stimuli; The Role of Stimulus Generalization and
    Discrimination; Generalization, Discrimination, and Language
Attention to the Stimulus
A Unit to Which the Stimulus Can Be Attached
    Attachment Units Versus Component Parts; How Learning Feeds on
    Learning

MEMORY

Short-Term and Long-Term Memory
Improving the Memory

LEARNING,
REMEMBERING,
AND FORGETTING

We learn. Some kind of new mediational unit (the term used in this book for what could also be called an engram, an association, or a bond) is formed inside us. Sometimes the mediational unit persists; it continues to exist—and we say that we remember. Sometimes it seems to disappear—and we say that we have forgotten.

At one time you learned the name of your first-grade teacher. Do you remember it now, or have you forgotten it? If you have forgotten the name, do you still remember the face? And could you perhaps remember the name if something happened to "jog your memory," as people say?

Are there any general rules that govern what we will learn, and under what circumstances, and how fast and how well? Can we in any way predict what we will remember and for how long and what we are likely to forget?

These last questions have a practical as well as a scientific importance. In popular language, learning means a planned and deliberate attempt to improve one's skills in one way or another. Thus the college student talks about learning chemistry or mathematics and learning to be a doctor, a lawyer, a teacher, or a businessman. A baseball pitcher, eager to move up from the minor leagues to the majors, sets about learning to throw a slider and a change of pace. A mother learns how to keep her children happy and properly fed. In all kinds of everyday events, learning in the popular sense of the word is important for self-improvement and self-satisfaction.

The principles of learning described in Chapter 2 were derived largely from the study of hungry animals that learned to perform a motor response, such as pressing a bar or running a maze, to obtain the reward of food. Most human learning takes place under quite different circumstances. Usually we are not hungry; we learn verbal rather than motor responses; our reward is not food but some token of approval from the teacher or experimenter or the kind of self-approval that accompanies a successful performance. To a far greater extent than any animal, we learn by imitation—a kind of learning that occupies a special place of its own. Nonetheless, some of the basic principles established through the study of animals are important in all kinds of learning. The ambitious college student as well as the hungry rat obeys the principles of reinforcement, partial reinforcement, stimulus generalization, stimulus discrimination, and extinction.

There has turned out to be a very close relation between scientific laboratory studies of learning—even those made with rats and more primitive organisms such as the cockroach and the paramecium—and the kind of goal-directed human learning referred to outside scientific circles. We now have a sizable set of rules and theories about the processes of learning, remembering, and forgetting. These not only explain a great deal about the modification of behavior but also have many practical implications for learning in the popular sense. Thus the material in this chapter and the following chapter has a double significance. While you learn about learning (in the scientific sense of the word) you also will learn how to achieve more efficient learning (in the popular sense of the word).

The Tools of an Early Learning Experiment   In a reproduction of an old telegraph office, an operator sends a message over the kind of equipment used in the Bryan-Harter study of learning. Telegraphers had to learn to hold the key down a fraction of a second for dots and a longer fraction for dashes. They also had to learn to interpret the clicks made by the receiving instrument (to the left of the photo), which was an electromagnet that moved a bar when the operator at the other end of the line touched his key. In the code used by telegraphers, dot-dash stands for *A*, dash-dot-dot-dot for *B*, and so on; the much used *E* is represented by a single dot and the much used *T* by a single dash.

FIGURE **3.1**

One of the most significant experiments in human learning was reported more than seventy years ago. At that
time the telegraph operator, tapping out messages in dots and dashes, was
an important man in America, responsible for most of the nation's long-
distance communication. The radio had not yet been invented, and there
were scarcely more than a half million telephones in use; it was the telegrapher who sent vital business messages and news dispatches from city to
city and from one railroad station to the next. Learning how to send
messages on a telegraph key and how to interpret the clicks of the receiving
instrument (see FIGURE 3.1) was a matter of much practical significance,
and two investigators named Bryan and Harter set out to study the process.

Telegraphy as it was then practiced was a complicated skill in which the
operator had to learn the code, to manipulate the key fast enough to send
at least sixty-six letters per minute, and to understand messages being sent
at a rate of seventy-two letters per minute or more. Fortunately the skill
was easy to measure. As new apprentices set about learning the trade, Bryan
and Harter listened in on their wires and counted the number of letters the
apprentices could send or understand per minute. When the results for
sending were plotted in graph form, Bryan and Harter obtained the learning curve shown in FIGURE 3.2.

FIGURE 3.2   *A Telegrapher's Learning Curve*   A typical apprentice's progress in
sending messages is shown by this curve. From zero ability at the start,
the apprentice made steady and rapid progress for the first eight weeks,
at the end of which he could send about 80 letters per minute. After
that, his progress slowed down. In the next eight weeks he added only
40 letters per minute, bringing him to the speed of 120 letters per
minute. Improving from 120 per minute to his ultimate level of 140
per minute took an additional twenty-four weeks. (1)

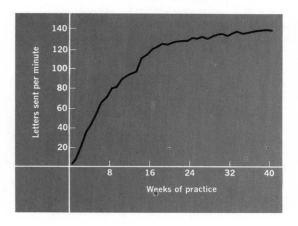

87

The Learning Curve of Decreasing Returns

This curve is called a *learning curve of decreasing returns;* it is typical of many kinds of learning that involve complicated motor skills. At first, progress is quite rapid; each new trial produces a substantial improvement. Then the curve starts to level off. Each new trial produces less and less improvement, until at last there is almost no progress at all.

The fact that so much learning takes place in the pattern thus discovered long ago by Bryan and Harter probably accounts for the many occasions on which we become discouraged in trying to acquire new skills. When we take up something such as tennis or bridge, we make considerable progress at the start; we feel that we are really getting somewhere. Then the improvement slows down, to the point where it seems almost nonexistent. We feel that we have virtually stopped learning and find it difficult to continue our efforts.

The Learning Plateau

When Bryan and Harter charted the speed at which apprentices could receive (rather than send) messages, they made the interesting discovery shown in FIGURE 3.3. During the "plateau" period of the curve the young telegrapher made almost no progress at all for ten weeks, a discouragingly long time. He was still below the required seventy-two letters per minute during this entire period, and we can assume that he must have been sorely tempted to give up the task as hopeless. Then, quite suddenly, he began to improve again. The explanation seems to be that the telegrapher learned

A Learning Plateau   In the first fifteen weeks the apprentice's speed at receiving messages rose rapidly until it was close to seventy words per minute. For about ten weeks thereafter he showed almost no improvement. Once this "plateau" had been passed, however, his speed again began to increase sharply. For the explanation, see the text. (1)

FIGURE **3.3**

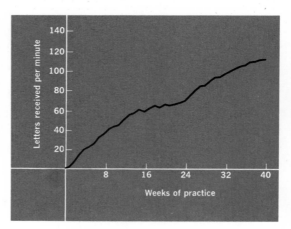

at the beginning to listen to messages letter by letter. He soon reached the upper limit of speed for this method, and no further progress could take place. Then, as his familiarity with the sounds of the code increased even though his speed did not, he suddenly began to listen in larger units—he heard not letters but entire words and even the combination of several words into familiar phrases. Using these new working methods, he again began to improve.

Learning plateaus apparently can also be caused by a loss of motivation or by boredom. But they occur most frequently in learning such things as telegraphy, typing, or the use of a musical instrument, where the original working methods are likely to have severe limitations but where new and better working methods can be developed. The moral of FIGURE 3.3, in learning of this kind, is not to despair and give up too soon.

Other Learning Curves

Three other kinds of learning curves are illustrated in FIGURE 3.4. In the *curve of equal returns,* progress is made at a steady rate, with each new trial producing an equal amount of improvement. This kind of straight-line "curve" is sometimes found in the learning of a poem or the vocabulary of a new language. As a matter of fact, the curve shown in FIGURE 3.2, plotted for the apprentice telegrapher's progress at sending messages, is an almost perfect curve of equal returns for the first eight weeks.

In the *curve of increasing returns,* the learner is in for a pleasant surprise.

FIGURE 3.4   *Other Types of Learning Curves*   In a learning curve of equal returns, progress moves at a steady rate, and each trial produces an improvement of equal size; the "curve" therefore takes the form of a straight line. In the curve of increasing returns, progress is slow at first, then rapidly increases; after a time, more learning occurs in each new trial than in many trials at the start. The S-shaped curve is a combination of increasing returns, equal returns, and decreasing returns. Progress is slow at the start, then increases to a straight line, but later slows again.

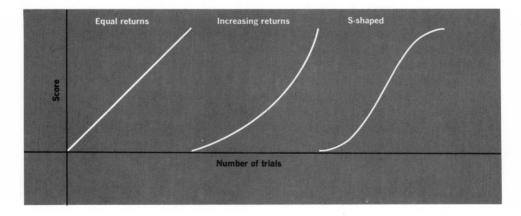

If he can just get by the early trials, in which progress is very slow, he will start improving by giant steps in the later trials. Unfortunately this kind of learning is rare. It seems to occur only in the learning of unfamiliar tasks that bear almost no relationship to anything we have ever done before, such as building an electronic amplifier or walking a tightrope.

The *S-shaped curve* would probably hold for almost all learning if only we could catch the learning process at the very beginning. For example, let us suppose that we could find a would-be apprentice telegrapher, as in the Bryan-Harter study, who had never before sat in a chair and had never made any of the muscular movements required for holding his arm on a table and touching and pressing the telegraph key. In that case, if he started the task completely from scratch, it seems quite likely that his progress would take the form of the S-shaped curve, with very slow progress at the start, then a speedup to straight-line progress for a time, and at last the gradually slowing progress of a curve of decreasing returns.

The theory that the S-shaped curve represents the basic and underlying pattern of all learning of complicated skills will probably never be proved, for it seems impossible to devise any kind of task to which the organism does not bring some previous experience. However, the learning curves appear to tell us these things:

1. The more unfamiliar the task to be learned, the more likely it is that progress will be slow at the start and will then increase.

2. In most learning of complicated skills, there is at least one period, short or long, in which each new trial produces an improvement of equal size.

3. As we approach the ultimate limit of learning, progress slows down, and it takes many trials to produce even a small amount of improvement.

We can see how these rules apply in everyday life if we think of a woman who takes up golf after a nonathletic childhood in which she has never gripped a golf club or even a baseball bat, has never swung at a baseball or tennis ball, and has never tried to throw a horseshoe to a pin. At first she is going to have a hard time hitting the golf ball at all, much less making it travel in a straight line or for any distance. Her progress will be painfully slow and she may be tempted to give up the game. If she persists, however, there will come a day when she starts learning rapidly.

A man with a more athletic background can learn golf much more quickly; he may be breaking 100 while the woman is still struggling to hit her first straight tee shot. But for both of them there will eventually come a time when further progress seems almost nonexistent. The man may break 100 quickly but spend the rest of his life trying vainly to get down to 90. The woman may make rapid progress from 150 to 115, then work for years to break 110.

It is impossible to talk about learning without at the same time talking about forgetting, because what we learn will not affect our behavior if it is forgotten. At this point, therefore, the discussion must turn to another classic experiment—this one performed in the nineteenth century by a German named Hermann Ebbinghaus, the first influential student of memory. Ebbinghaus wanted to study remembering and forgetting in the purest possible form, unaffected by any emotional factors or any other aspects of personality or past experience. He sought to have his subjects learn something that had no meaning to them—and no possible connection with their feelings or with anything they had learned in the past—and then to find how much of it they remembered for how long. He therefore used the nonsense syllable, which experimenters have been using ever since. He drew up twelve lists of thirteen syllables each, like the two shown in FIGURE 3.5. Using himself as a subject, he memorized the twelve lists to the point where he could repeat them twice without error, keeping track of the amount of time this took him. Once he had learned the lists he waited until he had forgotten them to the point where he could no longer repeat them without error. Then he set about relearning them, again keeping track of how long this took. The difference between the amount of time it took to learn the lists originally and the amount of time it took to relearn them was a good measure of how much he remembered.

A Study of Forgetting   In his classic study of forgetting, Ebbinghaus memorized lists of thirteen nonsense syllables similar to those shown here, then measured his memory for the lists by noting how long it took him to relearn them perfectly. The graph he constructed from his study showed very rapid forgetting immediately after the learning. After twenty minutes, he remembered only 58 percent and after about an hour only 44 percent. After the initial sharp dip, however, the curve flattened out. After one day he remembered about 34 percent and after two days about 28 percent. Although the graph line does not extend that far, he still remembered 21 percent after a month. (2)

FIGURE 3.5

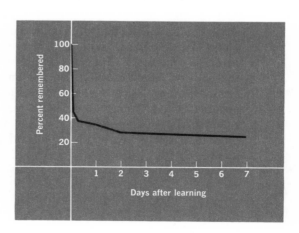

FIGURE **3.6**

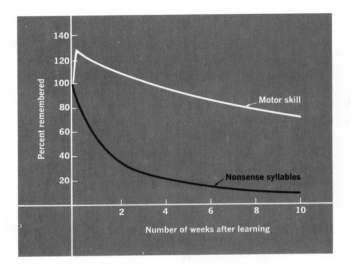

Verbal and Motor Forgetting   In the experiment illustrated by this graph the same subjects learned a rather simple motor skill (holding a pointer on a circle that was rotating as on a record player) and a list of nonsense syllables. The curves of forgetting show that the subjects remembered the motor skill much better than they remembered the nonsense syllables. For an explanation of the strange jump at the beginning of the curve for the motor skill, see the text. (3)

Using many different lists and varying the time between original learning and relearning, Ebbinghaus came up with the graph shown in FIGURE 3.5, the typical *curve of forgetting*. Other studies of forgetting have produced the same kind of curve time and time again—always showing a very large amount of forgetting immediately after learning and much smaller amounts of forgetting thereafter. The curve of forgetting tells us this: *When we learn something new, we quickly forget much of what we have learned, but we remember at least some of it for a long time.*

Two other curves of forgetting are shown in FIGURE 3.6. They illustrate the general principle that we tend to remember what we have learned about motor skills considerably better than we remember such verbal learning as nonsense syllables. Both curves resemble the classic Ebbinghaus curve, but the one for motor learning declines much more slowly than the one for verbal learning. Thus we tend to retain a good deal of the skill we once acquired as children at such motor tasks as swimming, riding a bicycle, roller skating, or sewing with a needle and thread. On the other hand we tend to forget many of the childhood jingles and poems that we once knew well.

The sharp rise at the start of the curve of motor forgetting in FIGURE 3.6

illustrates a phenomenon that has often been observed but is still not completely understood. In this case the subjects learned to keep a pointer on a rotating target to a degree of skill that was arbitrarily called 100 percent, then stopped practicing. The first time they were tested afterward, it turned out that they had not forgotten any of their skill but on the contrary had improved; they actually did much better than before. This often happens in the learning of motor skills; a common example is the golfer who takes a lesson, learns to hit the ball pretty well by the end of the lesson, then does even better the first time he picks up the club the next day. It also happens at times in verbal learning that has not been carried to completion. For example, you may try to memorize a poem and quit after you seem to have learned about 75 percent of it. The next time you try to recite it, you may find that you can recall more than 75 percent.

This phenomenon is called *reminiscence*. One possible explanation for reminiscence is that we get tired at the end of a learning period and cannot perform as well as we can later, after a rest.

Up to this point, the discussion of learning curves and curves of forgetting has been presented as if it were possible to measure the speed of learning and the speed of forgetting. It must now be pointed out that in actual truth these things cannot be measured —for a reason that has greatly handicapped the study of learning.

Let us say that two girls in elementary school are taking the same arithmetic course. They listen to the same explanations by their teacher and study the same textbooks. Now one day the teacher gives a written examination. Girl A gets 90. Girl B gets 70. The logical conclusion is that girl A learned her arithmetic very well and remembered it and that girl B either learned it rather badly or quickly forgot it.

The truth, however, is that we do not really know. All we are actually justified in saying is that girl A *performed* much better on the examination than did girl B. It may very well be that girl B had learned addition, subtraction, and the multiplication tables backward and forward and did badly on the examination because these subjects were so old hat to her that she was bored when asked to show how well she could perform.

Learning and Performance

Since we cannot measure learning directly, we have to adopt the best available substitute, which is to measure the behavior—or *performance*—that results from learning. If we want to measure how well a pianist has learned a new piece of music, we must ask him to perform it. If we want to measure how well a student has learned the Gettysburg Address, we have to ask him to recite it. And the performance will not necessarily be an accurate reflection of how much has been learned. A brilliant school girl may do badly on an examination. A golfer may have learned to be a sensational putter when he is alone on a practice green yet miss even the short ones in a match.

This is because performance requires not only the actual learning but also a motive to perform and the absence of conflicting behavior.

MOTIVE FOR PERFORMANCE   The reason the girl who knew her mathematics so well did badly on the examination was that she had no motive to perform. She was bored. She was satisfied in her own mind that she knew the answers, and she did not bother to prove it.

By providing her with a motive, we could doubtless have persuaded her to perform better. In return for a perfect examination paper we could have promised her a new dress or a new bicycle. We could have appealed to her pride or to her desire to please her teacher or her parents.

Performance often depends as much upon a motive as upon the learning itself. One person, with strong motives to compete and excel, makes the most of his learning; he gets good grades, wins athletic contests, gets ahead in his job and in his community. Another person may actually learn more, yet, because of strong motives to remain inconspicuous and to avoid the envy or hostility of others, get poorer grades, lose at games and contests, and never rise to a position of prominence or power.

ABSENCE OF CONFLICTING BEHAVIOR AND PERFORMANCE   The golfer who does well in solitary practice but badly in an actual match demonstrates the other requirement for performance. He has learned how to putt and he has a strong motive (let us say) to putt well and to win. But he gets stagefright in actual competition. He wants to putt well but his stagefright creates another kind of behavior—nervousness, tension. the inability to concentrate. This behavior gets in the way.

Stagefright, which is a form of anxiety, often gets in the way of performance. Many students consistently do badly in examinations, even though they know the material. All of us, after attending some kind of social function, have lain awake afterward thinking of all the brilliant things we might have said or done had we not been more or less paralyzed by tension at the time.

Many other kinds of conflicting behavior also get in the way of performance. Neither the student, the golfer, the pianist, nor anybody else can do his best under circumstances in which he cannot help engaging in such covert behavior as thinking about catching a plane, or about the illness of someone close to him, or about the fact that he does not have enough money to pay a bill due that day.

The Three Measuring Rods

Keeping in mind the warning that learning can be measured only indirectly by measuring performance, let us now enumerate three methods that can be used to make the measurement.

RECALL   One way to prove you have learned the Gettysburg Address is to recite it—which means to demonstrate that you can *recall* it. In school, a common use of recall as a measurement of learning is in the essay type of examination. When a teacher asks questions such as "What is classical conditioning?" he is asking you to recall and write down what you have learned.

RECOGNITION   There are many situations in which we cannot recall what we have learned, at least not completely, but can prove that we have learned something about it by being able to recognize it. For example, if you ask a school child to recall the Gettysburg Address, he may prove unable to do so. But if you show him the words "Fourscore and seven years ago our fathers brought forth on this continent" and ask him what begins with these words, he may immediately recognize the Gettysburg Address, thus demonstrating that he has certainly learned something about the speech.

You can probably think of many examples from your own experience. Someone asks, "Do you remember the name of the textbook we used in high school algebra?" and you reply, "No, but I'd recognize it if I saw it." You might give the same reply to questions such as, "Do you remember what dress Mary Smith wore to the dance last year?" or "Do you remember the number of the house we used to live in?"

Multiple choice examinations are a test of recognition; you are asked to choose the right answer from among several possible answers and thus to prove that you recognize it. Because recognition is easier than recall, many students would rather take a multiple choice than an essay examination.

RELEARNING   The most sensitive method of measuring learning is one that is seldom used. This is the method of *relearning*, which is accurate but cumbersome. All of us once learned the Gettysburg Address, or, if not that, then some other well-known piece of writing such as the funeral oration in Shakespeare's *Julius Caesar*. We may not be able to recall them now. Our ability to recognize them proves that we learned something but is not a very precise measure of how much. If we set about relearning them, however, the length of time this takes us will serve as a quite accurate measure of how much we learned the first time. (Note that this was the method Ebbinghaus chose.)

FIGURE 3.7 shows the results of an experiment that measured the same kind of learning by each of the three methods just discussed. The subjects

FIGURE **3.7**

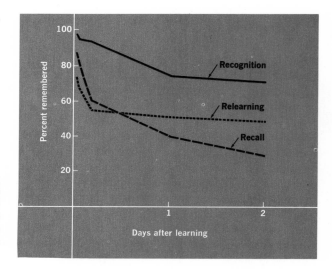

The Three Measures of Learning
The three forgetting curves were obtained by using all three measures of learning to test a group of subjects who had learned lists of nonsense syllables. (4)

made the highest scores—in other words, showed the least forgetting—when tested for recognition. The next highest scores were made for relearning and the lowest scores for recall.

Note, however, that in FIGURE 3.7 the curves for recognition and relearning are beginning to approach each other at the end of the two-day period. The curve for recognition is still declining noticeably, though slowly, while the curve for relearning is flattening out. If the experiment had been continued for a longer period of time, it can be assumed that the curve for recognition would eventually have dipped below the curve for relearning. Indeed it is possible that, when relearning is used as the measure, we never completely forget anything we have learned. Ebbinghaus, for example, once memorized some of the stanzas of Byron's poem *Don Juan*. After a lapse of twenty-two years he could not recall anything about these stanzas. But, when he set about relearning them, he found that this took him less time than it took him to learn some stanzas that he had never memorized before. As measured by relearning, the curve of forgetting had not dropped to zero even after all those years.

Redintegration: A Special Kind of Remembering

There is a fourth way of demonstrating learning that is worthy of mention even though nobody has ever figured out a way to use it as a measurement. Sometimes a stimulus will bring back a whole flood of detailed memories of some event that took place in our lives. For example, the sight of a Chinese restaurant may remind us of a day in childhood when our parents bought food at a Chinese restaurant and took it home for a family feast. We may remember driving to the restaurant in the family car; we may recollect the sight and smell of the restaurant and the paper cartons in which the food was carried home; we may even recollect the clothes we were wearing, the people who sat at the table, and much of the conversation. Similarly, a few words of a poem we learned in elementary school may remind us not only of the entire poem but of the day on which we learned it; we may recollect the schoolroom, the face of the teacher, and the schoolmates who sat near us. This rather special kind of remembering, in which we seem to reconstruct the entire incident from beginning to end, is called *redintegration.*

Redintegration is different from recall—for we can recall a poem or the face and name of a friend without remembering all the circumstances under which we first learned the poem or met the friend. It is also different from recognition and relearning, for it is a strangely rich kind of remembering in which we seem almost to relive an incident from the past. Though it is not used as an index of learning, it constitutes an interesting sidelight on learning and remembering.

ONE-TRIAL LEARNING

In the discussion of learning and forgetting up to this point we have been dealing with tasks and skills that have to be learned over a period of time. A motor skill such as telegraphy cannot be learned at once and neither can lists of nonsense syllables or a stanza of *Don Juan.* Learning of this sort, which requires a number of trials, is called *incremental learning.* The phrase comes from the word *increment,* which means an increase; *incremental learning* is the kind that takes place in a series of steps in which the amount of learning increases, sometimes quickly and sometimes slowly, until the learning is complete.

Learning also takes place in a different way that is very well illustrated by *syzygy,* that unusual word mentioned in Chapter 2. Although *syzygy* is hardly worth remembering, the chances are that you remember it very well. If you tried the experiment that was suggested and presented *syzygy* out of a clear sky to a friend, in all probability he also remembers it. The fact that this strange word was learned so quickly and is now remembered so well deserves consideration.

The important thing about *syzygy* was that *the word was learned in one trial.* Your friend did not have to practice, and you did not have to repeat the word. He learned it then and there.

One-trial learning takes place frequently among human beings, less frequently among lower organisms. It ordinarily requires certain special circumstances. Instead of using the word *syzygy,* suppose we had tried the experiment with the French word *aujourd'hui* (which is roughly pronounced oh-zhoor-dwee) or the German word *Schneeglöckchen* (the pronunciation of which can hardly be rendered into English letters at all). Or, to make the point even more clearly, suppose we had used a Chinese or Japanese word. In that case it is highly unlikely that the friend, after hearing it only once, would have been able to repeat it a half hour later, much less now.

Why should this be? The answer is that all the component parts of the word *syzygy* are already familiar to any American of college age. All of us have often used the sounds *syz*, as in *scissors; i*, as in *it*, and *jee*. as in *jeep*. They are a part of the repertory of language sounds we have already learned. They are mediational units that we already carry around in our heads. To form them into the new word *syzygy*, all we have to do is build one new mediational unit—an association among the three familiar syllables. When we deal with foreign words made up of unfamiliar sounds and syllables, we cannot learn so quickly, because we do not have the same kind of building blocks for learning already present in the form of previously learned mediational units.

Another example of one-trial learning is the way we build our vocabularies. Take, for instance, the word *horizon*. If you try to teach the meaning of this word to a four-year-old child, you will find the task impossible. But the average ten-year-old child who has never heard the word before needs only one explanation to grasp the meaning and add the word to his vocabulary. By the age of ten, he has learned the various mediational units—concepts of space, earth, and sky—that are component parts of the meaning of *horizon*. All he needs to do is form one more mediational unit—a bond between these previously learned units and the word *horizon*. He can form this new mediational unit, the bond, in a single trial.

Even in learning that cannot be accomplished in a single trial, component parts are significant. For a young child, learning to ride a bicycle is difficult because he has not yet mastered any of the component parts; he has to learn how to balance himself, how to steer, and how to pedal. If that same boy later buys a motorcycle, however, he quickly learns to ride the new machine. He already knows how to balance and steer; all he now needs to learn is the mechanical operation.

A young man from Africa who has never thrown a baseball would have a hard time learning to be a big-league pitcher. But the minor leaguer who aspires to the big leagues already knows how to hold the ball, release it as a fast ball or a curve, and aim it over the plate; he already knows many of the component parts of throwing a slider and a change of pace.

Memorizing the Gettysburg Address would be a difficult task for a child in the lower grades; he would first have to learn to recognize and pronounce words such as *conceived, dedicated,* and *consecrated.* The older child, already familiar with the words, finds it much easier to link them together.

The role of component parts in learning explains what would otherwise be a rather baffling fact about schoolwork. Insofar as can be measured, a fourteen-year-old child in the eighth grade has matured to the point where he seems to have all the nervous and physical equipment that makes learning possible. His innate capacity for learning will not increase very much; he is already just about as smart, to use the popular term, as he will ever be. Yet everybody knows that high school freshmen can learn things that would be beyond an eighth-grader; high school seniors can learn even more difficult things; and college students can go a long step beyond. The reason is that each year the student acquires more of the component parts of higher learning—a bigger vocabulary, more concepts, more mathematical symbols.

In learning any kind of complex behavior the speed of learning seems to vary directly with the number of component parts of the behavior that have been previously learned. From a practical standpoint, this means that learning feeds on learning. The more we know, the more we are likely to learn.

THE REQUIREMENTS FOR LEARNING

Learning sometimes seems to occur spontaneously, without any effort and almost by accident. Such is the case in latent or incidental learning, which was discussed on page 72. (The example given was this: A friend drives you to Smithville in his automobile. You have no intention of ever returning to Smithville and make no effort to learn the route. Yet, if for some reason you have to drive to Smithville at some time in the future, you may find that you learned a good deal about the route and the landmarks.)

At other times, learning does not take place no matter how hard we try— or think we try. We may attempt to become a good bridge player and fail utterly. We may try hard to learn some elementary words of Spanish, in preparation for a trip to Mexico, and have no success whatever. There probably are many reasons for failures of this kind, not all of which are as yet understood. But at any rate we can be sure, from both everyday observations and laboratory experiments, that learning does not take place unless certain requirements are met. In our lifetimes we see millions of sights and hear millions of sounds; we read innumerable pages of books, magazines, and newspapers; we look at many road maps and street signs. We remember only a very small percentage of all these things.

Perhaps many requirements must be met for learning to take place, but three of them seem to be basic. It appears that *learning is most likely to take place when there are 1) a distinctive stimulus, 2) attention to the stimulus, and 3) a unit of innate or previously learned behavior to which the stimulus can be attached.*

The Distinctive Stimulus

Unless a stimulus is *distinctive*—that is, unless it somehow stands out, is prominent, is capable of registering—it is not likely to attract enough attention for learning to take place.

All of us have listened to a lecturer from whom we learned absolutely nothing, because he spoke in such a monotonous voice and with so little emphasis on the points he was trying to make that there seemed to be no distinctive stimuli at all in his talk. As we often state it, "the words all ran together." Equally ineffective is the kind of fire-and-brimstone lecturer who shouts every word at us, never once lowering his voice. The best lecturer is the one who places sharp emphasis on the points he wants to make—that is, the special stimuli to which he wants to attract our attention. He makes these stimuli distinctive by using a different tone of voice and perhaps by gestures or by writing his main points on a blackboard, and often he repeats them for added emphasis.

Closely related to the requirement that the stimulus be distinctive is the fact that learning takes place most effectively in the absence of distraction. When Pavlov set about conditioning his dog, he used a cage in which there were no sights or sounds of any kind except the unconditioned stimulus of food and the conditioned stimulus of sound. One reason he did this was to make sure that no other factor would influence the learning process. But he also prevented distractions. If at the same time he presented the sound of the metronome he had also sounded a bell and a whistle, flashed a red light and a green light, sprayed perfume into the cage, shaken the dog's platform, and hit the dog's flanks with a paddle, the dog would have had a difficult time learning to respond to the metronome alone.

COMPLEX LEARNING STIMULI   In many learning situations the stimulus is simple and direct—such as Pavlov's metronome or the sight of the bar in the Skinner box. In many other situations, however, particularly in human learning, the stimulus is quite complex.

Let us consider, for example, what a quarterback learns to do on the football field. In scrimmage he calls a pass play, takes the ball from the center, and drops back waiting to make the throw. He already knows how to hold the ball, how to throw it, and how to run with it. To what stimulus must he now learn to attach these previously learned units of behavior? The answer gets extremely complicated. If any opposing players come charging through the line, he has to learn to sidestep them. If his primary receiver gets into the clear, he must learn to throw the ball way downfield. If not, he must learn to spot and throw to his secondary receiver. If there seems to be no chance at all of completing the pass, he must learn to run with the ball and also to run in a way that gives him the best chance to go as far as possible before he is tackled. It might be said that he must learn to attach his behavior to many stimuli—all the sights and sounds occurring on the field. Or it can be said that in cases such as this the entire situation is the stimulus, which seems the simpler way of putting it.

In a great deal of learning, the stimulus is the entire situation or a considerable part of it. The fire chief learns what kind of behavior is best calculated to cope with a fire depending on the sight of the flames, the sound of the crackling, and even the smell of the smoke. The lecturer learns to size up his audience and change his speech accordingly—sometimes speaking in simple terms, sometimes in more complicated ones, at times using jokes and at other times being dead serious.

The fact that the word *stimulus* can mean so many different things often confuses students. If you will remember that a stimulus is indeed a form of energy that excites the nervous system—but that this energy can vary from a single quick flash of light to everything that is going on at once on a football field or in the halls of Congress or even the sight of the entire earth as seen by an astronaut in space—you will avoid the confusion.

THE ROLE OF STIMULUS GENERALIZATION AND DISCRIMINATION   Stimulus generalization affects a great deal of real-life learning. Probably a good many of the apparently irrational fears that all of us exhibit are due to the kind of stimulus generalization shown in the experiment with the child Albert and the rat (pages 55–56). So is the fact that we often feel attracted to a person at first sight or find ourselves violently disliking him for no logical reason. The person for whom we acquire an instant affection may resemble an uncle or an aunt whom we liked in childhood; the person whom we automatically dislike may remind us of somebody who frightened or mistreated us when we were small.

A second aspect of stimulus generalization becomes apparent if we think for another moment about the football quarterback. The situation on the field, to which he must react with appropriate behavior, is probably never the same twice. If he had to learn to attach his behavior to every possible stimulus—every specific situation in which so many linemen were charging him, his possible receivers were in such and such a position, and the defenders were doing thus and so—his job would be hopeless. Only by generalizing, by behaving in a way he has learned was successful under similar though not identical circumstances, can he operate satisfactorily.

Most human behavior takes place under conditions that resemble those on the football field. The bridge player is never likely to find the cards in exactly the same position twice. The mechanic works on many different kinds of automobiles. When we drive a car we never find conditions on the road exactly the same twice; even the traffic lights vary in shape and position from one place to another. All of us, if we had to learn to behave appropriately

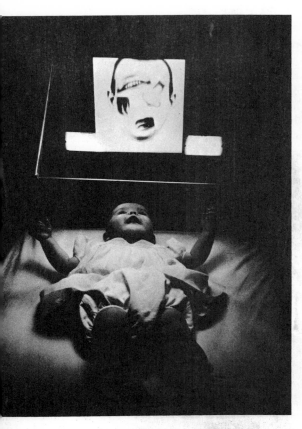

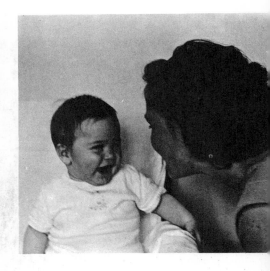

A Baby Develops Stimulus Discrimination The very young baby who has just learned about faces may smile at anything at all resembling the human face (*left*). The older baby (*above*) smiles when he sees the face of his mother, not a distorted face or the face of a stranger.

FIGURE 3.8

to every separate stimulus that assails us from childhood to old age, would be hard put to live our lives. It is stimulus generalization that makes the task possible.

Stimulus discrimination also plays a role in many kinds of learning. A human baby, when he first acquires the ability to smile, smiles at everybody; he will even smile at a mask resembling the human face. By the time he is eight months old, he smiles more selectively at his parents (see FIGURE 3.8).

GENERALIZATION, DISCRIMINATION, AND LANGUAGE To the lower animals, stimulus generalization and stimulus discrimination are based on physical characteristics—on the similarities or differences among sounds, shapes, brightnesses, sometimes colors. As shown in FIGURE 3.9, a duck can learn that food is always found underneath a three-sided figure and never under a figure with four or more sides, regardless of the exact shape of the figures. But for the duck or a rat this is a slow and laborious process. The animal eventually acquires a concept of triangularity that enables it to generalize and to discriminate, but the process takes a long time.

Let us suppose that we tried to teach a rat that it would find food behind any of the objects in the left-hand column below but not behind any of the objects in the right-hand column:

Cap pistol	Revolver
Building block	Brick
Small rubber ball	Orange
Beach ball	Cantaloupe
Teddy bear	Sponge
Drum	Barrel
Tricycle	Motorcycle
Doll	Child
Small wagon	Vacuum cleaner
Molding clay	Putty
Paint set	Cigarette case

Now the rat is really in trouble. It can learn only by trial and error. Even if it manages to learn, one by one, that food is found behind the objects at the left, it will again be baffled if we introduce a miniature xylophone or piano, a rag doll, a stuffed tiger, a rattle, or a toy train.

To the rat and indeed to any animal except man, a shiny metal cap pistol is a far different stimulus from a red rubber ball, a brown and shaggy teddy bear, or a flesh-colored plastic doll. To the human child, as soon as he has learned the word *toy* and the concept for which it stands—on the average at about the age of four—most toys represent a similar stimulus. Thus does language result in stimulus generalization between two objects as vastly different in physical size, shape, color, and texture as a little black

FIGURE 3.9   *Generalization and Discrimination by Shape*   After many trials the duck has learned that food is always found underneath some kind of three-sided figure. It can now generalize all triangles and discriminate between triangles and other geometrical figures.

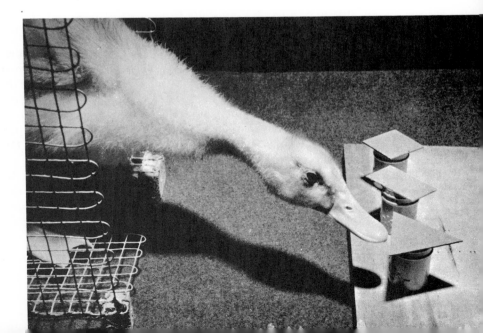

stub of crayon and a giant stuffed tiger. The process is called *mediated generalization*—because it depends upon the mediational units of language, resulting in the association of objects that do not of themselves possess any physical similarities.

Language is also the basis of much human stimulus discrimination. To a baby an orange looks like a rubber ball, and, if he has learned to play with a ball, he will also try to play with the orange. It is mostly on the basis of language that he learns to discriminate between a spherical object that is a toy and a spherical object that is food.

Attention to the Stimulus

One cannot learn the contents of a classroom lecture if he is not paying attention, if he is thinking about something else. Even when the stimulus is distinctive, there is the further requirement that attention actually be paid to it. Attention provides the bridge between the first of the requirements for learning (a distinctive stimulus) and the third (the inner unit to which the stimulus becomes attached). It makes possible a clear association between the two and thus a definite and lasting learning connection.

Although attention is obviously one of the requirements for learning, little is known about the dynamics of attention. This is partly because it has not been studied until recently; the early experimenters in learning concentrated on reinforcement, which is closely related to attention, rather than on attention itself. Moreover, it is very difficult to measure the amount or degree of attention a person invests while he is learning something. But new developments in physiological psychology offer hope that sensitive assessment of heart activity, breathing, and brain potentials may some day provide an objective index of this somewhat murky but important concept.

A Unit to Which the Stimulus Can Be Attached

In the last analysis, all learning is a matter of establishing new connections between previously unconnected items. One of these items, the stimulus, comes from outside the organism. The other must exist inside the organism. Pavlov's dog could not have learned to salivate to the sound of the metronome, for example, had it not had the innate capacity to salivate. The inner unit to which the outside stimulus is attached can be actual physical behavior, as in the case of Pavlov's dog, or it can be a mediational unit that has previously been learned, such as the concepts that go to make up the meaning of *horizon*.

The fact that we learn and remember only when the outside stimulus can readily be attached to some already existing unit is especially important in human learning, and most of all in learning that depends upon language.

A college student of a generation ago, reading a newspaper story about some event in Southeast Asia, would probably not have learned very much or remembered the story very long. He would not have had any previously learned mediational units—any knowledge about Southeast Asia or its importance in world affairs—to which the news story could be attached. More recent students, however, are likely to know a great deal about Southeast Asia's geography, people, politics, armies, and world importance. They can readily remember the contents of a new article about Southeast Asia because they possess many mediational units to which the new article can be attached.

ATTACHMENT UNITS VERSUS COMPONENT PARTS   Is the attachment unit the same thing as component parts of learning? No, it is not, although it may sound rather similar and is indeed rather closely related. To illustrate, let us consider the following incident.

A kindergarten teacher who has gone to Europe for the summer takes two coins to her class. "This one," she says, passing it around to her pupils, "is an English shilling." Then she passes the other around and says, "This is a French franc."

Now there is nothing very complicated about learning the words *shilling* or *franc*. As far as knowing the necessary components is concerned, every pupil in the class starts on equal terms.

Let us further suppose, however, that there is one pupil in the class whose family has frequently gone traveling in Europe. This boy has often heard his parents talk about England and France and about exchanging American dollars for foreign money. In addition he has been entrusted with sums of money that he has been permitted to spend for himself; he knows the difference between a United States nickel and a United States quarter or half dollar. On the other hand, there is a little girl in the class who has never heard the words *England* or *France* mentioned in her home. She does not know that there is any nation in the world except the United States, and she has never had any money of her own to spend, so that she does not know what a coin is.

Which of these two pupils is likely to remember, on the following day, which of the two coins the teacher holds up is the shilling and which is the franc? Naturally the boy is more likely to learn and remember; he possesses mediational units to which the words *shilling* and *franc* can be attached. With the girl, the words tend to fall on deaf ears. She simply has nothing inside her to which the words can readily be attached.

HOW LEARNING FEEDS ON LEARNING   For an analogy to the significant role played by the inner units to which a new stimulus can be attached, let us imagine the following situation.

We are facing a cork wall that is almost completely covered by small squares of hard tile, with only a few gaps of cork showing between the tiles. At this wall we start throwing darts. When the dart hits cork, it naturally sticks to the wall. When it strikes a tile, it does not stick, but let us say that it does knock the tile away, exposing another area of cork. At first, not many of our darts will stick to the wall. Later, as more and more tiles are knocked away and more and more gaps of cork appear, more and more of our darts will sink home.

This is the way learning takes place. Just as the dart sinks home only when it hits an area of cork to which it can stick, so the new stimulus is learned only when it gets attached to some unit already present inside the organism. The larger the area of cork, the more likely that any given dart will stick; similarly, the more units already present inside the organism, the greater the chance that the new stimulus will be learned.

In practical terms, we have here another demonstration of how learning feeds on learning. Just as the possession of component parts makes learning easier and faster, so does the possession of mediational units to which a new stimulus can be attached—as the word *shilling* can be attached to words and concepts such as *England, travel, money, coin,* and so forth. Each new unit we learn helps us in turn to learn others.

This is one reason children from underprivileged families often have a difficult time in school, thus continuing a vicious circle that leads one generation after another to have trouble getting along in the world. A child whose parents had very little education and use a limited vocabulary starts school with a severe handicap. There are hundreds and perhaps even thousands of words and concepts that he has never heard of but that are already familiar to children his age who come from more privileged homes. He simply does not have the mediational units required for the attachments between new and old that come easy to children whose parents speak a richer language. Many underprivileged children give up and eventually drop out of school, even though they may have a great deal of inborn learning ability and, if they once started building a vocabulary, might quickly acquire a storehouse of mediational units and catch up by leaps and bounds.

MEMORY

People differ widely in their inborn ability to learn and to remember; this capacity is one important aspect of the trait we call *intelligence.* Some people are even blessed with a valuable memory aid called *eidetic imagery,* which means the ability to recall an image that is an exact copy. For a demonstration of eidetic imagery, turn to FIGURE 3.10 and look at it for about thirty seconds before returning to your place in the text.

Do you still see the picture that you examined in FIGURE 3.10? Can you describe it in the present tense, as if it were still before you? Most people cannot. But a few can; they may even be able to count the number of leaves and blossoms on the plants and the number of rings on the cat's tail. An occasional college student has reported that while taking an examination— for example, while being asked to define and discuss eidetic imagery—he could actually see a textbook page like this one and read off the words he needed to answer the questions. This is a rare gift, and even the people who possess it seldom retain it past childhood. It tends to disappear about the time of adolescence and is rarely found in people beyond college age.

Some people who are otherwise quite unintelligent, sometimes to the point of being feebleminded, possess an unusual ability to remember certain things. One example, reported in 1965, was the case of twin brothers who had spent most of their lives in a New York home for retarded children. Although they were twenty-six years old, they looked much younger and were unable to answer the simplest kind of elementary school questions. When asked how much change they would get if they bought a thirty-five-cent box of candy with a dollar bill, they concentrated in a puzzled sort of fashion and at last agreed that the answer was fifty cents. But, when asked about any date on the calendar, all the way back to the year 1 and forward to years for which no calendars have as yet been written, they did something quite amazing. Asked the date of the first Wednesday in July 1901, they would correctly reply, in unison and at once, that it was July 3. One of them was able to answer such questions instantly for any day or date back to the year 1 and forward to the year 7000; the other was similarly infallible

FIGURE 3.10

A Test of Eidetic Imagery   To take the test, look at the picture for about thirty seconds, then return to your place in the text. (5)

over a period of 2000 years. One of them could also describe the weather perfectly, in great detail from morning until night, for any day within the past five years. Asked how they knew all these things, they replied that they had no idea.

In other cases, feebleminded people have shown strange ability to memorize railroad timetables or to play complicated musical selections on a piano after hearing them just once or to design and execute complicated crochet patterns. Such a person is called an *idiot savant*, a French phrase meaning idiot-scholar. It is difficult to imagine such an odd combination, and there have in fact been very few such people. The secret of their abilities is not known.

Short-Term and Long-Term Memory

Many of the things we learn stay in our memories for a long time, perhaps forever. Others, however, seem to stay for only a very short period and then to be lost completely. For example, if you have to ask the information operator for a telephone number and cannot write the number down for lack of a pencil or paper, you generally remember it only long enough to make the call; if you get a busy signal and are forced to dial it again, you often find that you have already forgotten it. Similarly, the cashier in a supermarket remembers only briefly that she must give the customer $3.76 change from a ten-dollar bill; by the time she starts checking out the next customer, the figure $3.76 has already vanished from her memory. When we add a column of figures such as:

$$
\begin{array}{r}
37 \\
49 \\
65 \\
\underline{22}
\end{array}
$$

we say to ourselves (adding the right-hand digits from the top down) 16, 21, 23; then write down the 3 and start over on the left-hand numbers, 5, 9, 15, 17; thus we get the answer 173. All the intermediary numbers that flash through our consciousness—the 16, 21, 23, 5, 9, and 15—disappear almost as rapidly as they are formed.

The rapidity with which we can forget some of the things we have learned is a valuable asset. The supermarket cashier would be hopelessly confused by the end of the day if she recalled every transaction starting with the first one of early morning. The addition of long columns of figures would be impossible if we recalled every step of the process; the numbers would get hopelessly in one another's way.

This rapid forgetting is the subject of much speculation. Perhaps it points to the existence of two separate and distinct kinds of memory process. We may have two kinds of storage mechanisms for our mediational units—one a preliminary kind of short-term memory, the other a long-term memory to which some but not all of our learning is transferred. To use a very loose figure of speech, we might say that our learning may go originally into a sort of in-basket such as one might find for the mail arriving in a large business office. But this basket has a very limited capacity and must be emptied out every few minutes. The important mail is transferred to permanent filing cabinets; the unimportant is thrown out.

The "memory experts" who perform on the stage make a specialty of remembering for a long time the things that the ordinary person would quickly forget. Some of their accomplishments are quite startling. For example, they may meet each member of a television studio audience just once before a program, then call off each person's name correctly a half hour later, as many as forty or fifty or even a hundred names in all. This is a trick performed with the aid of what is called a *mnemonic system*, after the Greek word for remembering. In a mnemonic system the user has an elaborate set of memorized symbols to which he can connect new things in some kind of logical order, and he can therefore remember them longer than short-term memory would ordinarily operate. "I left port" is a mnemonic device that countless beginning sailors have used to help them remember the confusing and easily forgotten difference between port (the left side of the ship) and starboard. The jingle that begins "Thirty days hath September" is another mnemonic device. The self-help books that promise to improve your memory are full of them. Mnemonic systems make for good parlor tricks and are indeed helpful in remembering unconnected and miscellaneous facts such as the names and faces of strangers at a party, or telephone numbers. They may also help in remembering rote facts in a college course.

Improving the Memory

The secret of acquiring a good memory—that is, of using one's capacity to remember to the maximum—is something quite different. It requires building up a large number of mediational units to which a new stimulus can be attached and organizing these units into logical patterns to which new associations seem to "stick" almost as a matter of course. William James put it beautifully many years ago:

> *The more other facts a fact is associated with in the mind, the better possession of it our memory retains.* Each of its associates becomes a hook to which it hangs, a means to fish it up by when sunk beneath the surface. Together, they form a network of attachments by which it is woven into the entire tissue of our thought. The "secret of a good memory" is thus the secret of forming diverse and multiple associations with every fact we care to retain. . . . Most men have a good memory

for facts connected with their own pursuits. The college athlete who remains a dunce at his books will astonish you by his knowledge of men's records in various feats and games, and will be a walking dictionary of sporting statistics. The reason is that he is constantly going over these things in his mind, and comparing and making series of them. They form for him not so many odd facts but a concept-system—so they stick. So the merchant remembers prices, the politician other politicians' speeches and votes, with a copiousness which amazes outsiders, but which the amount of thinking they bestow on these subjects easily explains. The great memory for facts which a Darwin and a Spencer reveal in their books is not incompatible with the possession on their part of a brain with only a middling degree of physiological retentiveness [by which James means inborn ability for remembering]. Let a man early in life set himself the task of verifying such a theory as that of evolution, and facts will soon cluster and cling to him like grapes to their stem. Their relations to the theory will hold them fast; and the more of these the mind is able to discern, the greater the erudition will become. (6)

The following chapter will discuss *management of learning*, the term used to describe the various ways in which learning can be made more efficient. All the aspects of management of learning are important and have considerable practical value, but no other has such a basic and all-pervasive significance as the one described in these words of William James. It is our storehouse of mediational units—those areas of receptive cork to which a new stimulus can stick like a dart sinking home—that determines more than anything else how well we will learn and remember.

SUMMARY

1. When improvement in a newly learned habit is plotted on a graph, we sometimes find *curves of equal returns*, and at other times find *curves of decreasing returns, curves of increasing returns*, or S-*shaped curves*.

2. It is generally believed that the S-shaped curve is the basic pattern of learning. It shows very slow progress at the start, then faster progress for a time, and at last slower progress (or decreasing returns) as the ultimate limit of learning is approached.

3. Some kinds of learning show a *learning plateau*: early progress is followed by a period in which progress seems to have stopped; this plateau period eventually gives way to a new period of progress. Plateaus usually indicate that the original working methods have reached their limit and must be replaced by better working methods before progress can resume.

4. *Curves of forgetting* show that when we learn something new we very quickly forge much of what we have learned but remember at least some of it for a long time.

5. Since it is impossible to measure learning directly, we are forced to use the best available substitute, which is to measure *performance*. Since performance requires not only the actual learning but also a) a motive to perform and b) the absence of conflicting behavior such as stage-fright, it does not always accurately reflect how much was learned.

6. Three measures of learning (as reflected by performance) are *recall, recognition,* and *relearning*. Recognition is usually easier than recall.

7. *One-trial learning* takes place when a new stimulus is attached in a single pairing to mediational units already present. One-trial learning demonstrates the importance of previously acquired *component parts*.

8. Learning is most likely to take place when three requirements are met: a) a distinctive stimulus, b) attention to the stimulus, and c) a unit of innate or previously learned behavior to which the stimulus can be attached.

9. Stimulus generalization and stimulus discrimination play an important part in learning—and particularly in human learning, where they are most often based on language labels.

10. Learning and remembering depend to a great extent on the number of previously learned mediational units to which a new stimulus can be attached. What this means in practical terms is that learning feeds on learning. The more we already know, the more we are likely to learn.

11. Memory—or the ability to remember an event—is subject to wide individual variations, including *eidetic imagery* (the ability to recall an image that is an exact copy).

12. Many investigators believe that there are two kinds of memory process —*short-term memory* (for things remembered only briefly and then discarded) and *long-term memory* (for things retained more or less permanently).

RECOMMENDED READING

Bartlett, F. C. *Remembering: a study in experimental and social psychology.* New York: Cambridge University Press, 1932 [1961].

Ebbinghaus, H. *Memory: a contribution to experimental psychology.* New York: Teachers College, Columbia University, 1913 [reprinted by Dover, New York, 1964].

Hall, J. F. *The psychology of learning.* Philadelphia: Lippincott, 1966.

Hilgard, E. R. and Bower, G. H. *Theories of learning,* 3rd ed. New York: Appleton-Century-Crofts, 1966.

Osgood, C. E. *Method and theory in experimental psychology.* New York: Oxford University Press, 1953.

Underwood, B. J. *Experimental Psychology,* 2nd ed. New York: Appleton-Century-Crofts, 1966.

THE IMPORTANCE OF ATTACHMENT UNITS

Familiarity with the Stimulus
Meaningfulness
Learning by Rote Versus Learning by Logic
The Role of Guidance

ATTENTION TO THE STIMULUS

Motives
Feedback
Rewards
Punishment
Novelty

THE DISTINCTIVE STIMULUS

Whole Versus Part Learning
Combination Methods
Overlearning
Distribution of Practice
Recitation

TRANSFER OF LEARNING

Positive Transfer
Negative Transfer
Mediated Transfer
Development of Learning Sets

THEORIES OF REMEMBERING AND FORGETTING

Retroactive Inhibition
Proactive Inhibition
Implications of Proactive Inhibition

EFFICIENCY IN LEARNING

Let us suppose that you have just been elected president of some campus organization. You have written an acceptance speech. Now you want to memorize the speech, so that you can deliver it without notes.

Will you be better off trying to learn the speech a paragraph at a time and then putting the paragraphs together—or learning the whole thing as a unit?

Will you learn more quickly if you read the speech a few times and then attempt to recite it—or if you just keep rereading?

Is it more efficient to keep studying without any breaks—or to study for a number of short periods, with rests in between?

Questions such as these come up constantly in learning. They are important to someone who wants to memorize a speech in the least possible time and to the student who wants to learn as much as he can in the time he has available to devote to his books. They are important to school teachers, who would want to add a few questions of their own. Will a student learn more if punished for his mistakes or if rewarded for his successes? Is there any advantage in keeping the student continually informed of how well he is doing? What kind of guidance, if any, is the most helpful?

The answers to these questions have been sought in the interests of pure science, but they have also been put to immediate practical use and have become one of the largest fields of applied psychology. Since they are used mostly by teachers and in classroom situations, they are called by the term *management of learning,* which means the attempt to arrange the most favorable possible conditions for learning to take place.

Previous chapters have discussed the elements of learning, from the simple reflex to complex mediational units such as motives and emotions, and some of the laws that govern the ways in which we learn, remember, and forget. This final chapter on the learning process will discuss the management of learning—a subject that will lead to a description, toward the end of the chapter, of theories on why we remember and how and why we forget.

Discussion of favorable conditions for learning is bound to revolve around the three requirements for learning: 1) a distinctive stimulus, 2) attention to the stimulus, and 3) some unit of innate or previously learned behavior to which the stimulus can be attached. It is only by manipulating these three requirements that learning can be managed and made more efficient. The first part of this chapter, therefore, can best be organized around the requirements for learning—taken up, for reasons of convenience, in reverse order.

THE IMPORTANCE OF ATTACHMENT UNITS

As William James realized long ago and as new knowledge of one-trial learning and component parts has again emphasized, nothing is so vital to the learning process as the storehouse of information we already possess, into which we can integrate and associate the new. That general principle has already been discussed in some detail. Some specific ways in which the principle has been shown to work can now be added.

Can Familiarity Breed Learning?   A group of rats was raised from birth in a cage that had circles and triangles on the walls. The geometric figures had no relation to the rats' feeding or other activity; they were simply present as a sort of decoration, like the pictures hanging on a living room wall. After the rats had grown up, they were asked to learn, as one is shown doing in the drawing, that food would always be found behind the triangle but not behind the circle, or vice versa; in other words, they were asked to learn to discriminate between the two geometric forms. The same task was also given to another group of rats that had grown up under the same conditions in a cage exactly the same except that the walls were blank. Question: Which group learned faster? For the answer, see FIGURE 4.2.

FIGURE **4.1**

Familiarity with the Stimulus

The purpose of the experiment shown in FIGURE 4.1 was to discover whether familiarity can help learning. The finding, shown in FIGURE 4.2, was that it most certainly can. Just being around the two stimuli while growing up helped the rats learn to discriminate between them later.

When the automobile was first introduced, many people had difficulty learning to drive. Today's generations, familiar with the automobile from childhood, have far less trouble. Children who grow up in houses that contain musical instruments seem to learn to play them more easily than other children, and children who have watched their parents read newspapers and magazines and books seem to learn to read more easily. Americans, living in a nation full of all kinds of machinery, can usually learn to operate a new factory machine or military vehicle more easily than can the native of a South Pacific island who has never seen any machinery more complicated than a water wheel. All of us who grew up with the English language can learn French, which uses the same alphabet, more easily than Russian or Chinese, which do not.

In school, the best teacher is generally the one who can relate new and unfamiliar material to the things his students already know and who explains it in the most familiar language possible.

Meaningfulness

FIGURE 4.3 illustrates an experiment that you can try for yourself by following the instructions given in the figure. If you do this, the scores you make on each of the four lists will probably be quite similar to the results found in the original experiment, which are shown in FIGURE 4.4.

It should come as no surprise that list 1, composed of actual three-letter words, should be the easiest of all the lists to learn. But why is list 2 easier to learn than list 3 and list 3 in turn easier than list 4? The answer is that the lists were drawn up in an attempt to discover how the degree of *meaning-*

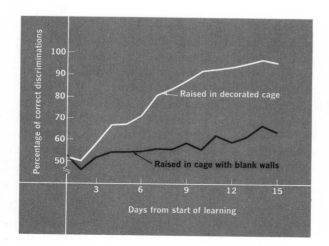

FIGURE 4.2

Results of the Familiarity Experiment The graph charts the results of the experiment shown in FIGURE 4.1. The rats that had grown up in the cage with circles and triangles on the walls learned much faster and much better than the other rats. (1)

Which List Is Easiest to Learn? These were the kinds of lists used in a well-known learning experiment, which you can repeat for yourself. Study list 1 for two minutes, then test yourself to see how many of the ten items you remember. Now do the same for each of the other three lists. To find how your scores compare with those found in the original experiment, see FIGURE 4.4. (Nonsense syllables, 2)

FIGURE 4.3

List 1	List 2	List 3	List 4
SIT	DOZ	SIQ	ZOJ
HAT	RAV	CUK	JYQ
BIN	ROV	BYS	XUY
COW	SOF	NOK	QOV
RIM	HOL	GEV	GIW
RAN	SUR	RYS	VAF
MET	LIF	CYP	CEF
POT	GYM	FYS	XYH
HUG	RUF	JAL	VYQ
FIG	BEV	QAT	ZYT

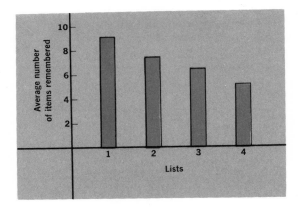

FIGURE 4.4

One Group's Scores on the Lists These are the scores made by the subjects in the original experiment. For an explanation of why there was such a large variation in how much was learned from the four different lists, see the text. (3)

fulness influences learning. Each of the nonsense syllables in list 2 is meaningful in the sense that it tends to remind almost everyone of some actual word —that is to say, all of us already have some word in our vocabulary with which the nonsense syllables of list 2 can easily be associated. In list 3, about half the words have this sort of meaningfulness. In list 4, none of the syllables do; in this list, all the syllables are truly "nonsense" in that they do not suggest associations with actual words. Thus the results shown in FIGURE 4.4 —and probably your own results if you tried the experiment—demonstrate how the meaningfulness of the material to be learned affects ease of learning.

Many other experiments have produced similar results. In one of the earliest experiments, subjects were asked to memorize a list of 200 nonsense syllables, a list of 200 digits in random order, a 200-word passage of prose writing, and 200 words of poetry. The results are shown in FIGURE 4.5. Note that the nonsense syllables were hardest of all to learn—even harder than the list of random digits. This is probably because the nonsense syllables were completely unfamiliar combinations of letters, whereas the digits, even though in meaningless order, did possess the quality of familiarity. But note also the great gap in degree of difficulty between both the nonsense syllables and the nonsense arrangement of digits as compared to the actual, meaningful passages of words in the prose and poetry. Poetry—which has not only meaningfulness but also a sort of internal logic and organization provided by the cadence and rhymes—proved easiest of all to learn.

The more meaningful the material we try to learn, the more readily it can be associated with something that we already know. To go back to the analogy of the darts and the wall that was used in the previous chapter, we might say that a meaningful stimulus is like a well-aimed dart directed toward an area of cork where it can sink home. If in addition the material has some organization and logic of its own—that is, if it tends to form its own internal associations and "hang together" as does poetry—the job of learning becomes easier still.

Learning by Rote Versus Learning by Logic

Closely related to the matter of meaningfulness is another well-established fact about learning: we learn more easily and remember longer if we learn by logic than if we learn by rote. An experiment that neatly demonstrates this is illustrated in FIGURE 4.6. Most of the students who worked on the numbers shown in the right-hand photograph, it should be mentioned, managed to discover the principle that lay behind the arrangement. You may want to try to discover it also before reading on to the next paragraph.

The pattern—as you may have figured out for yourself—is that the numbers following the first number 5 are obtained by regularly adding 3–4–3–4–3–4–3–4 to the preceding number. Thus 5 is followed by 8 (which is 5 plus

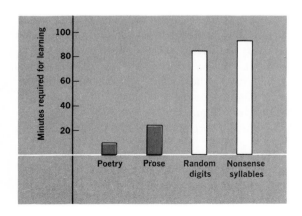

FIGURE 4.5

Meaningful Versus Meaningless Material   The length of the bars demonstrates how much more easily subjects in one experiment learned meaningful writing than meaningless lists of nonsense syllables and random digits. (4)

FIGURE 4.6

Rote Versus Logic In both these classes the students are asked to memorize the numbers on the blackboard. In the class at left the instructor suggests that the easiest way to remember them is in groups of three, as he has arranged them. In the class at right the instructor points out that the two lines of numbers are not arranged in random order but according to a definite and logical pattern, with the pattern

3); 8 is followed by 12 (which is 8 plus 4); 12 is followed by 15 (which is 12 plus 3); and so on. Number 26 at the end of the first line is followed by 29 (26 plus 3) to start the second line, and 29 is then followed by 33 (29 plus 4).

As the experiment was set up, the first class was in effect asked to learn the numbers by rote—that is to say, by sheer repetition, mechanically, without any regard to meaning. The second class learned by logic—with an understanding of the meaningfulness of the pattern. The two classes, as it happened, learned about equally well. When tested a half hour later, 33 percent of the students in the first class and 38 percent of the students in the second class recalled the numbers perfectly, exactly as shown on the blackboards. But their ability to remember the numbers for a period of time was sharply different. Three weeks later, not one of the students who had learned the numbers by rote remembered them correctly. Of the students who had learned by a logical rule, 23 percent still knew the numbers perfectly (5).

Most of the learning we do in school is a combination of rote and logical rule. There is no easy way for the elementary school pupil to learn his multiplication tables; he has to memorize them one step at a time, by rote. But he learns long division by grasping the logic of it. When we learn a foreign language, we have to acquire the vocabulary largely by rote—though, as we learn more and more words, we see certain patterns and sometimes figure out the meaning of a word that we hear or see for the first time. For conjugating the verbs and declining the nouns we can learn logical rules.

Although the multiplication tables are an exception, for a special reason that will be explained later, we tend to forget rather quickly the things we

the same for both lines. The students are left to find the pattern for themselves (as you may also want to try to do). The experiment was designed to see which class would learn the numbers more easily. For an explanation of the pattern of the numbers and the results of the experiment, see the text.

learn in school by rote. The logical principles that we have grasped tend to stay in our memories. Five years from now, for example, you may very well have forgotten words from this course such as operant and eidetic. But the general pattern of how learning takes place and modifies behavior will probably have stuck with you. A study that demonstrates what college students tend to remember from a course is shown in FIGURE 4.7.

One psychologist has suggested the useful term *chunking* as a description of the process of learning by logic. Material that has a logical set of principles tends to hang together like a chunk of wood or stone, in a tightly bound mass that resists the erosion of forgetting.

The Role of Guidance

From everything that has been said in the past few pages it follows that learning can be made easier by anything that helps us find elements of familiarity and meaningfulness in new material and learn it by logic and principle rather than by rote. Hence *guidance* plays an important role in the management of learning.

A textbook is one form of guidance. An enterprising student could find every fact and every theory in this book somewhere else in a library; he would find all the experiments reported in some psychological journal, and he could read the original books by the pioneers who have been mentioned here, such as Wundt, Galton, James, and Watson. But this would be the hard way to read about the science of psychology. The student who tried it would probably have considerable difficulty in relating Pavlov's experiments on conditioned reflexes to Skinner's experiments on operant conditioning.

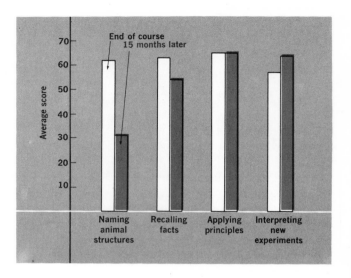

FIGURE 4.7

What College Students Remember   These scores were obtained by testing college zoology students, first at the end of their course and again more than a year later. They show that the students had forgotten about half the terminology they had learned for animal structures and many specific facts. But they still knew the principles as well as ever and could apply them to new situations. On the matter of interpreting experiments that they had never heard of before, they were actually better than at the end of the course. This improvement was probably due to the greater general knowledge and maturity acquired in an additional year of college. (6)

He might not see any connection between the learning of nonsense syllables, which seem such a far cry from reality, and actual learning in the classroom or the learning of such aspects of personality as motives and anxieties. Many of the words he found in the literature would be completely unfamiliar. Much of the material would at first glance seem meaningless. The underlying principles would not be apparent for a long time, and he would therefore have to make a dogged attempt to memorize many things by rote.

Every textbook represents an attempt at the management of learning by providing guidance. Textbook authors try to introduce new material in such a way as to relate it to what is already familiar. They try to point out the meaning of the many facts in their field and to relate the facts to general principles. Even so, textbooks are not always easy to read or to study. One reason is that the authors do not know the students who will be reading the book. They cannot be sure how much previous knowledge the students will bring to the subject. They may take for granted that the students are familiar with things that are in fact not familiar at all. Or they may make the opposite mistake and bore their readers by belaboring the obvious.

Far better than even the best textbook is the kind of guidance that can be provided, in person, by a good teacher. As President Garfield put it many years ago in a speech on education:

> I am not willing that this discussion should close without mention of the value of a true teacher. Give me a log hut, with only a simple bench, Mark Hopkins [the eminent president of Williams College] on one end and I on the other, and you may have all the buildings, apparatus, and libraries without him.

In modern America, the one teacher–one student relationship is unthinkable; classes must of necessity be much larger. But a teacher's guidance is still the most effective form of management of learning that is known. The art of teaching revolves largely around the manipulation of familiarity, meaningfulness, and learning by logic and principles—in other words, around the formation of associations between the new and the old that constitutes the third requirement of learning. It can also be applied to the other requirements for learning.

ATTENTION TO THE STIMULUS

When we pay attention—eagerly and single-mindedly—learning tends to be easy. When we do not pay close attention, learning tends to be difficult or even impossible. But, as every student knows, these simple facts are not in themselves very helpful. Try as we may to pay attention, we often fail. Listening to a classroom lecture, we find ourselves giving our attention not to the words but to the sound of rain on the windowpanes. Reading a textbook, we find ourselves thinking how pleasant it would be to have a hamburger or to go to sleep. What, then, are the factors that sometimes help us pay attention and sometimes turn our thoughts elsewhere? What, if anything, can we do to control these factors?

Motives

One powerful aid to paying attention is motivation. Some people seem to have an almost insatiable thirst for knowledge—any kind of knowledge. They find it easy to pay attention regardless of the subject matter. Some students who are motivated mostly by the desire for good grades also pay close attention regardless of whether they are studying psychology, philosophy, or ancient history. Most of us, however, are somewhat more selective; we are strongly motivated to learn some things, less strongly motivated to learn others. We are most likely to pay attention when the learning stimulus seems to satisfy our own particular and rather specialized motives.

A college woman who plans to become a teacher in an elementary school may find it easy to pay attention to a subject such as psychology, particularly when the specific topic of discussion is children, and difficult to pay attention to a subject such as Elizabethan literature. A woman about to get married is likely to pay more attention to home economics than to history. The man who hopes to be a high school coach pays close attention to physical education; the man who hopes to go into business, to economics and mathematics.

If the subject matter can somehow be related to a person's motives, attention can be sharpened. Thus the study of Spanish becomes easier if the student keeps reminding himself that he is quite likely to be traveling or even working some day in a Spanish-speaking country. The most successful teachers are those who manage to relate their subjects to the hopes and ambitions of their students.

Feedback

Earlier in the chapter it was pointed out that a person who tried to master a college subject by going to a library and starting to read would have great difficulty—the reason being lack of guidance in relating the various facts to one another and to the underlying principles of the subject. But suppose that a person of college age collected all the best textbooks he could find—in psychology, chemistry, economics, history, and any other subject he wanted to learn about—and then stayed home and studied these books. Could he acquire a college education through his own efforts, without going to school but with the help of books especially written to provide guidance?

It has actually been done. Many people who were unable to go to college for one reason or another but were strongly motivated to learn have managed to educate themselves and have as much knowledge as any graduate. Again, however, this is the hard way to learn. One reason—the fact that a teacher's guidance is better than a textbook—has already been discussed. Another lies in the importance of what is called *feedback*, a term borrowed from the field of automation.

Feedback means information on how well the learning process is going—how the learner is progressing, how much he has learned, how many mistakes he is making, and what kind of mistakes. A good example of feedback is demonstrated by teaching machines. The student studies a subject in a series of brief steps, writes down the answer to a question presented by the machine, and is told immediately by the machine whether he is right or wrong. This immediate feedback is perhaps the major advantage of the teaching machine.

One reason feedback helps the learning process is that it enables the learner to correct his mistakes quickly. This is especially apparent in motor learning. The beginning golfer who tries to learn by swinging a club at the grass blades in his back yard may be doing it all wrong and acquiring bad habits that he will have to correct later. If he swings on a practice range, the flight of the ball shows him his mistakes and he can then try to correct them at once.

The other reason—perhaps even more important—is that feedback helps capture and hold attention. Whatever the motives for paying attention and learning, they can generally be satisfied only by some kind of evidence that learning is actually taking place. Thus feedback serves as a strong reinforcement in the learning process.

In accordance with the principle of delay of reinforcement (page 63), the more rapid the feedback the more effective it is. For example, freshman chemistry students at one college were divided into two matched groups. Each time the instructor gave an hour examination, arrangements were made so that the papers could be graded immediately. The students in one group got their papers back before they even left the classroom where the test was given and learned right away which of their answers had been right and which had been wrong. The other group got the results at the beginning of the next class session. Even this difference in speed of feedback, which one might not expect to have any practical effect, proved important. The students who had seen the test results immediately did significantly better on the final examination (7).

Rewards

Perhaps the most frequently used tool in the management of learning is a reward. Laboratory rats are rewarded with food pellets for learning to press a Skinner bar, trained whales with pieces of fish for learning to jump out of water. Babies are rewarded for each new accomplishment with a smile and a pat on the head. Older children are rewarded with gold stars, candy, and trips to the movies. Even college students are rewarded for learning—with good grades and eventually diplomas from their teachers and sometimes with increased allowances or automobiles from their parents.

All these tokens of success, from food pellets to college diploma, are *external rewards* (also sometimes called *extrinsic rewards*). They are in a sense merely bribes provided by another person, but they can be effective and useful. Many an adult has been happier and more successful because of knowledge originally acquired mostly for the external reward of good grades and praise from a parent. Many a man is glad that he learned to play the piano as a boy—something he would never have done without the external reward of a new bicycle or a fishing trip.

A second group of rewards, more difficult to control, is *internal rewards* (also sometimes called *intrinsic rewards*). Internal rewards are feelings of satisfaction. An example is a boy learning to ride a bicycle. In part his attention may be drawn by external rewards, such as the respect of his friends. But the rewards are primarily internal—pleasant feelings arising from the satisfaction of his desire to prove his ability and from the sense of power derived from traveling faster on wheels than he can travel on foot. Other examples are adults who try very hard to learn to dance, to play a musical instrument, or to take beautiful photographs. Their attention is absolutely riveted on the learning situation—not because they seek any external reward but because they want the internal reward of learning a new skill, the reward that comes from meeting an internal standard of perfection.

In many learning situations, both internal and external rewards help recruit attention. The musician may learn both for his own pleasure and for praise from his friends. The mechanic may learn more about automobiles partly because of the inner satisfactions of his job and partly because he wants more pay. Of the two kinds of rewards, however, the internal seem to be the more effective and lasting aid to attention. In the management of learning, the teacher who can make his students eager to know for the inner satisfaction of knowing wields a powerful tool.

Punishment

Another frequently used tool is punishment. Just as we are rewarded for our successes from the early days of childhood, so are we punished for our failures. Babies are punished by a slap on the hand if they threaten to knock over a lamp and sometimes by a slap on the bottom if they seem to cry too much. Older children are punished if they are "sassy," get into fights or the cookie jar, or make poor grades at school. The punishment comes in a wide range of severity—from a mere "No!" stated in a firm tone of voice to a harsh spanking.

In elementary school, teachers punish pupils by keeping them after hours, by making them write essays on the evils of laziness, and by sending them to the principal's office for a stern lecture. In college, the punishment is more subtle. Poor grades are in themselves a kind of punishment and being flunked out is the ultimate.

Although our society quite frequently relies on punishment, the effectiveness of punishment in management of learning is a matter of considerable controversy among psychologists. For many years the consensus was that punishment was not effective at all. This opinion was based in part upon an experiment in which students who had no knowledge of Spanish listened to a Spanish word and five English words, then were asked to guess which of the English words meant the same thing as the Spanish word. For example, they might be given *casa* as the Spanish word, and *horse, house, cask, cattle,* and *rifle* as the English words. If they correctly guessed *house*, they were rewarded with an enthusiastic "Right!" If they guessed wrong, they were punished with a disappointed "Wrong!" It was found that the rewarded responses tended to be learned and repeated. But punishment did not seem to discourage an incorrect response. An answer that had been declared "Wrong!" was just as likely to occur again as any unpunished answer (8).

On the other hand, punishment has proved clearly effective in other situations. One example is the familiar one of housebreaking a dog, which is best accomplished by punishing the animal with a slap with a rolled-up newspaper when it makes mistakes. There is considerable evidence that punishment is most effective when the wrong response is punished and the correct response rewarded. In the case of housebreaking, for example, punishment for wetting the rug is best accompanied by clear indications to the animal that the same act is acceptable outdoors. When a rat is placed at the entrance of a T-shaped maze, it will learn very quickly to turn right instead of left if it is punished with an electric shock if it turns left and rewarded with food if it turns right. Many other kinds of animal experiments have also shown that punishment often results in rapid and long-lasting learning (9).

There is a growing belief that the effectiveness of punishment in the management of learning is too complicated a topic to permit of any categorical answers. Effectiveness appears to depend upon many factors—among them the nature of the learning task, the individual characteristics of the learner, the type and severity of punishment, and the timing of the punishment.

Novelty

FIGURE 4.8 illustrates one professor's somewhat unorthodox efforts at management of learning. Certainly students are not likely to fall asleep in a classroom where such things are known to happen, and, if they should fall asleep, they will soon be jolted back to consciousness. The professor's methods represent an attempt to capture attention through *novelty*. The new and unexpected always contains a certain amount of built-in capacity to attract attention. People used to run outside their houses to watch one of the new automobiles drive by or to see that curious new invention known as the airplane pass overhead. When television was new a few decades ago, people stared for minutes on end at the test patterns. Children in southern California are excited by rain, and children from the northern states are fascinated by their first palm tree. A blonde woman walking down the street in southern Italy stirs a ripple of interest, as does a brunette walking down the street in Sweden. The unexpected and surprising seems to recharge the attentional system, and thus novelty is another useful tool in the management of learning.

The tool must be used with caution. If wielded too flamboyantly or too

FIGURE 4.8

Novelty in the Classroom
Puffed rice goes flying in a
physics class at El Camino
Junior College as Professor
Julius S. Miller, an advocate of
dramatizing the subject matter,
demonstrates a principle of
air pressure.

often, it may do the opposite of what is intended—it may *dis*tract attention
from the real business of learning at hand. Even when carefully used it has
only a temporary effect, for novelty soon wears off. But the teacher who
employs it skillfully is like a long ball hitter who can also bunt; the students,
like the infielders in the ball game, are likely to stay on their toes.

THE DISTINCTIVE STIMULUS
In this discussion of the management of learning,
organized around the three requirements for learning,
one more requirement remains—the need for a distinctive stimulus. The
question that must now be asked is: How can the learning stimulus be made
more distinctive and helped to sink home like a dart in a cork wall?

Here we get into such questions as whether it is better to try to learn a
speech as a whole or by paragraphs, whether it is better to read only or to
read and recite, and whether it is better to study for one long, unbroken
period or for a series of shorter periods. In other words, we must consider
techniques of study—for all techniques of study are in essence an attempt to
manipulate the stimulus and present it in the most efficient way and on the
most efficient time schedule.

Before we get into specifics, let us consider two findings that have a
bearing on this problem. One of them is another of the contributions made
by Ebbinghaus, illustrated in FIGURE 4.9. As the curve shows, doubling the
amount to be learned does not just double the time required for learning

The More to Learn, the Progressively Harder **The** way in which learning becomes progressively more difficult as the amount of material increases is demonstrated by this curve, constructed from another of the experiments performed with nonsense syllables by Ebbinghaus. Note the steep rise in the curve from the time it took Ebbinghaus to learn each of the syllables in a list of seven (a mere 0.4 second) to the time it took him for each syllable in a list of thirty-six (22 seconds).

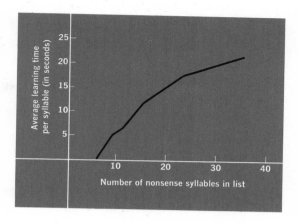

FIGURE 4.9

but increases the time by much more than double. When Ebbinghaus increased the length of his list of nonsence syllables from seven to thirty-six, or to slightly more than five times the original length, the time required for learning per syllable increased by fifty-five times!

The other finding is shown in FIGURE 4.10, which is an experimental demonstration of a fact you may have noticed in your own studies and classroom work. When we listen to a lecture, we usually remember the first part of it very well and also, although slightly less well, the last part. The middle is much harder to remember. The same thing happens in many other situations. If we listen to a fifteen-minute news broadcast and someone asks us afterward to tell about the news, we tend to remember the first items and the last ones but to forget the ones in the middle. If we make out a shopping list and lose it, we are more likely to remember the first and last items than the middle ones. In any series of stimuli, *serial position* helps determine which are learned best.

The *law of primacy and recency* states that out of a series of stimuli we find it easiest to remember the ones that came first (which had primacy) and the ones we encountered last (which had recency). This law, of course, holds only when the stimuli in the series are of approximately equal familiarity and meaningfulness. The results in FIGURE 4.10 would have been far different if the series of syllables had been XIL, PYB, JIW, BIV, CAT, DOG, HAM, CAR, KUG, LOD, GYS, NUR. In that case the familiar syllables in the middle of the list would have been learned first. All other things being equal, however, the law of primacy and recency holds for a wide range of situations and has an important application to the management of learning through manipulation of the stimulus.

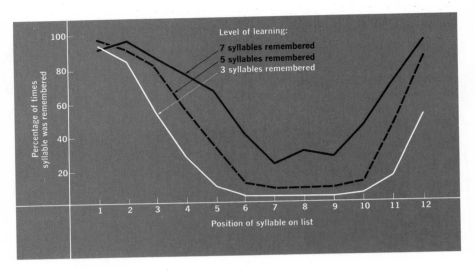

FIGURE **4.10**

The Law of Primacy and Recency The graph shows what happened when subjects were asked to study a list of twelve nonsense syllables and were tested at various stages of the learning process to see how many syllables they remembered—especially *which* ones they remembered. To interpret the graph, note first the white line that shows what had happened by the time the subjects had reached the level of learning where they knew three of the twelve syllables. In almost all cases the subjects were successful at remembering the first syllable on the list; well over 80 percent of the time they remembered the second syllable. The third syllable on the list was remembered about half the time, as was the last syllable on the list. Very few of the subjects remembered the fifth through the tenth syllables on the list. By the time the subjects had learned seven of the twelve syllables they still favored the ones at the beginning of the list and to a lesser extent those at the end. The seventh, eighth, and ninth syllables stuck in their memories least of all. The findings demonstrate the *law of primacy and recency*, which is explained further in the text. (10)

Whole Versus Part Learning

We are back now to the question of whether it is better to learn a speech as a whole or in parts. As a start toward answering it, let us see if we can apply what has just been said.

If we try to learn the speech as a whole, it follows from the law of primacy and recency that we will learn the beginning and the end of it first; we will know these parts by heart long before we master the middle. Score one point for the part method—for it seems a waste of time to keep working on the beginning and end of the speech long after we have mastered them.

As we know from the fact that difficulty of learning increases disproportionately with the amount of material, it will take us much longer to learn a ten-paragraph speech than it would take to learn ten separate paragraphs. Score another point for the part method.

Going back to what was said in the preceding section of this chapter, we know that feedback and reward are important in preserving attention. If we learn the speech a paragraph at a time, we will get faster feedback; we will be able to notice the results more quickly. As we learn each paragraph the knowledge that we have accomplished something will serve as a reward to keep us going. Score another point for the part method.

However . . .

We must also consider the role of meaningfulness and the importance of logical versus rote learning. Does the speech as a whole tend to hang together? Does it have more meaning as a whole than when broken up into individual paragraphs? If so, score a point for the whole method.

Similarly, we must consider the problem of transitions. If we learn the speech a paragraph at a time, studying each paragraph over and over until we know it, the last words of each paragraph tend to become associated with the first words of the same paragraph. If we are to avoid repeating ourselves when we deliver the speech, like a record player with a stuck needle, we must break these associations and establish new associations between the end of each paragraph and the start of the following paragraph. This is not always easy—so score another point for the whole method.

How does the score add up? It all depends. Generally speaking, the whole method seems to be indicated when the material to be learned is relatively brief and has a logical theme that ties it into a meaningful unit. The Gettysburg Address, for example, can probably be learned most efficiently by the whole method. The Amendments to the Constitution, however, can probably be best learned by the part method, because they are relatively long and are made up of twenty-three discrete units that do not form a meaningful whole, though each possesses its own internal logic. The question of who is doing the learning must also be taken into account. In general, the whole method works best for people who have had considerable practice with it and who are above average in intelligence and in background of learning—factors that help in making new material more meaningful.

Combination Methods

Often a combination of the two methods seems most efficient. In studying a chapter in a textbook, for example, one good system is to begin by skimming through it quickly, trying to grasp the general pattern and logic without paying very much attention to the details. Usually the introductory paragraphs and the summary are especially helpful. Sometimes, indeed, it is possible to get a good idea of the sense of a chapter simply by reading the first few paragraphs, glancing at the various headings and the words and ideas emphasized by italics or heavy type, and then reading the summary. Once this feel for the chapter as a whole has been acquired, a slower and more detailed study of the individual parts is in order—with particular attention to the parts that seem difficult to remember.

In learning a speech or any other material that has to be remembered word for word, there often seem to be definite advantages to the *progressive part method*, as it was termed by the psychologist who first suggested it (11). In this method, you learn the first paragraph (or first stanza or whatever unit seems natural). Then you learn the second. Next you learn to put the first and second together. Once you have these two down pat, you put them aside and learn the third, then combine the first, second, and third into a unit—and so on to the end. This method seems to combine many of the virtues of both whole and part learning and to minimize some of the disadvantages.

One of the troubles, of course, is that you still spend more time than is necessary on the early paragraphs or stanzas, particularly the first one. You *overlearn* these parts. But overlearning, it should now be pointed out, is not necessarily bad.

Overlearning

Adults are often surprised by how well they remember something they learned as children but have never practiced in the meantime. A man who has not had a chance to go swimming for years can still swim as well as ever when he gets back in the water. He can get on a bicycle after several decades and still ride away. He can play catch and swing a baseball bat as well as his son. A mother who has not thought about the words for years can teach her daughter the poem that begins "Twinkle, twinkle, little star" or recite the story of Cinderella or Goldilocks and the three bears.

One explanation is the *law of overlearning*, which can be stated as follows: Once we have learned something, additional learning trials increase the length of time we will remember it. A laboratory demonstration of this law is shown in FIGURE 4.11.

In childhood we usually continue to practice such skills as swimming, bicycle riding, and playing baseball long after we have learned them. We continue to listen to and remind ourselves of jingles such as "Twinkle, twinkle, little star" and childhood tales such as Cinderella and Goldilocks. We not only learn but overlearn.

Earlier in the chapter, it was mentioned that the multiplication tables are an exception to the general rule that we tend to forget rather quickly the things that we learn in school by rote. An explanation was promised later—and now, of course, you have it, for the multiplication tables are another of the things we overlearn in childhood.

FIGURE 4.11

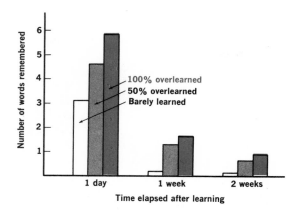

100% overlearned
50% overlearned
Barely learned

Time elapsed after learning

How Overlearning Aids Remembering These are the results of an experiment in which subjects learned a list of twelve single-syllable nouns. Sometimes they stopped studying the list as soon as they were able to recall it without error—in the words used in the chart, as soon as they had "barely learned" the words. At other times they were asked to continue studying the list for half again as many trials as bare learning required (50 percent overlearned) or to continue studying for the same number of extra trials as the original learning had required (100 percent overlearned). Whether measured after a day or at later intervals, the subjects who had overlearned by 50 percent remembered considerably more than those who had barely learned, and the subjects who had overlearned by 100 percent remembered most of all. (12)

The law of overlearning explains why cramming for an examination, though it may result in a passing grade, is not a satisfactory way to learn a college course. In cramming, we learn the subject barely well enough to get by on the examination. Shortly afterward, we are likely to forget almost everything we learned. A little overlearning, on the other hand, is usually a good investment toward the future.

In some cases, overlearning has disadvantages, as is demonstrated by the experiment shown in FIGURE 4.12. The explanation of the results obtained in this experiment seems to be that the children who studied the drawings longest learned to expect to see them in a definite order. They were set to see the umbrella after the elephant and the tricycle after the umbrella. Thus they recognized the partial clues very readily when these were presented in the same order as the original pictures. But their sets made it difficult for them to recognize the partial clues when the order was changed. The children who did less studying of the original pictures did not develop this kind of set and were more "open minded" when they saw the partial clues. The experiment shows that overlearning can produce sets that interfere with

131

The Negative Side of Overlearning   A series of drawings such as those at the left were shown to two groups of children. One group "barely learned" the drawings by looking at them five times. The other group overlearned them by looking at them twenty times. Later the children were tested to see if they could recognize the partial clues shown at the right. The group that had overlearned did better when the partial clues were shown in the same order as the original pictures but did not do quite so well as the other group when the order was mixed up. For an explanation of what this experiment demonstrates about overlearning, see the text. (13)

FIGURE **4.12**

using the knowledge in a new and unfamiliar way. The person who has overlearned remembers the material longer but in some cases may be less flexible about applying it.

Distribution of Practice

Another argument against cramming is that it represents an attempt to learn through what is called *massed practice*—that is, a single long learning session. Studies of a wide range of situations involving both human and animal learning have indicated that massed practice is generally less efficient than *distributed practice*—that is, a series of shorter learning periods. As FIGURE 4.13 shows, the same total amount of time spent in learning is often strikingly more efficient when invested in short, separated periods than all at once.

Three possible explanations have been suggested for the superiority of distributed practice:

1. Distributed practice reduces the fatigue that often accompanies massed practice in motor learning and the boredom that often occurs in massed practice in verbal learning.

2. In the intervals between learning in distributed practice the learner may continue to mull over the material he has learned, even without knowing that he is doing so. This process is called *covert rehearsal* and results in what is called *consolidation* of what has been learned.

3. In many kinds of learning it seems likely that we learn not only what

FIGURE 4.13

Massed Versus Distributed Practice

This graph shows the results of an experiment in which the eyelid blinking reflex, produced by a puff of air directed at the eye, was conditioned to a light. More conditioned responses were obtained when there were 90-second intervals between trials than when the intervals were shorter or, to put it another way, when the practice was more massed. (14)

This graph shows the results of an experiment in which the subjects learned to substitute numbers for letters. Progress was slowest in a single massed session of 120 minutes of practice, higher when the subjects worked in three 40-minute sessions spread over six days, and highest of all when twelve 10-minute sessions were spread over six days. (15)

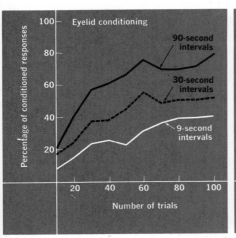

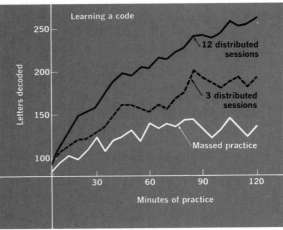

we want to learn but a number of useless and irrelevant habits that may actually interfere. A man learning to drive a golf ball, for example, might at the same time learn to grit his teeth, squint, and blink his eyes at the moment of impact—habits that do not help his swing but hurt it. During the intervals of distributed practice these extraneous habits may be forgotten more quickly than the basic subject matter of the learning. The process is called *differential forgetting*.

It must be added, however, that distributed practice does not always give such spectacular results as shown in FIGURE 4.13. It seems less helpful in learning by logic than in learning by rote, possibly because logical learning involves less boredom. In learning situations that require a lot of "cranking up" time—getting out several books and notebooks, finding some reference works on the library shelves, and finding a comfortable and well-lighted place to work—short practice periods may be less efficient than long ones. Moreover, distributed practice does not appear to have much effect if any upon how well the learning is remembered; even where it results in substantial savings of the time required for learning, it does not seem to improve retention. But the general idea of distributed practice is a useful tool in the management of learning. Probably all learning tasks can be best accomplished through some pattern of distributed practice—in some cases many short periods separated by long intervals, in some cases fewer and longer periods separated by shorter intervals, and in some cases perhaps a combination. The trick is to find the pattern that best suits the situation.

Recitation

We come now to the last of the questions posed at the beginning of the chapter: Is it better just to keep reading when you study or to read for a while and then attempt to recite? An answer will be found in FIGURE 4.14.

Experimenters have found that it makes no difference whether the subjects are children or adults or whether the material being learned is nonsense syllables, spelling, mathematics, or a foreign vocabulary. In every case it is more efficient to read and recite than to read alone.

Let us say that you have eight hours to devote to learning this chapter and that reading through the chapter takes you two hours. The least efficient way to spend your study time would be to read through the chapter four times. Perhaps the most efficient way would be to read it once, then try to recite to yourself or write down what you remember, then return to the book to devote more study to the points you had forgotten or that were hazy in your mind, then recite again. As FIGURE 4.14 shows, devoting as much as 80 percent of study time to recitation may be more efficient by far than mere reading.

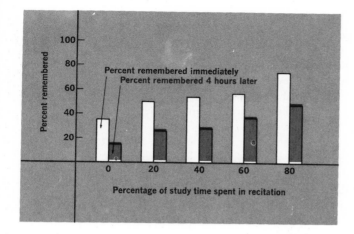

FIGURE 4.14

The Value of Recitation   The subjects were elementary school pupils and university students who studied a list of sixteen nonsense syllables. The total time spent in study was the same for all the subjects. Some subjects, however, spent the entire time reading the material, while others spent 20 to 80 percent of the time reciting. When the various groups were tested immediately and four hours later, the results were as shown here. (16)

Recitation seems to assist learning in a number of ways. It certainly helps make the stimulus more distinctive; it casts a telling searchlight on what you have grasped quickly and what you have not, on what you understand and what you still find obscure. It provides a form of feedback that sharpens your attention. It helps you find meaningfulness and logical principles in the material. Of all study techniques, recitation is the one of most clearly proved value.

TRANSFER OF LEARNING

Most educators once believed firmly that learning Latin and ancient Greek would exercise and discipline the mind. The beneficial effects, it was thought, would *transfer* to other kinds of learning: once a person had studied Latin and Greek, he would be that much better at learning anything from basket weaving to higher mathematics. A large-scale survey reported in the early 1920's demolished this theory of general transfer. In the survey, 13,000 high school students were tested for learning ability, then tested again a year later. Careful records were kept of the subjects they studied in the meantime. For example, some of the students took algebra, history, English, chemistry, and French, while some took algebra, history, English, chemistry, and Latin. If this second group had shown a substantially higher increase in learning ability than the first group, it would have seemed reasonable to attribute the improvement to the superiority of Latin over French. In the same way, using different groups from the big sample, it was possible to study the effects of all kinds of different subjects. Most closely connected with an increase in learning ability, it turned out, were the high school courses in mathematics (algebra, geometry, and trigonometry), with the social sciences and psychology not far behind. Latin was well down the list, nowhere near the top. At the bottom were biology and dramatic art (17).

All the differences from the very top of the list to the bottom were quite small; the students who took mathematics improved somewhat more in learning ability than students who took biology and dramatic art but hardly enough to be worth mentioning. Much more significant, in determining how much the students improved, was the amount of learning ability they started with. The students who were brightest to begin with improved the most; the students at the bottom improved the least. The investigators who conducted the survey concluded that the chief reason mathematics stood at the top of the list was simply that it tended to attract the ablest learners. In the days when the transfer theory was popular, it can be assumed, the best students were attracted to Latin or Greek (or persuaded by their teachers to take these subjects); it was the quality of the students, not the subject matter, that made Latin and Greek seem so stimulating to the mind.

Although the old general theory of transfer has been disproved, nonetheless it is true that certain specific kinds of transfer do take place, sometimes making new learning easier and sometimes making it more difficult.

Positive Transfer

One significant experiment in transfer is illustrated in FIGURE 4.15. The results of the experiment can be predicted from what has already been said about learning. List 1 is a clear case of forming simple connections between

An Experiment in Transfer   Subjects first learned the pairings in list 1, so that when presented with the stimulus of REQ they responded with KIY and when presented with TAW they responded with RIF. Some of them then learned list 2, in which the responses are the same and the first syllables in the list are quite similar to those in list 1. Others learned list 3, in which the responses are the same but the first syllables are totally different. Question: Did learning list 1 help in learning lists 2 and 3, and, if so, which did it help more? For the answer, see the text. (18)

FIGURE **4.15**

List 1		List 2		List 3	
REQ	KIY	REF	KIY	FIZ	KIY
TAW	RIF	TAS	RIF	MIP	RIF
QIX	LEP	QIL	LEP	BUL	LEP
WAM	BOS	WAP	BOS	NIC	BOS
ZED	DIB	ZEL	DIB	CAJ	DIB

a stimulus, namely the first of each pair of syllables, and a response, namely the second word. In list 2, the responses remain exactly the same, and the stimuli are only slightly different from those in list 1. From what we know about stimulus generalization, we would expect anyone who had learned list 1 to do very well on list 2. This indeed proved to be the case. It took the subjects only 44 percent as many trials to learn list 2 perfectly as it took subjects who had not learned list 1, which means that the *positive transfer* of learning from list 1 to list 2 was 56 percent—a very substantial amount.

But what about list 3? Here, though the responses remain the same, the stimuli are totally different. Stimulus generalization cannot operate. What can operate, however, is something else that has been discussed at considerable length—that very important role played in learning by units of innate or previously learned behavior to which a new stimulus can become attached. All the responses required by list 3, being the same as those in list 1, have already been learned. To learn list 3, the responses need merely become associated with new stimuli. It should come as no surprise, therefore, that the amount of positive transfer from list 1 to list 3, though smaller than to list 2, was also substantial—37 percent.

As a sort of shorthand helpful in discussing matters such as these, the symbol S_1 is often used for the original learning stimulus and R_1 for the original learning response. Learning ordinarily consists in forming the association S_1–R_1. When a new learning situation calls for the same response to become associated with a new stimulus, as in the experiment in FIGURE 4.15, the formula becomes S_2–R_1. Learning S_1–R_1 generally makes it easier to learn S_2–R_1—in other words, results in positive transfer—and the more similar S_2 is to S_1, the greater is the amount of transfer likely to be.

There are many everyday examples. Early in life we learn to turn on a water faucet. Later on, we encounter faucets of all sizes, shapes, and colors but have no trouble adjusting to them. Learning to use the handlebars of a tricycle helps us later to use the handlebars of a bicycle and still later the steering wheel of an automobile.

The principle of positive transfer has been of great practical value to many industries and particularly to the military services, which have found that they can often use inexpensive training aids to teach people to operate the most complicated and expensive kind of machinery. For example, the Air Force was once faced with the problem of training repairmen for a new bombing device that weighed a ton and cost around $250,000. Rather than tie up several of these expensive devices for a training program, the Air Force called in a psychologist, who managed to build a simple little substitute that cost only about $4000 yet enabled repairmen to learn almost as well as if they had worked on the real thing. The Navy's Link Trainer, a training aid that simulates the cockpit of a plane and teaches blind flying without ever leaving the ground, provided another impressive example of

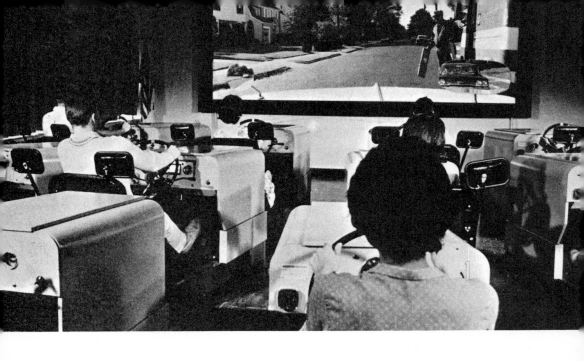

FIGURE **4.16**   *Some Training Aids with Positive Transfer*   Some relatively inexpensive training devices that have proved effective in learning are mock-ups of automobile controls used in conjunction with a motion picture of traffic, a "spaceship" that gives astronauts the sensations of flight while remaining on the ground, and piano keyboards with no strings attached.

positive transfer. A group of students who did their preliminary learning in this trainer before actually getting into an airplane was compared with a group who learned in an actual plane from the very start. The Link Trainer group reached the same level of efficiency after seven hours less time in the air than the other group—with important savings in air-time operating expenses and wear and tear on expensive equipment (19). Some other training devices are shown in FIGURE 4.16.

Negative Transfer

FIGURE 4.15 was a classic demonstration of what happens when S_1–R_1 is followed by S_2–R_1. What happens, however, when S_1–R_1 is followed by S_1–R_2—in other words, when the learning task calls for the same stimulus to become associated with a new response?

The same investigator responsible for the experiment in FIGURE 4.15 went on to study the S_1–R_2 situation as illustrated in FIGURE 4.17. This time, it developed, learning list 1 did not help the new learning but actually hindered it. There was a *negative transfer* amounting to 9 percent.

In another experiment with the S_1–R_2 situation, rats were placed in a simple T-maze. They started at the bottom of the T. At the point where they had to turn to either the right or the left, a light gave them the clue. If the light was on, they found food to the right. If the light was off, they found food to the left. They learned this, on the average, in 286 trials. Once they had thoroughly acquired this S_1–R_1 pattern, the task was reversed; when the light was on, the food was to the left, and, when the light was off, the food was to the right. In the new S_1–R_2 pattern, R_2 was exactly the opposite of R_1. The result was so much negative transfer that the rats required 603 trials to master the new S_1–R_2 situation (20).

Negative transfer causes considerable trouble in everyday situations. Having grown up with faucets that we turned, we may have trouble with some of the new faucets that must be pressed. Being used to faucets that we turn to the left, we run the risk of scalding or freezing ourselves in some of the new showers where the cold water faucet has to be turned in one

FIGURE 4.17

List 1		List 2	
REQ	KIY	REQ	SEJ
TAW	RIF	TAW	BOC
QIX	LEP	QIX	PUW
WAM	BOS	WAM	GIT
ZED	DIB	ZED	LIM

A Demonstration of Negative Transfer Again, as in FIGURE 4.15, the subjects first learned the pairings in list 1. Then they learned list 2, in which it will be noted that the first syllables remain the same but call for totally new responses. For an explanation of how learning list 1 affected learning list 2 in this case, see the text. (18)

direction and the hot water faucet in the other. Knowing how to steer a bicycle and an automobile only confuses us when we first try to operate the tiller of a boat.

Mediated Transfer

If the experiment illustrated in FIGURE 4.17 is varied slightly, it gives some interesting and at first puzzling results. Let us say that we ask students to learn pairings of nonsense syllables with some real words. For example, they learn:

S_1	R_1
XAL	moon
LAN	Detroit

Now we ask them to learn a new response to the same nonsense syllable:

S_1	R_2
XAL	pomegranate
LAN	window

Since S_1-R_1 is followed by S_1-R_2, we would expect to find negative transfer, and indeed this proves to be the case. However, we can get a different result by using slightly different real words as our R_2 responses. Suppose, for example, we give the same S_1-R_1 associations to a new group of subjects:

S_1	R_1
XAL	moon
LAN	Detroit

This time, however, we ask our subjects to learn the following new responses:

S_1	R_2
XAL	Roquefort
LAN	traffic

In this case there may be only a slight negative transfer or none at all. Indeed there may be some positive transfer. Why should this be?

The reason lies in some rather subtle associations that surround words such as *moon* and *Detroit*. Almost everybody has heard the old saying that the moon is made of green cheese. Thus it is easier to follow the learning of the S_1-R_1 pairing of XAL–moon with the S_1-R_2 of XAL–Roquefort than with the S_1-R_2 of XAL–pomegranate. Similarly, it is generally known that Detroit is the center of automobile production, and thus it is easier to learn the S_1-R_2 of LAN–traffic than the S_1-R_2 of LAN–window. There is a transfer of learning from *moon* to *Roquefort* and *Detroit* to *traffic* but not from *moon* to *pomegranate* and *Detroit* to *window*. The transfer occurs even though the students in the experiment may be entirely unaware that they are making any association of moon, cheese, and Roquefort or of Detroit, automobile, and traffic.

This special kind of transfer is known as *mediated transfer*. The term comes from the fact that a previously learned mediational unit—the association between moon and cheese and between Detroit and automobile—accounts for the transfer. This is just another of the ways in which the possession of a rich storehouse of previously learned mediational units aids the learning of new materials—sometimes in ways of which we are not even conscious.

Development of Learning Sets

The classic experiment demonstrating the development of learning sets is illustrated in FIGURE 4.18. The monkey in this experiment, asked to perform a long series of learning tasks that were similar in general but different in detail, got better and better at learning as the series went on. As is shown in FIGURE 4.19, toward the end the animal was able to master each new problem in a single trial. Whether or not it found the food on the first trial, it went almost unerringly to the correct object on the second and subsequent trials. In most convincing fashion, it had learned to learn.

Similar results, though not always such spectacular ones, have been ob-

A Monkey "Learns to Learn"   A monkey in a cage learns to discriminate between two objects, one of which has food beneath it. Sometimes, as in this photo, the food was always under the funnel and never under the cylinder. Sometimes it was under a circle but not a rectangle, a cube but not a sphere, or a black object but not a white object. In all, the monkey was asked to learn to discriminate between more than 300 different pairs of objects. Question: Did the animal learn faster toward the end of the series than at the beginning? For the answer, see FIGURE 4.19.

FIGURE 4.18

FIGURE **4.19**

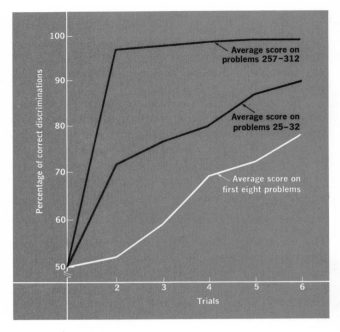

The Monkey's Progress   On each of the learning problems the monkey
had a 50–50 chance of finding the food on the first trial, and its score
on this trial averaged 50 percent. On the first eight problems the
animal made rather slow progress and still was averaging less than 80
percent correct on the sixth trial. Note, however, how much more
rapidly it learned on problems 25–32 and especially on problems
257–312. (21)

tained in many experiments with human beings. For example, students have
been shown to learn to learn even when the material is meaningless, such as
lists of nonsense syllables. If lists of equal difficulty are drawn up and students
are asked to learn a series of them, the second list will be learned more
quickly than the first list, on the average, and the fourth list more quickly
than the second. On more meaningful material, such as schoolwork, students
develop various kinds of learning sets that make them far more efficient
learners in high school than they were in elementary school and more
efficient in college than in high school.

THEORIES
OF REMEMBERING
AND FORGETTING

At one time the most generally accepted theory of
remembering and forgetting centered around the phrase
memory trace. According to this theory, learning left some kind of trace in
the organism resembling the marks of a pencil or a path worn into a plot

of grass. Perhaps the trace was basically electrical in nature and somehow set up where one nerve connects with another in the complicated switchboard of the brain. Perhaps it was chemical. At any rate it could be kept functioning through use, as a pencil mark can be emphasized by tracing and retracing and a pathway can be kept clear by continuing to walk over it. Without use, the memory trace tended to fade away, as a pencil mark fades with time and a pathway becomes overgrown when abandoned.

How then, however, to explain the fact that some memory traces never seem to disappear at all? How can we explain why Ebbinghaus should have remembered those stanzas from *Don Juan*—as measured by relearning—after twenty-two years of disuse? How can we explain the vivid remembrance of events believed to have been long since forgotten that occurs under hypnosis or electrical stimulation of the brain?

At our present state of knowledge, the memory trace theory can be neither proved nor disproved. But what has been learned about the transfer of learning, and especially about negative transfer, has suggested another theory that is currently more popular. This is the idea that the mediational units set up by learning are permanent, or more or less permanent, and do not tend to fade away with the passage of time. They are not just traces that are prone to decay. Rather, to use a figure of speech, they are like iron filings; they are virtually indestructible. But, like iron filings in a magnetic field, they cluster in certain patterns and can be pulled apart and rearranged when other filings are introduced into the field. The pattern of old filings helps determine where the new ones will cluster. But the new filings also influence and shift the old.

According to this theory, the reason we forget can be summed up in the single word *interference*—interference between and among old and new mediational units. Something we have learned in the past interferes with a new association we are trying to establish. Or what we learn now interferes with some old associations. To go back to our figure of speech, the old patterns of filings keep the new filings from going where we want them. Or the new filings disrupt the patterns we once had established. We forget not because any of our mediational units have faded away but because they have grouped themselves in different clusters of association.

Retroactive Inhibition

Whatever the nature of the forgetting process, it is well established that new learning can and does interfere with the ability to remember the old. This phenomenon, which has been studied for a long time, is called *retroactive inhibition*. Retroactive means affecting something that occurred in the past. Inhibition means the act of restraining or stopping. *Retroactive inhibition is the partial or complete blacking out of old memories by new learning.*

A laboratory demonstration of retroactive inhibition is illustrated in FIGURE 4.20. Many other experiments of this kind have produced similar results. When the learning of task 1 is followed by the learning of task 2, memory for task 1 is always less than it would otherwise be, and, the more similar task 2 is to task 1, the greater is the amount of interference.

In fact any kind of activity, not just learning, can cause retroactive inhibition, as has been demonstrated in the experiment shown in FIGURE 4.21. The person who is asleep, and thus as near to a state of suspended animation as possible, forgets less rapidly than the person who is awake and active.

A later refinement of the sleeping-waking experiment demonstrated another aspect of retroactive inhibition. In this case several subjects took part. Instead of nonsense syllables they were asked to memorize some meaningful material—some short stories that had been carefully constructed so that each one contained twelve elements that were essential to the plot of the story and twelve elements that were not essential. The subjects were then tested eight hours later for their recall of the stories, sometimes after sleeping and sometimes after going about their usual daytime activities.

As far as the nonessential elements of the stories were concerned, the results were much the same as in the earlier experiment with nonsense syllables. The subjects who had slept for the eight hours recalled 47 percent of these nonessential elements. Those who had been awake for the eight hours recalled only 23 percent. But the results for the essential elements

FIGURE 4.20   *Retroactive Inhibition*   The recall scores were obtained ten minutes after the subjects had learned a list of adjectives. During those ten minutes most of the subjects were kept busy at new learning tasks, but one group merely rested by reading jokes. The difference between this last group's high scores and the other groups' lower scores demonstrates the effect of retroactive inhibition. Note that the more similar the new learning is to the original, the greater the amount of retroactive inhibition. (22)

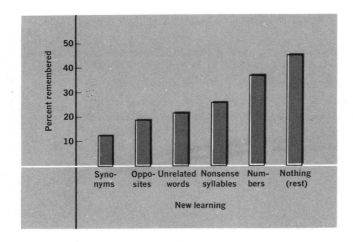

FIGURE **4.21**

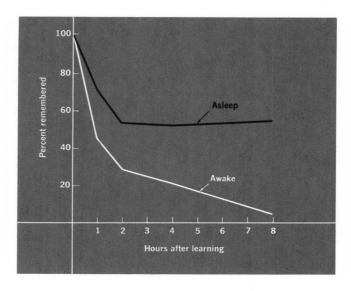

Forgetting Curves When Asleep and Awake   The black forgetting curve was obtained from a subject who learned lists of ten nonsense syllables immediately before going to bed and was wakened for testing at various times of the night. The white curve is for the same subject, but in this case he learned the lists in the morning, went about his usual waking activities, and was tested at various times of the day. Question: Why does the curve drop so much more sharply during waking hours than during sleep? For the answer, see the text. (23)

of the plots were strikingly different. The sleepers recalled 87 percent, the others 86 percent—scores that are virtually identical (24).

The findings in this experiment help explain the study, reported earlier in the chapter, in which it was found that college zoology students tended to remember the principles of the subject much better than such details as the terminology. Retroactive inhibition obviously has a greater effect upon the meaningless, the nonessential, and the specific detail than upon the basic principles that underlie meaningful learning. To return again to the figure of speech used earlier, the iron filings that cluster together in the firm associations formed around logic and understanding tend to stick together. It is the less tightly bound filings—the mediational units learned by rote, the unimportant, the details—that are likely to be shaken loose by later learning.

Proactive Inhibition

In retroactive inhibition, as we have seen, the new interferes with memory for the old. When the opposite happens and the old interferes with ability to remember the new, the process is called *proactive inhibition*.

145

FIGURE 4.22

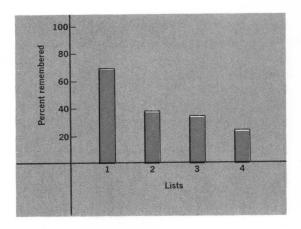

Proactive Inhibition The subjects learned a list of paired adjectives. Two days after learning they were tested for their recall of list 1 and asked to learn list 2. Two days later they were tested on list 2 and learned list 3. Two days later they were tested on list 3 and learned list 4. Two days later they were tested on list 4, and the experiment ended. The recall scores, which decline with each list, show the effect of proactive inhibition resulting from the learning of the prior lists. (25)

Proactive inhibition is demonstrated by the experiment illustrated in FIGURE 4.22, where the learning of previous word lists was found to interfere sharply with the ability to remember new lists. Similar results have been found in many experiments using nonsense syllables—a fact that points to an interesting contrast between learning ability and the ability to remember. We noted earlier that a subject who learns a number of nonsense lists usually improves as a learner; he can learn the tenth list more rapidly than the first list or the fifth list. But his ability to remember for any length of time decreases with each successive list. Like retroactive inhibition, proactive inhibition seems to have a stronger effect upon the remembering of meaningless materials and details than upon the remembering of meaningful material and general principles.

Implications of Proactive Inhibition

In many situations, proactive inhibition and negative transfer seem to work together; the mediational units acquired in learning task 1 make it more difficult to acquire the units of task 2 and also more difficult to remember them. Certainly the two processes are very closely related. To put the matter in everyday language, we might say that the first habits we acquire make it more difficult to learn new habits, particularly when the new habits conflict in some way with the old. Moreover, even when we think we have acquired the new habits, the old ones are likely to interfere and break in at any time.

Because so many people of recent generations in the United States have received a better education than did their parents and grandparents, there are many adults who learned more or less ungrammatical English in their homes and then learned later, in school and college, to speak correct English. Quite often a person with this kind of background, though well educated, will slip and make the most awkward kind of grammatical error, particularly when forced to speak rapidly and without thinking. Men who have been widowed or divorced and then remarried occasionally call their new wives by the first wife's name (a fact that a sociologist who has studied second marriages calls one of the hazards they present). Drivers who learn in an automobile with automatic transmission and then switch to stick shift sometimes go back to their old habits and neglect to put in the clutch and change gears.

In general, proactive inhibition and negative transfer explain why there is a good deal of truth in the old adage that it is hard to teach an old dog new tricks and why it is harder still to get him to remember the new.

SUMMARY

1. The attempt to arrange the most favorable possible conditions for learning to take place is called *management of learning.*

2. It is easiest to make new learning associations when the stimulus is *familiar, meaningful,* and can be *learned by logic and general principle rather than by rote.*

3. *Guidance*—as furnished by a textbook or preferably in person by a teacher—is the most effective form of management of learning because it points out the elements in the learning situation that are familiar, meaningful, and possible to learn by principle.

4. In attracting attention to the learning stimulus, one important factor is motivation. Attention is sharpened when the subject matter can be related to the individual's motives, whatever these may be.

5. *Feedback*—or knowledge of the results of learning—is important because it helps the learner correct his mistakes and also helps capture and hold attention. The quicker the feedback, the more effective it is.

6. *Rewards* also capture attention and are effective in the management of learning. *External rewards* (also called *extrinsic rewards*) are those provided by another person, such as praise, good grades, or cash payments. *Internal rewards* (also called *intrinsic rewards*) are the learner's own feelings of satisfaction resulting from successful learning.

7. *Punishment,* another tool frequently used in management of learning, appears to be effective in some situations and ineffective in others. Its

usefulness depends upon many factors and is a subject of controversy.

8. *Novelty* helps attract attention and is a useful tool in management of learning.

9. Two characteristics of the learning stimulus that have an important effect on the learning process are the following:

   a. *Amount.* As the amount to be learned increases, the difficulty of learning it increases disproportionately, so that doubling the amount more than doubles the difficulty.

   b. *Serial position.* In any series of learning stimuli the first ones are most easily learned, the last ones next most easily; the ones in the middle are learned last. This is called *the law of primacy and recency.*

10. Study techniques are attempts to manipulate the learning stimulus so as to present it in the most efficient way on the most efficient time schedule. Among the findings about study techniques are the following:

    a. Learning something *as a whole* has certain advantages, such as making the material more meaningful and more susceptible to learning by logical principle. *Part learning* provides more rapid feedback and avoids the overlearning of portions of the material. Often a combination of the two methods is most efficient.

    b. The more trials on which we continue to learn after learning to the point where we can barely achieve recall, the longer we tend to remember. This is called *overlearning.*

    c. *Distributed practice,* in which the learning process is broken up into separated periods, is generally more efficient than *massed practice.*

    d. *Recitation* has been demonstrated to be the most effective of all study techniques. It is far better to spend as much as 80 percent of the study period in an active attempt to recite than to spend the entire period reading the material.

11. The old theory of general transfer of learning, which held that learning subjects such as Latin and Greek "improved the mind" and made future learning easier, has been somewhat discredited.

12. In many cases, however, learning task 1 makes it easier to learn task 2. This is called *positive transfer.* It occurs most often in situations where task 2 calls for making the same response to a different stimulus (the S_1–R_1 / S_2–R_1 situation).

13. In other cases learning task 1 makes it more difficult to learn task 2, and this is called *negative transfer.* It occurs most prominently in situations where a new response must be made to an old stimulus (S_1–R_1 / S_1–R_2).

14. Two special forms of transfer are *mediated transfer* and the *development of learning sets,* both of which assist the learning process.

15. One theory of how we remember and forget is that learning creates some kind of *memory trace* that fades away through disuse.

16. A more generally held theory today is that the mediational units set up in learning do not fade away but become rearranged through the interference of other learning. In *retroactive inhibition* the ability to remember something learned in the past is reduced by new learning. In *proactive inhibition* the ability to remember new learning is reduced by something learned in the past.

RECOMMENDED READING

Bruner, J. S. *Toward a theory of instruction.* Cambridge, Mass.: Harvard University Press, 1966.

Deese, J. E. and Hulse, S. *The psychology of learning,* 3rd ed. New York: McGraw-Hill, 1967.

Fry, E. *Teaching machines and programmed instruction.* New York: McGraw-Hill, 1963.

Gage, N. L., ed. *Handbook of research on teaching.* Chicago: Rand McNally, 1963.

McGeoch, J. A. and Irion, A. L. *The psychology of human learning,* 2nd ed. New York: McKay, 1958.

Melton, A. W., ed. *Categories of human learning.* New York: Academic Press, 1964.

Smith, D. E. P., et al. *Learning to learn.* New York: Harcourt, Brace & World, 1961.

INTERPRETIVE BEHAVIOR

To the physicist, this book you hold is not at all what it seems to be: it is a collection of tiny bits of matter called protons and electrons, separated by relatively large amounts of empty space. These bits of matter are spinning in constant orbit like the planets around the sun. They have no color, not even black or white; if they seem to, it is only because they have a certain characteristic way of absorbing or reflecting the form of electromagnetic energy called light. This apparently solid, stationary, colored, black-and-white book is in physical fact largely empty space and a whirlpool of constant motion, and it has no color or brightness at all.

What the physicist knows about the true nature of this book and the world in general, however, has very little importance to the study of behavior. The organism behaves in accordance not with what the environment really is but with what it seems to be.

The way in which we view our environment depends partly upon the limitations of our senses. (Our eyes are not sharp enough to detect anything so small as protons and electrons; we can only discern large aggregations of them in the form of apparently solid matter.) Even more important than the evidence of our senses, however, is the manner in which we interpret the evidence and thus build up our own impressions of all the stimuli that the world presents to us. For example, your own behavior at this moment depends not so much on the fact that you see this book as a solid object as on the fact that you regard it as a college textbook. A child, though seeing the book exactly as you see it, might interpret it as something to draw on or to build into piles like blocks. To the organism called a bookworm, the book presumably also seems to be a solid object but it is something to eat rather than something to study or to play with. Thus the same book can have far different effects upon the behavior of a student, a child, and a worm.

The way in which we interpret our environment is the subject of this third section of the textbook. Chapter 5 deals with perception, the process through which we become aware of the stimuli in our world. Chapter 6 deals with the further step in which we use language and concepts to help make our interpretations, to think about the environment, and to manipulate the environment through the higher order mental process called problem solving. These chapters are, of course, closely related to learning, for among the most important of all the things we learn, as was mentioned at the end of Chapter 2, are perceptual expectations, words, and concepts.

PERCEPTION VERSUS SENSATION

Real Versus Perceived Movement
The Autokinetic Illusion
Other Sensory Illusions

SELECTION AS AN ELEMENT OF PERCEPTION

Stimulus Characteristics and Selection
    Change; Contrast; Movement; Size; Intensity; Repetition
The Perceiver and Selection

ORGANIZATION AS AN ELEMENT OF PERCEPTION

Inborn Tendencies in Organization
    Figure and Ground; Closure; Continuity; Proximity; Similarity;
    Common Movement
Learned Tendencies in Organization
    Shape Constancy; Brightness Constancy; Color Constancy; Location
    Constancy; Size Constancy; When Size Constancy Fails
Size and Distance
Other Clues to Distance
    Binocular Vision; Interposition; Perspective; Shadowing
Perception of Height and Depth
Perceptual Conflicts

THE PERCEIVER AND PERCEPTION

Early Experience
    Perceptual Expectations
    Influences on Perceptual Expectations
    The Influence of Language

5

PERCEPTION

We human beings move around the world confidently, secure in the belief that we understand the nature of our environment. When we look out a window, we know without thinking that it is a rectangular pane of transparent glass and that through it we see a nearby shrub, a long stretch of grass, a roadway, and other houses down the block. We know that the houses are three-dimensional and that behind their fronts lie rooms. We know which is farthest from us and which is closest. We know that one pedestrian is walking toward us and that another is walking away. When we look at an automobile, it does not matter whether we see a motionless hood and windshield, a motionless rear window and rear bumper, or a silhouette streaking across our field of vision. We know what we are looking at; if it is moving, we know in what direction and approximately how fast. A sound comes to our ears, and we know that it is an ambulance siren. Another sound comes to our ears, and we know that it is a voice; the sounds form a natural pattern of words and meaning without any effort on our part. We notice a smell and know that an apple pie is baking and that dinner time is near.

All this we take for granted. Actually, it represents a quite remarkable accomplishment, as can be realized if we think for a moment of how the world must have seemed to us when we were babies.

The baby can see and hear; he can smell and taste food; his skin is sensitive to pressure and to warmth and cold; he receives sensations from his own body that arise from such states as hunger and thirst. In other words, he has all the equipment of the senses; and his senses operate, if not nearly so efficiently as they will a little later, at least well enough to bring him many sensations from the outer world and from inside himself. The main difference between the baby's world and an adult's world is not so much that the baby's sensations lack clarity as that he has not learned what they mean.

When the baby's mother approaches, the image of her face that reaches his eyes grows larger. But quite possibly he is not aware that this means she is moving; her head may merely seem to be expanding, like a balloon being

153

inflated. To him, movement may be something entirely different; perhaps every time he moves his head the whole world seems to swing about. When his mother turns away, she may seem to disappear and to be replaced by another totally different image, that of her back, which the baby has not as yet discovered to have any connection at all with her face. When he looks at his own hand and happens to put it under a blanket, quite possibly the hand no longer seems to exist.

The baby has no idea, at first, that the palm of his hand also has a back; he does not know that the bars of his crib have an opposite side or that beyond the walls of his room lie other rooms. The window must seem like a sort of painting drawn on the wall, for the baby can have no idea that beyond the window is a three-dimensional world full of trees and grass and other houses down the block. To him the world is a strange panorama in which objects appear and disappear, grow smaller and larger, and vanish entirely when he closes his eyes. He is unaware of any connection between the movement of his mother's lips and the sounds that simultaneously reach his ears; even when he himself cries, as a reflex response to hunger sensations, he does not recognize that he is the source of the sounds he then hears.

The baby grows up and becomes a mature human being who sees the world and interprets its sights, sounds, and other sensations much as all of us do, yet also in a way that is probably individual and unique. His adult impressions of the world around him are governed by two factors: 1) the laws of *perception*, which is the subject of this chapter, and 2) *concepts* of the environment built up through the exercise of language, thinking, and problem solving, which are the subjects of the next chapter.

Perception is another term that is extremely difficult to define; in making the attempt, we can best start with an example that most of us have experienced. We are riding along a highway. Ahead of us, at the side of the road, we see a dead dog. Then, as we draw closer, we find that we do not see a dead dog at all. It is a piece of rumpled cloth. At one moment there is no doubt in our minds that we are looking at a dog. The next instant we know that we are looking at a piece of cloth. The fact is that we did not see a dog. We did, however, *perceive* a dog. In perception, we scan the stimuli in our world much as an electronic computer in a bank might scan the face of a check, looking for the numbers that will identify it. We seek to identify and "make sense" out of the objects in the environment. The process is rapid and more or less automatic; we seem to leap to our conclusions, some of which, when based on insufficient evidence as in the case of the nonexistent dog at the side of the road, are incorrect.

Perception, then, is *the process through which we become aware of our environment by organizing and interpreting the evidence of our senses.* Our perceptions are usually immediate and made without any apparent effort or deliberate thought. We perceive the mythical dog, for example, without trying, in fact almost in spite of ourselves, for perception is often a process over which we have little or no conscious control.

Perception influences our entire impression of the world around us, including all the sights and sounds that the world presents to us. It also influences our impressions of other people and their behavior. For example, at the end of a day one student might say to another, "My professor sneered at me today." Did the professor really sneer, or did the student merely perceive his facial expression that way? Or the student might say, "My girlfriend was delighted with the present I bought for her birthday." Was she really delighted, or did the student merely perceive her behavior that way?

PERCEPTION VERSUS SENSATION

As strange as it may seem at first thought, many of the things we seem to see and hear in the world are not really there, or at least not there in exactly the form we believe them to be. The "dog" at the side of the road is by no means unusual in human experience. Many of the illustrations in this chapter will show how easily the perception of an event can be in error. Identical objects seem to be of different size; stationary objects seem to be moving. Many of the ways other people apparently behave toward us—the affection or dislike that they seem to show or the criticism, anger, envy, disapproval, approval, warmth, or praise that they seem to express—are not realities but merely our own biased and incorrect perceptions.

Our senses of vision, hearing, touch, smell, and taste are constantly being bombarded by many kinds of stimuli from the outside world—by light waves, sound waves, the mechanical energy of pressure, and the chemical energy of the things we smell and taste. We are also bombarded by many stimuli from inside ourselves—by the energy generated when we move a muscle or when food passes through our alimentary canals or when our glands secrete behavior-influencing chemicals.

Energy impinges upon our bodies or is generated inside our bodies. Out of the stimuli formed by this energy we organize our impressions of an endlessly varied yet stable and consistent world of space and time and three dimensions. To realize how perception modifies the evidence of the senses, you need only glance at a tree. Look first to the left of the tree, then move your gaze slowly to the right. As you do this, the image of the tree that reaches your eyes definitely moves; the stimuli coming from the tree fall first on one part of your eyes, then cross over to another part. As far as the evidence reaching your sense of vision is concerned, that tree has moved just as surely as if it were an automobile passing across your field of vision as you held your eyes stationary. But the tree does not seem to move. It stays in place. Your perceptual organization of the world says that a tree is a stationary and motionless object, and this is the way you perceive it. This is something that you have learned, as you can tell if you look at the tree again through a pair of binoculars. Since you have never had the opportunity or necessity to build up a perceptual organization of the world as seen through binoculars, the images seen through the lenses catch you by surprise. As you swing the binoculars from left to right, the tree seems to move.

Real Versus Perceived Movement

Motion pictures do not really move; they are simply a series of still pictures like snapshots, flashed on the screen at the rate of about twenty per second. When we think we see an automobile crossing the motion picture screen, we actually see it for about one-twentieth of a second at one spot on the screen, then for one-twentieth of a second a little farther along, and so on. We ourselves "fill in" the gaps and seem to see a continuous movement. Our eyes are the victims—or perhaps one should say the beneficiaries—of the phenomenon called *stroboscopic motion,* meaning apparent motion produced by a rapid succession of images that are actually stationary. The simplest form of stroboscopic motion, called the *phi phenomenon,* is illustrated in FIGURE 5.1.

Another example of stroboscopic motion is shown in FIGURE 5.2. Here, as is explained in the caption, the flashing of four stationary lights in quick succession apparently results in a moving circle, but for some unexplained reason the circle seems smaller than if the lights were actually rotating. In our perception of the lights and the apparent movement we presumably make some kind of compromise between the reality and the illusion.

Another form of apparent movement takes place when a light, seen at some distance in a dark room, is made brighter, then dimmed to its original brightness. As it gets brighter, it seems to grow larger and to move closer.

FIGURE 5.1   *Perceived Movement in the Phi Phenomenon*   When a light is flashed behind opening 1 in a screen and an instant later behind opening 2, the bar of light seems to move as shown by the arrows; we perceive light moving across the screen between the two openings even though no light is actually there. When a light at opening 3 is quickly followed by a light at opening 4, the light seems to flip over and move in three dimensions, as if the page of a book were being turned. These are two examples of the apparent motion called the *phi phenomenon.*

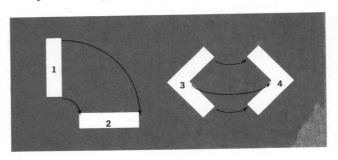

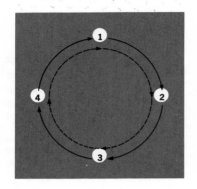

An Apparent Circle Lights 1, 2, 3, and 4 are flashed on in rapid succession. A person watching them in a dark room seems to see a band of light traveling in a circle. For some reason, however, the circle takes the form indicated by the dashed arrows—smaller than the circle of solid arrows that would be formed if the lights were actually rotating.

FIGURE 5.2

As it dims, it seems to grow smaller and to move away. This apparent movement is called the *gamma phenomenon*. It can sometimes be observed on the roads at night, if you come across a light that is blinking on and off to warn of a barricade. As the light goes off and its brightness drops to zero, it seems to move away. As it flashes on again, it seems to approach.

The Autokinetic Illusion

Ask a person to enter a dark room. Then turn on a pinpoint of light somewhere in the room, instruct him to stare at the light as steadily as he can, and ask him if he sees any movement. Although the light is in fact motionless, he will soon perceive it as making all kinds of movements—large and small, up, down, and sideways. If he is a suggestible person, and you tell him that the light is going to trace a word, he may actually perceive the motions of handwriting. This phenomenon is called the *autokinetic illusion*, meaning the illusion of self-generated movement that a stationary object sometimes creates.

Other kinds of autokinetic illusions have been produced by modern artists who are practitioners of what is often called "op (optical) art." Two examples are shown in FIGURES 5.3 and 5.4. The illusory motion in such paintings is obvious even in the small reproductions shown here and is quite startling when they are seen in full size. The explanation is not fully understood. You will probably note, however, that, though the effect is striking when you look with both eyes, it is reduced and perhaps even eliminated when you look with one eye only.

Other Sensory Illusions

If you ever had to sit toward the very side of a moving picture theater, down front close to the screen, you no doubt noticed that the men and women on the screen seemed distorted—very tall and thin, like figures seen in an amusement park mirror. This is indeed the pattern of visual stimuli

157

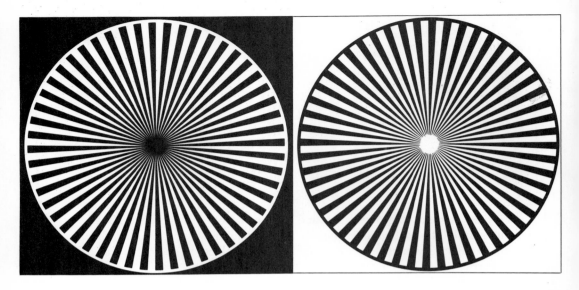

FIGURE **5.3**   *An Artist's Illusion of Motion*   Note the illusory movement at the center of the circles. This modern art work, by Wolfgang Ludwig, is titled "Cinematic Painting."

FIGURE **5.4**   *A Stationary Painting that Pulses*   Here the illusory movement in a modern painting takes the form of strange pulsations and flickers. This is "Current," by Bridget Riley.

reaching your eyes at that unusual angle. After a time, however, the distortion probably disappeared; the people on the screen began to look normal again, as if you were sitting in a better seat. The visual stimuli had not changed: what you saw halfway through the picture was distorted just as at the beginning. But somehow your perception of the stimuli had changed. You had made allowance for the distortion and now saw the people on the screen as having the normal shape that you know people to have. Much the same thing happens when you watch television. A television picture ordinarily contains considerable distortion; the lines forming the edges of buildings and doors are not quite straight, and the faces are somewhat lopsided. You perceive the picture, however, as perfectly symmetrical.

In hearing, the sound of a foreign language is at first a senseless jumble. If you study the language and become familiar with it, the same sounds begin to form a meaningful pattern, which you come to understand without even trying. When the language spoken is English, you perceive the same words and same meanings even if the sounds arrive at your ears in such vastly different forms as a Boston accent, a Midwest twang, and a Southern drawl. If a pianist plays the first six notes of "The Star-Spangled Banner" in the key of A flat major and then repeats them in the key of C major, the six sounds that reach your ears are entirely different, yet you recognize the melody as the same. Unless you have a good musical ear and some training, indeed, you may not perceive any difference at all.

If you touch someone on the back, then touch him again about a tenth of a second later at a spot a few inches away, he often perceives a movement across his skin—the sense of touch's equivalent of the phi phenomenon. Or, in a variation of this illusion, you can pick out three spots on his back, the middle one halfway between the other two. Touch spot one, then, rather quickly, the middle spot. Allow a slightly longer pause and touch spot three. He will almost surely feel certain that the last two spots were farther apart than the first two.

In perception we not only see, hear, and feel what is not there or something different from what is actually there but also sometimes add up our sensations in rather strange and unpredictable ways. As is demonstrated by the experiment illustrated in FIGURE 5.5, in perception two plus two does not always equal four!

Some other illusions that help explain the process of perception will be described later. The significant point to be made now is that there is by no means a perfect correspondence between the evidence of the world that reaches our senses and our perception of the world. Perception is an active process in which we greatly modify the evidence of our senses and manipulate it in various ways. In perception, we select which sensory stimuli to consider and then organize those selected stimuli into our own patterns of meaning. These two processes, *selection* and *organization,* are the key factors in perception.

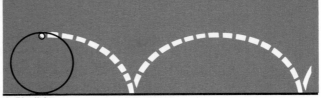

A. Rim light

B. Hub light

C. Theoretical combination

D. Actual perception

FIGURE 5.5   *A Sum of Sensations That Does Not Equal Its Parts*   One light is attached to the rim of a wheel, a second light to the hub. With the rim light on (A), the wheel is rolled along a table in a room that is otherwise totally dark. A person looking at the light perceives it as moving in the pattern shown by the dotted line, which is in truth the path followed by the light. Now the rim light is turned off and the hub light turned on (B). When the wheel moves, the light is seen as moving in a straight line. Finally, both lights are turned on, and the wheel is rolled along the table again. Theoretically, the observer should see a combination of the two sensations (C). Actually, he perceives what is shown at the bottom of the drawing: one light rotating around another light that moves in a straight line (D). This perception can hardly be called an illusion, because it represents what is actually happening, but it certainly is not the sum of the eyes' sensations. (1)

**SELECTION AS
AN ELEMENT
OF PERCEPTION**
During every waking moment our senses are bombarded with a barrage of miscellaneous stimuli. At this instant, for example, your eyes are receiving stimuli not only from this page of the book but also from many other objects that are within your field of vision— the light by which you are reading, the walls of the room, many objects of

160

furniture, perhaps the outdoors as seen through a window. To your ears come many sounds—the crackle of a page as you turn it, someone talking, an automobile going past, perhaps a radio playing softly in the distance. The smell of food cooking may be reaching your nostrils, and on your tongue may linger the taste of a salted peanut. Your skin senses feel many things— the pressure of clothing, the warmth of a sweater, the coolness of a draft blowing across the back of your neck. Sensory impressions arising from inside your body may be telling you that you are hungry or thirsty or that you are mildly upset over the fact that you want to get these pages read and learned in a hurry so that you can be on time for a social appointment.

You cannot pay attention to all these stimuli at once. You have to select some to which you will give your attention and thrust the rest into a sort of neutral gray background of which you are only dimly aware or perhaps not aware at all. As long as you attend to the words on the page you do not perceive all the other visual stimuli that strike your eyes. You do not perceive the voice talking, the automobile going by, or the radio playing unless you shift your attention. You are not aware of smells or of the pressure of your clothing unless you deliberately choose to pay attention to them.

Driving an automobile often furnishes striking examples of the selective nature of perception. As you drive along a highway where the traffic is light, you are listening to a football game on the radio. It is an interesting game and you are paying close attention, following every word and every play. Then suddenly an intersection looms ahead. Other cars are moving into the intersection; the lights are changing; you have to slow down, veer into a different lane, watch out for a car that has moved slowly into your path. When the traffic crisis is over, you start listening to the game again and find to your surprise that the score has changed. While your attention was directed elsewhere, a touchdown was scored without your ever knowing it. The radio was on just as loud as before, but you did not seem to hear it.

Stimulus Characteristics and Selection

Some of the factors that determine whether we will select one particular stimulus, out of all the many around us, appear to be inborn tendencies to be attracted to certain stimulus characteristics. Among them are the following.

CHANGE   This is the most compelling stimulus characteristic of all. Our sensory apparatus is so constructed that it adjusts rather rapidly to any steady and continued level of stimulation and quits responding. The technical word for this process is *adaptation*. Our senses adapt to a certain level of illumination or to a certain level of sound. When they have adapted, they stop sending messages to our brains. Any change in the stimulation, however, immediately produces a new response. For example, when a radio is playing softly in the next room, we soon adapt to the sound and no longer hear it, but we notice at once if the sound stops. We are instantly aware of the change when a light dims because a filament has burned out or when it becomes brighter because of a sudden surge of electricity.

Besides being attracted to a change in the intensity of a stimulus, we are attracted to any change in its quality. For example, we are in a restaurant where a number of people are talking at once, all around us. After a while we hear only the conversation at our table; the rest is just background noise to which we have adapted and stopped responding. But now a baby cries in the room. The cry does not make the background noise any louder or softer than before, but we are immediately aware of it.

CONTRAST   This characteristic, closely related to change, can be shown to influence even a baby less than two full days old. If a small black triangle is placed in the baby's field of vision and a photographic record is kept of his eye movements, it turns out that he spends most of his time focusing on a point or apex of the triangle—the spot where there is the sharpest contrast between the black of the triangle and the light background (2). Indeed the baby's early interest in the human face, especially the face of his mother, is dictated largely by the strong effect of contrast as an attention-getter. What he notices particularly in the human face is the high degree of contrast between a light face and dark eyes or between a dark face and the whites of the eyes and the teeth.

Some other examples of the role of contrast are these. One mountain among many does not necessarily attract our attention; the same mountain on an otherwise level plain would attract us at once. A six-foot man stands out in a room full of smaller men because he is so tall and at a meeting of basketball players because he is so short. A sports jacket with black and white checks is far more conspicuous than a jacket with checks in two shades of blue.

MOVEMENT   This characteristic, too, is related to change and can also be seen in very young babies, who try their best to follow any kind of moving object. If we adults look at a pasture full of horses, those that are running about attract our attention more than those that are quietly grazing. An advertising sign that uses stroboscopic motion is a better attention-getter than a sign whose message remains stationary.

SIZE   In general, a large object is more likely to attract attention than a small object. Driving along a strange highway, we tend to pay more attention to a river than to a creek. A mountain that looms on the horizon is a more compelling stimulus than a hill. When we look at the front page of a newspaper, we are attracted to the biggest headlines first.

INTENSITY   All other things being equal, it is the brightest or loudest stimulus that is likely to attract our attention. If we are driving at night through a downtown street where all the advertising signs are by some coincidence of equal size, the brightest of them seems the most compelling. The blasting noise of a sound truck passing by is likely to draw our attention away from the softer sounds of conversation or of a radio. Similarly, we are more likely to pay attention to a sharp poke in the shoulder than to a gentle tug at the elbow.

REPETITION   A television commercial seen for the first time may go virtually unnoticed. Repetition, however, sooner or later brings it sharply to our attention. If we are walking down a city street where all the newsboys are calling out the latest headline, we may ignore the words the first time or so, but eventually we notice them.

All these factors are important of their own accord; there is something about them that is basically appealing to the attention of the human organism (and in many cases apparently to lower animals as well). We naturally and automatically select stimuli that display these characteristics. These rules of perception are either learned very early or are somehow built into the organism, like the reflexes.

The Perceiver and Selection

There are other important factors influencing selection that are not so automatic and that have little to do with the characteristics of the stimulus itself. To a considerable extent, what is selected for attention depends upon which individual is doing the perceiving and upon what he has learned in the past and what his physical condition and emotional state are at the moment.

It is a well-known fact, which you doubtless have observed yourself, that people who go through the same situation often perceive different things. A family goes out for an automobile ride. The husband, who is thinking about trading in his automobile, concentrates his attention on the new cars on the highway. The wife is hardly aware of the other cars but keenly aware of all the details of a new shopping center. A son who wants a bicycle perceives the afternoon as a succession of children riding various types of bicycles. A daughter with a new dress and shoes perceives the afternoon as a succession of other girls whose clothes she can compare with her own.

A husband and wife attend a movie. Afterward the husband talks about the strength of character of the hero, the wife about the wardrobe of the heroine. Two sisters, living at college, go home for a weekend visit. After an evening of talking to their mother, one sister has noticed that the mother smiled on several occasions, which she takes to mean that the mother is in a happy mood. The other sister has noticed several frowns, which she takes to mean that something is troubling the mother. Thus does perceptual selection depend upon the perceiver.

ORGANIZATION AS AN ELEMENT OF PERCEPTION

The "dog" at the side of the road mentioned earlier in the chapter is eloquent proof of how, in the process of perception, we organize the evidence of our senses into patterns. We do not perceive the world as the chaotic and miscellaneous collection of stimuli that reaches our senses. On the contrary, the perceptual process organizes these stimuli into meaningful objects. We see not mere patches of light but houses, people, trees, and roadways. (And sometimes, because an error has been made in organizing the pattern, we see a nonexistent dog lying at the side of the road.) We hear not miscellaneous sound waves but voices, musical tunes, and doorbells.

For a further demonstration of the part organization plays in perception, you can try an old experiment that requires no more equipment than a few

FIGURE 5.6   *Perception of Hidden Figures*   The drawing contains a number of hidden objects that you are not likely to see at first glance. After you look long enough, however, you will perceive the objects so clearly that they will almost seem to leap out at you.

headlines cut from today's newspaper. All must be of the same size, and you must not have seen any of them before. Have a friend determine the farthest distance at which you can read the type by testing you with a new headline each time he moves back. Once he has reached a spot just beyond your range of vision, so that you cannot make out the words, have him read the headline out loud and then show it to you again. After you have heard the words, you will find you can read them so easily that you will wonder why you ever had any trouble with them. Here knowledge of the stimulus received through the sense of hearing has helped you organize the visual stimulus into a pattern, and your perception, at first a blur, is now sharp and meaningful. Much the same thing happens when you look at a drawing or photograph containing a hidden object, as in FIGURE 5.6. Once you have established the pattern and perceived the hidden object, it is almost impossible *not* to see it.

Study of the organization of perceptions began with Wilhelm Wundt. In his experiments with the sensations aroused by the sound of a metronome, Wundt noted that the clicks were always perceived in some kind of pattern, even though each of them was of exactly the same loudness and presented after exactly the same time interval. One person might perceive them in march time: *click*-click, *click*-click, *click*-click. Another might perceive them in waltz time: *click*-click-click, *click*-click-click, *click*-click-click. Or the sounds might be perceived in more complicated patterns such as CLICK-click-*click*-click, CLICK-click-*click*-click. At any rate, some kind of pattern was always perceived in sounds that of themselves had no pattern.

An early experimental tool in the field of visual organization was the checkerboard shown in FIGURE 5.7. Here, much as in the case of the metronome, all the colored squares are of equal size and are equidistant from one another. There is no inherent pattern in the drawing. As we look at it,

FIGURE 5.7

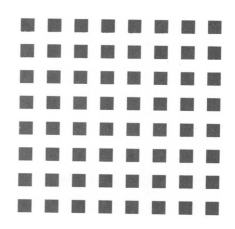

The Checkerboard Pattern As you look at this collection of colored squares of uniform size and spacing, what do you see? Look at it closely for a time, letting your eyes shift from one part of it to another if you are so inclined, and compare your perceptions with those described in the text.

however, we tend to perceive various kinds of patterns, which shift as we continue to stare at it and move our eyes from one point to another. We may perceive horizontal lines, vertical lines, or diagonals. Or we may perceive various patterns in which the individual squares seem to be arranged in pairs or in groups shaped like rectangles or squares.

Inborn Tendencies in Organization

In one way or another, then, we organize our sensory stimuli, often imposing a pattern where in fact none exists. Like the way we select, the way we organize is partly a matter of inborn tendencies, partly a matter of learning. Let us consider the inborn factors first.

FIGURE AND GROUND   One of the ways we organize our sensory stimuli is demonstrated by what you perceive as you read this paragraph. In terms of light waves it is composed of many irregularly shaped splotches of white and of black. But you do not perceive a mere jumble of white and black. You perceive letters and words of black, against a background of white. You organize the stimuli into figures that are seen against a ground.

FIGURE 5.8

The Figure-Ground Phenomenon To most people, the drawing at right is first perceived as a white goblet against a dark background. It can also be perceived, however, as two dark faces in profile against a white sheet. The drawing below is usually perceived as a series of rather strange black figures against a white ground. If you look at it long enough, however, the figure and ground shift into something quite different.

This tendency to organize visual stimuli into *figure and ground* is one of the basic rules in perception. A picture on the wall is perceived as a figure against a ground. So is a chair, or a person, or the moon seen in the sky. The figure hangs together; it has shape; it is an object. The ground is primarily a neutral and formless setting for the figure. What separates the two and sets the figure off from the ground is a dividing line called a *contour*.

One interesting example of how we organize visual stimuli into figure and ground is shown in FIGURE 5.8, where the contours can be interpreted in two different ways. In the drawing at the top you can perceive a white figure against a dark ground, the goblet, or a dark figure against a white ground, the faces. But you cannot perceive both at once. When you perceive the goblet, the faces recede into a formless background. When you perceive the faces, the goblet fades. In the drawing at the bottom the stimuli are meaningless until you organize them into figure and ground; then you clearly see *TIE*.

The tendency to perceive figure and ground is built into the organism. But what is perceived as figure and what is perceived as ground can be modified by learning and perceptual expectations, as is demonstrated in FIGURE 5.9.

CLOSURE   To perceive a figure, we do not need a complete and uninterrupted contour. If part of the contour is missing, our perceptual process

FIGURE **5.9**   *The Effect of Expectation on Figure-Ground*   To demonstrate how the organization of figure and ground is affected by perceptual expectancies, show drawing A to a friend, keeping the other two covered. Then let him look at drawing B. Almost surely, he will perceive drawing B as the face of the pretty young woman in A. To another friend, show drawing C before you let him look at B. This friend will probably perceive drawing B as the face of the old hag in C. (3)

A

B

C

Some Examples of Closure Though the figures are incomplete in one way or another, we perceive them at once for what they are. (Drawing of cat, 4)

FIGURE **5.10**

fills it in. Indeed we tend to fill in any of the gaps that might interfere with our perceiving an object. This perceptual process, called *closure,* is illustrated in FIGURE 5.10. An interesting example of the effect of closure in combination with our tendency to perceive contours separating figure and ground is shown in FIGURE 5.11.

CONTINUITY   Closely related to closure is *continuity,* which is illustrated in FIGURE 5.12. We tend to perceive continuous lines and patterns, and in any complex visual field we tend to perceive the organization that hangs together with the greatest continuity. The two lines shown at the left of FIGURE 5.12 have their own kind of continuity, but when they are put together a more compelling kind of continuity makes us perceive them quite differently.

Every beginning photographer has had the embarrassing experience of taking what he thought was a fine snapshot of a friend, only to discover, when the film was developed, that a telephone pole could be seen growing out of the friend's head. At the time the picture was taken the photographer was completely unaware of the pole. This is partly the effect of figure and ground, for a photographer perceiving his friend as figure tends to ignore the rest of the visual field as merely a neutral ground. But it is also partly the result of the continuity factor. When we look at a person's head, we perceive a continuous curved line and are not aware that—seen another way—the curved line merges into the straight line of a telephone pole.

FIGURE **5.11**

Is There a Contour or Not? Between the two semicircular patterns we perceive a white stripe. It seems to have contours—straight lines that separate it from the two patterns—though in fact no such contours exist. The drawing is another early contribution to the study of perception made by Friedrich Schumann, the inventor of the checkerboard that was shown in FIGURE 5.7.

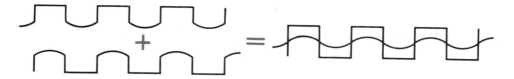

FIGURE 5.12   *Continuity in Perception*   At the left we clearly perceive two continuous lines that are combinations of straight and curved segments. When the two lines are put together as at the right, however, we find it difficult to perceive the original pattern. Instead we now perceive a continuous wavy line running through another continuous line of straight horizontal and vertical segments.

PROXIMITY   If Wundt had used not a metronome giving out a steady series of clicks but a device that varied the intervals between the clicks, his results would have been somewhat different. When we hear click-click . . . click-click . . . click-click (with the dots indicating a pause), we organize the sounds into pairs. When we hear click-click-click . . . click-click-click, we perceive patterns of threes. Indeed, several quite different sounds presented this way, such as click-buzz-ring . . . click-buzz-ring . . . click-buzz-ring, would still be perceived in groups of three.

Such is the effect of *proximity;* we tend to make patterns of stimuli that are close together. This is true not only of sounds presented close together in time but also of visual stimuli that are close together in space, as can be seen in FIGURE 5.13.

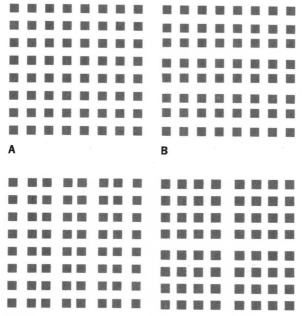

A

B

C

D

FIGURE 5.13

The Effect of Proximity   Checkerboard A is a repetition of FIGURE 5.7. Note what happens to our perception of it when some of the squares are moved closer together as in B, C, and D.

169

SIMILARITY   Much in the same way that we make patterns of stimuli that have proximity, we make patterns of those that have *similarity*. This is demonstrated by the checkerboard variation in FIGURE 5.14. Except that some of the colored squares have been changed to white squares or white circles, the checkerboard is the same as in FIGURE 5.7. Theoretically it is still possible to perceive many kinds of patterns. But in fact it is very difficult to perceive anything except the lines and groupings dictated by similarity. The white cross in FIGURE 5.14C, for example, fairly leaps from the page at us.

COMMON MOVEMENT   Let us try to imagine ourselves in a clearing in an Indian jungle, looking toward a dense growth of brightly colored trees and foliage. Somewhere in our field of vision is a tiger, poised motionless. Try as we will, we cannot see it. Its stripes blend in so perfectly with the jungle pattern that it is totally camouflaged. Then it moves. Immediately the stimuli become a pattern of their own. The tiger is now an object, and we perceive it clearly.

This is the result of the perceptual factor called *common movement*—the fact that, when stimuli move together, we tend to organize them into a pattern of their own. FIGURE 5.15 illustrates a popular laboratory demonstration of the effect of common movement and shows that it influences our perception even in that form of apparent movement known as the phi phenomenon.

FIGURE 5.14

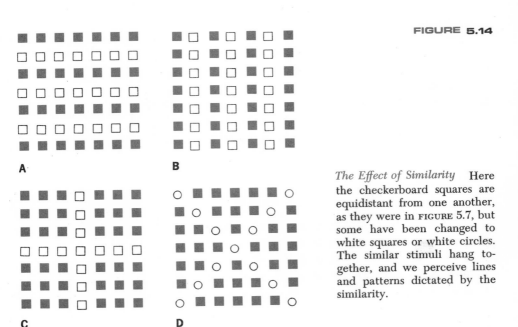

A

B

C

D

The Effect of Similarity   Here the checkerboard squares are equidistant from one another, as they were in FIGURE 5.7, but some have been changed to white squares or white circles. The similar stimuli hang together, and we perceive lines and patterns dictated by the similarity.

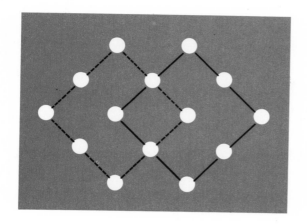

FIGURE 5.15

Organization Through Common Movement In a darkened room, nine lights in the positions shown at the left side of the drawing are turned on. The observer sees them in the pattern of the square indicated by the dotted line. Then they are turned off and the nine at the right turned on. As we might guess from what we know about the phi phenomenon, the observer perceives the square as moving to the position shown by the solid line. He does not perceive that four of the lights contained in the second square are simply repetitions of lights that were also present in the first square. (5).

Learned Tendencies in Organization

All the factors in organization discussed up to this point seem to be unlearned; they appear, at least in large part, to be an inborn characteristic of the human organism and to operate automatically. There are many other important factors, however, where learning does play a large part. Most of them can be grouped under the term *perceptual constancy*—the fact that we learn to perceive a stable and consistent world even though the stimuli that reach our senses are inconsistent and potentially confusing.

Consider, for example, a simple dinner plate. Unless we deliberately pick up the plate and hold it in a vertical position in front of our eyes, we almost never see it as a circle. Ordinarily the image of the plate reaches our eyes at an angle; the image is not a circle but an ellipse. Yet we perceive it, whatever the circumstances, as a round plate.

We may see the Empire State Building from the sidewalk right in front of it, looking up. We may see it as a tower in the distance or from a new angle when we are in an airplane or even as a tiny photographic image on a printed page. Yet we perceive it as constant and unchanging. When a friend extends his hand toward us, the image of his hand on our eyes is far bigger than the image cast by his entire body when he is a half block away from us, yet we perceive him as of constant size and proportion. The camera,

171

FIGURE **5.16**

What We Really See　To the human eye, as to the camera, a close view of the horse presents an enormous muzzle, an elongated head, giant eyes and ears, and legs that are tiny by comparison. But we *perceive* the horse in proper proportion, without the distortion that the camera records.

which does not possess the perceptual process, "sees" all kinds of distorted images, as is shown in FIGURE 5.16. We *see* the same kind of images, but we *perceive* them without the distortion.

To add to the complications, many of the stimuli that reach our eyes are moving or changing. Our friend is walking toward us across a room or past us on the sidewalk, or he is riding by in a rapidly moving automobile. Often we ourselves are moving and thus altering our relation to all the stimuli in our field of vision. Part of the visual field is in brightness; part is covered by shadows. The illumination changes from the bright sunshine of noon to dim twilight. All this makes very little difference to us. We perceive our friend as the same person despite all the confusions of motion or lighting. The snow seems just as white in the shadow of the house as in the open.

Once we have learned about the objects in our world, we perceive them as constant and unchanging—in shape, brightness, color, location, and size.

SHAPE CONSTANCY　We perceive the dinner plate as round even though its image seldom reaches our eyes as a circle. Similarly, we perceive a door as a rectangle not only when we are directly facing it but also while it is swinging open toward us and its image is continually changing. In other

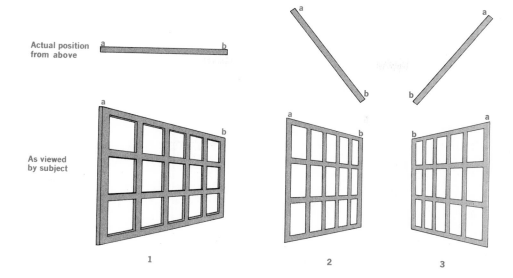

Actual position from above

As viewed by subject

1   2   3

FIGURE 5.17   *A Window Designed to Fool the Eye*   The "window" in this experiment is not a window at all but a specially constructed trapezoid in which edge *a* is considerably longer than edge *b*. In position 1, you are looking straight at the "window," but you perceive it as being at an angle, with edge *a* closer to you than edge *b*. In 2, the window has been rotated so that edge *a* is farther away than edge *b*, but edge *a* still seems to be closer. In 3, the window has been moved still farther, and you now incorrectly perceive it as being opposite to its position in 2; you do not realize that edge *a* is now on the right. If you could see this trick window rotate, you would perceive it not as turning but as moving back and forth, with the left edge coming closer and then backing away. Question: Does the trapezoidal "window" fool everybody? For the answer, see the text.

words, we perceive objects as retaining their shape regardless of the true nature of the image that reaches our eyes—a fact that is called *shape constancy*.

Shape constancy explains the optical illusion illustrated in FIGURE 5.17. The trick window used in the illusion fools almost all Americans and Europeans. But experimenters who took such a window to Zululand, in South Africa, made an interesting and at first puzzling discovery. When the illusion was tried on native boys who had never been away from their rural Zulu environment, fewer than half of them were fooled (6). The explanation seems to be that there are no rectangles in the Zulu environment; the Zulus live in round huts and build circular enclosures. Never having seen

173

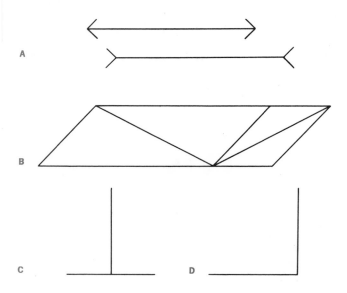

FIGURE 5.18

Optical Illusions Related to Environment   Are the two lines in each drawing the same length, and, if not, which is longer? (In B, the lines in question are the two diagonals—one extending downward from the upper left-hand corner, the other downward from the upper right-hand corner.) The answer is that each pair of lines is exactly the same. Americans and Europeans are more likely to be fooled by A and B than are African natives—again, as in FIGURE 5.17, presumably because of greater experience with rectangular objects and squared-off corners. But African natives are more likely than Americans and Europeans to be fooled by C and D, perhaps because of their greater experience with open fields where vertical lines such as trees are perceived as figure and the horizontal line of the earth as ground. (7)

squared off corners and rectangles, many of the Zulus had not developed the kind of shape constancy on which the illusion depends.

Some other optical illusions that have been shown to be more effective in some parts of the world than in others—presumably because of different learning experiences—are illustrated in FIGURE 5.18.

BRIGHTNESS CONSTANCY   Another kind of constancy can be demonstrated with the experimental setup shown in FIGURE 5.19. The spotlight is focused on the black circle so that the entire circle is illuminated but no light spills over to the background. The ceiling light and any others in the room are then dimmed until the two circles are of equal brightness. The amount of light reflected from each circle is now the same, and they would register as equal on a photographic light meter. Moreover, to a person who walks

174

into the room and cannot see the concealed spotlight, they look exactly the same; they are seen as two dimly lighted white surfaces. But the instant the observer becomes aware of the spotlight—for example, if a puff of smoke is blown into its beam or a hand moved into the beam—he suddenly sees that one circle is black. It looks completely and startlingly different. When the smoke or hand is removed from the spotlight beam, the two circles again look alike.

A similar thing happens in real-life situations. The light reflected from a black shoe in the sunshine may be as bright as the light reflected from a patch of snow in the deep shade. A light meter would "see" them as the same. But to us the shoe looks definitely black and the snow definitely white. *Brightness constancy*, as this phenomenon is called, greatly influences our perceptions.

COLOR CONSTANCY   Just as we tend to perceive objects to be of the same brightness regardless of the amount of light they actually reflect, so do we tend to perceive colored objects as displaying *color constancy*. One of the best demonstrations of this fact was an experiment in which small pieces of gray paper were cut in the shapes of familiar objects such as a banana, a lemon, a carrot, and a tangerine. The papers were then mounted on blue-green backgrounds and covered with finely ground glass screens. Because of the principles of color contrast, the gray figures against the blue-green

An Experiment with Brightness   A concealed spotlight and two cardboard circles suspended from the ceiling, one black and one white, provide the tools for an experiment that usually startles the subjects. For an explanation, see the text. (8)

FIGURE 5.19

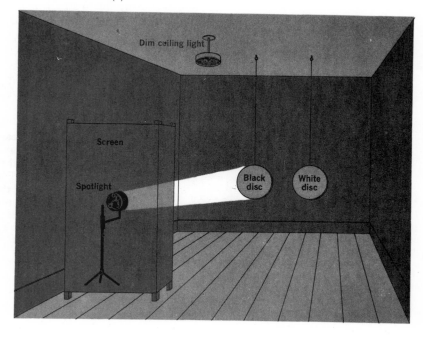

background looked brownish orange. All, however, should have seemed to be the same color. But when subjects were shown the banana-shaped paper and told that it was a banana, they tended to perceive it as yellowish; and when shown the tangerine-shaped paper and told that it was a tangerine, they tended to perceive it as reddish orange. Similarly, they perceived the lemon as yellowish and the carrot as orange (9).

LOCATION CONSTANCY   What happens to a person who wears a pseudophone—a laboratory device illustrated in FIGURE 5.20—is of considerable importance in the study of perception. Our sense of direction for sound depends on the fact that sounds coming from the left strike the left ear a tiny fraction of a second before they strike the right ear, while sounds from the right strike the right ear first. One would suppose, therefore, that the pseudophone would turn sounds completely around.

So it does—at first. The person wearing it sees an automobile traveling from left to right but hears its sound as moving from right to left. A knock at the front door seems to be coming from the back of the room. But after a few days, this changes. The wearer adjusts his perceptual process and perceives the sounds to be in the proper location.

A similar experiment with vision was performed many years ago by an investigator who built an elaborate system of lenses that completely reversed his visual field, turning the world he saw upside down and right to left. It was a bulky and heavy device, but he persisted in wearing it during his waking hours for eight days. At first he was confused and helpless. Every time he moved his head the world swam about (a fact we might expect from what happens when we look at a tree through binoculars). He had trouble recognizing even the most familiar surroundings and found it almost impossible to feed himself. Gradually, however, the world began to straighten out. Toward the end he was able to function quite well; he could avoid

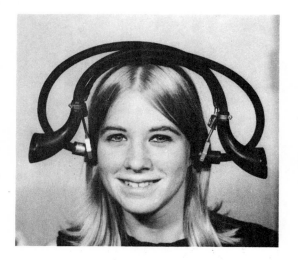

FIGURE 5.20

A Device to Fool the Ear   The young woman wears a pseudophone, a laboratory device that carries the sounds that would ordinarily reach her right ear to her left ear instead and the sounds that would ordinarily reach her left ear to her right ear. For an explanation of how she perceives the world, see the text.

bumping into objects and could perform acts such as eating almost without thinking about them. The world no longer moved when he moved his head. Most of it still looked upside down, but he had adjusted his perceptual processes and perceived the location and movement of objects more or less automatically. Indeed he had established new perceptual patterns so thoroughly that, when at last he took off the lenses, he again was confused and disoriented for a time (10).

The pseudophone and the inverted lenses demonstrate that even under the most difficult circumstances we manage to establish *location constancy,* which enables us to perceive objects as being in their rightful and accustomed place and as remaining there even when we move.

A more recent experiment with a different kind of lens sheds some additional light on location constancy. In this experiment the lenses shifted the visual field to the right. A person wearing them would reach out to touch a doorknob, for instance, and miss it by nearly a foot. When two students, a man and woman, put on the lenses, both were equally inaccurate when they tried to touch objects, always erring on the right. Then the woman, still wearing the lenses, stepped into a wheelchair. The man, still wearing the lenses, began pushing her around the campus. After this had gone on for a time, they were again tested for accuracy at reaching toward objects. The woman still missed as before. The man touched them unerringly (11). This would indicate that location constancy is developed at least in part by moving around in the world and learning to combine perception and motor coordination, just as the pseudophone indicates that it is also partly a result of cooperation among the senses.

SIZE CONSTANCY   The final type of object constancy can be demonstrated with an experiment that requires no more equipment than a full-sized dinner plate and a salad plate of the same pattern, the same in every respect except that it is much smaller. Put the dinner plate on a table, trying not to look at it. Now stand above it, hold the salad plate in front of your face, and look down toward the table. Keeping one eye closed, move the salad plate away from you until it just blots out the dinner plate—in other words, to the point where, if you moved it any farther away from your eye, you would begin to see an outline of the dinner plate.

What you have done, as is shown in FIGURE 5.21, is set up a situation where the visual images of the two plates are exactly the same size. Now move the salad plate to one side and open both eyes. What you perceive, without question or doubt, is a small plate fairly close to you and a large plate on a table. The dinner plate looks big; the salad plate looks small. You cannot perceive them any other way.

This simple but convincing experiment demonstrates *size constancy*—the fact that we tend to perceive objects in their correct size regardless of the size of the actual image they cast on our eyes. When you look at a distant tree or at the Empire State Building from a distance, the images of these objects on your eyes may be much smaller than the image of the hand you are holding out toward them; you can blot them out by moving your hand in front of them. Yet you still perceive a large tree, a giant skyscraper, and a relatively small hand.

Under ordinary circumstances, size constancy operates with remarkable accuracy. For example, the Air Force once made tests of how well pilots could judge the height of stakes planted in a field. Even when a stake about 6 feet high was nearly a half mile away, the subjects erred by an average of less than 4 inches (12).

WHEN SIZE CONSTANCY FAILS   One well-known experiment with size constancy was conducted as follows. The subject sat at the corner of a building where two hallways met at right angles. Glancing to his left, he could look down one hallway. Glancing to his right, he could look down the other. Ten feet away from him, in hallway 1, was an adjustable cardboard circle that he could make larger or smaller by remote control. In hallway 2, the experimenter presented cardboard circles of equal brightness but different sizes and at different distances. Some of the circles were placed a mere 10 feet away, some as much as 120 feet away. In each case, however, the combination of size and distance was regulated so that the size of the actual image on the subject's eyes was exactly the same—like the images of the two plates in FIGURE 5.21. The subject was asked to look carefully at each

FIGURE 5.21

Which Plate Looks Larger?   Both plates cast images of exactly equal size on the young woman's eye. When she moves the plate she is holding so that she can see both, do they look the same size or does one look larger? You can try the experiment yourself or find the answer in the text.

circle in hallway 2 as it was shown to him, estimate its size, and regulate the size of the adjustable circle in hallway 1 accordingly.

The results were much the same as in the experiment with the two plates. Even though the actual image of each circle in hallway 2 was exactly the same size, the subject perceived the larger but more distant circles as large and the smaller but closer circles as small. As shown by his estimates with the adjustable circle in hallway 1, he judged the actual size of the circles with extremely good accuracy and did so nearly as well when looking through only one eye as with both eyes.

Next, however, he was asked to look at the circles in hallway 2 with only one eye and through a small peephole. Under these circumstances, his accuracy fell off sharply. Finally, a long tunnel of black cloth was placed the length of hallway 2, and the circles were shown to him inside this tunnel. His accuracy was now further reduced. He perceived the circles in hallway 2 as much smaller than before. For example, the circle shown 100 feet away, which he had originally judged with good accuracy to be about 2 feet in diameter, now appeared to be only about a half foot in diameter. Looking through the peephole had removed some of the perceptual clues on which size constancy depends. Looking through the tunnel had removed still more of the clues. Without them, the subject's perception of size began to depend primarily upon the size of the actual image that struck his eyes (13).

Much the same effect can be obtained when you are watching television. A face seen in close-up on the screen or a person seen full-length looks quite large. But make a loose fist and look through it, holding the circle formed by your thumb and forefinger against your eye and making as small a peephole as possible with the curve of your little finger. (Close the other eye, of course.) You will probably be startled to discover how small the face or figure on the screen suddenly becomes.

Just as a face on the television screen is ordinarily seen as quite large, so is the full moon when it is just coming up over the horizon. When the moon is high above you, it looks quite small, like the television picture seen through your fist. Yet, strangely, if you turn your back to the horizon moon, bend over, and look at it through your legs, it becomes small. If you lie flat on your back to look at the moon that is high in the sky, it becomes large. The moon illusion has puzzled men for centuries and is still a matter of debate, but it depends in some way upon the perceptual clues that make up size constancy, clues that sometimes fail us.

Size and Distance

There are perhaps many clues to our perception of size; the most important of them is demonstrated in FIGURE 5.22. Before you go on to the next paragraph, look at the figure and try to answer the question that is posed in the caption.

Now that you have studied the figure, have you decided that the ball was as far away as the head at the left? Or perhaps the third head? Whatever you decided, you undoubtedly went through the following perceptual process.

A head is a head, always the same size. Since the head at the extreme left looks large, it must be the closest. Each succeeding head is smaller and must therefore be farther away. The ball is of unknown size; it could be anything from a pingpong ball to an enormous beach ball. Where you placed the ball, therefore, depends on what you perceived it to be. If you look again at the figure, you will note that a pingpong ball would seem to be about as far away as the first head and a baseball as far away as the second, while a basketball seems to "fit" the third head, and a beach ball the fourth.

The head and the ball are a good illustration of the close connection between perceived size and perceived distance. When we look at an object of unknown size, such as the ball in FIGURE 5.22, its perceived size is a function of perceived distance. A further demonstration of this fact is shown in FIGURE 5.23.

Similarly, we use objects of known size as a clue to perceived distance. At least in part, we judge how far away a basketball or the Empire State Building is by how large it seems. Our perception of distance can be thrown off badly if we misjudge size. For example, experiments have been conducted with specially made playing cards much larger or much smaller than the kind people ordinarily use for bridge or poker. When seen in a room that affords no other visual clues, the oversized cards always seem closer than they really are, the undersized cards farther away.

Where Is the Ball?   Is the ball as far away as the head at the extreme left, the head at the extreme right, or one of the heads in between? Compare your answer with the answer given in the text. (8)

FIGURE 5.22

Other Clues to Distance

Although perceived size is an important clue to perceived distance, it is by no means the only one. Other factors that help us perceive distance in a three-dimensional world are the following.

BINOCULAR VISION   Since our eyes are about $2\frac{1}{2}$ inches apart, they receive different images—a fact that you can demonstrate for yourself by looking at some object in the distance while holding a finger a foot or so in front of your nose. If you close first your left eye and then your right, your finger seems to move, because the image it casts on one eye is in a noticeably different part of the visual field from the image it casts on the other eye.

Ordinarily we focus both eyes on the same object, and the two images are somehow put together in the brain. (Although sometimes, if we are ill or have had too many drinks, this process is disturbed and we "see double.") The slight difference between the two images greatly assists our perception of distance. This fact is the secret of the three-dimensional or stereoscopic camera, which simultaneously takes two pictures through two different lenses and on two different pieces of film that are about as far apart as the human eyes. When the two pieces of film are seen through a viewer that presents one to the left eye and one to the right, we perceive a vivid and unmistakable three-dimensional effect.

Focusing our eyes also requires movements of the muscles that control the position of the eyeballs and the shape of the lens of the eye. It is believed that the sensations produced by these movements may also provide clues to distance perception.

Perceived Size as a Function of Perceived Distance   The lamppost and block of wood at the far right look much bigger than the lamppost at the far left and the block of wood in the foreground. We perceive them as larger because we perceive them as farther away. Actually— as measurement with a ruler will show—the two lampposts and two blocks of wood are exactly the same size. (14)

FIGURE 5.23

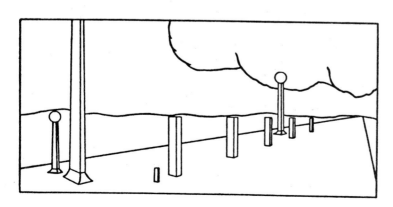

INTERPOSITION   This is the term used for the fact that nearer objects interpose themselves between our eyes and more distant objects, blocking off part of the image. The manner in which interposition serves as a clue to distance—such an important clue that when manipulated in the laboratory it can completely fool the eye—is illustrated in FIGURE 5.24.

PERSPECTIVE   Artists learned many centuries ago that they could convey the impression of distance and three dimensions on a flat piece of canvas by following the rules of *perspective,* which all of us use in real life as clues to distance.

Artists speak of two kinds of perspective. One, *linear perspective,* refers to the fact that parallel lines seem to draw closer together as they recede into the distance. A good example is railroad tracks or the edges of a highway seen on a level stretch of ground. *Aerial perspective* refers to the fact that distant objects, because they are seen through air that is usually somewhat hazy, appear less distinct and less brilliant in color than nearby objects. If you have lived within sighting distance of mountains or the skyscrapers of a large city, you may have noticed that the mountains or buildings seem much closer on days when the air is unusually clear.

Another factor in perspective is *gradient of texture,* which you can best observe by looking at a large expanse of lawn. The grass nearby can be seen so well that every blade is distinct, and therefore its texture looks quite coarse. Farther away, the individual blades seem to merge, and the texture becomes much finer. This and the other aspects of perspective as a clue to distance are illustrated in FIGURE 5.25.

Interposition and Distance Perception   Two playing cards are arranged as shown in A and are the only objects visible in an otherwise dark room. An observer looking at them through one eye has visual images as illustrated—one large card and one small card. The relative size tells him clearly that the smaller card is farther away. Now a corner is clipped from the near card, as shown in B, and the stands are arranged so that the images are seen as in C. The cue of interposition now makes the observer think that he is looking at a small card, close to him, and a larger card farther away. (1)

FIGURE 5.24

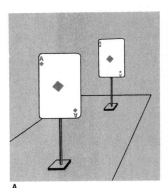 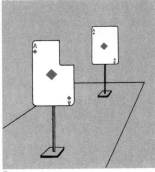 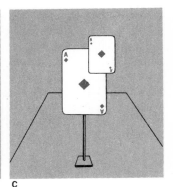

A   B   C

FIGURE 5.25   *Perspective and Distance*   Serving as clues to distance in this single photograph are all three kinds of perspective—linear, aerial, and gradient of texture.

SHADOWING   The pattern of light and shadow on an object often offers clues that aid in perception of three-dimensional quality. FIGURE 5.26 illustrates how the addition of shadowing turns what we perceive as a circle on the printed page into a ball. FIGURE 5.27 demonstrates how an unexpected pattern of shadows can mislead our perception.

Perception of Height and Depth

One special kind of distance perception concerns the vertical dimension of our world. We are standing on a high diving board. At what height are

FIGURE 5.26

How Shadows Create the Third Dimension   The mere addition of shadowing turns the flat circle into a three-dimensional ball. (12)

we? Or, to put it another way, how deep is the space beneath us? And how do we know?

Some interesting facts about the perception of height and depth have been disclosed by experiments with the apparatus shown in FIGURE 5.28. This device, which its inventor has termed a "visual cliff," is a piece of heavy glass suspended above the floor. Across the middle of the glass is a board covered with checkered cloth. On one side of the board the same kind of cloth is attached to the bottom of the glass, making this look like the solid or shallow side of the cliff. On the other side the cloth is laid on the floor, and to all appearances there is a drop at that side.

As is shown in FIGURE 5.28, a six-month-old baby crawls without hesitation over the shallow-looking side but hesitates to crawl to the deep side. Animals also show this tendency. A baby chick less than twenty-four hours old avoids the deep side. So do baby lambs and goats tested as soon as they are able to walk. Evidently this behavior is based on an ability to perceive depth that is an inborn characteristic, requiring no experience or learning.

By manipulating the various clues on which depth perception on the visual cliff might be based, it has been found that the essential one is *motion parallax.* This refers to the fact that, when we move our heads, near objects move across our field of vision more rapidly than objects that are farther away. You may have noticed this when on a moving train: the telephone poles along the tracks seem to race past the window, while buildings in the distance do not. When the baby or animal on the visual cliff moves its head, the checks on the cloth at the shallow side move rapidly across its

FIGURE 5.27

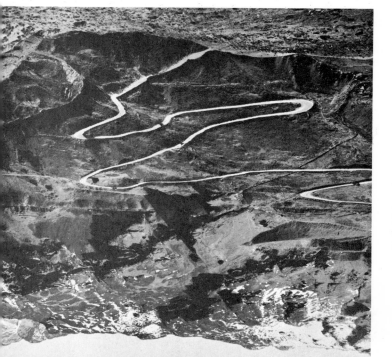

An Illusion Formed by Shadows The road seems to be winding down a long hill. But turn the page upside down to see what this really is.

FIGURE **5.28**

A Baby and the "Visual Cliff" At top, a six-month-old baby fearlessly crawls toward his mother on the glass covering the shallow-looking side of the visual cliff. But, at bottom, he appears afraid to cross over the glass covering the "deep" side. (15)

field of vision; the checks on the deep side do not. This inborn clue to depth perception appears to be the secret of how animals—particularly those like goats that are born into an environment full of mountains and sharp drops—manage to avoid falls.

Perceptual Conflicts

One more experiment on organization of perception deserves mention. Subjects were asked to look at a small square of white plastic through what looked like an ordinary pane of glass but was actually a lens that made the plastic square look like a rectangle, twice as high as it was wide. While they looked, they were also asked to reach behind the "glass" and feel the plastic square; they did this through a piece of black cloth that prevented them from seeing any distortion of their hand. Thus they did not catch on that the "glass" was really a lens.

Here was a situation in which two different senses brought two different kinds of evidence. The subjects *saw* a rectangle. At the same time they *felt* a square. How did they actually perceive the piece of plastic?

The answer is that they perceived the plastic as a rectangle. Most of them were not even aware that there was any conflict between the apparent appearance and the actual feel of the plastic (16). The sense of vision was dominant—an indication that whoever coined the phrase "seeing is believing" was more correct than he probably ever realized.

THE PERCEIVER AND PERCEPTION The factors discussed up to now operate in very much the same manner for everyone. All of us seem to have our attention attracted to stimuli by change, contrast, movement, size, intensity, and repetition. All of us seem to organize the stimuli in accordance with the rules of figure-ground, closure, continuity, proximity, similarity, and common movement. We all perceive objects as having constancy of shape, brightness, color, location, and size. Except when it is affected by some kind of physical handicap, one person's accuracy at distance perception is pretty much like another's and apparently based on the same kind of clues afforded by perceived size, binocular vision, interposition, perspective, and shadowing.

There are also many factors in perception that depend upon who is doing the perceiving and upon his prior experience, learning, and physical and emotional state at the moment. These factors can vary greatly from one person to another, so that two people exposed to exactly the same stimuli may perceive them in entirely different ways.

Early Experience

A chimpanzee named Kora, born in the late 1940's, is well known among psychologists for her contribution to knowledge of the importance of early experience to perception. For the first seven months of her life Kora was raised in darkness, with the exception of an hour and a half a day of vague illumination. (This was necessary to prevent actual degeneration of the nerve tissue of the eyes.) At no time in these seven months did she have an opportunity to see any kind of patterns in her visual field. At the end of that period she was tested for perception of visual patterns.

Compared with other chimpanzees of that age, she proved to be severely retarded. She did not blink when a moving object approached her eyes. She could not fix her gaze on a stationary person or a moving person or even follow the movements of a feeding bottle. It took her six days to learn to blink, thirteen days to fix her gaze on a stationary person or follow a moving person, and twenty days to follow the movements of the bottle. She had considerable trouble learning to avoid a mild electric shock that was paired with the presentation of a large disc prominently striped in yellow and black. Most chimpanzees learn this in one or two pairings, but Kora required two pairings a day for thirteen days (17).

Another chimpanzee, named Rob, was deprived of experience with the sense of touch: his forearms, hands, lower legs, and feet were covered, first with bandages and later with cardboard tubes. When Rob reached the age of thirty-one months, the experimenters removed the covers and tried to teach him to distinguish his right hand from his left. When his right index finger was squeezed, he was rewarded if he turned his head to the right; when his left index finger was squeezed, he was rewarded if he turned his head to the left. Another thirty-one-month-old chimpanzee, raised normally, learned this in about 200 trials. Rob showed very little sign of learning it even after 2000 trials. He performed normally, however, on learning tasks based on visual perception (18).

Among human beings, evidence of the role of early experience has been provided by cases in which people blind from birth because of cataracts were able to see for the first time after the cataracts had been removed by surgery. Reports of these cases indicate that the patients could immediately and without any opportunity for prior training perform three perceptual acts: 1) they could fix their gaze on a stationary object, 2) they could follow a moving object, and 3) they immediately perceived figure-ground relationships. But they had difficulty recognizing objects: for example, they had trouble distinguishing a circle from a triangle or a ball from a cube. Even after they had learned to recognize and identify a cube of sugar held in someone's hand, they could not recognize it when it was suspended on a string. They even had trouble learning to recognize the faces of their relatives, friends, and doctors; one patient, though of well above average intelligence, could recognize only four or five faces two years after the operation (19).

The evidence indicates strongly that human beings and higher animals require a considerable amount of early sensory experience if they are to show normal ability at making even the simplest kind of perceptual discriminations and performing tasks based on these discriminations.° In particular, they appear to need experience with stimuli showing a high degree of contrast. Fortunately, most of them receive this experience, and it is only under unusual circumstances that the retarding effect of early sensory deprivation can be observed.

For lower animals early sensory deprivation does not seem to be so damaging. Rats raised in darkness, for example, demonstrate normal size and distance perception as soon as they are moved into light and catch up quickly with other rats on tests involving the discrimination of visual patterns. You will recall, however, what happened when rats were raised in cages with circles and triangles on the walls (page 114). These rats performed better than others on tests requiring discrimination between circles and triangles. In another experiment, newly born rats were divided into three groups. One group was raised in regular wire cages, from which they could observe all the angles of the walls and doors in the laboratory room. The other two groups were raised in cages entirely enclosed by milk glass, which admitted light but did not permit them to see out. For one group the milk-glass walls were decorated with curved lines and for the other group with lines meeting at angles. When the groups were tested for discrimination between triangles and squares, the group raised inside milk-glass walls with curves did poorly. But the group raised inside milk-glass walls with angles did just as well as the group raised in normal cages. Experience with angles—of whatever nature—seemed to be the key factor (20).

In the experiment in sensory deprivation shown in FIGURE 5.29, note that the two kittens had an equal amount of exposure for three hours a day to the visual contrast and patterns provided by the striped walls. At the end of the experiment the kitten that had done the walking showed normal perception; for example, it blinked at approaching objects and put up its

---

° For the benefit of students who will go on to take advanced courses, it should be pointed out that perception is the subject of one of the liveliest and most fascinating of scientific debates. It can be argued that the cases just cited do not prove anything about the subjects' perception but only about their inability to coordinate other behavior with their perceptions. Perhaps the cataract patient perceives the cube of sugar and the human face just like anyone else. Perhaps Kora had no trouble perceiving the yellow-and-black disc and Rob no trouble perceiving which finger was squeezed. It may have been only their learning of suitable responses to these perceptions that was retarded. There are many such subtle and controversial problems, making the study of the finer points of perception much more complicated than the broad general outline presented in this chapter.

paws to avoid collisions. The kitten that rode in the gondola was perceptually retarded. This experiment is somewhat reminiscent of the one mentioned earlier in which two students wore lenses that shifted their visual fields toward the right. In that case, you will recall, the student who rode around the campus in a wheelchair did not adjust to the lenses, but the one who pushed the wheelchair was able to reach accurately toward objects. Perhaps the experiment with the kittens is further indication that the development of normal behavior depends upon moving around in the world and learning to combine perception and motor coordination; many psychologists have so concluded.

Just as sensory deprivation can cause retardation, so enriched sensory experience can help the organism improve the perceptual process. It has been found, for example, that most babies start reaching for objects when they are about five and a half months old. But when babies are surrounded from birth by large numbers of interesting visual objects, such as mobile toys of various shapes and colors hanging in their cribs, they tend to reach for objects sooner than usual (21). It appears that enriched experience is more effective very early in life than if it comes later.

FIGURE 5.29   *The Kitten that Hitched a Ride*   Two kittens were raised in darkness except for three hours a day in this apparatus. One kitten always did the walking; the other always got a ride. But note that the harness and the gondola are connected in such a way that the kitten that rides faces the striped walls at exactly the same angle as the kitten that walks. For a comparison of the perceptual abilities of the two kittens after ten days of using the apparatus, see the text.

Perceptual Expectations

Among the important mediational units we acquire through learning are those special forms of set known as *perceptual expectations*. All other things being equal, we tend to perceive what we expect to perceive.

Some demonstrations of this fact have been made with a laboratory tool called the tachistoscope, a device with which words or pictures can be shown to a subject for very brief exposure times, as small a fraction of a second as the experimenter desires. Many experiments with the tachistoscope have shown that a subject who knows in general what to expect can recognize words and objects much faster than a subject who has no idea what is coming. If a subject is told that he will be shown the names of fruits or vegetables, for example, he perceives them much more readily than does a subject who has no clue about the nature of the words.

In one of the early experiments with the tachistoscope, one group of subjects was told to expect words dealing with birds or animals and another group to expect words dealing with transportation and travel. Among the words that were then shown, each for a mere one tenth of a second, the experimenter slipped in some collections of letters that were not words at all, though they resembled real words. The first group had a strong tendency to perceive them one way, the second group a very different way. *Pasrort* was often seen as parrot by members of the first group and passport by members of the second group; *dack* as duck and deck; *wharl* as whale and wharf; and *sael* as seal and sail (22). Thus did that important form of set called perceptual expectations influence what the subjects perceived.

A different kind of experiment was once performed in a classroom. At the beginning of the hour the students were told that they would have a substitute instructor that day. To prepare them for the substitute (so they were told), slips bearing a written description of him were passed around. Half the slips described the substitute as "a rather cold person, industrious, critical, practical, and determined." The other half said "a rather warm person, industrious, critical, practical, and determined." The changing of only one word—*cold* to *warm*—had some interesting effects. The students who had received slips calling the substitute "warm" took more part in the classroom discussion that day than did the others. Afterwards, asked their impressions, they described the substitute as having more traits that go along with a "warm" personality than did the others (23). Again, perceptual expectations had influenced what the students perceived.*

Perceptual expectations play an important role in many of the interpretations we make of the environment. When we are around a relative who

---

* Here, too, a word of warning is called for: many psychologists would say that reactions to another person depend upon too many factors to be labeled perception.

has a reputation for being cranky and critical, we notice his more acid remarks and may not even be aware that a good deal of his conversation is just as pleasant as that of anyone else. Indeed we may interpret as sarcastic many remarks that, said in exactly the same words and tone by someone else, would probably strike us as harmless or perhaps even good-natured. When we are around someone we know likes us and from whom we expect warmth and acceptance, we may be totally unaware of a momentary outburst of anger or hostility.

Influences on Perceptual Expectations

Many different factors inside the organism can affect perceptual expectations and therefore what is actually perceived. Among them are biological drives such as hunger and thirst, motives such as a desire for achievement or acceptance, emotions such as anger and fear, and interests and values. Presumably all these factors operate by the same process. We tend to be preoccupied with them; we *think* about them; and our thoughts create a form of mental set.

A number of experiments have demonstrated the effect of these various influences on perception. In one of them, three groups of people were asked to describe "pictures" that they were told they would see dimly on a screen. Actually there were no pictures, merely blurs or smudges, but the subjects did their best to perceive some sort of pattern. One group had gone only an hour since eating, another group four hours, and the third group sixteen hours. It turned out that the subjects who had gone four hours without eating thought they saw more objects related to food than did those who had gone merely an hour and that the subjects who had gone sixteen hours without eating "saw" the most food-related objects of all (24).

In another experiment, two groups of subjects were used—one group highly motivated for achievement, the other group with low motivation for achievement. Both groups were tested on words shown with a tachistoscope, some of which, such as *strive* and *perfect*, were related to achievement and others of which were not. It was found that the subjects who had high achievement motivation could recognize the words related to achievement more rapidly than could the other subjects (25).

Another experiment using the tachistoscope was performed with six groups of people who had a high level of interest in religion, politics, economics, society, the arts, or theory. It was found that most of them were quicker to recognize words relating to these special fields than other words. The subjects interested in religion were quick to recognize *sacred*, for example, and those interested in economics were quick to recognize *income* (26).

The effect of values was demonstrated in an experiment performed with a group of children aged three to five, who were asked to manipulate an adjustable circle of light until it seemed to them to be the same size as a poker chip. Afterward some of them were taught to regard the poker chip as valuable; they could use it to obtain a piece of candy from a vending machine. When tested again for their perception of the size of the chip, these children estimated it to be significantly larger than before. After ten days the experimenter changed the situation so that the poker chip no longer operated the vending machine. The children's perception of the size of the chip then returned to the level it had been at the start (27).

Another experiment using an adjustable circle of light has indicated that children from poor families perceive the size of coins to be larger than do children from rich families (28). In a variation of this experiment, performed with adult subjects under hypnosis, a metal slug was perceived as larger when the subjects were told it was silver than when they were told it was lead, still larger when the slug was represented as being white gold, and largest of all when it was called platinum. In the same experiment, subjects who had been hypnotically persuaded that they were poor perceived the size as larger than did subjects persuaded that they were rich (29).

As has been said, we tend to perceive what we expect to perceive, and the experiments just cited demonstrate that we tend to expect to perceive what we would like to perceive at the moment or what we, in general, value most highly. In everyday terminology, our perceptual expectations are dependent on our state of mind, and our state of mind, in turn, depends upon the situation of the moment and upon all kinds of prior experience and learning.

The Influence of Language

In the next chapter the influence of language on behavior will be discussed at length. As a concluding word on the subject of perception, however, it should be pointed out that this is one of the areas of behavior in which language plays a significant role. Having a definite, clear-cut language label for an object in the environment is one of the important factors in creating the state of mind—the perceptual expectation—that makes it easy to perceive that object.

Some languages use a different system from ours for naming the colors. Some have a single word that stands for both green and blue and the entire range of greenish-blues in between. Others use a single word to lump together all the shades of red and purple. Indeed there is a language used in Liberia that has only two words to describe color; one of them (*hui*) covers all the blues and greens and the other (*ziza*) covers all the reds and oranges. People using these languages would react in very different fashion to an experiment in perception of colors.

On some matters, other languages are much richer than ours. Where we use the single word *snow*, the Eskimos have three different words, each for a different kind of snow. One Philippine tribe has dozens of different words for varieties of rice. When a feature of the environment is important, people seem to coin more words for it. Possessing the words makes possible perceptual discriminations that would go unnoticed by someone who uses the single words *snow* and *rice*.

One final example: in English, we speak of "picking up" an object, regardless of what the object is. The Navajo Indians, however, have several different verbs for the act of picking something up; the verb they use depends upon whether the object is round, square, or long and thin like a pencil. This fact led to an interesting experiment in which the investigator gathered a large collection of brightly colored objects of different shapes. He showed these to a group of English-speaking children of Navajo descent and asked them to sort out the objects that seemed to "go together." These children tended to sort the objects by color. Then he tried the same thing with children who spoke the Navajo language. These children tended to sort the objects by shape (30). The Navajo language, with its different verbs for the act of lifting objects of different shape, appeared to have focused their perceptual process on form.

Language serves as a sort of system of lenses that helps us select and organize. Where most of us perceive only a bird, the expert who has acquired a rich language of birdlore perceives a female western tanager. Where most of us perceive only that a friend looks a little below par, the physician with a rich language of medical knowledge may perceive the unmistakable symptoms of a specific disease. Where most of us perceive just a haze in the sky, the meteorologist perceives cirrostratus clouds that will affect tomorrow's weather. Outsiders often complain about the jargon of the various sciences and the law (and even sports), but the jargon is actually a language system that makes possible perceptions and perceptual discriminations that are essential to understanding the full richness and subtlety of these fields.

SUMMARY

1. Perception is the process through which we become aware of our environment by organizing and interpreting the evidence of our senses.
2. Our perceptions often differ from the actual sensory stimuli on which they are based. For example, we sometimes perceive motion when the stimuli are in fact stationary—as in the *phi phenomenon,* the *gamma phenomenon,* and the *autokinetic illusion.*

3. The key factors in perception are *selection* and *organization*. We pay attention to only some of the stimuli that reach our senses, and we organize these selected stimuli into our own patterns of meaning.

4. The organism has an inborn tendency to select certain stimuli in preference to others. Among the stimulus characteristics that automatically affect selection are *change, contrast, movement, size, intensity,* and *repetition*.

5. The tendency to organize sensory stimuli is so compelling that we tend to perceive patterns in stimuli that do not of themselves possess a pattern, such as the steady clicks of a metronome or a uniform mass of checkerboard squares.

6. One of the strongest influences in perceptual organization is *figure-ground*. We tend to see an object as a figure set off from a neutral ground by a dividing line called a *contour*.

7. Other largely inborn factors that influence organization are *closure, continuity, proximity, similarity,* and *common movement*.

8. An important learned factor in organization is *object constancy*, which refers to the fact that we tend to perceive objects as constant and unchanging even though the image of them that reaches our senses varies because of changing angle and distance.

9. Object constancy includes *shape constancy, brightness constancy, color constancy, location constancy,* and *size constancy*.

10. Size constancy plays a significant role in perception of distance, because perceived distance varies with perceived size.

11. Other perceptual clues to distance and depth are *binocular vision* (the slightly different images received by the two eyes), *interposition, perspective,* and *shadowing*.

12. Human beings and higher animals seem to require a considerable amount of early experience with sensory stimuli if they are to acquire normal perception (or at least the normal responses to what they perceive).

13. The *perceptual expectations* (a form of set) that have been learned are a strong influence on perception. All other things being equal, we tend to perceive what we expect to perceive.

14. Among the factors that help create perceptual expectations are drives, emotions, motives, interests, and values.

15. *Language* is an important influence on the way human beings select and organize in perception. Having a clear-cut language label for an object in the environment is one of the prominent factors in creating perceptual expectations that make it easy to perceive the object.

Allport, F. H. *Theories of perception and the concept of structure.* New York: Wiley, 1955.

Broadbent, D. E. *Perception and communication.* New York: Pergamon Press, 1958.

Dember, W. N. *The psychology of perception.* New York: Holt, Rinehart and Winston, 1960.

Forgus, R. H. *Perception: the basic process in cognitive development.* New York: McGraw-Hill, 1966.

Gibson, J. J. *The perception of the visual world.* Boston: Houghton Mifflin, 1950.

Gregory, R. L. *Eye and brain: the psychology of seeing.* New York: McGraw-Hill, 1966.

Hochberg, J. *Perception.* Englewood Cliffs, N.J.: Prentice-Hall, 1964.

Segall, M. H., Campbell, D. T., and Herskovits, M. J. *The influence of culture on visual perception.* New York: Bobbs-Merrill, 1966.

Teevan, R. C. and Birney, R. C., eds. *Color vision.* Princeton, N.J.: Van Nostrand, 1961.

WORDS AND CONCEPTS

The Development of Concepts
Some Kinds of Concepts
Concepts in Education
The Concepts of Adults
The "Salient Characteristic" of Concepts
Concept Hierarchies
Systems of Concept Hierarchies
Concepts and Connotations
Concepts and Personality

THINKING

The Elements of Thinking
      Images; Symbols; Facts and Premises
Thinking as a Process
      Logical and Mathematical Rules; Mediational Clusters
Undirected Versus Directed Thinking

PROBLEM SOLVING

Steps in Problem Solving
      Step 1: Defining the Problem; Step 2: Evaluating the Definition;
      Step 3: Holding the Problem in Memory; Step 4: Searching for
      Hypotheses; Step 5: Choosing the Best Hypothesis; Step 6: Evaluat-
      ing the Hypothesis; Step 7: Implementing the Hypothesis
Barriers to Problem Solving
      Persistence of Set; Functional Fixedness
Persistence of Set, Daily Living, and Creativity
The Role of Prior Knowledge

LANGUAGE,
THINKING,
AND PROBLEM SOLVING

The one kind of behavior above all that distinguishes man from other organisms is the use of language. Every human society ever studied, no matter
how remote and isolated from other societies, has been found to have a
language. No animal society has ever developed one. Indeed all attempts
to teach the use of language to animals have been failures. Experimenters
have raised chimpanzees in their homes just like their own children; the
chimps have learned such manlike traits as eating with a spoon and brushing
their teeth, but they have never learned to speak more than a few simple
words (1). Attempts have been made to teach language to dolphins, which
seemed promising subjects because they have brains that closely resemble
the human brain; these attempts also failed. Birds such as parrots and para-
keets can "speak" by imitating the sound of the human voice, but they show
no evidence of attaching any meaning to the sounds.

This is not to say that other organisms cannot communicate with one
another. Bees that have found a new food supply go back to the hive and
perform a dance, the nature and speed of which "tell" the other bees where
the food supply is (2). Birds sing their characteristic songs to attract mates
and discourage interlopers. Dolphins make sounds to one another, and chimpanzees use sounds and gestures to threaten other chimps or alert them to
danger. But there are only a limited number of sounds and gestures that
any other organism can use. Man's language is a special technique that permits him to communicate an infinite number and variety of messages and to
pass along all his accumulated knowledge to new generations through the
spoken and written word.

Why man alone should use language is somewhat puzzling. Chimpanzees
and other mammals have vocal cords; birds can make many of the sounds
of human language. Dolphins show many signs of great intelligence. But
apparently there is something about the organization of the human brain—
the dynamics of how it operates—that makes man unique.

Experience, of course, is essential; we have to learn not only the meanings of the sounds of language but also how to make these sounds. Some years

ago a six-year-old girl was found in a secluded home in Ohio; she had been brought up by a deaf-mute mother and had never been around any other human being. She could not talk and in fact made no sounds at all except croaking noises. But after a week around people who used language she began to imitate their voices, and in two years her speech and her use of language were normal for her age (3).

Language is so important to the study of human behavior that it has already been mentioned twice: in Chapter 3 as a basis for stimulus generalization and discrimination in learning and in Chapter 5 as an influence on perception. Now it must be discussed in detail, as a form of behavior that affects all the rest of our behavior and makes possible that special form of higher mental behavior called thinking and problem solving.

WORDS AND CONCEPTS

Man, like all other organisms, is quite limited in the number of sounds he produces. This may seem hard to believe, in view of the apparent richness and variety of all the sentences that can be heard in the halls of the United Nations Building—English, French, Spanish, German, Russian, and all the languages of Asia and Africa— but it is true. No language contains more than eighty-five different basic sounds. English has forty-five, and the simplest language known has fifteen. These basic sounds are called *phonemes* and are the building blocks of language. All the English vowels are phonemes—for example, the *a*, pronounced as in *cake*. The beginning sounds of most of the consonants are phonemes—for example, the sound of *b* at the beginning of the word *butter*. Other English phonemes include such sounds as the *th* in *the*, the *ch* in *chip*, and the *sh* in *shop*.

The phonemes are combined into syllables, some of which are themselves short words, such as *do, at, the, by,* and *new*. The syllables are then combined into words, and words into sentences. Babies learn very quickly to utter the phonemes and to combine them into syllables and words, and by the age of one or two they are already talking in simple sentences such as "Baby drink." At first they tend to use only nouns and verbs, the two kinds of words that carry the most important meanings. Later they start adding adjectives and, still later, articles—*a, an,* and *the*. By about the age of six, children have learned all the basic rules of grammar, which is the formal system by which sentences are constructed.

Some words are mostly symbols for objects—*water, aspirin, penny*. Even these very basic words give human behavior a range and flexibility that are denied to all other organisms. We can communicate our need for water or an aspirin tablet without the actual presence of these objects. Imagine the difficulties you would encounter if you were in a strange country where you did not know a single word of the native language and none of the natives knew a word of English. You would be able to shop only in stores that had the goods on display, so that you could point. And how would you go about ordering even so much as a piece of bread and an egg in a restaurant?

Most words, however, are not just symbols for objects. They represent a much more complicated symbol called a *concept*, which can best be defined as a symbol that stands for *a common characteristic or relationship shared by objects or events that are otherwise different.* The word *money* is a concept that includes all coins from a penny to a dollar and all paper currency, not only the coins and currency used in the United States but those used in other nations as well. *Medicine* is a concept that includes everything from aspirin to all the more unfamiliar and complicated drugs taken to relieve illness or improve physical condition. Abstract words such as *justice, freedom,* and *patriotism* are all concepts. As a matter of fact, since we cannot possibly have a separate word for everything in the universe, all words including even the most specific are usually used as concepts. A word of apparent simplicity such as *water* stands for the drinkable fluid that comes out of a kitchen faucet, the salty fluid that makes up the oceans, and the drops that fall from the sky as rain. *Aspirin* stands for a certain kind of drug, regardless of whether it comes in a tablet, a powder, or a fluid. *Penny* stands for coins of a certain value, regardless of the date or particular design printed on them.

It is the use of concepts that accounts for the richness of the mental processes of the human organism and enables him to perform outstanding feats of thinking and problem solving.

The Development of Concepts

It is an old joke that if a child is asked "What is a hole?" he is likely to reply, "A hole is to dig." To adults this seems funny, but it demonstrates the workings of concept formation in the child.

When children first start finding some kind of common thread of similarity linking otherwise dissimilar objects, they often build their concepts on the basis of *function*. To the child, the shared similarities depend on what one does with an object or what the object does. He learns that *paper* is a word that stands for objects that look different in many ways; paper can be white, green, red, or yellow, and smooth or rough, and large or small. What gives these objects the common name of *paper*, as far as the child is concerned, is that they are all "something to write on." Envelopes, of whatever color or size, are "something you put letters in." A big yellow collie and a little white poodle are both dogs because a dog is "something that barks." Food is "something you eat."

Another basis on which children lump objects together is *location*. Ask a child "What is furniture?" and he is likely to reply, "Furniture is what is in the living room." "What are flowers?" "Flowers are in the yard." "What is an animal?" "An animal is what you find in a zoo." These two aspects—location and function—are among the first symbolic similarities that the preschool child finds among the objects in his environment.

A little later, the developing child begins to build concepts out of combinations of *attributes*, such as the material that things are made of and how they look, feel, or taste. The older child, for example, might say that furniture is "something you sit on and you find it in the living room and it's made of wood and it's hard." Here he is defining his concept on three different bases —the function ("something you sit on"), the location ("you find it in the living room"), and also two physical attributes ("made of wood" and "hard"). He might now say that "fruits are things that you eat and they grow on trees and they're sweet." To similarities in function and location he has now added the physical attribute of sweetness. He also begins to notice similarities in *component parts*. Asked to define birds, he might reply, "Things that have feathers and wings." Or he might say that flowers "have stems and petals."

Similarities of function, location, physical attributes, and component parts are the simplest bases for concepts. A more sophisticated kind of concept involves *relationships*. These can be physical—as in experiments where a child or an animal learns that a reward will always be found under the smaller of two objects. They can be mathematical, such as the relationships implied by the letters and numbers in an algebraic equation. Or they can be as abstract as the relationships between schools of philosophy.

Some Kinds of Concepts

One investigation into the way concepts are formed is illustrated in FIGURE 6.1. Here, in essence, the subjects were asked to learn the meanings of the concepts that the experimenter had arbitrarily assigned to nonsense words. If you try the experiment yourself, you will probably learn the definitions of a LING, FARD, and so on just from studying the information available in the figure. (If not, you may want to try again with the additional clue that the drawings in column three are, from top to bottom, a LETH, MANK, FARD, LING, STOD, PILT, MOLP, RELF, and PRAN.)

The subjects in the experiment tended to be quickest at learning that a RELF was a face, a LETH a building, and a MOLP a tree. Next they learned that FARD meant circular, PRAN meant two diagonals crossed by another diagonal, and STOD meant a loop. The fact that LING was two, PILT five, and MANK six was usually most difficult to learn. In other words, the subjects first learned the concepts of definite objects, then of shapes, and last the more abstract concepts of numbers.

An Experiment in Concept Formation   These drawings were shown one at a time on a revolving drum, starting from the top to the bottom of the first column, then from the top to the bottom of the second column, and so on. After the final drawing in the last column the entire series of drawings was shown again. For each picture the experimenter spoke a nonsense word, as shown in the boxes in the first two columns. The subjects were asked to learn the name of each drawing and, as soon as they had learned it, to say it before the experimenter spoke. They were told that the experiment was merely a study of memory, and they did not know that any concept formation was involved. At some time in the course of showing the second column of drawings, however, most subjects noticed that the nonsense words were being repeated and caught on that there must be some general rule for naming the drawings. The reader is invited to fill in the empty boxes, then turn to the text to check the answers. (4)

FIGURE **6.1**

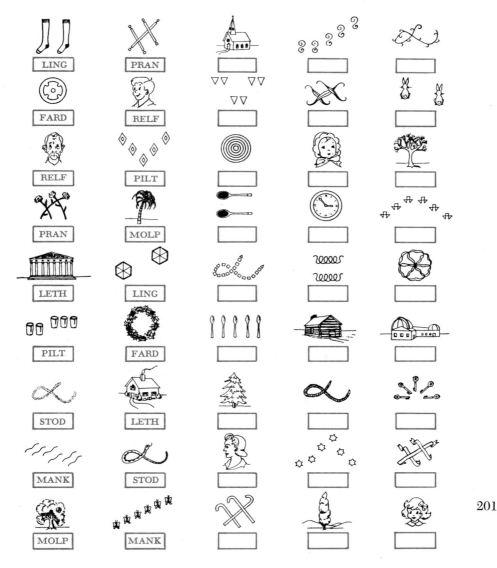

201

It appears that children—like subjects confronted with these nonsense words—first learn concepts of concrete objects and of shape and only later learn more abstract concepts such as mathematical relationships. But this is probably because they encounter more concrete stimuli than abstract concepts; they constantly respond to such objects as clothing, food, toys, furniture, human faces, and buildings and less frequently to abstract ideas. Moreover, as has been pointed out, learning a concept such as *horizon* requires the prior learning of a number of component parts; the child of four does not possess these component parts and cannot learn the meaning of horizon, whereas the child of ten can learn it on a single trial. Under some circumstances, even young children often prove capable of developing concepts that are very abstract.

Concepts in Education

A great deal of the educational process is concerned with the teaching and learning of concepts. In the lower grades we learn such concepts as nouns, verbs, and adjectives; addition, subtraction, and multiplication; latitude and longitude; continents and nations. Later we learn the concepts that form the subject matter of algebra, law, chemistry, economics, the social sciences, philosophy. This raises the question of whether it is better for a teacher to explain the concept first and then cite examples or to present the examples and let the student discover the concept for himself. The first of these methods is called *learning through exposition,* or *didactic learning;* the second is called *discovery learning.*

An example of discovery learning is shown in FIGURE 6.2. Here the concept to be learned is the meaning of the nonsense word PLAM, which is defined as a certain kind of nonsense figure. Examples are shown of figures that are PLAMS and other figures that are not PLAMS, and the student is left to discover the concept for himself. In general, this kind of learning has many advantages. It gets the learner involved and thus attracts and holds his attention. It also increases his confidence in his ability to make discoveries and encourages the kind of independent thinking that is one of the goals of the educational process.

FIGURE 6.2

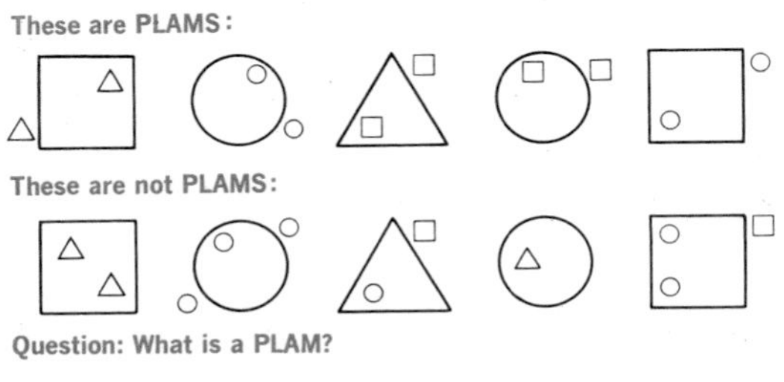

These are PLAMS:

These are not PLAMS:

Question: What is a PLAM?

A Problem in Concept Formation
Looking at this theoretical problem in concept formation, the college student has no difficulty discovering that a PLAM is a geometrical figure with a smaller figure inside it and another exactly similar small figure on the outside. For comment on how a pupil in the lower grades might best learn the meaning of PLAM, see the text.

Discovery learning, however, is most appropriate with learners who are sufficiently mature and intelligent to cope with the problems of concept formation and who are motivated to make the discovery. It is less appropriate in the lower grades of elementary school, where children lack maturity and motivation. It is particularly inappropriate for the duller young pupils and those who tend to be impulsive, to leap to the wrong idea, and to become discouraged by failure. In these cases a teacher may do better to use the didactic method and explain what a PLAM is before showing the examples.

FIGURE 6.2 also has bearing upon another question that has frequently been debated among educators—namely, is it easier to form concepts from positive examples (in this case, from seeing PLAMS) or from negative examples (in this case, from seeing non-PLAMS)? In general, the answer seems to be that positive examples are more helpful than negative examples but that a combination of the two is the most helpful of all. For instance, if we are trying to teach a child the concept *fog*, we can hardly accomplish our purpose by pointing to all the things that are not fog. It is much better to show a positive example, some actual fog. But even then the child might tend to confuse fog and smoke—so the best procedure is to show him several examples of fog and several examples of smoke and to point out the differences.

The Concepts of Adults

By the time we have reached adulthood so many factors have gone into our building of concepts that it is impossible to trace or list them. Even our concepts of physical objects often involve recognizing complex and subtle kinds of similarities and differences. Furniture, for example, is no longer just "something to sit on," "found in a living room," "made of wood," or "hard." Instead it is anything that falls into a group of objects that contribute to the convenience or decorative aspects of living in or near a building—regardless of whether it is used to sit on or to eat from, is found in a home or in an office, is made of wood, metal, or plastic, or is hard or soft.

Most of the words we use as adults involve concepts within concepts and therefore are extremely difficult to define in a simple or straightforward way. What, for example, do we mean by *man?* At the most sophisticated adult level, we tend to have a concept of man as the highest (another concept) of all mammals (still another concept!)—a mammal being a particular kind of organism (another concept!) that produces its young inside the body of the mother (another!), who nurses (another!) the baby (another!) after birth (another!). On the other hand, we can still think of man, on a more primitive level, in the kinds of terms children use to form their first concepts. For our concept of man includes similarities of function (he is something that walks and talks and drives automobiles), location (he lives on Earth; he is found in cities), component parts (he has arms and legs), and physical attributes (he is solid and covered with skin).

As a figure of speech, it might be said that the adult's concepts are like the catalogue file of a library, indexed and cross-indexed so that a search starting with a word such as *man* can lead almost anywhere. One card lists man's functions; it leads in turn to other cards that list the details of all his past and present activities. Another lists the places where he is found; it leads in turn to detailed lists of the characteristics of the continents, cities, and physical circumstances in which man dwells. Another lists his component parts and another his physical attributes. Beyond these four cards there are innumerable others that list more abstract and sophisticated attributes of man—that talk about him in terms of history, philosophy, and science and include his aspirations, triumphs, doubts, and failures.

One of the measures of how much a person has learned is how many cards there are under each concept in this mental filing system. To a child, for example, there is no association between the concept *man* and the concept *whale*, but the educated adult knows that these two very dissimilar organisms are related in that both are mammals. To the young child, the concept *man* never calls up an association with an ancient Egyptian Pharaoh or with the lamas of Tibet; to an adult, it may very well do so. The richness of our adult concepts depends upon how many similarities we have found to exist among all the apparently diverse elements in our environment and our history.

The "Salient Characteristic" of Concepts

We can follow the trail of cross-indexed concept cards almost anywhere. In our thinking and problem solving we often rummage through them at length and in depth. Most of the time, however, we tend to ignore the great bulk of the cards and to think of a particular concept in terms of what we consider its one outstanding feature. To a theologian, for example, the word *man* might ordinarily call up the concept of a creature of God, possessing a soul. To a physician, *man* might ordinarily mean a functioning collection of physiological apparatus, all subject to various diseases. To the zoologist, it might mean simply another kind of animal; to the policeman, an adult as opposed to a juvenile; to the military officer, a soldier; to a romantic young woman, a person whom one might marry.

Thus each of us has his own primary definition of each particular concept he uses, based on what to him is the *salient characteristic* of the various objects, events, or ideas that are included in the concept. A group of adults may be well aware that *salt* is a concept that means a certain kind of chemical compound, found in various forms in nature, in the laboratory, and in the human body. But to a cook in the group the salient characteristic of salt is that it is a seasoning used on food. The chemist usually thinks of it as a compound in which the hydrogen of an acid has been replaced by a metal. The physician thinks of it as a component of the human body. This tendency to concentrate on the salient characteristic and ignore other aspects depends in part upon a feature of concept formation that is called *concept hierarchies.*

Concept Hierarchies

In any list, one item must be at the top and the others must then follow in order to the bottom. So it is with the various lists in our filing system of concepts. This can best be illustrated in the case of a concept such as *vegetable.* Most of us, asked to draw up a list of vegetables, would think first of the very familiar ones such as tomato and potato. Only much later, if at all, would we think of such seldom encountered ones as artichoke or kale. Asked to draw up a list of animals, most of us would not think immediately that man is the most familiar animal of all; we might head our list with dog or cat or, if we happened to come from ranch country, horse. Way down toward the bottom of the list would come such unfamiliar animals as aardvark and lynx. Asked to list colors, most of us would start with red and take a long time to get to puce and cerise.

The term used to describe this fact is *concept hierarchies*—a hierarchy being a power structure in which the rank of each individual is clearly defined, from bottom to top, and each individual is subordinate to the one above him. In concept hierarchies the links between the concept and the associations at the top of the list are very powerful; the links between the concept and the associations toward the bottom of the list are weaker.

Systems of Concept Hierarchies

One of the interesting facts about concept hierarchies is that they tend to vary depending upon the situation and the subject. When we talk about inanimate objects such as buildings or furniture, for example, concepts based upon a similarity of component parts are usually well up in the hierarchy. Thus we tend to talk about buildings as being made of brick, steel, or wood and as having windows and doors. But we do not describe people this way. When we talk about a person, we do not usually concern ourselves with the fact that he has freckles or arms and legs. Instead we tend to think of his overall physical attributes; the fact that he is tall or short, heavy or slim, ranks high in the concept hierarchy. Above all, we tend to think of what might be called his personality characteristics. We term him aggressive or meek, ambitious or easygoing, hostile or friendly.

We build these concepts of a person just as we develop our other concepts—by noticing similarities. For example, we notice over a period of time that a person on one occasion argues over who has the right to a parking space, on another occasion pushes his way to a crowded store counter, and on still another occasion dominates the conversation at a party. These are all different kinds of behavior, taking place in different situations, but they all have a common thread that fits into the concept *aggressive*. We note that another man seems a little shy in company, prefers to stay home and read rather than go to a football game, and spends a good deal of his time alone. In these different forms of behavior we find a similarity, and we call him an introvert.

Our concepts of our own selves form a still different hierarchy. We tend to use evaluative concepts; we think of ourselves as good or bad, smart or stupid, popular or unpopular. Thus do our concept hierarchies vary according to the subject at hand. We use one system of hierarchies for inanimate objects, another for people, and still another for ourselves.

Concepts and Connotations

In the system of concept hierarchies that we apply to ourselves, as has just been stated, we frankly make evaluations. But, even in situations where we think we are being objective and using neutral concepts, we are also making evaluations of a sort. This is because most words—and particularly the words used as concepts—not only have the meaning that is apparent on the surface but also carry other implied meanings known as *connotations*. That is to say, they connote (or imply or suggest) certain qualities and values. A good example is the concept word *landlord*. Its dictionary definition is "a person who owns property and rents it to others." That is its plain and simple meaning. But the word also has some highly unpleasant connotations; one may think of a landlord as grasping, unkind, and miserly.

Knowledge of the importance of connotations in the concepts we use is the contribution of C. E. Osgood, who devised the type of scale shown in FIGURE 6.3. Each line of the scale, you will note, contains seven steps from an adjective such as "weak" at one end to its opposite such as "strong" at the other. To large groups of subjects, Osgood presented a wide variety of words, which they were asked to rate somewhere along each of the lines on his scale, only ten of which are included in FIGURE 6.3. As it turned out, there were considerable individual differences in the way people rated the words, but the average ratings made by one group were remarkably similar to the average ratings made by another group at a different time and place.

The scale is what Osgood called the *semantic differential*. It measures difference in meaning—not in the dictionary sense of meaning but in terms of the patterns of qualities and values that words connote. To a majority of people, for example, the word *success* proved to have strong connotations of being strong, large, active, good, hot, healthy, and happy. To a somewhat lesser extent, it suggested young and smooth. Other words turned out to have dissimilar patterns on the semantic differential, as can be seen for *fate* and *death* in FIGURE 6.3.

Osgood found that the most important line of all on his scale was good–bad. A very large number of words carry connotations of goodness or badness —more than carry any other kind of connotation. To enlarge upon the figure of speech used earlier, one might say that our catalogue file of concepts, with its cross-indexed hierarchies, is also organized in another way—as if the "good" concepts were printed in black ink on white paper, the "bad" concepts in white ink on black paper. Our tendency to think in terms of good and bad starts in childhood: among the "good" concepts are mother, father, friend, day, obedience, present, warmth; among the "bad" ones are stranger, night, disobedience, spanking, cold. As adults, we still think of a common thread of goodness running through such different concepts as health, angels, cleanliness, food, bed, work, Sunday, peace, freedom, wealth. We find a common thread of badness running through such varied concepts as sickness, devil, dirt, hunger, fatigue, idleness, war, slavery, poverty.

The second most important line on the scale, Osgood found, was strong–weak; this line accounted for the second largest number of connotations. Success is strong; so are concepts such as father, war, and devil. Mother is weak; so are such varied concepts as poem and illness. The third most important line was active–passive: many concepts have connotations of activity (such as success, social, and play), and many others have connotations of passivity (such as fate, death, introvert, and water.)

A great majority of all words and concepts have significant connotations on one or more of the top three scales. This has proved true not only for Americans speaking the English language but also for other peoples speaking different languages. Different cultures may disagree as to what particular

FIGURE 6.3

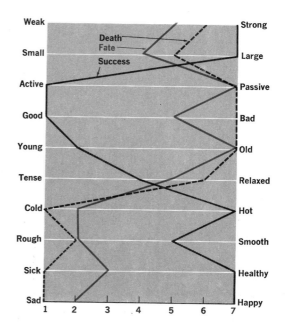

A Scale of Connotations The lines show the ratings given by one subject for three different words on ten lines of the Osgood *semantic differential.* For an explanation of what the ratings indicate, see the text. (5)

things are good or bad—for example, a Polynesian would regard work as "bad" and idleness as "good," in contrast to many Americans. In some societies the father is "weak" and the mother is "strong." But all people everywhere seem to use goodness, strength, and activity as important dimensions along which to organize most of their concepts.

Concepts and Personality

Although Osgood's work shows some significant similarities in the way all human beings develop and organize their concepts and concept hierarchies, it must also be pointed out that there are many individual differences. As was mentioned earlier, we form our concepts on the basis of our experiences. The similarities to which we are exposed most often are the ones that we notice first; they are also the ones that tend to be bound together by the most powerful associations and to occupy a high place in our concept hierarchies. The mechanic's son builds strong and persistent concepts of a mechanical nature; to him an automobile and a boat powered by the same kind of engine may seem more alike than two automobiles with different engines. The philosophy professor's daughter tends to form highly abstract concepts; her concept of an automobile may involve close associations with Phoebus' chariot in Greek mythology.

In one experiment, subjects were asked which word did not belong among the following four:

prayer, skyscraper, temple, cathedral

As you will note, this is an ingenious grouping of words. A person who has a tendency to respond with religious concepts can argue that *skyscraper* is different from the other words. A person who responds to the words as belonging to a hierarchy of architectural concepts can argue that *prayer* is out of place. As it happened, 70 percent of the subjects in the experiment chose *skyscraper* as being the word that did not belong. Then the same words were presented to another group but in different order:

skyscraper, prayer, temple, cathedral

This time the number who chose *skyscraper* dropped to 40 percent (6). Obviously the decrease was caused by the set created by the first word in the series. When *prayer* was the first word, most subjects were set for religious concepts; when *skyscraper* was the first word, most were set for concepts involving buildings. But even the effect of *skyscraper* in creating a set did not influence all the subjects. Many subjects' own concept hierarchies, with religious concepts occupying a prominent place, still led them to associate *prayer, temple,* and *cathedral* and to consider *skyscraper* the wrong word in the series.

As this fact indicates, each of us has his own catalogue file—to use that figure of speech again—with its own system of lists and cross-indexing. The same stimulus—the same word, the same action by another person, the same event taking place before our eyes—may set off entirely different lines of search through the files of different people, leading each of them eventually to take down a different book from the shelves—that is, leading them to engage in very different kinds of behavior.

To put it another way, the concepts we have learned and the way we have built them into hierarchies and have related and interlocked them one with another constitute our own personal system of organizing our environments. They influence what we select to pay attention to in our environments and how we organize our perceptions. Moreover, most of our concepts carry connotations of goodness and badness, strength and weakness, activity and passivity. We use our system of concepts to label and understand ourselves, our fellow men, and the objects and events in our environments; the labels themselves help determine whether we approve or disapprove, admire or deplore. In our development from infant to adult we have learned not only concepts but ways of responding to these concepts. Thus does language—in particular, the system of concepts each of us has built out of language—determine much of our behavior.

THINKING

The most important of all covert behavior is *thinking,* a word that all of us understand but that is difficult to define precisely. Perhaps it can best be described as *the covert manipulation of images, symbols, and other mediational units.* Sometimes thinking manipulates objects that are physically present in the environment, as does the thinking of a carpenter while he is working with tools and lumber to build a cabinet. But note that the carpenter does not just move these objects about; he thinks about their uses and measurements in relation to the as yet unfinished product he is building. In other cases, thinking is entirely independent of physical objects; we can think about objects that are not present, about events that occurred in the distant past, or about abstract concepts that have no physical reality at all. Thinking is an important form of behavior and a useful tool of mankind precisely because it can range so widely and is so free from restrictions imposed by the immediate environment. In the process of thinking we can manipulate any or all of the mediational units acquired in our lifetimes.

Like overt behavior, thinking ranges from the simple to the very complex. If someone tells you, "Think of an apple," you are likely to respond with the image of an apple; some sort of mediational unit is aroused and you seem to see an apple. If someone tells you, "Think of the name of a fruit," you may respond by thinking of the word *apple.* This is the simplest form of thinking—the arousal of a single mediational unit that is an image or a word. Ordinarily, however, thinking occurs in chains of mediational units—sometimes short and simple chains, sometimes long and complicated chains. The image of the apple may be followed by an image of eating the apple; this is a two-stage chain. Or it may be followed by a number of mediational units—additional images or words—which represent going to a store, buying apples, baking an apple pie. Now the chain has many links or stages. Chains of thinking are built from simple mediational units just as chains of complicated motor behavior are built from simple muscular movements.

The Elements of Thinking

In talking about overt behavior, one must speak of such units as simple reflexes, conditioned reflexes, free operants, and conditioned operants. Similarly, the elements that go into thinking must now be considered in detail.

IMAGES   A certain amount of thinking can be done with images, which, as was said earlier, are recollections of sensory experiences. Dreaming is this kind of thinking. When we dream, we seem to see a series of events happening much as if we were watching a moving picture. Besides the visual images, our dreams also contain images of sounds; we often seem to speak or be spoken to. Certain kinds of thinking of a high level of complexity and discipline are also possible through the manipulation of images. Mathematicians often think in "pictures" of space and of intersecting planes. Some musicians can compose or orchestrate by manipulating the images of sounds that they "hear" only inside themselves; Beethoven, for example, wrote many of his greatest works after he became deaf and could not actually hear tones at all.

SYMBOLS   The fact that animals seem to be capable of manipulating some kinds of symbols has already been mentioned. Human thinking, too, sometimes uses symbols other than words. The mathematician manipulates the wide range of symbols found in mathematical formulae. The musician manipulates symbols standing for notes and keys, In most human thinking, however, the richest source of building blocks is the symbols of language. Words, as has been said, enable us to label the objects and events in our environment and to manipulate them without seeing or touching them. Concepts enable us to treat them as groups containing various similarities and relationships.

FACTS AND PREMISES   The third group of elements of thinking is made up of relationships that we believe hold true for the objects and events of our environment. We have discovered, for example, that holding a finger in a flame causes pain and if continued long enough causes physical damage. We know from experience that if we slip off an edge we will fall. In thinking about fire and about mountain climbing, these facts are among the elements we manipulate.

When we have great faith in a relationship, we term it a *fact*. Thus we consider it a fact that fire burns flesh or that gravity causes falls. Many of what we accept as facts come from our own observations. Others represent the pooled observations of many people in our society—the kind of pieces of information found in various handbooks of fact in our libraries. Our thinking about the desirability of various cities as places to live, for example, might take into account such facts as that New York City is the largest in the United States, that the average annual rainfall in Oregon is high, or that the sun shines in Miami, Florida, on most days of the year. We may base our thinking about automobiles on various facts about the horsepower and miles per gallon of different models.

Other facts come from the empirical observations of science. When we think about the sky and the solar system, we take for granted the astronomer's observation that the moon revolves around the earth and that the earth and the other planets revolve around the sun. We accept the physiologist's observation that the blood stream carries oxygen from the lungs to the cells of the body, the finding of medical science that surgery is the best cure for appendicitis, the chemist's finding that an alkali neutralizes an acid.

We also accept as fact the axioms, definitions, and formulae of mathematics. We know that mathematics is not an empirical science, that it is entirely theoretical, yet we do not question that the circumference of a circle equals $2\pi r$ or that the square of the hypotenuse of a right-angled triangle equals the sum of the squares of the other two sides.

What we believe to be a fact may in truth be wrong. Just as we now take for granted that the earth is round and revolves around the sun, people at one time believed it to be a fact that the earth was flat and that the sun revolved around the earth. Some of the accepted "facts" in our own society may eventually prove to be equally incorrect. Nonetheless we give them full faith as constituting lasting relationships in our environment. We consider them to be "proved" and use them constantly to organize our thinking associations.

A *premise* is a belief that we accept even though it cannot be demonstrated so convincingly as the relationships we call facts. Some of our premises come from the sciences. The theory of evolution, for example, is only a set of premises. Many advanced mathematical theories are still only premises. In psychology the notion that intelligence is inherited is merely a premise, and so are most of the ideas about the learning process that were discussed in Part 2. But the premises we adopt from the various sciences are in accord with the best observations currently possible, and they have at least a certain claim to factual basis.

Other premises are the result of individual experiences and learning. They are not necessarily based on objective observation, and they may vary greatly from one person to another. One person, from what he has heard and observed, believes that most people are honest; much of his thinking about other people includes this firmly held premise. Another person holds just as firmly to the premise that most people are dishonest. One person bases much of his thinking (and overt behavior) on the premise that it is wise to keep one's nose to the grindstone, another on the premise that all work and no play makes Jack a dull boy. The importance of individual differences in premises as an element in thinking will become apparent in a moment.

Thinking as a Process

This section on thinking started by pointing out that covert behavior, like overt behavior, ranges from simple units to long and complicated chains. The elements of thinking, it has been shown, are images, symbols (especially words and concepts), facts, and premises. But what about the process that builds the elements into chains? Is there a process in thinking that is akin to the process by which overt behavior is molded? The answer is that just as complex overt behavior is built up by learning (such as classical and operant conditioning) so is thinking built up through learning processes. The processes take two forms, each of which deserves detailed discussion. They are: 1) association through logical and mathematical rules and 2) a far less precise, far more personal kind of association that can best be described by the term *mediational clusters.* Let us start with the more formal of the two.

LOGICAL AND MATHEMATICAL RULES   All of us know, at least in a general way, what it means to think logically. It means to be sensible and reasonable and to draw conclusions that are justified by the evidence. In logical thinking we add up the facts and conclude that two plus two equals four, not three or five.

The application of mathematical rules is one of the best examples of logical thinking. The circumference of a circle is always $2\pi r$, and π is defined as 3.1416. Therefore, if r (the radius) is 5 feet, the circumference has to be 31.416 feet. To reach any other conclusion would be totally illogical.

Outside the field of mathematics, a well-known example of logic is the *syllogism,* a three-step kind of thinking that goes as follows:

1. All men are mortal.
2. I am a man.
3. Therefore I am mortal.

In the syllogism, statement 1 is known as the major premise, statement 2 as the minor premise, and statement 3 as the conclusion. If the major premise and the minor premise are taken for granted, the conclusion follows inescapably.

Note that the syllogism is an argument from the general to the particular. It is logical to think:

> All mammals nurse their young.
> A whale is a mammal.
> Therefore a whale nurses its young.

It would not be logical to think:

> Some mammals live on land.
> All whales are mammals.
> Therefore some whales live on land.

People often fall into errors of logic. A young woman may decide to become a schoolteacher as a result of this line of thought: "My mother says she was extremely happy when she was teaching school; therefore I will be happy teaching school." The fallacies here are that the young woman may have very different tastes and that schoolteaching may have changed as a profession in the meantime. A man with a stomach ache takes a pill that was once prescribed for a friend on the ground that "the pill helped him; therefore it will help me." But the present stomach ache may be of an entirely different kind and may only be aggravated by the medicine.

Often when we accuse people of being illogical, however, we are wrong. Their logic is sound, granted their premises, and it is the premises that we disagree with. For example, the navigators of the Middle Ages were quite logical in believing that anybody who kept sailing due west from Europe would eventually fall off the earth. Their reasoning was as follows:

> All flat surfaces have edges.
> The earth is flat.
> Therefore the earth has edges and anyone who sails that far will fall off.

The logic was sound, but the minor premise was wrong: the earth is not flat. On a more commonplace level, men often consider women illogical; husbands cannot understand why their wives buy an oversupply of fresh peaches just because peaches happen to be unusually cheap. The wife's reasoning may go:

> All bargains are good and should be taken advantage of.
> Peaches are a bargain today.
> Therefore I will buy as many peaches as possible.

The logic is perfect. Where husband and wife disagree is on the first premise.

Many of the world's arguments and misunderstandings, among statesmen and nations as well as between husbands and wives, are caused not so much by fallacies of logic as by belief in different premises. One government economist, using faultless logic, may reach the conclusion that taxes should be raised this year. An equally brilliant economist, using equally flawless logic, may conclude that taxes should be lowered. One person decides, after much reasonable thought, that capital punishment should be abolished. Another person decides that it is essential. Which economist and which of the two opinions on capital punishment is right, and which is wrong? We cannot really say, because we have no way of establishing the validity of most of the premises that various people hold. We cannot be sure that a premise is wrong unless it clearly violates proved fact, and this is seldom the case. We know now for a fact, as the navigators of the Middle Ages did not know, that the earth is spherical rather than flat. And, if a man claims to be Napoleon, we know that he is definitely and unquestionably wrong, and we label him a psychotic. Mostly, however, we hold our premises more or less on faith; we can agree or disagree with another person's premises but cannot usually prove them right or wrong. Thus, even though rules of logic such as the syllogism are formal and well disciplined, people adhering to the rules can reach very different conclusions.

MEDIATIONAL CLUSTERS   In sharp contrast to formal logic is the other kind of thinking process—the kind best described by the term *mediational clusters*. These are dependent upon all the various kinds of associations that were discussed under the heading of language and particularly of concepts. We carry around with us, as has been said, elaborate systems of concepts based on function, location, similarity of component parts, physical attributes, and relationships. The concepts are arranged in hierarchies and are connected to one another by a sort of cross-indexing; moreover, the concepts carry powerful connotations of such qualities as goodness, strength, and activity. When we tap any part of this store of knowledge, we in effect tend to tap all of it. To go back to a figure of speech that was used earlier in the book, the learning process is like a cork wall in which new stimuli—new words, new ideas—sink home and become attached, like darts. Now, when we try to pull out one of the darts, a whole section of the wall, containing a cluster of numerous other darts, comes away.

Let us say that we ask a college student to think of the word *angel* and to report every word and idea that it suggests. As the student digs out the dart for *angel*, all kinds of associated words and thoughts pull loose. The student may start by describing the attributes of an angel (the white robe, the benign expression), then functions (playing a harp), location (in heaven), and connotations (good, weak, passive). The student may then move on to the concept of religion and the concepts that this word arouses in turn and at last to the opposites that *angel* suggests, such as the word *devil* and all its evil associations and connotations.

This kind of thinking is simply based on the clustering together of mediational units and the connections between clusters such as angel–good and their opposites such as devil–bad. It is the kind of thinking that is often called free association or stream of consciousness. Yet the associations are not altogether "free." The way each person has organized his concepts into hierarchies and systems of hierarchies, with some associations powerful and others weak, helps dictate each new link in his chain of thinking. A priest, starting with the word *angel*, might forge a chain of thought directly to the philosophical implications of the newest papal encyclical. A musician might make a chain of associations from angel to harp to his own special musical interests. An athlete might link angel–fly–fly ball–baseball.

Most chains of thinking involve associations dictated by mediational clusters rather than by logic. Indeed mediational clusters play a dual role in that they are the source of most of the premises upon which we base even our logical thinking. Premises such as those mentioned earlier—that most people are honest or that most people are dishonest, that hard and unremitting work is the source of success or of dullness—are not so much the result of objective observation as of the clustering of mediational units and their connotations.

Undirected Versus Directed Thinking

The discussion has proceeded from the elements of thinking to the two methods by which associations are made and linked together into chains of thinking. Now it must be pointed out that there are two very different kinds of thinking: 1) *undirected thinking*, which takes place spontaneously and with no goal in view, and 2) *directed thinking*, in which we try to forge a chain of associations that will reach a definite goal.

One example of *undirected thinking* is dreams, where we have no conscious control whatever over the chain of associations. The psychoanalysts maintain that dreams have an unconscious goal of some kind and represent the acting out of wishes we are afraid to express openly. But on the conscious level, at least, dreams seem to occur whether we want them or not and to proceed without rhyme or reason. Even in our waking moments a somewhat similar kind of thinking takes place. We look out the window and see a dog trotting across the yard. Immediately a long chain of images and thoughts occurs to us. The chain is undirected and uncontrolled. The sight of the dog seems to set it off almost automatically, much as the physician's hammer sets off the knee reflex. We start thinking because we cannot help it, along lines of associations that seem to proceed of their own accord.

Directed thinking, on the other hand, is something that we deliberately set into motion and that we discipline toward a goal. Directed thinking is aimed at 1) finding a solution and 2) recognizing the correct solution once it has been found. This is the kind of thinking we do when we try to answer questions such as: "Shall I go to college?" "Which college?" "What courses shall I take?" "What kind of job do I want?" And, later on in life: "Shall I buy or rent a house?" "What kind of insurance should I buy?" Or, on a more philosophical plane: "What political candidate shall I vote for?" "What is my obligation to the community?" "What are my ultimate aims in life?" "What values do I want to try to instill in my children?"

Much directed thinking takes the form of *problem solving*, which can be considered now as a topic of its own.

PROBLEM SOLVING   Many years ago an experimenter put cats into a number of what he called puzzle boxes—little cages from which the cats could escape only by lifting a latch or pulling a loop of string. Outside each box he placed food. The cats had a goal—namely, to get out of the box and get the food. But how? This was the problem.

It developed that the cats could solve the problem only through the method called *trial and error*. They made all kinds of movements; they stretched, bit, and scratched. Eventually, by chance, they stumbled upon the solution and made their escape (7).

The chimpanzee shown in FIGURE 6.4 is also faced with a problem. High above its head hangs a bunch of bananas. Its goal is to reach them. But how?

A Chimp Does Some Thinking   The chimpanzee is in a cage with a bunch of bananas hanging high above its reach and with three boxes, none of which is high enough in itself to enable the chimp to climb up and reach the bananas. After looking the situation over for some time, it starts to pile one box atop another for additional height and thus manages to reach the bananas.

FIGURE 6.4

The Chimp and the Sticks   This chimpanzee was confronted with some
sticks that posed a problem. The very short stick was within reach but
was too short to pull in the piece of fruit. The very long stick that
would pull in the fruit was well out of reach. At last the animal has
caught on and is using the shorter sticks to reach the longer ones; it
will have the fruit in a moment.

FIGURE 6.5

The solution to the problem, as the chimp has just discovered, is to pile the
boxes one atop another and climb up. In this case the animal caught on; it
got the idea; the solution came to it not after long and laborious trial and
error but in a sudden flash of what is called *insight.*

The chimpanzee in FIGURE 6.5 has solved a different kind of problem
through insight. In both cases there may have been some trial and error in
the sense that the chimps thought of other possible ways to try to solve the
problems and had to discard these methods as impracticable. But, if there
was trial and error, it took place covertly, through the manipulation of
symbols. In a way that is beyond the capacity of lower animals the chimpanzees solved their problems by thinking. Exactly how they did it—what
kind of symbols they used and how these symbols were linked—we of course
cannot know.

Steps in Problem Solving

The process of problem solving in human beings has been studied in detail.
It appears to require seven separate steps for maximum efficiency.

STEP 1: DEFINING THE PROBLEM   Sometimes, especially in school situations,
this is done for us. For example, a question on an examination may pose a

217

definite problem: "If a circular lake is ten miles across and a man walks at the rate of four miles an hour, how long will it take him to walk around the lake?" Other examination questions, however, may require that we define a large part of the problem ourselves. We may be asked an extremely abstruse question such as, "How do the aphorisms of Sartre derive from the metaphysics of Hume and Nietzsche?" Here we have to break down the problem into units we can comprehend; we must ask ourselves the meanings of the words *aphorism* and *metaphysics* and what we know about the writings of the men mentioned in the question. In situations outside the classroom the problem may be something like, "How can I become more popular?" Here we must decide: What is popularity? What is there about my present situation that bothers me and makes me feel the need for more popularity? Not until we have a grasp of the problem can we start to solve it.

STEP 2: EVALUATING THE DEFINITION   Once the problem has been defined, the proper next step is to pause and ask: Have I defined it correctly? Failure to make this check may make all the rest of the problem solving process a waste of time, for many of us have a tendency to jump to the wrong conclusions about the nature of the problem.

STEP 3: HOLDING THE PROBLEM IN MEMORY   We cannot solve the problem unless we remember it—and remember it accurately. This seems obvious, but failure to take this step is very common. Many students come up with the wrong answers on examinations because somewhere along the line they forget exactly what the question was. For example, a student cannot correctly solve the problem of the man and the lake if he forgets that the man was walking at the rate of four miles an hour and uses five miles an hour instead.

STEP 4: SEARCHING FOR HYPOTHESES   A hypothesis is a theory—in problem solving, a theory as to how the problem might be solved. In step 4, the object is to follow all possible chains of thought—by logic or by examining mediational clusters—in a search for all possible methods of solution. A person who poses the problem, "How can I become more popular?" might come up with many hypotheses: Change my style of dress. Learn to dance. Practice conversation. Join clubs where I can meet new friends. Act more cheerful. And so on.

STEP 5: CHOOSING THE BEST HYPOTHESIS   In the case just mentioned, the popularity seeker might decide that several of his theories would help solve the problem. In most cases, however, one hypothesis is clearly best, and sometimes only one hypothesis will work at all. There is usually only one correct answer, for example, to a mathematical problem or a multiple choice question. There was only one way for the chimpanzees in FIGURES 6.4 and 6.5 to reach the food.

STEP 6: EVALUATING THE HYPOTHESIS Once a hypothesis has been chosen, another check is in order. The problem solver must pause and ask if he has considered all the possibilities and is really sure, on second thought, that the hypothesis will work. Many of us tend to be impulsive and to favor the first hypothesis that comes to mind. Or we may choose an unsatisfactory hypothesis simply because we are loath to do the additional work that is involved in seeking for additional theories. Thus, before we commit ourselves, we had better take another look.

STEP 7: IMPLEMENTING THE HYPOTHESIS This is the final step—the behavior based on the problem solving process. On an examination we write down the answer. In situations outside the classroom we undertake the actions that we have decided will make us more popular or will enable us to reach whatever other goal we are seeking.

Barriers to Problem Solving

A failure at any one of the seven steps of problem solving can result in the failure of the entire process. Fortunately, however, efficiency at most of the steps can be improved through practice, and one can learn to become a better problem solver just as one can learn anything else. The step that is often most difficult to improve is step 4, searching for hypotheses. At this step the problem solver runs into two built-in barriers that often frustrate all his efforts. One is *persistence of set,* the other a special form of set called *functional fixedness.*

PERSISTENCE OF SET One of the best known experiments on the difficulties caused by persistence of set is shown in FIGURE 6.6—which asks some questions that you may want to tackle yourself before reading the explanation in the next paragraph.

As you may have worked out for yourself, problems 1 through 6 in FIGURE 6.6 are solved by filling the largest of the water jars first, then measuring off some of this water by pouring it into the smaller jars. In 2 through 6, the solution is always to fill jar B, then from this jar fill jar A once and jar C twice, leaving just the number of quarts you want. Problems 7 and 8 can also be solved this way, but it is much easier to use a different method. In 7, you need only fill jar A, then pour off three quarts into jar C. In 8, you need merely fill jars A and C. Yet even when the subjects in the original experiment were warned, "Don't be blind," some of them tended to stick to the old method, for which they had become set while working problems 1 through 6. When subjects received no warning, all of them continued to use the old method.

Most of us have this strong tendency toward *persistence of set.* We learn to apply certain hypotheses to the solving of problems; these hypotheses

FIGURE 6.6

	Size of jars (in quarts)			Quarts of
Problem	A	B	C	water needed
1	29	3	—	20
2	21	127	3	100
3	14	163	25	99
4	18	43	10	5
5	9	42	6	21
6	20	59	4	31
7	23	49	3	20
8	15	39	3	18
9	28	76	3	25
10	18	48	4	22
11	14	36	8	6

The Water Jar Problem The problem is to measure out the number of quarts of water in the final column, using jars of the sizes shown in columns A, B, and C. In problem 1 the solution is to fill jar A, then remove nine quarts from it by filling jar B three times. In the original experiment the subjects were advised after problem 6, "Don't be blind." If you work out the solutions yourself, remember this warning after problem 6. The solutions are discussed in the text. (8)

work for us; and we build up the habit of continuing to apply them—often at the expense of applying different hypotheses that would be much more efficient. It is persistence of set that makes it so difficult for most of us to solve brain-teasers that require a fresh new approach to familiar situations. For example, there is the old puzzle about the man who lived on the top floor of a nine-story apartment building. Every morning, when he went to work, he got on the elevator at the ninth floor. But in the evening, returning home, he got off at the eighth floor and walked up the remaining flight. Why? A somewhat similar puzzle concerns the man, bitter about life, who planned one last grim joke on humanity; his body was found hanging, with his feet a good 24 inches from the floor, in a locked closet that had no furniture or boxes. How did he manage to hang himself? Only by a determined effort to avoid persistence of set can we come to the answers.°

FUNCTIONAL FIXEDNESS The special form of set called *functional fixedness* —a tendency to think of objects as functioning in one certain way and to ignore their other possible uses—has been demonstrated by the experiment shown in FIGURE 6.7. The experiment poses a problem that is somewhat difficult to solve from a photograph but that most people manage to solve when they can work with the actual objects shown. For the solution, turn the page to FIGURE 6.8.

As is explained in FIGURE 6.8, the subjects in the experiment were divided into two groups. One of them had to start by using the pliers to loosen a wire and unfasten the wooden bar from the board, as has been shown here. The other group did not have to use the pliers in this way. The result of the experiment was that group 2 had considerably better success at solving the problem than did group 1. Using the pliers to loosen the wire seemed to

° The man in the elevator was a midget who could reach only as high as the button for the eighth floor. The man who hanged himself stood on a cake of ice that had melted by the time his body was discovered.

serve as a reminder to the subjects in group 1 that the function of a pliers is to loosen or tighten wires, turn bolts, or pull nails—not to serve as the legs of a flower stand. Their ability to solve the problem was seriously hampered by their tendency to think of the pliers in terms of its usual functions and not its possible other functions. They were victims of what is called *functional fixedness*.

This particular problem was one of several used in the same experiment; some of the other solutions depended upon using a box as a platform instead of a container or bending a paper clip and using it as a hook. The subjects who had to begin by using the objects in the normal way—the pliers to untwist wire, the box to hold things, the paper clip to fasten papers together— managed to solve 61 percent of the problems. The subjects who did not start this way and thus had less functional fixedness to overcome solved 98 percent.

Another example of functional fixedness is shown in FIGURE 6.9. Here the problem illustrated in the photograph was preceded by what the subjects were told were speed tests; the experimenter gave them the diagrams and parts for an electric circuit and asked them to build it as fast as possible. One group of subjects built a circuit containing the microswitch shown in the photograph. The other group's circuit contained the relay. When the two groups moved on to the problem of tying the strings together, a significant number of the subjects who had just used the microswitch as part of an electric circuit passed it by and chose the relay as the weight for the string. The subjects who had just used the relay in a circuit did the opposite.

Functional fixedness is of course a type of negative transfer—a classic case of S_1–R_1 followed by S_1–R_2. Having learned to use the pliers or the

An Experiment in Problem Solving   Subjects were asked to arrange any or all of these objects so that the board would stand firmly on two supports and could serve as a stand for a vase of flowers. The problem is difficult to solve from a photograph, without actually manipulating the objects, but you may be able to visualize the solution before turning to FIGURE 6.8, which demonstrates how the job can be done. The first step, of course, is to use the pliers to loosen the wire and detach the wooden bar. (9)

FIGURE 6.7

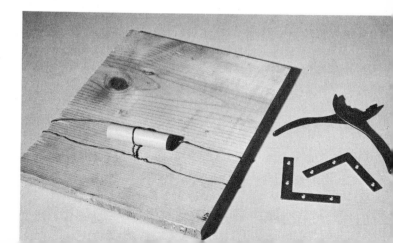

FIGURE 6·8   *The Solution to the Flower Stand Problem*   The problem posed in FIGURE 6.7 can be solved only by using the pliers in an unusual way, as two "legs" for the flower stand. The metal joints go unused. In the original experiment with this problem, the subjects were divided into two groups. One was confronted with the objects exactly as shown in FIGURE 6.7. The other group found the wooden bar loosely tied to the board and could remove it by simply untying a knot. Question: Which group made the better score? For the answer, see the text.

The·String Problem and Functional Fixedness   The problem is to tie the two strings together. It can be solved by attaching an object to one of the strings and setting it swinging so it comes into reach while you are holding the other string. Only two of the objects—the microswitch (A) and the electric relay (B)—are heavy enough to do the job. For an explanation of which subjects chose the microswitch and which chose the relay and the light this casts on functional fixedness, see the text. (10)   **FIGURE 6.9**

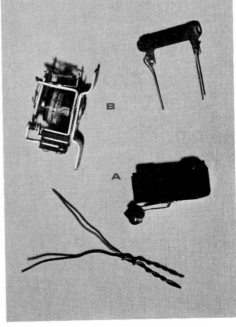

microswitch in one way, we find it difficult to cast aside the S_1–R_1 association and use them in an entirely different S_1–R_2 fashion. The old associations keep cropping up and interfering with the establishment of the new.

In many real-life situations, functional fixedness reduces our efficiency at solving problems. A nail file is for filing nails; we may overlook entirely the fact that it might help us tighten a screw and thus repair a broken lamp. A goldfish bowl is for fish; the first person who used one as a terrarium for growing house plants had to break some powerful old associations. Similarly, we have a tendency to think that things that perform the same functions should look alike. As old photographs show, the first automobiles strongly resembled buggies.

Persistence of Set, Daily Living, and Creativity

Although persistence of set and functional fixedness often interfere with problem solving, nonetheless they have certain important advantages in meeting the routine problems of daily living. We are set to use many of the articles around us in certain ways—the soap and toothbrush in the bathroom, our clothing, the knives and forks on the table. These sets help us bathe, dress, and eat breakfast almost without thinking about what we are doing. We are set to start an automobile in the routine way, to stop at red lights and start at green lights, to step on the brake when something gets in our path. Sets are particularly valuable when we must react quickly, as when avoiding another automobile or a pedestrian, and do not have time to ponder all the possible hypotheses of what action might be best.

On the other hand, it is persistence of set and functional fixedness that account for the fact that truly creative thinking is so rare. Before the airplane was invented, many brilliant men tried to fly with contraptions that imitated the shape of kites or the wings of a bird. It took the Wright brothers, who put all the old hypotheses aside and invented the entirely new principle of the aileron, to succeed. Historians of science have made a good case that the theory of relativity should have been invented by a French mathematician named Poincaré, who had all the factual and theoretical background required for putting the theory together. But Poincaré for all his brilliance was temperamentally not prepared to synthesize this creative idea, and the theory remained for Einstein to discover.

Studies of creative people have disclosed that they tend to have a number of traits in common that are not shared by most other people. Generally speaking, they were lone wolves in childhood; they either were spurned and rejected by other children or sought solitude themselves. If being different from other children caused them anxiety, they eventually overcame it; they grew up with no need to conform to the people and the ways of life around them. In fact creative people tend to *want* to be different and original and to produce new things. They are not afraid of having irrational or bizarre thoughts, are willing to examine even the most foolish-seeming ideas, and are not worried about success or failure. Many of them are aggressive and hostile, not at all the kind of people who win popularity contests of elections (11).

Creativity of any kind—the invention of a new mechanical device such as the airplane, the discovery of a new scientific principle, the writing of a great and original poem or novel—demands superior intelligence. But of the people who have the required intelligence perhaps not even as many as 1 percent are in fact creative. Even more than intelligence, creativity demands the kind of personality that scorns the tried and true, does not get imprisoned by persistence of set, but on the contrary seeks out new and unusual hypotheses even in the face of failure and ridicule.

Attempts have been made to devise tests that would spot creative people early in their school careers, so that they might receive special treatment that would encourage their talents. Two such tests are shown in FIGURE 6.10 and FIGURE 6.11. Unfortunately, it is easier to test and study sheer originality of response than other qualities that are also necessary for true creativity. Mere novelty is not enough. Besides being new and unusual, a creative hypothesis must also be *appropriate*. A new scientific theory must, like Einstein's, be in accord with the known facts. The person who looks at a creative painting or hears creative music must have an immediate perception of aptness, of a disciplined relationship to the world as he knows it, if he is to consider the work of art esthetically pleasing. Hence the critical debate over modern abstract art and modern music that uses dissonances and unusual sources of sound such as whistles and electronic devices. This kind of art and music is undoubtedly novel. But many critics believe that it is merely bizarre and fantastic rather than truly creative.

A Test of Creativity   These drawings are shown to fifth-grade children, who are asked to try to imagine what they might look like when completed. Most children make routine responses, but a few come up with original and creative ideas. The usual responses are: **A** the sun, **B** table with glasses on it, **C** two igloos, **D** raindrops, and **E** three people sitting at a table. Unusual responses would be: **A** a lollipop bursting into pieces, **B** a foot and toes, **C** two haystacks on a flying carpet, **D** worms hanging, and **E** three mice eating a piece of cheese. (12)

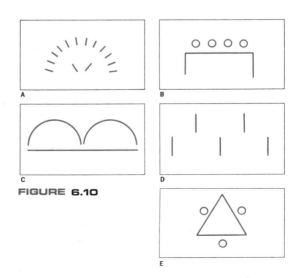

FIGURE 6.10

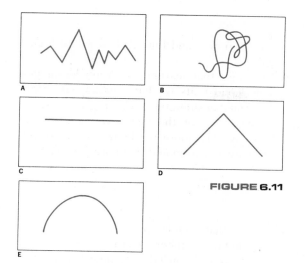

FIGURE 6.11

A Variation of the Creativity Test In this variation of the creativity test, children are asked what these lines suggest to them—the lines as a whole, not just in part. Ordinary responses would be: **A** mountains, **B** string, **C** stick, **D** arrow, and **E** rising sun. Unusual and original responses would be: **A** squashed piece of paper, **B** squeezing paint out of a tube, **C** stream of ants, **D** alligator's open mouth, and **E** fishing rod bending with a fish. (12)

The Role of Prior Knowledge

In FIGURE 6.12 we are asked to solve the problem of the relationships between various words, concepts, and numbers. To reach the solutions, we have to come up with some rather ingenious hypotheses; we have to notice some relationships that we might not ordinarily think of. In question 1, for example, we have to think of *hate, each, love,* and *evil* as collections of letters rather than as meaningful words. Only when we note that *each* begins with the last letter and ends with the first letter of *hate*—and that *evil* also begins with the last letter and ends with the first letter of *love*—can we find the solution.

In questions 2 through 5, we must also get an insight into the relationships. But, in addition, we must have some prior knowledge if we are to come up with the correct hypotheses. To solve question 2, we must be aware of the geographical facts that Nevada is east of California and that St. Louis is east of Denver. In question 3, we must know that the blood stream carries oxygen and that computers use tapes. In question 4, we must know that arthropod is a primary division of the animal kingdom to which flies belong and that a peso belongs to the family of currency. To solve question 5, we

FIGURE 6.12

UNDERLINE ONE.

1. *Hate* is to *each* as *love* is to: (a) evil, (b) sane, (c) good, (d) only.
2. *Nevada* is to *California* as *St. Louis* is to: (a) New York, (b) Washington, D.C., (c) Denver, (d) Detroit.
3. *Blood* is to *oxygen* as *computer* is to: (a) machines, (b) buttons, (c) people, (d) tapes.
4. *Fly* is to *arthropod* as *peso* is to: (a) Spain, (b) dollar, (c) shilling, (d) currency.
5. *81* is to *3* as *16* is to: (a) 1, (b) 2, (c) 3, (d) 4.

A Test in Problem Solving This difficult "test," on which few people would manage to get all the answers right, has been devised to illustrate some important facts about problem solving. The correct answers are a, c, d, d, and b. For an explanation, see the text.

must know that 81 is 3 to the fourth power and that 16 is 2 to the fourth power.

It has been mentioned several times that learning feeds on learning—the larger the storehouse of mediational units we have already acquired, the easier it is for a new stimulus to make meaningful and lasting associations. FIGURE 6.12 is an eloquent demonstration of the fact that thinking and problem solving also feed on learning. The more we know, the more hypotheses we can think of to meet a new situation and the more problems we can solve.

SUMMARY

1. Language is a special technique that enables man—alone among all organisms—to communicate an infinite number and variety of messages and to pass along all his accumulated knowledge to new generations.

2. The building blocks of language are *phonemes*—basic sounds that are combined into syllables and words. English uses forty-five phonemes, and no language uses more than eighty-five.

3. Some words are used mostly as symbols for a specific object, such as *water* or *aspirin*.

4. Other words are used as *concepts*. A concept is a *symbol for a common characteristic or relationship shared by objects or events that are otherwise different.*

5. Some of the simplest bases for concepts are similarities of *function, location, physical attributes,* and *component parts.*

6. A more sophisticated basis for concepts recognizes similarities in *relationships*—either physical, mathematical, or entirely abstract relationships.

7. Two classroom methods of establishing concepts are called 1) *learning through exposition* (also known as *didactic learning*), in which the teacher explains the concept and then cites examples, and 2) *discovery learning,* in which examples are presented and the student then discovers the concept for himself.

8. The concepts of adults embrace many kinds of shared similarities, some based on function and location like the concepts of children and others formed on a more sophisticated basis. Ordinarily each person's primary definition of a concept is based on what to him is the *salient characteristic* of the various objects, events, or ideas that are included in the concept.

9. The associations that make up concepts are arranged in *concept hierarchies,* meaning that some of the associations are very strong and likely to be thought of immediately, while others are weaker and less likely to be used.

10. Besides their surface or dictionary meaning, most words and concepts also have implied meanings called *connotations,* particularly of qualities that can be described as good–bad, strong–weak, and active–passive.

11. There are many individual differences in the way people learn concepts, build them into hierarchies, and relate and interlock them. Thus each individual has his own personal system of organizing his environment and responding to it.

12. *Thinking* is the covert manipulation of images, symbols, and other mediational units.

13. Just as simple muscular movements and reflexes are built into chains of *overt behavior,* so are the elements of thinking built into chains of *covert behavior.*

14. The chief elements of thinking are *images, words, concepts, facts,* and *premises.*

15. The elements of thinking are linked into chains by *logical associations* and by *mediational clustering.*

16. Two types of thinking are *undirected thinking,* which takes place spontaneously and with no goal in view, and *directed thinking,* the most important form of which is *problem solving.*

17. In human beings, problem solving is most efficient when performed in seven stages: a) defining the problem, b) evaluating the definition, c) holding the problem in memory, d) searching for hypotheses, e) choosing the best hypothesis, f) evaluating the hypothesis, and g) implementing the hypothesis.

18. A common barrier to problem solving is *persistence of set,* including a special type of set called *functional fixedness.*

19. Possession of a large storehouse of previously learned knowledge is an important factor in suggesting hypotheses and making it possible to solve problems successfully.

RECOMMENDED READING

Bartlett, F. C. *Thinking.* New York: Basic Books, 1958.

Berlyne, D. E. *Structure and direction in thinking.* New York: Wiley, 1965.

Brown, R. W. *Words and things.* New York: Free Press, 1958.

Bruner, J. S., Goodnow, J. S., and Austin, G. A. *A study of thinking.* New York: Wiley, 1956.

Bruner, J. S. and Olver, R. R. *Studies in cognitive growth.* New York: Wiley, 1966.

Jacobvits, L. and Miron, M. *Readings on the psychology of language.* Englewood Cliffs, N.J.: Prentice-Hall, 1967.

Mandler, G. and Mandler, J. M., eds. *Thinking: from association to gestalt.* New York: Wiley, 1964.

Osgood, C. E., Suci, G. J., and Tannenbaum, P. H. *The measurement of meaning.* Urbana, Ill.: University of Illinois Press, 1957.

Piaget, J. *The language and thought of the child.* New York: Harcourt, Brace & World, 1926 [reprinted by World, Cleveland, 1955].

Singer, J. L. *Daydreaming.* New York: Random House, 1966.

Wallach, M. A. and Kogan, N. *Modes of thinking in young children.* New York: Holt, Rinehart and Winston, 1965.

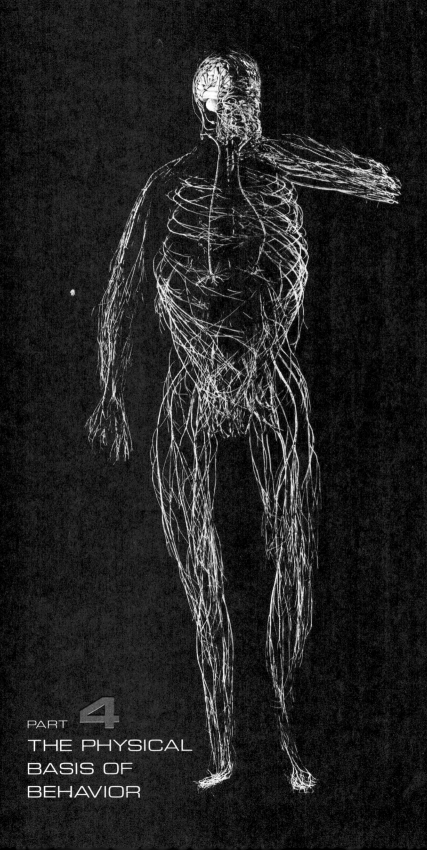

PART 4
THE PHYSICAL
BASIS OF
BEHAVIOR

Part 1 discussed the wide range of behavior. Part 2 described the all-important process through which behavior is learned. Part 3 described interpretive behavior—the manner in which we perceive our world, think about it, and solve the problems that it sometimes presents. Now, before going on to consider in detail such other elements of behavior as motives, emotions, emotional conflicts, and anxieties, the book must make a sort of detour into a subject that at first glance may seem somewhat out of place in a psychology textbook.

Even the language in this section of the book is in sharp contrast to the language of Parts 1, 2, and 3 and also of the sections to follow. You will find that Chapter 7, "The Genes, Glands, and Nervous System," sounds very much like part of a physiology book. Chapter 8, "The Senses," is a combination of physiology and some elementary physics describing the nature of the stimuli to which our organs can respond. One way of putting it would be to say that this section discusses the mechanics that underlie behavior, whereas the rest of the book discusses behavior in a functional sense.

The reason we must concern ourselves with the physical basis of behavior is that psychology deals not with behavior in the abstract but with the specific behavior of living organisms. To a very important extent, behavior is molded and limited by the nature of the organism. The paramecium, for example, is sensitive to light and dark and to heat and cold, and it can move toward or away from them. But its behavior is not at all influenced by many of the things that influence human beings; it is unaware of the existence in the environment of colors and the rise of the moon, of sounds and words, of newspapers and books. Its behavior is limited to a few such simple functions as moving, feeding, and its own primitive kind of reproduction.

But human beings too cannot rise above their physical limitations. No human being is ever likely to swim like a fish, fly like a bird, or run as fast as a race horse. We cannot respond to sound waves that we are unable to hear or to light waves that we are unable to see. (And, as will be discussed in Chapter 8, there are many such sounds and sights.) We are driven by such physical states as hunger, thirst, and sleepiness, and we must work in various ways to protect ourselves from heat, cold, and pain. Our emotions are closely tied in to the activity of the glands inside our bodies. Our ability to learn depends in large part upon the kind of nervous system we possess. It is impossible to understand many aspects of human behavior without knowing something about the human body.

THE GENES: KEY TO HEREDITY

Where We Get Our Genes
How Sex Is Determined
Dominant and Recessive Genes
Some Experiments in Heredity
The Implications of Heredity

HOW THE GLANDS AFFECT BEHAVIOR

The Endocrine Glands Defined
      Pineal; Pituitary; Thyroid; Parathyroids; Pancreas; Adrenal Glands;
      Ovaries; Testes
The Role of the Glands
The Endocrine Glands and Stress

THE NERVOUS SYSTEM

The Nerve Cell
The Nervous Impulse
How Neurons Fire
The Synapse
The Three Kinds of Neurons
Multiple Nerve Connections
How Pathways Are Determined
The Nerve Paths and Learning

THE CENTRAL NERVOUS SYSTEM

The Cerebral Cortex
How the Hemispheres Work Together
Other Forebrain Structures
The Brain Stem
The Electroencephalograph
The Brain and Behavior
The Brain in Learning and in Homeostasis

THE AUTONOMIC NERVOUS SYSTEM

Functions of the Sympathetic System
Functions of the Parasympathetic System

7

THE GENES,
GLANDS,
AND NERVOUS SYSTEM

In the physical equipment they possess, all organisms are more or less like the others of their species. The rats studied in the laboratory may differ somewhat in size, color, and such traits as excitability and ability to learn, but by and large they are more alike than different. Cats are a breed of their own. So are monkeys. Human beings, since they are more complicated and highly developed than other organisms, show greater individual differences than do other species; they vary considerably in size, strength, color of skin, facial characteristics, and intelligence. Nonetheless, the human race varies only within limits. As a poet once said, we are all brothers and sisters under the skin. The British nobleman and the jungle savage, the dwarf and the giant, the Einstein and the high school dropout, all have more in common than they have in contrast.

Why are we all alike, yet each one different? This is a question that must be answered before any attempt is made to describe the physical basis for behavior.

Human life starts, of course, when the egg cell of the mother is penetrated and fertilized by the sperm cell of the father. In this process the two join into a single cell. For about a full day this cell is quiescent. Then it divides into two living cells. The next day each of these two cells again divides, and now there are four cells. Within two weeks the original fertilized egg cell has grown by the process of division into a hollow ball of many cells, already formed into three separate layers destined to play vastly different functions in life. The outer layer of cells will eventually develop into the skin, the sense organs, and the nervous system. The middle layer will develop into bones, muscles, and blood. The inner layer will develop into all the organs of the digestive system.

The original fertilized egg cell must somehow have contained the whole key of life. Something inside it must direct the entire development from

**THE GENES:
KEY TO HEREDITY**

embryo stage to the baby at birth (whose body contains about 200 billion cells) and beyond that from infancy to fully matured adult. Something in it must also determine the inherited characteristics of the individual to be born—the color of the eyes, the shape of the facial features, the potential size, the learning capacity.

Will the child look like the mother or the father, or neither? Will his skin be light or dark? Will he be big-boned or delicate, strong-muscled or weak, short or tall? Will he be a genius or will he be feebleminded? The answer to these questions lies in the tiny structures shown in FIGURE 7.1 as seen under a powerful microscope. These are the forty-six *chromosomes* found in the cells of the human body. Their source is the original fertilized cell. As this cell splits and divides in two to start the process of growth, each of the chromosomes also divides in two, so that each of the two cells contains forty-six chromosomes as before. When the new cells divide, the chromosomes also divide again. Thus the cells of the fully-grown human body contain exactly the same forty-six chromosomes as were present in the fertilized egg cell in which life began. The chromosomes are the key to the development of the human adult and are the carriers of heredity.

Each chromosome, though tiny in itself, is composed of still tinier substances; it is like a string of beads, or a knotted rope, made up of hundreds of structures called *genes*. Each gene is made up of a chemical called *DNA* (deoxyribonucleic acid) and is believed to have the complicated structure shown in FIGURE 7.2.

As molecules go, the genes are quite large, but they are not large enough to examine and count, even under the strongest microscope. The estimate is that there are at least 20,000 of them in each human cell and perhaps as many as 125,000. Each one is believed to be responsible—sometimes by itself but more often in combination with other genes—for some particular phase of

FIGURE 7.1

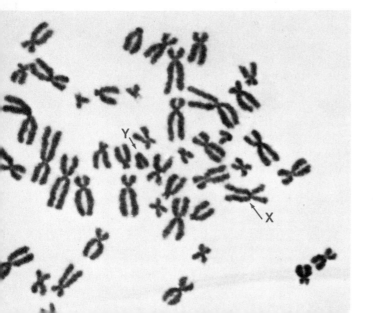

The Human Chromosomes When enlarged 1500 times, the human chromosomes look like this. These are from a man's skin cell, broken down and spread out into a single layer under the microscope. The labels point out the X- and Y-chromosomes, the special importance of which is discussed on page 235.

FIGURE 7.2

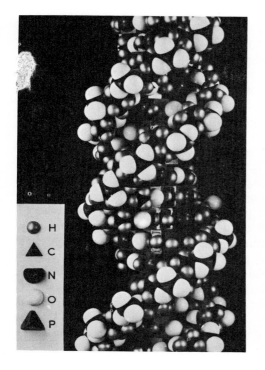

A Model of the Human Gene Each gene of each chromosome in the human cell is believed to have a chemical structure something like this. As shown in the code at lower left, the units represent atoms of the hydrogen, carbon, nitrogen, oxygen, and phosphorous making up the gene. The atoms are arranged in two long strands twisted together in intertwining spirals. The position of the individual atoms along the strands lends itself to a tremendous number of variations and is believed to constitute a sort of "code" that determines the role each individual gene plays in human development.

development. The genes direct the process by which some cells of the body grow into skin and others grow into nerves or muscles and also the process by which cells become grouped into organs such as the heart, the stomach, and the liver. They control such aspects of development as the color the eyes become and the length of the bones.

Our heredity depends on those many thousands of genes, organized into our forty-six chromosomes. It is the particular kind of genes present in the original fertilized egg that makes us develop into human beings and into the individual kind of human being that each of us is.

Where We Get Our Genes

In the living cell, it must now be emphasized, the chromosomes are not arranged as in FIGURE 7.1, where they were deliberately separated and spread out to pose for their microscopic portrait. Instead they are arranged in pairs—twenty-three pairs of chromosomes. In each pair the two chromosomes are similar in structure and function and are composed of genes of similar structure and function. For purposes of exposition, we can think of them as pairs A_1–A_2, B_1–B_2, C_1–C_2, D_1–D_2, and so on.

In growth, the twenty-three pairs of chromosomes with their matched genes duplicate themselves exactly, so that each new cell also has pairs A_1-A_2, B_1-B_2, C_1-C_2, D_1-D_2, and so on. But the cells of reproduction—the mother's egg cell and the sperm cell of the father—are formed in very different fashion. Here the pairs split up. Half of each pair goes into one egg or sperm cell, the other half into another cell. Thus each egg or sperm cell has only twenty-three chromosomes, not twenty-three pairs.

When two cells of reproduction are formed by this process, it is a matter of chance whether cell 1 will receive A_1 or A_2, B_1 or B_2, C_1 or C_2, and so on. Cell 1 may receive A_1, B_2, and C_1, in which case cell 2 will receive A_2, B_1, and C_2. Or cell 1 may receive A_2, B_2, and C_1, in which case cell 2 will receive A_1, B_1, and C_2. This random splitting of the twenty-three pairs can itself result in 8,398,608 different possible reproductive cells with different combinations of the two halves of the original pairs. Moreover, the splitting has a further complication. Sometimes A_1, in breaking away from A_2, leaves some of its own genes behind and pulls away some of the A_2 genes. Any of the twenty-three chromosomes can and often does behave in this way, with anywhere from one to several hundred genes from its paired chromosomes. All in all, there are many billions of possible combinations of the original pairs of chromosomes and genes.

An egg cell containing one of these combinations of the chromosomes and genes present in the mother is fertilized by a sperm cell containing one of the combinations of the chromosomes and genes present in the father. The chromosomes and genes pair up, and life begins for another unique human being. Never before, unless by a chance so mathematically remote as to be almost impossible, did the same combination of genes ever exist. Never again is it likely to be repeated.

The one exception to the fact that each human being is unique is in the case of identical twins. Here a single egg cell, fertilized by a single sperm cell, develops into two individuals. They have the same chromosomes and genes in the same combination, and, as all of us have noted, they tend to be very much alike in every basic respect. Their differences are due to events that occurred after conception—possibly starting with different positions in the womb and slight variations in the food supply they received there and certainly including their varied learning experiences, food intake, and chance encounters with disease germs or physical accident after birth.

How Sex Is Determined

One of the twenty-three pairs of chromosomes present in the fertilized egg cell plays a particularly important role in development: It determines whether the egg will develop into a boy or a girl. In FIGURE 7.1 you will note that two chromosomes are pointed out by arrows. One of them, as the caption states, is called an X-chromosome, the other a Y-chromosome. Despite their different appearances, they constitute a pair—the only exception to the rule that paired chromosomes are similar in structure. You will also note that the chromosomes in FIGURE 7.1 are from a cell taken from a male. The X-Y pairing always produces a male. When there is an X-X pair, the result is always a female.

This, then, is how sex is determined. When the mother's X-X pair of chromosomes splits to form an egg cell, the result is always a cell containing an X-chromosome. When the father's X-Y pairing splits to form two sperm cells, however, the X-chromosome goes to one of the cells, the Y-chromosome to the other. If the sperm cell with the X-chromosome fertilizes the egg, the result is an X-X pairing and a girl. If the sperm cell with the Y-chromosome fertilizes the egg, the result is an X-Y pairing and a boy.

Sperm cells containing the Y-chromosome appear to be more active and therefore more likely to reach and fertilize the egg cell; it is believed that perhaps as many as 150 or 160 boys are conceived for every 100 girls. However, in capacity to survive, the male of the species is the weaker of the two sexes from the moment of conception. Many fertilized egg cells containing the Y-chromosome do not develop into babies, and actual births number only about 106 boys for every 100 girls.

Dominant and Recessive Genes

If a man with blue eyes marries a woman with blue eyes, we can predict with absolute certainty that all their children will also have blue eyes. When a man with brown eyes marries a woman with brown eyes, we can never be sure. All we can say is that their children have a greater chance of being brown-eyed than blue-eyed. The fact that we cannot rule our the possibility of a blue-eyed child has some important implications for our study of heredity.

Eye color is determined by one particular pair of genes or perhaps by a particular group of paired genes. For convenience, let us assume that a single pair is involved, and let us call the pair GEC_1–GEC_2—meaning that gene for eye color 1 was inherited from the father and gene for eye color 2 from the mother. If GEC_1 and GEC_2 are both for brown eyes, there is no problem; the eyes will be brown. If GEC_1 and GEC_2 are both for blue eyes, the eyes will be blue. Sometimes, however, GEC_1 is for brown and GEC_2 for blue, or vice versa. What happens when the genes for blue and for brown compete?

The answer is that the gene for brown eyes always prevails; it is a *dominant gene*. The gene for blue eyes is a *recessive gene*, and its effects are always suppressed by the dominant gene. The person with one GEC for brown and one GEC for blue will always have brown eyes. But when his chromosomes and genes split to form reproductive cells, half the reproductive cells will carry the GEC for brown, the other half the GEC for blue. If one of the reproductive cells containing the GEC for blue happens to fertilize or to be fertilized by another reproductive cell containing the GEC for blue, the result will be a blue-eyed child. Thus can a person pass along a trait which he himself does not possess. The mechanics of the process are illustrated in FIGURE 7.3.

Among the genes known to be dominant in producing physical characteristics, besides those for brown eyes, are those that cause baldness in men, dwarfism, and cataracts of the eye. Certain recessive genes carry color blindness and some rather rare forms of hearing defects and feeblemindedness.

Most of the characteristics of the organism—human or animal—are determined not by a single pair of genes but by two or more pairs, often many. Human skin color and height, for example, are believed to be controlled by several pairs of genes. Many other physical traits such as facial characteristics, muscular strength, and speed of reactions, as well as psychological traits such as intelligence and emotional tendencies, are also controlled by many genes—a fact that helps account for the wide range of human physical appearance and personality.

FIGURE 7.3   *How Eye Color Is Inherited*   All blue-eyed people have inherited genes for blue from both parents; when a blue-eyed man marries a blue-eyed woman, their children always have blue eyes. Some brown-eyed people have inherited genes for brown from both parents; their children will always have brown eyes. When a man with two genes for brown marries a woman with two genes for blue, the children inherit one brown and one blue gene; since the brown gene is dominant, the children have brown eyes. When a brown-eyed man with one gene for brown and one for blue marries a brown-eyed woman who also has one gene for brown and one for blue, the probability is that three of their children will have brown eyes and one will have blue eyes.

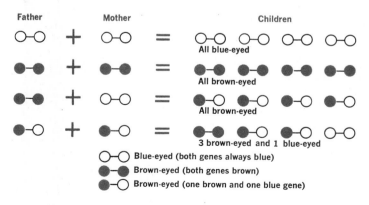

Some Experiments in Heredity

An experiment on the effect of heredity was once conducted with a group of laboratory rats of mixed ancestry. From this random group the experimenters undertook to breed a "bright" strain of rats, as measured by ability to learn a maze, and a "dull" strain. The rats that made the best maze scores were interbred, as were those with poorer scores. This selective mating of "bright" with "bright" and "dull" with "dull" was continued for many generations, with the quite remarkable results illustrated in FIGURE 7.4.

Many similar experiments have been performed. Rats have been selectively bred to produce one group that was extremely active and another group

FIGURE 7.4   *An Experiment in Selective Breeding*   These graphs illustrate the results of an experiment that started with 142 laboratory rats that, as the top graph shows, made a wide range of scores in a maze learning task. The rats with the best scores were then mated, as were those with poorer scores. This interbreeding of "bright" with "bright" and "dull" with "dull" continued in successive generations. As the middle graph shows, two very different groups had begun to emerge by the second generation. By the seventh generation (bottom graph) the "bright" and "dull" groups were quite distinct, and the average score of the "dull" group was only a fourth as good as the average score of the "bright" group. The effect of the selective breeding was about as strong by the seventh generation as it ever became; graphs for the eighth through eighteenth generations looked much the same. (1)

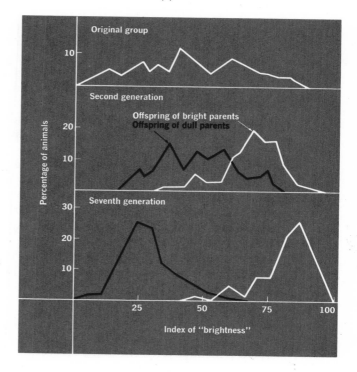

that was lethargic and to produce one group that was much more emotional (in popular language, "nervous") than another (2). Fruit flies have been selectively bred to produce one group that was strongly attracted to bright light and another group that was not (3).

What selective breeding does, of course, is increase the chance that the newer generations will receive genes that act to produce such traits as brightness at learning a maze, emotionality, and a tendency to move toward light. The result is a greater percentage of individuals that show the trait to a pronounced degree. Note, however, that selective breeding has its limits. In the experiment illustrated in FIGURE 7.4, the "bright" group showed no further improvement when interbreeding was continued after the seventh generation. Moreover, no individual in the "bright" group ever greatly surpassed the performance of the brightest member of the original group of rats. Selective breeding does not produce superindividuals, but only a greater percentage of individuals that perform close to the upper limits for the trait.

In the breeding of race horses, for example, selective mating has been practiced for many years, with the fastest colts of each generation bred to the fastest mares. The result has been a great number of fast horses but not any progressive increase in the top speed of which a horse is capable. Many experts in this field believe that Man o' War, born in 1917, many generations ago for horses, was as great a race horse as ever lived or ever will live.

The Implications of Heredity

Men are born, live their lives, and die. But the chromosomes and the genes are passed on from generation to generation, from parent to child. All of us carry around, in every cell of our bodies, the genes that have influenced human development and behavior since the beginning of man's appearance on earth. They guarantee that we will grow up in the image of our ancestors rather than into apes or fish. Yet the particular combination of genes that each of us carries is unique, coming from a grandfather here, a great-grandmother there, and so on back from countless individuals in countless generations.

So complicated is our inheritance of genes, so vast the possible combinations, that it would have been very difficult to predict, at the moment of conception, what any of us would be like. Two parents who are below average in intelligence can produce a genius. A brilliant husband and brilliant wife may have feebleminded children. In a family of twelve children no two may look at all alike.

Even if experiments in selective breeding were possible among human beings, it would take an impossibly long time to achieve any results. Our inheritance of those forty-six chromosomes and 20,000 to 125,000 genes is far more complicated than the heredity of rats or fruit flies and much less subject to any kind of manipulation. For example, it used to be a popular theory that we could eliminate feeblemindedness by sterilizing all feeble-minded people, thus preventing them from passing on their own particular genes. But the theory ignored the fact that the same kind of genes, though in different combination, are often carried by normal people as well. One scientist has estimated that even if we sterilized all the feebleminded of the next sixty-eight generations, a project that would take until about the year 4000, the human race would still be producing a great many feebleminded individuals, perhaps around 10 percent as many as now.

From what has been said here about heredity, it should now be clear what was meant by the statement that psychology, although it tends to lean toward the notion that the mind of the human baby is a *tabula rasa* or "blank tablet," does so with reservations. The particular combination of chromosomes and genes that comes together at the moment of conception constitutes a master key for the development of the new individual's body— his potential size, his appearance, his internal organs, his nervous system, his glands. And all of us, as will now be seen, are to a considerable extent the creatures and prisoners of our bodies.

For a simple but dramatic example of how our bodies affect our behavior, let us consider the *thyroid gland,* **HOW THE GLANDS AFFECT BEHAVIOR** a double-lobed mass of tissue lying at the sides of the windpipe. You have probably seen people who were suffering from goiter, in which the thyroid gland becomes enlarged, sometimes to extreme size. In one type of goiter the gland not only grows to giant size but also becomes extremely active. The patient's eyes often bulge, giving him a "pop-eyed" expression. He often loses weight and sometimes has muscle tremors. His heart beats faster than normal. His behavior changes markedly. He becomes excitable and over-active. We might say that he seems all wound up. He has trouble sleeping. His nerves seem to be on edge.

You may also have known people with an underactive thyroid gland. They tend to be placid. They tire easily; they are often sleepy; they have very little of what is popularly called "get up and go." Often they gain weight; they become fat and lazy. Thus does this single small gland, when it is either overactive or underactive, cause striking and important changes in behavior.

This is because the thyroid gland produces a chemical substance that plays a prominent role in providing bodily energy. The human body is in a sense an enormously intricate engine. We take in fuel, in the form of food. Our digestive system breaks the food down into simple chemicals that can pass through the walls of the digestive tract and into the blood stream, which carries them to all parts of the body, to every one of the billions of living cells. Inside the cells, the chemicals are combined with oxygen, which is also distributed by the blood stream, and burned off to provide energy. Or they are built up into living protoplasm, to become part of the cells, and the protoplasm itself can later be burned off. This never-ending chemical process, in which food is converted into protoplasm and energy, is called *metabolism*. It is the basic process of life. Metabolism begins when the egg cell of the mother is fertilized; when it stops we are dead.

All human behavior involves the process of metabolism. It is the energy thus provided that enables us to move our muscles, to walk, to talk. Metabolism also provides the energy with which we think. Thinking does not take very much energy; the fuel value of a single peanut is enough to run the brain at top speed for several hours—but of course this energy is vital.

When the thyroid gland manufactures too little of its chemical, the metabolic process is slowed down. When the thyroid manufactures too much, the metabolic process is speeded up. Thus whether we behave in sluggish, normal, or overexcited fashion depends largely upon this gland. Conversely, the sluggishness caused by an underactive gland can be relieved by daily doses of thyroid substance taken from animals; and the keyed-up behavior caused by an overactive gland can be relieved by surgery that removes the excess thyroid tissue.

The Endocrine Glands Defined

The thyroid is one of several glands in the body that affect behavior. All these glands have a common characteristic: they possess no ducts, such as the ducts of the salivary glands or the tear glands of the eye, for delivery of the substances they produce. Instead they discharge their substances directly into the blood stream, which then carries them to all parts of the body. For this reason, they are sometimes called the *ductless glands*. They are also known as *endocrine glands*, which means glands of internal secretion. The positions of the important endocrine glands in the body are illustrated in FIGURE 7.5.

The substances produced by the endocrine glands and poured into the blood stream are called *hormones*, meaning activators. The hormones are complicated chemicals that trigger and control many kinds of bodily activities and behavior, as can be seen from the following list of functions performed by the various glands.

PINEAL   This is the smallest of the glands, only a quarter of an inch long. It was not recognized as an endocrine gland until recently, and its functions

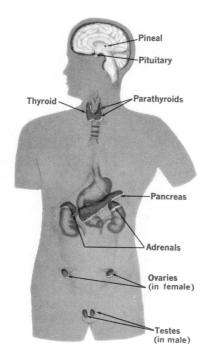

FIGURE 7.5

The Human Endocrine Glands These are the endocrine glands most important to human behavior. For their functions, see the text.

are not well understood. Its activity appears to be affected by light and darkness, and the hormones it produces appear to help control the female sexual cycle.

PITUITARY   This is the master gland, secreting a number of different hormones that have a profound effect upon the life process. In the early years the pituitary secretes a growth hormone that regulates the development of the body. As is illustrated in FIGURE 7.6, if the gland produces too little of this hormone, development is arrested and the child becomes a dwarf, while too much of the hormone causes the child to grow into a giant. At the time of puberty the pituitary secretes another hormone, which activates the sex glands, which in turn take over and control the change from child into mature man or woman. The pituitary also produces hormones that speed up or inhibit the activity of the thyroid and other glands.

THYROID   As was explained earlier, this gland controls the metabolic process and thus influences the general level of bodily activity, susceptibility to fatigue, and body weight.

PARATHYROIDS   These glands, lying around the larger thyroid gland, help maintain a normal state of excitability of the nervous system by regulating the balance of calcium and phosphorus in the blood.

241

FIGURE 7.6

Effects of the Pituitary Gland
The result of defects of the pituitary is dramatically illustrated in this photograph from Britain of a dwarf (underactivity of the gland) and a giant (overactivity).

PANCREAS   This large gland, lying below the stomach, secretes hormones that are essential in maintaining the proper level of blood sugar and in the metabolism of blood sugar to provide energy, especially for the brain. One of them is the well-known hormone called *insulin*. An underactive pancreas results in the disease called diabetes, which was invariably fatal before the discovery that injections of insulin from animals could be used as a substitute for the body's own hormone.

ADRENAL GLANDS   These two glands lie atop the kidneys. Each of them has two parts with quite different functions. The inner part, or *adrenal medulla*, secretes powerful stimulants called *adrenalin* and *noradrenalin*. These two hormones tend to affect the rate of heartbeat, raise the blood pressure, and cause the liver to release increased quantities of sugar into the blood to provide additional energy. They also tend to relax the smooth muscles of the digestive system, tense the striped muscles of movement, shift the flow of blood away from the digestive organs and toward the muscles, and act as a clotting agent that makes the blood coagulate more quickly if exposed to air, as in case of injury. The outer part of the glands, or *adrenal cortex*, produces a number of hormones called *steroids*, which are so essential to the body's functions that a lack of them would quickly cause death. Among the important functions of the steroids are to maintain a suitable salt balance in the body and to turn the body's proteins into sugar for a readily available supply of energy. One of the steroids is called *cortisol*—a name you will recognize as being similar to cortisone, the synthetic drug used widely in the treatment of such diseases as rheumatism and arthritis.

OVARIES   In addition to producing the female egg cells, the ovaries are glands of internal secretion. When activated by the pituitary gland, they secrete hormones that bring about the bodily changes known as secondary sex characteristics—for example, the development of the breasts. Their hormones also control menstruation, the production of egg cells, and the course of pregnancy after an egg cell is fertilized.

TESTES   In addition to producing the male sperm cells, the testes are also glands of internal secretion. They bring about such secondary male sex characteristics as the growth of facial hair and change of voice. Hormones from the testes also play a part in male sexual arousal.

The Role of the Glands

Considered as a whole, the endocrine glands constitute an elaborate and efficient system for integrating many bodily activities. The hormones they produce travel to all parts of the body via the blood stream. They regulate growth and sexual development. They help keep the rate of heartbeat and blood pressure at suitable levels. They control the metabolic process and thus the rate of bodily activity.

Of particular interest is the role they play in regulating behavior in times of emergency. When danger threatens, they rapidly secrete hormones that make the heart pound, raise the blood pressure, lift the level of blood sugar, and in many other ways prepare the body to take rapid and drastic action.

As will be seen in Chapter 10, these internal bodily changes are closely related to the emotions of fear and anger but in rather complex ways that need not concern us just now. For the moment, let us merely point out that the man in the grip of fear or anger is a man whose endocrine system is working at top speed and who is therefore capable of extraordinary levels of physical activity. The soldier afraid for his life can perform feats of strength and endurance that would ordinarily be beyond his capacity. The angry man can fight harder than he ever realized was possible, and, should he be injured, his body will minimize the damage, because his blood will clot faster than under ordinary circumstances.

The endocrine glands constitute an integrating mechanism that quickly mobilizes all our physical resources for "fight or flight." They enable us to fight for our lives harder and longer than would otherwise be possible or to run away from danger faster and farther. Indeed they go into action to counteract any kind of stress, a fact that in modern life constitutes a rather mixed blessing.

The Endocrine Glands and Stress

The word *stress* is very popular nowadays. Often it is used in conjunction with the word *strain;* people speak of the "stress and strain" of modern life. Most people, however, would be hard put to give an accurate definition of the word.

In the broadest sense, a stress is any stimulus that causes the organism to become more active and burn more energy than usual. In this sense, a great deal of normal living is a stress. Getting hungry before mealtime is a stress; it makes us active and edgy, until we at last get food. Climbing stairs is a stress. So is any form of work, from mowing a lawn to studying a textbook. Watching a moving picture—especially an exciting one with a lot of suspense —is a stress.

As the word is usually used in psychology and medicine, stress means *a stimulus that threatens to damage the organism.* Some common examples of purely physical stresses would be the invasion of the body by disease germs, a physical injury, prolonged exposure to extreme heat or cold, overwork, or excessive fatigue. Some common examples of psychological stresses would be the soldier's fear in battle or the anger felt by a man who wants to fight back against an insult. (Note that in both cases there is an actual or imagined threat of damage to the organism—being wounded in battle or being hurt in the fight that may erupt.)

Some interesting and significant experiments with stress have been performed in recent years by Hans Selye, a biologist at the University of Montreal. Selye has subjected various laboratory animals to many kinds of stress, including exposure to cold and the injection of poisons in doses not quite strong enough to kill. What invariably happens, he found, is that the endocrine glands immediately spring into action as the body automatically tries to defend itself. The adrenal glands in particular show some striking changes. They become enlarged and produce more adrenalin. They discharge their stored-up supply of steroids, a process that causes them to change in color from yellow to brown. Because of this intense activity of the adrenal glands, numerous changes occur in the body. Tissue is broken down to become sugar and provide energy. But the sugar is burned off so rapidly that the level of sugar in the blood, as well as the salt level, falls below normal.

In Selye's experiments, animals were subjected to the same high level of stress over a prolonged period. After a few days they seemed to adapt. The adrenal glands returned to normal size, began to renew their supply of stored-up steroids, and changed back to their normal yellow color. The level of sugar and salt in the blood rose to normal or even higher. To all intents and purposes, the animals had adjusted to the stress and were perfectly normal; they seemed just like any other animals in the laboratory.

The recovery, however, was only temporary. After several weeks of continued stress the adrenal glands again became enlarged and lost their stores of steroids. The level of sugar and salt in the blood fell drastically. The kidneys, as a result of receiving an excess of hormones, underwent some complicated and damaging changes. Eventually the animals died, as if from exhaustion. They had been killed, so to speak, by an excess of the hormones they had produced in their own defense.

Another of Selye's important findings was that, even during the period of apparent recovery, the animal was not so normal as it seemed. If a second kind of stress was added in this period, the animal quickly died. One might say that, in attempting to adapt to the original stress, they had used their defenses to the maximum and were helpless against a second form of stress (4).

For the sequence of events involved in prolonged stress—the initial shock or alarm, the recovery or resistance period, and at last exhaustion and death —Selye has coined the phrase *general adaptation syndrome*. (To physicians the word *syndrome* means the entire pattern of symptoms and events that characterize the course of a disease.) There are many indications that the general adaptation syndrome that Selye found in animals also occurs in human beings under prolonged stress and that to human beings psychological stress can be as damaging as any of the physical kinds of stress used in the Selye experiments.

When people talk about the "stress and strain" of modern life, they are recognizing that all of us are under certain pressures caused by competition (for such things as grades in school, acceptances to colleges, and, in the business world, jobs and promotions), as well as by social demands, worries about economic security and the possibility of war, the struggle to get through traffic jams and reach our appointments on time, and emotional conflicts and anxieties. It has been known for a long time that these psychological stresses, when severe and prolonged, can cause actual physical diseases, which are known as *psychogenic*, meaning born of psychological causes. The general adaptation syndrome seems to show how the endocrine glands serve as the mechanism that produces psychogenic physical ailments—among which, it now appears, can often be numbered such widely different conditions as kidney trouble, high blood pressure, heart and circulatory diseases, arthritis, and stomach ulcers.

Just as our physical equipment influences and limits our behavior, it appears from what we know of the general adaptation syndrome that our behavior can influence and sometimes even destroy our physical equipment. For some further light on this interplay between the body and behavior— even behavior that we ordinarily think of as being purely mental—let us now turn to the physical equipment that plays the greatest role in making human beings behave so differently from other organisms.

A one-celled animal does not, of course, possess a nervous system. The entire "body" of the paramecium, for example, is somehow sensitive to light and heat and capable of initiating its own movements. All the more complicated animals, however, do possess specialized nerve cells—fibers that convey messages from one part of the body to another. In the lowly little sea creature called the coral, there is simply a network of nerves, with no particular central point. The nerves and the various parts of the body work together much like the government of a loose federation of states, each preserving considerable independence. Higher up in the scale of evolution, the network of nerves becomes more complicated, and the beginnings of a central nervous system appear. The organism, it might be said, now has the beginnings of a strong central government, exercising control over all its parts. In man, the central nervous system has reached its peak of development: a large and enormously complex brain serves as a center of power and decision that regulates the behavior of all parts of the body in the most complicated and delicate fashion.

Unlike the paramecium, we would be helpless without a nervous system. We would be unable to react to stimuli from the outside world. We would not even be able to move our muscles. Indeed we could not live at all, for our hearts would not beat and our lungs would not breathe. When we go to the dentist and he blocks off the nerves of our gums with a local anesthetic, we cannot feel the tooth he is working on. If we are in an accident and sever the nerves that send impulses to the muscles of our legs, we can never again walk. If certain parts of our brains are destroyed by disease, we lose our ability to speak.

The Nerve Cell

The basic unit of the nervous system is the individual nerve cell, technically called *neuron*, an example of which is shown in FIGURE 7.7. Some of these fiber-shaped neurons are quite long; for example, the motor neurons that enable us to wiggle our toes extend all the way from the lower part of the spinal column to the muscles of the toes. Others, particularly in the brain, are only the tiniest fraction of an inch in length.

The neuron's *cell body*, which contains the chromosomes and genes that caused it to grow into a nerve cell in the first place, performs the work of metabolism. The *dendrites* are the neuron's "receivers"; when they are stimulated, they start a nervous impulse that travels the length of the fiber to the end of the *axon*. The speed at which the impulse travels depends partly on the size of the neuron; the greater the diameter of the fiber, the greater the speed. It also depends, to a much greater extent, on whether the

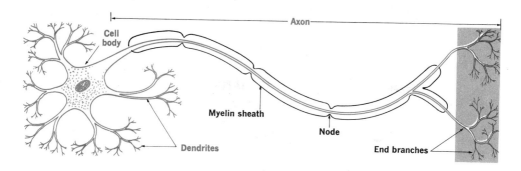

A Nerve Cell (Neuron) Like this motor neuron, all neurons are fiber-shaped cells with a *dendrite* or *dendrites* at one end, an *axon* at the other end, and a *cell body* somewhere in the middle. Stimulation of the dendrites sets up a nervous impulse that travels the length of the neuron to the end of the axon. In the case of this motor neuron, the *end branches* of the axon would be embedded in a muscle fiber, and the nervous impulse would make the muscle contract. The *myelin sheath* is a whitish coating that protects many neurons but not all. The *nodes* are constrictions of the sheath that act as relay stations to improve transmission of the nervous impulse. (5)

FIGURE 7.7

neuron possesses a *myelin sheath,* as does the one shown in the figure. In neurons that have the sheath, the impulse often travels slightly faster than 300 feet a second, compared to a more typical speed of only a little more than 3 feet a second in neurons without the sheath.

The Nervous Impulse

The nature of the nervous impulse is so foreign to anything else in our ordinary experience that it is somewhat difficult to describe or to comprehend at first. It is a tiny charge of electricity passing from one end of the fiber to the other, but it does not travel like the electricity in the wires of a house—as might be guessed from the fact that electricity travels not at a mere 3 to 300 feet a second but at 186,000 miles a second. The charge can be compared to the glowing band of fire that passes along a lighted fuse, except that no combustion takes place in the neuron and that the neuron, far from being destroyed by the nervous impulse, quickly returns to its normal state and is ready to fire again.

In its normal or resting state the neuron has a negative electrical potential in relation to the surrounding body fluids, which carry a positive potential. These two tiny electrical potentials are kept apart by the membrane that encloses the cell body and fiber of the neuron. When the neuron fires, however, something happens to the membrane—a chemical change of some kind. At the dendrite end of the neuron, where the stimulus has been applied, the membrane briefly loses its ability to keep the two electrical potentials apart, and the positive charge of electricity from outside the neuron jumps to the inside. This change in the membrane lasts only the briefest instant, but it passes along the entire length of the fiber, like the glow of a fuse, letting positive electrical charges into the neuron as it goes. If we could stop the nervous impulse along the way and make electrical measurements, we would find this: at the exact spot the impulse has reached, the membrane is letting the positive electrical charges jump into the inside of the neuron. Behind this point, the membrane has regained its ability to keep the electrical potentials apart and the normal negative charge is again building up inside the neuron. Up ahead along the fiber, the membrane and the normal negative charge inside the neuron have not yet been affected. Although the nervous impulse cannot in fact be stopped, its progress can be measured as shown in FIGURE 7.8.

FIGURE 7.8   *Progress of a Nervous Impulse* The progress of a nervous impulse can be recorded by placing two electrodes on the neuron, connected to a sensitive instrument for detecting minute changes in electrical voltage. In the top drawing the nervous impulse has not yet reached the first electrode. In the next drawing it has reached the first electrode and the needle swings left. It then moves on to a point between the two electrodes; the membrane beneath the first electrode has now recovered, and the needle returns to zero position. In the bottom drawing the impulse has reached the second electrode, causing the needle to swing again, this time in the opposite direction.

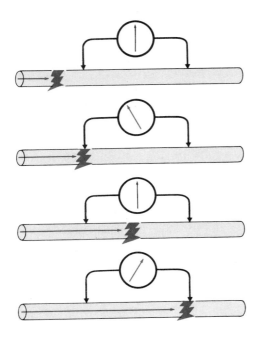

How Neurons Fire

The neuron ordinarily operates on what is called the *all or none principle*. That is to say, if it fires at all, it fires as hard as it can. Too weak a stimulus will not set off the nervous impulse at all. All stimuli of sufficient power set off the same kind of impulse, of exactly the same strength in every case. The voltage of the impulse as measured in FIGURE 7.8 is the same for a stimulus barely strong enough to fire the neuron as for a much stronger stimulus. For each neuron the voltage depends upon the same factors that determine the speed of the impulse—diameter and the presence or absence of a myelin sheath.

Once the neuron has fired, it requires a brief recovery period before it can fire again. This recovery period has two phases. During the first phase the neuron is incapable of responding at all. During the second phase it is still incapable of responding to all the stimuli that would ordinarily make it fire, but it can respond if the stimulus is powerful enough. Some neurons have a fast recovery rate and can fire, when sufficiently stimulated, as often as 1000 times a second. Others recover much more slowly and have a top limit of only a few per second.

FIGURE 7.9 shows the actual sequence of nervous impulses in a neuron over a period of several tenths of a second. Note that each impulse was of equal strength, as measured by the height of the jump it made in the lines. Stronger stimuli, however, made the neuron fire more often.

Records of a Neuron's Activity   These are tracings from electrodes that were placed on the neuron of a rat according to the plan illustrated in FIGURE 7.8. Only the passage of the nervous impulse past the first electrode was recorded, so that each upward jump of the lines shows a separate impulse. The neuron was from the rat's tongue, and the stimulus was salt solution in varying strengths. The response of the neuron to the weakest salt solution is shown in the top line. In the center line the stimulus was ten times stronger and in the bottom line a hundred times stronger. (6)

FIGURE 7.9

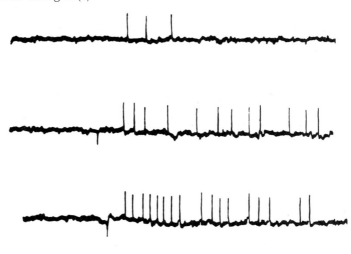

As remarkable as it may seem, those little jumps in the lines in FIGURE 7.9 are much of the story of what goes on inside the human nervous system. The neurons fire off their tiny waves of electricity, barely enough to jolt the needle of the most sensitive recording device. For each neuron, each wave is always the same size; the only possible difference is in the number and rapidity of the impulses. Yet somehow these impulses—by the way they are routed through the nervous system and the patterns they form—manage to tell us what our eyes see and our ears hear; they enable us to learn and to think; they direct our glands and our internal organs to function; they direct our striped muscles to perform such intricate and delicate feats as driving an automobile or playing a violin.

How they do all this will perhaps remain something of a mystery. There are, however, some important clues to the process, which will be the subject matter of the rest of this chapter.

The Synapse

The way one neuron connects with another is shown in FIGURE 7.10. The junction point, or *synapse*, marks the end of one nervous impulse and the start of a new one. The impulse of the first neuron cannot leap across the synapse; it can go only as far as the end of the axon and no farther. What happens, however, is that, when the electrical impulse reaches the end of the axon, a chemical called *acetylcholine* is released into the space between the two neurons. This chemical makes contact with the dendrite of the second neuron and causes it to fire. This method of contact at the synapse is now known to be the way the "message" from one neuron is passed along to another (7).

The Synapse The junction between the axon of one neuron and the dendrites of another neuron is called a *synapse*. For an explanation of what happens at the synapse, see the text.   FIGURE 7.10

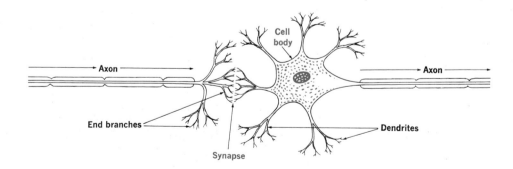

The Three Kinds of Neurons

The neurons of the human body, which are believed to number more than ten billion, come in many different lengths, diameters, and shapes. They can, however, be divided into three classes.

1. *Afferent neurons.* These are the neurons of the senses. The word afferent is derived from the Latin words *ad,* which means to or toward, and *ferre,* which means to bear or to carry. The afferent neurons carry messages toward the central nervous system—from our eyes, ears, and other sense organs.

2. *Efferent neurons.* These carry messages *from* the central nervous system. Their axons end in either muscles or glands. Their impulses make the muscles contract or activate the glands.

3. *Connecting neurons.* These are middlemen between other neurons. They are stimulated only by the acetylcholine discharged at a synapse by another neuron. They do not end in muscle or gland tissue but only in other synapses where they stimulate other neurons to fire. Most of them, though not all, are found within the central nervous system.

A simple example of how these three kinds of neurons work together is provided by the infant's grasping reflex, illustrated in FIGURE 7.11. As will be seen, the nervous messages that produce the reflex begin with stimulation of an afferent neuron, which in turn stimulates a connecting neuron, which in turn stimulates an efferent neuron—whose impulses cause the muscle to contract.

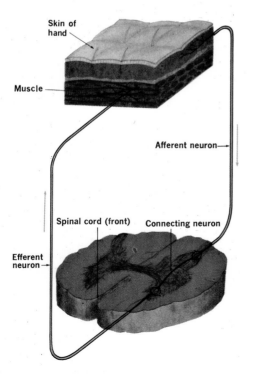

Skin of hand

Muscle

Afferent neuron

Spinal cord (front)   Connecting neuron

Efferent neuron

FIGURE 7.11

Connections for the Grasping Reflex Stroking the palm of the baby's hand stimulates an afferent neuron whose axon ends inside the spinal cord at a synapse with a connecting neuron. This connecting neuron, in turn, ends at a synapse with an efferent neuron. The impulses from the afferent neuron stimulate the connecting neuron, which in turn stimulates the efferent neuron, which makes the muscle of the hand contract. Note that the afferent neuron enters the spinal cord from the back, and the efferent neuron leaves from the front. This is always the case.

Multiple Nerve Connections

Most neurons and most synapses are not nearly so simple as those we have shown up to now. The afferent neurons usually have a number of fibers branching off from the main axon, all with numerous end branches forming synapses with the dendrites of not just one but many connecting neurons. The connecting neurons have numerous dendrites and can be stimulated not just by one but by many other neurons. They also have elaborate axon branches that form synapses with many, many other neurons. The efferent neurons often have numerous dendrites forming all kinds of synapses with a great number of connecting neurons.

Thus the nervous impulses set up by stroking the palm of the baby's hand and carried to the spinal cord do not ordinarily stimulate just a single connecting neuron leading to a single efferent neuron. They stimulate a number of connecting neurons—some of which connect to efferent neurons and some of which connect, directly or through synapses with additional connecting neurons, to the brain, where all kinds of further connections are made.

To add a further complication, the stroking stimulates not just a single afferent neuron but many, each one having its own complicated system of synapses. Even a simple reflex usually involves a considerable number of afferent neurons, connecting neurons, and efferent neurons and a whole elaborate network of synapses between them.

Still another complication is the fact that the cell body of a neuron, as well as the dendrites, is itself sensitive to stimulation and can itself fire off nervous impulses. Thus many additional synapses can exist right at the cell body and often do, particularly in the cells of the brain. One such brain cell is shown in FIGURE 7.12. Note the large number of other neurons that can stimulate the cell body—even aside from all the neurons that may form synapses with the cell's dendrites. This drawing—illustrating the complicated connections at just one part of a single neuron out of the more than ten billion neurons in the human body—is a good indication of the astronomical number of possible pathways that exist for a nervous impulse once it has got started.

How Pathways Are Determined

Helping determine the actual pathways of nervous impulses is the fact that a connecting neuron cannot ordinarily be fired by a single nervous impulse arriving at its cell body or one of its dendrites. The firing process at any complex connection requires what might be called multiple stimulation—a group of nervous impulses arriving at once or in quick succession from several or perhaps even a great many other neurons. The brain cell in FIGURE 7.12, for example, would not respond to a single impulse arriving at a single

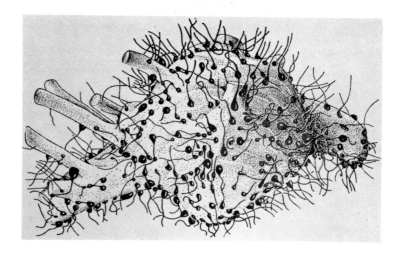

Synapses at the Cell Body Each of the threadlike lines in this diagram represents an axon branch from a different neuron, ending in a little enlargement called a *synaptic knob*. These knobs form a great many synapses directly connecting to the cell body of the brain neuron. Coming into the cell body from the left are its dendrites, and leading away to the right is its axon. Any of the synaptic knobs, as well as stimuli at the dendrites of the brain neuron, can induce the neuron to fire. (8)

FIGURE 7.12

synaptic knob. It might not respond even to impulses at two, three, or four synaptic knobs or perhaps even a half dozen. To make it fire at all, a considerable number of the synaptic knobs might have to be stimulated; to make it fire with any rapidity, the pattern of stimulation might have to be even larger and quite sustained.

But some of the various impulses arriving at a synapse may tend to inhibit rather than stimulate any further activity, and these impulses may cancel out the effect of impulses that are attempting to "get through." Thus every multiple synapse in the nervous system is a complex switching point. The nervous impulses arriving at the synapse may not "get through" at all; they may be too few in number or too far apart in time to fire any of the connecting neurons, or impulses tending to fire the connecting neurons may be canceled out by impulses tending to inhibit further transmission. At times the nervous impulses arriving at the synapse may be of such a number and such a pattern as to fire one of the connecting neurons but no more. At other times several connecting neurons may be fired. The particular ones that are stimulated into activity may vary. The number of impulses they fire and the rate at which they fire may also vary.

Thus no new impulses may be set off at all at the synapse, or new impulses may travel in any one of many directions or in several directions at

253

once. The new impulses that go along to the next switching point or points in the nervous system may be few or many, slow or rapid. Small wonder that the human nervous system is capable of so many accomplishments. By comparison, the nation's telephone network is just a child's toy.

The Nerve Paths and Learning

As has been mentioned, the physical basis for learning is not known. There are, however, some possible clues, which can be considered now that the workings of the nervous system have been discussed.

One theory, popular for a long time, maintains that the synapse is the important structure in learning. When we learn, we obviously route nervous impulses over a particular pathway, going through a number of synapse switching points in a particular pattern. When this happens, the theory goes, the synapses are changed in some manner—probably chemically. This change makes it easier for nervous impulses to travel the same route again. The pathway set up by learning becomes, so to speak, a path of least resistance.

The theory of chemical change at the synapse has received support from recent discoveries about acetylcholine, the chemical that is produced at the synapse and is responsible for stimulating the second neuron. In one study, a group of rats was raised from birth under conditions where they were more or less constantly occupied with learning tasks. Another group of similar rats did no learning at all except what came naturally in their lives in a cage. When the rats were put to death, an analysis of their tissues indicated that there had been considerably more acetylcholine in the brains of the rats that had done the learning (9). Thus learning certainly appears to increase the brain's production of this chemical.

One interesting fact about the human brain is that all its nerve cells are present at birth; the number never increases. Yet the brain grows substantially, from about eleven ounces at birth to over two pounds in adulthood. Part of this added weight is made up of sheaths that develop on some of the neurons and part by the addition of supporting cells (not neurons) that develop in the brain after birth. But the nerve cells themselves also grow in size, and they have been shown to develop additional dendrites much as a young tree develops new branches. This growth process appears to be stimulated by learning. For example, if one group of rats is raised in ordinary cages and another group in an enriched environment containing numerous visual stimuli and toys, examination after death shows that the rats from the enriched surroundings have substantially larger and heavier brains (9). This fact may also be some kind of clue to the mechanism of learning.

In recent years, many investigators have been exploring the possibility that learning may involve a chemical called RNA, which is similar to DNA, and, like DNA, is found in all cells of the body. These investigations were touched off by a report by a scientist in Sweden that learning appeared to cause permanent changes of the RNA molecules in the neurons of mice (10). Some experimenters have concluded that the memory trace is coded inside the RNA molecules in neurons much as the pattern of heredity is coded in the DNA molecules of the genes. The evidence, however, has been inconclusive and in many cases contradictory (11).

All that can be confidently said at the moment is that obviously *something* happens in the nervous system when we learn; it may happen at the synapses or inside the neurons or both. As a name for the repeatable pattern of nervous activity that is created by learning, there is no better term as yet than *engram*—which means a lasting impression made upon the protoplasm of the organism. Learning lays down an engram somewhere in the nervous system; this engram can be reactivated and thus remembered. But the nature of the engram is still a mystery.

As indicated in FIGURE 7.13, the neuron fibers of the human nervous system extend to all parts of the body. **THE CENTRAL NERVOUS SYSTEM** Traveling together in groups of fibers that are called *nerves*, they carry messages to and from the face, the arms, the entire trunk and the digestive organs, the legs, and the feet. The outlying nerves and the individual neurons that make up these nerves are called the *peripheral nervous system*. All of them eventually connect to that marvelous coordinating device known as the *central nervous system*—the *spinal cord* and the *brain*. The afferent neurons and nerves of the peripheral system carry their impulses inward to the central nervous system, where they account for what we call our sensations, such as hearing and the feeling of pain. The efferent nerves, originating in the central nervous system, deliver their impulses outward and thus control the glands of the body and muscles as far away as the fingers and toes.

The afferent nerves of the head—for example, the nerves that serve the receptors for taste in the tongue—connect directly or through connecting neurons to the brain. The efferent nerves of the head, such as those that control movements of the tongue and lips, also have direct connections to the brain. In all parts of the body except the head, the afferent and efferent nerves connect with the spinal cord.° As was noted earlier, the spinal cord itself provides the connections for simple reflexes. Mostly, however, it is a sort of central transmission channel, with a vast number of connecting neurons that carry nervous impulses to and from the brain, the master control center of the nervous system.

° There is one exception that, although it has no particular significance for the study of behavior, must be mentioned for the sake of accuracy. One of the twelve pairs of cranial nerves extends to the heart, blood vessels, and internal organs. Students who have taken courses in physiology will recognize that this is the so-called vagus nerve.

The Human Nervous System Like the tributaries that form a river, individual neuron fibers at all the far reaches of the body join together to form small *nerves*, which is the name for bundles of neuron fibers traveling together. The small nerves join with others to form larger nerves, at last becoming the very large ones that join with the central nervous system—the brain and the spinal cord. Twelve *cranial nerves*, in pairs going to the left and right sides of the head, connect directly with the brain. There are also thirty-one pairs of large *spinal nerves*, connected with the spinal cord at the spaces between the bones of the spine. In many of these nerves, afferent and efferent neurons travel together. The spinal nerves, however, are divided into two just outside the spinal cord. The afferent fibers (as was pointed out in FIGURE 7.11) enter the spinal cord from the back, while the efferent fibers leave from the front.

FIGURE **7.13**

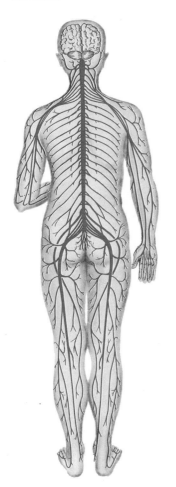

FIGURE **7.14**

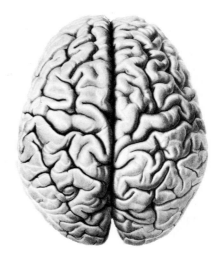

A Top View of the Brain This is the human *cerebral cortex*, the surface of the *cerebrum*, as seen from above. Note how it is divided into two hemispheres of similar size and appearance. Note also the many folds and fissures that add to its area. No other organism except the porpoise has such a large, intricately convoluted, and highly developed cerebral cortex. (12)

The Cerebral Cortex

If we could look down through the top of a transparent skull, we would see the human brain as shown in FIGURE 7.14. We would be looking at only a single one of its many parts—but, as it happens, the very part that most distinguishes man from the lower animals. This is the extremely large, highly developed *cerebral cortex,* the surface of that section of the brain called the *cerebrum.* The cerebral cortex can best be described as a sort of carpet of densely packed neurons with cell bodies, dendrites, and axons forming a closely knit fabric with innumerable connections and interconnections. This "carpet" contains so many nerve cells and is so big in area that it could not find room within the skull except for the fact that it is elaborately folded and refolded. We can see only about a third of the cortex; the rest is hidden because of the convolutions.

In appearance, the outstanding features of the cerebral cortex are these convolutions, the fact that it is divided into two separate halves called the *left hemisphere* and the *right hemisphere,* and its color. Because it is made up mostly of neuron cell bodies and dendrites, the cerebral cortex is gray, the color of unsheathed neuron tissue. It is the color of the cortex that has made "gray matter" a popular synonym for intelligence.

A side view of the cerebral cortex is shown in FIGURE 7.15. Note that there is a particularly prominent fissure extending downward from almost the very top of the cortex. On either side of this fissure lie two important areas of the cortex that seem to be the control points for our sensory impressions and our motor movements. The *sensory area* lies to the rear of the fissure. The *motor area* lies to the front.

The sensory area has been mapped through electrical stimulation of human patients who have had brain surgery under local anesthetic. When various parts of this area are stimulated, the patients report sensations of pressure or movement in parts of the body corresponding to the exact place where the stimulation is applied. As shown in the figure, the body is represented in the sensory area in upside-down position—with the feet and legs at the top of the area and the head at the bottom.

Stimulation of the motor area causes contraction of the muscles in various parts of the body, which, as in the sensory area, is again represented upside down.

The *visual area,* as FIGURE 7.15 shows, is at the very rear of the cortex. Stimulation of this area produces various kinds of visual sensations, and destruction of the area seems to destroy the ability to perceive visual patterns. When the visual area is surgically removed from animals, they cannot distinguish a circle from a triangle.

The *auditory area* lies just below another prominent fissure, which curves diagonally upward from the bottom left of the cortex toward the upper

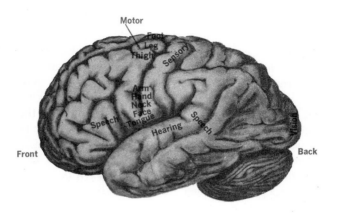

Motor

Foot
Leg
Thigh

Sensory

Arm
Hand
Neck
Face
Tongue

Speech

Hearing

Speech

Vision

Front

Back

FIGURE 7.15   *The Cortex and Its Functions*   On this side view of the cerebral cortex the areas that are known to have special functions have been mapped. (12)

right. The two areas marked *Speech* in FIGURE 7.15, though rather widely separated, both seem to be essential to speaking and to understanding the speech of others.

The ability to learn, to remember what has been learned, and to think does not appear to be localized in any special part of the cerebral cortex or indeed in any other part of the brain. Sometimes the destruction of parts of the brain will cause an apparently total loss of memory for some particular kind of knowledge—for example, the knowledge of language. But ordinarily the knowledge can be relearned, as if several or many parts of the brain are capable of taking over for the same kind of task. In general, intellectual abilities seem to be affected less by the special part of the brain that is destroyed than by the extent of the damage. A man whose brain is damaged very slightly by accident or illness usually manages, after perhaps a period of relearning, to function as well as before. If the damage is more extensive, he will never be able to function quite so efficiently, and he may be very seriously handicapped.

How the Hemispheres Work Together

As has been noted, the cerebral cortex is divided into two hemispheres. So, indeed, is the entire cerebrum, that large part of the human brain of which the cerebral cortex is merely the surface, though presumably the most important part.

As it happens, the afferent and efferent nerves of the left side of the body, except for the head, cross over to the right side of the brain. Similarly, the afferent and efferent nerves of the right side of the body cross to the left side of the brain. Thus stimulation of the sensory area of the left hemisphere causes feelings of pressure or movement in the right side of the body, and stimulation of the motor area of the left hemisphere causes movements of the right arm or right leg. To cause the same kind of sensations or movements in the left side of the body, the areas in the right hemisphere must be stimulated.

The nerves of the head are quite different. With the exception of the nerves of vision from the eyes, all the nerves of the head go to both hemispheres of the cerebrum; thus stimulation of the auditory area of either hemisphere causes the sensation of sound as coming from both ears at once. The nerves of vision split in a way that can be demonstrated if you close your left eye, look straight ahead with your right eye, and hold a pencil vertically in front of the eye, dividing the field of vision into two equal halves. When you do this, everything that you see to the left of the pencil is "registering" on the right hemisphere of the cerebral cortex, and everything you see to the right of the pencil is made up of nervous impulses that are reaching the left hemisphere. The same thing is true of the left eye. In other words, the nerves for the left half of the field of vision in both eyes go to the right hemisphere of the brain, and the nerves for the right half of the field of vision for both eyes go to the left hemisphere of the brain.

The two hemispheres of the cerebrum are connected by a large nerve bundle called the *corpus callosum*. (The corpus callosum cannot be seen in FIGURE 7.14 because it lies deeper down in the brain, well below the cerebral cortex. It will be shown in FIGURE 7.16.) The corpus callosum seems to enable the two hemispheres to cooperate.

Almost invariably, one hemisphere is dominant—usually the left hemisphere. (This is almost always true of right-handed people, as might be expected, but it also seems to be true of most left-handed people.) Most physical skills, reading, writing, and speech are controlled by the dominant hemisphere. Yet a medical case reported in 1966, of a forty-seven-year-old man whose entire left hemisphere had to be removed because of cancer, seems to indicate that these functions can be taken over by the other hemisphere when necessary. Less than a year after the operation the patient had relearned how to walk, eat, help with the dishes, do arithmetic problems, and express himself in speech.

Other Forebrain Structures

A sectional view of the brain, pointing out the structures of most interest, is shown in FIGURE 7.16. The cerebrum, which makes up such a large part of the entire brain mass, is the most prominent feature of what is called the *forebrain*—the highest part of the brain. The other important parts of the forebrain are the *thalamus* and the *hypothalamus*.

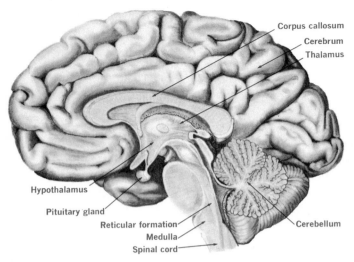

Corpus callosum
Cerebrum
Thalamus

Hypothalamus

Pituitary gland

Reticular formation
Medulla
Spinal cord

Cerebellum

FIGURE 7.16 *A Sectional View of the Brain* The functions of the brain structures shown in this drawing are discussed in the text. (12)

The *thalamus* is the brain's major relay station, connecting the cerebrum with the lower structures of the brain and the spinal cord. In the thalamus lie the cell bodies of important connecting neurons for the various senses. Nervous impulses that originate in the senses arrive eventually at the thalamus and from there are sent on to the cerebrum. Disruption of the operations of the thalamus has been shown to have some far-reaching effects—as was shown by a remarkable operation first performed on a human patient in 1965. This patient, dying of cancer, suffered pain so severe that it was not relieved even by narcotics. Surgeons placed electrodes in his thalamus, connected to a small power pack that he could carry in his shirt pocket. When the pain struck, he could send an electrical stimulus to his thalamus simply by pressing a button. The current brought relief from the pain within twenty minutes and, if kept on for about an hour, gave him continued relief for as long as eight hours, enough to permit him to sleep through the night. Presumably the current disrupted the activity of the thalamus, much as a bolt of lightning might short circuit and knock out an electrical transmission station, and thus prevented the pain impulses carried by the nerves of his body from reaching consciousness.

The *hypothalamus* has connections to both the higher and lower parts of the brain, to the pituitary gland, and to the autonomic nervous system. It is an important link to the endocrine glands and plays a significant role in emotions, the drives of hunger and thirst, sexual behavior, metabolism, and the preservation of a constant body temperature. It also helps direct sleeping and wakefulness. When a particular small part of the hypothalamus called the sleep center is destroyed in experimental surgery on animals, the animals stay awake until they die of exhaustion. When another small part called the waking center is removed, the animals spend most of their time sleeping (13).

The hypothalamus helps regulate many bodily activities. In turn, the hypothalamus is itself affected by many bodily changes—for example, changes in the blood that show the need for food or water—and by the hormones. One experiment showed that placing female sex hormones in the hypothalamus of a female rat caused her to remain in sexual heat constantly for a period of more than sixty days. Moreover, it has been found that, if female rats receive large doses of the male sex hormone during their first five days of life, they are less likely to show normal female sexual behavior when they are adults and indeed are likely to try to behave like male rats (14).

The Brain Stem

The forebrain, composed of the cerebrum, thalamus, and hypothalamus, rests atop other brain structures that are collectively called the *brain stem*. Four parts of the brain stem are of particular interest.

The *medulla* is the connection between the spinal cord and the brain. It is an important connecting tract for nervous impulses to and from the higher parts of the brain. It also contains centers that regulate heartbeat, blood pressure, and breathing. These centers, though they play no part in what are usually thought of as mental processes, are so essential that damage to them causes death.

The *cerebellum* controls body balance; it is the part of the brain that accounts for our posture and keeps us right side up. It also assists in coordinating our bodily movements and keeping them rhythmic and accurate.

The *pons* is a group of nerve fibers lying underneath and connecting the two sides of the cerebellum. Until recently, the functions of the pons were not known. New experiments indicate that the pons helps to regulate breathing (15) and is responsible in part for the nervous impulses that cause the rapid eye movements of a person who dreams during sleep.

The *reticular formation* gets its name from the fact that under a microscope it appears as a criss-crossed (or reticulated) network of rather short neurons connecting to other neurons in the brain stem and the hypothalamus. The afferent pathways carrying nervous impulses from the senses to the cerebral cortex have side branches that enter the reticular formation. Nervous impulses originating in the sensory receptors and traveling through these side branches appear to stimulate the reticular formation to send impulses of its own to all parts of the cortex, keeping the cortex in a general state of arousal and activity. When an electrode is placed in the reticular formation of an animal, the animal can be abruptly awakened from deep sleep by a mild electrical stimulus (16).

The Electroencephalograph

The brain has been studied in many ways. In animals, parts of the brain have been removed surgically and the effects noted, and electrodes have been planted in various places to determine what happens when electrical stimulation is applied. In human beings, the effects of electrical stimulation have also been studied during brain operations or in special cases such as that of the cancer patient in whose thalamus electrodes were planted. Moreover, scientists have had the opportunity to study the behavior of many people who have suffered brain damage of varying location and amount as the result of disease or accident. To this list of methods must now be added the use of the *electroencephalograph,* or EEG for short, a delicate instrument with electrodes that can be placed on the outside of the skull at any desired spot. This device produces tracings of the electrical activity in those parts of the brain lying below the electrodes.

Some typical EEG tracings are shown in FIGURE 7.17. As they indicate, some form of nervous activity goes on constantly in the brain, even when a person is sound asleep. The activity changes in nature, however, when a person is busy in one way or another—even when he merely dreams while asleep. The EEG is a promising tool for further studies but as yet is not very

FIGURE 7.17

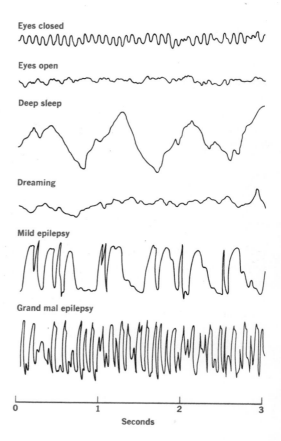

Some EEG Tracings   These are reproductions of actual EEG tracings made under various circumstances. The brain "at rest," when eyes are closed, characteristically shows steady waves of about ten per second, called *alpha waves.* These are replaced by faster waves of lower amplitude when the brain receives sensory stimuli (as when the eyes are open). In deep sleep the alpha waves are replaced by a slower rhythm, which is broken up when the subject dreams. In patients suffering from mild (or petit mal) epilepsy, the waves are characterized by spikes. Grand mal attacks of epilepsy display bursts of violent activity. (Tracings for sleep and dreaming, 17; others, 18)

well understood. Its chief value up to now has been in the diagnosis of certain abnormalities in brain activity, such as occur in epilepsy.

The Brain and Behavior

Some of the specific ways in which the brain has been shown to control behavior have already been mentioned—among them, the role of the cerebral cortex in sensations and in the control of motor behavior and speech and (in Chapter 2) the fact that a rat will learn to press the bar of a Skinner box for what seems to be the sheer pleasure of certain types of brain stimulation.

Perhaps even more significant are some other experiments that have resulted in the control of emotional behavior—one might almost say the personality. As shown in FIGURE 7.18, stimulation of one part of the brain makes an animal unusually docile, while stimulation at another spot makes the animal hostile and aggressive. Electrodes placed at other points in the brain make the animal act as if it is hungry or thirsty or cause extreme sexual arousal.

The most valuable thing we know about the brain, however, goes far beyond this knowledge of the functions of its various specific parts. In a

FIGURE 7.18

Electrical Control of Behavior   The cat in the photograph at top is made so friendly and docile by an electrical stimulus applied deep in the front part of its cerebrum that it happily ignores its traditional prey. The cat at right, electrically stimulated in the region of the hypothalamus, is enraged by the very presence of a laboratory assistant whose attentions, were it not for the stimulation, would be most welcome.

normal organism, with an intact and undamaged brain and with no artificial stimulation coming from electrodes, the brain acts as a unit; it works as an entity to integrate behavior and especially as the instrument through which behavior is modified by learning. We know that the engrams of learning laid down in the brain are the real controllers of behavior; they influence how we will interpret and respond to the stimuli that reach our senses; they influence what we find pleasant and what we find unpleasant; they determine what we find psychologically stressful and to what we will react emotionally; they, even more than real physical needs, influence our habits of sleep, hunger, thirst, and sexual behavior.

The central nervous system is an elaborate control mechanism with various parts that play more or less specialized roles in organizing and directing all our behavior from the continued beating of our hearts during sleep to the elaborate physical defenses we set up against danger in times of stress and from the simple reflex that draws our hand away from fire to the almost incredibly complicated intellectual activity that goes into the composition of a symphony. An important feature of the entire mechanism is the brain's store of learning.

In the day-to-day life of the normal organism the engrams of learning act very much as do the electrodes or the surgical knife that, in experiments, can make the organism move muscles, sleep, wake, act hungry or thirsty, and behave docilely or aggressively. It is as the instrument of learning that the brain is most important in psychology.

The Brain in Learning and in Homeostasis

In general, the cerebrum and especially its cortex seem to be the center of learning and the related higher mental processes—thinking, sensory discrimination, the use of language and speech, and the giving of executive orders to the muscles with which we perform such feats as playing games, operating a typewriter, and driving an automobile. The lower parts of the brain, generally speaking, are involved in what is called *homeostasis*—which means the maintenance of a more or less constant internal environment, with such bodily states as blood circulation, blood chemistry, breathing, digestion, temperature, and so on kept at optimal levels for our survival as living organisms. Our internal organs cannot operate without instructions, and it is the job of the lower parts of the brain to deliver these instructions.

Thus the lower parts of the brain can be thought of as operating much like the electronic equipment in a modern skyscraper that keeps the temperature at a comfortable level, circulates warm or cool air, runs the elevators, and turns the necessary lights on at night and off in the morning. In carrying out these functions they work in conjunction with another important part of the nervous system, the autonomic nervous system.

It was mentioned earlier that the hypothalamus, an important link from the central nervous system to the body, has connections to what is called the *autonomic nervous system*. This is a complicated nerve network that connects the central nervous system with the glands and the smooth muscles of the body.

The word *autonomic* means independent or self-sufficient, and the autonomic nervous system gets its name from the fact that in many ways it operates like a completely independent integrating system, regulating many bodily activities over which we have very little conscious control. We cannot ordinarily, for example, will our hearts to beat faster or the glands of our skin to start or stop perspiring; we cannot order our stomachs to digest our food or to stop the process of digestion so that the flow of blood can be directed away from the stomach and toward other parts of the body. The nervous impulses that give the body such commands are distributed by the autonomic nervous system—a process that goes on constantly, even during periods when we are asleep or in the deep coma caused by an anesthetic or a brain injury.

The autonomic nervous system is composed of centers called *ganglia*, which are masses of nerve cells and synapses forming complex and multiple connections, just as in the brain itself though on a much smaller scale. Some of the neurons originating in these ganglia have dendrites that receive messages from the central nervous system. Other neurons send messages via their axons to the glands and the smooth muscles, as shown in FIGURE 7.19.

There are two parts of the autonomic system, and they are quite different in structure. In the *sympathetic division* the ganglia lie in long chains extending down either side of the spinal cord, all connected and interconnected. Many of the axons extending outward from these chains of ganglia meet again in additional ganglia, where they form complicated interconnections with the neurons that at last carry the messages of the sympathetic division to the glands and smooth muscles. One such second-stage ganglion (the singular of *ganglia*) is particularly well known to boxing fans and is called the solar plexus. It lies just behind the stomach and is vulnerable to blows in the region below the breastbone; a punch there, delivered with sufficient force, can cause a knockout.

The ganglia of the *parasympathetic division* are more scattered; most of them lie near the glands or muscles to which they deliver their messages. For this reason the parasympathetic division tends to act in piecemeal fashion, delivering its impulses to one or several parts of the body but not necessarily to all. The sympathetic division, with its more central connections and interconnections, tends to act as a unit, delivering its impulses simultaneously to all the glands and smooth muscles.

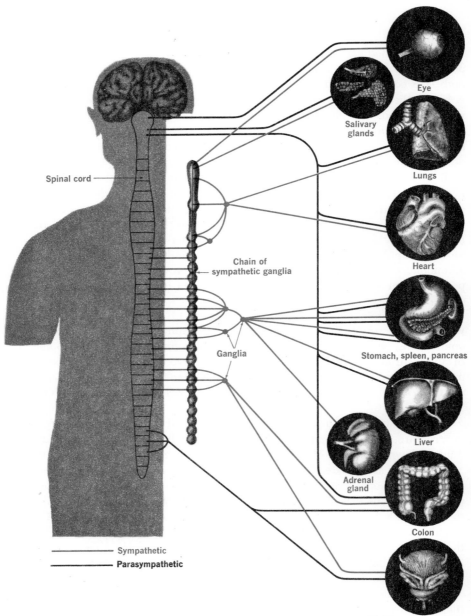

Spinal cord

Chain of
sympathetic ganglia

Ganglia

Eye

Salivary
glands

Lungs

Heart

Stomach, spleen, pancreas

Liver

Adrenal
gland

Colon

Bladder and sex organs

——— Sympathetic
——— **Parasympathetic**

The Autonomic Nervous System   The *parasympathetic division* of the
autonomic nervous system connects to the brain and to the lower part
of the spinal cord. The *sympathetic division* is composed of long chains
of ganglia, one on either side of the spinal column, which connect to
the spinal cord in the region of the trunk and the small of the back.
Both divisions have fibers extending to the smooth muscles and glands
of the body as shown. (19, 20)

FIGURE 7.19

Functions of the Sympathetic System

Earlier in the chapter it was pointed out that the pituitary and adrenal glands spring into action in situations of danger, flooding the blood stream with chemicals that prepare the organism for "fight or flight." What the endocrine glands do through the blood stream, the sympathetic division of the autonomic nervous system does directly. Where its neurons end in glands and in the muscles of the various organs of the body, the axons give off not the chemical acetylcholine but another chemical, very similar to adrenalin and noradrenalin, which stimulates the glands and muscles into action. One might say that the body has two parallel systems for integrating and mobilizing its resources in times of emergency—one by way of the circulatory system and one by way of the nervous system—both capable of performing the same job and usually working in combination. Like the endocrine glands, the sympathetic system is part of the apparatus of emotion and of reaction to stress.

When the sympathetic division goes into action, it enlarges the pupils of the eyes and stops the flow of the salivary glands. ("Wide eyes" and a dry mouth are characteristic of strong emotion.) It activates the sweat glands, contracts muscles at the base of the body hairs (causing the hair to rise on animals and in human beings causing gooseflesh), and changes the size of the blood vessels—enlarging those of the heart and striped muscles and constricting those of the stomach and intestines. It stimulates the lungs to breathe harder and the liver to release sugar into the blood for quick energy. It also stimulates the adrenal glands and pancreas, resulting in increases in the level of blood sugar and the rate of metabolism. It causes the spleen, a glandlike organ in which red corpuscles are stored, to release more of them into the blood stream, thus enabling the blood to carry more oxygen to the body's tissues.

Functions of the Parasympathetic System

The parasympathetic division is also active at times in situations of emergency, although in ways that are not yet entirely clear. In general, it seems to play its most important role as a regulator of bodily functions during those frequent periods when no danger threatens and the body can relax and go about the ordinary business of living. Impulses from the parasympathetic division constrict the pupil of the eye, stimulate the salivary glands, and lower the blood pressure. They also activate the stomach and intestines, thus setting into motion the normal processes of digestion, and they facilitate the functions of elimination from the intestines and bladder.

Considered as a whole, the autonomic nervous system is a valuable adjunct to the central nervous system. More or less independently and automatically, it directs many of the body's functions while we are asleep as well as while we are awake, and it moves quickly to help mobilize our functions in times of emergency. It relieves the central nervous system from the necessity of issuing all the continuing demands necessary to keep the body functioning at an optimum level. As will be seen in Chapter 10, it is also an important part of the physical basis for that rich, colorful, and sometimes exasperating form of behavior called emotion.

SUMMARY

1. The mechanisms of human heredity are the twenty-three pairs of *chromosomes,* forty-six in all, found in the fertilized egg cell and repeated through the process of division in every cell of the body that grows from this cell.

2. The chromosomes are made up of a large number of *genes,* which are composed of a chemical called DNA. The pattern of atoms inside these genes constitutes a "code" that directs the growth of cells into parts of the body and also accounts for the individual differences we inherit.

3. Egg and sperm cells are created through a splitting process that sends half of each pair of chromosomes and genes to one cell and the other half to another cell, in a random manner that makes each egg and sperm cell different, permits of billions of variations, and virtually guarantees that every individual will be unique (except for identical twins, who develop from the same egg cell).

4. A *recessive gene,* such as for blue eyes, inherited from one parent will give way to a *dominant gene,* such as for brown eyes, inherited from the other parent. But a recessive gene can be passed along to the next generation.

5. The *endocrine glands,* or *ductless glands,* influence behavior by secreting chemical substances called *hormones* into the blood stream. The important endocrine glands are:

   a. *Pituitary:* a master gland that secretes hormones that control growth, cause sexual development at puberty, and regulate other endocrine glands.

   b. *Thyroid:* regulates the rate of metabolism and affects the body's activity level.

   c. *Parathyroids:* regulate the balance of calcium and phosphorus in the blood, an important factor in maintaining a normal state of excitability of the nervous system.

   d. *Pancreas:* secretes *insulin,* which burns up blood sugar to provide energy.

e. *Adrenals:* composed of an *adrenal medulla,* which secretes the powerful stimulants *adrenalin* and *noradrenalin,* and an *adrenal cortex,* which secretes *steroids* that are essential to many bodily processes.

f. *Ovaries:* control the development of the secondary female sexual characteristics.

g. *Testes:* control the development of the male sexual characteristics.

h. *Pineal:* appears to help control the female menstrual cycle; seems to be affected by light and darkness; is not yet well understood.

6. The endocrine glands cause many of the bodily changes associated with emotions and also appear to be the mechanism through which physical or psychological stress can result in diseases such as heart trouble, high blood pressure, and stomach ulcers.

7. The nervous system is made up of fiberlike cells called *neurons,* which are stimulated through their *dendrites* and pass along a nervous impulse to the end of their *axons.* The nervous impulse is a tiny wave of electricity traveling at 3 to 300 feet a second.

8. The junction point between the axon of one neuron and the dendrite of another neuron is a *synapse.* Most synapses, especially in the central nervous system, are multiple connection points where arriving impulses may not get through at all or may set off few or many impulses traveling in any one (or more) of many different directions.

9. *Afferent* neurons carry impulses from the sense organs to the central nervous system. *Efferent* neurons carry messages from the central nervous system to the glands and muscles. *Connecting* neurons are the middlemen between other neurons.

10. There is evidence that the passage of nervous impulses may cause actual molecular changes inside neurons—which is a possible though highly controversial explanation for learning and remembering. Another theory is that the passage of impulses over a particular pathway changes the synapses in some way that makes it easier for nervous impulses to travel the same path again.

11. The central nervous system is made up of the *brain* and the *spinal cord.*

12. The spinal cord provides the connections for simple reflexes but is mostly a central transmission channel carrying nervous impulses to and from the brain.

13. Important parts of the *forebrain* are:

a. The *cerebral cortex,* highly developed in the human being, a dense and highly interconnected mass of neurons and their cell bodies. It contains areas that seem to account for our sensory impressions and to initiate movements and speech.

b. The *cerebrum,* the large brain mass of which the cerebral cortex is the surface.

    c. The *corpus callosum,* a large nerve tract connecting the *left hemisphere* and *right hemisphere* of the cerebrum and enabling the two hemispheres to cooperate and share in duties.

    d. The *thalamus,* the way station between the rest of the brain and the cerebrum.

    e. The *hypothalamus,* which serves as a sort of mediator between the brain and the body, helping control sleep, hunger, thirst, body temperature, and sexual behavior, and is also concerned with emotions.

14. Important parts of the *brain stem* are:

    a. The *medulla,* the connection between the spinal cord and the brain. It is vital to life because it helps regulate heartbeat, blood pressure, and breathing.

    b. The *cerebellum,* which controls body balance and helps coordinate bodily movements.

    c. The *pons,* a structure of neurons connecting the opposite sides of the cerebellum. The pons helps regulate breathing and is apparently the source of the nervous impulses that cause rapid eye movements during dreaming.

    d. The *reticular formation,* a way station through which messages from the nerves of the senses pass, setting up nervous impulses that are sent to the cerebral cortex and keep the cortex in a general state of arousal and activity.

15. Electrical stimulation of various parts of the brain has been shown to affect behavior in many ways, such as by causing rage, docility, sexual arousal, hunger, thirst, pleasure, and pain.

16. The *autonomic nervous system* connects the central nervous system with the glands and smooth muscles of the body. Acting more or less independently and automatically, it helps regulate such activities as breathing, heart rate, blood pressure, and digestion; and in times of emergency it works in conjunction with the endocrine glands, mobilizing the body's resources for drastic action by speeding up the heartbeat, directing the flow of blood away from the digestive organs and toward the muscles of movement, and stimulating the liver to provide additional blood sugar for quick energy.

17. The autonomic nervous system is composed of two parts: a) the *sympathetic division,* which tends to be active in case of emergency, and b) the *parasympathetic division,* which is most active under ordinary circumstances. Both divisions are made up of *ganglia,* or masses of neuron cell bodies, that have dendrites coming from the central nervous system and axons traveling out to the glands and smooth muscles. The ganglia of the sympathetic division lie in long chains along both sides of the spinal column. The ganglia of the parasympathetic division are more scattered, lying near the glands and muscles they affect.

Altman, J. *Organic foundations of animal behavior.* New York: Holt, Rinehart and Winston, 1966.

Brazier, M. A. B. *The electrical activity of the nervous system,* 2nd ed. New York: Macmillan, 1961.

Fraser, A. S. *Heredity, genes and chromosomes.* New York: McGraw-Hill, 1966.

Fuller, J. L. and Thompson, W. R. *Behavior genetics.* New York: Wiley, 1960.

Gardner, E. *Fundamentals of neurology,* 4th ed. Philadelphia: Saunders, 1963.

Isaacson, R. L., ed. *Basic readings in neuropsychology.* New York: Harper & Row, 1964.

Landauer, T. K. *Readings in physiological psychology: the bodily basis of behavior.* New York: McGraw-Hill, 1967.

McGuigan, F. J. *Biological basis of behavior: a problem.* Englewood Cliffs, N.J.: Prentice-Hall, 1963.

Morgan, C. T. *Physiological psychology,* 3rd ed. New York: McGraw-Hill, 1965.

Teitelbaum, P. *Physiological psychology.* Englewood Cliffs, N.J.: Prentice-Hall, 1967.

Vandenberg, S. G. *Methods and goals in human behavior genetics.* New York: Academic Press, 1965.

HOW THE SENSES OPERATE

The Range and Limits of the Human Senses
Why We Study the Senses
The Sensory Threshold
The Difference Threshold
Sensory Adaptation

TASTE

SMELL

THE SKIN SENSES

HEARING

The Physical Nature of Sound
    Frequency = Pitch; Amplitude = Loudness; Complexity = Timbre
Locating Sounds
The Ear and Its Receptors
How Do the Hearing Receptors Work?

VISION

The Structure of the Eye
    The Receptors of the Eye; Why We Wear Glasses
Visual Adaptation
Eye Movements
The Physical Nature of Light
    Wave Length = Hue; Intensity = Brightness; Complexity = Saturation
Mixing the Hues
Color Blindness
Afterimages

BODILY MOVEMENT

EQUILIBRIUM

CHAPTER

8

THE SENSES

To those of our ancestors who thought about the matter, the human senses were one of life's most puzzling mysteries. Here you stand, and out there, many yards away, totally unconnected in any apparent way with your body or your eyes, is a tree. How can you manage to see that tree? Why does its trunk look brown and its leaves green? Why are the roses near it red and the marigolds yellow?

A friend standing near the tree opens his mouth, and you hear words. What has happened—and why does his voice sound different from the voice of anyone else you know? Why does a piano sound different from a violin, and a violin from a trumpet?

Those roses you see out in the yard smell entirely different from the marigolds. Sugar does not taste at all like lemon juice or quinine. Some objects that you touch seem cold; some seem warm and some so hot that you have to draw your hand away in pain. Why?

For centuries nobody knew the answers to these questions. Even the best informed of men could only guess. Some of the guesses, as we now know, came fairly close to the truth. For example, one Greek philosopher who lived around 400 B.C. speculated that all objects gave off some kind of invisible substance that penetrated our eyes or the pores of our skin and then traveled to our brains. Not until recently was there any better explanation.

As you sit reading this book you are demonstrating the two basic principles now known to be involved in the operation of our senses.

HOW THE SENSES OPERATE

First, there must be a *stimulus*. As the Greek philosopher rightly guessed, something must actually impinge upon our bodies. In this case it is the light waves reflected off your book in the form of dark, white, and colored patterns. Turn out the light and darken the room, thus removing the light waves, and you can no longer see the book, even though it is still there.

Second, there must be *receptors* that are sensitive to the stimulus. The philosopher was wrong in thinking that anything could enter our pores and then travel to the brain. What happens is that the stimulus activates the receptors—in this case the light-sensitive nerve endings in your eyes—which then send nervous impulses to the brain, where they are translated into conscious sensations. Block off the receptors by closing your eyelids, and again you cannot see the book. You cannot see with your skin or your ears, because they do not possess any receptors that respond to the stimulus of light.

A *stimulus* has already been defined as any form of energy capable of exciting the nervous system; among the sensory stimuli are light waves, sound waves, the chemical energy that causes the sensations of taste and smell, and the mechanical energy that we feel through the skin as pressure and pain. A *receptor* can be defined as a specialized nerve ending capable of responding to energy.

The Range and Limits of the Human Senses

All organisms, even those without any specialized receptors, can respond to certain kinds of sensory stimulus. The one-celled paramecium can distinguish between warmth and cold and between light and dark. In the human being the senses have been developed to a high degree. Our eyes are so sensitive that, on a night when the air is clear but the moon and stars are blacked out by an overcast, a man sitting on a mountain can see a match struck fifty miles away. Our noses can detect the odor of artificial musk, a perfume base, in such low dilutions as one part musk to thirty-two billion parts of air.

Even so, our senses are by no means perfect. Owls can see far better in the near-dark than we can. Hawks, soaring high in the air, can see mice that we would never be able to distinguish at such a distance. Bees can see ultra-violet light (the rays that produce sunburn), which we cannot see at all. Dogs and porpoises hear tones that go unheard by the human ear. (You can buy whistles that will call your dog without disturbing your neighbors.) The minnow, which has taste receptors all over its body, has a far sharper sense of taste than we do. Bloodhounds are used to track down criminals because they have a far sharper sense of smell.

In some ways the deficiencies of our sense organs are a blessing. Light waves, as the physicists have shown, are one form of electromagnetic radiation. So are many other things, such as cosmic rays, X-rays, radio and television signals, and the electric currents passing through the wires of our houses. The length of the wave determines which of these forms the radiation takes. Light waves, the only wave lengths to which our eyes are sensitive, are a tiny fraction of the entire range. If we could see all the wave lengths—everything from cosmic rays to the radio and television signals passing through the air and the flow of electricity—we would surely be completely confused. Our eyes would give us a hopeless jumble of impressions.

Why We Study the Senses

Although it is hard for anyone in our present scientific age to believe, the philosophers of the past spent a lot of time wondering whether there really was any such thing as a tree or whether trees were just an illusion of the human mind. They argued interminably about questions such as these: Does the world look the same to any two people? If a tree falls in a lonely forest, where nobody is around to listen, does the tree make a sound? Where does reality end and the human mind create its own imaginative world?

Not until the discovery of the nature of light and sound waves and some of the facts about the human nervous system could anyone be sure of the answers. Now we know that of course there is a tree, reflecting light waves of a certain length and pattern, which all people see in more or less the same fashion. If the tree falls, it creates sound waves regardless of whether or not someone is there to listen. And we know that our senses reflect reality—though in an imperfect and sometimes incomplete way.

If we regard the human organism as a sort of computer, then our senses provide our inputs. They tell us what kind of world we are living in and how the world is changing from moment to moment. Without the evidence provided by our senses, all the rest of our complicated physical and nervous equipment would be useless—just as a modern heating system would be useless without the sensitive element in the thermostat that says the building is now warm and the heat must be turned off, or the building is getting cold and the heat must be turned on. Our sensory inputs relay the fact that the traffic light up ahead has turned red, and by a complicated process of mental and motor activity we step on the brake and stop the automobile. Our sensory inputs inform us that the weather has turned cold, and we put on more clothing lest we freeze to death.

The Sensory Threshold

At some time in your childhood you doubtless took the simple test of hearing in which a doctor or nurse holds a watch somewhere in the vicinity of one ear. The watch is constantly ticking away, sending out sound waves. But sound waves decrease in volume as they travel through the air; and, if the watch is too far away, you cannot hear it at all. As it is moved closer, eventually there comes a spot at which you can hear it clearly. At one distance the sound waves are too weak to make the receptors in your ear respond. A little closer the waves are strong enough; now the receptors send signals to your brain and you hear the watch. The test is a crude measurement of the *absolute threshold* of that ear—in other words, the minimum amount of stimulus energy to which the receptors will respond. By comparing your threshold to that of other people, the doctor or nurse gets a rough idea of whether your sense of hearing is average, sharper than average, or below average.

Measurements establishing the precise absolute thresholds for the various senses under various conditions have been made with procedures known as *psychophysical methods*—techniques of measuring the psychological equivalents of changes in the physical strength of a stimulus. In a typical psychophysical experiment a subject is placed in a dark room and brief flashes of light are presented, with the exact candlepower of the light controlled down to the tiniest fraction. Some flashes are so weak in intensity that the subject never sees them. Other stronger flashes are seen every time. In between, there is a sort of twilight zone of intensities at which the subject sometimes sees the flash and sometimes does not.

There are many reasons for this "sometimes" factor. The human body is constantly at work: the heart is beating, the lungs inhaling or exhaling air. Each cell of the body, including the sensory receptors, is being fed by the blood stream and is throwing off waste materials. All sorts of spontaneous nervous activity are constantly going on in the brain. Sometimes all these conditions work together in favor of detecting a weak stimulus; sometimes they work against it. So the absolute threshold is not really "absolute." It is arbitrarily considered to be the intensity at which the subject sees the flash exactly half the time.

A synonym for threshold is the word *limen;* a *subliminal* stimulus is below the threshold, a *supraliminal* stimulus above it. Hence the phrase subliminal advertising, which has been a matter of considerable controversy in recent years. The theory behind subliminal advertising is that brand names, flashed on a television or motion picture screen so briefly as not to attract any conscious notice, can nonetheless be effective in influencing purchasers. This idea is as yet unproved.

The Difference Threshold

Let us return for a moment to the psychophysical method of measuring a subject's absolute intensity threshold for a brief flash of light. This time let us change the experiment and present two lights to the subject, side by side. We start with two lights of exactly equal intensity; and the subject, as we would expect, sees them as exactly the same. Now we show him the two lights again, but this time we have added a tiny fraction of a candlepower to the light on the right. To the subject, they still look the same. We show him the same light on the left but double the intensity of the light on the right, and now he sees a difference very clearly. If we continue the experiment long enough, keeping the left-hand light at the same intensity and varying the intensity of the right-hand light, sometimes by very small amounts and sometimes by larger amounts, eventually we will discover the smallest possible difference that his eyes are capable of recognizing 50 percent of the time. This is the *difference threshold,* or *difference limen,* an important concept in sensory psychology.

The difference threshold—often called the *just noticeable difference* or j.n.d. for short—is a measurement of our basic capacity to discriminate among different stimuli, and, as such, it has innumerable applications to the study of human behavior. Suppose, for example, that it should turn out that the human eye could see only black, white, red, green, blue, and yellow, always as pure colors and with no shadings of any kind. In that case artists would never attempt to put any subtlety into the coloring of their paintings, and horticulturists would be wasting their time if they tried to breed a flower in a delicate new shade of pink or purple. Suppose that all the foods we ate could be divided into merely three classes, one tasting like raw potatoes, one like an apple, the third like buttered bread. There would be no point in having all the variety of foods that now appears on supermarket shelves, and there would be very little difference between a meal at a cheap roadside hamburger stand and a meal in a fine restaurant.

Psychophysical measurements have shown that if the left-hand light in our experiment has an intensity of 1 candlepower, the right-hand light must have an intensity of 1.016 candlepower to be recognized as different. If the left-hand light is 10 candlepowers, the right-hand light must be 10.16 candlepowers. If the left-hand light is 100 candlepowers, the right-hand light must be 101.6 candlepowers. In other words, the difference in intensity between two lights must be 1.6 percent before it can be recognized. For sound, the just noticeable difference is about 10 percent.

This rule that the difference threshold is a fixed percentage of the original stimulus was discovered more than a century ago and in honor of its inventor is called *Weber's Law.* The law does not apply at very low intensities or at very high intensities, but it holds generally over the greater part of the range of stimulation. In practical terms, it means this: The more sensory stimulation to which the human organism is being subjected, the more additional stimulation must be piled on top of this to produce a recognizable difference. In a room where there is no sound except that of a mosquito buzzing, you can hear a pin drop. Even on a noisy city street you can hear the honk of an automobile horn but may be completely unaware of the fact that a friend is shouting to you from down the block. At an airport where jet planes are warming up, a small cannon could go off close beside you without making you jump.

Sensory Adaptation

At this moment, unless you happen to be sitting in a draft or in an unusually hot room, you almost surely are not conscious of feeling either hot or cold. And you probably feel the same all over; you are not conscious that your feet are cooler or warmer than your hands or that the skin on the calves of your legs is any cooler or warmer than the skin on the small of your back. Yet careful measurements of your skin temperature would probably show small but significant differences for your feet, which are encased in socks or stockings and shoes; your uncovered hands; your calves, covered by a pair of trousers or by nylon stockings; and the small of your back, covered by several layers of clothing and a belt and pressed against the chair.

Nor are you conscious of any special pressures against your skin. But wherever your clothing touches your skin, there certainly is pressure; and at places the pressure is made quite intense by a wristwatch band or by a belt, to the point where you may find marks on your skin tonight when you undress.

Why do you not feel these stimuli? The answer lies in the principle of *sensory adaptation*, which means that after a time the sensory receptors adjust to a stimulus—they "get used to it," so to speak—and stop responding.

The classic example of sensory adaptation is this simple experiment. Fill a bowl with water of just about skin temperature—water that feels neither hot nor cold to your hand, water that we may say has a neutral temperature. Fill a second bowl with cold water and a third bowl with water that feels quite warm to the touch. Now put your left hand in the bowl of cold water and your right hand in the bowl of hot water. After a minute or two, put both hands in the bowl that contains water at the neutral temperature. Even though you know perfectly well that both hands are in the same water, your left hand will feel warm, your right hand cool. The receptors in your left hand have become adapted to cold water, and water of neutral temperature now seems warm. The receptors in your right hand have adapted to warm water, and water of neutral temperature now seems cold.

In some ways, the tendency of our senses to adapt to stimuli makes them less accurate than they would otherwise be. The human skin would make a poor thermostat for a heating system; what we want in a heating system is a thermostat that will invariably turn the heat on when the room temperature drops to 69 degrees and turn the heat off as soon as the temperature rises to 71 degrees. But in everyday living, sensory adaptation is generally an advantage. It would be distracting indeed if we were conscious all day of the pressure of every garment we wear and of every slight temperature change from one patch of our skin to another. If our noses did not gradually get used to the odors about us and stop sending signals to our brains, the people who work in fish markets and gas plants would be a lot less happy than they are now.

Because of the principle of sensory adaptation, some scientists like to define a stimulus as a *change in energy* capable of exciting the sense organs. Such a definition is not literally correct, because we never adapt completely to a pressure strong enough to cause severe pain, and we continue to feel uncomfortably warm in a 110-degree room no matter how long we stay there. But the definition is nonetheless useful to keep in mind, because it emphasizes the fact that our sensory apparatus is best equipped to inform us of changes in our environment, and it is awareness of change in the environment that is most valuable to us.

With these general principles of the operation of the senses in mind, let us now examine our senses separately and in detail. It is popularly assumed that we are gifted with five senses; the best order in which to explore the five is to start with the simplest and least efficient one, which is *taste,* and proceed to *smell,* the *skin senses, hearing,* and *vision.* Even after we have examined the so-called five senses, however, it will be necessary to add two more—*bodily movement* and *equilibrium*—to explain the full range of human sensory apparatus.

TASTE

In view of the variety of foods we recognize and either enjoy or reject, it may seem strange to call the sense of taste our simplest and least efficient. What is generally called the "taste" of food, however, turns out to depend only in small part on our sensory receptors for taste. Much of the sensation depends on other factors—on warmth, cold, the consistency of the food, the mild pain caused by certain spices, and above all on smell. When our noses are stuffed up by a cold, food seems almost tasteless.

If you examine your tongue in a mirror, you will note that it is covered with little bumps, some very tiny, others a bit larger. Inside these bumps, a few of which are also found at the back of the mouth and in the throat, are the *taste buds,* which are the receptors for the sense of taste. Each bump contains about 245 taste buds, and each taste bud in turn contains about twenty receptors sensitive to chemical stimulation by food molecules. Food in solution spreads over the tongue, enters small pores in the surface of the bumps, and sets off chemical changes that depolarize the receptors and thus set off nervous impulses that are sent to the brain. Apparently the receptors respond to four basic qualities: *sweet, salt, sour,* and *bitter.* Some of the taste buds respond to only one of these qualities, others to two or three of them, and some to all four.

Our knowledge of the taste receptors explains why people who quit smoking often find that food tastes better and why older people often find they have to use much more salt and spice to make food taste as good as it did in their youth. Tobacco smoke temporarily reduces the sensitivity of the taste receptors (and also of the receptors for smell). In people past middle age the number of sensitive taste buds begins to decline so that older people simply do not have as many taste receptors capable of responding. People who live to extremely advanced ages sometimes lose the sense of taste entirely.

Animals—at least some of them—apparently have a very different sense of taste from the human kind. Cats do not seem to be sensitive to sweetness; they show no fondness for candy. Dogs usually like candy and horses seem to prefer a lump of sugar to any other kind of taste.

SMELL

At the very top of the nasal passages leading from the nostrils to the throat, as can be seen in FIGURE 8.1, lies the *olfactory epithelium,* the membrane that contains the receptors sensitive to smells. As we breathe normally, the flow of air from nostrils to throat takes a direct route, as the chart indicates, but a certain amount rises gently to touch the olfactory epithelium. When an odor is strong enough—as in a freshly painted room or in a kitchen where garlic is cooking—we quickly become aware of it, without effort. For fainter odors we need to stir up the air in the nasal passages, so that more of the stimulus comes into contact with the olfactory epithelium. This is why we sniff when trying to determine by sense of smell whether milk is fresh or sour or how much we like a new brand of cologne.

The receptors for smell are sensitive only to gases and to volatile substances that become dissolved in the air much as sugar dissolves in water. An actual molecule of the substance must touch the smell receptors; this is the stimulus that fires the receptors and sends nervous impulses to the brain.

It has been known for a long time that substances with a very small molecular size have very little odor and that very large molecules are not volatile and therefore have no odor at all, while the molecules of in-between

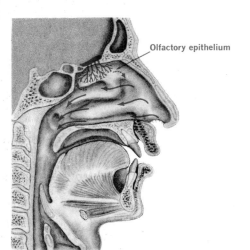

Olfactory epithelium

FIGURE 8.1

The Receptors for Smell A cross section of the human head shows the position of the *olfactory epithelium,* containing the receptors for the sense of smell. The normal passage of air through the nasal passages is indicated by the arrows.

size have the strongest odor. Recent studies seem to indicate that not only the size but also the shape of the molecule may determine how a substance smells. According to one theory, the smell receptors have very tiny slots or hollows of varying shapes, into which molecules of different shapes fit like a plug into an electric socket or a jigsaw piece into a puzzle; when a receptor is "filled" by the appropriate kind of molecule, it fires and sends its message to the brain. Proponents of the theory have suggested that there appear to be seven basic classes of molecules producing seven basic odors: camphorlike, musky, flowery, pepperminty, etherlike, pungent, and putrid. Some molecules apparently fit into more than one kind of receptor and thus produce the more complex sensations that result from combinations of the seven basic odors (1).

THE SKIN SENSES

One of the tools developed for studying the sensitivity of the human skin is the *esthesiometer,* shown in use in FIGURE 8.2. If the two points of the esthesiometer are close together, they feel like the touch of a single object. If they are far enough apart, they feel like the two separate objects that they in fact are. In other words, the esthesiometer measures what is called the *two-point threshold* for the sense of pressure.

Experiments with the esthesiometer make it immediately apparent that the two-point threshold differs widely for various parts of the body. To be felt as two objects, the points have to be thirty-four times as far apart on the middle of the back as on the fingertips and twice as far apart on the fingertips as on the tip of the tongue.

From what has already been said about stimuli and sensory receptors, we know what the esthesiometer is telling us. In the first place, there must be receptors capable of responding to the stimulus of pressure in the skin of each part of the body. In the second place, the receptors in parts of the body

FIGURE 8.2

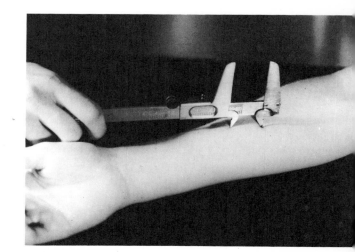

Two Sensations or One? With an instrument developed for this special purpose, an experimenter determines how far apart two pressure stimuli must be before the subject can feel them as two separate sensations instead of as one.

such as the fingertips and tongue must be more numerous, more sensitive, or both than the receptors in places such as the middle of the back.

But which is it? Are the pressure receptors at the tip of the tongue and in the fingertips more numerous, or are they more sensitive? Or are they both?

One way of answering these questions is to try to map the surface of the skin, searching point by point for spots that are sensitive to pressure and using different degrees of pressure to measure the absolute threshold at these points. The technique is shown in FIGURE 8.3.

When the skin is mapped in this fashion, it turns out that there are more spots sensitive to pressure at the tip of the tongue and in the fingertips than on the back. Moreover, the absolute threshold at these spots is far lower at the tip of the tongue and at the fingertips. We have our answer: in the regions of the body where the two-point threshold is lowest, the pressure receptors are *both* more numerous and more sensitive.

If we continue to explore the skin with other stimuli, we make a further discovery. The stimulus of pressure has given us one kind of map. A warm stimulus shows a very different kind of map for the spots sensitive to warmth. A cold stimulus gives a third kind of map, and a needle used to elicit pain gives a fourth pattern. The four different kinds of maps are illustrated in FIGURE 8.4. As the figure shows, the number of sensitive spots varies greatly from one part of the body to another for pain, cold, and warmth as well as for pressure; but in any single area there are usually more pain spots than pressure spots, always more pressure spots than cold spots, and always more cold spots than warmth spots.

A strange thing about the cold spots is that they respond not only to a stimulus colder than skin temperature but to a very warm stimulus. When one of these spots is touched by a rod heated to 110 degrees Fahrenheit or more, we actually feel a strong sensation of cold at that point. This phenomenon is known as *paradoxical cold*—and it seems to explain how we distinguish a hot stimulus from a merely warm stimulus. When we touch a

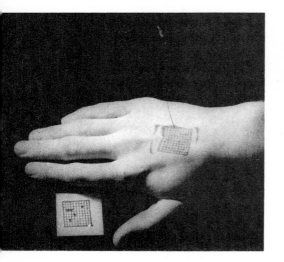

FIGURE 8.3

Mapping Skin Sensitivity   A grid is printed on the skin, and the experimenter goes over the grid searching for spots sensitive to the pressure of human and animal hairs of different thicknesses. These are pressed against the skin just hard enough to make them bend, and the exact pressure exerted by each thickness of hair can be measured by pressing it in similar fashion against a delicate weighing balance. Sensitive spots are recorded on a copy of the grid. The same area can also be mapped for spots sensitive to pain, warmth, and cold—often giving results as shown in FIGURE 8.4.

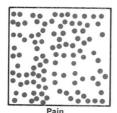

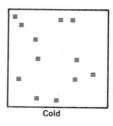
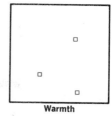

| Pain | Pressure | Cold | Warmth |

The drawings show the typical results when the same small area of skin is mapped for sensitivity to pain, pressure, cold, and warmth.

FIGURE **8.4**

The Results of Skin Mapping

The number of sensitive spots usually found per square centimeter varies considerably depending upon which part of the body is mapped. (2)

	Spots per square centimeter			
	PAIN	**PRESSURE**	**COLD**	**WARMTH**
Tip of nose	44	100	13	1.0
Forehead	184	50	8	0.6
Chest	196	29	9	0.3
Back of hand	188	14	7	0.5

surface heated to more than 110 degrees Fahrenheit, both the warmth receptors and the cold receptors respond and send their nervous impulses to the brain, and it is this mingling of both that results in the sensation of heat. This can be demonstrated by the dual coils shown in FIGURE 8.5. When cool water is passed through both coils, the device naturally feels cool to the touch. When warm water is passed through both coils, it feels warm. But when one coil is warm and the other cool, the device suddenly—and to the amazement of anyone who touches it—feels hot.

From the various experiments we know that the skin really has four

FIGURE **8.5**

To warm and cold water supply

Warmth Plus Cold = What? Warm water can be passed through both coils, or cool water can be passed through both, or warm water can be passed through one coil and cool water through the other. For a description of the unexpected result of passing warm water through one coil and cool water through the other, see the text.

separate senses—pain, pressure, cold, and warmth, with a combination of the last two producing the sensation of heat. As it happens, the nerve endings in the skin come in four general forms—some in little branches (called free-ending nerves), some in globular bulbs, some in egg-shaped corpuscles, and some in the form of "baskets" surrounding the roots of the hairs. This fact naturally has suggested the possibility that each type of nerve ending might be a receptor for each of the four sensory stimuli, and a great deal of experimental work has been done in an attempt to establish a connection. All the efforts have thus far failed.

It is interesting to note that the center part of the cornea of the eye—the transparent "window" over the pupil—is supplied only with nerves of the free-ending type, and this area seems to be sensitive only to pain, not to pressure, cold, or warmth. But this proves only that the free endings are exclusively receptors for pain in this particular small area of the body. In other areas they may respond to other stimuli as well, and other types of nerve endings may also respond to pain.

We have pain receptors in all our muscles and internal organs as well as in our skin, and some of the most excruciating pains come from cramps or from distension of the intestines by gas. Yet most of the internal organs do not respond to the ordinary stimuli for skin pain. The intestines, for example, can be cut or even burned without arousing any sensation of pain.

Although pain seems to be one of the crosses that we must bear, it actually serves a purpose. Without the warning given us by pain we might hold our hands in a flame until the tissues were destroyed or cut off a finger while peeling an apple. Even the pain of headache, which cannot be attributed to any specific outside stimulus, is probably a warning that we have subjected ourselves to too much physical or psychological stress; by forcing us to slow down or even take a day off, the headache takes us away from a situation that, if continued, might cause some serious damage to the tissues of our bodies or to our mental stability.

Just as we sometimes ignore pain, as in the heat of an athletic contest, we sometimes add to the amount of pain we feel. Many experiments have shown that the expectation and fear of pain add greatly to the discomfort we feel from a painful stimulus. The person who goes to the dentist's office expecting to grin and bear it manages to get through the experience with a minimum of discomfort. The person who goes in fear and trembling is likely to suffer agonies.

HEARING

When you hit the key for middle C on a piano, a hammer strikes the string for middle C, the string vibrates, and you hear a sound. Not just any sound, but a very definite sound. You can distinguish it from other notes on the piano; it seems higher than the B just below it and lower than the D just above it. It also sounds different from the middle C on other musical instruments; if someone in the room were playing the same note on a clarinet, you would recognize at once that the sounds were alike yet somehow different.

If you hit the key a little harder now, the sound, though remaining the same in every other respect, is louder. Hit the key a little more gently, and the sound is softer.

If you had an old-fashioned 78 rpm recording of that same middle C on the piano, it would again sound the same but different; you might describe it as less rich, or "tinnier." On a modern high-fidelity recording the note would sound much more natural.

Striking the piano key is a start toward exploring some of the basic facts about the sense of hearing. Sound is an extremely complicated stimulus, ranging from the lowest notes of a tuba to the highest notes of a shrill whistle, changing in volume from the merest hint of a whisper to the most deafening clap of thunder, taking such diverse and varied forms as the click of two coins in a pocket, the human voice, and the blended richness of a hundred different instruments in a symphony orchestra. The receptors in the human ear have to be very sensitive indeed to respond to such a wide range of stimuli.

The Physical Nature of Sound

The stimulus for sound is sound waves, rippling unseen through the air. Sound waves are roughly analogous to waves on water. If you throw a stone into a quiet pond, waves start to radiate out. It looks as if the surface of the water is moving away from the stone, forming circles of ever increasing size. Actually, as you can tell if there are some twigs or fishing corks floating on the surface, this is not true. The twigs and corks stay in the same spot and merely bob up and down.

What happens when the stone hits the surface of the pond is that it puts pressure on the water. The surface is pushed up, then falls, and in so doing passes the pressure along to the adjoining water. The rising and falling motions continue outward in ever widening circles, with the ripples getting smaller and smaller as the pressure of the stone's impact is absorbed.

When you hit that middle C on the piano, something very similar happens in the air. The piano string starts to vibrate. As it vibrates in one direction, it compresses the air, just as an accordion player compresses the air inside the instrument by pushing the ends together. As the string vibrates in the other direction, it expands the air and creates a partial vacuum, as the accordion player does when he pulls the ends of the instrument apart. These alternations of pressure and expansion are passed along through the air, growing weaker in volume as they go, until at last there comes a point where the energy from the string's vibration is used up and the waves disappear. The sound waves, then, are ripples of compression and expansion of the air. Regardless of how loud or soft they may be or whether they are high sounds or low sounds, they travel through the air at a standard rate of speed; the speed of sound, which we hear discussed so often in these days of fast airplanes, is around 750 miles an hour, or 1100 feet per second.

FREQUENCY = PITCH   Fortunately for our study of sound waves, it is possible to turn these unseen air ripples into pictures that tell us a great deal about them. This is done with a device called a cathode-ray oscilloscope, as shown in FIGURE 8.6. The wavy lines that flicker across the screen of the oscilloscope are one of our most useful tools for exploring the varied nature of sound waves.

The kind of picture we see on the oscilloscope screen is shown in FIGURE 8.7. Note how the characteristic called *frequency*, meaning the number of waves per second, determines the *tone* or *pitch* that we hear.

The difference threshold for frequency varies considerably from one person to another. Some people can easily tell that one tone is higher than another when the frequency difference is less than that between a C and a C♯. Other people have trouble telling whether a C or a D is higher, or even a C or an E. A few people are almost entirely tone deaf. This is why not everyone can be taught to play a musical instrument and why some people persistently sing off key.

AMPLITUDE = LOUDNESS   The drawings in FIGURE 8.8 illustrate the second important characteristic of sound waves, called *amplitude*, which determines the loudness that we hear. It has to be pointed out, however, that amplitude and loudness are not entirely synonymous. If tones of 100 cycles, 1000 cycles, and 10,000 cycles are sounded at exactly the same amplitude and therefore

FIGURE 8.6

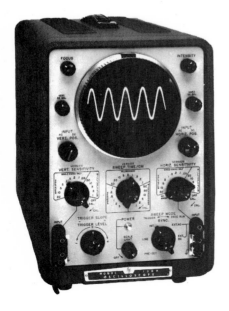

Turning Sound Waves into Pictures   Sound waves picked up by a microphone are converted into electric currents and fed into an *oscilloscope*, which has a screen similar to a television screen, where "pictures" of the waves can be studied.

FIGURE **8.7**

How Sound Varies in Frequency

A pure tone of middle C would look like this on the oscilloscope screen. As the air is compressed the line rises; then the line drops back to the base line and continues downward as the air expands. A single cycle of the curve is shown in color on the graph. For middle C, 256 of these cycles flash across the oscilloscope screen every second; in other words the *frequency* of the sound wave for middle C is 256 cycles per second.

The C above middle C, sounded at exactly the same degree of loudness, would look like this. Here the waves flash across the screen exactly twice as fast, for the frequency of the C above middle C is 512 cycles per second. Thus the oscilloscope screen demonstrates that the higher the frequency of the sound waves, the higher the pitch we hear. The height of the waves, however, remains the same.

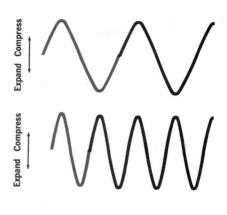

FIGURE **8.8**   *How Sound Varies in Amplitide*

Here again is the oscilloscope picture of a pure tone of middle C, sounded as before in FIGURE 8.7. A single cycle is shown in color.

Here the same tone is sounded with double the force. The frequency of the wave remains the same, but it is now twice as high as before. The height of the waves is called their *amplitude,* and the oscilloscope screen demonstrates that it is the amplitude of the waves that determines how loud they sound to our ears.

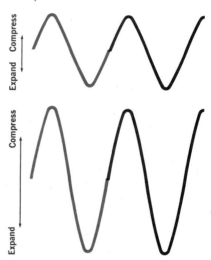

seem exactly the same in volume to the oscilloscope, to our ears the middle tone sounds much louder than the high tone, and the high tone sounds louder than the low tone. The absolute threshold of hearing follows the same pattern. We can hear small amplitudes at 1000 cycles that we could not hear at 10,000 cycles and can hear amplitudes at 10,000 cycles that we could not hear at 100 cycles.

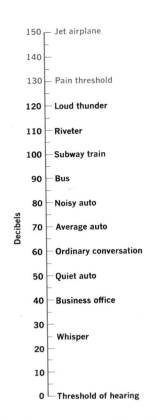

Decibel Scale of Loudness The zero point on the decibel scale is set at the absolute threshold of hearing, and from there the readings go up to the neighborhood of 60 decibels for the sound of ordinary conversation, around 120 for a clap of thunder, and 150 for a jet airplane engine. (3,4)

These last facts raise an interesting question. If our sense of hearing is least sensitive of all to very low tones, why is such a low tone used for foghorns? The answer is that sound waves of low frequency travel much farther than waves of high frequency. High frequency waves are absorbed much faster by the air through which they travel and by any objects that get in their way, while low frequency waves travel on and on. The next time you hear a band playing in the distance—as when a parade is approaching or when you are driving toward a football stadium—notice that it is the tubas you hear rather than the flutes.

A familiar measure of amplitude is the *decibel;* the decibel scale is shown in FIGURE 8.9. You will note, of course, that this is not an absolute scale; a clap of thunder at 120 decibels is far more than twice as loud as conversation at 60 decibels. But it is an ingenious scale (of the type mathematicians call logarithmic) that condenses the entire range of possible amplitudes of sound into meaningful numbers. Sound-sensitive devices that give readings expressed in decibels can be used to measure everything from the applause at television shows to the effectiveness of a sound-absorbent ceiling in reducing the noise level in a business office. An absolute scale of amplitude would have to use numbers going all the way up to 500,000, for the smallest amplitude we can hear is just about 1/500,000 as great as the largest amplitude.

Very loud noises, of course, are extremely unpleasant and eventually reach the point where they actually cause pain. Sounds with a decibel rating of 80 or more are generally unpleasant, and those with a rating of 130 or more are painful.

COMPLEXITY = TIMBRE   In the previous diagrams of sound waves as they are seen on the oscilloscope screen, we have been showing pure tones. In fact, however, pure tones do not exist outside sound laboratories; the closest thing to a pure tone, in real-life situations, is the sound made by that very simple musical instrument, the flute.

The sound waves that actually reach our ears have a third characteristic, in addition to frequency and amplitude, that is called *complexity*. When you strike that middle C on the piano, as has been mentioned, the string vibrates at a frequency of 256 cycles a second, creating its characteristic pitch. However, it also vibrates in other and more complicated ways. Each half of the string vibrates separately, at a rate of 512 cycles a second. Each third of the string vibrates, at a rate of 768 cycles a second. And each quarter of the string also vibrates, at a rate of 1024 cycles a second. These additional vibrations are called *overtones*. They have less amplitude than the fundamental tone, but they play an important role in changing the shape of the sound wave that comes from the piano.

The complexity of the sound wave determines what is called its *timbre*. Each musical instrument has its characteristic pattern of overtones, and the note of middle C struck on a piano therefore has a noticeably different timbre from the middle C of a violin or a clarinet. Timbre, as well as pitch, helps account for the ease with which we distinguish one voice from another.

The complexity of sound waves and the resulting sensation of timbre also account for the fact that modern high-fidelity records and record players sound so far superior to the old 78 rpm equipment. The old records reproduced tones of 100 to 5000 cycles per second; thus they faithfully reproduced most of the fundamental tones that come from musical instruments, which range from about 30 cycles at the bottom of the piano keyboard to the 4608-cycle note at the very top. But they could not reproduce all the overtones. Present-day high-fidelity equipment covers practically the full range of frequencies to which the human ear is sensitive, about 20 to 20,000 cycles per second.

The really avid high-fidelity fan likes to turn the volume way up; he does this, though he does not usually understand why, because of the already noted fact that our absolute threshold of hearing is higher at high frequencies than at middle frequencies. To hear all the overtones and thus fully appreciate the timbre, the volume control has to be set way up. Older listeners have to turn the volume up highest of all, because for some unknown reason the absolute threshold for high frequencies rises each year after a person reaches the age of about twenty-five.

Locating Sounds

You are walking across the campus and someone behind you, where you cannot see him, calls to you. You know immediately that he is toward your left or toward your right; you turn in that direction without even thinking. Or you are sitting in a room, not looking out the window. An automobile passes by and you know without thinking that it is moving from left to right. Something about the sound waves gives the receptors in the ears some important clues about the direction from which the sound is coming and the direction in which it is moving. What are the clues?

Old experiments with the pseudophone point to the answer. As has been mentioned, the pseudophone is a set of earphones that capture the sound waves at the right ear and transfer them over to the left ear and send the sound waves that would ordinarily reach the left ear to the right ear. When a person wears the pseudophone and keeps his eyes closed, the automobile that goes past from left to right sounds as if it is moving in the opposite direction, from right to left.

Obviously the stimulus that arrives at one ear is not the same as the stimulus that arrives at the other ear. Under ordinary circumstances, a sound wave from the left reaches the left ear a tiny fraction of a second before it reaches the right ear. It is in an earlier phase of the curve from compression to expansion of the air. It is also a tiny bit louder than after it has passed around the head to the right ear. And its overtones are slightly different. The clues to locating sounds thus are *timing, phase, amplitude,* and *timbre.*

The Ear and Its Receptors

As can be seen in FIGURE 8.10, the ear has three parts. Sound waves enter the outer ear and set up vibrations in the eardrum. These vibrations then pass through the middle ear, which is an air-filled cavity containing three small bones that conduct and amplify the vibrations, and finally to the inner ear. Here they reach the *cochlea,* a bony structure shaped like a snail's shell, which contains the receptors for hearing.

The cochlea is filled with fluid, and stretched across it, dividing it more or less in half, is a piece of tissue called the *basilar membrane.* Sound waves are transmitted to the *oval window* of the cochlea, where they set up motions of the fluid that bend the basilar membrane. Lying on the membrane is the *organ of Corti,* a collection of hair cells that are the receptors for hearing. The cells are bent as the membrane bends and are thus stimulated to fire.

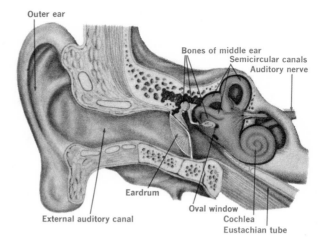

Outer ear

Bones of middle ear
Semicircular canals
Auditory nerve

Eardrum

Oval window

External auditory canal

Cochlea

Eustachian tube

Structure of the Ear   Sound waves reaching the outer ear pass through a short canal across which the eardrum is stretched. Vibrations of the eardrum are then conducted and amplified by the three bones of the middle ear, the last of which connects to the *oval window* of the *cochlea*. The receptors for hearing lie in the cochlea. The *Eustachian tube* connects with the air passages of the mouth and nose and keeps the air pressure in the middle ear the same as the pressure outside. (It is when this tube is temporarily blocked that we feel a sense of pressure against the eardrum when going up or down in an elevator or airplane.) The *semicircular canals* of the inner ear play no part in hearing but will be discussed later for their role in the sense of equilibrium. (5)

FIGURE 8.10

How Do the Hearing Receptors Work?

Despite many years of experimentation, this subject still has to be approached in the form of a question.

The earliest theory was based on the shape of the basilar membrane, which is very narrow at the end nearest the oval window, gradually gets wider, and reaches its maximum width at the other end. This suggested that the membrane might operate somewhat like a harp, with short "strings" tuned to high frequencies and long "strings" to low frequencies. A high-pitched sound would cause one particular narrow part of the membrane to vibrate, thus firing the hearing receptors at that particular place. A sound pitched a little lower would fire the receptors at a slightly wider place. Our sensation of pitch would depend on which receptors sent their messages to the brain.

More recent study of the inner ear, however, has shown that the basilar membrane does not work at all like a harp. When sound waves are transmitted to the cochlea through the oval window, the entire basilar membrane responds, with some very complicated wavelike motions that move along its length and breadth (6). It is true, however, that these motions sometimes reach

291

their greatest intensity at one part of the basilar membrane and sometimes at another. Apparently the frequency of the sound waves determines which part of the membrane moves the most, and it seems quite possible that our sensation of pitch depends upon which particular part of the membrane receives the most stimulation. This is called the *traveling wave theory* of hearing. There is some evidence that the sensation of pitch also depends, at least at times, on the number of receptors stimulated and on the combined frequency of the nervous impulses that they send to the brain (7).

VISION

One of the first things we learn about sensory stimuli in elementary or high school—without realizing at the time that this is what we are learning—is that there is a great difference between sound waves and light waves. You doubtless remember some of the examples. A boat whistles in the distance, and we see the blast of steam before we hear the sound. We see the lightning flash before we hear the thunder. From these observations we realize that light travels much faster than sound.

Sound waves, as has been mentioned, are alternations of pressure and expansion of the air; they travel at a speed of around 750 miles an hour. Light waves, on the other hand, are pulsations of electromagnetic energy, closely related to such other wavelike forms of energy as cosmic rays, X-rays, radio waves, and electricity. They do not create any motion of the air and indeed can travel through a total vacuum, as they do when light reaches us across the vast expanses of empty space from a star. If you could arrange to make two coins hit together inside a vacuum tube, you would hear no click, because sound waves cannot be formed in a vacuum. But the light waves from a filament inside a vacuum tube shine brightly. They travel at a speed of 186,000 miles a second, the fastest speed known and presumably the fastest possible. (If a light wave could be reflected around the world, it would get back to the starting point in less than one-seventh of a second.)

In the daytime, light waves of such intensity as to illuminate our entire landscape reach us from the burning fires and explosions of the sun. At night, they reach us by reflection from the moon and, at much lower intensities, from the more distant suns that we call stars. Light waves can be produced by burning a candle or by using electricity to heat a light bulb's filament.

The Structure of the Eye

The receptors for the sense of vision lie in a small patch of tissue at the back of each eyeball, called the *retina*. Each retina, if flattened out, would appear as an irregular circle with a diameter of a little less than an inch and a total area of only about three fourths of a square inch—about the size of a quarter.

Yet with these two very small pieces of sensory apparatus we can clearly see the much larger pages of a book such as this and indeed an entire room; from an airplane we can see thousands of square miles of the landscape.

This would be impossible unless the eye, in addition to its receptors, had some sort of equipment for bending light waves and focusing them sharply on the retina, much as a fine camera takes a sharp photograph of a wide sweep of landscape by focusing the light waves on a small piece of film. The structure of the human eye, indeed, greatly resembles a camera. If you have ever taken photographs, particularly with one of the more complicated cameras that must be focused and set before each picture, you will feel right at home with the diagram of the eyeball in FIGURE 8.11, which should be studied in detail before continuing to the next paragraph.

The iris and pupil of the eye resemble the diaphragm at the front of a

A Cross Section of the Eye   Light waves first strike the *cornea*, a transparent bulge in the outer layer of the eyeball. The cornea serves as a sort of preliminary lens, gathering light waves from a much wider field of vision than would be possible if the eyeball merely had a perfectly flat window at the front. The waves then pass through the *pupil*, which is an opening in the *iris*, a circular arrangement of muscles that contract and expand to make the opening smaller in bright light and larger in dim light. (When you look at your eyes in a mirror, the pupil is seen as the dark, almost black circle at the center; the iris is the larger circle around it and contains the pigments that determine eye color.) Behind the pupil lies the transparent *lens*, the shape of which is controlled by the *ciliary muscles*. The lens focuses the light rays on the *retina*, which contains the light-sensitive receptors of the eye; the most sensitive part of the retina is the *fovea*. Messages from the receptors are transmitted to the brain by way of the *optic nerve*, which exits from the back of the eyeball, a little off center. Attached to the eyeball are muscles that enable us to look up, down, and sideways. The space inside the eyeball is filled with a transparent substance, as is the space between the cornea and the iris. (8)

FIGURE 8.11

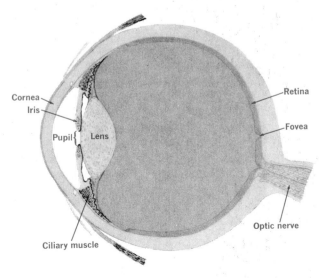

Cornea
Iris
Pupil{ Lens
Ciliary muscle
Retina
Fovea
Optic nerve

camera; when the pupil is opened to its maximum size, it admits about seventeen times as much light as when it is contracted (in photographic terms, "stopped down") to its smallest size. The lens of the eye serves the same purpose as the lens of a camera but in a way that would not be possible with even the most carefully designed piece of glass. The lens of a camera has to be moved forward and backward to focus on nearby or faraway objects. The lens of the eye remains stationary but changes shape. The ciliary muscles flatten it out to bring faraway objects into focus and squeeze it into a thicker shape to focus on nearby objects.

Any experienced photographer would tell you that the lens of an expensive camera is at least as sharp as the lens of the human eye and that the camera diaphragm has a much wider range than the iris. But a comparison of the very best camera film to the retina is something else again. It takes two different kinds of camera film to take pictures in color and in black and white. The retina, however, does both jobs at once; it is sensitive both to colors and to black and white. Moreover, the retina is sensitive to very low intensities of light that would not register at all on photographic film and at the same time it can function under very high intensities of light that would completely burn out a photographic film. Most important of all, it responds continuously, without any winding from one frame to the next. At this instant you see these words on the page; if you raise your eyes slightly you immediately see the wall of the room; if you shift your eyes again you look out the window and see the landscape—all in one continuous and uninterrupted series of visual sensations. In photographic terms, the retina is a highly versatile "film" capable of constantly renewing itself.

THE RECEPTORS OF THE EYE   Packed into the small area of each retina are about 125,000,000 receptors. Most of them are rather long and narrow in shape, a fact that has given them the name *rods*. About 5 percent of the receptors are somewhat thicker and are tapered; these are called *cones*. The rods are the receptors for light intensity, especially low intensities, providing sensations of white, gray, and black but not of color. The cones are the color receptors, although they too are sensitive to differing light intensity.

The cones are most numerous toward the center of the retina; indeed there is one small area at the very center, called the *fovea*, that contains only cones, packed together more tightly than anywhere else. The fovea is the most sensitive part of the retina. When we read or do anything else that requires a very clear image, we manage to look at the object in such a way that its light waves fall on the fovea.

The manner in which light waves stimulate the receptors of the retina was discovered many years ago when physiologists managed to extract a substance known as *visual purple* from the rods. Visual purple is highly sensitive to light, which bleaches it at a rate depending upon the intensity and wave length. It is generally accepted that light waves striking the retina act directly upon the visual purple and that chemical changes in the visual purple then cause the rods to fire (9).

More recently, research workers have reported finding substances somewhat akin to visual purple in the cones; one of these substances appears to be most sensitive to red light, a second to green light, and a third to blue. Moreover, some extremely delicate experiments with individual receptors in the eyes of animals have indicated that some cones have a special sensitivity to red, others to green, and still others to blue (10). These facts seem to bear out the *Young-Helmholtz theory*, which has been widely accepted for many years. Young and Helmholtz noted that the entire range of hues that we see can be produced by combining red, green, and blue (as will be explained later) and therefore speculated that there must be three kinds of cones differentially sensitive to these wave lengths.

It must be noted, however, that the receptors in the retina, when they are fired, discharge their messages into a highly elaborate network of very short nerve fibers at the back of the retina, as shown in FIGURE 8.12. Messages from the cones in the fovea have their own individual routes to the optic nerve and thence to the brain; but most of the cones outside the fovea, and the rods, share a route to the brain with other receptors. Thus the network shown in FIGURE 8.12 serves partly to funnel the messages from the 125,000,000 receptors in the retina to approximately 1,000,000 fibers in the optic nerve. But the network also makes possible all kinds of cross-stimulation between nerve fibers, in which one nerve impulse can be piled on top of another impulse or can cancel it out. The messages that leave this network for the brain travel as if in two separate channels, one carrying information for red and green, the other for blue and yellow. This fact is reminiscent of another view of color vision called the *Hering theory;* it was Hering's belief that the eye had cones that produced the sensation of red when they acted in one direction and of green when they acted in the opposite way, and also cones that produced blue at times and yellow at times. Hering was probably wrong about the cones themselves but right in terms of the total pattern of nervous impulses set up in the network at the back of the retina.

At the point where the optic nerve exits from the eyeball it creates a small gap in the retina; there are no rods or cones at this point. The area is almost completely insensitive to light and is therefore known as the *blind spot.* We are never aware of this blind spot in ordinary life, but you can discover it by examining FIGURE 8.13.

WHY WE WEAR GLASSES   Everybody has heard the phrase *20/20 vision.* A person with 20/20 vision, sitting in a chair 20 feet away from an eye chart, can distinguish as many letters on the chart as can the normal person. Some people have above normal vision; those who can distinguish letters from 30

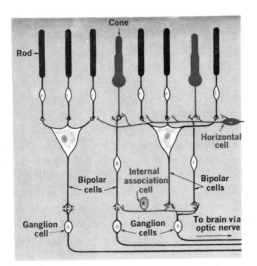

FIGURE 8.12

The Retina's Rich Network of Nerves This is a simplified diagram of the elaborate network of nerves through which messages from the rods and cones of the retina are transmitted to the optic nerve and thence to the brain. The cone at the center, like all cones in the fovea, has its own individual and direct route, through a tiny *bipolar cell*. The rods and also the cones outside the fovea send their messages to bipolar cells that have several endings and thus receive messages from several receptors. The receptors and the bipolar cells are also interconnected through nerves known as *horizontal cells* and *internal association cells*. When you remember that there are about 125,000,000 rods and cones in each retina, constantly being fired by light waves and discharging their messages into this kind of network, you can appreciate the very complicated pattern of nervous activity that goes on at the back of the retina and the wide variety of messages that can then be transmitted through the fibers of the optic nerve. (11)

feet away that the average person can see only at 20 feet, for example, are said to have 30/20 vision. Many people are below normal; they may for example be able to distinguish only as many letters at 20 feet away from the chart as the average person sees from 40 feet, in which case they are said to have 20/40 vision.

FIGURE 8.13

A Demonstration of the Blind Spot Hold the book about a foot in front of you, close your right eye, and look at the face on the right. Now move the book slowly closer. When the image of the cat at the left falls on the blind spot of your left eye, it will disappear. To demonstrate the blind spot of the right eye, repeat with the left eye closed and your gaze concentrated on the cat at the left.

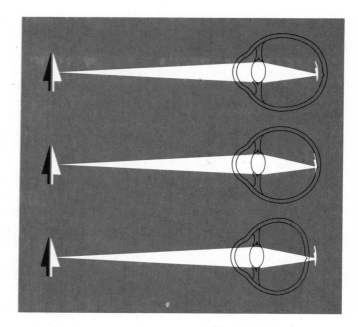

The Normal and Defective Eyeball   The eyeball in the middle, shaped
like an almost perfect sphere, is the normal eyeball, in which light waves
from both near and far can be focused sharply on the retina. The nearsighted eyeball (*top*) is too long from front to back; the lens can focus
nearby objects on the retina but cannot flatten enough for distant objects,
the images of which are focused at a point in front of the retina. The
farsighted eyeball (*bottom*) is too short; the lens can focus faraway
objects on the retina but cannot bulge enough for nearby objects, the
images of which are focused at a point behind the retina.   **FIGURE 8.14**

Most defects of vision are caused by irregularities in the shape of the
eyeball, as shown in FIGURE 8.14. Nearsighted people do all right at reading
and with other close-up objects but need glasses to help bring faraway objects
into better focus. Farsighted people can see all right at a distance but need
glasses to help bring nearby objects into better focus. There is also a defect
known as *astigmatism,* not shown in FIGURE 8.14, caused by irregularities
in the shape of the cornea or lens that bend some of the incoming light waves
into a distorted pattern. Astigmatism can also be corrected with glasses.

Most people over the age of forty-five have to use glasses for reading.
The explanation is that the lens of the eye starts to harden gradually, beginning almost at birth and continuing constantly as we grow older. By the
mid-forties the lens has grown so hard that the ciliary muscles can no longer
squeeze it into as large a bulge as is required for the sharp focusing of a
nearby object such as a book, and even the normal eye now needs the kind
of help that the farsighted eye has needed all along.

Visual Adaptation

Everybody knows, from everyday experience, that the eyes can function under an extremely wide range of illumination. For example, you are walking down a street in the glare of the summer sun; then you enter a moving picture theater where there is hardly any light at all. At first the inside of the theater seems pitch-black, and you have trouble finding your way down the aisle and into an empty seat. But after a while, as your eyes get used to the dark, you find that you can clearly see the aisles, the seats, and the people around you—so well that if you happen to have sat down next to a friend you will easily recognize him.

During about the first ten minutes of adjusting to the dark, we see with the cones. Then they finish adapting as much as they can, and the rods take over, continuing to adapt until they reach their own much lower absolute threshold after about an hour. At this point, the eyes are about 100,000 times more sensitive to light than they were in the bright sunlight.

One proof that the rods are much more sensitive then the cones to low intensities of light is the fact that we do not see colors in a dimly lighted theater—nothing but shades of gray. Another proof can be established by finding a very dim star in the heavens at night. If you look directly at the star, so that the light waves fall on the cones in the fovea, the star will disappear. But if you glance a little to the side, so that the star's light waves fall on a part of the retina supplied with rods, the star will reappear.

As was mentioned earlier, all sensory receptors adapt to a steady intensity of stimulation and eventually stop responding. Yet, no matter how hard we stare at something, it never disappears from view. While our eyes are open our field of vision never goes blank. Does this mean that the rods and cones are an exception to the rule and never stop responding to a stimulus?

No, the rods and cones are not an exception. They do adapt and stop firing. The reason we are not aware of the fact is that our eyes are constantly moving. As you read this book, for example, you gaze first at a word or two at the beginning of the line; then your eyes "jump" to the next word or words and so on until you have reached the end of the line, when they jump to the start of the next line. In a line of print the width of this one, your eyes make five to fifteen jumps and stops. When you look at a landscape or even a fairly simple photograph, your eyes jump from point to point, as shown in FIGURE 8.15, at the rate of three to four jumps a second. Besides these jumps, the eyes also make tiny but rapid movements, like very fast pendulum swings, at the rate of 30 to 100 per second.

These eye movements constantly shift the incoming light waves from one part of the retina to another, so that the stimulus for each rod and cone does not long remain the same. Moreover, each time you blink your eyelids you give the entire retina a brief rest.

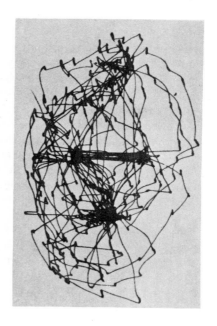

FIGURE 8.15

A Pattern of Eye Movements   The pattern of lines was made by bouncing a light beam off the white of the eye of a man looking at the photograph of the girl, thus recording his eye movements. Note how many of the movements took place and how they trace all the important elements of the photograph.

With laboratory equipment using an arrangement of mirrors and lenses, experimenters have managed to keep an image falling on exactly the same group of rods and cones despite eye movements; the equipment is so designed that every time the eyeball moves the image moves with it. These experiments have demonstrated that the receptors of the eye adapt and stop firing rather quickly. A fine line viewed through such an apparatus, for example, seems to disappear within a few seconds (12). Another investigator has obtained the same results with a sort of "slide projector" so tiny that it can be mounted directly on the cornea, where it throws its picture on the same part of the retina no matter how much the subject moves his eyes (13).

Eye Movements

The pattern of eye movements shown in FIGURE 8.15 demonstrates one very important way in which the human eye differs completely from a camera. You can point a camera at a landscape and within a fraction of a second make a photographic record of everything that is in that landscape; you can study it later and count how many horses and cows are in the picture, how many trees shade the farmhouse, how many windows the house has. If one thinks of the film in terms of human attributes, it "remembers" everything.

The next time somebody is driving you through the countryside, close your eyes as the automobile goes over the top of a hill, open them, take a quick look at the new landscape that spreads out in front of you, close them again—and discover for yourself how little your eyes have really told you about that landscape. Perhaps you know that you saw some horses and cows —but how many? Were they moving or grazing? How many houses did you see? What color were they? Did the road ahead of you curve to the right or to the left?

You will probably be surprised to realize how few such questions you can answer; you thought you saw the landscape, but you actually saw very little of it. This is because your eyes did not have time to make the kind of movements shown in FIGURE 8.15.

Our eyes never give us a single, unified, complete picture, as does a photographic film. As FIGURE 8.15 indicates, they receive an impression of one part of the scene in front of us, then another, and another, on and on until we have seen the whole as a succession of many different parts. We might compare the process to the creation of a mosaic. The receptors in the retina fire off a message about one small piece of the mosaic, then another. The visual centers of the brain, probably with the help of the network of nerves at the back of the retina, then put the pieces together into a unity. Study of the structure of the eyeball and of the rods and cones of the retina tells us many interesting and important things, but in the last analysis these represent only the mechanics of vision. The ultimate nature of the seeing process, like life itself, is still a mystery about which we can only speculate and marvel.

On the other hand, research into eye movements has had one very practical result. It has shown how people who are slow readers—a great handicap in learning and in the enjoyment of literature—can learn to read much faster.

As FIGURE 8.16 shows, reading speed depends upon the number of eye movements; the fewer jumps you make per line, the faster you read. The fast reader's secret is that he takes in a larger number of syllables or words at each glance and thus requires fewer jumps. Fortunately this skill can be learned, at least within limits.

The basic method of developing reading speed is to practice reading as fast as you can without losing all sense of what the words mean. The best way to do it is with the help of a specialist in this kind of teaching. But you may even be able to increase your speed yourself, if you can persuade a friend to time you and question you afterward to make sure you have understood the words. Choose something that is easy to read: a sports story in

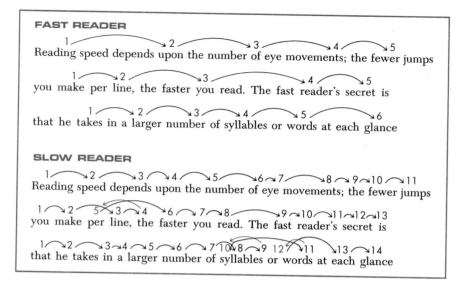

FAST READER

Reading speed depends upon the number of eye movements; the fewer jumps

you make per line, the faster you read. The fast reader's secret is

that he takes in a larger number of syllables or words at each glance

SLOW READER

Reading speed depends upon the number of eye movements; the fewer jumps

you make per line, the faster you read. The fast reader's secret is

that he takes in a larger number of syllables or words at each glance

Eye Movements of Fast and Slow Readers   A reader's eyes jump from point to point along a printed line as indicated by the arrows, stopping at spots indicated by the numbers. The fast reader makes few jumps, taking in a considerable amount of the printed line at each pause. The slow reader makes many jumps and sometimes, as indicated by the colored lines and numbers, goes backward instead of proceeding forward.

FIGURE 8.16

the newspaper, a short story in a magazine. Have your friend tell you when to start and stop you after exactly a minute. Push yourself as hard as you can, even if you feel that you are in danger of losing the sense of what you are reading. (Usually you will be surprised to find that increasing your speed does not lessen your comprehension at all and indeed often improves it.) Practice like this a few times a day, keeping track of the number of words you read per minute while still making sense of them, and, unless you were a fast reader to begin with, you should find the total going up. If you were a slow reader at the start, you may eventually find yourself reading three or four times faster or even more.

The Physical Nature of Light

Although light waves are very different from sound waves, there is a close parallel in the way the two kinds of waves produce sensations. Sound waves, it will be remembered, vary only in frequency, amplitude, and complexity, yet variations in these three characteristics produce a wide range of pitch, loudness, and timbre. Light waves also have three variables. They vary in *wave length,* which is the distance between the peaks of the waves. (The shortest light waves are about 16/1,000,000 inch long; the longest are about twice that length.) They vary in *intensity,* which is the amount of energy they possess. And they vary in *complexity*—that is to say, the light that reaches our eyes may be composed of waves of only a few different lengths or it may be composed of many lengths. As in the case of sound, these three differences account for the range of sensations produced by light waves.

WAVE LENGTH = HUE   Just as the frequency of the sound wave determines its pitch, so does the wave length of the light wave determine its *hue*—the scientific name for the characteristic usually called color. The hues range from violet, for the shortest of light waves, to red, for the longest. They include what are ordinarily called "all the colors of the rainbow." But hue is the proper term for them because many of the sensations ordinarily described as colors depend upon other factors than wave length, as will be noted a little later.

As is indicated in PLATE I°, light that appears white to us is actually a mixture of the wave lengths of all the hues. When a white light such as a sunbeam is broken down into its components, as by the prism in PLATE I, the wave lengths are separated and the result is a *spectrum* of all the wave lengths and corresponding hues from shortest to longest.

INTENSITY = BRIGHTNESS   The harder we strike a piano key, the more amplitude we produce in the sound wave and the louder the sound we hear. In vision, the strength of the light wave is called the intensity, and the sensation that the intensity produces is called *brightness.* A 100-watt electric light bulb produces light waves of stronger intensity than does a 50-watt bulb and thus looks brighter. Or, much as a band sounds louder when it is close than when it is far away, the light from the sun looks much brighter than the light from other, more distant stars, even though some are much bigger.

Just as was noted for hearing, however, the intensity of light waves does not fully account for all the degrees of brightness we see. The cones are most sensitive to the green and yellow at the middle of the spectrum, and under good illumination these hues look brighter than violets or reds of equal intensity.

COMPLEXITY = SATURATION   The third way in which light waves vary is illustrated in PLATE II. Note that in the squares of PLATE II the hue of red does not change. Nor does the brightness. But as more and more gray is added—thus mixing in wave lengths of all the other hues—the red that we see becomes what might be called "less red," or "duller," or "muddier."

° The color plates can be found between pages 306 and 307 in this chapter.

This characteristic of the visual stimulus is called *saturation*, which can be defined as the amount of pure hue present as compared to the amount of other wave lengths mixed in. You will note that again there is a parallel of sorts with hearing. In hearing, the complexity of the sound wave determines timbre. In vision, the complexity of the mixture of light waves determines saturation.

Mixing the Hues

Every school child who owns a paint set knows that, if you have no green, you can produce it by combining blue and yellow, but every school child is wrong. If you combine the wave length of blue with the wave length of yellow, you do not get green at all. Until fairly recently, as a matter of fact, nobody had ever combined any of the various hues. You cannot do this with paint, for the following reason.

As was demonstrated in PLATE I, the white light from the sun, which illuminates our world by day, is a combination of all the wave lengths of the spectrum. So is the artificial light by which we see at night, though in an imperfect way. (Candlelight and electric light are both yellowish.) The reason that black paint looks black is that it absorbs nearly all the waves, of all lengths, and reflects almost no waves at all back to our eyes. Blue paint looks blue because it absorbs most of the wave lengths except those in and around the blue portion of the spectrum, including, since no paint is a pure blue, some of the green waves. Yellow paint absorbs most of the waves except those in and around the yellow part of the spectrum, including some of the green waves. When you add blue and yellow paint together, you get a mixture that now absorbs all the wave lengths of the spectrum except the greenish ones that both the paints happen to reflect. But this is not *adding* light waves; it is more like *subtracting* them.

It was not until the invention of some modern devices that the addition of one light wave to another became possible. One of these devices is the color filter, shown in PLATE III, which permits only waves of a certain length to get through. With two slide projectors equipped with two different kinds of filters, hues of two wave lengths can be thrown on the same white screen and thus mixed. Another device is the color wheel, on which papers of different hue can be rotated so fast that they fuse into a single image on the retina. Even these devices are not completely accurate, for it is almost impossible to make a filter or colored paper that transmits only one pure frequency or wave length. But the devices do actually add different wave lengths together, with sufficient accuracy to disclose some interesting facts about color mixtures and how our eyes respond to them.

Starting at the top of PLATE III, note what happens when the wave length of violet, taken from the shortest end of the spectrum, is mixed with the wave length of red, taken from the longest end of the spectrum. The result is a purple. For some unknown reason, it looks like a hue in its own right, even though it can be produced only by a mixture of wave lengths.

Mixing blue and green gives a result that seems to have some of the characteristics of each. (The same is true for a mixture of green and yellow.)

When red and green are mixed, the result is yellow.

When blue-violet is mixed with yellow, the result is not the green that the school child with his paint set would expect—but a hueless and neutral gray.

Let us now try to find a hue that we can combine with green to produce a gray. Search where we will among the wave lengths of the spectrum, we cannot find such a hue. The only way we can neutralize green into gray is shown by the final example in PLATE III. It must be combined with the purple produced by combining violet and red.

These observations are summarized in PLATE IV. From this circle, composed partly from nature's own spectrum of wave lengths and hues and partly from the man-made purples, we can predict what will happen when any two hues are mixed. Hues opposite each other on the circle combine into a neutral gray and are known as *complementary hues*. Any two hues not opposite each other will mix into a hue midway between them.

But the circular guide is just another of the discoveries that ask more questions than they answer. When we mix a violet wave length with a green wave length, we do not fool the prism, which can still separate the two wave lengths. But our eyes see the combination as a greenish-bluish hue that looks exactly the same as a certain wave length of light lying midway between the two hues we have mixed.

Color Blindness

Turn now to PLATE V, take a quick look at the two circles, note the numbers you see there if any, and then read the caption.

Many students have had the surprise of their lives when they came to a test like this for color blindness. Perhaps it happened to you. If not and you yourself passed the test, then you might try showing the test to your friends. Since color blindness is a much more common visual defect than is generally supposed, you should soon come to one who fails the test and will have an experience that is worth going to some trouble to obtain. It seems almost unbelievable that you can look at the circle and clearly see one number, while a friend clearly sees a different number or is absolutely sure that there is no number at all—especially if the friend, as so often happens, has never before suspected that he was color blind and still insists that he can see color just as well as anybody else.

How can a person be color blind and not know it until he takes a test?

Total color blindness, in which the whole world is seen only in shades of gray, like a black-and-white photograph, is extremely rare. In a nation such as the United States, with a population of around 200,000,000, there probably are no more than 5000 people in all who are totally color blind. Also quite rare are people who have normal vision for red and green but have trouble with blues and yellows. These blue-yellow deficiencies seem to be caused by some unusual kind of disease.

The common type of color blindness takes the form of red-green deficiencies; the person who suffers from it has normal vision for yellow and blue but has trouble with reds and greens. It is caused by an inherited defect, the nature of which is not known. The deficiency can range from a total inability to distinguish reds and greens to a weakness that makes it difficult to distinguish them at low saturations or brightnesses.

In real-life situations, the person who suffers from red-green color blindness gets considerable help from other clues. He is helped to distinguish between red and green traffic lights, for example, by the fact that manufacturers of the lights, knowing how common his deficiency is, have used glass that lets through many yellow waves along with the red and many blue waves along with the green. He also has all the clues afforded by variations in brightness and saturation. Moreover, the colors seen in real life are almost never pure hues but instead are mixtures. Grass, although predominantly green, also reflects some yellow and blue wave lengths. A red apple also reflects some yellow and blue, in different proportions from grass. The color-blind person soon learns that the particular mixture of hues, brightness, and saturation that he sees when he looks at grass is called green and that the mixture he sees when he looks at an apple is called red.

Tests such as those in PLATE V eliminate the clues usually afforded by the impurity of the colors ordinarily seen and by brightness and saturation. Thus they reveal deficiencies that might ordinarily never be noticed.

Only about one woman in a thousand suffers from color blindness, but about seven men in a hundred have some form of it. Except in extreme cases it is not much of a handicap. The color-blind person may be unable to appreciate all the beauty of a sunset or of the autumn foliage, but, in a world that provides the normal eye with millions of different visual sensations, the color-blind man can afford to miss some of them.

Afterimages

There is one way in which our visual sense seems to differ from all the other senses. This is illustrated in PLATE VI, and you should experiment with this figure, according to the instructions, before you continue to the next page.

What PLATE VI demonstrates is the phenomenon known as the *afterimage*. As you stare fixedly at the pattern of colors, you provide a prolonged stimulus to the retina. When the stimulus is then withdrawn (as you withdrew it by transferring your gaze to another part of the page), you see an afterimage that is in complementary colors to the original stimulus. If you follow the instructions carefully, the afterimage should be so vivid as to startle you—if not on the first try, at least after a little practice.

Presumably various parts of the retina are constantly sending afterimages to the brain, but ordinarily they are so faint and fleeting that we do not notice them. The experiment in PLATE VI provides a stronger afterimage than usual, because you fix your gaze on the color pattern rather than making your usual constant eye movements. The experiment also enables you to see the afterimage more clearly, because you then transfer your gaze to an empty space rather than to a space already filled with other patterned stimuli. You can get the same effect anywhere by staring fixedly at a color or a pattern of colors and then quickly transferring your gaze to a blank surface such as a ceiling or a plain gray wall.

In actual fact, although this is difficult to show except under laboratory conditions, there are two afterimages. Immediately after the stimulus is withdrawn you continue to see a *positive afterimage,* in the same color as before. But this quickly vanishes and is replaced by a *negative afterimage,* in which the complementary colors appear. The generally accepted explanation is based on the action of visual purple and the substances sensitive to hue that are believed to be present in the retina. The chemical changes produced in these substances by the light stimulus would presumably continue briefly even after the stimulus is removed. Then an opposite chemical change would occur as the substances "return to normal," so to speak. This change in the opposite direction could serve as the stimulus for sensations of the complementary color.

BODILY MOVEMENT

Exploration of the "five senses" has now been completed, but, as was pointed out earlier, there are two other senses that are less prominent and less obvious but equally important in enabling us to function.

Perhaps the most vital of them is our sense of bodily movement—a sense that most people never even realize they possess. One way of demonstrating the existence and importance of this sense is as follows. Close your eyes and then point a finger straight up toward the ceiling, down toward the floor, off to your due left, and then to your due right; stand up; raise your left knee and touch it with your right hand.

What you have just done may not seem very remarkable; it is something that we take for granted. But think about it for a moment. How did you

Plate I   THE HUES OF THE SPECTRUM

A beam of white light passing through a prism is turned into a *spectrum*. The explanation is that sunlight is a mixture of all the wave lengths to which our eyes are sensitive; the prism, bending each wave length at a slightly different angle, separates the mixture into all the component wave lengths, each of which has its own color or, to use the more scientific term, *hue*. The violets are the shortest wave lengths to which our eyes are sensitive, the reds the longest.

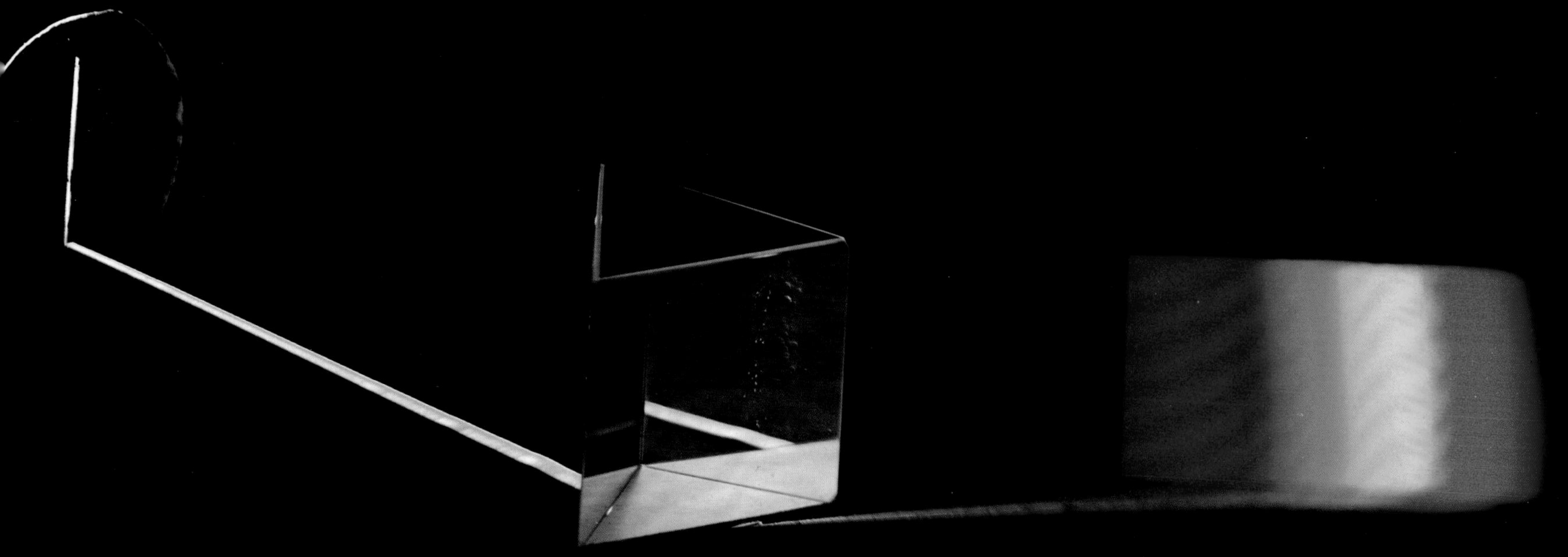

The laws of color mixture can be summarized by bending the spectrum into an incomplete circle, as shown here, and filling in the gap with the purple that is also seen as a very distinct hue. (Purple is a combination of the wave lengths at the red end of the spectrum and the wave lengths at the violet end.) To find what hue a mixture of any two colors will produce, draw a line between them. If the line passes through the center of the circle, the result will be gray. If not, the result will be the hue midway between the two hues being mixed.

Plate V A TEST OF COLOR BLINDNESS

In the circle at left, people with normal color vision see the number 92; in the circle at right, they see a 23. Totally color-blind people see no number at all in either circle. These are two of the ingenious combinations of hues and brightnesses that make up the Dvorine Pseudo-Isochromatic series of color-blindness tests. (14)

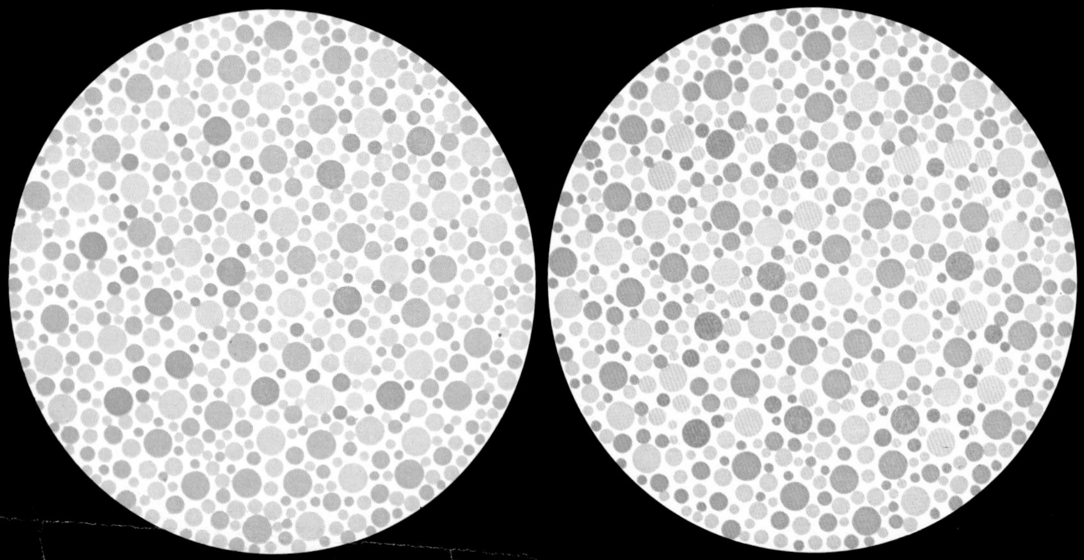

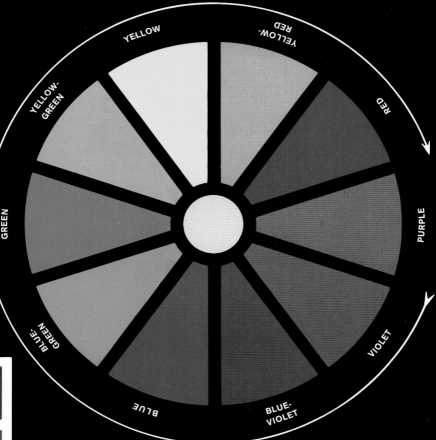

HUES OF THE SPECTRUM

YELLOW-GREEN

GREEN

BLUE-GREEN

BLUE

YELLOW

YELLOW-RED

RED

PURPLE

VIOLET

BLUE-VIOLET

Plate IV A CIRCULAR GUIDE TO THE HUES

Plate II SATURATED VERSUS UNSATURATED COLOR

This series of colors shows what happens if we start with the purest possible red wave length and then gradually add more and more gray of equal brightness. The square at the extreme left is said to be completely saturated. The square at the extreme right is the least saturated red that can be distinguished from pure gray.

Plate III COLOR MIXTURE

When light waves are combined by projecting filtered light waves onto a screen, some of the results are these. One projector provides the hue at left, the other the hue at right. The mixture of the two hues is in the center. For an explanation, see Plate IV and the text.

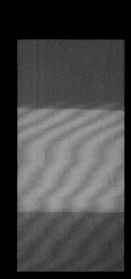

Plate VI   THE VISUAL AFTERIMAGE

The principle of the afterimage produces a startling effect in this modern paint-ing. Look at the top rectangle for about half a minute, fixing your gaze on the white spot in the center. Then shift your eyes quickly to concentrate on the dark spot in the lower rectangle. (This painting, ''Flags,'' is by Jasper Johns. Oil on canvas with raised canvas, 1965. Collection: the artist.)

know where your arm was to begin with, and how did you know when you had moved it so that your finger was pointing up, down, or to the sides? How did you know where your left knee was and how to move your right hand to touch it?

None of your "five senses" helped you do this; they had no way of telling you about the position of your arms and legs and could only verify the fact, through the pressure receptors of the skin, that you had actually succeeded in finding and touching your knee. You could never have done what you did without the sense of bodily movement, which keeps us constantly informed of the position and movement of our muscles and bones.

The receptors for the sense of bodily movement are nerve endings found in three parts of the body. The first are in the muscles, and they are stimulated when the muscle stretches. The second are in the tendons that connect our muscles to our bones; they are stimulated when the muscle contracts, putting pressure on the tendon. The third, and apparently most important of all, are in the linings of the joints between our bones, and they are stimulated by movement of the joint.

Without these receptors we would not be able to walk without great difficulty; we would have to keep constant watch with our eyes to help guide the motions of our legs and feet. Even with the help of our eyes we could never perform the rapid and closely coordinated movements required to dance or to play baseball.

EQUILIBRIUM

When we walk, we walk erect, not at an angle to the ground; when we lose our footing and start to fall, we catch our balance through reflex action, without even thinking about it. Standing in a closed elevator and unable to see any motion, we nonetheless know when we start to move and whether we are moving up or down; and we also know when we stop. If we sat blindfolded in a totally silent swivel chair, we would know immediately when someone began to rotate the chair.

All these facts depend upon our sense of equilibrium, the receptors for which are in the inner ear. If you look back at FIGURE 8.10, you will note that the cochlea, containing the receptors for hearing, is only one part of the inner ear. The rest of the inner ear is made up of three *semicircular canals,* extending out from a *vestibule.* The canals are filled with liquid, and the liquid in one or more of the canals is set into motion any time we move in any direction whatever. The movement of the liquid stimulates hairlike receptors with which the canals are equipped. In the vestibule, which is also filled with liquid, the hairlike receptors are matted together and tiny pieces of stonelike crystal are embedded in the mattings. The little crystals put pressure on the receptor cells in the direction of the force of gravity and keep us oriented to an upright position even when we are not moving. Between them, the receptors of the canals and the receptors of the vestibule are constantly aware of the position of the head and any change in position, thus providing the messages needed to keep us in balance and oriented to the force of gravity. The messages operate by reflex action to produce the muscular movements required to preserve our equilibrium.

Perhaps the most dramatic evidence of how the sense of equilibrium operates is an old experiment involving a lobster—chosen because its equivalent of the human inner ear is readily accessible when the lobster sheds its shell. For the stones that are the lobster's equivalent of the crystals in the human vestibule the experimenters substituted iron filings. These worked just as well as the stones, and the lobster had no problem of equilibrium. But when a magnet was placed above the lobster, exerting a stronger upward force on the iron filings than the downward force of gravity, the lobster turned right over on its back.

SUMMARY

1. The role of the senses in human behavior is to keep us informed about the kind of world we live in and especially how the world around us is changing from moment to moment.

2. The two essentials of sensation are a *stimulus* (any form of energy capable of exciting the nervous system) and a *receptor* (a nerve ending capable of responding to a particular stimulus).

3. To cause a receptor to fire, a stimulus must be of an energy above the *absolute threshold* of the receptor, and a change in stimulus must be above the *difference threshold*. The thresholds are affected by *adaptation*, which is the tendency of all receptors to stop responding to a continued level of stimulus.

4. Taste receptors are sensitive only to sweet, salt, sour, and bitter. Most of what we call "taste" depends on the sense of smell.

5. The receptors for smell appear, according to some recent investigators, to be sensitive to seven basic classes of molecules producing seven basic odors, which are then combined into all our various sensations of smell.

6. The skin has patterns of four kinds of spots—presumably related to nerve endings immediately beneath or near the spots—sensitive to pressure, pain, warmth, and cold. A temperature over 110 degrees Fahrenheit stimulates both warmth and cold spots and produces the sensation of heat.

7. The stimulus for hearing is sound waves, which are alternations of pressure and expansion in the air. Sound waves vary in *frequency, amplitude,*

and *complexity*. The frequency determines the *pitch* we hear; the amplitude determines the *loudness* (although not entirely), and the complexity determines the *timbre*.

8. Our ability to tell whether a sound is coming from the left or right is based on the fact that the sound wave arrives at one ear before the other ear. When it arrives at the second ear, the wave is slightly different in *timing, phase, amplitude,* and *timbre*.

9. Sound waves strike the eardrum and are amplified and conducted by the bones of the middle ear to the *cochlea* of the inner ear, where they set up complicated wavelike motions of the *basilar membrane*. The receptors for hearing are the hairlike cells of the *organ of Corti*, lying on the basilar membrane; these cells are stimulated by motion of the membrane.

10. The stimulus for vision is light waves, a pulsating form of electromagnetic energy closely related to cosmic rays, X-rays, radio waves, and electricity. Light waves enter the eyeball through the transparent *cornea* and the *iris* and then pass through a transparent *lens*, which is changed in shape by the *ciliary muscles* to focus the waves sharply on the *retina* at the back of the eyeball. The receptors for vision are nerve endings in the retina called *rods* and *cones*.

11. The rods are sensitive only to differences in light intensity (and thus provide sensations of white, gray, and black); the cones to both light intensity and color. The rods contain *visual purple*, a substance that is bleached by light; presumably it is the chemical reaction of the visual purple to light that causes the rods to fire. The cones apparently contain substances that are chemically sensitive to blue, red, or green.

12. One outstanding quality of the human eye is the wide range of intensities to which it is sensitive. When the eye is completely adjusted to the dark, its absolute threshold declines to the point where it will respond to a stimulus with only 1/100,000 of the intensity required to cause a response under sunlight conditions. At low intensities only the rods function, and color vision is absent. The cones have a much higher absolute threshold.

13. Under ordinary circumstances, our eyes make a rapid and constant series of movements, focusing on one part of the field of vision, then jumping to another. These fragmentary "pictures" or pieces of mosaic are then put together, by the brain and presumably also by the elaborate network of connecting nerves at the back of the retina, into a unified pattern, so that we seem to be seeing the entire field of vision as a single whole.

14. In reading, the eye makes a series of jumps from the left of the line to the right, taking in a certain number of syllables or words at each pause. Reading speed can be improved by learning to increase the span taken in at the pauses.

15. Light waves vary in *wave length, intensity,* and *complexity of mixture*.

Wave length determines *hue;* intensity determines *brightness* (although not entirely); and the complexity of the mixture of waves determines *saturation.* White light is a mixture of all the wave lengths, as can be demonstrated by passing it through a prism and obtaining a *spectrum* of the hues.

16. Some degree of color blindness, usually for red-green, is suffered by about 7 percent of men and much less frequently by women. Many color-blind people learn to use such clues as variations in brightness and saturation to make up for their deficiencies and are thus unaware of them.

17. In addition to the "five senses" we ordinarily think of, we have two other important senses. The sense of *bodily movement,* the receptors for which are nerve endings in the muscles, tendons, and joints, keeps us informed of the position of our muscles and bones and is essential for the coordination of such complex movements as walking. The sense of *equilibrium,* the receptors for which are hair cells in the inner ear, keeps us in balance and oriented to such forces as movement and gravity.

18. The stimuli and receptors of the human senses are as follows:

SENSE	STIMULUS	RECEPTOR	SENSATION
Vision	Light waves	Rods and cones of retina	Colors, patterns
Hearing	Sound waves	Hair cells of organ of Corti	Sounds, tones
Skin senses	Mechanical energy, heat	Nerve endings in skin	Pressure, warmth, cold, pain
Smell	Molecules of volatile substances	Nerve endings in olfactory epithelium	Odors (camphor-like, musky, flowery, pepperminty, etc.)
Taste	Molecules of soluble substances	Taste buds of tongue	Flavors (sweet, salt, sour, bitter)
Bodily movement	Mechanical energy	Nerve endings in muscles, tendons, joints	Position and movement of muscles and bones
Equilibrium	Mechanical energy and gravity	Hair cells of semicircular canals and vestibule	Movement in space, pull of gravity

Békésy, G. v. *Experiments in hearing.* New York: McGraw-Hill, 1960.

Evans, R. M. *An introduction to color.* New York: Wiley, 1948.

Geldard, F. A. *The human senses.* New York: Wiley, 1953.

Gregory, R. L. *Eye and brain: the psychology of seeing.* New York: McGraw-Hill, 1966.

Helson, H. *Adaptation-level theory.* New York: Harper & Row, 1964.

Hirsh, I. J. *The measurement of hearing.* New York: McGraw-Hill, 1952.

Judd, D. B. and Wyscecki, G. *Color in business, science, and industry,* 2nd ed. New York: Wiley, 1963.

Mueller, C. G. *Sensory psychology.* Englewood Cliffs, N.J.: Prentice-Hall, 1965.

Teevan, R. C. and Birney, R. C., eds. *Color vision.* Princeton, N.J.: Van Nostrand, 1961.

PART

5

THE MOTIVES AND FEELINGS
THAT UNDERLIE BEHAVIOR

Most of us spend a great deal of our energies pursuing some kind of goal. The goal may be a simple one, such as making an A in a college course or finding time to watch a favorite television show every week. It may be a complicated and long-term goal, such as becoming a nurse or owning one's own business or getting rich. It may be an abstract goal, such as being a good citizen and good parent and leaving the world a better place than we found it. Indeed we may have many goals, some simple and immediate, others complex and long-range.

Closely related to our goals are our day-to-day and minute-to-minute feelings about life, for we generally feel good when we achieve our goals and bad when we fail to achieve them. Depending upon how things are going at the moment, we may feel mildly confident, buoyant, or even elated; on the contrary, we may feel depressed, panicky, or grief-stricken. Usually our feelings take a pattern that is characteristic of us. We may be inclined to be cheerful or pessimistic; our friends may think of us as emotionally stolid or emotionally excitable.

Chapter 9, on motives, discusses the wishes and desires that often direct one person's behavior toward goals far different from those of a person who has acquired different motives. Chapter 10, on emotions, discusses the various kinds of feelings that events in the world can arouse in us—often, again, resulting in individual differences in behavior. Between them, motives and emotions go far to account for and clarify the variety and richness of human personality.

DRIVES

Hunger
Thirst
Sleep
Sex
Other Drives
A Definition of Drive

STIMULUS NEEDS

The Need for Sensory Stimulation
The Need for Stimulus Variability
The Need for Physical Contact

MOTIVES

Certainty
Attachment and Affiliation
Dependency
Independence and Achievement
Social Approval
Escape from Unpleasant Feelings
Hostility
Domination
Living up to Standards
Cognitive Consonance

MOTIVES AND BEHAVIOR

Motivational Dispositions and Aroused Motives
Motive Strengths
Requirements for Behavior
Guessing Another Person's Motives
The Principle of Functional Autonomy

MOTIVES

Of all the words used by the relatively new science of psychology, perhaps the one that has achieved the quickest and widest popularity is *motives*. It is a word heard almost every day in remarks such as: "I wonder what her motive is?" "I don't trust his motives." "I didn't seem to help the situation, but at least my motives were good."

Now that the word has become so popular, everybody feels free—and competent—to analyze the motives of others. We see a young man who spends as much time as possible around girls and has a date nearly every night, and we say that he is "highly sexed," meaning that he has a strong sexual motive. We notice that another young man swears a great deal, even around girls, and we call him "hostile." A young woman is constantly asking her boy friend for help with her studies, and we term her "dependent." Another young woman studies until late every night, and we call her "ambitious."

Motives operate in a much trickier fashion, however, than is generally supposed. Every one of the judgments in the preceding paragraph could be wrong. The young man who dates every night may not have strong sexual motives but merely a desire to impress his friends as a man about town. The young man who swears may do so not out of hostility but out of a sexual motive; he may think that this kind of behavior makes him seem more masculine and therefore more sexually attractive. The young woman who asks her boy friend for help with her studies may also have a sexual motive rather than an urge to be "dependent"; she may feel that the appearance of needing help makes her seem more feminine and attractive. The young woman who studies hard may well be the dependent one; she may be not ambitious but merely afraid of losing the approval of her parents if she fails to get good grades.

It is extremely difficult to judge motives from behavior. As a matter of fact, motives may never result in observable behavior. A man who has been eagerly following the developments in space exploration may have a strong motive to go to the moon. Yet the goal is unattainable for him, and he makes no attempt to attain it. On a more commonplace level, many people talk wistfully about going to Europe yet never try to save the money or make the time for the trip. Many people say they want to write; they have a motive to become a famous author. But they never put a word on paper. People who are strongly motivated by hostility may never show it except in hidden and devious ways.

Though the subject is full of difficulties and confusions, motivation is a key issue in psychology. We are used to thinking in terms of cause and effect. Astronomy tells us *why* the sun rises in the morning and sets at night. Physics tells us *why* a piano sounds different from a saxophone. Chemistry tells us *why* wood burns and iron does not. It is only natural that we should also search for some kind of underlying causes of behavior.

Why do young people—despite discouragements, fatigue, financial problems, and occasional illness—keep going to school year after year? Why do people undertake such awesome projects as building cities or exploring space? Why do people marry, rear families, cooperate with their neighbors, and sometimes quarrel? Why do some women seek a career and others devote themselves to their families? Why do some men strive all their lives to be President and others to have the neatest lawn on the block? Why do people get into trouble and nations go to war?

For many centuries the "why" of behavior was attributed to the human soul, which was thought of in part as a force that initiated, organized, and directed the individual's activities. A number of the early psychologists, on the other hand, believed that the explanation lay in inherited instincts. These men were impressed by the inborn and unlearned tendencies of the robin to build the characteristic nest of its species and of the salmon to migrate from river to ocean and back to the river to spawn. Since man is also an animal, they reasoned, he too must behave in accordance with instincts. William James theorized that there were no less than seventeen powerful human instincts: toward imitation, rivalry, pugnacity, sympathy, hunting, fear, acquisitiveness, constructiveness (the urge to build), play, curiosity, sociability, shyness, secretiveness, cleanliness, jealousy, love, and mother love (1).

It is now known, of course, that human beings have few if any instincts, and the forces inside the human being that often initiate, direct, and organize behavior are instead called motives. Motives take all the forms mentioned by James as instincts and many others; indeed the list of possible human motives seems almost endless.

The definition of a motive is this: *A motive is a desire for a goal that, through learning, has acquired value for the individual.* This desire for a goal often leads the person to learn ways of gratifying the motive. The motive for recognition by others can lead a young boy to improve his skill at football; the motive for a romantic relationship may lead a girl to learn how to flatter a young man without his awareness. Thus the cause of some behavior rests with motives.

In the early weeks of life, before the child has learned to value certain goals, most of his behavior is unlearned, caused by biological drives and certain kinds of stimuli. The infant cries when he is hungry, makes sucking motions when his lips are stimulated, watches a moving light. However, although the biological drives—such as hunger and thirst—initially elicit an unlearned response, with development the child *learns* a new set of behavioral responses to these drives. The five-year-old asks for food when he is hungry or for soda when he is thirsty. Soon he may develop a motive to drink a particular type of soda, even when he is not very thirsty. Thus there is an intimate connection between biological drives and motives, and a discussion of motives can best begin with an explanation of the biological drives.

On the surface, the operation of the drives seems quite simple. We get hungry. Therefore we eat. Once we have eaten enough, we know that we no longer feel hungry. Therefore we stop.

DRIVES

Yet this seemingly obvious sequence of events contains some underlying puzzles. What makes us "get hungry"? How do we know that eating will relieve the feelings of hunger? Why, once we have eaten, do we stop feeling hungry? Why do most of us eat just enough to keep at more or less normal weight, not too thin and not too fat?

Hunger

Common-sense observation tells us that we have hunger pangs and that these pangs come from the stomach; often we can even hear our stomachs growl as if demanding food. In 1934 the experiment shown in FIGURE 9.1. seemed to prove once and for all that the common-sense version of hunger was correct. For a long time the experiment was accepted as the final word on the nature of the hunger drive, and then evidence to the contrary began pouring in. One experimenter operated on a rat and severed all the sensory nerves leading from the stomach to the brain, yet the rat ate as before (3). In another operation the entire stomach of a rat was removed, yet the rat continued to show signs of hunger (4). Cases were reported in which the human stomach had to be removed, without any pronounced effect upon the desire for food (5). A new method was devised for measuring stomach contractions electrically, with electrodes placed on the skin of the abdomen, and this time no particular connection was found between the contractions and feelings of hunger (6). All these new findings indicated that the results of the experiment shown in FIGURE 9.1 were misleading. Presumably the stomach had attempted to digest the balloon, thus setting up an artificial pattern of contractions and "pangs."

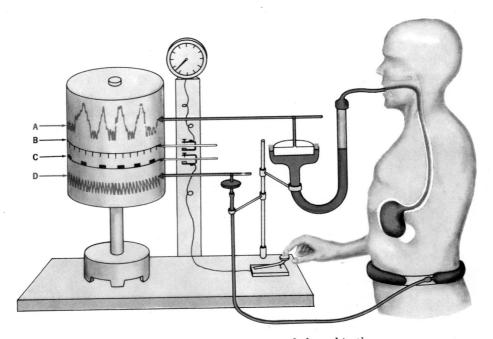

An Experiment with "Hunger Pangs" Contractions of the subject's stomach force air out of a balloon he has swallowed, causing jumps in line A on the recording drum. Line B shows elapsed time. Line C records when the subject presses the telegraph key, as he was instructed to do whenever he felt hunger pangs. Line D is a record of abdominal movements caused by breathing. Note that the recording drum shows the subject feels hungry each time his stomach contracts. But see the text for a warning against drawing false conclusions about the source of hunger sensations. (2)

FIGURE 9.1

It is now believed that the primary basis of the hunger drive rests with the chemical composition of the blood, which changes after a period of not eating. This is indicated by the fact that, when blood from a hungry dog is transferred into the veins of a dog that has just eaten, the well-fed dog starts looking for food again (7). There may also be some sensory clues from the stomach and elsewhere, but these do not appear to be essential.

Changes in the blood caused by lack of food appear to stimulate directly one area in the brain (specifically, in the hypothalamus), and this area seems to control the hunger drive and the sensations it arouses. When the area is surgically destroyed, an animal loses practically all interest in eating (8). Another nearby area seems to be responsible for satiation; when this area is destroyed, an animal eats constantly and becomes grossly fat (9).

Food itself—not the mere act of eating—is the goal of the hunger drive. In one experiment a rat received an injection of milk directly into the stomach if it went to one arm of a T-shaped maze, an injection of salt solution if it went to the other arm. The rat soon learned to prefer the arm in which it received the milk injection (10). In another experiment a tube was attached to the ear of a rabbit so that fluids could be pumped directly into the blood stream. In the rabbit's cage were three plates. If it sat on one plate, salt solution was pumped into the blood stream. On the second plate it received artificially sweetened water with no food value. On the third it received a solution of sugar. After a while the rabbit began spending most of its time on the plate where it received the sugar (11). The drawing in FIGURE 9.2 illustrates a similar experiment.

Aside from man and the animals he has domesticated, few animals tend to become overly fat. Their hunger drive operates in such a manner as to give them the amount of calories they need to keep their body weight constant. Moreover, they develop hungers for the specific kinds of foods they need. They tend to eat a balanced diet of carbohydrates, proteins, fats, minerals, and vitamins. If they have been deprived of any of these substances for a period of time, they will eat it in preference to anything else, even if they are otherwise fully satiated with food. These regulatory mechanisms also appear to be related to blood chemistry.

Hunger, of course, is one of the most powerful of the drives. A hungry animal may be driven to a frenzy of action, and it will search tirelessly until it finds food and satiates the drive. In our well-fed modern Western world

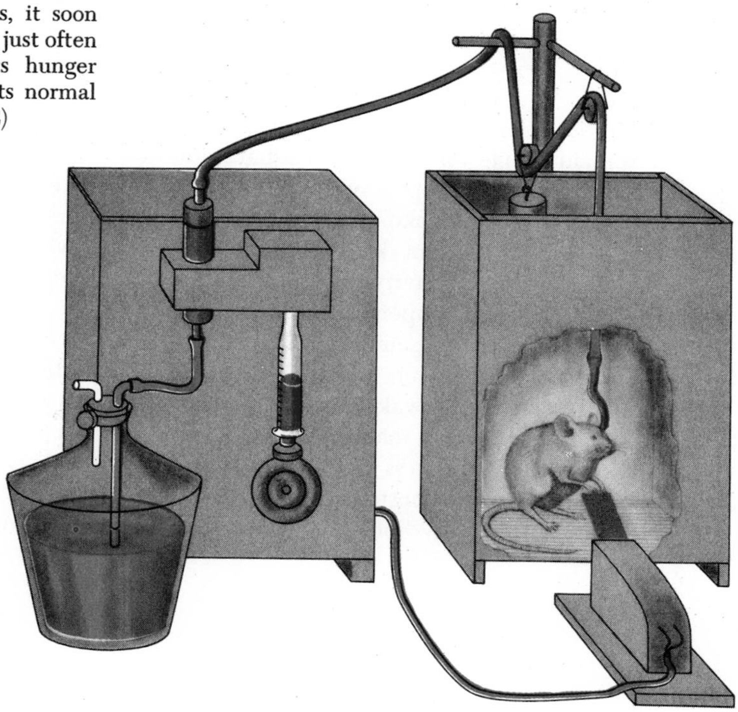

A Well-Fed Rat That Never Eats
When the rat presses the bar, a squirt of liquid food is delivered directly to its stomach. The rat never smells, tastes, or swallows the food. Nonetheless, it soon learns to press the bar just often enough to satisfy its hunger drive and maintain its normal intake of calories. (12)

FIGURE 9.2

most of us seldom see the full effect of the hunger drive among human beings. But under conditions where men are deprived of food, as in wartime concentration camps, they will steal, fight, and even kill to get it.

Thirst

When we drink, water passes quickly through the stomach and into the small intestine, where it is absorbed into the blood stream at a rate that depends largely on its salt content. (Water containing a small amount of salt is absorbed rapidly, water with a heavy concentration of salt more slowly.) The blood stream, in turn, delivers it to all the cells of the body. When we go without drinking for a time, the process is reversed and water is drawn from the cells of the body into the blood stream, which must maintain a constant minimum level of water. People who talk about being "dehydrated" when they are very thirsty are using the correct word. The cells and tissues of their bodies are actually suffering from the effect of losing too much water.

It appears that the thirst drive is controlled by an area in the hypothalamus that is sensitive to changes in water level and pressure. (Nerve cells do not lose water except in the most extreme cases, but those in the "thirst center" presumably are sensitive to changes in the supporting cells and body fluids around them.) Sensory messages from the mouth, throat, and stomach also seem to play a part, though a minor one, in stimulating the area. Much as in the case of hunger, the goal of the thirst drive is water, not the act of drinking. When the experiment that was shown in FIGURE 9.2 is changed so that the animal receives water rather than food directly in the stomach, it soon learns to take in the normal amount of water even though it never drinks.

Sleep

Surgical destruction of one area in the hypothalamus causes an animal to remain awake until it dies of exhaustion; destruction of another area causes the animal to sleep almost constantly. Thus there appear to be a "sleep system" and a "wakefulness system" in the brain. Exactly what stimulates these centers is not known, though sleep and wakefulness appear to be associated with activity of the highest part of the brain, with muscle tension, and with body temperature.

Under ordinary circumstances the sleep drive induces most people to sleep six to nine hours a day. We ordinarily associate sleeping with the darkness of night and wakefulness with the brightness of day. But people who live in the far north maintain much the same rhythm of sleep and wakefulness during the six months of the year when the sun shines constantly as during the six months of constant darkness (13). People who are forced to stay awake for as long as fifty hours can usually continue to perform short and simple tasks efficiently, but their ability to perform more complicated tasks is seriously affected and their judgment impaired (14). Prolonged deprivation of sleep is believed to be a basic element in the "brain-washing" techniques that have been so widely discussed in recent years.

All of us have a physiological rhythm related to our sleeping habits. During sleep, body temperature reaches its low point of the twenty-four-hour day, and the release of hormones by the glands is at a minimum. Temperature and glandular activity are at their peak when we are widest awake. For some people the peak comes right after waking; for others, considerably later in the day. This accounts for the fact that some of us are "day people" who wake up full of energy, do most of our day's work by noon, and are tired early in the evening, while others of us are "night people" who have a hard time dragging ourselves out of bed, do our best work late in the day, and like to stay up late.

A sudden change in sleeping hours upsets the rhythm and often produces changes in behavior. In this age of jet transportation many people fly to parts of the world where the time is as much as eight hours earlier or later than at home. Recent studies have shown that they usually suffer at first from physical discomfort and reduced physical and mental efficiency—to the point where it is unsafe for a pilot to fly another plane immediately or for a diplomat or a businessman to make a critical decision.

Sex

Among the lower animals sex appears to be as direct and primitive a drive as hunger or thirst. At most times the female sex drive is quiescent, and the female is not sexually attractive to the males of her species. She has regularly recurring periods of heat, however, in which large amounts of hormones are released from her sex glands and trigger some sort of sex control mechanism in the central nervous system. During these periods, which vary in frequency and length from species to species, the female actively seeks sexual contacts and engages in the kind of courtship and copulatory behavior characteristic of the species. A female in heat is usually apparent to the male of the species through various cues such as odors, the sex "calls" of the cat and other animals, and reddening of the sexual skin in monkeys and birds.

For most organisms, sexual behavior is unlearned; birds and lower animals raised in isolation demonstrate normal sexual behavior at the first opportunity. But monkeys raised in isolation do not (15). And among human beings sex can hardly be considered only a biological drive. The desire and ability of the human female to perform the sex act are not significantly dependent upon her hormone cycles; nor is her sexual attractiveness to the male. Sex is of course a powerful force in human affairs, but much of this influence derives from its motivational rather than its drive qualities.

Other Drives

Four other biological drives deserve brief mention. The *pain* drive leads to such reflex behavior as pulling the hand away from fire and such learned behavior as swallowing medicine to relieve a headache. The *breathing* drive goes unnoticed under ordinary circumstances, but a man who is drowning or being suffocated will fight as hard for air as he might fight for food when facing starvation. The *elimination* drive—to get rid of the body's waste products—is important mostly because of the social customs and taboos that have grown up around it.

The *temperature* drive is common to all warm-blooded animals; in human beings its goal is to maintain the body at about 98.6 degrees Fahrenheit. This is usually accomplished without conscious effort, on warm days through the evaporation of perspiration, on cool days through shivering and the constriction of blood vessels in the skin. Yet the drive can have pronounced effects upon behavior. A rat in a Skinner box where the temperature is near freezing will learn to press the bar for the reward of brief warmth from a heating lamp (16). A considerable amount of human activity is devoted to making clothing, building houses, and designing central heating and air conditioning systems that help satisfy the temperature drive.

A Definition of Drive

From what has been said about the specific drives, some generalizations can now be made. A drive is a special type of physiological condition that occurs when the organism is in a state of deprivation (that is, in need of food or water) or imbalance (too warm or too cold or needing to sleep or to eliminate its waste products). The physiological condition serves as the stimulus for a special pattern of nervous activity in the lower part of the brain. In human beings the pattern results in a sensation, such as the feeling of hunger, thirst, or fatigue. The pattern also frequently serves as an energizing force that leads to behavior. When we are hungry, we go to the vending machine for a candy bar or to a restaurant for a meal. When we are thirsty, we go to a water fountain. When we are tired, we go to bed. By so doing, we attain a goal that brings about an end to the physiological condition, stops the pattern of nervous activity, and thus satisfies the drive.

Strictly speaking, a drive consists merely of the physiological condition and the resulting pattern of nervous activity; it does not always affect behavior. But in the study of psychology, drives are most usefully discussed in terms of three separate but intimately related factors: 1) internal stimulation of the organism by physiological conditions, 2) external objects that alter the physiological conditions and come to serve as incentive stimuli, and 3) behavior that is elicited by the incentive stimuli and ends when the drive is satisfied. (The meaning of *incentive* will be enlarged upon later in the chapter.)

The biological drives are powerful and dramatic forces.
All of them except the sex drive lead to the learning of
behavior essential to keeping the organism alive and intact, and the sex drive
is essential to the survival of the species. When the drives go unsatisfied, they
often result in intense sensations of discomfort and eventually in death.
Naturally the biological drives have long been recognized and studied as
primary sources for the energizing of behavior. For many years they were
considered the only basic and inborn sources, from which all motives were
derived.

In recent years, however, more and more evidence has indicated that
the basic nature of the organism demands certain other satisfactions. Food,
water, sleep, and the other goals that satisfy the biological drives do not
seem to be enough. In addition, the organism seems to have inborn tendencies
to seek certain kinds of stimulation. Exact understanding of these tendencies
is incomplete, and there is not even full agreement as to what they should
properly be called. Some investigators believe that they are closely allied to
the drives and should bear the same name; these investigators would add to
the list of biological drives such others as a curiosity drive, an activity drive,
and a manipulation drive. Other investigators, noting that these tendencies
seem to spring from the nature of the central nervous system rather than
from any other physiological conditions, have called them psychological needs.
The term used here, *stimulus needs*, may eventually require revision as more
is learned about them. The term has been chosen for two reasons. First, the
goal of all these tendencies seems to be some kind of stimulation or change
in stimulation. Second, the tendencies do not have the life-and-death urgency
of the drives, and their goals are not so specific and clear-cut as goals such
as food and water; use of the word *needs* instead of the word *drives* suggests
that there are important differences between the two.

There appear to be several different kinds of stimulus needs, which deserve
individual discussion.

The Need for Sensory Stimulation

This need has already been mentioned, although not by name. In Chapter 5,
on perception, the importance of early sensory experience for the development of normal perception was discussed. It was also mentioned that the
human baby, when less than two days old, tends to focus his eyes on the
apex of a black triangle that is seen against a light background—the exact
spot at which the contrast between black and white is the greatest. Thus
the baby seems to exhibit an inborn tendency to seek increased *sensory
stimulation*.

Some experiments demonstrating the strange effect that lack of sensory stimulation has upon adults have also been described. In these experiments volunteer subjects remained in bed in a soundproof room, wearing goggles that let them see only a dim haze and casts that covered their arms and masked the sense of touch. Or they wore a soundproof diver's helmet and were suspended in water held at skin temperature. The result was that many of them were unable to think logically, their memories were disorganized, and sometimes they had hallucinations and delusions (page 11).

Why a lack of sensory stimulation should have such drastic effects is not completely understood. One possibility is suggested by what has been discovered about the reticular formation of the brain. Nerve impulses from the sense organs pass through the reticular formation on their way to the sensory areas of the cortex, or highest part of the brain, where they result in conscious sensations. As they pass through, they seem to set off other impulses, which are sent by the reticular formation to all parts of the cortex, keeping it in a general state of arousal and activity. Without a constant barrage of impulses from the reticular formation, perhaps the cortex cannot function normally. This seems to be a possible explanation of the need for sensory stimulation.

The Need for Stimulus Variability

As was also stated in the chapter on perception, there is something inherently attractive about a *change* of stimulus; this is the most important factor of all in attracting perceptual attention. To this statement it should now be added that organisms appear to display a definite need for *stimulus variability;*

FIGURE 9.3   *A Response to Change*   In the trial run a rat enters the T-maze at the bottom and is stopped by the glass panels, at a point where it can see that the left arm is dark and the right arm is white. In test 1 the glass panels are removed and both arms are dark; the rat shows a strong tendency to enter the arm that was formerly white. If the trial run is followed by test 2, the rat shows a strong tendency to enter the arm that was formerly dark. As is explained in the text, this behavior is dictated by a preference for a change in stimulus. (17)

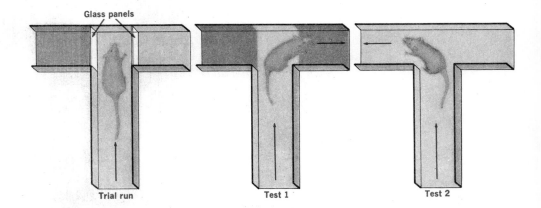

Glass panels

Trial run   Test 1   Test 2

given the opportunity, they show an innate preference for a change in stimulus and tend to seek it out. This has been demonstrated in the experiment shown in FIGURE 9.3. Even in this simple T-maze the rat shows a strong tendency to go to the arm that represents a change of stimulus—the dark arm that was originally white or the white arm that was originally dark.

The experiment with the rat and the T-maze fits in with many other observations of animal and human behavior. If rats have a choice between two mazes, one where food is always found in the same place in the final alley and the other where they have to search for the food after reaching the final alley, they generally choose the one where they have to search (18). Monkeys will learn to open a window, as in FIGURE 9.4, for the reward of seeing what is happening on the other side (19). Presented with the hooks and latches shown in FIGURE 9.5, a monkey will work hard to open them even though he has discovered that doing so leads nowhere. Human babies seem irresistibly attracted to play with a rattle, a toy hanging over the crib, or their own fingers. Adults gladly pay for the kind of stimulus change represented by a jukebox record or the lights flashing in a pinball game.

It may turn out that there are such things as activity and manipulation drives, as some investigators have speculated, and that curiosity is also a

FIGURE 9.4

The Curious Monkey   The monkey, a prisoner in a dimly lit box, learns to push open the window solely for the privilege of watching a toy train in operation for 30 seconds. (19)

FIGURE 9.5

Work for Work's Sake   Do the latches unlock anything? No. Does the monkey know this? Yes. Then why does it work so hard to open them? For the answer, see the text.

drive in its own right. It seems more probable, however, that all these forms of behavior are undertaken as a result of the need for stimulus variability. Such a need has an obviously useful role for the organism. Every stimulus change represents a new source of information about the environment, and information about the environment is essential to successful adjustment and at times even survival. An organism with an inborn need for stimulus variability has a biological advantage over an organism without it.

One aspect of stimulus variability that deserves special mention is *stimulus complexity*. A very young baby, to whom a toy rattle represents a strange and complicated stimulus, will play with it for a long time. An older infant will put it aside more quickly, and a school child will not play with it at all. To the school child a game of tag is endlessly fascinating; the college student will settle for nothing less than football. To satisfy the organism's needs, the stimulus must have a certain amount of complexity—a factor that is closely related to variability. On the other hand, a stimulus that is too complex is not attractive. A child is more attracted to a nursery rhyme than to a Shakespeare sonnet.

One important experiment in stimulus complexity is shown in FIGURE 9.6. When rats were placed in the maze shown at the left, some spent most of their time in the loop with plain white walls, others in the horizontally striped loop. When rats were placed in the maze shown at the right, some spent most of their time in the horizontally striped loop and some in the vertically striped loop. These results seem to indicate that various individuals have different levels of stimulus complexity with which they are most "comfortable" and for which they show a preference.

After the initial preferences of the rats had been noted, they spent several sessions a day in the mazes, for a number of days. Now it was found that sometimes their preferences changed. If so—and this was the most significant finding of the experiment—they always moved from a less complex stimulus to a more complex stimulus, never in the other direction.

The results of the experiments with the loops and with the T-maze that was shown in FIGURE 9.3 have led to the formulation of an important new psychological idea called the *theory of choice.*° The theory holds that every stimulus object has a certain complexity value, which is also its information value. Moreover, every individual organism has his own *ideal level* of complexity—that is, the level for which he has a preference. The individual will seek out objects of his ideal level of complexity, will choose them from among other objects, will work for them, and will learn what he has to do to obtain them. He will also explore objects of a somewhat higher complexity called *pacer stimuli*. As he masters the new level of complexity of the pacer stimuli,

---

° The term was coined by William N. Dember, the psychologist who directed the experimental work.

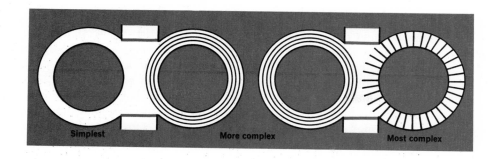

A Test of Complexity Needs   The two mazes, shaped like figure eights, were designed to test the preferences of rats for levels of stimulus complexity. The animals enter from either top or bottom by pushing open swinging doors (represented by the colored lines). In the maze at the left the animal has a choice of spending its time in a loop with plain white walls or a loop with walls striped horizontally in black and white. In the maze at the right the animal has a choice between a loop with horizontal stripes and a loop with vertical stripes. The white loop is the simplest of the three stimuli. The loop with vertical stripes provides the most rapid changes from black to white, as the animal runs through it, and is therefore the most complicated of the three. Question: Where did rats introduced into these mazes spend the most time? For the answer, see the text. (18)

FIGURE 9.6

his own ideal level rises, and he is now ready to deal with new pacers and again raise his own ideal level. Thus the need for stimulus variability provides a basis and reinforcement for increasingly complicated kinds of learning.

The Need for Physical Contact

FIGURE 9.7 shows what happened in a much discussed series of experiments by Dr. Harry F. Harlow, who took baby monkeys from their own mothers and gave them substitutes that he called "surrogate mothers." As the photos show, the babies based their preferences on the kind of tactual stimulation that the surrogates provided; they greatly preferred the comfort of snuggling against the softness and warmth of a "mother" built of sponge rubber and terrycloth, even when a "mother" who provided less pleasing physical contact gave them their food.

The Harlow experiments, of course, are reminiscent of the way human babies can be observed to cling not only to the softness of the mother's body but also to objects such as an old piece of blanket or a teddy bear that presumably represent physical comfort and perhaps security. The organism apparently has an inborn need for a special kind of stimulation, often involving softness and warmth, that can be called *physical contact* or *tactual comfort*.

An unexpected by-product of the Harlow experiments was the finding that

327

the monkeys raised by surrogate mothers, when they grew up, turned out to have many symptoms of maladjustment. They were unfriendly, aggressive, and sexually incompetent. Along similar lines, it has been observed that human babies who were abandoned at birth and brought up in busy and crowded institutions where they spent almost all their time alone in a crib, infrequently handled by any human adult, tended to grow up into maladjusted and neurotic children and adults (20). Obviously tactual comfort is not enough to enable the newborn organism to develop to normal maturity. One is tempted to say that the infant has a need for large amounts of handling by adults; indeed there is a strong temptation to go a step further and use the word *love*. But whether the facts indicate the existence of an actual need or merely an interference with the normal learning process is not known. Babies brought up without contact with their real mothers—or a flesh-and-blood substitute—miss much of the experience, guidance, and discipline that would normally teach them the ways of their species.

FIGURE 9.7

Baby Monkey and "Surrogate Mothers" The baby monkey has been taken from its mother and placed with two "surrogate mothers." The baby receives its milk from the mother made of wire; yet it shows a strong preference for the mother made of terrycloth and even holds on to her while nursing from the other mother. At the bottom right, the baby clings to its terrycloth mother just as it would to a real mother while exploring strange and at first frightening objects.

Behavior undertaken to satisfy stimulus needs is molded
and modified by learning. For example, the need for
stimulus variability requires more and more complicated stimuli for satisfaction, and this leads to behavior that displays a preference for more complicated stimuli. Similarly, the behavior set into motion by the biological drives is often affected by learning. The organism has to learn to find the food that is the goal of the hunger drive; indeed baby mammals, after being fed by their mothers' milk in the early days of life, must learn that solid foods can be a substitute and also how to eat solid food. But both the stimulus needs and the biological drives are in themselves unlearned; they are inborn characteristics of the organism.

Motives, on the other hand, are learned. It would be impossible to list all the human motives, for the number of goals that we can learn to desire is almost infinite. It is useful, however, to describe some categories into which many motives seem to fall and to trace the possible sources.

Certainty

Quite early in life the child begins to show a desire for the kind of *certainty* represented by his own bed, his own toys, the presence of familiar objects and people in his environment. As he gets a little older, he likes to have rules set for his conduct; he likes the certainty of knowing what he is permitted to do and what he is not permitted to do. The prospect of uncertainty—sleeping in a strange house, being taken care of by a strange baby sitter, going to school for the first time—is likely to upset him.

Adults, too, tend to be motivated toward the known and away from the unknown. For some of us, such as explorers and astronauts, other motives prove stronger, but, in general, the desire for certainty operates strongly in most of us at most times. We like to feel that we know how our relatives and friends will act toward us, what is likely to happen tomorrow in the classroom or on the job, and where and how we will be living next year. Just as children are often upset by new experiences, adults are often upset by such uncertainties as the possibility of unemployment or war.

The motive for certainty has been demonstrated in experiments in which college men volunteered to receive a series of electrical shocks of varying intensity and at varying time intervals. By pressing one button they could learn when the next shock would be administered, and by pressing another button they could learn how intense it would be. They pressed the buttons oftener when there was a high degree of uncertainty about the timing and intensity of the next shock than when there was a low degree of uncertainty (21).

Attachment and Affiliation

The baby soon learns to associate the satisfaction of hunger and thirst and the relief of pain, as well as pleasant sensory stimulation, with the presence of the mother. Thus a desire for the mother's presence seems to become the first of the motives the infant acquires. He smiles when she approaches and may cry when she leaves. Out of this early motive develop the adult motives that can be categorized as desires for *affiliation*—the motives to be around other people, to be close to people, to join clubs and be part of a group, and other goals that center around pleasant social relations.

Human sexuality belongs in part to this category. To the human being, the desire for companionship and affection is often as important as the desire for the sex act itself.

Dependency

Closely allied to the baby's desire for the presence of the mother is the desire for help. Since he cannot feed himself, protect himself from the cold, or escape from the pain caused by an open safety pin, he learns to actively desire *dependency*—the satisfaction of his drives and wishes by others. As he grows older, his parents usually discourage this motive and encourage him to rely instead on his own efforts. Yet the dependency motive usually persists. Most of us continue as adults to have strong urges to lean upon our parents for advice and financial help, to take our problems at work to the boss, to rely upon columnists and television commentators to interpret the world's events for us, and to give enthusiastic allegiance to political leaders who have strong personalities.

Society frowns upon dependent behavior by the male but considers a certain amount of it to be appropriate, "feminine," and rather attractive for the female. Thus dependent behavior is more often apparent in the responses of women than of men. This does not mean, however, that the motive is necessarily any less strong among men. They may merely suppress it or exhibit it only in hidden ways.

Independence and Achievement

In the process of discouraging the growing child from dependent behavior, parents teach him another motive—the desire for *independence*, which appears to originate in attempts to please the parents by acting like a "big" boy or girl. Despite the apparent contradiction, which sometimes causes conflict, the motives for dependency and independence exist side by side in most of us.

Closely related to independence is the motive for *achievement*, the desire to perform well and to succeed. Studies of people rated high in achievement motive have shown that their mothers demanded considerable independence.

These individuals were expected very early in life to go to bed by themselves, to entertain themselves, and later to earn their own spending money and choose their own clothes. Moreover, they were rewarded for these accomplishments with warm displays of physical affection. The mothers of those rated low in achievement motive did not demand the same kind of independence until much later. The striking difference in the kind of training received by people with high and low achievement motive is illustrated in FIGURE 9.8.

People high in achievement motive tend to try harder and to attain more success in many kinds of situations. In studies where they have been matched with other people of equal ability but weaker achievement motive, they have been found to do better on tests of speed at mathematical and verbal tasks (23) and on intellectual problems (24). They also make better grades in high school (25) and college (26). As is shown in FIGURE 9.9, they are more likely to move upward in society and rise above their family origins.

In general, the achievement motive is much stronger among Americans than among the people of many other societies, such as, notably, the natives of the tropical lands. An American who visits a South Seas island is likely

Early Training and Achievement Motive   A group of boys was divided into those who tested high and low for achievement motivation. Their mothers were then asked at what ages they had demanded that the boys show twenty different kinds of independent behavior, such as staying in the house alone, making their own friends, doing well in school without help, and doing well in competition. All mothers agreed that they had made all twenty demands by the time their sons were ten. But the mothers of sons with high achievement motivation made about as many demands at the age of two as the mothers of sons with low achievement motivation made at the age of four and about as many at the age of five as the other mothers at the age of seven. (22)

FIGURE 9.8

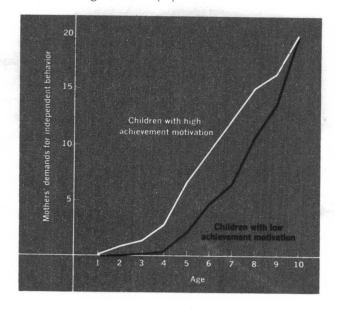

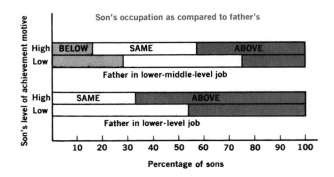

Achievement Motive and Upward Mobility Sons whose fathers had lower-middle-level or lower-level jobs were found more likely to rise above the father's level if they were high in achievement motive, more likely to remain at the same level or drop to a lower level if they were low in achievement motive. (27)

FIGURE **9.9**

to think of the natives as shiftless and lazy, while, to the islander, Americans seem to be wasting their lives in a frenzy of meaningless accomplishment. The difference is dictated in part by cultural standards that belong in the area of social psychology (Chapter 16). But there appears to be a relationship between these cultural standards and practices in child rearing. A study of other societies has shown that, where the achievement motive is strong, parents encourage early independence. In societies where the motive is weak, parents make less rigorous demands and make them later. Perhaps there is a circular relationship in which less demanding parents produce children with lower achievement motive, who in turn produce a society in which child-rearing practices tend to be less demanding.

Social Approval

To the baby, a kiss or a pat on the cheek is a goal in itself. The older child —say, by about the age of three—has learned to value these gestures as a sign of approval. With the help of the language symbols he has begun to learn, he has discovered that these gestures mean his parents value him; they like him; he is "good." Later the desire for signs of approval from the parents becomes generalized into the motive for *social approval.*

This motive takes various forms and results in many kinds of behavior among adults. A woman may want to become president of the PTA not so much for the sake of the job as because she regards it as a sort of vote of approval by her friends and neighbors. A man may be motivated to become a good teacher or doctor by a desire for signs of approval from his students or patients. Actors are notoriously eager for applause. Even the man who accumulates riches may be motivated less by a desire for the things money can purchase, including security, than by his belief that money is a symbolic proof of society's approval.

Escape from Unpleasant Feelings

The young child, to escape from the frightening sight of a stranger in the house, runs to his mother and hides his head in her skirt. He may also struggle to avoid dark rooms, cats, dogs, and any other objects or events that have become associated with fear. Among adults the desire to *escape from unpleasant feelings*, notably fear and anxiety, can be one of the strongest of motives. Soldiers sometimes run away from battle, and most of us run away at times from an argument or a social situation that has made us anxious. We also develop a closely related motive for *avoidance* of unpleasant feelings. We may refuse to ride in airplanes or even elevators or to get up and speak in public. We may prefer to feel underpaid rather than experience the anxiety attached to asking for a raise, and some of us would rather live alone than risk the fear attached to approaching the opposite sex.

Hostility

This is a motive that most of us do not like to admit but that all of us possess. Evidence of it first appears in the child at about the age of two. Up to then, all that he has seemed to want from other people is their presence and the stimulation, help, and approval they provide. But at this stage he begins to want something else from them. He wants—at times—to see them display signs of worry, fear of discomfort, actual pain. Later he may hope that misfortune will befall them and that he will have the gratification of knowing about it.

Hostility appears to result from the fact that the child cannot have everything he wants. Some of his desires are bound to be frustrated by the rules of society and by the conflicting desires of other people. He cannot always eat when he wants to. He has to learn to control his drive for elimination except when he is in the bathroom. He cannot have the toy that another child owns and is playing with. His mother cannot spend all her time catering to his whims. Other children, bigger than he, push him around.

Hostility often leads to the type of behavior called *aggression*, which takes such forms as argumentativeness, scorn, sarcasm, physical and mental cruelty, and fighting. Yet, while most people are motivated at some time by hostility, not everyone displays aggression. Boys and men are more inclined to do so than are girls and women, for society approves of a certain amount of aggression in the male but discourages it in the female. Just as dependent behavior is peculiarly a female prerogative in our society, so is aggression largely a male prerogative.

Domination

The desire for *domination* is the urge to force other people to behave in accordance with one's own wishes, to make them give in. This motive is clearly apparent in the behavior of the first-grade bully. In later life it is often generalized into a desire for *power* or symbolic proof that other people are respectful and can be dominated. Just as one man may be motivated to accumulate money as a guarantee of certainty and another because he regards money as a symbol of social approval, so may a man strive for money as a symbol of power. When a businessman says contemptuously of a rival, "I could buy and sell him," he really means, "I have more money than he. Therefore I am more powerful. Therefore I can dominate him and he cannot stand in my way; he must be submissive toward me."

Living up to Standards

One of the last of the motives to develop in the growing child is *living up to standards*—that is, to rules that the individual sets for his own behavior. The motive is slow to be learned because the individual cannot have standards until he has acquired some fairly sophisticated concepts of what society expects and values, such as independence, responsibility, attractiveness, rationality, kindness, friendliness, bravery, skill, neatness, honesty, fairness, manliness, femininity, and many others.

Exactly how standards are acquired is not known. Presumably, when we are very young, the environment seems unordered and unpredictable. We do not know what to expect or what is expected of us. We are motivated toward certainty; therefore we search for stable rules by which we can judge our own thoughts and our own conduct. We seem to learn many of the rules through reward and punishment; certainly this is the way we first learn that it is "good" to control our drive for elimination and "bad" to destroy property. We also learn by observing the conduct of other people, particularly our parents, and the beliefs they express. Few if any nine-year-old girls have ever been punished for being unattractive, yet somehow they have learned that attractiveness is valued by society and have set certain standards of attractiveness for themselves. Boys that age have already set standards of manliness, partly at least as the result of constantly hearing their parents say, "Don't cry."

Standards are also acquired through the process of *identification*. All of us, in the course of growing up, come to think of ourselves as being almost one and the same person as our heroes—usually our parents, sometimes another adult, an older brother or sister, or an older child whom we greatly admire. We think of ourselves as being like them and especially as having their skills and their power. Their virtues and their triumphs are like our own; we rejoice in them and attempt to imitate them. And we set ourselves the standards that seem to be our heroes' standards, for, if we follow their rules, then surely we will attain the marvelous goals that they seem to have attained, and we will be admired as much as we admire them.

Our standards form what is often called our *ego ideal*—our notion of how, if we were as perfect as we would like to be, we would always think and behave. Many of us acquire such high standards that we cannot possibly live up to all of them at all times. In fact some of our standards demand that we suppress other motives, which may be quite powerful at times; they tell us that we should not take food from another person even if we are hungry, that we should be kind even to people to whom we feel hostile, that we should play fair no matter how much we want to win, and that we should always obey society's rules about sexual behavior. As a result, we often have feelings of shame and guilt, over our thoughts if not actually our conduct. In popular terms, our consciences hurt. The pangs of conscience, when we fail to meet our standards, can be painful indeed. It has been observed that men who have committed crimes frequently behave in such a way that they are almost sure to be caught and convicted; apparently they prefer punishment by imprisonment to the kind of self-punishment that results from a serious failure to live up to one's own standards.

Cognitive Consonance

It is a rather strange and amusing fact of human behavior that a person who goes to an expensive restaurant and pays a ridiculously high price for a meal is almost sure to insist afterward that the meal was magnificent. A student who drives a hundred miles and sits through a blizzard to watch a football game in which his team is beaten 42–0 is likely to insist afterward that the drive was pleasant, the weather not especially bad, and the game much closer than the score would indicate. Are such people merely making excuses and trying to save face? Perhaps—but there is some evidence that they may actually believe what they say.

Although the idea is fairly recent and still controversial, many investigators believe that there is a motive for what has been called *cognitive consonance* —that is, for being consistent and rational in one's thinking and for preserving agreement and harmony among one's thoughts, beliefs, and behavior. Conversely, there is a desire to avoid *cognitive dissonance,* or lack of consistency and agreement. The following experiments and studies will help clarify the way these motives operate.

1. In one study, investigators found a group of sixty-five people who had bought new automobiles four to six weeks earlier and another group of sixty people from the same neighborhood who had not bought new cars for at

least three years. A survey was made of what kind of automobile advertisements they had been reading. If cognitive consonance is truly a motive, the investigators reasoned, the people who recently had bought automobiles would tend to read advertisements that would justify their purchases, and they would shun advertisements suggesting that they should have bought a different kind. The owners of old cars would read any and all ads that struck their fancy. The results bore out this hypothesis. Of the owners of new automobiles, about two thirds had recently read advertisements describing the virtues of the cars they had purchased. Only about one third had read advertisements for competing makes. The owners of old cars did not show any preference (28).

2. In an experiment with college students the subjects were asked to work for a long time at a boring task. They were then divided into three groups. The first, or control, group was asked to rate the task on a scale ranging from "extremely dull and boring" to "extremely interesting and enjoyable." As expected, the control group gave the task a quite negative rating on this scale. The other two groups were placed in a situation designed to produce cognitive dissonance: they were asked to tell other students waiting to take part in the experiment that the task had in fact been extremely interesting and enjoyable. In other words, they were asked to say something that they presumably did not believe. Members of group 2 were paid twenty dollars to do this. Members of group 3 were paid only one dollar each.

The hypothesis in this experiment was that group 2 would consider the twenty-dollar payment a sufficient justification for telling an untruth and therefore would experience only a low degree of cognitive dissonance. The results appear to bear out the hypothesis. When asked later to tell what they really thought of the task by rating it on the scale of "dull and boring" to "interesting and enjoyable," they gave it much the same unfavorable rating as had the control group. The hypothesis also dictated that members of group 3, paid only the nominal sum of one dollar, would experience a high degree of cognitive dissonance, which they would be able to reduce only by deciding that the task was in fact rather interesting. As it turned out, they did give the task a positive rating on the scale; they claimed that in fact it had been almost as "interesting and enjoyable" as they had told the waiting subjects (29).

3. Another experiment with college students produced results that appear to violate all the rules of common sense but offer considerable support to the theory that there is a motive for cognitive consonance. This provocative experiment is described, and the results are illustrated, in FIGURES 9.10 and 9.11. As FIGURE 9.10 shows, the experiment compared the amount of pain felt by four groups of students who received electric shocks while studying word lists. Note that the subjects who experienced "high dissonance"—because they had rather foolishly volunteered to learn list 3 and thus continue

		Level of shock while learning		Felt level of pain	
		LIST 2	LIST 3	LIST 2	LIST 3
Subjects who had no choice but to learn LIST 3	GROUP I	severe	severe	painful	painful
	GROUP II	severe	moderate	painful	much less painful
Subjects who volunteered for LIST 3	GROUP III ("low dissonance")	severe	severe	painful	painful
	GROUP IV ("high dissonance")	severe	severe	painful	less painful

Cognitive Dissonance and Felt Pain   The subjects, after learning list 1 of words under normal conditions, were subjected to two painful shocks per trial while learning list 2. They were then divided into the four groups listed above. Groups I and II had no choice but to continue with the experiment and learn list 3. Groups III and IV were told they had fulfilled their obligation and were free to leave but that they could volunteer to learn list 3 if they so chose. The hypothesis of the experiment was that the act of volunteering for a painful experience would produce cognitive dissonance. For the volunteers in group III the dissonance was reduced to a low level by the experimenters' explanation that their action was of great service to science and to the space program. No such reassurance was given to the volunteers in group IV, whose dissonance therefore presumably remained high. Note that the members of group IV—presumably in an attempt to reduce the dissonance—said they felt the pain of the shocks on list 3 as considerably less than on list 2. For further discussion of this experiment, see the text and FIGURE 9.11. (30)

FIGURE 9.10

FIGURE 9.11   *Effect on Learning of Cognitive Dissonance*   The graphs show the number of trials required for learning the three word lists in the experiment that was introduced in FIGURE 9.10. Note the remarkable similarity of the curves for group I and group III and for group II and group IV. All four groups of subjects performed about equally well on list 1, then were about equally hampered by the severe shocks administered while they were learning list 2, to the extent that they required nearly twice as many trials. On list 3, however, the story was quite different. For what is believed to be the explanation, see the text. (30)

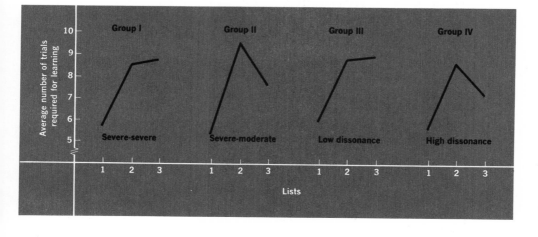

a painful experiment of whose value they were doubtful—said that the pain of the shocks was substantially reduced from that felt while studying list 2. Presumably they could reduce their cognitive dissonance only by believing that the shocks became less severe.

FIGURE 9.11 demonstrates that not only the subjective perception of pain by group IV but also the group's learning performance was affected by the high amount of cognitive dissonance. Members of this group actually performed on list 3 as if the amount of painful shock *had* been reduced. They did just about as well as (in fact slightly, though not significantly, better than) group II, for whom the amount of shock was in fact reduced. Thus members of group IV, experiencing a high degree of dissonance and presumably attempting to reduce it, not only said the pain was less but behaved as if it actually *were* less. The experiment seems to show that their perception of pain—not just their verbal report—was decreased by their attempt to reduce cognitive dissonance.

These three experiments cast a new light upon some factors in human behavior that have heretofore been unexplained. The experiments indicate that human beings are motivated to go to considerable lengths to prove that they are rational and sensible and, if they do something foolish, to find some means of explaining it away.

MOTIVES AND BEHAVIOR   Since motives grow out of biological drives and stimulus needs that are common to all human beings and since they are molded by childhood learning experiences that are more or less common to all people in our society, it appears likely that everyone possesses, at least in some degree, each of the motives that has just been mentioned. That is to say, all of us are motivated toward certainty, attachment and affiliation, dependency, independence and achievement, social approval, escape from unpleasant feelings, hostility, domination, living up to standards, and cognitive consonance.

Yet no two of us ever behave exactly alike. Why?

Motivational Dispositions and Aroused Motives

One reason is that motives, like the other mediational units acquired through learning, are not always in active awareness. Most of the time our motives lie somewhere in our storehouse of memories, waiting, like our knowledge of the multiplication tables or the telephone number of a friend, to be drawn upon at the appropriate time. It follows that motives are not always in operation. At times a college woman may be strongly motivated to get good grades, but this motive is not in her awareness when she is on a date watching a basketball game. Conversely, the cluster of sexual and social motives that preoccupies her on a date is not in her awareness when she is concentrating on her studies (although it may crop up when she is unsuccessful at concentrating on them).

A distinction must be made between *motivational dispositions,* which represent the sum total of all the motives we have learned and sometimes think about, and *aroused motives,* which are those we are thinking about at any given moment. Motivational dispositions are *potential* influences upon our thinking and behavior. Aroused motives are *active.* An aroused and active motive is more likely to affect behavior than a motive that is not aroused, although many psychologists believe that a motive can be completely unconscious and still affect behavior.

The concept of unconscious motives, which is perhaps one of the thorniest problems in psychology, was emphasized by Sigmund Freud. It was Freud's belief that people have wishes and desires of which they are never aware but which influence their behavior nonetheless, sometimes to a striking and dramatic degree.

One example of what appears to be an unconscious motive is the phenomenon known as posthypnotic suggestion. The hypnotist tells the subject that after he awakens from his trance he will go and raise a window the first time the hypnotist coughs but will not remember that this instruction has been given to him. The subject comes out of the trance, the hypnotist coughs, and, sure enough, the subject opens a window. If asked why, he is likely to say that the room was getting stuffy or that he felt faint. He has no suspicion that the real reason was simply to comply with the hypnotist's demand.

Other examples appear to be all around us. A mother seems to believe in all sincerity that she has the most generous, affectionate, and even self-sacrificing motives toward her daughter, yet an unprejudiced observer can see clearly that the mother's real motives are to dominate the daughter, keep her from marrying, and have her as a sort of maidservant. A man earnestly denies that he has any hostile motives, yet we can see that in subtle ways he performs many acts of aggression against his wife, his children, and his business associates. A person may feel genuinely motivated to go to the dentist or keep a date with an old friend who is coming to town, yet conveniently "forget" the appointment.

The chief unsolved question is how a desire that is unconscious can actively operate to produce relevant behavior. Perhaps there is no really sharp division between what is conscious and what is unconscious. Although the notion of unconscious motives is puzzling, it appears to be valid, and it indicates that we will often find it as difficult to analyze our own motives as to know the motives that direct the behavior of others.

Motive Strengths

Like many other forms of learning, motivational dispositions exist in hierarchies. Some are strong and easily aroused. Others are much weaker and seldom aroused. A man who has a strong motivational disposition toward hostility may be aroused to hostile desires and aggressive behavior by such mild frustrations as a broken shoelace, a cashier who is slow making change, or a telephone caller who has the wrong number. A person with a weaker disposition toward hostility might find such happenings merely amusing and might not be aroused even by a deliberate social snub or by a driver who comes charging through a stop sign and bangs into his fender. Each of us has his own thresholds for the kinds of events that will activate a motivational disposition and make it leap into awareness as an aroused motive.

The strength of a motivational disposition appears to depend in part upon the number of occasions on which it is aroused but not gratified. Its intensity does not grow while it remains in the inactive and potential state and is out of awareness. Nor does it grow if, every time the motive is aroused to an active state, the goal is reached. This can perhaps best be illustrated by a rather minor motive all of us probably possess—the desire to win at table tennis. If we live and spend our vacations in places where there is no equipment for the game, we may go for many months without ever thinking about the motive. Then we go to a recreational hall where people are playing, and the motive is aroused. But if now we play the game with a friend whom we can beat easily, game after game without fail, we soon lose interest again. On the other hand, if we should move into a residence hall where the game was constantly played and if we should usually lose when we try our hand at it, our motivational disposition might grow in strength substantially.

Requirements for Behavior

Even when a motivational disposition is strong and the motive is easily and frequently aroused to the active state, there may still be no effect whatever on behavior. A motive leads to goal-related behavior only when certain requirements are met.

1. *Knowledge of how to satisfy the motive.* Just as we acquire the motive itself by learning, we must also learn the kind of behavior that is likely to result in attaining the goal. A child may have a strong motive for affiliation and affection yet not know how to go about obtaining them. Similarly, an adolescent boy may have strong motives for the companionship of girls yet not know how to make himself attractive to girls or ask for a date. An adult may want to earn a lot of money yet lack any skills that have high value in the economic marketplace. The adult who wants to write to satisfy his achievement motive may not know how to go about starting.

2. *Absence of conflicting motives.* As a student gets ready to eat his evening meal a number of motives may flash into the active state and crowd one after the other into his thoughts. The motive to get good grades, associated with other motives for long-term security and achievement, may suggest that he spend the evening studying. Social, affiliative, and sexual motives may point toward going out on a date. The dependency motive, as well as his standards for proper behavior of a son toward his parents, may point toward writing a letter home. Other motives may incline him toward such behavior as going to a movie, bowling, or even working out in the gymnasium to prepare himself for a possible fight with someone he hates.

Obviously he cannot satisfy all these motives. They are in conflict. Only one can prevail—usually the one that is strongest in the hierarchy at the moment. All the others, lower in the hierarchy, will give way. They have been aroused; they have reached the active state; but no behavior results. The rule is that a motive is most likely to result in behavior in the absence of conflicting motives of greater strength.

3. *Incentive.* Even when we have learned what kind of behavior is likely to gratify a motive and when conflicting motives are absent, we must also have an *incentive*—that is to say, the motive is triggered into behavior by an event that arouses it, an event that elicits thoughts of the desired goal. Let us say that the student at the end of the day, instead of being torn among a number of conflicting motives, has no particular desires at all concerning the evening's activities. Now a friend calls him and suggests that they go to an 8 P.M. tryout for parts in a college drama. Going to the tryout is a potential incentive to implement any one of a number of motives— desires for achievement and affiliation, possibly sexual motives. Whether the student will respond eagerly or turn down the invitation will depend in large part upon the *incentive value* that trying out for a drama has for him.

The incentive value of any event or object varies considerably from person to person. Two men may have equally strong motives to succeed at athletics, but one man's motive may center around golf, the other man's around tennis. For the first man, winning a golf tournament has high incentive value and winning a tennis tournament has low incentive value; for the other man, the opposite is true. Of two women with equally strong motives for affiliation and social approval, one may place a high incentive value on attending a dance, the other on joining a discussion group. If we offer two boys a dollar to mow the front lawn, the dollar may have sufficient incentive value for one of them but not for the other.

4. *A reasonable chance of success.* Even when the first three requirements are met, a motive is not likely to result in any behavior unless a person believes that he has a reasonable chance of success—that he can reach the goal and thus obtain satisfaction of the motive. Thus even if the student invited to try out for the college play places a high incentive value on

getting an acting part, he is likely to turn down the invitation if he believes that he has absolutely no chance of success. Or let us say that the motive aroused to the active state is the desire to call up a girl the student has seen in one of his classes and ask her for a date. He places a high incentive value on the date. But, if he is shy and awkward around girls and considers himself unattractive and uninteresting, he is hardly likely to try to satisfy the motive.

The fact that a motive does not usually produce behavior unless there is a reasonable chance of success is perhaps, in the last analysis, just another case of conflict of motives in which the motive to attain a goal gives way to the stronger motive to avoid the unpleasant emotions accompanying failure. But it is such a special case and of such importance in determining whether or not behavior will result that it deserves mention on its own.

An experiment that explores the role of both chances of success and incentive is illustrated in FIGURE 9.12. Note how much harder the young women in this experiment tried to win their "contests" when the prize—the incentive value of winning—was doubled. Note also that the lowest scores were

FIGURE 9.12   *The Effect of Incentive and Chances of Success*   The subjects in this experiment were college women, who were told they could win a small cash prize in a contest that involved two tasks—one working problems in arithmetic, the other drawing X's inside small circles. Some subjects were offered a $1.25 prize, the others a $2.50 prize. Both groups were divided into four additional groups. One was told that a single prize would be given for the top score among twenty students; in other words, they thought they had one chance in twenty of winning. Others were told that they were in competition with two other students (one chance in three) or with a single other student (one chance in two—or 50–50). A fourth group was told that equal prizes would be given to the top three scorers out of four (three chances in four). Note that the subjects with a chance at a $2.50 prize—in other words, a higher incentive— worked harder than the subjects whose possible prize was only half that amount. In both groups the highest scores were made by those who thought they had a 50–50 chance of winning. (31)

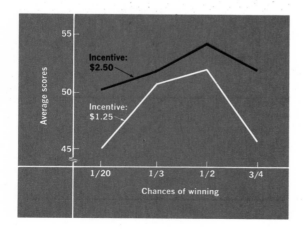

made by the women who believed that they had very little chance of winning. An interesting sidelight is the fact that the women who believed that winning was almost a sure thing also had low scores, particularly when the incentive value of the prize was low. The highest scores of all were made by those who thought they had a 50–50 chance.

5. *Freedom from anxiety.* The manner in which the vague fears and premonitions of anxiety may prevent motives from resulting in behavior can be observed even in very young children. If a child is separated from his mother for a long period of time and becomes intensely anxious over her absence, he may behave very strangely when he has the opportunity to see her again. Although he is strongly motivated to be reunited with her, he may at first actually avoid her rather than approach her.

Because of the different way the two sexes are brought up in our society, girls and women usually have particularly strong anxieties about their hostile motives, and boys and men about the desire for help. Therefore anxiety tends to play a particularly important role in inhibiting aggressive behavior on the part of women and dependent behavior on the part of men.

Sexual motives can generate considerable anxiety for both women and men, sometimes to the point of frigidity and impotence that completely block satisfaction or desire for the sex act. In an experiment on sexual anxiety, young men were asked what stories a series of pictures suggested to them; although many of the pictures had a strong sexual content, the men tended to ignore this fact in their stories. In fact they were less inclined to read sexual meanings into pictures where it was obviously present—presumably because these pictures aroused anxiety—than into "neutral" pictures. Then they had several drinks and were asked to invent stories for another similar series of pictures. This time—presumably because the alcohol had reduced their anxiety—their responses to pictures with a high sexual content were much more sex-oriented than before, and in some cases they were quite blatantly so (32).

Guessing Another Person's Motives

As the preceding paragraphs imply, it is very dangerous to assume that a person does not possess a motive just because he makes no overt attempt to gratify it. The motive may exist in considerable strength yet not result in observable behavior because the person has not learned how to satisfy it, because he has stronger conflicting motives, because the incentive does not exist, because he does not believe he can succeed in obtaining satisfaction, or because the motive arouses a crippling amount of anxiety.

There are many other difficulties in determining a person's motivation. For one thing, people learn different ways of satisfying their motives. One man may satisfy his hostility by getting into arguments, another by avoiding social contacts as much as possible. Hostility may indeed be one man's reason for becoming a professional prizefighter and another man's reason for becoming a soldier.

To a considerable extent, the kind of behavior with which we learn to satisfy our motives depends upon family patterns, social class, and even the part of the world where we happen to grow up. To a person brought up in one kind of home, a good deal of rough physical horseplay and loud verbal argument may express motives of approval and affection, which a person brought up in a more restrained home might easily mistake for extreme hostility. A mother on a farm in northern Norway who finds her four-year-old blocking a doorway does not ask him to move, does not in fact speak to him at all, but simply picks him up and silently sets him down out of the way (33). To an American mother this might seem a hostile act; in northern Norway it is simply the way an affectionate mother customarily behaves. To a Midwesterner who is in the habit of striking up conversations with strangers, a taciturn New Englander may seem hostile and contemptuous; to the New Englander, the talkative Midwesterner may seem to have some ulterior motive in mind.

A further complication lies in the fact that the same kind of behavior may spring, in different people, from very different motives. One young woman may work hard for good grades because of a strong desire for achievement, another to win the approval of her parents, and another because she is hostile toward her parents and knows that they will be jealous of her good grades.

Many kinds of behavior spring not from just a single motive but from many motives, working together. The physician may simultaneously be gratifying desires to follow in his father's footsteps, to acquire security, to gain signs of approval from others, to satisfy achievement motives, and to help and nurture other people.

Moreover, behavior that is originally undertaken to gratify one motive may later be switched to the service of another motive. This can best be explained by the following example. A young man on his first job may take a highly aggressive attitude toward his fellow workers because of hostility. Much later in life, when he has become successful, holds a position of authority, and has mellowed to the point where his hostile motive has virtually disappeared, he may continue to shout, pound his desk, criticize the people who work for him, and show many other signs of apparent anger and hostility. His motive now is that he has found—or thinks he has found—that such tactics keep his staff members on their toes and result in greater efficiency. Most people who observe such a man assume that he is still very hostile, but his closest friends often catch on to the change of motivation and say of him that "his bark is worse than his bite."

The Principle of Functional Autonomy

One aspect of motivation that was found puzzling for many years is illustrated by this frequent real-life occurrence. A young man from a humble background enters the business world and works with almost superhuman energy. By the time he is sixty he is successful and rich. Yet he continues to work as hard as ever. He may work himself into an early grave or, in the attempt to keep enlarging his business, lose everything he has made.

His hard work as a young man is easy to understand. We can assume that he had strong motives for certainty, achievement, probably also for power. But by sixty he is more successful and powerful than he probably had ever hoped, and he has more money than he can possibly spend. Why, then, should he continue to work so hard?

The explanation lies in a principle formulated by Gordon W. Allport, who has termed it *functional autonomy* (34). The principle holds that an activity which is originally a means to an end frequently acquires an independent function of its own and becomes an end in itself. The businessman starts out by working hard to gratify his motives for success, security, and power. But eventually the desire to work hard becomes a motive in its own right. His old motive has been transformed into a new one, which has a self-perpetuating power of its own.

Some other examples have been cited by Allport. A woman does not particularly like or want children; she does not possess the motive to nurture children that is commonly called maternal love. Nonetheless she treats her children well and lovingly because of various other motives centering around the approval of her neighbors and living up to her own standards of how a mother is supposed to behave. Eventually, as she practices devotion to her children, she begins to find that this is a valuable end in itself; the desire to nurture her children acquires functional autonomy. Another woman, in her youth, dresses well and uses cosmetics expertly for sexual motives. In her later years, although she is now a widow and has no intention of marrying again, she continues to show good taste in clothes and grooming because the desire for these things has become a motive in its own right. A man who makes custom-built furniture sets himself high standards of workmanship because he believes that this will bring him success and wealth. In later years he finds that this kind of workmanship is actually reducing his income because it takes more time than his customers are willing to pay for, but he continues to do a good job because the desire for craftsmanship has become a motive in itself.

The principle of functional autonomy appears to account for many human activities that seem far removed from the biological drives and stimulus needs and often do not even seem to serve any useful purpose. Desires that have acquired functional autonomy explain why the miser yearns for money he will never spend, the puzzle addict cannot sleep until he has solved the day's crossword, and the Englishman dresses for dinner (so at least legend has it) even when lost in the jungle.

SUMMARY

1. *A motive is a desire for a goal that, through learning, has acquired value for the individual.* Motives are believed to be derived, in part, through complicated learning processes, from the inborn desires for goals dictated by *biological drives* and *stimulus needs.*

2. The *biological drives* are hunger, thirst, sleep, sex, pain, breathing, elimination, and temperature.

3. A biological drive is a special type of physiological condition that occurs when the organism is in a state of deprivation (in need of food or water) or imbalance (needing to sleep or get rid of waste products). For the study of behavior, drives are regarded as comprising three factors: a) internal stimulation of the organism by physiological conditions, b) external objects that will alter the physiological conditions and therefore come to serve as incentive stimuli, and c) behavior that is elicited by the incentive stimuli and ends when the drive is satisfied.

4. In addition to biological drives, the organism appears to have tendencies to seek certain kinds of stimulation. These tendencies are often called *stimulus needs.*

5. Stimulus needs include the needs for general sensory stimulation, stimulus variability, and physical contact.

6. Studies of the need for stimulus variability have led to the hypothesis that every stimulus object has a certain complexity value (related to its information value); that each individual organism has his own *ideal level* of complexity; that the organism will seek out stimuli of this level; but that the organism will also explore objects of slightly greater complexity called *pacer stimuli.* As the organism masters the new level of complexity of these pacer stimuli, his ideal level rises; the organism is then ready to deal with new pacers and again raise his ideal level.

7. Among important motives are the desires for *certainty, attachment and affiliation, dependency, independence and achievement, social approval, escape from unpleasant feelings, hostility, domination, living up to standards,* and *cognitive consonance.*

8. *Motivational dispositions* are the sum total of all the motives that a person has learned; they are *potential* influences on his behavior. *Aroused motives* are those that the person is actually thinking about at the moment; they are *active* influences upon behavior.

9. Although the mechanisms are difficult to explain, it is generally believed that human beings may have *unconscious motives*, which influence their behavior even though they are unaware of them.
10. A motive results in overt behavior only when the following requirements are met: a) knowledge of how to satisfy the motive, b) absence of conflicting motives, c) incentive, d) a reasonable chance of success, and e) freedom from anxiety.
11. Motives are difficult to judge from behavior for the following reasons:
    a. A motive may not result in any behavior at all.
    b. The same motive may result, in different people, in different kinds of behavior.
    c. The behavior with which people try to implement motives depends upon family patterns, social class, and cultural influences.
    d. The same kind of behavior may spring, in different people, from different motives.
    e. Many kinds of behavior spring not from a single motive but from many motives, working together.
    f. Behavior originally undertaken to satisfy one motive may later be switched to the service of another motive.
12. *Functional autonomy* is the term for a principle which holds that an activity originally undertaken to implement a motive frequently acquires an independent function of its own and becomes an end in itself.

RECOMMENDED READING

Atkinson, J. W. *An introduction to motivation.* Princeton, N.J.: Van Nostrand, 1964.

Atkinson, J. W. and Feather, N. T., eds. *A theory of achievement motivation.* New York: Wiley, 1966.

Cofer, C. N., and M. H. Appley. *Motivation: theory and research.* New York: Wiley, 1964.

Festinger, L. *A theory of cognitive dissonance.* Stanford, Calif.: Stanford University Press, 1962.

Haber, R. N., ed. *Current research in motivation.* New York: Holt, Rinehart, and Winston, 1966.

McClelland, D. C., et al. *The achievement motive.* New York: Appleton-Century-Crofts, 1953.

Murray, E. J. *Motivation and emotion.* Englewood Cliffs, N.J.: Prentice-Hall, 1964.

EMOTIONS AND MOTIVES

Motives as a Source of Emotions
The Motivating Quality of Emotions

BODILY CHANGES IN EMOTION

Changes Controlled by the Central Nervous System
Autonomic Changes
Autonomic Changes and the Lie Detector
Pupil Size as a Measure of Emotion

PHYSIOLOGICAL THEORIES OF EMOTION

The Body in Anger and Fear
The Body in Other Emotional States

NEUROLOGICAL THEORIES OF EMOTION

THE "JUKE BOX" THEORY

The "Stooge" with the Hula Hoop
The "Angry Stooge"
Other Schachter Experiments
Implications of the Schachter Experiments
A Tentative Definition of Emotion

EMOTION AND LEARNING

Emotions as Reflexes
Conditioning Emotions
Learning the Labels for Emotion
The Importance of the Labels

INDIVIDUAL DIFFERENCES IN EMOTION

Glandular Differences
Differences in the Autonomic Nervous System

THE EMOTION OF ANXIETY

Sources of Anxiety
Some Effects of Anxiety
Anxiety and Risk Taking

10

EMOTIONS

At a World Series game, a dignified and usually soft-spoken judge jumps to his feet, boos the umpires, moans when the other team scores a run, and sheds tears of joy when his own team comes from behind in the ninth inning. In battle, a soldier who was cautious and timid in civilian life performs the most daring feats of bravery. In an emergency involving a sick child, a mother who had always considered herself physically fragile finds that she can stay awake and alert for forty-eight hours.

These are some of the more striking examples of how emotions influence behavior, as is another kind of human drama in which men in the grip of rage commit murders and men in panic push women aside to get to the life-boats of a sinking ocean liner. In more ordinary situations, emotions involving mild excitement or eagerness often help us learn faster or get a job done more efficiently. But emotions involving fear and anxiety can make us forget everything we knew while we are taking an important examination or strike us dumb when we get up and try to make a speech.

Emotions are among the most powerful of the forces that influence behavior. Generally speaking, we do not seem to have much control over them. They seem to boil up of their own accord; even in situations where we have determined in advance to remain calm, we find ourselves unaccountably angry, frightened, or anxious. They command our attention and we cannot ignore them. When we feel intensely emotional, we cannot concentrate on performing our jobs as we should, or choosing our words carefully, or even listening to music or reading a book.

Strong emotions—of the kind that made Oedipus gouge out his eyes, Juliet renounce her family for Romeo, and Hamlet kill his uncle the King—have been the chief subject of the world's literature, in all nations of all ages. Philosophers have always tried to understand them, and they have been an important field of psychological investigation ever since the earliest studies of Wilhelm Wundt.

We do not always feel angry, fearful, sad, lonely, or joyous. Indeed we experience one or another of these emotions during only a rather small part of our waking hours. This is one thing that distinguishes our emotions from other psychological processes, which go on more or less constantly while we are awake. During all our waking hours we are busy receiving the messages of our senses and selecting and organizing them into our perception of our environment. We are usually engaged in some kind of overt behavior, anything from talking to a friend to working in a factory. Much of the time we are engaged in the covert form of behavior known as thinking; thoughts and images are passing through our consciousness. But only some of our sensations and perceptions, only some of our overt acts and our covert thinking, can be regarded as emotional.

What is the origin of these emotional states, which, though rather infrequent, are among the most intense, memorable, and influential experiences of our lives?

Although many aspects of emotion are the subject of considerable controversy, most investigators would agree that *emotions are closely related to biological drives and learned motives* (1).

Motives as a Source of Emotions

A man stumbling across a desert without food or water is likely to grow intensely fearful that he will die of starvation or thirst, or bitterly angry at the circumstances that have put him there. If he now sees a town in the distance, with the promise of food and water, he is likely to experience the sharpest kind of relief and joy. A young woman who wants a certain young man to ask her for a date may become hopeful and fearful by turns; if he does not ask her, she may become angry or sad; if he does ask her, she is likely to experience emotions of happiness and tenderness.

Satisfaction of any motive can produce emotions—as we can infer from the behavior of a child who gets the doll she wanted for Christmas, the professional golfer who sinks a long putt to win his tournament, or the President-elect as he faces the television cameras on the morning after the election. Even mere anticipation of satisfaction can produce emotions—as we can infer from the antics of a child just promised a trip to the zoo or from the excitement of a young man looking at the automobile he is saving his money to buy. Similarly, frustration of a motive can produce emotions of anger or despondency, and mere anticipation of failure to achieve the goal can produce fear or anxiety.

Motives are not always accompanied by emotions. We may want to make a trip to see a friend without experiencing feelings of expectation or anxiety;

if the trip proves impossible, we do not necessarily become despondent. We may have the mild and emotionally neutral kind of hostility toward another person expressed in the words, "I don't really care much for him." But any *strong* motive arouses emotions, as a person reveals when he says he wants something "so badly that I can taste it" or says of another person, "I hate his guts." A strong motive can be defined, indeed, as one that is accompanied by emotion. The woman who is strongly motivated to nurture her children suffers with them when they get sick and rejoices with them when they are happy. The man who is strongly motivated toward success in business is fearful and anxious over his problems, elated when he solves them, and devastated when he fails.

The Motivating Quality of Emotions

The relation between motivation and emotions works both ways: the desire for pleasant emotions can become a motive in itself. We are motivated to go to a funny moving picture to enjoy the emotions associated with laughter. We play games—and sometimes do our life's work—partly for the joy of anticipation and the happiness that comes with success. We go surfing or ride a roller coaster partly because a certain amount of fear, if we know it will be followed immediately by relief, is pleasant.

We also are motivated to escape unpleasant emotions. In part, we make friends to escape from loneliness, work to avoid the painful emotions that accompany failure, are polite to other people and obey the laws to avoid the painful emotions that accompany violations of our standards. The desire to escape from the emotion of anxiety is an especially strong motive that influences many kinds of behavior.

How do emotions become attached to motives, and how do they sometimes become motives in their own right? The answer is through learning, in a manner that will be discussed later in the chapter. First let us examine the nature of emotions.

BODILY CHANGES IN EMOTION

Suppose that you are riding in a bus, minding your own business. The man next to you taps you gently on the arm, politely begs your pardon for interrupting you, and says, in a perfectly calm tone of voice and with a noncommittal facial expression that shows no sign that he is in any way upset or angry, "I don't like you." Then he turns away and quietly resumes reading his newspaper. If you were asked afterward whether he had displayed emotion (not just signs of eccentricity), what would you say?

Now suppose that you carelessly drive through a stop sign, run into another automobile, and badly damage the whole side of it. The other driver gets out and says, "It's all right; don't worry about it; everybody makes mistakes; anyway, I'm insured." You note, however, that his voice is quivering, his facial muscles are twitching, and his hands are trembling. Is he emotional or is he not?

To the first question most people would answer *no*, even though the kind of aggressive behavior involved in a remark such as "I don't like you" ordinarily is highly emotional. To the second question most people would answer *yes*, even though a matter-of-fact remark such as "It's all right" is usually considered to show the absence of emotion. Most scientific investigators of emotion would agree about the driver of the automobile. Before agreeing about the man on the bus they would want to make sure that he was really as calm inwardly as he appeared on the surface.

By scientific consensus as well as in popular usage, the words *emotion* and *emotional* are reserved for cases in which physiological changes accompany mental activity. The easiest cases to recognize are those in which the organism is quite obviously "stirred up." We assume that another person is emotional when we note that his voice is unusually high-pitched, when he blushes or gets pale, when his muscles grow tense or tremble. We know that we are ourselves emotional—even if we manage to conceal all outward signs—when we can feel that we are inwardly shaking or "hot under the collar" or that our mouths are dry, our pulses racing, or our stomachs "full of butterflies." But there are also quieter emotions in which the body almost seems to be "toned down." Such are the calm, peaceful, and contented feelings of a mother nursing a child or of a person enjoying a sun bath, a beautiful piece of music, or a cup of coffee after a satisfying meal. In these cases too, however, the physiological processes are affected in some manner.

The relationship between mind and body in emotion seems to work both ways. Think about something very pleasant, such as pitching a perfect baseball game, being elected queen of the homecoming celebration, inheriting a million dollars from an unknown relative, or anything else that appeals to you. Quite possibly you will soon *feel* pleasant. Think of something that angers you, such as a bad grade, a social snub, being blamed for someone else's mistake. Soon you may *feel* angry. Or try the opposite. Make a smile, hold it, and see if you do not begin to feel happy and have pleasant thoughts. Clench your fist, keep clenching it, and see if you do not begin to feel angry and have aggressive thoughts.

What does it mean to be "stirred up"? In search of the answer, investigators have used laboratory apparatus of many kinds, such as the device shown in FIGURE 10.1. Their measurements have shown that a wide variety of changes take place in the body in states of emotion (2).

FIGURE **10.1**

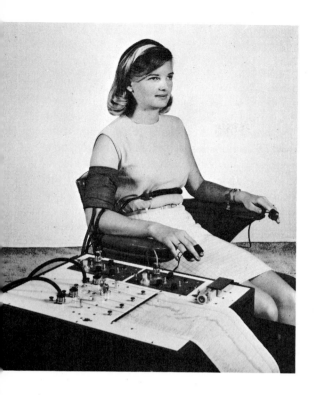

Measuring the "Stirred-up" State of Emotion A continuous record is kept by the machine of the young woman's rate of breathing (from the tube around her body), galvanic skin reflex or change in electrical conductivity of the skin caused by sweating (from electrodes attached to her hand), and heart rate and blood pressure (from the band around her upper arm). All these physiological activities and many others that can be measured by more complicated apparatus may be affected in states of emotion. This particular machine is a so-called lie detector, discussed in the text on page 354.

Changes Controlled by the Central Nervous System

Some of the bodily changes in emotion represent activities of the striped muscles, controlled by the central nervous system. One of them is *muscle tension,* particularly noticeable in states of anger when the teeth are clenched. Another, *tremor,* occurs when two sets of muscles work against each other. Many people, when emotionally excited, have a tendency toward *eye blinking* and *other nervous movements,* such as brushing back their hair or drumming their fingers on a desk. And many emotions result in *facial expressions of emotion,* such as frowns, grimaces, or smiles, or *vocal expressions of emotion,* such as laughter, snarls, moans, or screams.

Although all these forms of bodily activity are under the control of the central nervous system, they do not appear to be voluntary; they "just happen" as part of the general pattern of change that accompanies emotion. We seem to have no more conscious control over them than we do over the next and larger group of bodily responses.

Autonomic Changes

Autonomic changes are controlled by the autonomic nervous system (page 265) and by the endocrine glands (page 243), and we therefore have little

353

conscious control over them. In many emotional states the rate of heartbeat jumps, sometimes from the normal of 72 per minute to as high as 180. Blood pressure may also rise sharply, and blood is often diverted from the digestive organs to the striped muscles and surface of the body, resulting in flushed cheeks and the sensation of being "hot under the collar." The composition of the blood changes. The number of red corpuscles, which carry oxygen, increases markedly, and the secretion of hormones by the endocrine glands produces changes in the level of blood sugar, acidity of the blood, and the amount of adrenalin and noradrenalin (powerful stimulants secreted by the adrenal gland) in the blood stream.

The normal movements of the stomach and intestines, associated with the digestion and absorption of food, usually stop during anger and rage; in other emotional states they may show changes resulting in nausea or diarrhea. The body's metabolic rate tends to go up; food in the blood stream and the body tissues themselves are burned off at a faster rate, creating additional energy. Breathing may change in rate, depth, and ratio between time spent breathing in and time spent breathing out; we may gasp or pant. The salivary glands may stop working, causing the feeling of dryness in the mouth that is often associated with fear and anger. The sweat glands, on the other hand, may become overactive, as shown by the dripping forehead that may accompany embarrassment or the "cold sweat" that sometimes accompanies fear. The muscles at the base of the hairs may contract and raise gooseflesh. Finally, the pupils of the eyes may enlarge, causing the wide-eyed look that is characteristic of rage, excitement, and pain.

Autonomic Changes and the Lie Detector

Each of the physiological changes just mentioned, as has been said, is controlled by the autonomic nervous system. The changes generally take place without conscious control, whether we want them to or not. Only one of them, breathing, is regulated by the central nervous system as well as by the autonomic nervous system. In emotional situations we often can deliberately breathe more deeply or more slowly, but we usually cannot do much about our heart rate, our blood pressure, the activities of our sweat glands, or the other physiological changes.

This fact has led to the development of the lie detector. As shown in FIGURE 10.1, the lie detector usually measures rate of breathing, galvanic skin reflex, heart rate, and blood pressure—the four physiological changes that have been found most useful in spotting the emotions that in most people accompany the act of lying. An example of how the lie detector may disclose a falsehood is illustrated in FIGURE 10.2.

Although the lie detector test has been used for many years, on the assumption that the emotions accompanying the act of lying usually result in measur-

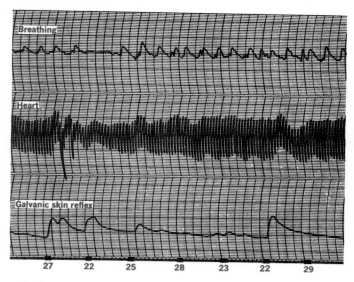

The Lie Detector Discloses a Falsehood These tracings were made in a lie detector test of a subject who had been asked to try to conceal which number he had chosen in advance of the test; the lines show his physiological reactions when queried about the numbers shown at the bottom. He had actually chosen the number 27; note the sharp changes in the tracings for heart and galvanic skin reflex when he heard this number and denied that it was the correct one. The subject attempted to produce a false impression of lying about the number 22; he did so by tensing his toes. Note that he was able to produce changes in the heart line and GSR. The line for breathing rate, however, reveals his deception by showing that he held his breath as he tensed his toes the first time he heard the number 22. (3)

FIGURE 10.2

able physiological changes, recent studies show that its use is subject to many errors. Some people appear able to suppress physiological responses to lying. Others are made so nervous by the test that they show changes in response to any kind of question (4). The lie detector is still used in criminal investigations, but the results cannot be introduced as evidence in court without the consent of both the prosecution and the defense.

Pupil Size as a Measure of Emotion

Some recent studies have indicated that changes in the size of the pupil may be an extremely sensitive measure of emotion, including active interest. In the experiment illustrated in FIGURE 10.3 a motor-driven camera was used to photograph the eye twice a second. As is shown in the figure, the diameter of one male subject's pupil increased 30 percent in four seconds while he was looking at a picture of a woman's face. In general, male subjects showed significant increases in pupil size when looking at pictures of women, especially pin-up pictures; female subjects showed pronounced increases when

355

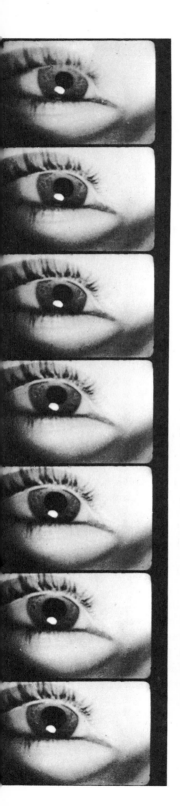

FIGURE 10.3

A Photographic Record of Pupil Response The subject was a man. The photographs of his eye were taken as he looked at a picture of a woman's face. Note the rather rapid increase in pupil size from the normal, at top, to the bottom, where the diameter is about 45 percent greater.

Why Do These Photos Produce Different Reactions? These were two of the pictures shown to male subjects while a motor-driven camera recorded any changes in their pupil size as in FIGURE 10.3. Both pictures produced increases in pupil size, and afterward the subjects said that the two pictures were exactly alike. For some reason, however, the picture at left produced twice as large an average increase in pupil size as did the picture at right. See if you can figure out why before turning to the text for the explanation.

FIGURE 10.4

looking at pictures of a baby and especially of a mother with a baby. When the subjects looked at pictures they found unpleasant, the pupil size did not increase, as when women looked at pictures of sharks (5).

As part of the same study, men were shown the two photos in FIGURE 10.4, with the intriguing results that are described in the caption. Before reading on, you may want to study the photos and the caption and try to figure out why the photo at left produced a stronger reaction than the photo at right.

The only difference between the two photos, as you may have discovered, is that the one at left has been retouched to make the young woman's pupils seem larger. This very slight change presumably was the cause of the greater response. It was not noted consciously by the subjects in the experiment—a fact that may indicate that pupil size can reveal reactions of which we ourselves are not even aware.

Pupil size has been found to increase reliably when a person is engaged in mental activity such as solving mathematical problems or trying to remember a telephone number, and the more difficult the problem the larger the pupil becomes.

PHYSIOLOGICAL THEORIES OF EMOTION

As has been noted, the stirred-up bodily states that are a part of emotion are highly diffuse. They include various kinds of tension, tremor, and other movements of the striped muscles controlled by the central nervous system, as well as many changes regulated by the autonomic nervous system and affecting the endocrine glands, blood chemistry, and the smooth muscles of the visceral organs, the blood vessels, and the iris of the eye. When we are emotional, it might be said, we tend to be emotional all over. In the adult human being, who has learned to control many of the outward signs of emotion, this fact may be apparent only to the delicate measuring apparatus of the laboratory. It is much more obvious in the case of animals, as is shown in FIGURE 10.5.

In the long history of scientific investigation of the emotions, these widespread and often dramatic forms of bodily activity have naturally received a great deal of attention. They were the basis of an influential theory of emotion proposed by William James, a theory that has particular interest because it completely reversed all previous thinking about emotions. Common sense says that we cry because we are sad, strike out because we are angry, tremble and run because we are afraid. James made the suggestion—startling to the scientific world of his day and even now to the person who hears it for the first time—that things were exactly the opposite.

James said that emotion occurs in this fashion. Certain stimuli in the environment set off the physiological changes. These changes in turn stimulate the various sensory nerves leading from the visceral organs and other parts

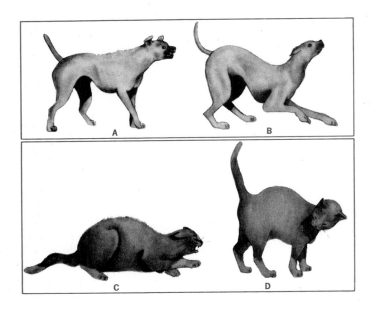

Emotional Postures in Dog and Cat The dog approaching an enemy exhibits many signs of stirred-up bodily state (A). The bristling hair and the wide and staring eyes are evidence of activity of the autonomic nervous system. The dog's entire posture has been affected: it walks stiffly, holds its tail high and pricks its ears forward, and growls. If it discovers that it is approaching not a hostile stranger but its own friendly master, the pattern immediately changes (B). The hair and pupils return to normal, and the dog may begin salivating. The muscles of its body relax; it lays back its ears and wags its tail. The cat's display of emotion is somewhat different—it crouches toward an enemy (C) and arches its back and purrs for its master (D)—but equally diffuse. (1)

FIGURE 10.5

of the body to the brain. It is these sensory messages from our aroused bodies that we then perceive as emotion. In other words, we do not cry because we are sad; on the contrary, we feel sad because we are crying. Similarly, we do not tremble because we are afraid but feel afraid because we are trembling (6).

This notion that the physiological changes come first and that the perceived emotion is a feedback from the change and comes afterward was also proposed at about the same time by a Danish scientist and persisted more or less unchallenged for many years as the James-Lange theory of emotion. Many physiologists and psychologists who take a physiological viewpoint still tend to equate emotion and bodily activity. In some scientific writings the word *emotion* is used as virtually synonymous with an aroused or stirred-up bodily state. In fact all of us use the word in this fashion when we apply it to animals, for all that we know about the animal is that it exhibits an aroused physiological state; we cannot be sure that this aroused state results in any feelings at all.

The Body in Anger and Fear

If perceived emotion is strictly a matter of feedback from aroused bodily states, then it follows that there should be a different pattern of bodily activity for each emotion, resulting in a distinctive and recognizable pattern of sensory feedback. Many studies have been made, therefore, of the physiological activities that accompany the various emotions.

For anger and fear, the findings have been along lines that the James-Lange theory would predict. In one study, subjects were placed in an apparatus similar to the one shown in FIGURE 10.1. Laboratory technicians then behaved in ways that angered or frightened the subjects, without disclosing that the actions were deliberate and a part of the experiment. Each subject was made angry on one occasion and fearful on another, and the combined results of the physiological measurements showed some significant differences. In anger there was a tendency for the heart rate to go down, blood pressure to go up, muscular tension to increase, and, most of all, for the number of galvanic skin reflexes to rise sharply. In fear there was a tendency toward faster breathing, peaks of muscular tension, and increased electrical conductivity of the skin (7).

The physiological changes found in this study to be characteristic of anger are the kind known to be produced by the hormone noradrenalin, and the changes found characteristic of fear are known to be produced by the hormone adrenalin. Thus it would appear that the adrenal gland is unusually active in secreting one of its hormones in anger and a different one in fear—a notion for which additional evidence has been found. In one study, a chemical analysis was made of the urine of players on a professional hockey team to learn how much noradrenalin and adrenalin they were secreting before and after a game. It turned out that the players actively taking part in the game, fighting to win, showed about six times as much noradrenalin after the game as beforehand. But two players who were injured, unable to play, and worried about their future with the team showed increased amounts of adrenalin. The coach sometimes showed more noradrenalin and at other times more adrenalin, depending upon how well his team had done in the game (8).

Along the same line, it has been found that animals such as lions, which survive by fighting and killing their prey, have large quantities of noradrenalin in their systems, while rabbits, which survive by running away, have large quantities of adrenalin (9). Thus it appears that anger and "fight" are associated with the physiological effects of noradrenalin and fear and "flight" with the effects of adrenalin.

The Body in Other Emotional States

Aside from the findings about fear and anger, however, there is not much evidence to support the view that each different emotion depends upon a unique pattern of bodily sensations. Certainly no experimenter has ever been able to find a hundred different physiological states to match the hundred different kinds of emotional experience described by our language. In general, the bodily changes in emotion are what recent investigators have called "rather diffuse and global in character" (10). It has proved very difficult to determine, from physiological measurements alone, what kind of emotion a person is experiencing. Indeed the same person, on two separate occasions when he says he feels joyous, may show different bodily changes. And different people may show quite different patterns when experiencing the same emotion: one person may tend to perspire a great deal, another to show muscle tension, another to have a rapid pulse (11).

In addition, the visceral organs, which James considered to be especially important in emotion, tend to respond rather slowly to impulses from the autonomic nervous system or to stimulation by the hormones. As was noted in FIGURE 10.5, a dog or cat sometimes changes almost instantly from a posture of rage to a posture of friendliness when it sees that what it thought was a hostile stranger is really its master; the pattern of sensations from the animal's visceral organs could not change that rapidly. Indeed the visceral organs are rather insensitive, and the sensory messages they send to the brain are often vague and indistinct (12).

For these reasons and others, the James-Lange theory began to fall into disfavor, and around 1930 a different kind of theory was proposed, based upon the rapidly expanding knowledge of how the brain works.

NEUROLOGICAL THEORIES OF EMOTION
An emotion can be triggered by electrical stimulation of the brain: if an electrode is planted in one area of the hypothalamus of a cat, for example, the animal can be made to behave as if enraged by the presence of an enemy. Other studies have also pointed to the importance of the hypothalamus in emotion. Even when the entire cerebral cortex of a dog is removed, the animal still displays most of his typical rage pattern; in fact the "rage" is produced by mild forms of stimulation that would not disturb a normal dog. The pattern persists in the absence of some other brain structures as well as the cerebral cortex. But it does not take place unless the hypothalamus is left intact (13).

It appears that the hypothalamus, with its close relationship to the autonomic nervous system and to the pituitary gland, plays a special role in emotion. This has led to the formulation of neurological theories of emotion, one of the oldest and best known of which is the Cannon-Bard theory. According to this theory, certain stimuli in the environment cause the hypothalamus to fire off patterns of nervous activity that arouse the autonomic nervous system and thus trigger the physiological changes that are associated with emotion. At the same time, the hypothalamus fires off patterns of messages to the cerebral cortex that result in the feelings of emotion. The Cannon-Bard theory, it will be noted, attaches no importance to the feedback of bodily sensations, which is the basic element of the James-Lange theory.

The most generally accepted neurological theory today, conceived in 1937, is the Papez-MacLean theory. This theory stresses the importance of the *limbic system*—a set of interconnected pathways in the brain that are related to the hypothalamus, some other subcortical structures, and some primitive areas of the cerebrum that have to do with such processes as the sense of smell, movements of the mouth associated with the kind of behavior through which lower animals explore their environments and find food, and sexual behavior. Surgery or electrical stimulation of areas in the limbic system has produced significant changes in the disposition of animals and in their sexual behavior. It is also in one of these areas—the "pleasure center"—that electrical stimulation serves as a reinforcement for learning, which an animal often prefers to food.

THE "JUKE BOX" THEORY

Some new studies raise the interesting possibility that both the physiological and the neurological theories of emotion are partially right but that neither offers the full explanation. Modern thinking about emotions has been greatly influenced by some new experiments performed by Stanley Schachter at Columbia University, which are so important that they deserve discussion here in full detail.

The "Stooge" with the Hula Hoop

In one experiment Schachter used a volunteer subject who agreed to submit to an injection of what he was told was a harmless drug whose effect on vision was being studied. The drug, so the subject was told, would produce certain physical effects—numbness of the feet, itching of the skin, and a slight headache. In truth the subject received an injection of that powerful stimulant adrenalin, in an amount sufficient to produce many of the stirred-up physiological changes that accompany strong emotion.

The subject was asked to sit in a waiting room for a time. In the room was another student, a "stooge" who had specific instructions from Schachter. The stooge began behaving quite strangely. He wadded up paper and used it like a basketball, with a wastebasket as his target. He found a hoop in the room and used it like a hula hoop, dancing around with gay abandon. He folded pieces of paper into toy airplanes and sailed them in all directions. In other words, he acted like a person who was a little out of his head with high spirits. When he invited the subject to join in the fun, the subject found himself unable to resist. Soon he too was gripped by a feeling of excitement and happiness and was sailing paper airplanes even more boisterously than the stooge.

The "Angry Stooge"

Another of Schachter's subjects received the same kind of injection and the same story about its effects and also found another student in the waiting room. This time the stooge behaved differently. Instead of acting happy he pretended to be angry; he was bitter and aggressive. Soon the subject, too, found himself feeling angry and behaving in an angry fashion.

The experiment with the two kinds of stooges was performed with a number of subjects. In general, the subjects whose bodies were stirred up with adrenalin felt happy and behaved in a giddy fashion when they were exposed to the happy stooge, and they felt angry and behaved aggressively when exposed to the angry stooge. In each case, presumably, the physiological effects of the adrenalin were more or less the same. The accompanying emotion depended on what was happening around them—the context in which they found themselves.

In another part of the experiment the subjects were treated in exactly the same fashion except that they were told the truth about what kind of physiological reactions to expect from the injections; they were correctly informed that they would experience a fast pulse, hand tremors, and a flushed feeling in the face. These subjects were much less inclined to be influenced by the mood of the stooge; they tended to hold themselves aloof from his high spirits or his anger. A control group of subjects who received a salt water injection also tended to resist the stooge (14).

Other Schachter Experiments

Two other experiments performed by Schachter must also be mentioned. In one of them he had three groups of subjects watch a slapstick movie. Before the movie was shown, group 1 received an injection of adrenalin, and group 2 received an injection of a tranquilizer that suppresses activity of the sympathetic nervous system and therefore has physiological effects that are generally the opposite of those produced by adrenalin. Group 3, the control group, received an injection of salt water. The subjects whose bodies were stirred up by the adrenalin showed the greatest signs of amusement while watching the movie and afterward gave it the highest rating for being funny.

The subjects whose physiological activity was suppressed by the tranquilizer showed the least amusement and gave the movie the lowest rating. The control group's reactions were in the middle (15).

The other experiment involved a classroom situation in which students had the opportunity to cheat, and it was based on the supposition that one powerful deterrent to cheating is emotions of fear and anxiety. Some of the students received an injection of tranquilizer; others did not. It developed that, of the students who received the tranquilizer and in whom the tranquilizer appeared to actually have the intended effect of reducing physiological activity, 40 percent cheated. Of the control group, only 20 percent cheated (16).

Implications of the Schachter Experiments

One conclusion toward which the Schachter studies seem to point is that changed bodily states are indeed an essential element in producing feelings of emotion and not just a side effect as the neurological theories of emotion have supposed. It was the subjects who were stirred up by adrenalin who reacted emotionally to the happy stooge and the angry stooge. It was the subjects injected with adrenalin who found the movie the most hilarious. Conversely, it was subjects whose physiological activity had been dulled by tranquilizers who found the movie the least funny and who appeared to have the weakest emotional barriers to cheating.

The James-Lange version of why feedback from bodily sensations is important, however, appears to be contradicted by the studies. The stirred-up bodily activity produced by the adrenalin injections did not by itself result in a specific emotion or even in any emotion at all. The subjects who had been correctly informed about what kind of bodily sensations to expect did not become giddy when exposed to the happy stooge or angry when exposed to the belligerent stooge. Those who had been misinformed became giddy in one context and angry in another context, even though, presumably, their bodily states were generally alike.

Schachter and his colleagues have concluded that emotions depend upon two factors: 1) physiological arousal and 2) a mental process by which the subject interprets or labels his physiological sensations. Thus a subject aroused by adrenalin may interpret his sensations as merely being the physical symptoms of rapid heartbeat and tremor that he was told to expect, and he may therefore experience no emotion at all. The subject aroused by adrenalin and aware of physiological sensations that he does not understand may interpret these sensations as a giddy happiness in one kind of context and as anger in another. Or he may have exaggerated feelings of amusement and joy when he sees a funny movie.

The Schachter findings point to what has been colorfully named the "juke box" theory of emotion (10). In normal situations the physiological arousal is caused by some stimulus in the environment rather than by an injection of adrenalin. The stimulus can be compared to the dime placed in a juke box. It presumably sets off patterns of brain activity, especially in the hypothalamus, that in turn activate the autonomic nervous system and the endocrine glands, causing a general state of physiological arousal. Sensory receptors in the body report these physiological changes to the brain. But the sensations are vague and can be labeled in many different ways, just as the juke box activated by the dime can be made to play any one of a number of different records depending on which button is pushed. We label the sensations on the basis of the environmental context and what we are thinking about at the moment. If they are caused by the sight of a snake we feel afraid; if they are caused by a slap in the face we feel angry.

In the juke box, we activate the mechanism by inserting the dime and select the record by pushing a button. In emotion, a stimulus activates physiological changes, and we ourselves decide what emotion these changes represent.

A Tentative Definition of Emotion

The Schachter findings lead to a definition of emotion that, though it must be advanced with caution, seems to cover many of the known facts: *An emotion is the interpretation of a change in level and quality of internal sensations in a particular context.* The internal sensations result from physiological changes caused by patterns of brain activity, especially in the hypothalamus, that act chiefly through the autonomic nervous system but also have a direct effect upon the striped muscles of the body. The interpretation is a psychological process that seeks to determine the relationship between the sensations and the environmental context and that accounts for our subjective feelings.

There is an interesting parallel between the psychological process involved in emotion and another process discussed earlier in the book. In Chapter 5, you will recall, perception was defined as the process through which we become aware of our environment by organizing and interpreting the evidence of our senses. In emotion, we organize and interpret the sensations from within our bodies. Just as perceptions are the patterns of meaning we find in external stimuli, so are our emotional feelings the patterns of meaning we find in internal stimuli—influenced, however, by our perception of the environmental context of the moment.

Note that the definition speaks of a *change* in internal sensations, not an absolute level of sensation. Just as our sense organs are most sensitive to a change in stimuli from the environment, so are the sensory nerves inside the body most sensitive to a change in internal conditions. Some emotions are based on a stirred-up condition of the body. Others such as sadness or loneliness may involve a lower level of activity, reduced heartbeat and blood pressure, and a lack of muscle tone rather than tremor. Similarly, a hard-driving executive may be more or less stirred up at all times yet unaware of any emotion except at such times as his high rate of physiological activity decreases for some reason.

As for the interpretation we make of the changes in our internal sensations, it is sometimes immediate and automatic. If we find a snake in our path, for example, everything seems to happen at once: our hearts jump, we feel afraid, and we exhibit fearful behavior by leaping back. At other times the interpretation takes longer and is less clear-cut, as can be seen in the following report of an experience that befell a university instructor:

> On a late afternoon recently, I became aware of some extremely unpleasant feelings, involving, among other things, nausea and headache. Something was wrong. But what?
>
> I tried to figure out the possibilities. At noontime, I had behaved badly toward my daughter; I had snapped at her over an incident that was unimportant and really not her fault. Was I perhaps feeling guilt and remorse over this occurrence?
>
> My income tax return was due in a few days; I had done some preliminary work on it and had been startled to find out how much additional paperwork was necessary and how much money I was going to have to pay the government. Was I angry and upset because of the tax?
>
> The third possibility seemed to be that I was physically ill. There was a virus going around the university and several people with whom I work closely had come down with it. I decided that this was the answer—I was getting the virus—so I took some aspirin and went to bed early. I do not know what the correct interpretation was; but my behavior was determined by the interpretation I chose.

A man who is aware of a changed pattern of visceral sensations while he is sitting in a hotel room in a strange city may decide that he is lonely. A man whose best friend recently died may interpret the same pattern of sensations as grief. A man who has an important and risky business deal coming up may interpret it as fear or anxiety, and another man who is making a long bus trip home after a hard day's work may decide that he is merely tired.

Typically, the person who becomes aware of changed internal sensations attempts to explain and understand them. He scans the environment and reaches a decision. Sometimes his decision is immediate and perhaps reached unconsciously. At other times it involves a longer and more deliberate search that is akin to problem solving; the person may select one hypothesis, test it, and discard it in favor of another. At the end of the search he applies an emotionally toned label to his feelings; he decides that he is happy or sad or angry.

The behavior that is undertaken because of emotion depends largely upon the label that is put upon it. Moreover, the labeling process itself appears in many cases to produce further bodily changes and intensified feelings. Once a person has decided that he is afraid, he is likely to have additional activity of the autonomic nervous system, intensified physiological changes, and a greater feedback, all which add to his feelings of fear.

EMOTION AND LEARNING Different investigators, approaching the study from different viewpoints, tend to think of emotion in four quite different ways. They may emphasize 1) the physiological changes, 2) the patterns of activity in the central nervous system, 3) the kind of overt behavior that is labeled emotional, or 4) the subjective feelings of emotion, such as the sensations of fear or anger. These subjective feelings are often called *affects* to distinguish them from the other meanings of emotion.

The baby exhibits emotion in the first of the four meanings of the word; his rate of breathing is sometimes very slow and sometimes very fast, and his rate of heartbeat may vary from 50 to 200 per minute (10). It can be assumed that he also shows changed patterns of activity in the central nervous system, associated with the physiological changes. Certainly he exhibits emotional behavior—by weeping and thrashing about or by smiling and cooing. It appears unlikely, however, that he experiences emotion in the fourth sense of the word; he probably does not have the subjective interpretive feelings that are called fear, anger, and so on.

Emotions as Reflexes

To the very young baby, what look like emotions are complex reflexes. Three kinds of stimuli are known to lead almost automatically to crying, thrashing, and other "intense" behaviors that are usually regarded as emotional. The three are: 1) painful stimuli, 2) sudden and intense stimuli such as loud noises, and 3) loss of support (such as would result, in adults at least, in the sensation of falling). Presumably these events cause some kind of patterns of activity in the limbic system, especially in the hypothalamus, and lead to discharge of the autonomic nervous system.

Other kinds of stimuli result in the kind of behavior associated with pleasure, such as smiling. Presumably these "pleasure" stimuli—which include warmth, tactual comfort, and feeding—also result in reflex physiological changes connected with patterns of nervous activity in the autonomic nervous system and the limbic system.

At any rate, the chain from stimulus to behavior in the baby is a fairly simple one, as is shown in FIGURE 10.6. An unconditioned stimulus sets off

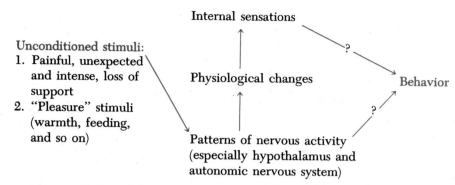

Unconditioned stimuli:
1. Painful, unexpected and intense, loss of support
2. "Pleasure" stimuli (warmth, feeding, and so on)

Internal sensations

Physiological changes

Behavior

Patterns of nervous activity (especially hypothalamus and autonomic nervous system)

Unlearned Connections in Emotion   Charted here are the simple reflex connections for emotion in the human body. The unconditioned stimuli set off patterns of nervous activity that trigger physiological changes. Afferent nerves of the internal organs and muscles then report the internal sensations to the central nervous system. The final two connections to behavior are in dispute. According to the James-Lange theory, the internal sensations set off behavior. According to the Cannon-Bard and other neurological theories, behavior occurs because of the nervous patterns, independently of the internal sensations.

FIGURE 10.6

activity in the central and autonomic nervous systems. These nervous impulses trigger reflex physiological changes, which in turn result in sensations carried to the brain by the afferent nerves of the internal organs and muscles. Only the final link between these various processes and the emotional behavior is in doubt. Perhaps there is a direct link from the patterns of nervous activity in the hypothalamus and elsewhere to behavior, as the Cannon-Bard theory would suggest. Or perhaps the baby's behavior is linked to the bodily sensations, as the James-Lange theory would suggest. This latter notion finds support from the fact that a baby's emotional behavior—such as crying in response to the painful stimulus of an open safety pin—sometimes occurs only after a fairly long time lag, as if indeed it depended upon a slow buildup of visceral changes and a feedback from these bodily changes (10). Either way, there is no need to suppose that the baby actually interprets the feedback from his body as the kind of emotional feelings—the affects—that are so well known to adults. These, as the Schachter experiments indicate, appear to be the result of learning.

Conditioning Emotions

The "Albert experiment" (page 55) demonstrates how the physiological reflexes can be conditioned to previously neutral stimuli. To review briefly, the eleven-month-old child Albert did not initially display any fearful behavior toward a rat; the rat was a neutral stimulus. The sight of the rat was then paired with an unexpected loud noise, an unconditioned stimulus to

367

which Albert did automatically respond with the physiological changes that accompany fear. After a number of pairings his reactions were conditioned to the conditioned stimulus of the rat. He now behaved fearfully toward the rat and, through stimulus generalization, to similar stimuli such as a rabbit or a man with a beard.

This is one of the ways in which learning influences emotions. The unpleasant physiological reflexes originally set off by the three kinds of unconditioned "fearful" stimuli mentioned above become conditioned to many other unconditioned stimuli. The physiological reflexes originally set off by a small number of unconditioned "pleasure" stimuli also become conditioned to many unconditioned stimuli. By the time we are adults we respond with physiological reflexes to such originally neutral stimuli as the sight of a rival or a loved one, a newspaper headline, or any of hundreds of other things that have at some time in the past been paired directly or indirectly with one of the unconditioned stimuli that cause the reflexes in the baby. Even thinking about an object of fear, love, or hate can produce these physiological reflexes, which explains the fact, mentioned near the start of the chapter, that if you think about something pleasant you may actually begin to *feel* pleasure and that if you think about something such as a social snub or being blamed for someone else's mistakes you may actually begin to *feel* anger.

Learning the Labels for Emotion

As the child grows older, he learns that people often describe themselves as being happy, angry, afraid, or sad. In other words he begins to learn the hundred different language labels that are applied by English-speaking people to their emotions. He acquires mediational units that are in effect interpretations of emotional situations and states.

When he is around the age of five or six, he tends to apply the words to the external situation rather than to his internal sensations. He is likely to say, "I am angry because you took my toy away" or "I am happy because you are going to get me a lollipop." His interpretations are based chiefly, we might say, upon the environmental context. It is only later that he begins to focus to an equal extent upon his internal sensations—the feedback from physiological changes—and to say, as adults often say, "I feel sad today" or "I feel afraid."

By adolescence the learning process has come to include all the complicated connections illustrated in FIGURE 10.7. As shown by the numbered route, events in the environment may act as conditioned stimuli that operate directly to set off the various kinds of central nervous system patterns involved in emotional behavior. The reactions in the limbic system trigger physiological changes that in turn are reported back to the central nervous system as internal sensations. The adult has learned to interpret the internal

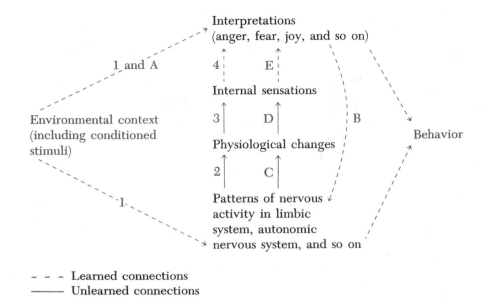

Interpretations
(anger, fear, joy, and so on)

1 and A   4 ;   E ;

Environmental context   Internal sensations
(including conditioned   3 | D | ; B   Behavior
stimuli)   Physiological changes

2 | C |

·1·   Patterns of nervous
activity in limbic
system, autonomic
nervous system, and so on

– – – Learned connections
——— Unlearned connections

Learned Connections in Emotion   Charted here are the connections
believed to represent the learned patterns of emotions in the human
adult. Feelings of emotion may be aroused either through the numbered
route or through the lettered route, as described more fully in the text.
The adult also possesses the simple unlearned reflex connections shown
FIGURE 10.7   in FIGURE 10.6

sensations—with the help of his knowledge of the environmental context—
as feelings of emotion. His interpretations—that is, his decisions as to what
emotion he is experiencing—affect his behavior; he will tend to behave in
ways that he has learned are appropriate to that emotion. His behavior may
also be more directly influenced, of course, by the patterns of nervous activity
set off by the environmental context.

The lettered route shown in FIGURE 10.7 describes an even more complex
way in which the environmental context may lead to emotional experiences
and behavior. In this case the environmental situation leads directly to an
emotional interpretation. For example, a person may be hiking alone in a
forest. He is enjoying the scenery and the exercise. Then it gradually dawns
upon him that the skies have been getting more and more cloudy, to the
point where he cannot see the sun and therefore is not sure of his directions.
At the same time, his watch tells him that he has been walking for hours and
that it is now late in the afternoon. He does not know where he is; night is
approaching, and a storm may be brewing. It occurs to him that he should
be afraid—and this interpretation of his environment, the process of thinking

about being afraid, can set off patterns of nervous activity in the limbic system and autonomic nervous system. The patterns of nervous impulses trigger physiological changes and internal sensations appropriate to fear. Feedback from the sensations strengthens his emotional interpretation, and he is now very definitely afraid.

The Importance of the Labels

The language labels used to interpret and describe emotions have an important effect upon the learning process and thus upon emotions and emotional behavior. For example, today's young people often say that they are "alienated" or "uncommitted"—two fairly new words used as labels for emotion. Presumably the internal sensations described by these words are the same as have been experienced by young people of previous generations. But previous generations did not possess such labels as "alienated" or "uncommitted" and therefore interpreted the sensations differently. To them, the internal sensations meant that they were restless, frustrated, impatient, ambitious, unhappy, lonely, or lovesick.

INDIVIDUAL DIFFERENCES IN EMOTION

Evidence of the wide range of individual differences in capacity for emotion lies all around us. We have friends who go into ecstasy over the receipt of a birthday card and others whom we would not expect to be greatly moved by the gift of a diamond. We have bad-tempered acquaintances who seem to be angry most of the time and good-natured acquaintances who never seem to be angry at all. We know happy people and sad people, brave people and fearful. One woman is terrified by a thunderstorm; another is not afraid to fight off and chase a purse snatcher. One shows signs of tension when her best friend drops in for a cup of coffee; another seems to stay calm while running an elaborate charity dinner.

The individual differences have two sources. Some of them are the result of learning; they depend upon differences in the kinds of experiences discussed in the preceding section of the chapter. Other individual differences, however, may depend upon characteristics of the nervous system, the glands, and other physical equipment; these differences appear to be largely inborn and determined by heredity.

Glandular Differences

One important individual difference among animals has already been discussed—namely, the fact that the adrenal glands of lions appear to produce large amounts of noradrenalin, while those of animals such as rabbits produce large amounts of adrenalin. In this connection, it has also been found that the adrenal glands of wild rats are much larger than those of rats that have been bred for generations in the laboratory (17).

In human beings, several individual differences have been found in the endocrine glands. Normal thyroid glands have been found to vary from 8 to 50 grams in weight, testes from 10 to 45 grams, ovaries from 2 to 10 grams. The output of human adrenal glands has been found to vary from 7 to 20 grams, of pituitary glands from 250 to 1100 milligrams (18). Although there is no direct evidence, it seems reasonable to suppose that a person with large and active endocrine glands would experience different physiological changes and therefore different emotions from a person with smaller or less active glands.

Differences in the Autonomic Nervous System

Generally speaking, women seem to be more fearful than men. The emotion of fear seems to be aroused more easily in women, by stimuli that do not have the same effect upon men. Moreover, women are more inclined to behave in a fearful manner. When there is a noise downstairs in the middle of the night, the wife traditionally hides her head under the covers; it is the husband who must venture to a meeting with what might be a burglar.

Of themselves, these facts do not necessarily tell us anything about innate differences. Our society teaches women that it is perfectly acceptable for them to become afraid and to act afraid; they are given full privilege to display the emotion of fear. Men, on the other hand, are not supposed to become terrified at the sight of a mouse; and, if the noise downstairs really is that of a burglar, they are supposed to do something about it. The apparent differences between men and women, therefore, might be strictly the result of learning and, indeed, might represent the suppression of fear in men rather than its absence.

Some animal experiments, however, indicate that there may in fact be some biological differences in emotion between the sexes. When male and female monkeys are raised in isolation, then placed with other monkeys for the first time, the females tend to act as if they are more afraid of their new companions than do the males. The females often run to a corner of the cage as if to hide or get away; the males generally do not (19). In an experiment with mice, the animals were placed in a cage, a tone was sounded, and a few seconds later an electric shock was administered. The cage was one from which escape was possible, and records were kept of how quickly the mice learned to get out of the cage when the tone was sounded and thus to escape the shock. Five different breeds of mice were used, and some noticeable differences in speed of learning were found among them. That is to say, one breed learned on the average to escape from the shock considerably more quickly than did another. In each individual breed, however, the female mice learned more quickly than did the males (20).

The experiment with the mice has been interpreted as meaning that the electric shock caused a clearer and stronger perception of unpleasant sensations for the females than for the males. Both this experiment and the observations of the monkeys raised in isolation may mean that the autonomic nervous system of the female may have a lower threshold for reaction than does the autonomic nervous system of the male and is more inclined to react more quickly, more intensely, and to weaker stimulation.

In human beings, indications of individual differences in the sensitivity of the autonomic nervous system have been provided by experiments with a drug called methacholine. This drug tends to lower the blood pressure but also stimulates the sympathetic nervous system, which has a tendency, as has been noted, to raise the blood pressure. Four quite different reactions to the drug have been noted, presumably indicating differences in the way the sympathetic nervous system responds. Some people show a sharp decrease in blood pressure, with no sign of a return to the previous level after fifteen minutes. Some show a decrease but a return to the previous level within fifteen minutes. Others show only slight changes in blood pressure. In still others the blood pressure may show an initial dip but then rises rather substantially. Presumably the sensitivity and activity of the sympathetic system are lowest in the first group, somewhat higher in the second group, still higher in the third group, and highest of all in the fourth (21).

It has also been found that people have characteristic patterns of physiological change in emotional situations. For example, one person may consistently show a rapid pulse, while another may show only a small change in pulse rate but a pronounced increase in skin temperature (22). These varying patterns may also point to individual differences in the activity of the autonomic nervous system.

Considering all the evidence about innate emotional factors, it seems reasonable to assume that people have pronounced constitutional differences in levels of glandular activity and in the sensitivity and activity patterns of their autonomic nervous systems. We might even speculate that there are constitutional differences in the central nervous system and especially in the way the hypothalamus and the limbic system operate.

This line of reasoning has led to a provocative speculation about the processes involved in psychoses. The suggestion has been made that people suffering from psychoses may have some sort of functional disturbances of the nervous structures involved in the physiological reactions to stimuli and that, because of these disturbances, they may have unusual patterns of physiological change and hence feedback of bodily sensations not generally experienced by other people (23). The person experiencing these sensations must try to interpret them, but the words and concepts he has learned from other people offer him no clues; therefore the interpretations at which he finally arrives may seem completely unintelligible and bizarre by ordinary standards. The strange feelings sometimes experienced by people under the influence of alcohol or drugs may be similar examples of bodily sensations, produced by unusual patterns of nervous activity, that defy rational interpretation.

One emotion that deserves special discussion is *anxiety,* **THE EMOTION** which is one of the most powerful of emotions and has **OF ANXIETY** far-reaching effects upon behavior. Anxiety is *a vague unpleasant feeling— a premonition that something bad is about to happen.* Anxiety is closely related to the emotion of fear; in fact it is very difficult to draw any sharp dividing line between the two. Generally speaking, fear appears to be a reaction to a specific stimulus and to have a "right now" quality about it. We see a snake and feel afraid; we know what we are afraid of and recognize that we are afraid right here and now. Anxiety is more vague; its cause is not always apparent. Moreover, as the definition states, it is a premonition of something that is about to happen—it is not concerned so much with the here and now as with the future.

In neurological terms, anxiety appears to be controlled, like other emotions, by patterns of nervous activity in the limbic system. Just as animals will learn to perform tasks for the reward of electrical stimulation of the "pleasure center" in the brain (page 72), so will they learn to work for the reward of having stimulation in certain other areas turned off. Since stimulation in some of these "displeasure" areas has been found to produce signs of fearful behavior (24), it is generally assumed that the animals are motivated by the desire to escape from fear or anxiety. In human beings an operation called a prefrontal lobotomy was formerly used as a last-resort treatment for extreme kinds of mental disease. The operation, which severed connections between the frontal lobes of the cerebral cortex and lower brain centers, tended to make patients so anxiety-free that they seldom worried about anything and often behaved in irresponsible fashion.

In physiological terms, anxiety often seems to be accompanied by muscular tension, especially in the back of the neck, by increased heart rate, and by a sweating of the palms producing the galvanic skin reflex. The physiological changes, however, have proved difficult to measure. In one study of adults who had been observed over a long period of time, the investigators divided the subjects into one group that appeared to display considerable anxiety over aggressive behavior and another group that did not seem to have this kind of anxiety. A recording in which the speaker talked about aggressive thoughts and actions was played to both groups, and their GSR and heart rate were measured. One might suppose that the anxious subjects would have shown stronger autonomic reactions, but the opposite proved to be true (25). Presumably the nonanxious subjects felt free to become involved in the recording and to respond to it. The anxious subjects, on the other hand, presumably were afraid to become involved; their anxiety made them turn a deaf ear, so to speak, to the recording. This is one of the problems that make anxiety difficult to study.

From the psychological viewpoint, anxiety is an extremely unpleasant experience and particularly difficult to cope with because of its vagueness. We usually cannot pin down the cause or even the precise nature of what we fear will happen. We can only describe the feeling in the most general kind of terms; we say we are worried, tense, "blue," moody, or "jumpy." The last word, though as vague as the others, is particularly appropriate because the person who is in the grip of anxiety has a lowered threshold for other kinds of emotional responses. He is likely to be quite irritable and quickly moved to anger; on the other hand, he may also overreact to pleasurable stimuli. He tends to have wide swings of mood and his behavior is often unpredictable.

Some investigators believe that the psychological experience of anxiety can exist independently of any physiological changes and bodily sensations. To these investigators, therefore, anxiety is not necessarily a physical condition at all but a cognitive process—what we might call a particular form of thinking or state of mind. The idea finds some support in the fact that many people seem to be more or less anxious almost constantly, certainly over longer time spans than are generally ascribed to emotions.

Sources of Anxiety

In children, especially between the ages of two and seven, anxiety usually seems rather clearly related to some kind of external event. Children are made anxious by a threat to their desire for presence of the caretaker. They are also made anxious by school tests, the prospect of spanking, and threats of physical harm such as are represented by strange animals, storms, and the dark.

The anxieties of adults are more generalized, and they center around events and possibilities that are much harder to define. Almost any motive can be accompanied by anxiety in the adult. Obviously the adult's sources of anxiety are mostly learned, though by what process is not definitely known. Some investigators think that the basic learning mechanism is fairly simple and revolves around the fact that the child is often punished or threatened with punishment when he attempts to satisfy his biological drives and his learned motives. He is punished (physically or verbally) for satisfying his biological drives by raiding the cookie jar or by soiling his pants and for satisfying his motives by engaging in aggressive behavior toward his parents or his friends, by performing forbidden sexual acts, and so on. Through conditioning, these various forms of behavior become associated with punishment; and perhaps, through the principle of stimulus generalization, any thought of implementing the motive, and thus the motive itself, may come to arouse thoughts and fears of punishment—hence anxiety. Other investigators, while conceding that punishment is a factor, also stress the role of learning experiences that teach the unpleasant consequences of failing to satisfy a biological drive or motive.

However anxiety is learned, its basic sources in adults often seem to be the following.

1. *Physical harm.* Almost everyone—even professional mountain climbers and racing drivers—experiences anxiety in situations of physical danger that threaten bodily harm. Many people have anxious feelings about possible illness or about being killed in a war.

2. *Rejection.* This centers around the social motives that spring from the child's original desire for presence of the caretaker. One reason that people frequently appear uneasy in social situations is anxiety over the possibility that people will not like them. Anxiety over rejection plays a large part in dating and in marriage.

3. *Uncertainty.* Lack of certainty is the source of the anxiety that most of us experience when we go to a new school, a new class, or a new job—particularly if the administrators of the school, the professor, or the boss are not very clear about what they expect us to do.

4. *Cognitive dissonance.* The manner in which people attempt to reduce cognitive dissonance and thus satisfy the motive for cognitive consonance was discussed in Chapter 9. Cognitive dissonance is usually accompanied by anxiety; this is the reason that a student who likes to think of himself as highly intelligent is upset when he gets a grade that tells him he is not, and that a person who likes to think of himself as generous is upset when he turns down a beggar.

5. *Frustration and conflict.* These two frequent sources of anxiety will be discussed in detail in the following chapter. The frustration of *any* motive—that is, roughly speaking, the failure to satisfy it—can result in anxiety. Conflicts between any two motives that cannot both be satisfied often result in anxiety.

Some Effects of Anxiety

Some of the ways anxiety affects behavior have already been discussed. It has been mentioned that anxiety often takes the form of stagefright, which makes the student perform badly and get a poor grade on an examination even though he has actually learned the material or which makes a golfer play below his optimum level of skill. It has also been pointed out that anxiety often interferes with the undertaking of behavior that would satisfy a motive—particularly when the anxiety is aroused by a conflict between a motive such as hostility or sexual gratification and the motive to live up to our own standards of what is right and wrong about aggressive or sexual behavior. The following chapter will discuss the various defenses—some useful and some harmful—with which people try to escape the distress of anxiety.

There is one effect of anxiety, however, that has particular significance for college students and deserves discussion at this point. This is the effect of anxiety on learning, which has been the subject of considerable experimentation. Unfortunately, no experiment on anxiety can be completely satisfactory, because it is extremely difficult to know either how much anxiety a particular person feels or the source of the anxiety. The experimenter usually has to rely on the subject's answers to some sort of questionnaire, and it is almost impossible to devise a questionnaire that will satisfactorily measure anxiety over uncertainty, cognitive dissonance, and particular kinds of frustration and conflict. Much of the experimental work on anxiety has involved the use of scales that attempt to measure the particular kind often called "test anxiety," which centers around violations of standards by failure at school tasks. On the basis of questionnaires, subjects have been divided as well as possible into groups with "high anxiety" and "low anxiety," and their learning of various tasks has then been studied—with results that, though not entirely conclusive because of the limitations just mentioned, are nonetheless interesting.

In one experiment, the learning involved conditioning the eyelid blinking reflex of college students to a previously neutral stimulus, and the findings were as shown in FIGURE 10.8. Note how much more quickly the conditioning took place among the "anxious" students than among the "not anxious." In another experiment, however, the results were quite different. In this case the students were asked to trace a path through a maze while blindfolded; the maze had ten places where the subjects had their choice of going to either right or left and had to learn which direction was correct. At this task, the "high anxiety" students learned more slowly than the others (27). One possible explanation for the results of these two experiments appears to be that students with "high anxiety" over achievement learn simple tasks more quickly because they become more involved but have trouble with more complicated learning, requiring the making of choices, because their anxiety interferes with intense concentration.

What about anxiety and performance in college? This question was explored by an investigator who selected a relatively "anxious" group and a relatively "not anxious" group of male students, and then examined their College Board scores, as an indication of their ability, and their actual grades in college. As is shown in FIGURE 10.9, the students with the lowest levels of

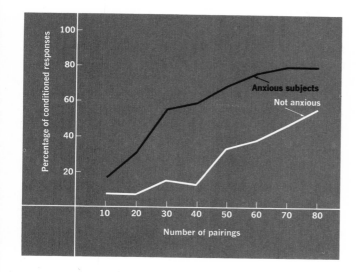

FIGURE **10.8**

Anxiety and Simple Conditioning Charted are the results of an experiment in conditioning the eyeblink reflex of two groups of students, one of which had a high level of anxiety and the other a low level of anxiety. Note that in all sets of trials from the first to the last, conditioning was more rapid for the anxious group. (26)

scholastic ability made much the same grades regardless of whether or not they seemed to be experiencing anxiety. So did the students with the highest levels of scholastic ability. But at the in-between levels of ability—where, of course, most students fall—the students who were relatively free from anxiety made significantly better grades than did the anxious students.

In a follow-up study an attempt was made to select "anxious" freshmen who were making low grades and were in danger of flunking out of college. One group of these freshmen took an active part in a counseling program in which they received advice about their problems in college, methods of study, campus life in general, and their relations with their professors—advice that presumably would reduce their anxiety about the college situation. Another group, matched as closely as possible for College Board scores, type

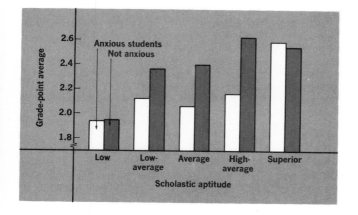

FIGURE **10.9**

Anxiety and College Grades The bars show the average grades made by relatively "anxious" and relatively "not anxious" students of different levels of scholastic ability as indicated by their College Board scores. Note the pronounced differences in the middle ranges of scholastic ability. (28)

of high school attended, and other factors that influence performance in college, did not receive counseling. From midterm to the end of the first semester the counseled group made an average improvement of more than half a grade point. The group that was not counseled improved by less than a tenth of a grade point (29). Anxiety about the college situation would appear to be a frequent—though perhaps correctable—cause of failure in college.

Anxiety and Risk Taking

FIGURE 10.10 illustrates the results of an experiment that offers some clues about the possible relationship between anxiety and the willingness to take risks. Note that the subjects who appeared to be relatively free from "test anxiety" tended to scorn the "sure thing" in this game; they made very few throws from the close distances at which they were almost certain to succeed but would receive only a low score. They also tended to avoid the high risk

FIGURE **10.10**   *Anxiety, Conservatism, and "Going for Broke"*   The curves show the strategies employed by three different kinds of subjects in a game where they tossed rings at a peg from any distance they chose. For ringing the peg from close distances they received very low scores, from far distances very high scores, and from middle distances middle scores. Subjects in group 1 had been classified on the basis of previous tests as being highly motivated toward achievement and low in "test anxiety." Group 2, though also highly motivated, was high in anxiety. Group 3 ranked low in achievement motivation and high in anxiety. For a discussion of the different strategies of the three groups, see the text. (30)

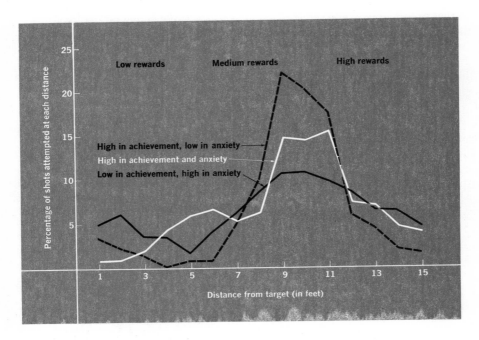

of gambling that they could score from the longest distances, which would have given them the highest scores. Subjects who appeared to be relatively high in "test anxiety" made many more shots from the short distances, but also "went for broke" more often by trying from the longest distances. This was particularly true for the subjects who were both high in anxiety and low in achievement motivation.

One might speculate, on the basis of this experiment, that people who are highly anxious about success and failure tend to adopt either a very conservative or a very risky strategy in life situations. They are inclined to settle for the "sure thing" and thus avoid failure that would add to their anxiety, or else they tend to take the kind of chances at which success is such a remote possibility that failure can readily be excused. All of us, certainly, have observed people who do not take many chances in life, settle for jobs that seem beneath their real abilities, yet occasionally take a flier in a gambling casino or in risky investments. Less anxious people, on the other hand, appear to have sufficient confidence to assume the middle-range risks that are most likely to lead to success in the long run.

Along similar lines, it has been observed that college students who appear to have a high amount of fear of failure tend to leave examination rooms early (31), as if to avoid the further anxiety of continuing to try on the examination. This strategy, of course, only increases the likelihood of the failure that they find such a disturbing prospect.

SUMMARY

1. Emotions are closely related to biological drives and learned motives. They often accompany the satisfaction or frustration of a motive or the anticipation of satisfaction or frustration.
2. The desire to obtain pleasant emotions or to avoid or escape unpleasant emotions can itself become a motive.
3. Emotions involve a wide range of physiological changes regulated by both the central nervous system and the autonomic nervous system and endocrine glands.
4. The bodily changes regulated by the central nervous system include a) muscle tension, b) tremor, c) eye blinking and other nervous movements, d) facial expressions of emotion, and e) vocal expressions of emotion.
5. The bodily changes regulated by the autonomic nervous system and endocrine glands include a) heart rate, b) blood pressure, c) blood distribution, d) composition of the blood, e) gastrointestinal activity, f) metabolic rate, g) breathing, h) salivation, i) sweating, j) gooseflesh and hair standing on end, and k) pupil size.

6. Recent studies indicate that changes in pupil size are a sensitive measure of some emotions. Pupil size has been found to increase noticeably when a person looks at an interesting photograph or when he engages in mental activity such as trying to remember a telephone number.

7. *Physiological theories* of emotion have emphasized the role of bodily changes. The *James-Lange theory* holds that stimuli in the environment set off these physiological changes, that the changes in turn stimulate sensory nerves inside the body, and that the messages of these sensory nerves are then perceived as emotion. According to this theory, we do not tremble and run because we are afraid but feel afraid because we are trembling and running.

8. *Neurological theories* of emotion have emphasized the patterns of activity of the central nervous system. The *Cannon-Bard theory* holds that stimuli in the environment set off such patterns of activity in the hypothalamus and thalamus; these patterns are then relayed both to the autonomic nervous system, where they trigger the bodily changes of emotion, and to the cerebral cortex, where they result in the feelings of emotion. The more recent *Papez-MacLean theory* emphasizes the role of the *limbic system*, a set of interconnected pathways in the brain related to the hypothalamus, some primitive parts of the cerebrum that have to do with the sense of smell and eating, and other structures.

9. Recent experiments by Schachter have indicated that physiological changes are essential for emotion but that the same pattern of physiological change can result in different emotional feelings in different environmental contexts. This has led to a new theory (sometimes called the "juke box" theory) that emotion depends upon both physiological arousal and a mental process by which the organism interprets the physiological sensations on a basis of the environmental context.

10. Thus the word *emotion* is used:
    a. By physiologists to describe various changes that take place inside the body.
    b. By neurologists to describe patterns of nervous activity.
    c. By psychologists to describe such behavior as weeping or laughing.
    d. To describe the subjective feelings—often called *affects*—that bear such familiar names as fear, anger, and so on.

11. Learning plays a triple role in emotion by a) determining what kind of external stimuli will cause physiological arousal, b) providing the words with which we label the feelings caused by the physiological changes (as fear, anger, and so on), and c) linking our feelings and interpretations with behavior.

12. Individual differences in emotion appear to be caused both by learning and by constitutional differences in glandular activity, sensitivity and

activity of the autonomic nervous system, and possibly also by different characteristics of the central nervous system.

13. People who have a tendency toward certain kinds of anxiety appear to learn faster in simple learning situations but more slowly than others when the learning demands the making of choices. In college, the presence or absence of anxiety does not appear to affect the grades of students of lowest or highest learning capacity. Of students in the in-between range of ability, however, those with a tendency toward anxiety appear to make significantly lower grades than those who do not suffer from anxiety.

14. Anxiety appears to be related to risk taking. People with high levels of anxiety over success and failure seem to adopt either a conservative strategy, in which they settle for lower rewards but minimize the chance of failure, or a "go for broke" strategy, in which they take chances at which success is such a remote possibility that failure can readily be excused. People with low levels of anxiety appear inclined toward the middle-range risks that usually are the most likely to lead to success in the long run.

RECOMMENDED READING

Candland, D. K., ed. *Emotion; bodily change, an enduring problem in psychology: selected readings.* Princeton, N.J.: Van Nostrand, 1962.

Darwin, C. *The expression of the emotions in man and animals.* New York: Philosophical Library, 1955.

Mandler, G. Emotion. In Brown, R., et al., eds. *New directions in psychology.* New York: Holt, Rinehart and Winston, 1962, pp. 267–343.

Sarason, S. B., et al. *Anxiety in elementary school children.* New York: Wiley, 1960.

Young, P. T. *Motivation and emotion.* New York: Wiley, 1961.

Discussion of motives and emotions leads naturally to a consideration of the human personality, for, in large part, each individual's personality depends upon the motives that characteristically influence his behavior and upon the kind of emotions that life's events tend to arouse in him. There are "strong personalities" (highly motivated toward independence and domination) and "weak personalities" (highly motivated toward dependency and submission). There are people with exuberant personalities (who appear to be constantly experiencing the emotion of joy): people with quarrelsome personalities (who appear to be constantly experiencing anger), and people with gloomy and frightened personalities (who seem to be constantly experiencing fear, anxiety, and guilt).

Personality is made up of many factors—indeed, of all the mediational units that the individual has acquired in his lifetime, including not only his motives and emotions but also his characteristic ways of perceiving the world, thinking about it, solving its problems, and making all the various kinds of adjustments that it requires. Thus many aspects of personality have already been discussed. This section of the book will point out how the threads already mentioned, and some additional ones, are woven into the richly varied fabric of human personality.

Chapter 11 treats frustration of motives and conflicts between motives, both of which play a prominent part in determining personality, and also describes the abnormalities of emotion and behavior to which frustration and conflict sometimes lead. Chapter 12 concerns the various theories of personality that have been developed by psychologists and psychoanalysts and also discusses the treatment of personality disorders.

FRUSTRATION

Sources of Frustration
  Physical Obstacles; Social Obstacles; Personal Obstacles
Intensity of Frustration
  Strength of the Frustrated Motive; Distance from Goal; Nature of the
  Obstacle; Number of Obstacles
The Relative Nature of Frustration
Tolerance of Frustration

CONFLICT

Conflicts with Standards
Conflicts over Goals
Approach and Avoidance
  Gradients of Approach and Avoidance; Other Influences on Approach
  and Avoidance

EFFECTS OF FRUSTRATION AND CONFLICT

Aggression
  Direct Aggression; Displaced Aggression; Criticism of Oneself
Withdrawal
Depression and Apathy
Regression
Stereotyped Behavior
Vacillation

DEFENSE MECHANISMS

Rationalization
Intellectualization
Projection

Repression
Denial
Identification
Reaction Formation
Substitution
The Role of Defense Mechanisms

ABNORMAL PSYCHOLOGY

What is Abnormality?
Stress and Abnormality
Influences on Abnormal Behavior
     Biological Factors; Sociological Factors; Psychological Factors

PSYCHONEUROSES

Anxiety States
     Anxiety Reaction; Asthenic Reaction; Hypochondriacal Reaction;
     Phobic Reaction
Hysteria
     Conversion Reaction; Dissociative Reactions
Obsessive-Compulsive Reactions
Neurotic Depression
Psychosomatic Disorders

CHARACTER DISORDERS

PSYCHOSES

Organic and Functional Pyschoses
     Schizophrenia; Manic-Depressive Psychosis; Paranoia
The Origins of Psychosis

11

FRUSTRATION AND CONFLICT

Students of behavior have sometimes speculated on what life would be like if we human beings were motivated by only one desire at a time, if we had learned exactly the kind of behavior designed to satisfy each motive, and if the world were so arranged that satisfactions for all our motives were there for the taking (1).

It is difficult to imagine such a situation. The closest thing to it, perhaps, exists among some of the societies of the tropical islands, where the climate is so warm that the simplest kinds of shelter and clothing are sufficient and where food can be picked off the nearest tree or scooped out of the ocean. Yet even the most primitive of human societies, living in the midst of the greatest natural abundance, seem to be plagued by conflicts of one kind or another. Their gods or the social taboos of the tribe frown on certain kinds of behavior. They have rules that regulate their eating habits, their expression of hostility, their religious rituals, their social relationships, and their sexual behavior. The rules are often very different from those of our own society and may seem quite lax by comparison. But they are rules nonetheless, and they sometimes prevent satisfaction of the motives of primitive man, though to us those motives may seem modest and uncomplicated.

Perhaps the frustration of motives is part of the price human beings must pay for the privilege of living together in a society. (No society could survive if its members freely satisfied their acquisitive motives by totally disregarding property rights and satisfied their hostile motives through murder.) Or perhaps man possesses some kind of divine discontent or sheer perversity that makes life in a conflict-free paradise intolerable.

Certainly our own kind of civilization makes frustration and conflicts of motives inevitable. We acquire motives that we cannot possibly satisfy—at least not at all times and in full—and we also acquire motives that are incompatible and thus bound to conflict. The frustration and conflicts give rise to various highly unpleasant emotions, particularly anxiety, which have a profound and sometimes devastating effect upon behavior.

A college basketball tournament provides a good example of frustration in the making. Eight teams and eight coaches are strongly motivated to win the tournament. Forty or more players would all like to be named most valuable player. But only one team can be the champion, and only one man can be most valuable player. All the other teams, coaches, and players are bound to be frustrated. If we watch the losers closely, we will see many kinds of emotional effects. Some of them will display hostility; they will slam the ball or a towel on the floor. Some of them may weep with disappointment. Some will display depression or apathy; they may be "down in the dumps" for days afterward and have a difficult time getting interested in food, studies, and social events. Even those who shrug off defeat and smilingly congratulate the winners will have some kind of emotional twinges, though they may hide them or quickly get over them.

Sources of Frustration

The word *frustration* has two different meanings, one based on external events, the other on internal feelings. The external definition is *the blocking of motive satisfaction by an obstacle.* The internal definition of frustration is *the unpleasant feelings that result from the blocking of motive satisfaction by an obstacle.* In either case the key word in the definition is *obstacle.* Several kinds of obstacles can cause frustration. Most of them fall into the following three groups, which are generally used to classify the sources of frustration.

PHYSICAL OBSTACLES   Some obstacles to motive satisfaction are inherent in our environment. The world was not designed for mankind's constant pleasure. Over much of the world the hunger drive is often frustrated by poor soil, drought, and other causes of crop failure. Even in the well-fed United States, our desire for physical comfort is often frustrated by heat, cold, and storms. Time can be an obstacle. There may simply not be enough hours in the day for all the things we would like to do. Many of the motives of the adolescent have to go unsatisfied until he is older and more mature.

Other physical obstacles are man-made but equally unavoidable. Our desire to get to class on time is frustrated by a broken alarm clock, a flat tire, or a traffic jam. Our desire to see a friend is frustrated by the fact that he attends a school a thousand miles away. We are constantly frustrated in small ways by broken shoelaces, stuck windows, wrong numbers on the telephone, and lack of seats on the bus.

387

SOCIAL OBSTACLES   Many frustrations spring from our relations with other people. A young man has a strong motive for acceptance and affection from a particular young woman, but she does not like him at all. A girl's desire to study music is frustrated by parents who have other plans for her. A workman's desire for higher wages is frustrated by his boss. A wife's desire to have a career is frustrated by a husband who is opposed to her taking a job.

Sometimes our motives meet obstacles imposed by society as a whole. Minority groups may be unable to satisfy their desires for social and economic advance because of prejudice. In some nations, people from lower social classes meet with obstacles if they try to rise above their origins; many jobs and professions are closed to them. One special kind of frustration that society often creates for the individual concerns the motive for certainty. The child likes to have rules set for him; he likes to know what he is permitted to do and not permitted to do. When the adults around him fail to set these guidelines, the child's motive for certainty is frustrated, and he often becomes extremely anxious. The desire of adults for certainty is often frustrated by such features of our society as economic changes, the draft, and the threat of war and destruction.

PERSONAL OBSTACLES   The last group of obstacles to motive satisfaction is made up of our own deficiencies. Some of us dream of being actors but lack the talent and the physical appearance. We want to be musicians but are tone deaf. We aspire to be atomic scientists but lack the intelligence. Our urges for acceptance and affection may be frustrated by characteristics we have that rub other people the wrong way.

Intensity of Frustration

Some frustrations can be quickly shrugged off; others persist and fester. In other words, there are degrees of frustration, varying from mild to severe. The intensity of frustration appears to depend upon the following factors.

STRENGTH OF THE FRUSTRATED MOTIVE   A student may be mildly motivated to win a bridge game to which he has been invited by his girlfriend's parents, but he is not likely to suffer much frustration if he loses. A student who is thinking of making bridge his career—and therefore has a strong motive to prove his superiority at the game—may be seriously frustrated by losing. In general, we suffer severe frustration over failure to satisfy strong motives such as those for achievement, acceptance, affection, and sexual experience. We are less frustrated by obstacles to motives that are less important to us.

The relationship between motive strength and degree of frustration has been demonstrated experimentally as follows. A baby was permitted to drink a half ounce of milk from his bottle. Then, while his hunger drive presumably was still very strong, the bottle was taken away. He began crying within five seconds. On another occasion, the bottle was taken away after he had drunk 2.5 ounces. This time he did not cry for ten seconds. On still another occasion he was permitted to drink 4.5 ounces, at which point his hunger drive presumably was reduced to quite a low intensity. This time he waited twelve seconds before crying (2). The common-sense notion that the effect of an external frustration on the person depends upon the strength of the motive blocked appears to be borne out even by the behavior of babies.

DISTANCE FROM GOAL   Another common-sense notion about frustration is that it is bound to be greater if an obstacle appears when the goal seems within reach than if satisfaction is thwarted when the goal is still distant. A young woman who wants to be a movie actress will probably be able to cope with her disappointment if she is told after a few casual lessons that she has no talent. But suppose that she goes to drama school, works hard, wins praise, stars in some of the school plays, is offered a movie test by a producer who has seen her and assures her that she has the potential for success—and then finds that for some reason she photographs so badly that she can never hope for a part. Her frustration is sure to be intense.

This factor has also been demonstrated experimentally. The behavior of rats in a maze has been found to be affected more by a barrier near the goal than one at the start (3). So has the behavior of college students trying to learn a maze (4). The results of an experiment in which school children were frustrated at various distances from their goal is shown in FIGURE 11.1.

NATURE OF THE OBSTACLE   Most of us can cope much better with physical obstacles—those that seem to be unavoidable quirks of nature or of mechanical failure—than with social obstacles raised by our fellow man. Even when the obstacles are social, we tend to be less frustrated if there appears to be some kind of sensible explanation than if the obstacle seems to be arbitrary and capricious. Our frustration at having to wait in a doctor's office is tempered by the fact that we see he has a waiting room full of other patients who also want to seek his advice. We are likely to feel considerably more frustrated by a filling station attendant who makes us wait while he has a long conversation with a young woman in a car at the other pump.

One investigator asked a group of college students how they would act if, for example, a date called up at the last minute to cancel out and either gave a valid excuse such as sudden illness or gave no reasonable explanation. Their response indicated substantially more frustration in the second case (6).

NUMBER OF OBSTACLES   Frustration has a cumulative effect. We may laugh at the first obstacle, shrug off the second, react only mildly to the third, but sooner or later, if the sequence continues, we lose patience. Let us say that

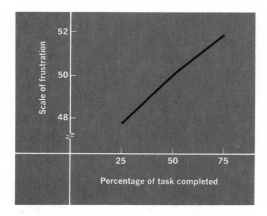

FIGURE 11.1

Frustration and Distance from Goal   The curve shows the results of an experiment in which children were asked to play a "game": they were supposed to place thirty-six marbles into the thirty-six holes of a game board. Sometimes they were permitted to complete the "game." At other times the experimenter interrupted them by activating a device that made the marbles already in the holes drop out of sight. Each time this happened a buzzer sounded. The child could turn off the buzzer by pressing on a plunger, and the pressure he applied was presumably a rough measure of his degree of frustration. Note how much greater it was when the child was interrupted when he was near the goal (75 percent completed) than when he was still far from the goal (25 percent completed). (5)

a young man is trying to get to a basketball game. He loses time because a shirt button pops off, then finds he must stop at a filling station for gas. His date keeps him waiting while she finishes dressing. He approaches a railroad crossing just as the gates go down, and a train that seems to be a hundred cars long slowly lumbers by. The highway to the field house is blocked by detour signs. On the detour the signs are so vague that he gets lost. Back on the right road, he runs into a traffic jam near the field house. The parking lot is full, and he has to drive around for ten minutes exploring the nearby streets. The closest parking place he can find is a half mile away from the arena, and all the while he is walking this half mile he hears shouts from inside that tell him the game has begun. When he arrives at long last, he finds that he left the tickets at home. At this point, which of us would not be almost beside himself with frustration?

The Relative Nature of Frustration

One interesting aspect of frustration has been demonstrated in an experiment in which children aged two to five were observed in a playroom that was equipped only with "half toys," such as a telephone without a transmitter and an ironing board without an iron. Despite the missing parts, they played quite happily—until the screen was removed and they saw much better toys in the other half of the room. Then, when a wire barrier was placed between them and the "whole toys," most of them showed signs of extreme frustration (7).

What people find frustrating, as this experiment shows, is a relative matter. "Half toys" are fun to play with, if there is nothing better at hand. When better toys lie just beyond reach, the "half toys" are no longer good enough. In adult life a man may be perfectly satisfied with his salary until his best friend gets a raise and with his old used car until his neighbor buys a new convertible. A woman who has never before wished for such possessions may feel frustrated when a friend shows up in a fur coat or moves into a new house. Many people who are quite successful and well liked suffer pangs of frustration because a brother or sister is even more successful and popular.

If a modern American were by some miracle transported to the America of a century ago, he would undoubtedly suffer all kinds of frustrations—from lack of central heating in winter and air conditioning in summer, from inability to get quick relief from a toothache, from lack of good lighting to read by at night. Yet the Americans who lived a hundred years ago probably suffered no more frustration than exists today. Among Negroes in America, indeed, there is probably more frustration today than ever before. Although the civil rights movement and increased economic opportunities have greatly improved the *absolute* level of the Negro's position in society, they have also served to emphasize the *relative* disadvantages under which he lives and thus have created more intense frustration.

Tolerance of Frustration

Even in childhood, human beings seem to display rather wide individual differences in the amount of frustration they can tolerate; this has been demonstrated experimentally, as illustrated in FIGURE 11.2. Apparently the child's tolerance can be increased to a certain extent through special training, as has been indicated by the experiment described in FIGURE 11.3.

Among adults, individual differences in frustration tolerance have been dramatically apparent under wartime conditions. Some men break down under the relatively mild frustrations of training camp and display the various symptoms of abnormal behavior that will be discussed later in the chapter. Others are able to withstand the much more severe frustrations of the battlefield and prisoner of war camps. Under more ordinary circumstances, all of us know people who have managed to carry on in normal fashion and even appear relatively cheerful despite serious physical handicaps or tragic disappointments and know others who are reduced to tears or temper tantrums if the breakfast bacon is burned.

FIGURE 11.2

Frustration Tolerance Among Children An intelligence test was given to two groups of children, one judged to be well adjusted and the other to be poorly adjusted. The test used was the Stanford-Binet, which ordinarily begins with easy items that the child usually gets all correct and progresses to more difficult ones that the child cannot answer. The experiment was designed on the hypothesis that to poorly adjusted children the usual progression might cause frustration and thus lower scores. Therefore the test was given twice—once in the

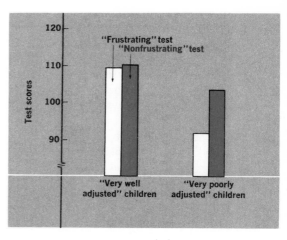

ordinary way (deemed "frustrating") and once by mixing up the easy and difficult questions and returning to an easy one every time the child experienced a failure (deemed "nonfrustrating"). On the average, the well-adjusted children made almost exactly the same scores both times. The poorly adjusted children made substantially higher scores on the "nonfrustrating" test—indicating that their performance on the other test was indeed affected by a lower threshold for frustration. (8)

FIGURE 11.3

Results of Training in Frustration Tolerance The length of the bars shows the amount of improvement in various kinds of behavior made by a group of a dozen children who were given special training in an attempt to increase their tolerance to frustration. The white bars represent the children's average score on the experimenter's scale of immaturity and maturity before training, the colored bars the average score after training. The children in the experiment were chosen after an initial test in which they demonstrated considerably more frustration when confronted with difficult situations than did other children, whose average scores on the maturity scale are represented by zero. Note that after training the group that originally behaved in an immature fashion actually made better scores on some aspects of behavior than did the more "normal" group. The experimenters trained the children by encouraging them to complete simpler tasks and thus to persist at tasks in expectation of eventual success and by showing them how to attack problems constructively and without the help of adults. (9)

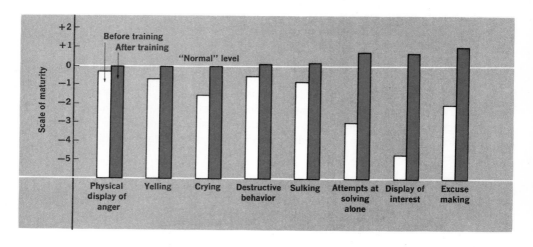

Although the word *conflict* can ordinarily mean many things, ranging from the struggle of two small children over a rubber ball to a world war, for present purposes it has only one meaning. *A conflict is the simultaneous arousal of two or more incompatible motives, resulting in unpleasant emotions.* The emotional factor is an essential part of the definition. For example, a person might be motivated to take a trip to Europe by boat and at the same time to make the trip by air. But this situation might not necessarily cause any emotional distress. Both prospects would probably be pleasant, and the decision betweeen them could be made by the casual flipping of a coin. Therefore the situation need not result in conflict. If, however, both wishes involve some unpleasant emotions— perhaps fear of seasickness on the one hand and fear of airplanes on the other—then a conflict would exist. The person will experience uncertainty, hesitation, and the feeling of being "torn" and distressed—elements that are an integral part of conflict and that make conflicts such an unpleasant part of life and a potential threat to normal behavior.

Conflicts fall into two general classes. One class includes conflicts between motives and standards; the other includes conflicts over incompatible goals.

Conflicts with Standards

Our standards, acquired through learning and identification with our childhood heroes, comprise our pattern of how we feel we should behave. When a motive urges us toward behavior that is incompatible with our standards, we have a conflict that often results in intense anxiety. The growing child, for example, may be motivated by hostility and the desire for independence to strike out in some manner against his parents. But these motives conflict with his desire to live up to standards that tell him he must be an obedient child and must respect his parents, causing him to experience shame or guilt. An adolescent or adult often experiences similar conflicts and anxieties over what would happen to his image in society or to his own self-respect if he struck out angrily against a teacher or a boss.

In bygone years a motive that appears to have conflicted very often with standards and to have generated intense anxiety was the sexual urge. But society today appears to take a somewhat more permissive attitude toward sexual expression; we are surrounded by books, movies, and television shows (all of which have an effect on standards) that seem to define sexual expression as desirable rather than shameful. In today's society a motive that appears to generate considerable anxiety among men is the desire to be dependent and passive. Among women the desire to be dominant (for example, by working in masculine occupations) often generates intense conflict and unpleasant emotion.

Conflicts over Goals

The other class of conflicts occurs when two motives for different and incompatible external goals are aroused at the same time. Most students experience frequent conflicts between the desire to get passing grades and the desire for affiliation and approval (as represented by socializing with one's friends). Many times during a school year these two motives conflict acutely and painfully. For example, it is the night before an examination. The motive to get good grades creates a strong pull toward locking oneself in one's room and studying. But friends call and suggest going to the movies or a party. Various motives for acceptance and affection, for being known as a good fellow and not as a bookworm, now pull strongly in the opposite direction. Only one of the two motives can be satisfied. An agonizing decision must be made.

To complicate the situation, the decision will arouse anxieties no matter which way the student turns. If he decides to study, he feels anxious about the loss of the goal of being with his friends and also about the possibility that their regard for him may be lowered and that they may be inclined to reject him. If he decides to go with his friends, he feels anxious over the possibility of failure on the examination and perhaps also over rejection by his teachers and his parents.

In life after college the same kind of conflict often occurs between the motive for success and wealth and the motive to be with one's family. Shall the young inventor spend the evening in his laboratory (and risk loss of affection from his wife and children) or spend the evening with his family (and risk failure as an inventor)?

Life is full of conflicts over pairs of goals that cannot both be attained. Shall I marry now (and lose my chance for other social experiences with the opposite sex) or wait (and risk losing the person I think I love)? Shall I try for a high-paying but difficult job (and risk failure) or settle for a more modest job (and give up the idea of being rich)? Shall I spend my money for an automobile (and skimp on food and clothing) or for more basic needs (and lose the pleasure that an automobile would provide)? Shall I spend everything I earn (and risk my future security) or save some of it (and miss out on things I want to buy now)? Shall I live in city or country? Shall I have a small family or a large one? The list of conflicts could be expanded almost indefinitely.

Approach and Avoidance

A useful way to categorize conflicts over goals—of special value because it provides a start toward studying some of the effects of conflict—is based on the concepts of approach and avoidance. Most conflicts over goals, it has been suggested, fall into one of three categories: 1) *approach-approach,* 2) *avoidance-avoidance,* or 3) *approach-avoidance* (10).

In an *approach-approach conflict* the aroused motives have as their objectives two desirable goals, both of which we want to approach. However, we cannot approach both goals at once, and attaining one of them means giving up the other. We cannot simultaneously satisfy the motive to watch the late movie on television and the motive to get a good night's sleep. We cannot simultaneously satisfy the motive to spend our money on a new tennis racket and the motive to spend it on a coat. The conflict in an approach-approach situation arises from the fact that attaining one desirable goal means giving up another desirable goal. We are torn between alternatives—each of which would be thoroughly pleasant except for our disappointment over losing the other.

In an *avoidance-avoidance conflict* there is simultaneous arousal of motives to avoid alternatives, both of which are *un*pleasant. For example, your automobile is very dirty, and you would like to avoid being seen driving it while it looks so disreputable. On the other hand, you would also like to avoid the trouble of washing it. Another example: You are too keyed up over tomorrow's examination—or golf match—to get to sleep. You would like to avoid the unpleasantness of tossing and turning in bed. But you would also like to avoid the grogginess you will suffer tomorrow if you take a sleeping pill.

In an *approach-avoidance conflict* we have mixed feelings about a single goal that has both desirable aspects (that make us want to approach it) and undesirable aspects (that make us want to avoid it). In the laboratory an approach-avoidance conflict can be set up by teaching an animal that if it goes to a certain spot in a maze it will receive food, but it will also receive an electric shock. In real-life situations we may be tempted to eat a pizza but know from experience that pizzas give us indigestion. We may want to go swimming with our friends but know that the water is much too cold for comfort. We may want to follow the school team to an out-of-town game but dislike the idea of driving so far.

Sometimes we are torn between two goals that both have their good points and their bad. This is true in the case of the student undecided between studying and going out with his friends. He wants to approach the goal of study because it will satisfy his achievement motive, and at the same time he wants to avoid it because it arouses anxiety over rejection by his friends. He wants to approach the goal of socializing with his friends because it satisfies his affiliation motives, but he wants to avoid it because it arouses anxiety over the next day's examination. The situation involves a *double approach-avoidance conflict.* Since any decision between two goals is likely to result in a certain amount of regret or anxiety over giving up the one that we decide against, most conflicts are double approach-avoidance.

GRADIENTS OF APPROACH AND AVOIDANCE   Caught in an approach-avoidance conflict—single or double—what is a person likely to do? It has been established that he will exhibit what is called a *gradient of approach* toward his goal (or toward each of his two goals in a double conflict). In other words, the strength of his inclination to approach a desirable goal will vary in accordance with certain factors. He also will exhibit a *gradient of avoidance*, or changing strength of inclination to avoid an unpleasant goal.

The two gradients have been demonstrated and plotted for certain kinds of animal behavior as shown in FIGURE 11.4. Note that the gradient of approach, though it rises as the goal is neared, does not rise very fast; it is not very steep. The gradient of avoidance, however, is much higher at and near the goal than farther away; this gradient is extremely steep. The lines demonstrate two general principles of the tendencies to approach a desirable goal or avoid an undesirable goal:

1. The gradients of approach and avoidance reach their highest level near the goal.
2. The gradient of avoidance is steeper than the gradient of approach.

In the right-hand graph in FIGURE 11.4 the gradients of approach and avoidance are shown together. In this situation one would expect an animal placed in the alley at point A to have a greater tendency to approach than to retreat from a goal that is simultaneously desirable and undesirable; one would expect it to move toward the goal until it reached the point at which the gradient of approach and the gradient of avoidance intersect and are equal. Similarly, one would expect an animal placed in the alley at point B to move away from the goal until it reached the point at which the gradients are equal, then to stop and hesitate. The experimental evidence suggests that this does indeed happen. It is theoretically possible to predict which direction an animal caught in this approach-avoidance conflict will take and where it will stop (12).

OTHER INFLUENCES ON APPROACH AND AVOIDANCE   On the basis of FIGURE 11.4 and the principles of the gradients of approach and avoidance, the factors that influence decisions in situations of conflict can now be summarized. Note, as you go through the following list, how similar these factors are to those discussed on pages 340–43 as helping to determine whether a motive will result in behavior.

1. *Distance in space from goal.* In the case of the student torn between going out with his friends and studying for an examination, we can presume that the pull toward joining his friends may well prevail if the friends are physically present. If the student is in his room with his books when the invitation comes, he may be pulled more strongly toward study. But if the

idea of studying arouses strong inclinations toward avoidance, the closer he gets to his books the more likely he will be to pull away from them and join his friends.

2. *Distance in time from goal.* If the student's conflict occurs a full week before the examination, the pull toward study is hardly likely to prevail against the pull toward his friends. But, if the decision has to be made the night before the test, the student is likely to resolve the conflict by studying, because the goal of passing the examination is so close in time.

3. *Strength of motive.* The importance of motive strength was experimentally demonstrated in the same study that is illustrated in FIGURE 11.4. If the rat was not very hungry—in other words, if his motive to obtain food was relatively weak—the entire line representing the gradient of approach was lowered. When he was very hungry, the gradient of approach was raised.

4. *Expectancy of goal attainment.* The final factor that influences the decision in case of conflict is expectancy of goal attainment. For the student the pull toward his friends will depend in part upon how successfully he

FIGURE 11.4   *Approach and Avoidance*   The graphs illustrate the results of an experiment on the tendencies of rats to approach a desirable goal or avoid an unpleasant goal. The animals were placed in a harness attached to a sort of leash, so that measurements could be made of how hard they would pull against an attempt to restrain them. In the part of the experiment illustrated in the graph at left, they ran down a narrow alley toward a goal at which they expected to find food. Note that the pull against the harness—measuring the gradient of approach—becomes gradually stronger as they near the goal. In the part illustrated at center, they had learned to expect not food but an electric shock at the goal; they were placed in the alley near the goal and permitted to run away. Note how much harder they pulled when near the undesirable goal than after they had got some distance away—in other words, how steep the gradient of avoidance is. In the graph at right, the two gradients are both shown, as a theoretical picture of what the situation might be if the animals had received both food and shock at the goal line. Note where the two gradient lines intersect. If an animal who expected both food and shock at the goal were placed at point A to the left of the intersection, what would it be likely to do? If placed at point B, what would it do? For the answer, see the text. (11)

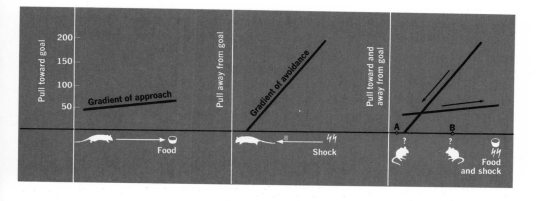

believes he can satisfy his motives for socialization by going out with them; his pull toward studying will depend in part upon how much chance he thinks he has of passing the examination.

EFFECTS OF FRUSTRATION AND CONFLICT By definition, frustrations and conflicts are unpleasant; they result in anxiety and other unpleasant emotions. The organism therefore tries to relieve the frustration or resolve the conflict in order to escape from the distress. Thus many forms of behavior—some of which, unfortunately, can result in even greater distress—are set into motion by frustration and conflict. Some are more likely to occur in situations of frustration, others in situations of conflict.

Aggression

When frustrated by some obstacle, the organism often fights back. It attacks the obstacle—whether this be a physical barrier, a person, or society as a whole. The hungry animal, barred from getting at food by a door, will try to gnaw through the wood. The child, frustrated by another child who takes his toy, will often attack with his fists. The adult, frustrated by high taxes, writes an angry letter to the editor of his newspaper. Thus *aggression* is one possible result of frustration. It may take several forms.

DIRECT AGGRESSION   In the experiment with the "half toys" many of the children made a direct assault on the wire barrier that separated them from the better toys that they wanted. This is a good example of direct aggression, which is focused on the obstacle that causes the frustration. Other examples would be the child's striking the other child who has taken his toy and the adult's organizing a political fight against the taxes that frustrate him. Direct aggression may be a rather futile outlet for the emotions aroused by frustration, such as weeping or angrily kicking at a tire that has gone flat, or it may be a form of operant behavior that attempts to get rid of the obstacle and relieve the frustration (see FIGURE 11.5). It is often learned through the imitation of other people.

DISPLACED AGGRESSION   In some cases, a direct attack upon the obstacle is impossible. But aggression is likely to result anyway and to take some rather strange outlets, as was demonstrated by the following experiment.

A group of young boys was organized into two handicraft clubs. One was directed by an adult leader who behaved in a friendly and democratic way, taking the boys into his confidence and letting them help make the group decisions. The leader of the other group deliberately ran it with an iron hand, giving the boys no voice in the proceedings and instead issuing arbitrary

Different Reactions to Frustration Even thirteen-month-olds show pronounced differences in reactions to frustration. When the boy is separated by a fence from his mother and toys, he displays active behavior by first trying to climb the fence, then trying to squeeze around it. The girl, in the same situation, bursts into helpless tears.

FIGURE 11.5

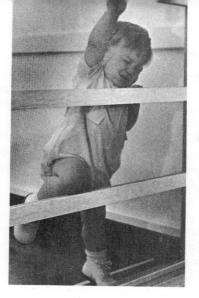

orders and presumably arousing considerable frustration. The behavior of the two groups was then observed after the leaders had left the room. The outstanding feature was that the boys who had been frustrated by their iron-handed leader began to release their pent-up aggression by directing it toward the members of the group who were least able to stand up and fight back (13).

This kind of *displaced aggression*—aroused by frustration by an obstacle that cannot be attacked directly and taken out on an innocent bystander—is very common. The man frustrated by a powerful boss goes home and behaves aggressively toward his wife and children. The child frustrated by his parents takes out his aggression on a smaller child or on a pet. Displaced aggression probably accounts for much booing of umpires at baseball games and for the popularity of Westerns in which the villain gets his comeuppance at the end.

CRITICISM OF ONESELF   A person who has made a tactless remark will sometimes say, "I could bite my tongue off." A person who has made a stupid mistake may say, "I could kick myself." In fact people actually pound their foreheads with their fists at times or bang their heads against a wall. Thus can the strong feelings born of frustration lead to criticism of oneself, a sort of angry self-derogation.

We are stranded on a country road because we forgot to check the gasoline gauge; we have failed an examination because we carelessly put down the wrong figure. We feel that we have been frustrated by an obstacle of our own making; we direct our anger against the part of ourselves that is to blame. In other cases we may be frustrated by someone we cannot attack or by a situation we do not quite understand, and we take out our aggression in the form of self-derogation. We often accuse ourselves of being stupid, ungrateful, unlovable—when in fact the cause of our frustration lies elsewhere. Self-derogation may take the form of a generalized self-hate that leads a person to punish himself (for example, by denying himself the pleasure of recreation or a good meal) or, in extreme cases, to commit suicide.

The three types of aggressive behavior—direct, displaced, and self-critical—may singly or in combination account for many types of violent behavior. Vandalism, juvenile delinquency, and crime are forms of aggressive behavior generally resulting from frustration.

Withdrawal

Another frequent reaction to frustration, especially when it continues over long periods, is *withdrawal*. Most of us have known people who seem to have lost all hope of overcoming their obstacles and have lapsed into inaction; we say of them that they have "given up" or "quit trying." They are trying to relieve their feelings of frustration by withdrawing from the attempt to attain their goals.

Withdrawal can take a number of forms. One of the most common is *fantasy*, in which the person tries to spend as much time as possible not in the real world of obstacles and frustrations but in a make-believe world of daydreams in which he imagines that he is attaining his goals. Reading is often a retreat into the world of fantasy; the shy and physically weak young man imagines that he is the conquering hero beloved by all the maidens who surround King Arthur's court; the shy and physically unattractive young woman imagines that she is the glamorous heroine of the newest novel about the international smart set.

Another kind of withdrawal has been called *nomadism*, in which the frustrated person wanders through life without ever putting down roots or devoting himself to the goals sought by most people. The old-fashioned hobo, who floated from town to town living on handouts, was displaying a form of nomadism. The modern beatnik, avoiding work and family responsibilities, may also be an example of nomadism.

Depression and Apathy

Closely related to withdrawal are *depression* and *apathy*. The victim of frustration may live his days in the kind of depression often called "a blue funk." He may become so apathetic that he seems to lose all interest in what happens to him and has a difficult time finding the energy for the ordinary chores of life.

In times of catastrophe and war, depression and apathy are common and often extreme. American soldiers in prisoner of war camps in Korea, forced to live day after day under conditions of privation and with no hope of being rescued in the near future, sometimes became so apathetic that they died of diseases they would quickly have thrown off under ordinary circumstances (14).

Regression

One of the most striking findings of the experiment with the "half toys" was that the frustrated children began to behave as if they were, on the average, seventeen months younger than their actual age. This kind of behavior—retreating toward types of activity appropriate to a lower level of maturity—is called *regression*.

The first-born child in a family often shows signs of regression when a baby brother or sister arrives; he may go back to such forgotten habits as thumb sucking, or he may want to be fed from a bottle. Frustrated adults may regress to weeping or temper tantrums, or they may try to return to their family homes and the arms of their parents, like the wife who goes home to mother after a quarrel. An extreme case of regression such as is sometimes found among psychotics is illustrated in FIGURE 11.6.

Stereotyped Behavior

Another reaction to frustration is the tendency to repeat some action over and over again, despite the fact that it appears to serve no useful purpose. This

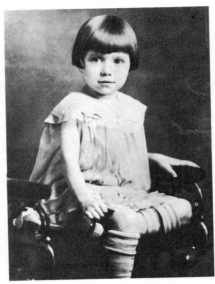

A *Case of Regression*   The girl at left, a seventeen-year-old psychiatric patient, found the old photograph of herself at center, taken when she was five. She then cut her hair and made every other possible attempt to look as she had at five, as shown in the photograph at right. (15)

FIGURE 11.6

is called *stereotyped behavior*. Among adults it has been observed to a pronounced degree in medical patients who have suffered brain damage that interferes with their speech or motor skills. Frustrated by their disabilities, many such patients keep placing their shoes and other belongings in certain definite places and patterns, and they become upset by any variation in the appearance or arrangement of their rooms or lockers. Many frustrated people have definite sterotyped patterns of conversation—phrases they keep repeating over and over again, whether they are appropriate to the discussion or not.

In a classic experiment on stereotyped behavior, a rat was placed on a stand from which it could jump toward either of two small doorways, one marked with a white circle on a black card, the other marked with a black circle on a white card. If the rat chose correctly, the door opened, and the rat entered a food compartment. If it chose incorrectly, it bumped into a locked doorway and fell into a net. After the rat had learned to discriminate between the white and the black circles, the problem was made insoluble; half the time food was placed behind the white circle and the door behind the black circle was locked, and the other half of the time this procedure was reversed. The rat's attempts to reach the food and to avoid the bump and fall were now frustrated. After a while it simply remained on the stand and refused to jump at all—a reaction resembling apathy. The experimenter then forced the rat to jump by applying a shock, a blast of air, or a prod with a stick. Under these circumstances the animal's behavior became highly

402

stereotyped; it tended to keep jumping time after time to the same doorway, regardless of the marking or whether it was rewarded or was punished by a fall. This stereotyped tendency to jump in the same direction every time persisted for as many as several hundred trials and sometimes continued even when the other doorway was left open so that the food behind it was clearly visible (16).

Vacillation

In conflict situations a frequent reaction is *vacillation*—the tendency to be drawn first toward one resolution of the conflict, then toward the other. The student torn between studying and going out with his friends may change his mind several times; at one moment he may lean strongly toward studying, at the next moment toward going out. In an extreme case of vacillation he may take so long making up his mind that he has very little time left for either of the two possibilities.

In an experiment on vacillation, children were shown two attractive toys and a clock that was set into motion by pressing either of two bars, one under each of the toys. The children were told to select the toy they wanted by pressing one of the bars. The clock would then run for a full minute, after which the toy they had selected would be theirs. At any time before the minute was up, however, they could change their minds and choose the other toy by pressing the other bar. Many children changed their minds at least once and often several times (17). They usually waited until the clock had run for about two thirds of a minute, at which time anxiety over losing the second toy presumably outweighed their desire to obtain the first toy.

As is shown in FIGURE 11.7, vacillation is accompanied by anxiety. The beginning parachutists in this study, who continued to vacillate between jumping and not jumping, showed a steady and pronounced increase in physiological signs of anxiety right up to the moment of making the jump. The experienced jumpers presumably felt committed to the jump much sooner, stopped vacillating, and showed no further increase in anxiety.

Among the effects of frustration and conflict, as has just been described, are aggression, withdrawal, depression **DEFENSE MECHANISMS** and apathy, regression, stereotyped behavior, and vacillation. In addition, frustration and conflict often result in a group of psychological processes that play such an important part in behavior that they deserve a section of their own. They are called *defense mechanisms*, and they act to reduce the anxiety that results from frustration and conflict. All defense mechanisms involve

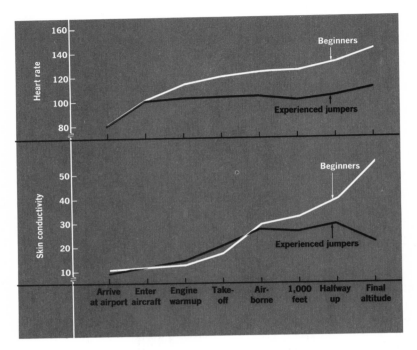

FIGURE 11.7   *Vacillation and Anxiety*   As indications of anxiety, records were kept of the heart rate and the electrical conductivity of the skin of parachute jumpers. Note that the heart rate of experienced jumpers increased only until they got into the aircraft, and the skin conductivity only until they were airborne. For the beginning jumpers, heart rate and skin conductivity continued to rise right up to the moment of jumping. One explanation appears to be that the experienced jumpers felt committed to jump as soon as they entered the plane, while the beginners continued to vacillate between jumping and not jumping until the last moment. (18)

self-deception and a distortion of reality, and it is generally believed that they operate unconsciously—that is, a person adopts a defense mechanism without being aware of it. These processes apparently operate in everyone at times; in psychotic people they are seen in extreme and exaggerated form.

Rationalization

This is perhaps the most common of defense mechanisms. It is familiar even to children, although not under its scientific name, through Aesop's fable about the fox who, unable to reach the grapes, consoled himself by deciding that they would have been sour anyway. *Rationalization* is an attempt to find logical excuses for disappointments or unseemly behavior.

As Aesop correctly perceived, people often use the "sour grapes" rationalization to explain away frustrations. A young man, frustrated because he was turned down by the college of his choice, convinces himself that he did not really want to go to that school anyway; it is too far from home or the student body is too snobbish. A young woman who has hoped in vain that one of her classmates will ask her for a date convinces herself that he is a sloppy dresser, wears his hair too long, and is arrogant and generally unattractive.

We also use rationalization at times to conceal from ourselves the fact that we have acted out of motives that conflict with our standards. A mother's real reason for keeping her daughter from dating may be jealousy; she rationalizes by saying that she is acting for the girl's own good. A student may cheat on an examination to avoid the work of studying, but he rationalizes by claiming that everybody cheats. The miser may rationalize his refusal to give money to good causes by claiming that charity weakens the moral fiber of the people who receive it.

Intellectualization

This word is applied to a defense mechanism that, though it somewhat resembles rationalization, is not quite the same. In rationalization, we explain away frustrations by deciding that we did not really want the goal, or we make excuses for our behavior by attributing it to desirable motives rather than to the real ones. In *intellectualization,* we are not concerned so much with goals or motives as with emotions, particularly anxiety; we try to analyze and explain away the unpleasant feelings themselves. The long discussions that take place in college dormitories and coffee shops over such questions as religion, sex, and morality are examples of intellectualization. Young people generally suffer anxiety related to these questions. By analyzing the questions intellectually and making them a matter of theory rather than of action, they reduce the anxiety that frequent thoughts about these subjects would otherwise produce.

Observations of prisoners awaiting execution have shown that they often manage, through some kind of intellectual process, to eliminate emotional reactions to their fate and to view it calmly and almost coldly (19). Similarly, in more ordinary situations, people often explain away their emotional reactions to personal reverses or to the death of their loved ones. In intellectualization, we remove ourselves from our problems and see them with a detachment that protects us from unpleasant emotional consequences.

Projection

The man who claims that everybody is dishonest and the woman who is convinced of the sexual immorality of the younger generation may have reached these conclusions through honest examination of the evidence. On the other hand, they may be exhibiting another common defense mechanism called *projection*, in which the individual foists off or projects onto other people motives or thoughts of his own that cause him anxiety. The man who talks too much about the dishonesty of mankind may very well be concealing his own strong tendencies toward dishonesty. The woman who talks too much about the immorality of young people may be concealing her own strong sexual desires, which cause her considerable anxiety.

In one experimental study of projection, the subjects were college fraternity brothers who lived under the same roof and knew each other well. Each subject was asked to rate his fraternity brothers on a scale that measured four undesirable traits: stinginess, obstinacy, disorderliness, and bashfulness. In the answers the experimenters found general agreement that some members of the fraternity were indeed quite stingy, obstinate, disorderly, or bashful. The subjects were also asked to rate themselves on these traits. These self-ratings showed that some of the men described by their friends as stingy or obstinate freely admitted that they possessed these traits, while others did not. The most significant finding was that the students who were in fact stingy or obstinate, but were unaware of it or unwilling to admit it, were the most inclined to attribute these traits to the others. The student whose fraternity brothers generally agreed was stingy but who described himself as generous was likely to rate his friends as possessing a high degree of stinginess (20). Presumably he was relieving his anxiety over possessing this trait by projecting it—by claiming that others, and not he, possessed it.

Projection plays a part in many disagreements in marriage. Many husbands complain that their wives are extravagant, although a disinterested observer can clearly see that it is the husband himself, not the wife, who is wasting money. Wives who are torn by sexual conflicts and urges toward infidelity may falsely accuse their husbands of having affairs. A marriage counselor who hears accusations by husband or wife of bad conduct or improper motives on the part of the other partner always looks for the possibility that the complaints represent projection rather than the truth.

Repression

In many cases, people who suffer anxiety over their motives seem simply to banish the motives altogether from their conscious thoughts; they cease to be aware of the motives. This process of pushing down motives (or conflicts) from consciousness into the unconscious is called *repression*, a concept taken from psychoanalytic theory. The phenomenon of repression is difficult to understand and to study and remains something of a mystery. Its effects, however, are frequently observed. A woman who at one time suffered severe conflicts and anxiety over sexual urges may now have repressed her motives to the point where she is not aware of any sexual desires or feelings at all. Many people seem to be entirely unaware that they possess such motives as dependency or hostility. Some cases of *amnesia*, or loss of memory, are believed to be exaggerated forms of repression, although amnesia can also be caused by brain damage.

Denial

Another defense mechanism, closely related to repression, is called *denial*, in which the person simply denies the existence of the events that have aroused his anxiety. A child whose father has died, for example, may refuse to believe it and insist that the father is on a long journey and will return some day. An eldest child, frustrated by the birth of a brother or sister, may deny that the baby really belongs in the family. Adults who are told that they are suffering from a serious disease may refuse to believe the doctor. In extreme cases, a psychotic mother may appear to believe firmly that a doll is a child who has died, or a psychotic criminal may appear fully convinced that he did not commit an act at which he was caught red-handed.

Identification

The term *identification* has already been defined as one of the processes through which the growing child develops his standards. The child comes to think of himself as being almost the same person as his parents and the other figures of authority in his life; he takes into himself their power, their virtues, and their triumphs, and he adopts their standards because he believes that this will help him attain the exalted position that they have attained. The process is often used as a defense mechanism, in one of two ways.

In its simpler form, identification as a defense mechanism represents an attempt by the individual to relieve anxiety over his own conflicts by assuming the virtues of an admired person or group that seems free of such anxiety. Thus a man who is anxious about his lack of courage may identify with an astronaut or a group of mountain climbers so that he can believe that he too possesses their courage. A young woman anxious about her own lack of charm and social skill may identify with the glamorous and outspoken heroines who marry and cast aside kings in the historical novels.

In a more complex form, an identification is established with a figure of authority who is resented and feared. Thus a young man may defend himself against the anxiety aroused by hostile feelings toward his boss by identifying with the boss; he may imitate the boss's mannerisms, mouth the same kind of opinions, and pretend that he possesses the same kind of power. This kind of identification may also be made with a group. Thus young people, anxious about their feelings of envy and hostility toward an in-group, may identify with the group and adopt its standards. A study of prisoners in German concentration camps in World War II showed that many of them began to imitate the characteristics of the very guards from whose brutality they were suffering (21).

Identification appears in some cases to be a conscious process; the person seems to be aware of his attempts to make himself similar to a model who possesses characteristics that would reduce his own anxiety. In other cases the whole process is unconscious, and the person is not aware that he is imitating another individual or a group.

Reaction Formation

When a person displays a trait to excess—that is, in exaggerated form that hardly seems called for by the circumstances—the possibility always exists that he is using the defense mechanism called *reaction formation*. That is to say, he is pretending to himself to possess motives that are the opposite of the real motives that are causing him anxiety. For example, a man appears to be overpolite; he is constantly holding doors open for other people, saying "Yes, sir," and "Yes, ma'am," always smiling, agreeable, and apologetic for his mistakes. This exaggerated politeness and concern for others may simply be a defense mechanism he has adopted to conceal the fact that he has hostile motives and is made anxious by his hostility. A woman who dresses in a sexually provocative manner and is constantly flirting and telling risqué stories may only be concealing her basic sexual inhibitions and fear of being unattractive.

Substitution

The college student who would like to be an athlete but cannot reach this goal because of lack of physical strength or because of his anxiety over competition may turn instead toward the goal of becoming a great painter. The young woman who would like to be the most popular girl on the campus but is unattractive or bashful may turn instead toward the goal of leading her class in grades. This defense mechanism is called *substitution*, in which an unobtainable or forbidden goal is replaced by a different goal.

The Role of Defense Mechanisms

In the last analysis, perhaps every person's defense mechanisms are unique. Certainly many investigators would want to add to the list of eight that have been mentioned here. Some investigators would use different names for them or perhaps lump some of those mentioned here under the same name. The important thing is that human beings show considerable ingenuity at adopting forms of self-delusion. In one way or another they persuade themselves that they did not really want the goals from which they have been blocked, that their motives are admirable, that they are living up to their own and society's standards, and that their disappointments are somehow bearable.

Because frustration and conflict are so frequent, all of us use defense mechanisms from time to time. Many of these mechanisms are, of course, irrational. Nonetheless, they often serve a useful purpose. They may help us through crises that would otherwise overwhelm and disable us. If nothing else, they may gain time for us—time in which we can gather the strength, maturity, and knowledge needed to cope more realistically and constructively with our anxieties. It is only in the more extreme cases that the use of defense mechanisms—like the other effects of frustration and conflict mentioned earlier in the chapter—slip over into the realm of abnormal psychology.

The dividing line between normal psychological processes and behavior on the one hand and abnormal psychological processes and behavior on the other is difficult to draw. All of us, as has been said, are irrational in our use of defense mechanisms. Moreover, we may also be moved to more or less irrational aggression, withdrawal, depression and apathy, regression, stereotyped behavior, and vacillation. Indeed a person who behaves normally most of his life and is ordinarily quite successful at his job and his relations with his fellow workers, his family, and his friends may go through periods when he behaves abnormally and may even require hospital treatment. Similarly, people who would be definitely classified as psychotic during much of their lives may have long periods in which their behavior and psychological processes appear to be normal.

ABNORMAL PSYCHOLOGY

What Is Abnormality?

It is virtually impossible to make any absolute definition of abnormal behavior. Is it abnormal for a young woman to faint from the excitement of attending a dance or the embarrassment of overhearing profanity? It was not so considered in Victorian England. Is it abnormal to believe in witches? It was not so considered by the American colonists. Is suicide abnormal? To most Americans, it may seem like the ultimate in abnormality. Yet the Japanese Kamikazes in World War II committed suicide willingly and eagerly and were regarded as national heroes. More recently, some of the Buddhists in Vietnam have committed suicide as a form of political protest and have been regarded as exhibiting strength of character rather than mental illness.

One approach has been to define abnormality as behavior that is statistically deviant—in other words, as behavior that is rather uncommon and unusual in any particular society. But this is an unsatisfactory criterion because the behavior of a great scientist or writer is just as deviant statistically as the behavior of an archcriminal or a suicide. Another approach is to say that behavior is abnormal if it results in poor adaptation to the particular culture in which one lives. This is a somewhat more satisfactory definition, but it puts a premium on conformity. It would mean that Jesus and Socrates, both of whom adapted so poorly to their societies that they were executed, were abnormal.

On a more theoretical level, abnormality has been thought of as the equivalent of strong anxiety and mental health as the absence of anxiety. But this definition too is unsatisfactory, for a certain amount of anxiety is inevitable. Most clinical psychologists, therefore, have now adopted a criterion relevant for our society; they say that abnormal behavior is anything that seriously interferes with a person's ability to work and to love.

Stress and Abnormality

It appears that all human beings, and animals as well, can stand a certain amount of frustration, conflict, and anxiety—all the forces that are often lumped together under the concept of stress. But, if the burden becomes too great, they may lapse into abnormality, ranging from the mild to the severe.

It has been known ever since the time of Pavlov that animals can be made to behave abnormally under laboratory conditions that produce frustration and conflict. Pavlov conditioned a dog to discriminate between a circle and an ellipse projected on a screen; the dog learned to salivate to the circle but not to the ellipse. Then the shape of the ellipse was changed gradually so that it became more and more like a circle. Even when the difference in appearance was quite small, the dog still made the discrimination. But, when the difference became too small for the dog to perceive and the discrimination became impossible, the dog began to behave strangely. At various times animals placed in this situation became restless, hostile, destructive, or apathetic, and they developed muscle tremors and tics (22).

Many similar experiments have also produced abnormal behavior in laboratory animals. Cats, for example, were taught various means of obtaining food and then, to create a conflict, were given an electric shock or air blast when they performed the act that was rewarded with food. They very quickly—after only one or two repetitions—began to show signs of restlessness, agitation, fear, and panic (23). Among human beings, a common kind of abnormal psychology produced by unusually stressful situations is "battle fatigue," the breakdown often experienced by soldiers who have coped successfully with many difficult problems in civilian life.

Influences on Abnormal Behavior

Some people have a low threshold for stress, others a much higher one. Three kinds of factors appear to determine which people develop the symptoms of abnormal behavior.

BIOLOGICAL FACTORS   As was mentioned in Chapter 10, there appear to be considerable individual differences in glandular activity, sensitivity of the autonomic nervous system, and, possibly, activity of the brain centers concerned with emotion—all of which may incline one person to be more easily aroused and more intensely emotional than another. Among the possible effects of these individual differences may be unusual patterns of physiological change, which produce sensations that cannot be interpreted by any ordinary standards. Any biological deficiency or abnormality in the emotional apparatus may lower the threshold for stress or cause distorted reactions to stress.

SOCIOLOGICAL FACTORS   Statistical studies of *schizophrenia*, the most frequent form of psychosis, appear to show that it is most common among the lowest social classes in large cities—the slum and near-slum dwellers (24). Perhaps people at that level of society experience more frustration and conflict than people at higher levels. But there is also a possibility that growing up in a lower-class home or belonging to a minority group may reduce a person's tolerance for stress.

PSYCHOLOGICAL FACTORS   The most important influence on the possible development of abnormal behavior is the individual's specific learning experiences in childhood and adolescence. For example, the person who acquires motives for power that he cannot gratify or whose motives for affiliation and approval are frustrated by the belief that other people dislike him becomes vulnerable to extreme anxiety. Particularly significant are the person's standards. An event that produces little or no anxiety in a person with relatively low standards of mastery and competence may produce an almost unbearable anxiety in a person with higher standards. Clinical psychologists sometimes are called on to treat people who appear to have suffered a crippling amount of anxiety over violations of standards of sexual behavior, honesty, hostility, or dependency that would seem trivial to most of us.

PSYCHONEUROSES

In a sort of twilight zone between normal behavior and the extreme abnormality of psychosis lie the conditions that are technically known as *psychoneuroses*, usually shortened to *neuroses* in popular usage. All psychoneuroses are characterized by high levels of stress and anxiety, lasting over a considerable period of time. They may be mild and cause little trouble, or they may be so severe as to verge on the psychotic.

In a sense, every psychoneurosis is unique—the product of one person's unique frustrations and conflicts, as they affect the tolerance for stress dictated by his own unique biological, sociological, and psychological background. However, the symptoms tend to fall into patterns that permit a useful system of classification often used by therapists (25).

Anxiety States

Although anxiety is characteristic of all psychoneuroses, it is a more obvious symptom in some of them than in others. *Anxiety states*, one rather large group of psychoneuroses, include the following.

ANXIETY REACTION   In this type the anxiety is the outstanding symptom. The individual often describes himself as "chronically uneasy," for reasons he cannot explain. At times the feeling becomes so intense that it resembles sheer panic. It may result in physical symptoms such as palpitation of the heart, cold sweats, and dizziness.

ASTHENIC REACTION   The victim of asthenic reaction is chronically tired, listless, and unable to concentrate or work efficiently. At one time the condition was called *neurasthenia*—a word that means weakness of the nerves—because it was thought to result from general exhaustion of the nervous system. But no actual physical disorder is present. The victim often has anxieties over strong but repressed feelings of hostility toward a husband or wife (or, in the case of children and adolescents, toward a parent). Or his anxieties may center around failure to attain his goals. The asthenic reaction is a way of excusing his failure to cope with his frustrations and conflicts on the ground that he lacks the physical and mental energy for decisive action.

HYPOCHONDRIACAL REACTION   The hypochondriac tends to excuse his failures not on the ground of weakness but on the ground of illness. The student who is faced with writing a difficult term paper or taking a difficult examination may develop all the physical symptoms of a severe stomach disorder or hope that the slight swelling in his neck is a sign of mononucleosis—diseases that would excuse him from the ordeal. Some people tend to be hypochondriacal in all situations, as a way of life. They will shun a doctor who tells them they are physically sound and able to cope with their problems and desperately search for a doctor who will agree that they are sick.

PHOBIC REACTION   In this case the anxiety takes the form of unreasonable fears. Two common ones are *claustrophobia* (fear of confinement in small places, which makes some people unable to ride in elevators) and *acrophobia* (fear of high places, which affects some people when they have to climb to a top row of a football stadium). But phobic reactions may be attached to any object at all. Some people are thrown into panic by a snake, an ambulance, or even a toy balloon.

Hysteria

As used to describe psychoneuroses, the word *hysteria* has a different meaning from the usual one. It refers specifically to the following two conditions.

CONVERSION REACTION   This form of hysteria results in strange and often dramatic physical symptoms that have no organic basis. The patient may suffer paralysis of the arms or legs and even blindness or deafness. He may lose all sensitivity in one part of the body. In one type called glove anesthesia he loses all sensitivity in the hand, as if it were covered by a glove; he cannot feel a pinprick or even a severe cut anywhere from fingertips to wrist.

DISSOCIATIVE REACTIONS   In dissociative reactions the patient sets himself apart in some manner from the conflicts that are troubling him. One type of dissociative reaction is *amnesia,* or loss of memory. Another, quite rare, is *multiple personality,* in which the individual seems to be split into two or more different selves that represent sides of his personality that he cannot integrate into a unity. *Sleep walking,* in which a person performs acts while asleep that he cannot remember after he wakes up, is also a dissociative reaction.

Obsessive-Compulsive Reactions

Obsessions are thoughts that keep cropping up in a persistent and disturbing fashion. Some psychoneurotics are obsessed with the idea that they have heart trouble or that they are going to die by a certain age. A common and mild form of obsession is the feeling of people starting out on a trip that they have left the door unlocked or the stove turned on.

Compulsions are irresistible urges to perform some act over and over again, such as washing one's hands dozens of times a day. The housewife who cannot bear to see a knife or fork out of line at the table and keeps emptying her guests' ash trays is exhibiting mild forms of compulsion.

Obsessive-compulsive reactions seem to represent an attempt to substitute acceptable thoughts or actions for the unacceptable desires that are causing conflict and anxiety.

Neurotic Depression

To all of us, life brings its disappointments and losses. It is only normal and natural to feel discouraged by a bad grade in school or by failure to obtain an intensely desired job and to feel grief when a loved one dies. Overreacting to such events, however, is characteristic of a psychoneurosis known as *neurotic depression.* The individual appears to be particularly sensitive to unhappy events, and his normal discouragement or grief is complicated and exaggerated by feelings of dejection, hopelessness, and guilt. Since neurotic depression is an abnormal reaction to a particular situation, it usually disappears eventually—either when the situation changes or when its impact wears off.

Psychosomatic Disorders

Frustration, conflict, and anxiety often result in actual physical symptoms in the form of various *psychosomatic disorders*—a phrase meaning ailments caused by interaction between mind and body. Among disorders that often appear to be psychosomatic are headaches, backaches, digestive disturbances, ulcers, skin ailments, asthma, and many others. The symptoms and the pain caused by them are very real. In the case of ulcers, indeed, actual damage to the tissues of the body is clearly apparent. Some psychosomatic disorders appear to be conditioned reflexes, others to be part of the general adaptation syndrome (pages 244–45). When stimulation of the autonomic nervous system and the endocrine glands by frustration and conflict continues too long, the high rate of glandular activity can result in injury to the glands themselves and to the bodily organs. Apparently some people, because of biological differences, are especially susceptible to damage of a certain kind; there are "ulcer types" and "headache types."

CHARACTER DISORDERS   In addition to psychoneuroses, the list of which has now been completed, there is another group of abnormal forms of behavior that lie between the normal and the psychotic. These are known as *character disorders,* sometimes also called *personality disorders,* and they are characterized by a failure to acquire efficient and mature ways of coping with the problems and stresses of adult life.

One well-known type of character disorder is *psychopathic personality,* the core of which is lack of a sense of social responsibility. The psychopath (as a person with this type of character disorder is called) seems to lack a conscience and to have no feeling for other people. The word is mentioned frequently in court cases, for the criminal who appears to experience no remorse for his deeds is a good example of the extreme psychopath.

In other forms of character disorder a person may show a tendency to exhibit temper tantrums like a small child or to be emotionally unstable and "fly off the handle" over minor incidents. Homosexuality and other sexual deviations are considered to be forms of character disorder, as is addiction to alcohol or narcotics.

Psychosis refers to the extreme forms of mental disturbance that are often known in popular terminology —and also in legal language—as insanity. A psychosis is any form of mental disturbance that is so severe as to make a person incapable of getting along in society. It has been estimated that, at any given moment, about a million Americans are suffering from psychotic disorders and that two-thirds of this number are being treated in hospitals, where they occupy about half of all the hospital beds available in the nation (25). It has also been estimated that about one child in ten born today will spend part of his life in a mental hospital (26).

Because of these high figures, many people assume that the "stresses and strains" of modern industrial civilization and city life have greatly increased the amount of mental disturbance, but this does not seem to be true. Court records have shown that there were about as many commitments to mental hospitals, in proportion to population, in the relatively rural Massachusetts of the nineteenth century as in the highly industrialized Massachusetts of the present century (26). The same types of mental disturbances found in the United States and other industrialized nations have also been observed in primitive societies throughout the world (27). If the rate of hospitalization for mental ailments is higher in America today than ever before or than in more primitive nations, this appears to be true only because we have more facilities for diagnosis and treatment.

Organic and Functional Psychoses

One way of classifying psychoses is into two groups: 1) *organic,* or caused by actual damage to the brain by disease or injury, and 2) *functional,* or having no apparent connection with any organic disturbance.

In the organic group the most common type is *senile psychosis,* caused by deterioration of the brain cells and other physiological changes due to aging. Since more people live to extreme old age today, senile psychosis has become increasingly frequent, and its sufferers occupy a large proportion of the beds in mental hospitals because the tissue damage they have sustained cannot be remedied. At one time, brain damage resulting from advanced stages of syphilis was frequent, but this kind of organic psychosis has been reduced by improved methods of treating syphilis. Other organic psychoses can be caused by excessive and prolonged use of alcohol, by some rather rare kinds of infectious diseases, and by accidental injuries to the head (which, though common, do not often result in psychosis).

Functional psychoses are divided into three types.

SCHIZOPHRENIA   This is the most common psychosis of all, accounting for perhaps as many as 25 percent of all first admissions to mental hospitals. It is particularly frequent among young adults in their twenties and is more common among men than among women. The patient appears to lose contact with reality and lives in a shell-like world of his own, sometimes refusing to talk or even answer questions and often displaying disordered thought and little or no emotion. Some schizophrenic patients act like small children; others sometimes stay frozen in the same rigid positions for long periods of time; and others may have *hallucinations* (imaginary sensations, such as seeing nonexistent animals in the room or feeling bugs crawling under the skin) or *delusions* (false beliefs, such as imagining that they are already dead). The symptoms can be so varied that some investigators believe schizophrenia to be not a single type of disturbance but a number of different types that may some day be classified and treated in quite different ways.

MANIC-DEPRESSIVE PSYCHOSIS   This is characterized, as the name indicates, by extremes of mood, and often by wild swings from intense excitement to deep melancholy. In the manic phase the patient tends to be talkative, restless, aggressive, boastful, uninhibited, and often destructive. In the depressive phase the patient may become so gloomy and hopeless that he refuses to eat. Some patients swing from the manic to the depressive, while others exhibit only one of the two phases, usually the depressive. Manic-depressive psychosis, particularly the depressive kind, is more common among women than among men. It is most likely to occur in middle adulthood.

Even without treatment, manic-depressive psychosis usually disappears— the manic phase ordinarily in about three months, the depressive phase in about nine. The patient then returns to normal, and about a quarter of all patients do not have a second attack. In other patients the psychosis recurs, often several times.

PARANOIA   This is the least common of the functional psychoses. It is characterized by delusions—sometimes by delusions of grandeur in which the patient believes that he is Napoleon or Christ and sometimes by delusions of persecution in which the patient believes that people are trying to kill him. The delusions of persecution are believed to be an extreme form of projection, in which the patient projects to the rest of the world his own hostile motives.

The Origins of Psychosis

As was said earlier, schizophrenia appears to be more frequent in urban slums than elsewhere. In general, the home and family background of people suffering from all types of psychosis appears to be less favorable than average, as is shown in FIGURE 11.8. However, most people who grow up even in the worst homes do not become psychotic, while many people who come from what appear on the surface at least to be the most privileged homes do become psychotic. Married people are less likely to become psychotic than unmarried people, but this is probably because people with psychotic tendencies are less likely to get married in the first place. For reasons not understood, men appear more subject to psychosis than women; the ratio of males to females among first admissions to mental hospitals is about 4 to 3.

Because of the possibility that psychoses may be related to abnormalities of brain chemistry, considerable research has been done with various drugs. *Psychedelic drugs* such as LSD have been found to produce mental states that in some ways resemble the psychoses. *Tranquilizers* relieve many of the symptoms of psychosis and have been used widely in mental hospitals to calm patients and make them amenable to other forms of treatment. But the majority of mental disturbances, so far as is known, fully deserve the label *functional*. Some people seem to be predisposed to them by inherited biological factors and others by unfortunate sociological backgrounds or learning experiences, but in the last analysis they appear to represent an extreme form of reaction to extreme levels of frustration and conflict—in other words, to a level of anxiety that the individual cannot cope with.

FIGURE 11.8   *Background of Normal and Psychotic Children*   The bars illustrate some of the more pronounced differences found in a study of the family backgrounds of a group of psychotic children as compared with a control group of normal children. (28)

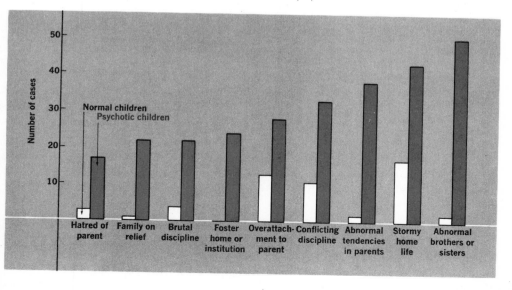

1. *Frustration* can be defined as a) the blocking of motive satisfaction by an obstacle or b) the unpleasant feelings that result from the blocking of motive satisfaction.
2. The obstacles that cause frustration may be a) physical, b) social, or c) personal.
3. The intensity of frustration experienced depends upon a) strength of the frustrated motive, b) distance from goal, c) nature of the obstacle, and d) number of obstacles.
4. Some individuals can tolerate relatively large amounts of frustration, while others react strongly to relatively small amounts.
5. A *conflict* is the *simultaneous arousal of two or more incompatible motives, resulting in unpleasant emotions.*
6. Two classes of conflicts are a) *conflicts between motives and standards* (for example, between hostility and inner standards that prohibit the display of hostility) and b) *conflicts over incompatible goals* (for example, between the desire for fame and the desire to be with one's family).
7. Conflicts over goals can be a) approach-approach, b) avoidance-avoidance, or c) approach-avoidance.
8. The *gradient of approach* toward a desirable goal becomes higher as the goal is approached. The *gradient of avoidance* of an undesirable goal is higher at and near the goal and is steeper than the gradient of approach.
9. Factors that help determine whether a motive will be implemented by behavior are a) distance in space from the goal, b) distance in time from the goal, c) strength of the motive, and d) expectancy of goal attainment.
10. Among the results of frustration and conflict are a) aggression, b) withdrawal, c) depression and apathy, d) regression, e) stereotyped behavior, f) vacillation, and g) defense mechanisms.
11. *Defense mechanisms* are psychological processes, involving self-deception and a distortion of reality, that act to reduce the anxiety resulting from frustration and conflict.
12. The defense mechanisms include a) rationalization, b) intellectualization, c) projection, d) repression, e) denial, f) identification, g) reaction formation, and h) substitution.
13. *Abnormal behavior* has been defined as a) behavior that is statistically deviant, b) behavior that causes poor adaptation to the culture, or c) behavior that results from extreme anxiety. None of these is entirely satisfactory, and perhaps the best definition is that abnormal behavior is *anything that seriously interferes with a person's ability to work and to love.*
14. Abnormal behavior is believed to result from stress beyond a person's threshold for stress, which is determined by a) biological factors such as

418

glandular activity and sensitivity of the autonomic nervous system, b) sociological factors such as those faced by the lowest social classes or by minority groups, and c) psychological factors, particularly a person's standards and anxieties over standards.

15. *Psychoneuroses* are forms of abnormal behavior that lie between normal behavior and the extreme abnormality of *psychosis*. They can be classified into:

    a. *Anxiety states,* including anxiety reaction, asthenic reaction, hypochondriacal reaction, and phobic reaction

    b. *Hysteria,* including conversion reaction and dissociative reactions

    c. *Obsessive-compulsive reactions*

    d. *Neurotic depression*

    e. *Psychosomatic disorders*

16. *Character disorders* (sometimes called *personality disorders*) also lie between the normal and the psychotic. They are characterized by a failure to acquire mature ways of coping with adult life.

17. Two types of psychoses are a) *organic,* or caused by actual damage to the brain, and b) *functional,* or having no apparent connection with any organic disturbance.

18. Three types of functional psychosis are a) schizophrenia, b) manic-depressive psychosis, and c) paranoia.

RECOMMENDED READING

Allport, G., ed. *Letters from Jenny.* New York: Harcourt, Brace & World, 1965.

Berkowitz, L. *Aggression: a social psychological analysis.* New York: McGraw-Hill, 1962.

Coleman, J. C. *Abnormal psychology and modern life,* 3rd. ed. Glenview, Ill.: Scott, Foresman, 1964.

Dollard, J. and Miller, N. E. *Personality and psychotherapy: an analysis in terms of learning, thinking, and culture.* New York: McGraw-Hill, 1950.

Freud, Anna. *The ego and the mechanisms of defence.* New York: International Universities Press, 1946.

Freud, S. *An outline of psychoanalysis.* New York: Norton, 1949.

Maher, B. A. *Principles of psychopathology.* New York: McGraw-Hill, 1966.

Miller, N. E. Liberalization of basic S-R concepts; extensions to conflict behavior, motivation, and social learning. In Koch, S., ed. *Psychology: a study of a science,* Vol. II. New York: McGraw-Hill, 1959, pp. 196–292.

Munroe, R. L. *Schools of psychoanalytic thought.* New York: Holt, Rinehart and Winston, 1955.

White, R. W. *The abnormal personality,* 3rd. ed. New York: Ronald, 1964.

WHAT IS PERSONALITY?
Personality Defined
The Personality Hierarchy

PERSONALITY THEORIES

PHYSIOLOGICAL THEORIES
Sheldon's Body Types
The Pro and Con of Sheldon's Theory

PSYCHOANALYTIC THEORY
Anxiety, Repression, and the Unconscious
The Id
The Ego
The Superego
Superego Versus Ego Versus Id
The Pro and Con of Freud
Jung's Theory
Adler's Theory
Horney and Fromm

SOCIAL LEARNING THEORIES
The Frightened Rat
The Aggressive Children
Conditioning and Reinforcement
Learning Theories and Psychoanalysis

OTHER THEORIES OF PERSONALITY
Maslow's Self-Actualization Theory
Rogers' Self Theory
Self-Image and Neurosis
Similarities and Differences Among the Theories

PSYCHOTHERAPY
Client-Centered Therapy
Psychoanalysis
Behavior Therapy
Other Types of Psychotherapy
The Value of Psychotherapy

MEDICAL THERAPY
Electroshock Therapy
Drugs
How Effective Is Medical Therapy?

12

PERSONALITY THEORY AND PSYCHOTHERAPY

The previous chapter has already touched upon the study of personality —for two critical characteristics of personality are a person's sources of frustration and conflict and his behavior when he is frustrated or in a conflict situation. The time has come, however, to take a more sharply focused look: What is personality? What are the ways in which individual personalities differ? What is known about the origins, the structure, and the dynamics of personality? In other words, the discussion must now turn to *personality theory* and to the various types of *psychotherapy,* or attempts to treat abnormal personalities, that are derived from personality theory.

WHAT IS PERSONALITY?

Personality is another word that everybody uses but few try to define. It is a concept that has been discussed at least since the time of the ancient Greeks, whose physicians believed there were four types of personalities, each related to different fluids inside the body. The *sanguine* person had a rich flow of blood, which made him happy, warm-hearted, and optimistic. The *melancholy* person had an excess of black bile, which accounted for his moodiness. The *choleric* or bad-tempered person had an excess of yellow bile. The *phlegmatic* person was slowed down and made listless by an excess of phlegm.

The human personality takes far more than four forms, and its origins are extremely complicated. But we might still describe the personalities of some of our acquaintances with the adjectives used by the Greeks. Some people are indeed sanguine, melancholy, choleric, or phlegmatic, at least a good deal of the time—and the tendency to display a particular behavior "a good deal of the time" is part of the modern definition of personality.

Personality Defined

Personality is *the total pattern of characteristic ways of behaving and thinking that constitute the individual's unique and distinctive method of adjusting to his environment.* There are four key words in the definition, most easily discussed by taking them up in this order: 1) *characteristic,* 2) *distinctive,* 3) *adjusting,* and 4) *pattern.*

A way of behaving or thinking, to qualify as a part of personality, must have some continuity over time and circumstance; it must be *characteristic* of the individual. We do not call a man bad-tempered if he "blows up" only once in ten years. We say that a bad temper is part of his personality only if he displays it many times under different circumstances.

To qualify as a part of personality, a way of behaving or thinking must also be *distinctive*—that is, it must distinguish the individual from other individuals. This eliminates such common American characteristics as eating with a knife and fork, placing adjectives before rather than after nouns, and carrying a driver's license—all of which are more or less the same for every American and do not distinguish one person from others.

A young woman might always wear a ring that is a family heirloom and the only one of its kind in the world; her wearing of the ring would therefore be both characteristic and distinctive. It would not, however, be considered a part of her personality, unless, perhaps, she attached some deep significance to the ring and acted as if it were an important symbol of personal worth and social acceptance. The word *personality* is ordinarily attached only to characteristics that play a major part in the individual's adjustment to his environment. A positive personality characteristic—such as a friendly manner—helps the individual adjust to the people and events around him; a negative one—fear of people—produces loneliness, failure, or anxiety. But *adjusting* is a relative word. A man who likes the solitude of nature and his own thoughts may be quite well adjusted as a forest ranger but poorly adjusted if he works as a salesman in a busy discount house. A young woman who is not concerned about stylish clothes and does not like to set her hair every night can be well adjusted at a school where informality is accepted but poorly adjusted at a finishing school where students are expected to look like fashion models at all times.

There are many kinds of personality characteristics; indeed the English language has at least 4000 words to describe them. Each individual possesses some but not all of them, and his personality is the *pattern,* or sum total, of the characteristics he possesses and displays. Thus one person's pattern of adjustment to his environment may be such that he is characteristically and distinctively cheerful, outgoing, optimistic, prompt, hard-working, and aggressive. Another person may tend to be depressed, introverted, pessimistic, tardy, lazy, and submissive. Still another may be cheerful but introverted, optimistic but tardy, and hard-working but submissive. A fourth person may be gloomy but extroverted, pessimistic but prompt, and lazy but aggressive. The possible combinations are endless and account for the many varieties of human personality.

The Personality Hierarchy

One important fact about personality is that, like so many other aspects of human behavior, the various possible thoughts and responses within a given personality exist in a hierarchy; some are strong and easily and frequently aroused, while others are weaker and less likely to occur. In a social situation, for example, there are many ways that an individual can try to adjust to the others in the group; he can be talkative or quiet, friendly or reserved, boastful or modest, bossy or acquiescent, more at ease with men or more at ease with women. One person may characteristically respond by withdrawing into the background, and we say that such a person is shy. Another may characteristically display warmth and try to put the others at their ease; we say that such a person is outgoing. Another may be talkative, boastful, and domineering, and we say that he is aggressive or "pushy." In each of the three individuals, certain responses are strong in the personality hierarchy and easily aroused.

Each person's hierarchy of actions and thoughts has a certain amount of permanence. The shy person behaves shyly under many circumstances, and the aggressive person has a consistent tendency to be boastful and domineering. However, the hierarchy may change considerably according to circumstances. A young person who is aggressive around people his own age may behave rather shyly in the presence of older people. A person who is usually shy may have one close friend with whom he is completely at ease. All of us, no matter how friendly or reserved we may be, are likely to have a strong tendency to make friends if we have been isolated for a long time, such as after an illness or a stretch at a lonely job. On the other hand, we are likely to want some solitude after a round of parties. The businessman who is ordinarily interested in his job and eager to talk about it may shun this kind of conversation when he gets home late at night after a hard day's work.

A personality theory is an attempt to organize the great **PERSONALITY THEORIES** variety of human behavior around some general principles that will help us understand why people are different. Such a theory attempts to explain which personality characteristics are the most important, the most likely patterns of relationship among characteristics, and the way in which these patterns are established. There are numerous theories of personality, which for the sake of convenience we can consider under the categories of 1) physiological theories, 2) psychoanalytic theory, and 3) social learning theories.

The theory of the physicians in ancient Greece was a *physiological theory* of personality; it presumed that its four types of human temperament were caused by physiological conditions. Among modern investigators the best-known proponent of a physiological theory of personality is William Sheldon, who has proposed that there are three basic types of body build that are closely related to three types of personality. His theory, although controversial, is interesting and provocative.

Sheldon's Body Types

After measuring the physical characteristics of many subjects, Sheldon decided that the three basic body types are the *endomorph, mesomorph,* and *ectomorph,* as shown in FIGURE 12.1. The names come from the three layers of specialized cells that begin to appear as the fertilized egg cell develops into an embryo—the endoderm, which turns into the visceral organs; the mesoderm, which turns into muscles, bones, and blood; and the ectoderm, which turns into skin, sense organs, and nervous system. Thus the endomorph is characterized by a strong digestive system; the mesomorph by strong muscles and bones; and the ectomorph by a skin area and nervous system that are large in proportion to his size.

Most people are mixed types; they are partly endomorph, partly mesomorph, and partly ectomorph. But in many people, one or another of the three types is predominant, often to a pronounced degree. Along with the pre-

FIGURE 12.1   *Sheldon's Body Types*   The *endomorph* (*left*) has well developed visceral organs and tends to be round in build, with relatively weak bones and muscles. The *mesomorph* (*center*) is the athletic type, with strong bones and muscles. The *ectomorph* (*right*) is the stringbean type, with long, slender arms and legs and light muscles.

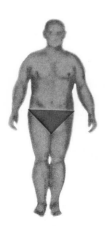 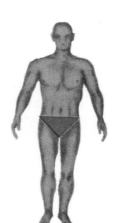 

dominant body type, says Sheldon, goes a characteristic type of temperament and personality. The endomorph can be described as *viscerotonic,* the mesomorph as *somatotonic,* the ectomorph as *cerebrotonic.* The personality traits theoretically associated with each type are shown in FIGURE 12.2.

The Pro and Con of Sheldon's Theory

One investigator who studied children aged two to four found that there was a pronounced tendency for boys classed as mesomorphs to be energetic, fearless, and assertive and for boys classed as ectomorphs to be quiet, aloof, cautious, and conforming (2). Sheldon has also reported very high relationships between the three body types and the three kinds of personalities he has listed. But other investigators have found smaller relationships and in some cases no significant relationship at all (3).

Sheldon's Temperament Types   These are some of the traits that Sheldon considers most characteristic of the three body types illustrated in FIGURE 12.1. (1)   **FIGURE 12.2**

Viscerotonic
(Endomorph)

- Relaxed in posture and movement
- Loves physical comfort
- Slow reactions
- Loves polite ceremony
- Loves social company
- Even emotions
- Tolerance
- Complacency
- Communicates feelings easily and smoothly

Somatotonic
(Mesomorph)

- Assertive in posture and movement
- Loves physical adventure
- Energetic
- Needs and enjoys exercise
- Competitive aggressiveness
- Bold directness of manner
- Physical courage for combat
- Unrestrained voice
- Overly mature in manner and appearance
- Loves risk and chance

Cerebrotonic
(Ectomorph)

- Restrained in posture and movement
- Loves privacy
- Overly fast reactions
- Mental overintensity
- Fear of society
- Self-conscious mobility of eyes and face
- Inhibited social expression
- Secretiveness and emotional restraint
- Quiet, vocally restrained
- Youthful in manner and appearance

One problem in verifying the theory is that accidents of disease or eating habits can make it difficult to ascertain a person's basic body build without making measurements throughout his early life. Whether or not Sheldon's theory bears the test of further research, it should be pointed out that virtually all theories of personality depend at least in part on physiology; there is general agreement among investigators that the structure of the glands and the autonomic nervous system, as well as intelligence and other inborn traits, have at least some effect upon personality. Sheldon's theory merely represents an extreme view of the connection between physiology and personality.

All physiological theories, it should be noted, hold that personality is determined to a large extent by various kinds of inherited predispositions. Thus they emphasize the role of heredity, rather than of environment, in the shaping of personality.

PSYCHOANALYTIC THEORY   The most influential personality theory during the past half century has been *psychoanalytic theory*, originally formulated by Sigmund Freud (see FIGURE 12.3). Freud began his career in Vienna in the 1880's as a physician and neurologist. He became interested in psychological processes as the result of his experiences with patients who were suffering from hysteria—that is, from paralysis of the legs or arms that seemed to have no physical cause. His final theories represent a lifetime of treating and observing many kinds of neurotic patients and also of attempting to analyze the unconscious aspects of his own personality.

FIGURE 12.3

The Founder of Psychoanalysis
Sigmund Freud introduced psychoanalytic theory to a startled and at first skeptical world about seven decades ago.

Freud himself was quite neurotic in his youth, suffering from feelings of anxiety and deep depression. He retained some neurotic symptoms all his life; he was a compulsive smoker of as many as twenty cigars a day, was nervous about traveling, and was given to what were probably hypochondriacal complaints about poor digestion, constipation, and heart palpitation. However, he managed to overcome his early inclinations toward depression and lived a rich professional, family, and social life—an indication that in his case the physician had managed to heal himself, at least in large part.

When Freud introduced his ideas around the turn of the century, they were bitterly attacked. Many people were repelled by his notion that man, far from being a rational animal, is largely at the mercy of his irrational unconscious thoughts. Many were shocked by Freud's emphasis on the role of sexual impulses and particularly by his insistence that young children have intense sexual motives. Over the years, however, the furor has died down. There is considerable controversy over the value of psychoanalytic methods in treating neurotic patients, but even those who criticize psychoanalysis as a form of therapy accept some of Freud's basic notions about personality and its formation.

Anxiety, Repression, and the Unconscious

Freud's ideas are very difficult to summarize; the student who hopes to understand them fully must be prepared to do extensive reading of both Freud's own writings and the psychoanalytic textbooks and commentaries that have been written by his followers. The discussion that follows here must of necessity omit many aspects of Freudian theory and confine itself to the ones that have had the most lasting influence—and even those must be somewhat oversimplified. No psychology textbook would be complete, however, without at least painting in broad strokes some of the many contributions Freud made to the theory of personality.

Some of Freud's most influential ideas concerned concepts so central to the study of psychology that they have already been prominently mentioned. One of them was the role of anxiety. Freud was a pioneer in emphasizing the importance of anxiety, which he believed to be the central problem in mental disturbance. Another was repression and the other defense mechanisms mentioned in Chapter 11. Freud believed that these mechanisms, and especially the process of repression, are frequently used to eliminate from conscious awareness any motive or thought that threatens to cause anxiety. Another influential idea was his concept of the unconscious mind, composed in part of repressed motives and thoughts. Freud was the first to suggest the now widely held theory that the human mind and personality are like an iceberg, with only a small part visible and the great bulk submerged and concealed. All of us, he maintained, have many unconscious motives of which we are never aware but which nonetheless influence our behavior. (An example cited in Chapter 9, where unconscious motives are first discussed, is the case of a man who sincerely believes that he has no hostile motives, yet who in subtle ways performs many acts of aggression against his wife, his children, and his business associates.)

The Id

The core of the unconscious mind, according to Freud, is the *id*, composed of raw, primitive, inborn forces that constantly struggle for gratification. Even the baby in his crib, Freud said, is swayed by two powerful drives. One is what he called the *libido*, embracing sexual urges and such related desires as to be kept warm, well-fed, and comfortable. The other is aggression—the urge to fight, dominate, and where necessary destroy.

The id operates on what Freud called the *pleasure principle*, insisting on immediate and total gratification of all its demands. Freud felt, for example, that the baby—though unable to think as yet like a human being and thus more like a little animal—wants to satisfy his libido by possessing completely everything he desires and loves and to satisfy his aggressive urges by destroying everything that gets in his way. As the child grows up, he learns to control the demands of the id, at least in part. But the id remains active and powerful throughout life; it is indeed the sole source of all the psychic energy put to use in behaving and thinking. It is unconscious and we are not aware of its workings, but it continues to struggle for the relief of all its tensions.

The Ego

The conscious, logical part of the mind that develops as the child grows up was called by Freud the *ego*—the "real" us, as we like to think of ourselves. In contrast to the id, the ego operates on the *reality principle*; it tries to mediate between the demands of the id and the realities of the environment. Deriving its energies from the id, the ego perceives what is going on in the environment and develops the operational responses (such as finding food) necessary to satisfy the demands of the id. The ego does our logical thinking; it does the best it can to help us lead sane and satisfactory lives. To the extent that the primitive drives of the id can be satisfied without getting us into danger or harm, the ego permits them satisfaction. But when the drives threaten to get us jailed as a thief or rejected by society as a brawler and a rake, the ego represses them or attempts to satisfy them with substitutes that are socially acceptable.

The Superego

In the ego's constant struggle to satisfy the demands of the id without permitting the demands to destroy us, it has a strong but troublesome ally in the third part of the mind as conceived by Freud—the *superego*. In a sense the superego is our conscience, our sense of right and wrong. It is partly acquired by adopting the notions of right and wrong that we are taught by society from the earliest years. However, Freud's concept of the superego represents a much stronger and more dynamic notion than the word *conscience* implies. Much like the id, the superego is mostly unconscious, maintaining a far greater influence over our behavior than we realize. It is largely acquired as a result of that famous process that Freud called the *Oedipus complex*, which can be summarized as follows.

According to Freud, every child between the ages of about two and a half through six is embroiled in a conflict of mingled affection and resentment for his parents. The child has learned that the outer world exists and that there are other people in it, and the id's demands for love and affection reach out insatiably toward the person he has been closest to—the mother. Although the child has only the haziest notion of sexual feelings, he wants to possess his mother totally and to take the place of his father with her. But his anger against his father, the rival with whom he must share her, makes him fearful that his father will somehow retaliate. To further complicate the situation, his demands for total love from his mother are of course denied, a fact that also arouses the aggressive drives of the id and makes him want to retaliate against his mother—so that he becomes overwhelmed with strong feelings of mingled love, anger, and fear toward both parents at once.

This period of storm and stress was named by Freud after the Greek legend in which Oedipus unwittingly killed his father and married his own mother and then, when he discovered what he had done, blinded himself as penance. Girls, according to Freud, go through very similar torments in the period from two and a half to six, except that their libido centers chiefly on their fathers, their aggression chiefly on their mothers.

The Oedipus conflict must somehow be resolved; the way this is done, according to Freud, is through identification with the parents. The child ends his mingled love and hate for his parents by becoming like them, by convincing himself that he shares their strength and authority and the affection they have for each other. The parents' moral judgments, or what the child conceives to be their moral judgments, become his superego. This helps him hold down the drives of the id, which have caused him such intense discomfort during the Oedipal period. But, forever after, the superego tends to oppose the ego. As his parents once did, the superego punishes him or threatens to punish him for his transgressions. And, since its standards were rigidly set in childhood, its notions of crime and guilt are likely to be completely illogical and unduly harsh.

In their own way the demands of the superego are just as insatiable as the id's blind drives. Its standards of right and wrong and its rules for punishment are far more rigid, relentless, and vengeful than anything in our conscious minds. Formed at a time when the child was unable to distinguish between a "bad" wish and a "bad" deed, the superego may sternly disapprove of the merest thought of some transgression—the explanation, according to Freud, of the fact that some people who have never actually committed a "bad" deed nonetheless feel guilty all their lives.

Superego Versus Ego Versus Id

The three parts of the human personality are in frequent conflict. One of the important results of the conflict is anxiety, which is produced in the ego whenever the demands of the id threaten danger or when the superego threatens disapproval or punishment. Anxiety, though unpleasant, is a tool that the ego uses to fight the impulses or thoughts that have aroused it. In one way or another—by using repression and the other defense mechanisms, by turning the mind's attention elsewhere, by gratifying some other impulse of the id— the ego defends itself against the threat from the id or superego and gets rid of the anxiety.

In a sense the conscious ego is engaged in a constant struggle to satisfy the insatiable demands of the unconscious id without incurring the wrath and vengeance of the largely unconscious superego. To the extent that a person's behavior is controlled by the ego, it is sensible and generally satisfying. To the extent that it is governed by the childish passions of the id and the unrelenting demands of the superego, it tends to be foolish, unrewarding, painful, and neurotic.

If the ego is not strong enough to check the id's drives, a person is likely to be a selfish and hot-headed menace to society. But if the id is checked too severely, other problems may arise. Too much repression of the libido can make a person unable to enjoy a normal sex life or to give a normal amount of affection. Too much repression of aggression makes him unable to stand up for himself and to hold his own in the give and take of competition. Too strong a superego may result in vague and unwarranted feelings of guilt and unworthiness, and sometimes in an unconscious need for self-punishment.

The Pro and Con of Freud

There can be little question that Freud was an important innovator who had a number of most useful insights into the human personality. He was the first to recognize the role of the unconscious and the importance of anxiety and defenses as a factor in personality. He also dispelled the myth, widely accepted before his time, that children do not have the sexual urges and hostile impulses that characterize adults.

One criticism of Freud is that he may have overemphasized the role of sexual motivation in personality. In Freud's nineteenth and early twentieth century Vienna, with its strict sexual standards, it is perhaps only natural that many of his neurotic patients should have had conflicts and guilt feelings centering around their sexual desires. In today's Western world, with its more permissive attitudes toward sexual behavior, this kind of conflict and guilt seems to be less frequent. Yet people continue to have personality problems, and the incidence of serious mental disturbance seems to remain about the same as ever. This would indicate that conflicts over sexuality cannot be the sole or perhaps even the most important cause of personality disturbances.

Another frequent criticism of Freud is that many of his ideas about the dynamics of human behavior can be explained more economically without using his concepts of the id, ego, and superego. This will be made clear in a moment, when the social learning theories of personality are discussed.

Jung's Theory

A number of Freud's disciples broke away from his theories to a greater or lesser degree and established psychoanalytic schools of thought of their own. One of the first of these was Carl Jung, who felt that Freud had overestimated the importance of the sexual drives. To Jung, the instinctive drive called the libido comprised far more than sexual urges; it was an all-encompassing life force that included deep-seated attitudes toward life and death, virtue and sin, and religion. Instead of Freud's id, ego, and superego, Jung emphasized what he called the functions of the personality—modes of viewing the events of the world and making judgments about them. Ideally, he believed, a person would grasp these events with what he called sensation (the evidence of the senses as to what the objects in the world were like at the moment) and also intuition (an understanding of their past and future potential). He would judge objects and events on the basis of both thinking (a more or less coldly logical view) and feeling (an emotional judgment of agreeable or disagreeable, right or wrong). But in most people the function of sensation tends to develop at the expense of intuition or vice versa, and the function of thinking at the expense of feeling or vice versa; the neglected functions are relegated to the unconscious mind and disharmony results.

It was Jung who invented the words *introvert* and *extrovert*—the former describing a person who tends to live with his own thoughts and to avoid socializing, the latter describing a person whose chief interest is in other people and the events of the world. Both introversion and extroversion, he believed, were necessary for fulfillment of the human personality; unfortunately, as in the case of the four functions, one of them tends to develop at the expense of the other. As this brief summary of Jung's ideas indicates, he tended to emphasize the intellectual and spiritual qualities of the human personality, rather than the primitive drives of sex and aggression.

Adler's Theory

Another early disciple who rejected Freud's emphasis on sexuality was Alfred Adler. To Adler, who was even more interested in social psychology than Jung, the most important factor in determining a person's motives and therefore his conflicts was the social context in which he grew up.

It was Adler who first used the term *inferiority complex*. One basic influence on human behavior, he believed, is the fact that the baby is born into the world completely helpless, dependent upon those around him, and therefore overwhelmed by feelings of inferiority that he must struggle for the rest of his life to relieve. If development is normal, the child acquires such personality traits as courage, independence, and wholesome ambition. If not, he may grow up with feelings of inadequacy implied by the term inferiority complex. Or he may overcompensate for his early helplessness and become aggressive and ambitious in the destructive sense.

Adler also suggested that each person develops his own style of life—a certain style of thinking and behaving that makes him unique in the way he attempts to attain his goals. To Adler, this style of life is more important than the particular goals that a person chooses.

Horney and Fromm

In more recent years a number of other writers have made substantial revisions of the original Freudian theories, and they may be considered to have established psychoanalytically based theories of their own.

Karen Horney, who practiced both in her native Germany and in New York, rejected Freud's concepts of the id, ego, and superego and his emphasis upon the sexual origins of neurosis. According to her theory, the central factor in human personality is what she called *basic anxiety*—the uncomfortable feelings that are aroused in the child by any threat to his security, such as a tendency by his parents to dominate him, overprotect him, disparage him, or fail to give him warmth, respect, and guidance. The insecure child, suffering from basic anxiety, tries in various ways to relieve his feelings of being isolated and helpless in a potentially hostile world. He may choose one or a mixture of three basic techniques, described by Horney as 1) moving toward people (showing a need for love), 2) moving against people (becoming powerful and dominant), or 3) moving away from people (becoming independent). In so doing, he may become the victim of any one or more of the ten "neurotic needs"—or irrational and unsatisfactory solutions to his problem of basic anxiety—shown in FIGURE 12.4.

Erich Fromm, another German-born psychoanalyst who has practiced in the United States, has revised Freud's theory along different lines. He believes that the key element in human personality is not sexuality but the

MOVING TOWARD PEOPLE

1. *The need for affection and approval* Indiscriminate attempts to please others and live up to their expectations; dread of unfriendliness and hostility.
2. *The need for a "partner" who will take over one's life* Submerging one's own personality and letting the "partner" take all responsibilities.
3. *The need to restrict one's life within narrow borders* Remaining inconspicuous; making no demands; being modest and belittling of self.

MOVING AGAINST PEOPLE

4. *The need for power* Craving for domination over other people; disrespect for others; admiration of strength and contempt for weakness; craving for intellectual superiority.
5. *The need to exploit others* Pride in exploiting people financially and sexually; dread of being exploited oneself and thus being made to seem "stupid."
6. *The need for social recognition or prestige* Friends and possessions evaluated solely according to their prestige value; dread of "losing face."
7. *The need for personal admiration* Attempts to live up to an inflated image of oneself and to be admired for it.
8. *The need for personal achievement* Relentless driving of oneself to greater achievements; need to be recognized as the very best worker, sportsman, lover, or whatever.

MOVING AWAY FROM PEOPLE

9. *The need for self-sufficiency and independence* Refusal to need anyone else or to be "tied down"; dread of closeness and love.
10. *The need for perfection and unassailability* Feelings of superiority over others; driving for perfection; worry over possible flaws or mistakes.

Horney's Ten Neurotic Needs These are the ten "neurotic needs" listed by Horney as types of unsuccessful attempts to solve the basic anxiety that is the central concept of her personality theory. (4)

FIGURE 12.4

fact that people have become isolated from nature and from other men. According to this theory, people have the five basic needs shown in FIGURE 12.5. These needs are impossible to satisfy in our present society (or in any other society as yet devised); therefore all of us tend to have frustrations and personality problems. It is society, Fromm has said, that is "sick," and the only lasting solution to personality problems is to create a different kind of society

in which man relates to man lovingly, in which he is rooted in bonds of brotherliness and solidarity . . . which gives him the possibility of transcending nature by creating rather than by destroying, in which everyone gains a sense of self by experiencing himself as the subject of his powers rather than by conformity (6).

433

1. *Relatedness*   This need stems from the fact that man has lost the union with nature that other animals possess; it must be satisfied by human relationships based on productive love (which implies mutual care, responsibility, respect, and understanding).
2. *Transcendence*   The need to rise above one's animal nature and to become creative.
3. *Rootedness*   The need for a feeling of belonging, best satisfied by brotherliness toward mankind.
4. *Identity*   The need to have a sense of personal identity, to be unique. It can be satisfied through creativity or through identification with another person or group.
5. *A Frame of Orientation*   The need for a stable and consistent way of perceiving the world and understanding its events.

FIGURE 12.5   *Fromm's Basic Human Needs*   According to the theory developed by Fromm, these are the five basic needs of human beings—frustration of which causes personality problems. (5)

A number of other personality theories that represent variations on Freud's work could be added. In general, the psychoanalysts who have modified Freud's original theories tend to play down his concern with sexuality and instead to emphasize other drives, motives, and the relevance of social factors.

SOCIAL LEARNING THEORIES   Social learning theories represent an entirely different kind of approach to the study of personality. Unlike the physiological theories, they are not particularly concerned with the role of inherited characteristics. Unlike the psychoanalytic theories, they do not stress the role of primitive drives, the Oedipus complex, or unconscious motives. Instead they hold that most personality traits are the result of learning—particularly the kind of learning that takes place in interaction with other people or, to put it another way, within a social context.

To the social learning theorists, personality is largely composed of habits—that is to say, of habitual ways of responding to situations. These habits are learned in accordance with the standard principles of learning; they are *learned responses to stimuli in the environment.* Thus social learning theories are also known as S-R (for stimulus-response) theories. Prominent among the originators of social learning or S-R theories are John Dollard and Neal Miller and more recently Albert Bandura and Richard Walters.

434

The Frightened Rat

One simple but impressive experiment devised by Miller is often cited in support of social learning theories. In the course of this experiment a rat is placed in a plain white compartment that contains a bar that can be pressed, like the bar in a Skinner box. There is nothing unusual about the compartment, nothing that would appear in any way frightening. Yet the rat shows signs of fear and immediately presses the bar—which permits it to escape into a black compartment alongside. For some reason the rat fears the white compartment and will work to escape into the black compartment. Why? Does it have an inborn fear? Or some kind of unconscious conflict? The explanation is quite simple. In a previous stage of the experiment the rat received an electric shock in the white compartment, from which it could escape only by learning to press the bar so that it could move to the black compartment. Its apparently neurotic fear of the white compartment is simply the result of learning. It learned to fear the compartment when it was shocked; it still fears the compartment although the shock is no longer present (7).

This experiment will perhaps remind the student of the "Albert experiment" described on page 55, in which a baby who had displayed no previous fear of a rat was conditioned to behave fearfully not only toward the rat but also toward other furry objects, such as a rabbit or the face of Santa Claus. Here, too, an observer who saw only the final stage of the experiment might be puzzled by Albert's behavior. In fact Albert had learned to respond with fearful behavior through simple classical conditioning.

The Aggressive Children

Bandura and Walters have shown that behavior related to personality characteristics is learned not only through conditioning but also through imitation or modeling. In other words, we learn to make the same responses that we have watched someone else make, particularly if that person is someone with whom we identify. In one experiment children at play were in a room where they could observe an adult. In some cases the adult worked quietly at assembling a sort of tinker toy. In other cases the adult performed some very aggressive actions toward a large doll—kicking it, hitting it with a mallet, and so on. Later the children were subjected to some mild frustration and then were placed in an observation room, behind a one-way mirror, where they too could play in any way they chose with a tinker toy or a large doll. Those who had watched aggressive behavior by an adult showed more aggression toward the doll than did those who had watched nonaggressive behavior. The results were the same when the children watched a movie rather than a real-life demonstration of aggression. (See FIGURE 2.16 on page 75.)

Conditioning and Reinforcement

As these experiments indicate, the social learning theories maintain that the wide range of human personality traits, including the abnormal ones, can be explained by the basic principles of learning. The child is born with a certain range of responses, both reflex and operant. Through conditioning and imitation these responses become attached to previously neutral stimuli. Through stimulus generalization they may be aroused by many kinds of situations.

The social learning theories place considerable emphasis on reward and punishment—particularly on the kind of rewards and punishments given by the family and by society. Responses that are reinforced by praise and social reward tend to be repeated and to become habitual; those that are punished by rejection tend to undergo extinction. Dollard and Miller have suggested that the individual moving through his cultural environment is like a complicated version of a rat moving through a T-maze. Only if we know in which arm of the T the rat will be rewarded by food and in which arm he will be punished by a shock can we predict his behavior. To predict an individual's behavior we would have to know which of his responses have been rewarded by society and which have been punished and in what way and to what extent (8). We would also have to know what kind of models he has chosen to identify with and to imitate.

Learning Theories and Psychoanalysis

Many of Freud's psychoanalytic concepts can be explained in somewhat different terms by the social learning theories. Dollard and Miller agree, for example, that unconscious conflicts are the basis of most severe personality problems. Their explanation, simpler than Freud's, is that most of these conflicts arise in the early years before the child has learned language labels for the stimuli in his environment and for his own visceral drives and reflexes—in other words, at a time when the child, lacking language, does not really have a consciousness. They also believe that many of what Freud calls unconscious desires are wishes that the person represses by the deliberate process of "not thinking" about them, because "not thinking" reduces the anxiety associated with them.

Freud's id, to the learning theorists, is a person's basic biological drives. The superego is a person's learned standards. Anxiety, rather than resulting from conflicts among id, ego, and superego, represents the sensations resulting from a reflex visceral reaction that has become attached, through learning, to many different kinds of environmental situations and to one's thoughts.

Many other theories of personality have been proposed, some resembling those already mentioned, others quite different. It is impossible to list all of them in a book of this length, much less to explain them. Let us, however, consider two that demonstrate the wide range of approaches that have been made.

OTHER THEORIES OF PERSONALITY

Maslow's Self-Actualization Theory

A psychologist named Abraham Maslow has proposed a theory that centers around the phrase *self-actualization*. In Maslow's view, most students of personality have been too impressed by the neurotic aspects of personality and have therefore taken too dark and pessimistic a view of human nature. He believes that men are innately good and that normal, healthy development would enable each person to actualize his own true nature and fulfill his potentialities. Thus self-actualization is the goal of life, and anything that blocks this goal makes a person frustrated and neurotic. Aggression and destruction are not the natural characteristics of mankind but only the result of an environment that prevents satisfaction of human needs.

What Maslow considers to be the true human needs are illustrated in FIGURE 12.6. He believes that these needs exist in every person, though those at the top of the hierarchy are often weak and easily thwarted by social pressures and other factors. Note that Maslow's theory, holding that human nature is essentially good, is in opposition to Freudian theory, which holds that man can be an acceptable social animal only when his ego holds the raw passions of his id in check.

Maslow's Pyramid of Human Needs According-ing to the Maslow theory of personality, human needs are arranged in this kind of pyramid. Those at the bottom are the most urgent and must be satisfied before those at the next highest level begin to operate. Thus people in primitive societies must fill their physiological needs before they can under-take the search for safety; and only in a wealthy and stable society can men begin to seek the higher goals to which human nature aspires. The need for self-actualization, at the top of the pyramid, means the desire for full realization of one's own potentialities and satisfaction of the thirst for knowledge and beauty. (9)

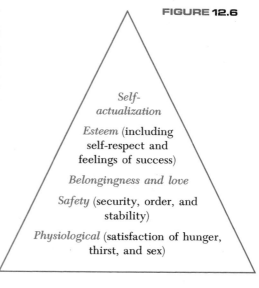

FIGURE 12.6

Self-actualization

Esteem (including self-respect and feelings of success)

Belongingness and love

Safety (security, order, and stability)

Physiological (satisfaction of hunger, thirst, and sex)

Rogers' Self Theory

In the large group of hypotheses about personality that are known as *self theories*, the best known has been formulated by Carl Rogers. Like Freud, Rogers developed his theories out of his treatment of disturbed people; his first position after receiving his Ph.D. was in the Rochester (New York) Guidance Clinic, and he has continued to spend much of his time in clinical work with patients seeking therapeutic help. Unlike Freud, however, Rogers was trained in psychology rather than in medicine, and the conclusions he has drawn from his observations are different from psychoanalytic theory.

Rogers' theory centers around the concept of the *phenomenal self*—that is to say, the image of himself that each person perceives in his own unique fashion, based on the evidence of his senses. The phenomenal self does not necessarily correspond to reality: many people who are clearly successful and highly respected nonetheless perceive themselves as unworthy failures. Nor is the phenomenal self necessarily the kind of self the person would like to be, as has been demonstrated by a study inspired by Rogers' theories.

In this study two groups of subjects received packets of cards each of which contained a statement about personality, such as, "I am likable," "I am a hard worker," "I am a submissive person." The subjects were asked to sort the cards along a line ranging from those that best described them to those that described them least well. After a record had been made of these sortings the subjects were asked to sort the cards again in a way that best described the kind of person they would like to be.

One group was made up of subjects who were seeking treatment for personality problems. The other was a matched control group of subjects who had not sought therapy and presumably did not consider it necessary. For the experimental group of patients there turned out to be no relation at all between what they considered to be their real selves and the kind of ideal selves they wanted to be. For the control group the relationship was quite high. The logical conclusion was that the patients seeking treatment were dissatisfied with themselves as they saw themselves, while the "normal" subjects were reasonably satisfied—a conclusion borne out by the fact that after treatment the patients showed much more correspondence than before between their real selves and their ideal selves (10).°

Self-Image and Neurosis

The experiment lends support to one important concept in Rogers' theory, which is that personality maladjustments are caused by a person's failure to

---

° The relationships were determined by calculating coefficients of correlation, as will be described in Chapter 13. The correlation between real self and ideal self for the patients was zero, for the control group .58. After treatment the correlation for the patients was .34.

integrate all his experiences, desires, and feelings into his image of self. This idea can best be explained by an example.

A young boy thinks of himself as being good and as being loved by his parents. However, he also feels hostility toward a younger brother, which he expresses one day by breaking his brother's toys. His parents punish him, and he now faces a crisis in integrating the experience into his image of self. He is forced to change the image in some way. He may decide that he is not a good boy but a bad boy and therefore acquire feelings of shame and guilt. He may decide that his parents do not love him and therefore feel rejected. Or he may decide to deny that he feels any hostility toward his brother, in which case he sets up a conflict between his true nature and his image of himself.

Each of us, says Rogers, attempts to perceive his experiences and to behave in a way that is consistent with his image of himself. When we are confronted with a new experience or new feelings that seem inconsistent with the image, we ordinarily can take one of two opposite courses.

1. We can recognize the new experience or feelings, perceive them clearly, and somehow integrate them into the image of self. This is a healthy reaction. The boy just mentioned, for example, could under ideal circumstances decide that he does feel hostility toward his brother; this is something he must reckon with; but the hostility does not make him "bad" or mean that he will be totally rejected by his parents and society.

2. We can deny the experience or feelings or perceive them in distorted fashion. Thus the boy may attempt to deny that he feels any hostility toward his brother and maintain that he broke the toys simply in retaliation for his brother's hostility (thus adopting what has been called the defense mechanism of projection).

According to Rogers, the maladjusted person is one who perceives any experience that is not consistent with his self-image as a threat, denies it to consciousness, and thereby sets up an ever widening gulf between his self-image and reality. His image of himself does not match his true feelings and the actual nature of his experiences; he must set up more and more defenses against the truth; and more and more tension results. The well-adjusted person, on the other hand, is one whose image of self is consistent with what he really thinks, feels, does, and experiences; instead of being rigid the self-image is flexible and constantly changes as new experiences occur.

Similarities and Differences Among the Theories

Although the various personality theories may seem in sharp conflict, actually they agree on many points. For example, they tend to agree that motives are basic forces in personality and that motives and habits learned early in childhood are important influences on adult behavior. They also tend to agree that identification (as Freud would say) or imitation (as Bandura and Walters would say) plays an important role—that children, and adults as well, adopt some of their motives, values, and forms of behavior from other people.

One basic difference among the personality theorists is a disagreement over which motives are the most important. To Freud, the basic motives are sexuality and aggression; to Adler, the motive for superiority; to Maslow, the need for self-actualization; to the social learning theorists, the need for praise and reward. This disagreement may reflect the kind of subjects from whom the various theories were developed. Freud, for example, dealt with middle-class patients in a place and time in which many people had sexual conflicts because society took a repressive view of sexuality. Maslow's more recent theories were developed from observations of college students at a time when society's view toward sexuality was more permissive and when America's affluence permitted more attention to a motive like self-actualization. Bandura and Walters have done much of their work with young children, for whom the desire for adult praise is a powerful motive and imitation of others a common phenomenon.

Another basic difference among the theories is that some of them (notably the psychoanalytic) emphasize covert behavior—the mental processes concerned with motives, conflicts, and anxieties. Others (notably the social learning theories) tend to emphasize overt behavior rather than mental processes. This disagreement is important because it has led to different approaches to the treatment of personality problems. As will be seen in the following section, psychoanalysis tries to deal with the dynamics of the mental processes that underlie behavior, while other forms of psychotherapy try to mold and change behavior more directly.

PSYCHOTHERAPY

Psychotherapy—the treatment of personality disorders and mental illness through psychological methods—is in a sense an ancient technique, dating back to the Greek physicians. For example, the Greeks often attempted to treat their maladjusted patients by removing them from their families, thus bringing about a change of environment—a method sometimes recommended today. For women suffering from hysteria the Greek physicians suggested marriage—an interesting form of treatment in light of modern discoveries that hysteria is often associated with sexual maladjustments and anxiety.

During the Middle Ages, however, the Greek approach to personality disorders was cast aside, and people suffering from the more intense and obvious forms of maladjustments and mental disease were punished as witches who were possessed by the devil. Even when the first so-called insane asylums were set up in the sixteenth century they were little more than prisons where the inmates were kept in chains and were "treated," if at all, by being whirled around in harnesses or having holes bored into their heads (see FIGURE 12.7). It has only been in the present century that mental hospitals have become humane institutions, where the most advanced medical and psychological methods are used in an attempt to help the mentally ill, and also that considerable numbers of physicians and psychologists have begun to devote themselves to giving treatment and guidance to the less seriously disturbed.

FIGURE 12.7

Old "Treatments" for the Mentally Ill In bygone centuries mental patients were treated by boring holes in the skull to release the "evil spirits" (*left*), by being stretched and whirled in harnesses suspended from the ceiling (*bottom right*), or by being chained virtually motionless to a wall (*bottom left*).

Client-Centered Therapy

Since Carl Rogers and his self theory were the last of the personality theories discussed, let us begin with the kind of treatment developed by Rogers, known as *client-centered therapy*. The central idea in client-centered therapy is for the therapist to display warmth and total acceptance toward the patient, thus providing a nonthreatening situation in which the patient is free to explore all his thoughts and feelings, including those that he has been unwilling to perceive clearly for fear of condemnation by others or by his own conscience. No matter what kind of hostilities the patient admits to or what kind of sexual desires, the therapist remains understanding and accepting; he is never surprised and never criticizes. Indeed he encourages the patient to help clarify and expand upon even the most negative aspects of his personality. In the safety of this relationship with the totally permissive therapist the patient is expected to gradually acquire the ability to resolve his conflicts.

The process, Rogers has said, takes three steps: 1) the patient begins to experience, understand, and accept feelings and desires that he has previously denied to consciousness; 2) he begins to understand the reasons behind his behavior; and 3) he begins to see ways in which he can undertake more positive forms of behavior. Ordinarily his image of self changes rather drastically; ideally he learns and becomes what he really is.

The patient is permitted to set his own pace in the course of treatment and to develop his own conclusions. At no time does the therapist try to set the goals of treatment or to suggest what values the patient should seek in life. His aim, as Rogers has written, is to convey the wholehearted impression that he regards the patient "as a person of unconditional self-worth; of value no matter what his condition, his behavior, or his feelings." The patient is also regarded as fully capable of eventually working out the positive answers to his problems and of deciding for himself when the therapy has succeeded and can be ended.

Many people who hear about client-centered therapy for the first time are struck by the question: If every person were encouraged to be completely himself, would the world not be suddenly filled with aggressive, brawling, murderous, sexually unrestrained, and self-seeking egoists? Rogers says not. Like Maslow, he uses the phrase *self-actualization;* he believes that people, if not twisted by conflicts between image of self and true self, tend to grow along wholesome and socially desirable lines.

Psychoanalysis

In the classical psychoanalytic treatment developed by Freud the chief tool is *free association.* The patient, lying as relaxed as possible on a couch, is encouraged to let his mind wander where it will and to speak out every thought that occurs to him—no matter how foolish it may seem, how obscene, or how insulting to the analyst. In this situation, as when drifting off to sleep, conscious control of the mind is reduced to a minimum, and unconscious forces have an opportunity to come to the surface. The analyst also studies the patient's dreams, which often represent unconscious desires, and any slips of the tongue the patient may make, which also are considered clues to the unconscious.

The analyst remains as anonymous as possible, not disclosing his own personality or his likes and dislikes. Indeed he usually sits to the rear and one side of the patient's head, so that the patient's flow of free associations will not be affected by his facial expressions. One reason for this mantle of anonymity is to encourage the phenomenon called *transference,* another tool that helps the analyst probe the patient's unconscious. Transference means, to the analysts, that all of us tend to transfer to the people we now know the emotional attitudes that we had as children toward such much-loved and much-hated persons as our parents and our brothers and sisters. In analysis, patients display these spontaneous emotional reactions toward the analyst; they may at times be overwhelmed by a desire to please him and be praised by him or by resentment and hatred of him. Because the analyst has done his best to be completely neutral, neither likable nor unlikable, he can presume that these feelings offer a good clue to the patient's unconscious.

Through the patient's free associations, dreams, tongue slips, and transferences—and even by noting what subjects the patient seems to avoid—the analyst gradually begins to get a picture of the unconscious problems that represent the patient's real difficulties. He then can help the patient acquire insights into the unconscious processes and gain control over them. The goal in analysis is to strengthen the ego and give the patient what one analyst has called "freedom from the tyranny of the unconscious" (11).

Behavior Therapy

A relatively new method of treating personality abnormalities is *behavior therapy,* which makes a direct attack upon the symptoms through the use of learning principles. Behavior therapy makes no attempt to probe the unconscious or to alter the general pattern of personality; instead it concentrates upon eliminating whatever particular kind of behavior or anxiety is bothering the patient. It does so by regarding the symptom as a conditioned response, which can be extinguished through some form of counterconditioning.

One behavioral therapist, for example, has reported the case of a patient who was a transvestite; he was unable to have sexual relations with his wife unless he first dressed up as a woman, and he frequently went out on the streets at night dressed in this fashion and wearing a wig. This symptom had become especially uncomfortable to the patient because he feared that his young son, as he grew up, would learn about it. The treatment prescribed was extremely simple. Electrodes were fastened into the woman's clothing that the patient habitually wore; he was encouraged to dress up but warned that at some point he would receive a painful shock or hear a buzzer and that the shock or buzzer would then be repeated at irregular intervals until he had removed the clothing. Each session of therapy included five starts at dressing followed by the shock or buzzer, with a one-minute rest period between each trial. After 400 trials, the treatment was considered ended. A follow-up report six months later showed that the patient had not returned to transvestism and reported that he was feeling less anxious than he had felt for many years (12). This particular type of behavioral therapy is known as aversive conditioning, because it associates the behavioral symptom with pain and punishment rather than with pleasure and reward. Aversive conditioning has also been reported successful in treating other forms of sexual maladjustment, such as homosexuality, and alcoholism.

One name prominently associated with behavior therapy is that of Joseph Wolpe, a physician who was born in South Africa, was at first a follower of Freud, and then broke away from psychoanalysis after studying psychological theories of learning. For the treatment of anxieties Wolpe has developed a technique called *reciprocal inhibition,* in which he attempts to associate the stimulus that has caused anxiety to some new response. One of his patients, for example, was a woman whose anxiety centered in part around death; she felt mildly anxious whenever she saw an ambulance or a hospital, much more anxious when she drove past a cemetery, and extremely anxious when she thought of her first husband lying in his coffin. With such a patient, Wolpe's technique is first to produce complete relaxation, either by teaching the patient to relax the muscles, by hypnosis, or by having the patient breathe a mixture of oxygen and carbon dioxide. While thus relaxed, as shown in FIGURE 12.8, the patient would be asked to think about the stimulus lowest on the list, the sight of an ambulance, and to stop thinking about it immediately if any feeling of anxiety occurred. According to Wolpe, this technique gradually associates the stimuli with relaxation rather than with anxiety, and the patient is able to think of what had been more and more disturbing stimuli for longer and longer times until finally treatment is complete.

In one study in which Wolpe treated thirty-nine patients who had various kinds of phobias and other anxieties, he reported successful results in thirty-five of the cases after an average of only eleven therapeutic sessions each; he managed to follow up twenty of these cases for anywhere from six months to four years and was able to report that there were no relapses and no new symptoms (13).

Other Types of Psychotherapy

As can be seen from the very substantial differences among client-centered therapy, psychoanalysis, and behavior therapy, the term psychotherapy covers a multitude of techniques. Still other methods include *psychodrama*, in which the patient is encouraged to act out his problems and fantasies in the company of other patients or therapeutic assistants who have been trained in the techniques of psychodrama; and *play therapy*, usually used with children, in which the patients can express their feelings by drawing pictures, modeling, or handling puppets or other toys.

Group therapy is the simultaneous treatment of several patients at a time; it has been used by many therapists of various schools of thought. The method is in part the child of necessity, for there are not enough trained therapists to treat all prospective patients individually. But it also seems to have some genuine advantages. The group situation may help relieve the individual

Relaxation in Behavior theory   Joseph Wolpe, a leading theorist and practitioner of behavior therapy, observes the reactions of a patient who is attempting to remain completely relaxed while thinking of stimuli that once produced feelings of anxiety.   **FIGURE 12.8**

patient's anxieties by demonstrating that there are other people with the same problems, and it also creates a kind of social give-and-take that is impossible in a face-to-face session with the therapist.

The Value of Psychotherapy

At this point the student is almost sure to be asking two questions: Does psychotherapy work? Which if any of the methods is the most effective?

These questions are the subject of the most intense kind of controversy in scientific and medical circles. Each type of therapy has its advocates and its critics. Some investigators believe that no method of psychotherapy is particularly effective, others that all the methods have considerable virtue.

The scientific method of answering the questions would be to select experimental and control groups—to find, say, fifty disturbed people and have them treated by a client-centered therapist, then send a matched group of fifty other patients to a psychoanalyst, another matched group of fifty to a behavior therapist, and so on, while preventing a matched control group of fifty from having any therapy at all. But this seems almost impossible, for who is to say how disturbed any individual is, and how can we match one disturbed individual with another? For that matter, how can we match the various therapists to make sure they are equally skillful? And how can we measure how much our subjects improve and how long their improvement lasts?

In the absence of any valid measure of the success of psychotherapy, what practical recommendations can be made about it? In other words, how could any one of us best advise a troubled friend or take action if we ourselves should feel troubled?

In the first place it appears quite likely that modern society has placed a little too much emphasis on personality disturbances. Although the early psychotherapists believed that they could aim toward an ideal of perfect adjustment and total absence of personality problems, this ideal now appears to have been unrealistic. It is not at all clear that there is a single standard of adjustment for all people in all cultures at all times. On the other hand, it does seem clear that everyone can expect to feel troubled and anxious from time to time. Perhaps this is simply part of the human condition.

Fortunately, some personality problems clear up spontaneously. The cause of the improvement is not known. Perhaps the situation that has caused the psychoneurotic behavior changes—as, for example, when a young woman who has suffered serious depression as the result of a broken engagement forgets her sorrow and becomes interested in another man. Or perhaps many of us manage, without outside help, to get insights into our conflicts or to recondition our behavior into more successful forms.

There seems to be little doubt, however, that there are many situations in which outside help can be valuable—perhaps in speeding recovery, perhaps in bringing about a more complete recovery than would otherwise take place. The exact form of the help may not matter as much as the fact that *some* kind of help is obtained. As a matter of fact there are fewer differences in the actual practice of psychotherapy than the theoretical differences among the various schools would indicate. One study has indicated that therapists tend to begin their professional lives by practicing their theories rather rigorously, but, after a certain amount of practical experience, tend to become more and more alike in the methods they use to treat patients (14).

MEDICAL THERAPY

To complete the discussion of treatment of personality disorders, it must be pointed out that there are three large groups of people who are especially concerned with this field, only two of which have been mentioned thus far. One group is the clinical psychologists. Another is the psychoanalysts, most of whom are physicians and all of whom have taken special training in psychoanalytic theory and practice. The third group is composed of *psychiatrists,* who are physicians who have taken special training in the treatment of mental disorders but have not specialized in the methods advocated by the psychoanalysts. All clinical psychologists, all psychoanalysts, and most psychiatrists rely totally or at least mostly on psychotherapy, though their methods of psychotherapy take various forms. There are some psychiatrists, however, who lean strongly toward biological theories of personality disturbances, particularly of the psychoses like schizophrenia, and who tend to rely heavily upon drugs as a method of treatment.

Medicine is of course not our concern in this book, but the medical approach to personality problems deserves mention. Many biochemists and other researchers believe strongly that personality disturbances, though they seem to be purely functional, have a physical cause. It has been suggested, for example, that schizophrenia may be associated with some chemical, as yet undiscovered. In the normal person, the suggestion goes, this particular chemical has no ill effects; but, in the person whose autonomic nervous system and stress apparatus are not working properly, the chemical environment of the brain is thrown off balance, and the chemical causes the symptoms of psychosis. Because of possibilities of this sort, many researchers are studying brain chemistry in an attempt to find changes that may accompany personality disturbances.

Even in the absence of any substantial proof of the medical theories of personality disturbances, psychiatrists have used several kinds of biological treatment, which have proved valuable for at least some patients though the reasons are not understood. The most generally used are 1) *electroshock therapy* and 2) various kinds of *drugs.*

Electroshock Therapy

When electrodes are fastened to a patient's head and an electric current roughly as strong as household electricity is passed between them for a fraction of a second, the patient goes into a brief convulsion and then is unconscious for a half hour to an hour. When he wakes up, he seems drowsy and confused, but no permanent harm seems to be done to his memory or his learning ability.

Electroshock has been used chiefly to treat patients suffering from depression, often with very good results. It has also been used to relieve manic symptoms, with somewhat less success, and has been tried for schizophrenia, with results that are controversial.

Drugs

A number of drugs, the effects of which have often been discovered more or less by accident, are also used in the treatment of personality disorders. They fall into four chief classes: 1) *narcotics,* 2) *tranquilizers,* 3) *energizers,* and 4) *psychedelic drugs.*

Chief among the *narcotics* is the drug *sodium amytal,* popularly known as "truth serum." Small injections of this drug produce a deep sleep, which is preceded by a period of drowsiness in which the patient seems able to recall and discuss experiences that he ordinarily represses. It is therefore often used in an attempt to learn about deeply unconscious problems.

The *tranquilizers* have been most useful in calming mental patients who previously were so noisy, hostile, and destructive as to be unmanageable. The tranquilizers may reduce or eliminate the patient's hallucinations and delusions as well as his anxieties. The use of these drugs has been of considerable help in changing the atmosphere of mental hospitals and making previously violent patients amenable to attempts at psychotherapy. Many patients, kept on the proper dosage, have been able to return to a more or less normal life. Milder forms of tranquilizers have been prescribed to relieve the tensions and anxieties of neurotic patients or of "normal" people who are facing unusually difficult situations in their lives.

The *energizers* are stimulants that heighten physical and mental activity; they have been used as a substitute for electroshock in treating depression.

Among the *psychedelic drugs* the best known is LSD, which is short for lysergic acid diethylamide. Taken by a normal person, LSD often produces visual hallucinations and a sense of detachment from one's own body; sometimes it produces feelings of joy, and sometimes it causes anxiety and even terror. In about 2 to 5 percent of users, it has been estimated, the drug causes extreme disturbances similar to psychosis (15). Some investigators suspect that the drug may produce permanent and potentially dangerous changes in brain chemistry.

In the psychotic patient LSD appears to increase the already high level of anxiety and tendency toward fantasy, and it may therefore be of value in inducing him to talk more freely to the therapist.

How Effective Is Medical Therapy?

As in the case of psychotherapy, the value of the various medical therapies is a matter of controversy. Electroshock, for example, has been credited with as much as 90 percent success in relieving severe depression and is believed by many psychiatrists to have saved patients who otherwise would probably have committed suicide. To many investigators, however, electroshock remains what one critic has described as "trying to fix an expensive watch by kicking it."

When the tranquilizers were first introduced in the 1950's, they were hailed as a breakthrough in the treatment of mental disturbance. Numerous studies have demonstrated their value in controlling the patient's moods and enabling him to behave more normally. But much of the original optimism concerning their use has disappeared. They are in no sense a cure for mental disease but merely a means of relieving the symptoms—or, as some have said, "masking" them. Some investigators believe that the chief value of tranquilizers lies in making the patient receptive to the methods of psychotherapy.

SUMMARY

1. *Personality* is the total pattern of characteristic ways of behaving and thinking that constitute the individual's unique and distinctive method of adjusting to his environment.

2. Three categories of theories that attempt to explain the origin and dynamics of personality are a) physiological, b) psychoanalytic, and c) social learning.

3. Sheldon's physiological theory divides people into three basic types: a) *endomorphs,* who tend to have a *viscerotonic* temperament; b) *mesomorphs,* who tend to have a *somatotonic* temperament; and c) *ectomorphs,* who tend to have a *cerebrotonic* temperament.

4. Freud's psychoanalytic theory emphasizes three aspects of the personality: a) the unconscious *id,* containing the person's instinctive drives toward sexuality (the *libido*) and aggression; b) the conscious *ego,* which is the person's operational contact with reality; and c) the largely unconscious *superego,* which threatens punishment for transgressions.

5. The superego is acquired in large part as a result of the *Oedipus complex*, a conflict of mingled love and hate toward the parents that every child is assumed to undergo between the ages of two and a half and six. The child resolves the conflict by *identifying* with his parents and absorbing what he considers to be their moral judgments, which form his superego.

6. *Anxiety*, another key concept in psychoanalytic theory, is said to be aroused when the environment or the demands of the id threaten danger or when the superego threatens disapproval or punishment.

7. Among successors of Freud who have proposed various kinds of variations of his theories are Jung (who introduced the concepts of *introvert* and *extrovert*), Adler (who introduced the concept of *inferiority complex*), Horney, and Fromm.

8. *Social learning theories*, also known as S-R theories, maintain that personality is composed of habitual ways of responding to stimuli in the environment. Social learning theories emphasize the reinforcements and punishments provided by society for certain types of behavior as well as the importance of imitating the behavior of other persons, called *models*.

9. Other theories of personality include Maslow's theory of self-actualization and Rogers' theory of the phenomenal self—or the self perceived by a person on the basis of internal and external sensory evidence.

10. Three influential schools of psychotherapy are a) Rogers' *client-centered therapy*, b) *psychoanalysis*, and c) *behavior therapy*.

11. In client-centered therapy the therapist attempts to provide a nonthreatening situation by displaying warmth and total acceptance toward the patient; in this permissive atmosphere the patient is supposed to be freed to explore aspects of himself and his experiences that he had previously repressed.

12. Psychoanalysis uses the techniques of *free association*, study of dreams and slips of the tongue, and *transference* to give the patient insights into his unconscious conflicts.

13. Behavior therapy concentrates on the symptoms of personality conflict, which are regarded as conditioned responses that can be eliminated through counterconditioning. Prominent among the behavior therapists is Wolpe, who devised the method of *reciprocal inhibition* for reducing anxiety.

14. Other forms of psychotherapy include *psychodrama, play therapy*, and *group therapy*.

15. Medical therapy is the treatment of personality disturbances through medical methods, among the most prominent of which are a) *electroshock* and b) *drugs*.

16. Drugs used in medical therapy fall into four chief classes: a) *narcotics* (such as "truth serum"), b) *tranquilizers* (used to calm disturbed people),

c) *energizers* (to combat depression), and d) *psychedelic drugs* (such as LSD, which produces some of the symptoms of psychosis in normal people).

RECOMMENDED READING

Adler, A. *Practice and theory of individual psychology.* New York: Harcourt, Brace & World, 1927.

Freud, A. *The ego and the mechanisms of defence.* New York: International Universities Press, 1946.

Freud, S. *New introductory lectures on psycho-analysis.* New York: Norton, 1933.

Fromm, E. *Man for himself: an inquiry into the psychology of ethics.* New York: Holt, Rinehart and Winston, 1947.

Hall, C. S. and Lindzey, G. *Theories of personality.* New York: Wiley, 1957.

Horney, Karen. *Neurosis and human growth.* New York: Norton, 1950.

Jung, C. G. *The basic writings of C. G. Jung.* New York: Random House, 1959.

McCurdy, H. G. *The personal world: an introduction to the study of personality.* New York: Harcourt, Brace & World, 1961.

Rogers, C. R. *Client-centered therapy.* Boston: Houghton Mifflin, 1951.

Sarason, I. G. *Personality: an objective approach.* New York: Wiley, 1966.

Wolpe, J. *Psychotherapy by reciprocal inhibition.* Stanford, Calif.: Stanford University Press, 1958.

All sciences are interested in both general laws and predictions about individual events. Thus chemistry is concerned with the general laws that explain what happens when a large number of molecules of an acid meet a large number of molecules of a metal, and it is also concerned with what happens when specific amounts of two specific substances are put together in a test tube under specific conditions of pressure and heat.

Psychology resembles the other sciences in this respect. It is interested in general laws of learning, perception, thinking, motivation, and emotions—all the psychological processes, common to most organisms, that have been discussed up to this point. As will be seen in this section, it is also concerned with individual differences.

It was Sir Francis Galton who first began collecting proof that no two individual human beings are ever exactly alike. He studied people's height, weight, hearing, sense of smell, color vision, ability to judge weights, and many other traits and abilities, and he found that all kinds of human characteristics vary over a wide range from small to large, weak to strong, and slow to fast.

To establish that differences exist, Galton had to make measurements and analyze his measurements statistically. Thus *measurement,* used to study individual differences, has been an important branch of psychology almost from the beginning.

Chapter 13 discusses general principles of measurement—the statistical methods used to analyze measurements and to draw inferences from them. Chapter 14, "Measuring Intelligence and Personality," describes the tests that have been devised to measure various kinds of human abilities and characteristics; it also discusses what measurement has disclosed about the nature and distribution of intelligence.

WHY THE STATISTICAL METHOD IS IMPORTANT

Probability
Coincidences

PROBLEMS IN MEASUREMENT

Ratio and Interval Scales
Ordinal and Nominal Scales
Is Psychological Measurement Valid?

THE NORMAL CURVE OF DISTRIBUTION

The Curve's Meaning
Other Uses of Statistics

DESCRIPTIVE STATISTICS

Number in Group
Average Measurement
Variability and Standard Deviation
Percentiles

INFERENTIAL STATISTICS

Population and Sample
Control Groups
Comparing Two Groups
 Standard Error of the Mean; Probability and "Significance"
Correlation
 Scatter Plots; Correlation and Prediction; Correlation, Cause, and Effect

THE MATHEMATICAL COMPUTATIONS

The Mean
The Standard Deviation
The Standard Error of the Mean
Differences Between Groups
Correlation
Contingency

13

MEASUREMENT

One of the questions that fascinated Sir Francis Galton was whether tall parents had taller than average children. Another was whether successful men tended to have successful sons. Since Galton's time, other investigators have explored many similar questions, such as: Do intelligent parents tend to have children of above-average intelligence? Do strict parents tend to produce children who are more or less aggressive than the children of parents whose discipline is more lenient? Do intelligent people tend to be more or less neurotic than people of less intelligence?

All these are important questions. None of them—as Galton discovered —can be answered satisfactorily without making some kind of measurements and then submitting them to statistical analysis. Both these processes are equally important. We cannot hope to deal with individual differences unless we can measure them. And we cannot understand the meaning of the measurements or the relationships they show among various traits of the organism unless we analyze them in accordance with sound statistical principles.

Thus *measurement* and the *statistical method* of analyzing measurements have been important branches of psychology ever since Galton's time. *Measurement* is defined as the assignment of numbers to traits, events, or objects, according to some kind of orderly system. The *statistical method* refers to the application of mathematical principles to the interpretation of the numbers. Since both processes involve a certain amount of mathematics, they are approached with distaste by some students. However, the mathematics are secondary. Measurement and the statistical method of analyzing measurements are, above all, what has been called a *way of thinking* (1)—a problem solving tool that enables us to summarize our knowledge of psychological events, make valid inferences about behavior, and avoid jumping to wrong conclusions, as people who do not understand statistical methods often do.

A person can understand the techniques of measurement and the statistical method and use them to great advantage in analyzing behavior without ever memorizing a single mathematical formula or making a single mathematical computation. On the other hand, the mathematics are interesting in their own right, are not particularly difficult to anyone who has had a high school algebra course, and are an essential tool in almost all types of psychological research. This chapter will talk first about the principles and uses of measurement and statistical analysis, without going into the mathematics any more than is absolutely necessary. A separate section at the end of the chapter will describe the mathematical computations.

WHY THE STATISTICAL METHOD IS IMPORTANT

Let us begin by considering two incidents that, though they concern medicine rather than psychology, are particularly dramatic examples of why the statistical method is an essential tool in science.

In 1965 a follow-up study of several million women who had been taking birth-control pills showed that a number of them had become victims of a dangerous disease in which blood clots form on the inside walls of blood vessels and sometimes break loose, travel to the brain or lungs, and cause death. In fact thirteen such deaths were reported among these women—raising the question of whether the pills were safe for human use. To some physicians the answer seemed perfectly clear. The women took the pills, and thirteen of them died from traveling blood clots; the pills obviously caused the ailment and should be taken off the market. But this was a case where physicians unacquainted with the statistical method had jumped to the wrong conclusion. Further study showed that, in any group of women of child-bearing age, a certain number die of traveling blood clots each year, whether or not they take the pill. Statistical analysis indicated that the death rate was actually lower among women who had taken the pill than among those who had not.

At about the same time, hospitals in many countries began reporting the birth of babies born without arms, without legs, or with badly deformed arms and legs. There were not very many cases. It would have been easy to say that they occurred by mere coincidence. Or they might have been interpreted as the result of radioactive fallout or (by a superstitious person) as the result of the position of the planets in the sky. As it happened, however, it was discovered that every mother of a deformed baby had taken a certain new kind of tranquilizer pill while she was pregnant. *Every* deformed baby was traced to the tranquilizer, and so far as was known no mother who had not taken the tranquilizer gave birth to a similarly deformed baby during the same period. Here the connection between the tranquilizer and abnormal babies was convincingly shown, by statistical standards, and the tranquilizer was taken off the market at once.

Probability

For another example of how we can profit from thinking in terms of the statistical method, examine FIGURE 13.1. This illustration tells a great deal about the statistical approach as opposed to the nonstatistical, and you are urged to try to answer the question it poses before you read on to the next paragraph.

Common sense says that the answer to the question in FIGURE 13.1 is the hand with thirteen spades. When a bridge player gets such a hand, the newspapers are likely to report it as a great rarity. The player is likely to talk about it the rest of his life. And, in all truth, a hand of thirteen spades is extremely rare. It occurs, as a mathematician can quickly calculate, on an average of only once in about 159 billion deals.

However, the other two hands shown in FIGURE 13.1 are *equally rare.* The rules of statistical probability say that the chance of getting *any* particular combination of thirteen cards is only one in about 159 billion deals. The reason a hand of thirteen spades seems rarer than any other is that bridge players pay attention to it, while lumping all their mediocre hands together as if they were one and the same.

Let us think about the hand of thirteen spades in another way. Since it occurs only once in 159 billion deals, is it not a miracle that it should ever occur at all? No, it is not. It has been estimated that there are about 25 million bridge players in the United States. If each of them deals twenty times a week, that makes 26 billion deals a year. The statistical method tells us that we should expect a hand of thirteen spades to be dealt on the average of about once every six years.

Which Hand Is the Rarest?   These three hands have all been dealt at various times in bridge games. Question: Which hand are you *least* likely to get if you play bridge tonight? For the answer—which casts considerable light on why and how statistics are important—see the text.

FIGURE 13.1

Coincidences

This last fact—that we must expect a hand of thirteen spades to occur with some regularity—explains many occurrences that would otherwise seem baffling. For a simple example, let us say that we go to a party tonight and find ourselves in a rather small group of twenty-three people. Someone at the party remarks, "Tomorrow is my birthday," and someone else says, in surprise, "That's funny; it's my birthday too." Does this seem a strange coincidence? Perhaps. But a mathematician can figure out that in any group of twenty-three people, the chances are better than even that two of them will have the same birthday.°

Every once in a while the newspapers report that someone shooting dice at Las Vegas made twenty-eight passes (or winning throws) in a row. This seems almost impossible, and in fact the actual mathematical odds are more than 268,000,000 to 1 that it will not happen to anyone who begins throwing the dice. These are very high odds indeed. Yet, considering the large number of people who step up to all the dice tables in Las Vegas, it is inevitable that sooner or later someone will throw the twenty-eight passes.

The laws of probability explain many of the coincidences that seem—to people who do not understand these laws—to represent the working of supernatural powers. A woman in Illinois dreams that her brother in California has died and next morning gets a telephone call reporting that he was killed in an accident. This may sound like an incredible case of some kind of mental telepathy, but the laws of probability offer a much simpler and more reasonable explanation. Most people dream frequently. Dreams of death are by no means rare. In the course of a year millions of people dream of the death of someone in the family. Sooner or later, one of the dreams is bound to coincide with an actual death.

Astrologers and other seers who claim to predict the future also profit from the rules of probability. If an astrologer keeps predicting that a "catastrophe" will occur, he is bound to be right sooner or later, because the world is certain to have some kind of tragedy, from airplane accident to tornado, in any given period. And a prophet who makes his reputation by predicting the death of a "world statesman" takes advantage of the fact that there are many world statesmen and that many of them are in an age bracket where death can be expected.

In a world as big as ours, all kinds of coincidences are certain to occur.

° For the benefit of mathematically inclined students it should be explained that the probability of finding two persons in the same room with the same birthday is given by the formula:

$$1 - \frac{365 \times 364 \times 363 \cdots (365 - N + 1)}{365^N}$$

N is the number of people in the room. With twenty-three people the formula gives the probability as 0.507, or slightly better than 50–50.

It would be a statistical miracle if they did not. Statistical analysis enables us to separate cases of sheer coincidence from cases in which some cause may be operating.

To make a measurement and thus get the data we need for statistical analysis, we must have some kind of scale **PROBLEMS IN MEASUREMENT** of numbers. Among such scales used in everyday affairs are length in inches and feet, weight in ounces and pounds, and temperature in degrees Fahrenheit. Without these scales of measurement we could only guess, and our guesses would in some cases be far off. Note the four photographs, for example, in FIGURE 13.2. Judging from what the people are doing and what they are wearing, we would surely guess that the weather was much warmer when the photo was taken of the young man lying on the beach than when the man in the topcoat was looking out to sea. Somewhere in between, we might guess, were the temperatures when the two children were playing in the sand and the older children at the playground. Actually all four photographs were made on the same January day, in and around New York City, at a time when the temperature as recorded by the weather bureau was an unseasonable 65 degrees. Various people reacted to the temperature in quite different ways; some felt that the 65-degree temperature was a heat wave while others still felt chilly.

Note also the photograph in FIGURE 13.3, and estimate the height of the young men as asked in the caption. After you have done so, turn to FIGURE 13.4. The two photos demonstrate how wrong our judgments of height can be when we lack a scale of measurement.

Ratio and Interval Scales

The most satisfactory type of measurement is made on what is called a *ratio scale*, an example of which is the scale of feet and inches. In measuring length we have a true zero point; we can conceive of a mythical point in space that has no length at all. Moreover, all the numbers on the scale fall into perfect ratios. An object that is three feet long is exactly three times as long as a one-foot object, as we can prove by lining up three one-foot rulers and measuring their total length with a yardstick. A man six feet tall is twice as tall as a boy who measures three feet. If we are driving at a steady speed, it takes us five times as long to travel five miles as to travel one mile.

The scale of weight is another ratio scale. An object that weighs two ounces is twice as heavy as an object that weighs one ounce, as can be demonstrated by putting a two-ounce weight on one side of a balance scale and two one-ounce weights on the other side.

Somewhat less satisfactory than a ratio scale, but nonetheless very useful,

FIGURE 13.2   *What Is the Temperature?*   Try to guess what the temperature was when each of these four photographs was taken. Then compare your guesses with the correct answers given in the text.

How Tall Are These Young Men? After studying this picture, how would you describe each of the three young men—as very short, short, average, tall, or very tall? After you have decided on the answers, check them against FIGURE 13.4 on the next page.

FIGURE 13.3

is an *interval scale*, the best example of which is a thermometer. The intervals on the thermometer are all equal; the liquid inside the tube must expand just as far to move from 49 to 50 degrees as from 99 to 100 degrees. However, no ratio is implied by temperature readings; one cannot say that 100 degrees is twice as hot as 50 degrees.

Ordinal and Nominal Scales

In psychology, unfortunately, ratio and interval scales are seldom applicable. The major use of ratio scales is in measuring the physical properties of stimuli —for example, the intensity of lights and sounds and the amount of pressure applied against the skin. Interval scales are used in measuring reactions to warmth and cold. In most cases psychology must do the best it can with less satisfactory scales.

Psychology frequently uses *ordinal scales*, which, as the name implies, are scales on which individuals are arranged in order of rank. A good example of an ordinal scale is the scores on a true-false test given as a classroom examination. Let us say that there are a hundred questions. One student, and one only, gets all hundred correct; he obviously stands number 1 in the class. The number 2 score is 95 correct, the number 3 score is 94, the number 4 score 90, and so on, down to a score of 25, which is the lowest in the

461

class. Note that the rating of 1 indicates only that this student was ahead of the next highest scorer; it does not say by how much. Indeed the number 1 student got five more answers correct than did the number 2 student, while number 2 had only one more correct answer than number 3. (Teachers often arrange examination results by rank order and arbitrarily give A's to the top 10 percent, B's to the next 20 percent, C's to the next 40, D's to the next 20, and F's to the lowest 10 percent.)

The numbers for intelligence quotient, or I.Q., obtained from intelligence tests constitute an ordinal scale, assigning a number of around 180 or 190 to the highest score made by any person who has ever taken the test and around 10 to 20 to the lowest score. The I.Q. is really nothing more than a measure of what rank order one person occupies among all the people who have taken the test. It does not mean that a person who scores 150 is twice as smart as one who scores 75. Moreover, the 5-point difference between a score of 150 and a score of 155 does not represent the same amount of intelligence as does the 5-point difference between 100 and 105. As on all ordinal scales, the differences between I.Q. scores do not have the quality of sameness possessed by the differences on a ratio scale like a ruler or an interval scale like a thermometer.

The simplest of all scales is a *nominal scale,* in which numbers are used to designate different categories. Nominal scales have been used frequently

FIGURE 13.4   *The Young Men's Actual Height*   Here a scale of measurement has been added to the photo shown in FIGURE 13.3—and we see that the young man at the left is of average height; the young man in the middle is taller than average; and the man at the right is very tall. They looked smaller in FIGURE 13.3 by comparison with the young woman, who, it can now be seen, is unusually tall for a girl. Thus do scales and numbers provide a far more accurate kind of measurement than is otherwise possible.

throughout this book in reporting experiments. For example, in the Schachter experiment on reactions to a funny movie (page 362), the subjects who received an injection of adrenalin were called group 1, those who received a tranquilizer group 2, and those who received salt water (the control group) group 3. The numbers given to the groups merely lump some of the subjects together because they are alike in some important respect, with no implication that the number 3 means that this group is in any way larger, smaller, better, or worse than the groups given the numbers 2 or 1. In a study of college students, similarly, the investigator might assign the number 1 to women and the number 2 to men, or he might want to separate students from different schools by assigning number 1 to those from school A, 2 to school B, 3 to school C, 4 to school D, and so on.

Is Psychological Measurement Valid?

Since psychology is forced to rely on ordinal and nominal scales rather than the much more sensitive interval and ratio scales, the psychologist is under much the same handicap that the physicist would face if he had no ratio scale of weights and could say only that something is very heavy, heavy, not so heavy, only slightly heavy, or not heavy at all. (Or that a cook would labor under if the recipes could only recommend a lot of this, a medium amount of that, and a small amount of the other.) This is a continuing problem in the science. Many investigators are trying to devise more adequate scales, and at least modest progress in psychological measurement is being made every year. But any discussion of psychological measurement must contain a warning that the scales on which we must now rely leave a great deal to be desired. We must not overestimate the accuracy of the numbers we use, and we must be modest about the conclusions that we draw from them.

It should also be pointed out, however, that no form of measurement is completely accurate. Even the measurements used in the physical sciences are subject to error. At what point, for example, does 99 degrees Fahrenheit cease to be 99 degrees and become 100? Or, if we are trying to make finer distinctions, at what point does 99.9 degrees become 100? At what point does a person cease to weigh 120 pounds and begin to weigh 121, and at what point does an automobile cease to travel thirty-five miles an hour and begin to travel thirty-six? (In cooking, how level is a "level teaspoon," and how heaping is a "heaping tablespoon"?) An engineer using the measurements of physical science may feel that he has a reasonably accurate idea of weights, tensile strengths, and possible loads, but he builds the bridge two or three times stronger anyway, to allow for possible errors.

We have to apply psychological measurements with caution—much more caution than is called for in using a yardstick or a thermometer. We must not fall into the error of thinking that our statistical analysis of the measurements is sacred just because it can be put into numbers and mathematical equations. But we have to try to measure psychological traits as best we can if we are to study and understand them. And statistical analysis, used with proper humility, is an invaluable tool in helping us comprehend the meaning of our figures and avoid generalizations that are too sweeping or mathematically false.

THE NORMAL CURVE OF DISTRIBUTION   Closely related to the rules of probability discussed earlier in the chapter is a statistical principle that has particular significance for the study of human behavior, as Galton was the first to notice. This can best be approached through another example taken from outside the field of psychology—an example that you can try for yourself if you like. Put ten coins into a cup, shake them, throw them on a table, and count the number of heads. Do this a number of times, say 100. Your tally will probably be roughly the same as the one shown in FIGURE 13.5.

What you have come up with is a simple illustration of normal distribution. When you toss ten coins 100 times—a total of 1000 tosses—you can expect 500 heads to come up, an average of five heads per toss. As the tally shows, this number of five heads came up most frequently. The two numbers on either side, four and six, were close seconds. The numbers farther away from five were increasingly infrequent. Ten came up only once, and zero did not come up at all. (Over a long period, both ten and zero would be expected to come up on an average of once in every 1024 tosses.)

The tally shown in FIGURE 13.5 can be converted into the bar chart shown in FIGURE 13.6, which provides a more easily interpreted picture of what happened in the coin tossing. And the bar chart can in turn be shown in the form of a smooth curve. In FIGURE 13.7 the curve shows what would happen if the coins had been tossed not just 100 times but 1024 and had come out exactly as the law of probability would predict.

This is the *normal curve of distribution*, sometimes called the *normal probability curve*, and it is one of the most useful tools in studying individual differences. Note that the curve is shaped like a bell. From its highest point, which is at the average, it declines rather sharply to both left and right, then begins to flatten out. At the extremes, both left and right, it slowly approaches zero.

FIGURE 13.5

A Tally of Coin Tosses   Ten coins were shaken in a cup and tossed on a table 100 times. A tally of the number of heads that appeared on each toss is shown here.

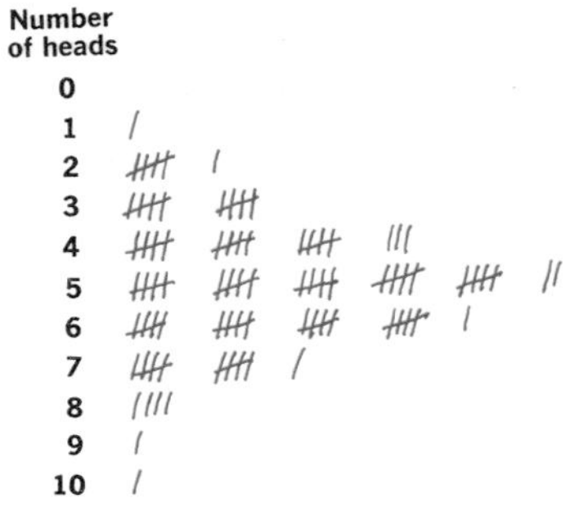

Number of heads						
0						
1	/					
2	⊬⊬	/				
3	⊬⊬	⊬⊬				
4	⊬⊬	⊬⊬	⊬⊬	///		
5	⊬⊬	⊬⊬	⊬⊬	⊬⊬	⊬⊬	//
6	⊬⊬	⊬⊬	⊬⊬	⊬⊬	/	
7	⊬⊬	⊬⊬	/			
8	////					
9	/					
10	/					

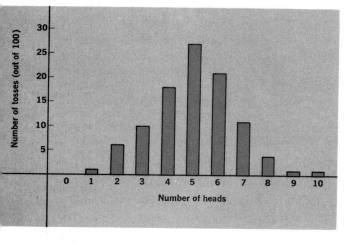

FIGURE **13.6**

The Tally in Bar Form Here the results of the coin-tossing experiment, which were shown in tally form in FIGURE 13.5, have been converted into a bar chart. Note the peak at the center and the rapid falling off toward each extreme.

FIGURE 13.7

A Normal Curve of Distribution If the coin-tossing experiment were continued until 1024 tosses had been made, the results would approximate this curve—which is a normal curve of distribution.

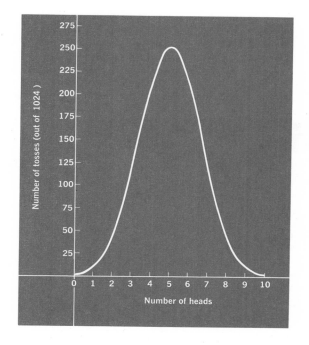

The Curve's Meaning

The important thing about the curve of normal distribution is that it provides a picture of the way many events are distributed in the world. The curve in FIGURE 13.7 resulted from a tally of coin tosses. Galton drew up a normal curve by constructing a device that was something like a pinball machine

465

held up perpendicularly; he poured gunshot into a funnel at the top center, and the round pellets fell past a series of pins to compartments at the bottom. The same sort of device, in more elaborate form, entertained visitors to the New York World's Fair of 1964–65, as can be seen in FIGURE 13.8. Like Galton's invention, it resulted in a chance distribution greatest in the center compartments and falling off to a smaller number in the end compartments.

In human affairs the normal curve applies to many traits. FIGURE 13.9 shows how men's height falls into the pattern. FIGURE 13.10 shows how the number of digits that can be remembered after a single presentation is distributed. Similar curves have been found for human weight, mechanical aptitude, and many other characteristics. Intelligence tests are based on the assumption that intelligence is also distributed in this fashion; the tests are then arbitrarily constructed to produce the curve shown in FIGURE 13.11. The message of the normal curve is that in many measurable traits most people are average or close to it, some are well below or above, and a few

FIGURE 13.8   *A Machine That Produces the Normal Curve*   The distribution of the balls in the compartments at the bottom of the machine—a close approximation of the curve of normal distribution—was obtained by chance as they fell from the top past a series of pins that directed most of them to the center, a few to the sides.

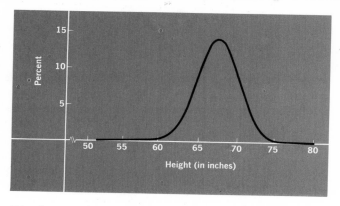

FIGURE 13.9   *Distribution of Men's Height*   Measurements of the height of more than 91,000 Englishmen called up for military service in 1939 gave this curve of distribution. The average height was 5 feet 7½ inches. Note how few men measured less than 5 feet or more than 6 feet 3 inches. (2) (In the United States today, the average height of men is nearly an inch taller than shown here.)

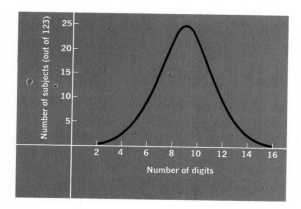

FIGURE 13.10

Distribution of Memory Span for Digits   The curve shows the distribution of the memory span for digits found in a group of 123 women students. The number of digits is the maximum that the students were able to repeat accurately after hearing them one time only. (3)

Distribution of Intelligence   This curve shows the distribution of intelligence in the United States, as determined by a Stanford-Binet test given to a large standardization group in 1937. A total of 46.5 percent of those measured had intelligence quotients between 90 and 109. Fewer than 1 percent scored below 60 and only 1.33 percent scored 140 or over. (4)

FIGURE 13.11

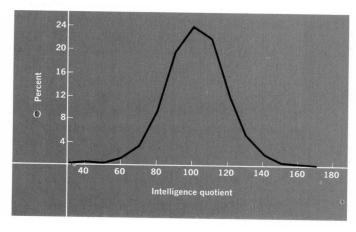

are very far below or above. Those who are about average have a lot of company. But some people are as rare in height or in the scores they make on intelligence tests as are the twenty-eight passes in a dice game.

Other Uses of Statistics

The normal curve is the basis for *descriptive statistics*, which provide a quick and convenient method of summarizing the characteristics of any group of people or animals. It is also the basis for *inferential statistics*, which enable us to make reasonably accurate generalizations from measurements. Let us say that we are interested in intelligence. We test 10,000 people. Now we have 10,000 raw scores. To pass along our knowledge of what we have learned about intelligence, we need not quote every one of the 10,000 scores. Through the use of descriptive statistics we can summarize and condense; with a few well-chosen numbers that will be explained in a moment, we can tell another person much of what he needs to know to understand our results. And through the use of inferential statistics we can make some valid generalizations that will probably hold true not just for our 10,000 cases but for the several billion people in the world.

DESCRIPTIVE STATISTICS   In order to describe the attributes of a group—say, the group of 10,000 people tested for intelligence—we must use three specific numbers. We must compute 1) the number of individuals in the group, 2) the average value (in this case the average I.Q. score), and 3) the variability of the measurements. Let us consider the three in order.

Number in Group

This is simply the total number of subjects in the sample. It is an important number because we can usually draw more confident conclusions from a large sample than from a small sample. If we test only three people for intelligence, we may happen to select three geniuses or three morons. A larger sample is likely to be more representative of the population as a whole.

Average Measurement

In everyday language, *average* means the sum of all the measurements divided by the number of subjects. For example, six students take an examination containing a hundred true-false questions and get test scores of 70, 74, 74, 76, 80, and 82. What is usually considered the "average" score is 456 divided by 6, or 76. This kind of arithmetic average is a useful figure statistically and is technically known as the *mean*.

Another useful kind of average is called the *median*, the halfway point that separates the lower 50 percent of scores from the higher 50 percent. In the example just given the median would be 75, because half the scores fall below 75 and the other half fall above. The median is an especially useful figure when the data include a small number of exceptionally low or exceptionally high measurements. Let us say, for example, that the six scores on the true-false examination were 70, 74, 74, 76, 80, and 100. The one student who scored 100 brings up the mean score quite sharply, to 79. But note that 79 is hardly an "average" score because only two of the six students scored that high. The median score, which remains at 75, is a better description of the data.

A third type of average is called the *mode*. This is the measurement or score that applies to the greatest number of subjects. In the case of the true-false examination it would be 74, the only score made by as many as two of the students. The mode tells us where the highest point of the curve of distribution will be found.

In a perfectly symmetrical curve of normal distribution, the mean, the median, and the mode are the same. When they are markedly different, it usually means that we are dealing with a *skewed distribution* like those illustrated in FIGURE 13.12.

Variability and Standard Deviation

Some of the examples already shown in the illustrations of this chapter demonstrate that the normal curve of distribution, even when perfectly symmetrical and preserving its characteristic bell shape, may take different forms. Sometimes it is high and narrow. At other times it is shorter and wider. This depends upon the *variability* of the measurements.

FIGURE **13.12**   *Skewed Distribution Curves*   The curve at the left is said to be negatively skewed. Note that more scores fall below the mode than above it. The curve at the right is positively skewed, with more scores falling above the mode than below it.

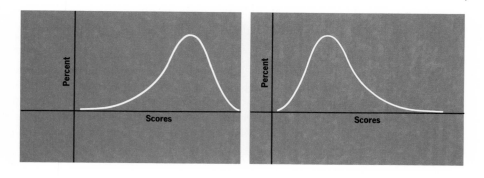

A crude way to describe the variability is simply to give the *range* of measurements—the highest minus the lowest. Another and much more sensitive description is provided by what is called the *standard deviation,* mathematically abbreviated to the initials SD. The standard deviation, which is computed from the data by a formula that will be discussed in the second section of the chapter, is an especially useful tool because it shows quite precisely how many measurements or scores will be found under any part of the curve. As is shown in FIGURE 13.13, in any normal distribution exactly 34.13 percent of all the measurements lie between the mean and 1 SD above the mean; 13.59 percent lie between 1 SD and 2 SD's above the mean; and 2.14 percent lie between 2 SD's and 3 SD's above the mean. Thus the SD provides an eloquent description of the measurements.

On the matter of the intelligence quotient, for example, the mean is 100 and the SD is approximately 15. Armed with this knowledge alone, plus the general statistical rule illustrated in FIGURE 13.13, we know that human intelligence is distributed according to the following table:

I.Q.	Percentage of people
145 and over	0.14
130–144	2.14
115–129	13.59
100–114	34.13
85–99	34.13
70–84	13.59
55–69	2.14
under 55	0.14

The SD is also used to compute what are called *standard scores,* or *z*-scores, which are often more meaningful than actual scores on a test. The *z*-score tells how many SD's a score is above or below the mean; it is obtained very simply by noting how many points a score is above or below the mean and then dividing by the SD. A *z*-score of 1 is one SD above the mean; a *z*-score of –1.5 is one and a half SD's below the mean.

Percentiles

There is one other term in descriptive statistics that deserves special discussion. This is *percentile,* which is used not so much to describe the nature of the distribution as to add further meaning to any individual score.

The meaning of percentile can best be explained with an example. Take the case of a college senior who wants to go on to graduate school and is

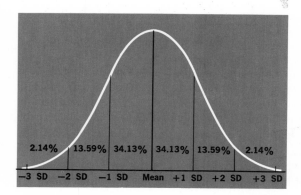

2.14% | 13.59% | 34.13% | 34.13% | 13.59% | 2.14%

−3 SD   −2 SD   −1 SD   Mean   +1 SD   +2 SD   +3 SD

Using the SD to Analyze Data   In a normal curve of distribution the standard deviation indicates how many measurements or scores will be found at various distances from the mean. As shown here, 34.13 percent of all measurements lie between the mean and 1 SD above the mean. Measurements that are between 1 SD and 2 SD's above the mean make up 13.59 percent of the total, and measurements between 2 SD's and 3 SD's above the mean make up 2.14 percent. The same percentages are found below the mean. Note that the figures do not quite add up to 100 percent. This is because 0.14 percent of measurements are found more than 3 SD's above the mean and another 0.14 percent are found more than 3 SD's below the mean. These various percentages hold for any normal distribution, although the size of the SD is of course quite different from one curve to another.

FIGURE 13.13

asked to take the Graduate Record Examinations, which are nationally administered aptitude tests often used to screen applicants. He makes a score of 460 on the verbal test and 540 in mathematics. By themselves, these scores do not mean much either to him or to the faculty of the school he wants to attend. But records kept of other people who have taken the test provide a means of comparing his scores with those of other college seniors. A score of 460 on the verbal test, the records show, lies on the 40th percentile for men. This means that 40 percent of all senior men who take the test make a lower score and 60 percent make an equal or higher score. The 540 score in math lies on the 66th percentile for men; in other words, 66 percent of senior men make a lower score, and only 34 percent make an equal or higher score. These percentile figures show the student and the school he hopes to attend how his ability compares with that of other prospective graduate students: he is well above average in mathematical ability (only a third of male college seniors make better scores) but below average in verbal aptitude.

Percentile ratings can be made for any kind of measurement, whether or not it falls into a normal distribution. A percentile rating of 1 means that no one had a lower score. A rating of 99—or, to be more exact, 99.999—is the highest. A rating of 50 is exactly in the middle, at the median.

471

When an investigator runs a rat through a maze, he is
not really interested in how that particular rat will
learn the maze. His primary interest is in discovering a general principle of
behavior that says something about the learning process of all rats and, by
implication, perhaps about learning processes in general. The investigator who
studies the performance of a group of subjects who memorize nonsense syllables or their behavior when they receive an injection of adrenalin and
watch a funny movie is not interested in these particular people. His ultimate
interest is in learning about the behavior of people in general. This is why inferential statistics—which permit us to make valid generalizations from our
measurements and to avoid false conclusions—are so important.

Population and Sample

Science is interested in what is called the *population* or sometimes the *universe*—that is to say, all people, all organisms, all objects, all events. But we
cannot study or measure the entire population. We cannot give an intelligence
test, for example, to every human being now on the face of the earth; even
if we could, we still would not have reached the entire population, because
many people would have died and many new people would have been born
in the meantime. We must settle for what is called a *sample*, a rather small
group taken from the population.

The rule is that a sample must be *representative* of the population we
wish to study. If we wish to make generalizations about intelligence, we
cannot use a sample made up entirely of men or a sample made up entirely
of women. Both sexes must be represented. If we want to discuss the political
attitudes of Americans, we cannot poll merely the Republicans or people who
live in big cities or people who belong to one kind of church or one kind of
social class. Our sample must be representative of all kinds of Americans.
The humiliating failure of the *Literary Digest* election poll of 1936 was
caused by taking a sample from the lists of owners of telephones and automobiles—a sample that contained only the richer citizens of the time and
was therefore not representative of the voting population as a whole.

An important aspect of a representative sample is that it must be chosen
at random: each member of the total population must have an equal chance
of being studied. The experimenter who wants to study the emotionality of
rats in a laboratory cannot reach into a cage and pull out the first dozen animals that are closest at hand. The very fact that they are close at hand may
mean that they are tamer than the others and have a different kind of emotional temperament. To ensure a valid sample, the experimenter might take
the first rat, reject the second, take the third, reject the fourth, and so on.

The political pollster might interview the man in every fifth house and the woman in every tenth house. One of the admitted weaknesses of the Kinsey studies of sexual behavior is that the sample was made up entirely of people who volunteered for interviews. Although this procedure was unavoidable, it does raise a question as to whether the kind of people who will volunteer to talk about their sexual behavior may not behave differently from people who hesitate to volunteer.

Control Groups

The use of a control group is standard experimental procedure. In Schachter's experiment with the funny movie, for example, he wanted to examine the effect of injecting adrenalin or a tranquilizer into his subjects. To make sure the drugs had any effect at all, he had to compare the behavior of his subjects with the behavior of a control group that underwent all the conditions of the experiment except one. The members of the control group had the same kind of needle stuck into their arms and then watched the same movie. The only difference was that the injection they received was salt water, which has no effect upon the body, rather than adrenalin or a tranquilizer, which do. In experiments on the effect of recitation upon learning, the performance of an experimental group that studies part of the time and recites part of the time must be compared to the performance of a control group that attempts to learn the same material under the same conditions (type of room, lighting, noise level, time of day, and so on) except for the absence of recitation. In other words, the experimental group must be matched with a control group for whom all conditions are the same except for the one experimental variable that is under investigation.

Ideally, every individual in the control group should be identical to a member of the experimental group. But this is of course impossible, because not even identical twins (who are too scarce anyway) are alike in every respect. The investigator must usually rely on a control group that, like the experimental sample, is representative of the population under study and randomly selected. Any individual used in the investigation should have an equal chance of being in the experimental group or the control group.

Comparing Two Groups

For an example of how inferential statistics are used to compare two groups, let us imagine an experiment in which we try to determine whether physical health affects the learning ability of high school students. We select an experimental group of sixteen representative, randomly chosen students, who agree to take part in a rigorous health program. We arrange a supervised diet and exercise, give them regular physical examinations, and promptly treat any defects or illnesses. We also select a control group of sixteen similar students, who do not receive any special treatment. At the end of a year, we find that the experimental group has a grade-point mean of 89, with a standard deviation of 3. The control group has a grade-point mean of 85, with a standard deviation of 4. Question: Is this difference of four points between the mean of the experimental group and the mean of the control group significant?

Although four points may sound like a lot, the question is not so easy to answer as it may seem. The reason is that *any* two samples of sixteen people each, taken from the high school population or any other population, are likely to have somewhat different means. Suppose we write the names of all the students in the high school (or in the city) on slips of paper and draw the slips from a hat. The grade-point mean for the first sixteen names we draw may be 85, for the next sixteen names 86, for the next sixteen names 87. If we pull twenty different samples of sixteen students each from the hat, we will find that the means of the samples vary over a fairly wide range. So the question now becomes: Is the difference between the mean score of 89 for the experimental group and the mean score of 85 for the control group larger than a difference we might get accidentally by pulling samples from a hat? In other words, is the difference statistically *significant*, or is it perhaps merely the result of chance?

STANDARD ERROR OF THE MEAN   Helping answer the question is the fact that the means of randomly chosen samples, like raw measurements or scores themselves, tend to fall into a pattern of normal distribution. From our control group of sixteen with a grade-point mean of 85 and a standard deviation of 4, we can figure out the distribution of all the means we would be likely to get if we continued to pick samples of sixteen students at random, and we find that the curve looks like the one shown on the left in FIGURE 13.14. We get the curve by using the formula (shown on page 481) for the *standard error of the mean*. For the control group the standard error of the mean comes to 1.0. We can also work out the standard error of the mean for the experimental group, which comes to 0.75.

The standard error of the mean is also known as the standard deviation of the mean, because it can be used just like the standard deviation of the distribution of scores. As is shown in FIGURE 13.14, we can use the mean and standard error of the mean of the control group to infer the range in which the true mean of the entire high school population must lie. We can also use the figures for the experimental group to infer the range in which the mean would probably have fallen if we had applied the experimental conditions to the entire high school population.

Having drawn these two curves, we can put them together as is shown in FIGURE 13.15. They show us that the probability is very high that there is a true difference between the grades of students who receive special medical

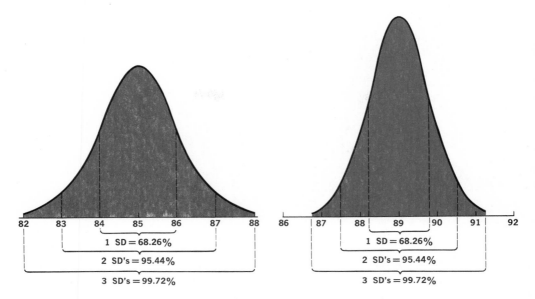

How Means Are Distributed   These graphs show how the standard error of the mean of a sample is used to infer the true mean that would be found if the entire population could be measured. In the control group of high school students, at left, the mean is 85 and the standard error of the mean is 1.0. Thus we know that the chances are 68.26 percent that the true mean lies between 84 and 86 (1 standard error above or below the mean of our sample), 95.44 percent that the true mean lies between 83 and 87 (2 standard errors above or below), and 99.72 percent that the true mean lies between 82 and 88 (3 standard errors above or below). In the experimental group, at right, the mean is 89 and the standard error of the mean is 0.75. Thus we know that the chances are 68.26 percent that the mean for the entire population under the special conditions of the experiment would have been found between 88.25 and 89.75; the chances are 95.44 percent that the mean would have been found between 87.50 and 90.50; and they are 99.72 percent that the mean would have been found between 86.75 and 91.25. Note how the two graphs utilize the same principle that was illustrated in FIGURE 13.13.

FIGURE 13.14

care and the grades of students who do not. The possibility that the difference we found is merely a matter of chance is represented by the small area that lies beneath the extreme right-hand end of the control curve and the extreme left-hand end of the curve for the experimental group.

PROBABILITY AND "SIGNIFICANCE"   The curves in FIGURES 13.14 and 13.15 demonstrate the principle that underlies the comparison of two groups through the standard error of the mean. In actual statistical calculation these curves need not be constructed. We can use the two means and the standard error

475

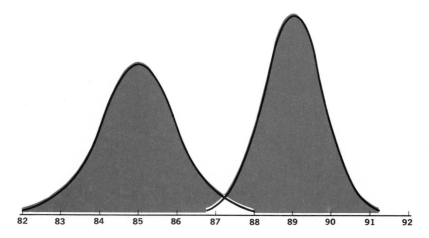

82 83 84 85 86 87 88 89 90 91 92

Is the Difference Significant? When the curves that were shown in FIGURE 13.14 are superimposed, they have only the small white area in common. The probability that the difference between the two means is due to chance is represented by this area; the probability that the difference is a real one is represented by the colored areas.

FIGURE 13.15

of each mean to work out what is called *the standard error of the difference between the means* (see page 481). This figure can in turn be used to work out the probability that the difference we found was due merely to chance. In the case of the mythical experiment we have been describing, the probability comes to less than .01.

It is an arbitrary rule of thumb in experimental work that a difference is considered *statistically significant* only when the probability that it might have been obtained by chance is .05 (5 chances in 100, or 1 chance in 20) or less.

In reports on experiments that can be analyzed with this kind of inferential statistics, the probability figure is always given; you will frequently find the note

$$p \leq .05$$

meaning that the difference would be found by chance only 5 times or less out of 100 and is therefore statistically significant. In all the experiments cited in this book, p was .05 or less.

Correlation

Galton's question—do successful fathers have more successful sons than other fathers?—is a problem involving another statistical device, called *correlation*. If success on the part of the father is often accompanied by success on the part of the son, then these two events are related to one another in some way. In statistical terms, they are *correlated*. Galton showed that there was

476

indeed a correlation between the two events; other investigators have shown that there are correlations between I.Q. and grades in school, between grades in school and economic success, between a parent's strictness and aggressive behavior in the child, and between many other psychological traits and forms of behavior.

Some correlations are *positive,* meaning that the higher a person measures on scale X (for example, I.Q.), the higher he is likely to measure on scale Y (for example, grades). *Negative correlations,* in which a high score on scale X is likely to be accompanied by a low score on scale Y, have also been found. For example, the frequency of premature births has been found to be negatively correlated with social class—meaning that there tends to be less prematurity among upper-class families than lower-class families. Negative correlations also exist between aggressive behavior in children and social class and between test anxiety and school grades.

The relation between the X- and Y-scales is expressed in mathematical terms by a *correlation coefficient,* calculated in several possible ways as explained on page 485. A correlation coefficient can range from 0 (no correlation at all) to $+1$ (a perfect positive correlation) or -1 (a perfect negative correlation.) But correlations of $+1$ or -1 are very rare. Even such physical traits as height and weight, which would seem to go together in almost perfect proportion, do not reach a correlation of $+1$. Some typical correlations that have been found are:

Between I.Q. and college grades	.50
Between parents' I.Q.'s and child's I.Q.	.49
Between I.Q. and ability at pitch discrimination	.00
Between boys' height at age two and height at age eighteen (5)	.60
Between boys' height at age ten and height at age eighteen (5)	.88

SCATTER PLOTS   A rough idea of the degree of correlation between two traits can be obtained by plotting each subject's score on scale X against his score on scale Y, as shown in FIGURE 13.16. A dot is put down for each person at a point that corresponds to both his scores, giving us what is called a *scatter plot.* When the dots are scattered completely at random, we can see that the correlation is 0. If we should run into one of those extremely rare cases where the dots form a straight line, moving diagonally up or down, we know that we are dealing with a correlation of $+1$ or -1. Most scatter diagrams take a form that lies somewhere between. If a fairly narrow oval would enclose most of the dots, the correlation is rather high. If the oval must be fatter to enclose the dots, the correlation is much lower.

The correlation coefficient is a statistical method of expressing the degree

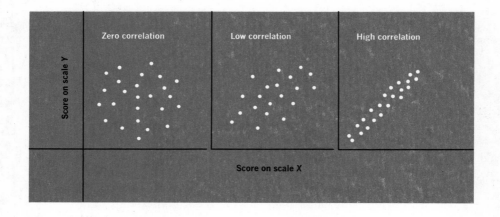

FIGURE 13.16

Scatter Plots of Correlations These scatter plots were obtained by making a dot for each subject at a point indicating both his score on scale *X* and his score on scale *Y*. (6)

of relation with great precision and without going to the trouble of constructing a scatter plot.

CORRELATION AND PREDICTION   One of the chief practical uses of correlation is in predicting. College administrators, for example, know that scores on any standard intelligence test or on a test like the College Boards are correlated with college grades. They can predict, therefore, that a young man or young woman with very high scores will probably get good grades and that a student with very low scores will probably fail. They may decide to limit enrollment, therefore, to students with scores high enough to indicate a reasonable chance of success.

Guidance counselors know that scores on certain kinds of aptitude and interest tests are correlated with success in various kinds of jobs and thus can offer young people the prediction that they will probably succeed or fail as computer programmers, accountants, auto mechanics, professional musicians, or whatever other job they may be considering.

It must always be kept in mind, however, that a coefficient of correlation is less accurate in making predictions than it sounds. Only when the correlation is very close to 1, as in the high correlation shown in FIGURE 13.16, does every subject tend to show a close relationship between score on scale *X* and score on scale *Y*. Even in a correlation of .75, which sounds high, there is a considerable amount of scatter, representing subjects who scored relatively low on scale *X* but relatively high on scale *Y*, or vice versa. Since most correlations found in psychological studies are lower than .75, we must be quite tentative in making predictions.

CORRELATION, CAUSE, AND EFFECT The correlation coefficient is especially useful for measuring relationships between psychological traits that cannot be studied through the preferred method of experimental manipulation, but only through less powerful methods such as naturalistic observation, tests, interviews, and questionnaires. (The advantages and limitations of these methods of investigation were discussed in Chapter 1.) If we want to study the effect of harsh discipline in the home upon tendencies to aggression, for example, we cannot deliberately force one group of children to submit to harsh discipline and permit another to grow up under more permissive conditions. We can only try to learn as much as we can about the home backgrounds of children who appear to display various levels of aggression. If we find no correlation between aggressive behavior and strict discipline in the home, we must conclude that the two factors are not related. If we do find a correlation, we are justified in concluding that there may be a connection between the two.

We must be careful, however, not to exaggerate the degree of relationship that is implied even by a rather high numerical value of correlation. And we must also avoid jumping to conclusions about cause and effect. Did the children become aggressive because the parents were strict, or were the parents strict because the children were aggressive? Is it possible that some third factor caused both the parents' strictness and the children's aggression? (For example, it may be that parents who are generally cold and rejecting of their children tend to be strict and that it is the coldness and rejection, rather than the strictness, that make the children aggressive.)

As a reminder of the danger of jumping to false conclusions on the basis of correlations, it is a good idea to keep in mind that there is a very high correlation between the number of permanent teeth that have erupted through the school child's gums and his raw scores on questions answered correctly on any kind of intelligence or aptitude test. But it would be foolish to conclude that his teeth make him smarter or that his scores make more teeth appear. Increased maturity produces both the teeth and the higher scores.

THE MATHEMATICAL COMPUTATIONS

As was said earlier, the mathematical knowledge required for statistical analysis is not particularly complicated. One need only be able to manipulate mathematical symbols, the most frequently used of which are explained in FIGURE 13.17, and to apply the few basic formulae presented in FIGURE 13.18.

The symbols and formulae are presented at the start of this section on computations so that they can be found all in one place for future reference.

N	Number of subjects from whom a measurement or score has been obtained
X	The numerical value of an individual score
Y	If each subject is measured on two scales, the numerical value of an individual score on the second scale
Σ	The Greek capital letter sigma, standing for "sum of"
ΣX	The sum of all the individual scores on scale X
M	The mean, which is the sum of the scores divided by the number of subjects
x	A deviation score; that is, the difference between an individual score and the mean for the group of which the individual is a member
y	A deviation score on the second or Y-scale
SD	The standard deviation of the scores
SE_M	The standard error of the mean; also called the standard deviation of the mean
D_M	The difference between two means; for example, the difference between the mean (M) of scale X and the mean of scale Y
SE_{D_M}	The standard error of the difference between two means, used as a measure of whether the difference is significant
p	Probability, expressed in decimals ranging from .00 (no chance) through .50 (50–50 chance) to 1.00 (100 percent chance). A result is considered statistically significant when $p \leqq .05$, meaning that there are only 5 chances in 100 (or fewer) that it was obtained by chance.
r	Correlation coefficient obtained by the product-moment method
ρ	Correlation coefficient obtained by the rank-difference method
z	A standard score, expressed in number of SD's above or below the mean.
C	Coefficient of contingency; type of correlation used to find relationships between events on a nominal scale.

FIGURE 13.17   *Some Useful Symbols*   These are the mathematical symbols used in the formulae presented in this chapter.

They may seem rather difficult when shown all together in this fashion, but their application should be readily apparent from the examples that will be presented as we go along.

The kind of measurement that an investigator often wants to analyze is illustrated in FIGURE 13.19. Here seventeen students have taken a psychological test and have made scores ranging from 60 to 97. The raw scores are a jumble of figures, from which we now want to determine the mean, the standard deviation, and the standard error of the mean.

1. For determining the mean:

$$M = \frac{\Sigma X}{N}$$

2. For determining a deviation score:

$$x = X - M$$

3. For determining the standard deviation:

$$SD = \sqrt{\frac{\Sigma x^2}{N - 1}}$$

4. For determining a z-score:

$$z = \frac{x}{SD}$$

5. For determining the standard error of the mean:

$$SE_M = \frac{SD}{\sqrt{N}}$$

6. For determining the difference between two means:

$$D_M = M_1 - M_2$$

7. For determining the standard error of the difference between two means:

$$SE_{DM} = \sqrt{(SE_{M_1})^2 + (SE_{M_2})^2}$$

8. For determining the critical ratio:

$$\text{Critical ratio} = \frac{D_M}{SE_{DM}}$$

9. For determining the coefficient of correlation by product-moment method:

$$r = \frac{\Sigma xy}{(N - 1)SD_x SD_y}$$

(In this formula, SD_x is the standard deviation of the measurements on the X-scale, and SD_y is the standard deviation of the measurements on the Y-scale.)

10. For determining the coefficient of correlation by rank-difference method:

$$\rho = 1 - \frac{6(\Sigma D^2)}{N(N^2 - 1)}$$

Some Statistical Formulae   These are some of the most frequently used formulae in statistical analysis. Their use is explained and illustrated in the text and in the following figures.

FIGURE 13.18

1.	78	4.	74	7.	92	10.	74	13.	70	16.	82
2.	97	5.	80	8.	72	11.	85	14.	84	17.	78
3.	60	6.	77	9.	79	12.	68	15.	76		

The Test Scores of Seventeen Students These raw scores, obtained by seventeen students on a psychological test, will be analyzed statistically in the text.

FIGURE 13.19

The Mean

The formula for the mean, as can be seen from FIGURE 13.18, is

$$M = \frac{\Sigma X}{N}$$

These symbols denote, as can be found in FIGURE 13.17, that the mean equals the sum of the individual scores divided by the number of subjects.

The way the formula is applied is illustrated in FIGURE 13.20. The sum of the individual scores, which are shown in column one, is 1326. The number of subjects is 17. Thus the mean is 78.

FIGURE 13.20

TEST SCORES (X)	DEVIATION SCORES (x)	DEVIATION SCORES SQUARED (x^2)
78	0	0
97	+19	361
60	−18	324
74	− 4	16
80	+ 2	4
77	− 1	1
92	+14	196
72	− 6	36
79	+ 1	1
74	− 4	16
85	+ 7	49
68	−10	100
70	− 8	64
84	+ 6	36
76	− 2	4
82	+ 4	16
78	0	0
$\Sigma X = 1326$		$\Sigma x^2 = 1224$

$$M = \frac{X}{N} = \frac{1326}{17} = 78$$

$$SD = \sqrt{\frac{\Sigma x^2}{N-1}} = \sqrt{\frac{1224}{16}} = \sqrt{76.5} = 8.75$$

Computing the Mean and the SD Using the formulae in FIGURE 13.18, we first compute the mean score (M) for the seventeen students, which comes out to 78. Once we have the mean, we can compute the standard deviation (SD)—starting by obtaining the deviation scores ($x = X - M$), then squaring these scores to get x^2.

The Standard Deviation

The method of finding the standard deviation is also illustrated in FIGURE 13.20. The formula for the standard deviation is

$$SD = \sqrt{\frac{\Sigma x^2}{N-1}}$$

This means that the standard deviation is the square root of the figure we get by dividing the number of subjects minus 1 into the sum of all the deviation scores squared.

The deviation scores shown in column two have been obtained by the formula $x = X - M$—that is, by subtracting the mean, which is 78, from each individual score. These figures in column two have then been squared to give the figures in column three. The sum of the x^2 figures is 1224, and this figure divided by 16 (our $N - 1$) comes to 76.5. The standard deviation is the square root of 76.5, or 8.75.

The Standard Error of the Mean

Finding the standard error of the mean for our group is extremely simple. The formula is

$$SE_M = \frac{SD}{\sqrt{N}}$$

We have found that the SD of our sample is 8.75 and our N is 17. The formula yields

$$SE_M = \frac{8.75}{\sqrt{17}} = \frac{8.75}{4.12} = 2.12$$

Differences Between Groups

For an example of how the formulae for analyzing differences between groups are applied, let us return to the mythical experiment mentioned earlier in the chapter. We had the school grades, you will recall, of an experimental group of sixteen students who took part in a health program; the mean was 89 and the standard deviation was 3. We also had the grades of a control group of sixteen students; the mean for this group was 85 and the standard deviation was 4.

The difference between the two means is easily computed from the formula

$$D_M = M_1 - M_2$$

which means that the difference between the means is the mean of the first group minus the mean of the second group—in this case, 89 minus 85, or 4. To know whether this difference is statistically significant, however, we must calculate the standard error of the difference between the two means. To do so, as FIGURE 13.18 shows, we must use the fairly complex formula

$$SE_{D_M} = \sqrt{(SE_{M_1})^2 + (SE_{M_2})^2}$$

Our first step is to compute SE_{M_1}, the standard error of the mean of our first or experimental group. We do so as shown earlier, this time with 3 as our standard deviation and 16 as our number of subjects.

$$SE_{M_1} = \frac{SD}{\sqrt{N}} = \frac{3}{\sqrt{16}} = \frac{3}{4} = 0.75$$

We also compute SE_{M_2}, the standard error of the mean of our second or control group, where the standard deviation is 4 and the number of subjects is 16.

$$SE_{M_2} = \frac{SD}{\sqrt{N}} = \frac{4}{\sqrt{16}} = \frac{4}{4} = 1.00$$

Thus SE_{M_1} is 0.75 and SE_{M_2} is 1.00, and the standard error of the difference between the two means is computed as follows:

$$SE_{D_M} = \sqrt{(SE_{M_1})^2 + (SE_{M_2})^2} = \sqrt{(0.75)^2 + (1)^2} = \sqrt{.5625 + 1}$$
$$= \sqrt{1.5625} = 1.25$$

To complete our analysis of the difference between the two groups, we need one more statistical tool—the *critical ratio*. This is given by the formula

$$\text{Critical ratio} = \frac{D_M}{SE_{D_M}}$$

In the case of our mythical experiment we have found that D_M is 4 and that SE_{D_M} is 1.25. Thus the critical ratio is

$$\frac{4}{1.25}$$

or 3.2.

The critical ratio gives us a measure of the probability that our difference was due merely to chance. For reasons that a mathematically minded student may be able to work out for himself but that need not concern the rest of us, the magic numbers for the critical ratio are 1.96 and 2.57. If the critical ratio is as high as 1.96 then $p \leq .05$, and the difference is considered statistically significant. If the critical ratio is as high as 2.57, $p \leq .01$, and the difference is considered highly significant. The critical ratio we found for our two groups, 3.2, is well over 2.57, and we can have some confidence that the difference was not the result of chance.

Correlation

There are a number of ways of computing correlation coefficients, depending upon the type of data that are being studied. The most frequently used is the *product-moment method,* which obtains a coefficient of correlation designated by the letter r for the relationship between two different numerical test scores. The formula is

$$r = \frac{\Sigma xy}{(N-1)SD_x SD_y}$$

To use the formula we have to determine the amount by which each subject's score on the first test, or scale X, differs from the mean for all scores on scale X—in other words the value for x, the deviation score, which may be plus or minus. We must also determine the amount by which his score on the second test, or scale Y, differs from the mean for all scores on scale Y—in other words, the value for y, which also may be plus or minus. We then multiply x by y for each subject and add the xy products for all the subjects in the sample. This gives us the top line, or numerator, of the formula. The bottom line, or denominator, is found by multiplying the number of subjects minus 1 $(N-1)$ by the standard deviation of the scores on the X-scale (SD_x) and then multiplying the product by the standard deviation of the scores on the Y-scale (SD_y). An example is shown in FIGURE 13.21.

In some cases it is convenient to use the *rank-difference method,* which produces a different coefficient of correlation called ρ (the Greek letter *rho*), which is similar to but not exactly the same as r. The formula is

$$\rho = 1 - \frac{6(\Sigma D^2)}{N(N^2-1)}$$

The method of applying the formula is demonstrated in FIGURE 13.22. Note that the D in the formula refers to the difference between a subject's rank on scale X—that is, whether he was first, second, third, or so on among all the subjects—and his rank on scale Y. ΣD^2 is found by squaring each subject's difference in rank and adding to get the total for all subjects.

Contingency

One other frequently used type of correlation is known as the *coefficient of contingency,* symbolized by the letter C. This is used to find relationships

SUBJECT	TEST SCORES		DEVIATION SCORES		PRODUCT OF DEVIATION SCORES (xy)
	X	Y	X	Y	
1.	60	81	-12	$+ 1$	$- 12$
2.	80	92	$+ 8$	$+12$	$+ 96$
3.	70	76	$- 2$	$- 4$	$+ 8$
4.	65	69	$- 7$	-11	$+ 77$
5.	75	88	$+ 3$	$+ 8$	$+ 24$
6.	85	96	$+13$	$+16$	$+208$
7.	60	64	-12	-16	$+192$
8.	75	75	$+ 3$	$- 5$	$- 15$
9.	70	77	$- 2$	$- 3$	$+ 6$
10.	80	82	$+ 8$	$+ 2$	$+ 16$
					$\Sigma xy = 600$

$N = 10$

For scale X, $M = 72$, and $SD_x = 8.56$

For scale Y, $M = 80$, and $SD_y = 9.98$

Thus

$$r = \frac{\Sigma xy}{(N - 1)SD_x SD_y} = \frac{600}{(10 - 1) \times 8.56 \times 9.98} = \frac{600}{768.9} = .78$$

Computing a Correlation   Note that in the sample of ten, four subjects who scored above the mean on scale X also scored above the mean on scale Y (subjects 2, 5, 6, and 10). Four subjects who scored below the mean on scale X also scored below the mean on scale Y (subjects 3, 4, 7, and 9). Only two subjects (1 and 8) scored above the mean on one test and below the mean on another. Thus multiplying the x-deviations times the y-deviations gives us eight positive products and only two negative products. Σxy, which is the total of the positive products minus the total of the negative products, comes to 600. The correlation coefficient comes to the rather large figure of .78.

The manner in which SD_x and SD_y were computed is not shown, but the student can check the figures of 8.56 for SD_x and 9.98 for SD_y by applying the formula for computing a standard deviation as shown in FIGURE 13.20.

FIGURE **13.21**

between events that can be measured only on what is called a *nominal scale* —where all we can say about them is that they belong to certain groups, to which we can give a name but no meaningful numerical value. For example, we can set up a nominal scale on which all college students taking a humanities course are grouped in class 1, all taking engineering are grouped into class 2, and all taking a preparatory course for one of the professional schools such as law or medicine are grouped into class 3. We might set

SUBJECT	TEST SCORES X	TEST SCORES Y	RANK X	RANK Y	DIFFERENCE IN RANK (D)	DIFFERENCE SQUARED (D^2)
1.	60	81	9.5	5	-4.5	20.25
2.	80	92	2.5	2	-0.5	0.25
3.	70	76	6.5	7	$+0.5$	0.25
4.	65	69	8.0	9	$+1.0$	1.00
5.	75	88	4.5	3	-1.5	2.25
6.	85	96	1.0	1	0.0	0.00
7.	60	64	9.5	10	-0.5	0.25
8.	75	75	4.5	8	-3.5	12.25
9.	70	77	6.5	6	-0.5	0.25
10.	80	82	2.5	4	$+1.5$	2.25
						$\Sigma D^2 = 39.00$

$N = 10$

Thus

$$\rho = 1 - \frac{6(\Sigma D^2)}{N(N^2 - 1)} = 1 - \frac{6(39)}{10(10^2 - 1)} = 1 - \frac{234}{990} = 1 - .24 = .76$$

Computing ρ   Here the same scores that were shown in FIGURE 13.21 have been used to find the rank-difference correlation, ρ, which comes out to .76—very close to the .78 that we found in FIGURE 13.21 for r. In computing ρ, we disregard the individual scores on scale X and scale Y and use merely the rank of each score as compared to the others on the scale. Note that subjects 2 and 10 are tied for second place on the X-scale. Their rank is therefore considered to be 2.5, halfway between second and third place.

FIGURE 13.22

up another nominal scale on which we designate the students as males or females. If we then want to determine whether there is any relationship between a student's sex and the kind of college course he is likely to take, we use the coefficient of contingency. Its meaning is roughly the same as that of any other coefficient of correlation.

SUMMARY

1. *Measurement* is the assignment of numbers to traits, events, or subjects, according to some kind of orderly system.
2. The *statistical method* is the application of mathematical principles to an analysis and interpretation of the measurements.
3. The statistical method is of special importance as a *way of thinking* reminding us that events take place in accordance with the laws of

probability and that many events that might appear to be remarkable coincidences are bound to happen by chance.

4. The most satisfactory kind of measurement is made on a ratio scale such as weight or height, where there is a true zero point and where the number 2 means exactly twice as much as the number 1, 6 means three times as much as 2, and so on. Other scales, in decreasing order of precision, are *interval scales* (such as a thermometer, where each degree represents an equal expansion of the measuring fluid but where 100 degrees cannot be said to be twice as hot as 50 degrees), *ordinal scales* (based on rank order), and *nominal scales* (in which numbers are simply assigned to different categories, as when men are assigned one number and women a different number).

5. Events that are distributed by chance, including many human traits, fall into the pattern of the *normal curve of distribution*, which is shaped like a bell. Most such events or traits cluster around the average, and the number declines approaching either the lower or the upper extreme.

6. *Descriptive statistics* provide a quick and convenient method of summarizing measurements. Important descriptive statistics are:
   a. The *number of subjects*, or N.
   b. Measurements of the *average*, including the arithmetic average, or *mean* (total of all scores divided by N), *median* (point separating the lower half of scores from the upper half), and *mode* (most frequent score in the group).
   c. Index of *variability*, including *range* (obtained by subtracting the lowest score from the highest) and *standard deviation*, symbolized by SD. In a normal distribution, 34.13 percent of the scores lie between the mean and 1 SD above the mean, 13.59 percent between 1 SD and 2 SD's above the mean, and 2.14 percent between 2 SD's and 3 SD's above the mean, while 0.14 percent lie more than 3 SD's above the mean. The same pattern of distribution exists below the mean.

7. *Percentiles* are used to describe the position of an individual score in the total group. A measurement on the 75th percentile is larger than 75 percent of the measurements, or, to put it another way, 25 percent of measurements lie on or above the 75th percentile.

8. *Inferential statistics* are procedures that allow us to make generalizations from measurements. They enable us to infer conclusions about a *population* or *universe*, which is the total of all possible cases, by measuring a relatively small *sample*. To permit valid generalization, however, the sample must be *representative*.

9. A set of findings is considered statistically *significant* when the probability that findings might have been obtained by chance is only 5 in 100 or less; the figure is expressed mathematically as $p \leqq .05$.

10. *Correlations* between two measurements—such as scores on two different tests—range from 0 (no relationship) to $+1$ (perfect positive relationship) or -1 (perfect negative relationship).
11. The symbols and formulae used in the statistical analysis described in the chapter are shown in FIGURES 13.17 and 13.18.

RECOMMENDED READING

Arkin, H. and Colton, R. R. *Tables for statisticians*, 2nd ed. New York: Barnes & Noble, 1963.

Edwards, A. L. *Experimental design in psychological research*, rev. ed. New York: Holt, Rinehart and Winston, 1960.

Guilford, J. P. *Fundamental statistics in psychology and education*, 4th ed. New York: McGraw-Hill, 1965.

Hammond, K. R. and Householder, J. E. *Introduction to the statistical method: foundations and use in the behavioral sciences.* New York: Knopf, 1962.

Hays, W. L. *Statistics for psychologists.* New York: Holt, Rinehart and Winston, 1963.

McCollough, C. and Van Atta, L. *Statistical concepts: a program for self-instruction.* New York: McGraw-Hill, 1963.

Siegel, S. *Nonparametric statistics for the behavioral sciences.* New York: McGraw-Hill, 1956.

REQUIREMENTS OF A TEST

Objectivity
Standardization
Reliability
Validity
A Word on Bad Tests
Types of Tests

INTELLIGENCE TESTS

The Stanford-Binet Test
Mental Age and I.Q.
The Wechsler Tests
Group Tests
The Virtues of Intelligence Tests
Weaknesses of Intelligence Tests

THE NATURE OF INTELLIGENCE

What Determines Intelligence?
    "Primary Mental Abilities"; I.Q. and Heredity; I.Q. and Environment;
    The Effect of Special Environments
Changes in I.Q.
    I.Q. and Educational Opportunities; Are People Becoming More
    Intelligent?; I.Q. and Age
I.Q. and Occupation
The Mentally Retarded
The Mentally Gifted

OTHER KINDS OF TESTS

Vocational Aptitude
Interests
Personality
    Objective Tests of Personality; Situational Tests; Projective Tests

14

MEASURING INTELLIGENCE AND PERSONALITY

The aspect of measurement called *testing* is one area where everybody, whether or not he ever takes a psychology course, is almost bound to come into contact with psychology. It is virtually impossible to grow up in the United States today without sooner or later taking a test that has been devised by a psychologist or at least in accordance with techniques originally developed by psychologists.

In the early grades many schools give their pupils some kind of intelligence test as a guide to how well they are likely to perform in their classes —and also as a clue to whether they are underachievers who are not living up to their true capacities or overachievers who are working exceptionally hard and doing better than might be expected. In the later grades most pupils take the Iowa Achievement Tests, which measure their progress (and the general level of progress at their particular school) against national averages. As part of the requirement for admission to many colleges, high school seniors take the Scholastic Aptitude Tests, which are a form of intelligence test.

The school child who has trouble adjusting may be asked to take various kinds of personality tests that will help identify the nature of his problems. The student who seeks vocational guidance is often asked to take tests for special aptitudes, such as mechanics or art, and tests that measure his interests and preferences. If he goes into the Army, he receives his assignment on the basis of the Army's own general intelligence tests and a number of aptitude tests designed to measure special abilities for work in radio, electronics, mechanical repair, and other fields. When he seeks a job, his prospective employer may test his intelligence, his specific abilities, and sometimes his personality characteristics.

Testing is an important branch of psychology in which many investigators have been hard at work for many years. It is the source of much of the data analyzed with the statistical tools described in the previous chapter. It has been especially useful in the study of human intelligence and has cast considerable light on the nature of intelligence and the relationship between intelligence and success in school or career.

Informal tests of human characteristics go back to the beginnings of history. Literature and mythology are full of stories of young men who had to slay dragons to prove that they were brave enough to deserve the hand of a princess or had to answer riddles posed by wise men to prove that they were intelligent enough to become rulers. In the modern world, informal testing continues. A college woman tries out for a campus musical and is asked to read some of the lines and sing a few bars of a song; on the basis of this sample of her talents the judges decide whether she will probably do well in the actual performance. A college man tries out for the basketball team and is kept on the squad or dropped depending on how well he performs at some of the skills required in an actual game. Even courtship is a form of informal testing. Most of us choose our future wives or husbands on the basis of what we can observe of their behavior.

Like informal tests, formal psychological tests are forced to rely on a limited sample of behavior, since it is impossible to measure how intelligently a person will perform on every possible kind of task or to observe all the behavior that might reflect his personality. Also like informal tests, they often are used to predict future behavior.

Intelligence tests are given in elementary school mostly to predict how much and how easily the child will learn; Scholastic Aptitude Tests are an attempt to predict how well the student will be able to handle the college curriculum. Personality tests are often used to predict the likelihood that a person will make satisfactory emotional adjustments under various conditions. They are sometimes used to help identify a need for psychotherapy and to discover what kind is likely to be most effective for a particular patient.

The ways in which formal psychological tests differ from informal methods of assessment can best be explained by describing the four quite strict requirements that they are expected to meet, insofar as it is at all possible. The psychological test should be 1) *objective,* 2) *standardized,* 3) *reliable,* and 4) *valid.*

Objectivity

The test should give results that are uncolored by personal opinion or prejudice. The person taking the test should get the same score regardless of who administers the test and who scores it. In fact the first intelligence test was an attempt to obtain a more objective measure of a child's ability to profit from classes in school than could be provided by the opinion of his teacher, which might be colored by the child's pleasant or disagreeable personality, his behavior in class, or his family's position in the community.

Standardization

The results of a test are most useful when they can be compared to the scores of other people. Thus tests are standardized, whenever possible, by administering them to a large and representative sample of the population. The score made by an individual can then be interpreted properly; it can be seen to be average, low, or high.

Reliability

An analogy can be made here between a test and a housewife's oven thermometer. If the thermometer is reliable—that is, if it gives the same reading every time for the same amount of heat—the housewife can count on her roasts and pies to come out cooked as she wants them. But, if the thermometer is damaged and unreliable, it may give a reading of 300 degrees on one occasion and 400 degrees the next, even though the actual temperature is exactly the same; in this case the results of cooking are likely to be somewhat disappointing.

A good test, like a good thermometer, must be reliable; the scores it yields must be consistent. One way of determining the reliability of a test is to compare the same person's score on all the odd-numbered items with his score on all the even-numbered items; these two scores should be similar. Another way is to give a person the same test twice, some time apart; again the scores should be similar.

Validity

The most important requirement for a test is that it be valid—that is, it must actually measure what it is intended to measure. This is unfortunately the most difficult of the requirements to fill and to explain. Perhaps the best approach is to discuss what is meant by the absence of validity.

Suppose that an investigator wants to develop a test that will predict which college women will make the best teachers in the first three grades of elementary school. On the notion that the ability to use words is important he devises a test that measures how good college women are at tasks such as defining words, completing sentences, remembering and repeating the content of paragraphs heard a single time, and so on. The test is objective; it is standardized on a large group of subjects; and tests and retests show it to be highly reliable. Thus it meets the first three requirements of a good test. But it is not necessarily valid. It may measure not teaching ability but only the ability to understand and manipulate words.

There are a number of ways to determine the validity of a test. Common sense is one of them; the items in the test must bear a meaningful relationship to the characteristics being measured. (For example, the thought of trying to assess musical ability by asking questions on major league baseball standings does not "make sense" and must be rejected). Another way is to observe the future behavior of people who have taken the test and determine whether they behave as their test scores predict. Thus, in the case of the test of teaching ability, the scores of a group of college women might be compared with later ratings of the quality of their teaching. Or, to save time, the test might be given to a group of teachers whose ability was already known. If there proved to be a close relationship between their test scores and their ratings as teachers, this would indicate that the test is valid. If there was no relationship or only a small relationship between the scores and the ratings of teaching ability, the test would have to be rejected as invalid.

A Word on Bad Tests

A comment is in order here about the many bad tests to which Americans are frequently exposed. In the sixty years since the first intelligence test was designed, testing has become a fad, and many tests have been devised by people who have no idea how much thought, effort, and discipline should go into their creation. A standard feature in today's newspapers and magazines is the so-called test of how good a husband we are or would make, how good a wife we are, how happy we are, and how we compare with the rest of the world on such traits as honesty, mental health, nervousness, tension, or tendencies toward alcoholism.

To judge the value of these tests, designed by journalists rather than by psychologists, note how they fail to meet the four requirements of a good test. They are not objective, for we are told to rate and score ourselves—an invitation to giving ourselves all the best of it. They have never been standardized; what the author calls an "average," "low," or "high" score is just his own guess. Their reliability and validity are unknown.

Types of Tests

Before discussing some actual tests, their uses, and what has been learned from them, it will be useful to describe some of the words that identify and distinguish among different kinds of tests. First, a distinction must be made between a *group test* and an *individual test*. The group test is administered to many people at once; it typically takes the form of printed questions, such as those shown in FIGURE 14.1, which are answered by making penciled notations. The individual test is given to one person at a time by a trained examiner; here the test items can call for a verbal answer or for the subject to perform some kind of task, as illustrated in FIGURE 14.2. Group tests have made possible the measurement of hundreds of thousands of soldiers and

Three of these things are alike in some way. Fill in the answer space beneath the one that is different.

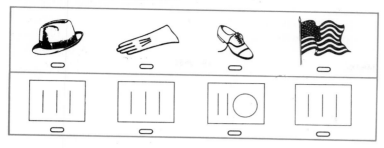

We say: "Boy is to trousers as girl is to what?"

The first two drawings are alike except the second one has a dot inside it. Which drawing goes with the circle in the same way as the first two drawings go together?

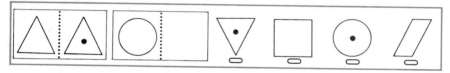

Find the picture that shows two boys running.

Find the circle that has the largest star inside it.

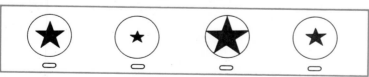

A Group Intelligence Test These are sample items for second- and third-graders from the Otis-Lennon Mental Ability Test. At this age level the person administering the test reads the instructions to the children taking the test. In all intelligence tests the sample items demonstrate how the questions should be answered and are not counted in the scoring. The actual items in this test range from about as difficult as the sample items to much more difficult. (1)

FIGURE 14.1

students each year—a job for which there would never be enough time or testers to use the individual method. They have a limitation, however. A low score on a group test may be caused by such factors as temporary ill health, poor vision, or lack of motivation—which would be apparent to a trained examiner administering an individual test.

Another distinction separates *aptitude tests* from *achievement tests*. An aptitude test attempts to measure a person's capacity to learn a new skill; an example is the Scholastic Aptitude Test, which, as the name indicates, measures the student's capacity to learn academic material in college. An achievement test measures how much a person has already learned, as of this moment. Thus the Iowa Achievement Tests measure what the student knows about the various subjects taught in school. Perhaps the distinction between aptitude and achievement tests is even clearer in the case of the Seashore Musical Aptitude Test, designed to measure a person's capacity to profit from musical instruction by assessing such basic elements of musical skill as pitch discrimination and rhythm discrimination. A person might make a high score on the Seashore test even though he knows nothing about musical scales and has never learned to play an instrument; such a person, however, would almost surely get a low score on a musical achievement test. On the other hand, a person who had forced himself to learn to play the piano might obtain a high score on a musical achievement test but a low score on the Seashore aptitude test. The sections that follow discuss in more detail tests designed to measure specific psychological characteristics. The three major areas of human functioning for which tests have been devised are 1) mental ability, 2) vocational aptitude and interests, and 3) personality factors such as motives and sources

FIGURE 14.2   *An Individual Intelligence Test* With colored blocks of various patterns, the young woman is asked to copy a design from the Wechsler-Bellevue Block Test. The examiner notes how fast she can perform this task.

of anxiety and conflicts. Most of the chapter will be devoted to intelligence tests, because up to now these tests have demonstrated greater reliability and more convincing validity than any other kind of test.

Intelligence tests are perhaps the most popular of psy- **INTELLIGENCE** chological procedures. Everybody has heard about them **TESTS** and about the I.Q., or *intelligence quotient,* that they produce. Intelligence tests have been widely used for years by schools, industry, and the military services. The results have been analyzed statistically in various ways, resulting in a considerable body of knowledge on how I.Q. is related to such factors as parents' I.Q., parents' schooling, father's occupation, and the I.Q. of brothers, sisters, and twins. Numerous studies have also been made comparing the I.Q.'s of various nationalities, races, and age groups.

The intelligence test began as a psychologist's answer to a specific and practical problem faced by Paris schools at the beginning of the century. Too many classrooms were crowded, and poor students were holding up the progress of the better ones. The solution, the school authorities decided, was to identify the children who lacked the mental capacity required by the standard curriculum and put these children in a separate school of their own. But how was the identification to be made?

This was a problem, the authorities felt, which could not safely be left to the teachers. There was too much danger that a teacher would show favoritism toward children who had pleasant personalities and would be too harsh on those who were bright enough but tended to be troublemakers. There was also the question whether a teacher could successfully identify a child who appeared dull but in fact could have done the work had he tried (2). The authorities called in a French psychologist named Alfred Binet, who solved the problem by developing a test that was first published in 1905, has been revised a number of times since, and is still widely used today.

The Stanford-Binet Test

In the United States one of the best-known current versions of Binet's original test is the 1960 *Stanford-Binet Intelligence Scale.* It is an individual test given by an examiner using the kind of equipment illustrated in FIGURE 14.3. The child is asked to perform certain tasks with this equipment and to answer questions that test his vocabulary, memory span for sentences and numbers, and reasoning ability. Some of the items used are shown in FIGURE 14.4.

As can be seen in FIGURE 14.4, the items are arranged by age levels; six tasks like those shown are listed for age two, six more difficult tasks for age three, and so on. One way of scoring the Stanford-Binet is as follows: The

FIGURE 14.3

Equipment for the Stanford-Binet Test These are the "props" used in administering the Stanford-Binet Scale to young children.

FIGURE 14.4   *Items in the Stanford-Binet Test*   Below are some of the items at various age levels on the Stanford-Binet Intelligence Scale. (3)

Two years old
- On a large paper doll, points out the hair, mouth, feet, ear, nose, hands, and eyes.
- When shown a tower built of four blocks, builds one like it.

Three years old
- When shown a bridge built of three blocks, builds one like it.
- When shown a drawing of a circle, copies it with a pencil.

Four years old
- Fills in the missing word when asked, "Brother is a boy; sister is a _____" and "In daytime it is light; at night it is _____."
- Answers correctly when asked, "Why do we have houses?" "Why do we have books?"

Five years old
- Defines *ball, hat,* and *stove.*
- When shown a drawing of a square, copies it with a pencil.

Nine years old
- Answers correctly when examiner says, "In an old graveyard in Spain they have discovered a small skull which they believe to be that of Christopher Columbus when he was about ten years old. What is foolish about that?"
- Answers correctly when asked, "Tell me the name of a color that rhymes with head." "Tell me a number that rhymes with tree."

Adult
- Can describe the difference between laziness and idleness, poverty and misery, character and reputation.
- Answers correctly when asked, "Which direction would you have to face so your right hand would be toward the north?"

examiner first finds the age level at which the child can perform all six of the tasks (or answer all the questions) correctly. This provides a basic figure for the child's mental age. The examiner then goes on to the next highest level and continues until he reaches a level where the child cannot pass any of the six items. He then adds up the score, giving credit of two months for each item passed successfully at levels above the basic mental age. For example, a child passes all six items at the six-year-old level, three at the seven-year-old level, one at the eight-year-old level, and none at the nine-year-old level. His final *mental age* (or MA) is determined by crediting him with a basic figure of six years, plus six months for the three questions answered at the seven-year-old level and two months for the single question answered correctly at the eight-year-old level; thus his mental age is six years and eight months.

After the items have been selected and pretested, they are assigned to the various age levels by the method illustrated in FIGURE 14.5. Each of the six items included in the test at the eight-year level, for example, will be passed by about 60 percent of all eight-year-old children. Some children who are younger than eight will also pass, and most of those who are older than eight will pass. Note in FIGURE 14.5 that the particular item illustrated

Age and Test Performance   The curves show the number of children, of chronological ages five through fifteen, who are able to pass three items at different levels of difficulty on the Stanford-Binet Scale. For the curve at the left, note that only about 20 percent of children age six can pass the item and only about 40 percent of children age seven. The item is passed, however, by about 60 percent of children age eight, by nearly 80 percent of those age nine, and by more than 90 percent of those age ten. On the basis of data like these, each item is placed at the age level where about 60 percent can pass; these three items will be found in the test form at ages eight, ten, and twelve. (3)

FIGURE 14.5

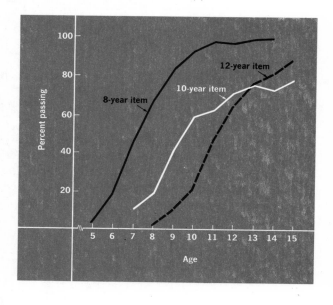

for the eight-year-level is passed by a few children as young as five and by nearly 20 percent of six-year-olds. On the other hand, nearly 20 percent of nine-year-olds fail on the item, and a few children fail it even at the ages of eleven, twelve, and thirteen.

Mental Age and I.Q.

The concept of mental age is based on the fact that as children mature they are able to pass more and more of the items on the Stanford-Binet. The test has been designed so that the average child will obtain a mental age corresponding to his actual chronological age. Thus the average seven-year-old child who takes the Stanford-Binet will show a mental age of seven; the average child of seven and a half years will show an MA of seven and a half, and so on. Those who have less intelligence than average as measured by the test will show an MA that is lower than their chronological age; those who have more than average intelligence will show an MA higher than their chronological age.

Intelligence quotient, or I.Q., is simply the relationship of mental age to chronological age; it is obtained by the formula

$$\text{I.Q.} = \frac{\text{MA}}{\text{Chronological age}} \times 100$$

As an example of how the formula is applied, we can consider the mental age of six years and eight months obtained for the child mentioned earlier. For convenience, the mental age is converted into months; six years and eight months equals eighty months. If the child's chronological age is also eighty months, his

$$\text{I.Q.} = \frac{80}{80} \times 100 = 1 \times 100 = 100$$

If he is only six years old (seventy-two months), his

$$\text{I.Q.} = \frac{80}{72} \times 100 = \frac{10}{9} \times 100 = 111$$

If his actual age is eight years (ninety-six months), his

$$\text{I.Q.} = \frac{80}{96} \times 100 = \frac{10}{12} \times 100 = 83$$

This is the general principle for computing the I.Q. on the Stanford-Binet. In actual practice, because it is quicker and easier, the I.Q. is usually determined from tables that make it possible to compare the child's raw score with the scores made by other children of the same age. This latter method is also the one used with all other intelligence tests. They are administered to large standardization groups of various ages. The average raw score of the standardization group is then equated with an I.Q. of 100; a raw score that is 1 standard deviation above the group's average usually represents an I.Q. of 115; and a score that is 2 standard deviations above average represents an I.Q. of 130.° This statistical method of computing the I.Q. is valuable because the concept of mental age or of I.Q. based on mental age is not meaningful for adults.

The Wechsler Tests

The *Wechsler Adult Intelligence Scale* (called WAIS for short) and the *Wechsler Intelligence Scale for Children* (WISC) are both in wide use. Like the Stanford-Binet, they are individual tests. Their distinguishing feature is that the test items are divided into two major categories, *verbal* and *performance*. The verbal items measure vocabulary, information, general comprehension, memory span, arithmetic reasoning, and ability to detect similarities between concepts. The performance items measure ability at constructing designs with blocks (as shown in FIGURE 14.2), completing pictures, arranging pictures, assembling objects, and substituting a set of unfamiliar symbols for digits.

The subject's I.Q. is calculated for the test as a whole or for the verbal items and the performance items considered separately. This technique is often an advantage in testing people with poor verbal background who may have trouble with the language items but demonstrate considerable ability on the performance items.

Group Tests

An example of a group intelligence test has already been illustrated. This is the *Otis-Lennon Mental Ability Test,* shown in FIGURE 14.1, which is actually a series of five tests of varying difficulty designed to cover the school years from kindergarten to college freshman. A well-known test for children in kindergarten and the first grade is the *Pintner-Cunningham Primary Test,* illustrated in FIGURE 14.6.

Prospective members of the Army and Navy take the *Armed Forces Quali-*

° For students who read this chapter before reading Chapter 13, it should be explained that the standard deviation is a statistical tool used to describe the distribution of measurements. For our present purposes, the standard deviation is important for two reasons: 1) It provides an accurate method of converting a score on one scale (such as here the raw score on intelligence test items) into a score on another scale (such as I.Q.). 2) It shows how many individuals in the population will make any particular score. As is explained in greater detail on page 470, about 34 percent of all individuals have an I.Q. between 100 and 114, while 14 percent have an I.Q. between 115 and 129 and 2 percent 130 or over. Similarly, 34 percent fall between 85 and 99, 14 percent between 70 and 84, and 2 percent under 70.

There are *two* things that belong together in this row. Let's see if we can find them. Put a mark on the fork. Now mark something that belongs with the fork.

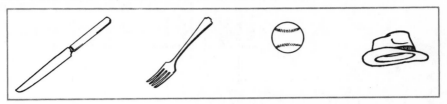

Look at the picture of the rooster. Find what is gone from the rooster and mark it.

FIGURE 14.6   *The Pintner Test*   These are sample items for kindergarten and first-grade pupils from the Pintner-Cunningham Primary Test. (4)

fication Test. The *Scholastic Aptitude Tests* (SAT) are also group intelligence tests but they have been standardized for high school seniors rather than the population as a whole. The average SAT score is 500, and the standard deviation is 100. Since the seniors who take the test are a rather highly selected group, a score of 500 represents an I.Q. of well over 100.

The Virtues of Intelligence Tests

All modern intelligence tests have a high degree of reliability. A person's I.Q. as given by one of the tests will be similar to his I.Q. as shown by another test or by the same test given after a reasonable interval.

Intelligence tests are also valid, for they have proved quite satisfactory at predicting success in school. In many studies of the relation between I.Q. and school grades, correlations of .40 to .60 have been found ° (5). Some forms of school achievement show a higher correlation than others, as is illustrated in FIGURE 14.7.

Students who have very low I.Q.'s tend to drop out of school before or

° Correlation, which was explained more fully in Chapter 13, is a statistical device for measuring the relation between two different scores—such as I.Q. and school grades. A correlation of 1 indicates a perfect relationship; 0 indicates no relationship; and the figures from .01 to .99 describe low to high levels of relationship.

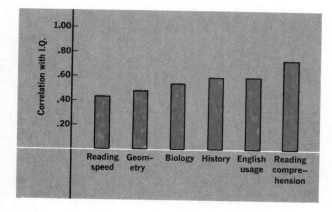

FIGURE **14.7**

I.Q. and School Achievement
These correlations between I.Q. and specific school subjects or skills were found in a study that used the Stanford-Binet Scale to measure intelligence. (6)

immediately after the twelfth grade, leaving a rather highly selected group to go on to college. One study made a generation ago showed that the average I.Q. of college freshmen was 118, of graduates 123, and of those who had obtained the Ph.D. degree 141 (7). Because a larger proportion of young people attend college today, the figures for freshmen and graduates now are probably somewhat lower. At universities with the highest entrance standards, however, the figures are very high.

Weaknesses of Intelligence Tests

One weakness of intelligence tests is the impossibility of devising a test of general mental ability that is purely an aptitude test rather than an achievement test. An intelligence test necessarily relies heavily upon the individual's current level of achievement—the vocabulary he has acquired, his knowledge of the rules of logic, his ability to manipulate numbers and visual symbols. If you study the items from the Stanford-Binet Test shown in FIGURE 14.4, you will note that many of the questions are based on what the subject has learned. To answer them correctly, the two-year-old child must have learned the meaning of hair, mouth, and hands; the four-year-old must have acquired some fairly rich concepts of houses and books; the adult must have learned the points of the compass.

The essential difference between intelligence and achievement tests is that the intelligence test attempts, insofar as possible, to measure the subject's ability to use his existing knowledge in a novel way. Thus the two-year-old is asked to apply his knowledge about his own lips and hair to a paper doll; the adult is asked to make a novel spatial orientation based upon his knowledge of the compass. Perhaps the best example of the difference between an intelligence test and an achievement test is the Stanford-Binet item at the nine-year level in which the child is asked to point out the absurdity in the statement: "In an old graveyard in Spain they have discovered a small skull which they believe to be that of Christopher Columbus when he was about ten years old." Finding the absurdity is a novel task, but it also requires the child to know that Columbus lived to be an adult and that people do not cast off their skulls as a snake casts off its old skin.

In constructing an intelligence test an attempt is made to base all the items on previously acquired knowledge or skills that everyone has had an equal chance to attain. It is assumed that every two-year-old has had an equal opportunity to learn the meaning of hair, mouth, and hands; every four-year-old knows the words *houses* and *books;* every nine-year-old knows that Columbus discovered America; every adult has been exposed to information about the points of the compass. No questions are included that can be answered only by a child who has had specialized training in summer camp about nature study or only by an adult who has taken a course in trigonometry or Spanish.

Nonetheless, despite the efforts of the test makers, there is a bias in the test that favors people who have grown up in a varied environment and have been exposed to a rich range of language. Thus city children tend to make higher scores than rural children (8). Children from middle- and upper-class homes make higher scores than children from lower-class homes (9). Whites make higher average scores than do Negroes, who have generally grown up in environments that do not stimulate language growth (10).

As a measure of actual innate intelligence the tests are probably unfair to rural children, children from lower-class homes, Negroes, and other groups who have grown up, by and large, with fewer intellectual advantages. If the I.Q. is considered solely as a measure of the likelihood that the child will get good grades in school, however, this criticism does not apply, for the same kind of impoverished background that tends to reduce a person's score on an intelligence test also hampers his progress in the school system.

The intelligence test, it must be remembered, was originally designed to measure the ability to learn school tasks, and this is what it still measures today. Perhaps it would be more accurate to say that the intelligence test provides an A.Q., or academic quotient, rather than an I.Q., or intelligence quotient.

THE NATURE OF INTELLIGENCE

Let us put aside all thoughts of intelligence testing and I.Q.'s for a moment and ask a more abstract question: Just what is intelligence? What does the word mean?

Many investigators would agree with the following definition: *Intelligence is the ability to profit from experience, to learn new pieces of information, and to adjust to new situations.* But is it a single ability or a combination of several different kinds of ability?

What Determines Intelligence?

"PRIMARY MENTAL ABILITIES"   One well-known investigation into the nature of intelligence was made by L. L. Thurstone, who gave dozens of different kinds of tests to school children and decided that intelligence is composed of seven recognizable factors, which he called *primary mental abilities*. The factors are:

1. *Verbal comprehension*—indicated by size of vocabulary, ability to read, and skill at understanding mixed-up sentences and the meaning of proverbs.
2. *Word fluency*—the ability to think of words quickly, as when making rhymes or solving word puzzles.
3. *Number*—the ability to solve arithmetic problems and to manipulate numbers.
4. *Space*—the ability to visualize spatial relationships, as in recognizing a design after it has been placed in a new context.
5. *Associative memory*—the ability to memorize quickly, as in learning a list of paired words.
6. *Perceptual speed*—as indicated by the ability to grasp visual details quickly and to observe similarities and differences between designs and pictures.
7. *General reasoning*—skill at the kind of logical thinking that was described in Chapter 6.

Thurstone noted, however, that a person who was above average in any one of these abilities also tended to be above average in the others. He concluded, therefore, that intelligence is composed of the seven primary mental abilities plus some kind of "general factor" that is common to all (11). Thurstone's description of intelligence, though useful, may be an oversimplification. One group of investigators has devised finely differentiated tests that indicate the existence of no less than 82 distinguishable factors that go to make up intelligence, and it is this group's theory that there are probably 120 such factors in all (12).

I.Q. AND HEREDITY   To what extent is I.Q. influenced by heredity? Some of the best evidence comes from studies of identical twins, whose development has been directed by exactly the same chromosomes and genes. In one study the correlation between the I.Q.'s of identical twins reared in the same home was found to be .91 (13). This is a high correlation indeed, especially when it is considered that even the same person's I.Q. scores, calculated at different times, do not show a perfect correlation. (When the same child takes the Stanford-Binet test at one-year or two-year intervals, the correlation is around .90.) Some other correlations between the I.Q.'s of members of the same family are shown in FIGURE 14.8.

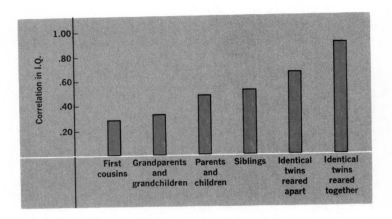

Family Resemblances in I.Q. Studies of members of the same families have shown correlations in I.Q. ranging from about .29 for first cousins to .91 for identical twins reared together. (Data on twins, 13; other data, 14)

FIGURE 14.8

The correlations offer evidence that I.Q. may be inherited. However, environment is also crucial.

I.Q. AND ENVIRONMENT   In the study in which the correlation between identical twins reared in the same home was found to be .91, figures were also obtained for a number of identical twins who, for one reason or another, had been separated and reared in different homes. For these twins the correlation was considerably lower—.77. In some cases one twin's I.Q. was as much as fifteen or twenty points higher than the other's. Presumably the twins started out life with a similar mental capacity, which was altered by the different environments in which they grew up.

Many studies have been made in an attempt to determine the effect of a foster home environment. In one case the subjects were children who had been placed in highly superior homes where they had remained for many years. The I.Q.'s of their real mothers were known to average 91. The children, tested at an average age of thirteen, proved to have a mean I.Q. of 109 or higher, depending upon the testing method used (15). Another study was made of cases in which two children, not related, had been adopted into the same foster home and had been reared together in the same environment. The correlation between I.Q.'s was .65 (16)—even higher than shown in FIGURE 14.8 for true siblings. These two studies seem to indicate that environment plays a large role in determining I.Q. Unfortunately we cannot know what the average I.Q. of the children in the first study would have been had they been reared by their own mothers. Nor can we be sure what the correlation in the second study would have been had the children been brought up apart.

FIGURE 14.9

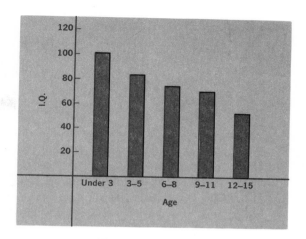

Effect of Poor Environment on I.Q. The bars indicate the average scores on intelligence tests made by the children of feebleminded mothers. Note that the youngest children proved about normal in intelligence but that the oldest children had an average I.Q. of only about 53. (17)

THE EFFECT OF SPECIAL ENVIRONMENTS   In extreme cases of very poor environment the effects on I.Q. have proved quite dramatic. FIGURE 14.9, for example, shows the results of a study made of the children of feebleminded mothers. Note that the older the child was—in other words, the longer he had been exposed to the impoverished environment provided by a feebleminded mother—the lower was the I.Q.

At the opposite extreme, special training programs providing enriched environments have been found effective in raising the I.Q., as in one study where the subjects were boys with an average I.Q. of 66. After several months of intensive training, in which an attempt was made to encourage ingenuity and to help the boys handle social situations and abstract problems, the average I.Q. of the group rose to 76 (18).

Changes in I.Q.

Even for children who remain in more or less the same kind of environment, the I.Q. often shows substantial changes over the years. In one study 140 children were tested every year from the ages of two to twelve. For about half of them the I.Q. showed little change; for the other half there were changes upward or downward that in some cases reached striking proportions. Some of the individual records from this study are illustrated in FIGURE 14.10. Note that one child's I.Q. rose from about 110 to 160, while another's dropped from about 140 to 110.

It was found that girls were more likely to show decreases in I.Q., boys more likely to show increases. Among the children who showed large increases there were twice as many boys as girls. When the children who gained were compared with those who declined, they were found to be more competitive, aggressive in conversation, and independent. They worked harder in school, showed a strong desire to master intellectual problems, and were persistent when faced with difficult tasks.

507

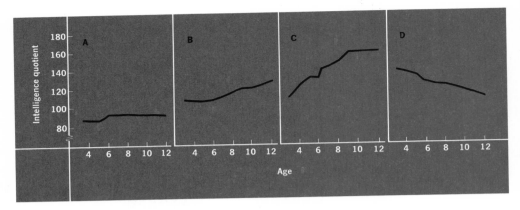

Changes in Children's I.Q.'s When children were tested annually for I.Q., these were some of the curves obtained. About half the children gave nearly straight-line results as in A, showing little change in I.Q. Some showed pronounced improvement as in B (from about 110 to about 130); some showed striking improvement as in C (from about 110 to about 160); and some showed substantial decreases as in D (from about 140 to about 110). (19)

FIGURE 14.10

What conclusions can be drawn from this study? First, it appears obvious that the I.Q. is by no means a constant and unchanging phenomenon like a person's fingerprints. Parents and teachers often take a child's score on an intelligence test too seriously; they give up on the child who has made a low score and expect too much from the child who has made a high score. Actually the young child with a low I.Q. may show gains (especially if he is a boy) and the young child with a high I.Q. may not continue to score so well (especially if she is a girl).

Second, it appears that intelligence tests as now designed measure achievement motivation as well as ability, for the strength of the child's desire for intellectual achievement seems to be closely related to upward or downward changes in I.Q. Parents who emphasize and reward intellectual accomplishment and independence and who provide a model of intellectual achievement with which the child can identify are the most likely to find their children gaining in I.Q. over the years.

The study raises another interesting question: Can a person improve his I.Q. through a deliberate effort toward better achievement? The answer is not known. But certainly some college students who make rather poor grades as freshmen suddenly begin making much better grades later. It may be that retesting of these students would show an increase in I.Q.

I.Q. AND EDUCATIONAL OPPORTUNITIES The I.Q. of the adult, it appears from the evidence that has been cited, depends upon a number of factors. It depends in part upon heredity, but it is also affected by environment and by motivation. One other factor, related to environment, must also be discussed—namely, the kind of formal educational opportunities that the person has had.

There seems to be little doubt that increased educational opportunities can result in higher I.Q. Even nursery schooling for the preschool child seems to produce changes; in a number of studies the average improvement in I.Q. among nursery-school children was found to be 5.6 points (20). There is considerable doubt, however, as to whether the increase persists or is only temporary.

In 1924, at a time when the schools in Hawaii were generally conceded to be inferior to those on the mainland United States, intelligence tests given in Hawaii produced scores far below those found in the city of Seattle; in 1938, by which time there had been vast improvements in the Hawaiian school system, the difference had virtually disappeared (21).

A study of Negro children who had lived in the South in the 1940's and then moved north to attend schools in Philadelphia gave the results illustrated in FIGURE 14.11. By the time they reached the ninth grade in Philadelphia the children showed substantial average increases in I.Q., and the change was greatest of all for the children who had gone through all nine grades in Philadelphia. Presumably the increases can be attributed to better educational facilities in Philadelphia as well as to the generally more stimulating environment of the big city as opposed to the impoverished rural areas where the children spent their early years.

ARE PEOPLE BECOMING MORE INTELLIGENT? There is one study that raises the interesting possibility that the average level of intelligence in the United States has risen quite substantially in the past half century—in other words, that an I.Q. of 100 represents a higher level of mental ability today than it did in the past.

In this study a large and representative group of World War II soldiers

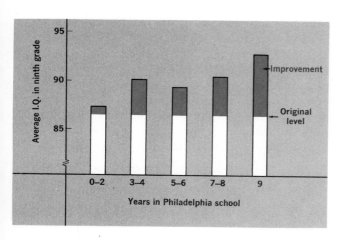

FIGURE 14.11

School Opportunities and I.Q.
The average I.Q. of Negro children from the South who entered the first grade in Philadelphia was 86.5, but by the time these children reached the ninth grade the average was 92.8. Children with fewer years in Philadelphia schools also improved but to a lesser degree. (22)

took a test resembling the group intelligence test used by the Army in World War I. Since they were an "average" group, their mean raw score on the test should have been the same as the mean score that had been made by World War I soldiers; it should have fallen on the 50th percentile of World War I scores. Instead their average score fell on the 83rd percentile—just about one full standard deviation above the World War I mean (23). If the two tests were in fact equally difficult and if these World War II soldiers were in fact as representative of the population as were World War I soldiers, the results would indicate that an I.Q. of 100 today may represent about the same actual level of learning ability as did an I.Q. of 115 at the time of World War I.

This seems at first glance to be a rather strange finding, but perhaps it is only logical in view of what is known about the factors that influence the I.Q. Since World War I vast numbers of American people have moved from the lower classes into the middle and upper. Millions of people have moved from rural areas into cities. Schools have been improved, and the number of students who complete elementary school, high school, and college has greatly increased. Radio and television have exposed children to verbal stimulation and variety. Thus the average young American today may very well possess more of the kind of abilities measured by intelligence tests than did the average young American of several generations ago.

I.Q. AND AGE   As the child's ability to pass increasingly difficult items on the Stanford-Binet clearly shows, intelligence grows rapidly during childhood. Some time after late adolescence, however, a change occurs, and a person's raw scores on an intelligence test no longer improve. This fact raises some interesting questions: At what age does the kind of ability measured by intelligence tests reach its peak? Once the peak is attained, does the ability then decline during middle and old age? Although the answers are not entirely clear, there is some evidence that is well worth discussing.

In one study the investigators managed to give intelligence tests to virtually all the inhabitants, aged ten to sixty, of a single community, using the Army's standard World War I test. The results are illustrated in FIGURE 14.12. Note that the total score on the test rose rapidly by age group to about eighteen, then began to decline and continued downward for all older ages at a fairly steady pace. The scores on different kinds of items making up the test, however, showed different patterns of changes. On items measuring reasoning ability there was a sharp decline in scores from ages eighteen to thirty and a steady decline thereafter. On items measuring vocabulary there was no decline at all. The scores rose rapidly from ages ten to twenty, then continued to rise slowly and were highest of all for the sixty-year-old group.

The Wechsler Adult Intelligence Scale has shown somewhat different re-

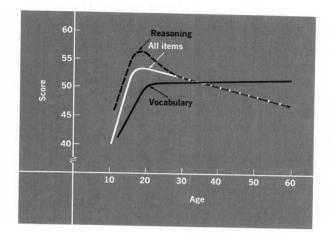

FIGURE **14.12**

Age and Intelligence The curves show the mean scores made by people of various ages on an intelligence test as a whole, on the vocabulary items in the test, and on reasoning, tested by items involving analogies. The subjects were the inhabitants of a New England village. (24)

sults. In standardizing the current version of this test, scores were obtained from representative samples of various age groups from sixteen through sixty-four; the results were as illustrated in FIGURE 14.13. Note that the total score continued to rise until it reached more or less of a plateau between the ages of twenty and thirty-four, then began a fairly sharp decline. On the verbal part of the test the plateau lasted longer, through the age of forty-four, and the decline afterward was relatively small. On performance items the decline began after the early twenties and was relatively steep.

When the New England study and the Wechsler figures are considered together, they indicate that young people make the best scores on intelligence tests—at somewhere between the late teens and the early thirties,

FIGURE **14.13** *WAIS Scores by Age* These are the scores made by various age groups on the Wechsler Adult Intelligence Scale. Note that the total score rises through the teens, remains fairly steady from age twenty through thirty-four, then begins to decline rather sharply. Much of the decline after thirty-four, however, is caused by lower scores on the performance part of the test. On the verbal part the plateau lasts through the age of forty-four and the decline after forty-four is relatively slight. (25)

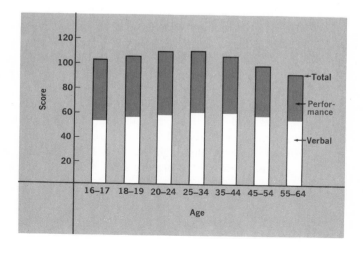

depending upon the kind of test. People over thirty-five make lower scores on all test items except those measuring vocabulary; the lower scores are especially noticeable on items that measure reasoning and performance. One must be careful, however, in drawing conclusions. Do the figures mean that the kind of ability measured by intelligence tests actually reaches its peak between ages seventeen and thirty-four and then declines? Or is there some other explanation?

One possibility is that young people of high school and college age are accustomed to taking tests and have developed certain strategies of question answering, while the older person, many years out of school, has forgotten these strategies. Another is that the older person may take the tests less seriously and have less motivation for a high score than a younger person. A third possibility, suggested by the evidence cited earlier indicating that the average level of mental ability may have increased in the past half century, is that more of today's young people than older people have grown up in environments favorable to high I.Q. scores.

One way to explore this third possibility would be to keep testing a large group of people, first in their late teens and then from time to time as they got older. Studies of this kind, which require that the investigator keep in touch with his subjects over a period of forty years or more, have naturally been rare. But a study has been reported in which a group of people who had taken the Army's World War I test when they were college freshmen took the same test again thirty years later. Their scores proved to be higher than their earlier scores on all items except those concerning arithmetic (26). Although the total mass of evidence is not conclusive, there does not seem to be any cause for despair over what will happen to our mental abilities as we get older.

I.Q. and Occupation

The classic study of the relationship between I.Q. and occupation was based on data available from the thousands of men who took the Army's group intelligence test in World War II. The results, illustrated in FIGURE 14.14, show some pronounced differences in the average I.Q. of men in various kinds of jobs, ranging all the way from 93 for miners and 94 for farmhands to around 120 for accountants, lawyers, and engineers. Even more interesting is the large range of I.Q.'s found in every occupation. Some of the miners and farmhands turned out to have I.Q.'s above the average for accountants, lawyers, and engineers.

The study seems to indicate that the various occupations demand a certain minimum level of I.Q. A man who is able to hold a job as a truck driver, for example, might not be able to hold a job as a teacher. In every occupation, however, there are some men with I.Q.'s well above average who presumably could hold their own in even the most demanding professions. One can assume that many of these men lacked the education, opportunity, or motivation to enter higher level jobs.

Aside from its effect in determining occupational choice, to what extent is I.Q. related to success in life? The evidence is somewhat indirect. One study of college graduates attempted to find the relation between college grades, which as noted earlier are correlated with I.Q., and success as measured by income. In general, A students were found to earn more than B students, and B students more than C and D students; but the differences were smaller than one might expect. Of the four income brackets used in the study, 50 percent of men who had been A students were in the top two, compared to 41 percent of men who had been C and D students. The differences in income for A, B, and C–D students were greatest for teachers,

I.Q.'s by Occupation   The bars show the range of I.Q.'s found for men in various occupations in the United States and also the average (mean) I.Q. for each occupation. Note that the average I.Q. of accountants was 121, of miners only 93, yet some miners had higher I.Q.'s than some accountants. (27)

FIGURE 14.14

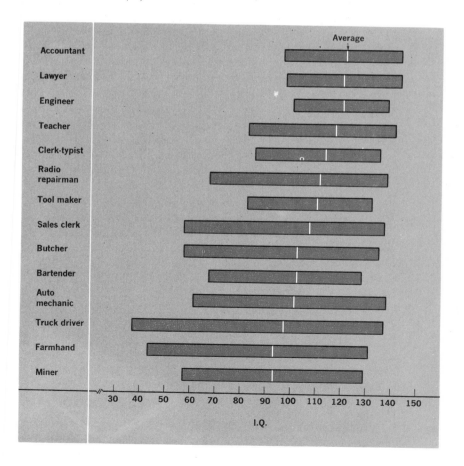

clergymen, artists, and government workers and lowest for businessmen (28).

Thus a high I.Q. does not guarantee financial success, and a relatively low I.Q. does not seem to doom a person to failure. In some occupations, indeed, a high I.Q. apparently can be a handicap. A study of young women employed in a chocolate factory, for example, found that the most intelligent among them were the most easily bored (29). A study of clerks employed at routine jobs showed that the turnover was highest among the most intelligent (30).

The Mentally Retarded

At the extreme low end of the curve of normal distribution of I.Q.'s lie the people whose I.Q.'s are below 70, the *mentally retarded*, who make up 2.28 percent of the population. This is a small percentage, but in a nation like the United States, with a population of around 200,000,000, it represents a large number of total cases. There are about 4,560,000 mentally retarded people in the United States, and retardation is therefore a widespread and serious problem.

The standard classification of the mentally retarded, from mild to profound, is shown in FIGURE 14.15, along with a description of their characteristics as infants, children, and adults. Fortunately most cases of mental retardation fall into the "mild" class. These people, though they have trouble in school and often do not get past the sixth-grade level in reading and arithmetic, can usually function adequately as adults; they manage to hold jobs, get along in society, and in general take care of themselves. At the other extreme are the cases of "profound" retardation; these people never learn to do much more than walk and talk a little, and they require care and supervision all their lives.

What causes mental retardation? Some cases stem from specific biological abnormalities. Among these are cases of *Mongolism*, apparently caused by the presence of an extra chromosome (making a total of forty-seven instead of the normal forty-six). In Mongolism the child has many other abnormalities besides mental retardation, including unusual bone structure in the hands, feet, and skull; the condition takes its name from the round face and slant eyes characteristic of its victims. Another form of serious retardation is *cretinism*, caused by an abnormally low level of secretion by the thyroid gland. If detected in time, this type of mental retardation can be prevented by giving the child thyroid substance. Other forms of retardation can be caused by biological abnormalities in metabolism, injury to the brain at birth, or brain damage caused by diseases, such as German measles, suffered by the mother during pregnancy.

There are many other cases, however, where no physical cause is apparent. Here one cannot be sure whether retardation is due to an undetected illness, a poor and unstimulating environment, or heredity.

The Retarded   This description of the characteristics of the mentally   FIGURE **14.15**
retarded—of various degrees and at various ages—was drawn up by
the U.S. President's Panel on Mental Retardation. (31)

Type	Characteristics from birth to adulthood		
	BIRTH THROUGH FIVE	SIX THROUGH TWENTY	OVER TWENTY-ONE
MILD (I.Q. 53–69)	Often not noticed as retarded by casual observer but is slower to walk, feed self, and talk than most children.	Can acquire practical skills and useful reading and arithmetic to a third to sixth grade level with special education. Can be guided toward social conformity.	Can usually achieve social and vocational skills adequate to self-maintenance; may need occasional guidance and support when under unusual social or economic stress.
MODERATE (36–52)	Noticeable delays in motor development, especially in speech; responds to training in various self-help activities.	Can learn simple communication, elementary health and safety habits, and simple manual skills; does not progress in functional reading or arithmetic.	Can perform simple tasks under sheltered conditions; participates in simple recreation; travels alone in familiar places; usually incapable of self-maintenance.
SEVERE (20–35)	Marked delay in motor development; little or no communication skill; may respond to training in elementary self-help—for example, self-feeding.	Usually walks barring specific disability; has some understanding of speech and some response; can profit from systematic habit training.	Can conform to daily routines and repetitive activities; needs continuing direction and supervision in protective environment.
PROFOUND (below 20)	Gross retardation; minimal capacity for functioning in sensorimotor areas; needs nursing care.	Obvious delays in all areas of development; shows basic emotional responses; may respond to skillful training in use of legs, hands, and jaws; needs close supervision.	May walk, need nursing care, have primitive speech; usually benefits from regular physical activity; incapable of self-maintenance.

Most people who are mentally retarded can profit from special training. Considerable advances in training have been made in recent years, and there are now many state institutions with a good record of preparing the retarded to function in society. A recent follow-up study was made of men and women twenty years after they had left a New York State institution. Among the findings were the following:

> Male, 37 years old, I.Q. 57. Has a license as practical nurse. Has made an "excellent adjustment," owns a car, and is saving money—but is reluctant to marry because he fears his children would be retarded.

> Male, 41, I.Q. 51. Has been employed by the same company for twenty years, currently as a tractor driver. Considered "an excellent and loyal" employee. Is married and buying a home.

> Female, 52, I.Q. 63. Has been employed as a domestic worker by the same family for twenty years. Does fine handwork, makes her own clothing, and is good at making repairs to plumbing and wiring.

> Female, 41, I.Q. 60. Was pregnant when admitted to institution at fifteen. Afterward worked and managed to support herself and her son. Now happily married and living on a farm; is a good housekeeper. (32).

The Mentally Gifted

At the opposite extreme from the mentally retarded are the 2.28 percent of the population (again 4,560,000 in all in the United States) who have I.Q.'s over 130. These are the *mentally gifted*. At the very top of the group are the people called *geniuses*, whose I.Q.'s may range up to 190.

A genius is capable of remarkable accomplishments, even early in life. Mozart, who surely would have scored near the very maximum had intelligence tests been invented at the time, began composing music when he was four and wrote a symphony when he was eight. John Stuart Mill, the nineteenth-century economist, read Plato in the original Greek before he was nine. In more recent times Norbert Wiener, the mathematician, graduated from high school at the age of twelve and from college at fifteen.

A classic study of the mentally gifted was begun in 1921 by Lewis M. Terman and continued by him and his associates for many years. He began with 1500 California school children who had I.Q.'s of 140 or more, and he managed to follow many of them into middle age.

The old belief that the genius is a sickly, maladjusted bookworm was dispelled by the Terman study. The gifted children were above average in height (by about an inch), weight, and appearance. They were better adjusted than average and showed superiority in social activity and leadership.

In later life, not all the gifted children lived up to their early promise. Some of them dropped out of school and wound up in routine occupations; some, even though they went to college, turned out to be vocational misfits and drifters. But these were the exceptions, and their records tended to show problems of emotional and social adjustment and low motivation toward achievement. On the whole the group was outstandingly successful. In large proportion, the gifted went to college, achieved above-average and often brilliant records, and went on to make important contributions in fields ranging from medicine and law to literature and from business administration to government service. Many achieved the recognition of a listing in *Who's Who* or *American Men of Science*. The average level of accomplishment was far higher than could be expected of a group chosen at random.

The gifted child can, however, meet serious problems—especially if he grows up in a home or attends a school that does not recognize his superior abilities. Because he is intellectually advanced for his years, he may seem to be a know-it-all and come to be resented by other children, teachers, and even parents. If he stays in the same grades as other children his age, he may be bored by the work and become lazy or difficult to discipline; if he skips grades, he may have trouble adjusting socially, though not mentally, to older children. In some ways the gifted child can benefit from specialized training just as much as the retarded child—as many schools have recognized by providing enriched activities such as that shown in FIGURE 14.16.

Although intelligence tests are the most widely used and generally the most valid, there are scores of other   **OTHER KINDS OF TESTS**
kinds of tests, devised for special purposes. Among them, and worthy of special note, are tests of *vocational aptitude*, *interests*, and *personality*.

A Special Project for Gifted Children   In a nursery class for gifted children a four-year-old learns to operate a typewriter—a skill not ordinarily taught until high school.   **FIGURE 14.16**

FIGURE 14.17

A Dexterity Test Using a tweezers, the subject is taking part of the Crawford Small Parts Dexterity Test.

Vocational Aptitude

Many tests have been devised in an attempt to measure the skills required for certain kinds of occupations—skills such as mechanical ability, the special kinds of manual dexterity involved in various factory jobs, the motor coordination required for operating complicated machinery, and the speed and accuracy at dealing with details required in clerical jobs.

In general, the present tests of vocational aptitude are considerably less satisfactory than intelligence tests in that their correlation with actual success on a job is usually much lower than the correlation between I.Q. and success in school. However, they often offer valuable clues about an individual's pattern of skills, and in the hands of trained counselors they serve as a useful adjunct to vocational guidance.

Some vocational aptitude tests measure actual performance, as does the manual dexterity test illustrated in FIGURE 14.17. Others, such as those il-

FIGURE 14.18

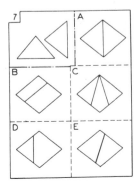
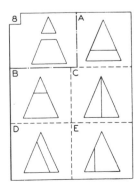

A Test of Mechanical Ability If the pieces shown separately were put together, which of the five figures lettered A through E would they make? These are sample items from the *Revised Minnesota Paper Form Board*, a paper-and-pencil test of mechanical ability. (33)

lustrated in FIGURES 14.18 and 14.19, are administered with paper and pencil.

One widely used test is in fact a battery of tests measuring several different kinds of vocational ability. It is called the *Differential Aptitude Tests,* the sample page of which is shown in FIGURE 14.20. As will be seen, it measures eight different kinds of ability, scores for which are calculated separately. The test provides a good indication of the abilities at which the individual is above average and those at which he is below average and thus serves as a general guide to the kind of jobs at which he would be most likely to succeed.

FIGURE **14.19**   *The MacQuarrie Test*   Below are sample items from the *MacQuarrie Test for Mechanical Ability,* another paper-and-pencil test. (34)

Follow each numbered line with your eyes to the square at right where it ends and write in its number.

Starting with the circled dot, draw lines between dots to copy the figure at the left.

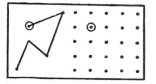

Next to each X, place the number of other blocks that this particular block touches.

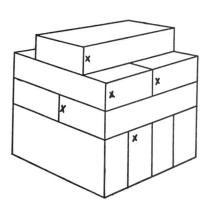

FIGURE 14.20 *The Differential Aptitude Tests* The sample items below illustrate the eight types of vocational ability measured by the Differential Aptitude Tests. (35)

VERBAL REASONING

Each of the fifty sentences in this test has the first word and the last word left out. You are to pick out words that will fill the blanks so that the sentence will be true and sensible.

For each sentence you are to choose from among five pairs of words to fill the blanks. The first word of the pair you choose goes in the blank space at the beginning of the sentence; the second word of the pair goes in the blank at the end of the sentence.

. . . . . . is to water as eat is to . . . . . .

A. continue —— drive
B. foot —— enemy
C. drink —— food
D. girl —— industry
E. drink —— enemy

NUMERICAL ABILITY

This test consists of forty numerical problems. Next to each problem there are five answers. You are to pick out the correct answer.

Add   13   A 14   Subtract 30   A 15
      12   B 25   20   B 26
                C 16   C 16
                D 59   D 8
                E none of these   E none of these

ABSTRACT REASONING

Each row consists of four figures called Problem Figures and five called Answer Figures. The four Problem Figures make a series. You are to find out which one of the Answer Figures would be the next, or the fifth one in the series. Note that the lines in the Problem Figures are falling down. In the first square the line stands straight up, and as you go from square to square the line falls more and more to the right.

PROBLEM FIGURES   **ANSWER FIGURES**

SPACE RELATIONS

This test consists of sixty patterns which can be folded into figures. For each pattern, four figures are shown. You are to decide which *one* of these figures can be made from the pattern shown.

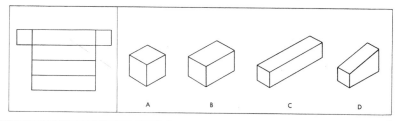

MECHANICAL REASONING

This test consists of a number of pictures and questions about those pictures.

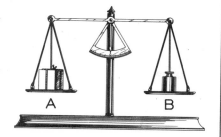

Which weighs more?

(If equal, mark C.)

CLERICAL SPEED AND ACCURACY

This is a test to see how quickly and accurately you can compare letter and number combinations. In each Test Item one of the five is *underlined*. You are to look at the *one* combination that is underlined, find the *same* one after that item number of the separate answer sheet, and fill in the space under it (as has been done here).

TEST ITEMS

V.	AB	AC	AD	AE	AF
W.	aA	aB	BA	Ba	Bb
X.	A7	7A	B7	7B	AB
Y.	Aa	Ba	bA	BA	bB
Z.	3A	3B	33	B3	BB

SAMPLE OF ANSWER SHEET

	AC	AE	AF	AB	AD
V.				▮	
	BA	Ba	Bb	aA	aB
W.			▮		
	7B	B7	AB	7A	A7
X.	▮				
	Aa	bA	bB	Ba	BA
Y.	▮				
	BB	3B	B3	3A	33
Z.					▮

LANGUAGE USAGE: SPELLING

This test is composed of a series of words. Some of them are correctly spelled; some are incorrectly spelled. You are to indicate whether each word is spelled right or wrong.

			R	W
W.	man	W.	▮	
X.	gurl	X.		▮
Y.	catt	Y.		▮
Z.	dog	Z.	▮	

LANGUAGE USAGE: GRAMMAR

This test consists of a series of sentences, each divided into four parts lettered A, B, C, and D. You are to look at each sentence and decide which part has an error in grammar, punctuation, or spelling. If there is no error in a sentence, fill in the space under the letter E.

X. Ain't we / going to / the office / next week?
　　A　　　　B　　　　C　　　　D

Y. I went / to a ball / game with / Jimmy.
　　A　　　B　　　　C　　　　D

	A	B	C	D	E
X.	▮				
	A	B	C	D	E
Y.					▮

Interests

In addition to ability there is another important factor to be considered in choosing a vocation. All of us, when we decide on our life's work, must ask: How interesting will the work be to a person like me?

The attempt to provide some kind of scientific answer for this question has resulted in what are called *interest tests*—which, as the name indicates, measure the subject's preferences in literature, music, art, science, school subjects, social affairs, kinds of people, and a wide range of activities ranging from butterfly collecting to repairing a clock or making a speech. The subject's pattern of interests can then be compared to the pattern shown by people who are already successfully holding various kinds of jobs.

One widely used interest test is the *Strong Vocational Interest Blank*, which contains 400 items on which the subject is asked to list his likes, dislikes, and preferences. His scores can be compared to those made by men in forty-seven different occupations, ranging from accountant to Y.M.C.A. secretary, and by women in twenty-eight occupations, including that of housewife. For each occupation that he is considering, the subject receives a score of A to C. A score of A shows a close correspondence between the subject's interests and those of people already in that occupation and is considered an excellent indication that the subject would like the job. A score of C shows a very low correspondence and is considered unfavorable. The in-between scores, from B+ to B−, are considered indecisive.

The *Kuder Preference Record* is an interest test in which various types of activity are presented in groups of three, as shown in FIGURE 14.21. The subject is asked to indicate which of the three he likes best and which he likes least. There are several forms of this test. The one that has been used longest and most widely is the Kuder Preference Record—Vocational, in which the subject's scores are compared with those made by the general population, resulting in a profile on ten separate groups of interests as shown in FIGURE 14.22. The test has been standardized separately for men and women and for high school, college, and adult groups. The Kuder Preference Record—Personal gives a profile of the subject's preferences in matters called Sociable (being in groups), Practical (dealing with familiar and stable

Items from the Kuder Test   In each set of three sample items on the Kuder Preference Record-Vocational the subject has punched a hole in the left-hand column to indicate which type of activity he would most like to engage in (for example, visit a museum) and a hole in the right-hand column to indicate which type he would least like to engage in (browse in a library). (36)

FIGURE 14.21

A Kuder Preference Profile As shown by the bars, this subject has an exceptionally high interest in the outdoors (where his score was on the 88th percentile), literary matters (99th percentile), and social service (97th percentile). In all the other seven fields his interest is below average—especially for mechanical matters (below the 2nd percentile), computational (11th percentile), and musical (13th percentile). Presumably he would be considerably happier in charge of library and story activities at a camp for the underprivileged than as an automobile mechanic or accountant. (36)

FIGURE 14.22

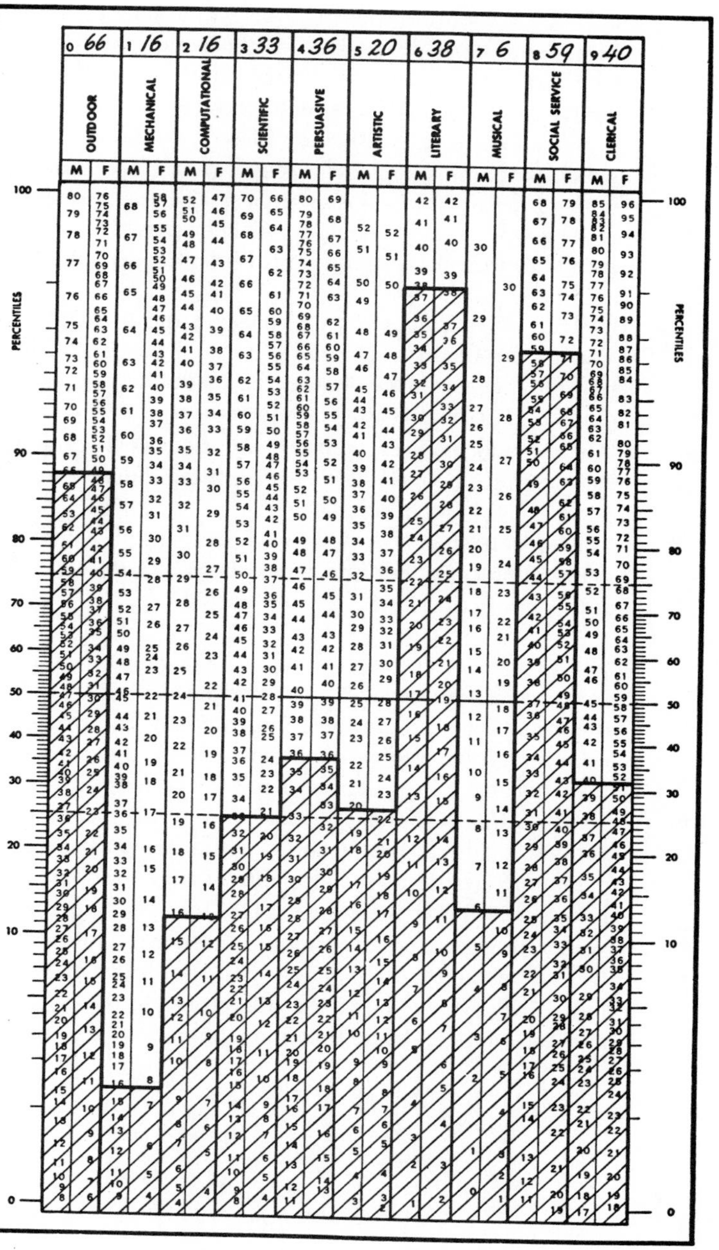

0 *66*	1 *16*	2 *16*	3 *33*	4 *36*	5 *20*	6 *38*	7 *6*	8 *59*	9 *40*
OUTDOOR	MECHANICAL	COMPUTATIONAL	SCIENTIFIC	PERSUASIVE	ARTISTIC	LITERARY	MUSICAL	SOCIAL SERVICE	CLERICAL

situations), Theoretical (dealing with ideas), Agreeable (avoiding conflicts), and Dominant (directing other people).

Personality

The search for reliable and valid measures of personality has been carried on intensively. A test that could accurately measure degree and type of anxiety would be an invaluable research tool, opening up almost infinite possibilities for further study. A test that could accurately distinguish between normal and neurotic personalities would enable clinical psychologists to find the people most in need of psychotherapy and to practice preventive psychotherapy on children near the danger line. It would also provide an objective judgment on the effectiveness of various kinds of psychotherapy and perhaps lead to the discovery of new methods. It would make comparisons possible among people who have grown up in different environments and with different kinds of experiences and thus greatly add to the knowledge of developmental psychology. Conceivably, by spotting certain kinds of disturbed personalities it could prevent tragedies like the assassination of President Kennedy.

Thus a great deal of time, energy, and ingenuity has gone into the creation of personality tests. But the goal has been elusive. Although current personality tests are valuable, the ideal kinds of measures have not yet been devised. Personality is a composite of many elements—the product of a tangled and endless web of experiences beginning at birth, continuing throughout life, and unique for each individual—and the difficulties in measuring it are staggering.

The personality tests now in use, all of which have some virtues and many limitations, fall into three classes: 1) *objective tests*, 2) *situational tests*, and 3) *projective tests*.

OBJECTIVE TESTS OF PERSONALITY   The *objective tests* get their name because they are administered and scored according to a standard procedure, and the results are not seriously affected by the opinions or prejudices of the examiner. Like group intelligence tests, they are usually paper-and-pencil tests that have been standardized for large groups of representative subjects.

The *Allport-Vernon-Lindzey Study of Values* is a measure of the subject's concern with six broad fields of human activity and thought—theoretical, economic, aesthetic, social, political, and religious. It is made up of questions like those shown in FIGURE 14.23, designed to reveal whether the subject values religion above economic matters or literature above sports. One of the interesting findings made with the Study of Values is illustrated in FIGURE 14.24, which shows the differences in the average scores made by men and by women. Note that men tend to place more value on theoretical,

PART I. In the boxes to the right, rate the two alternative answers 3 and 0 if you agree with one and disagree with the other; if you have only a slight preference for one over the other, rate them 2 and 1, respectively.

EXAMPLE

If you should see the following news items with headlines of equal size in your morning paper, which would you read more attentively? (a) PROTESTANT LEADERS TO CONSULT ON RECONCILIATION; (b) GREAT IMPROVEMENTS IN MARKET CONDITIONS.

PART II. In the boxes to the right, rate the answers 4, 3, 2, and 1 in order of personal preference, giving 4 to the most attractive and 1 to the least attractive alternative.

EXAMPLE

In your opinion, can a man who works in business all the week best spend Sunday in —
a. trying to educate himself by reading serious books
b. trying to win at golf, or racing
c. going to an orchestral concert
d. hearing a really good sermon

A Test of Values   In the Allport-Vernon-Lindzey Study of Values the subject is asked to give numerical values to his preferences among various activities and opinions. (38)

FIGURE **14.23**

Sex Differences in Values   On the six types of values measured by the Allport-Vernon-Lindzey Study of Values, these pronounced differences have been found in the mean scores of men and of women. (38)

FIGURE **14.24**

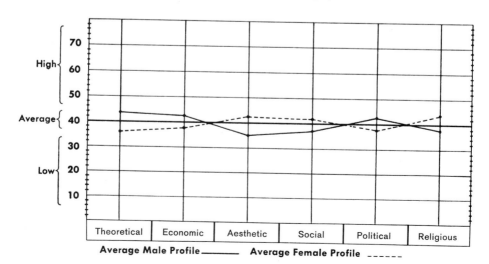

Average Male Profile ———   Average Female Profile - - - - - -

economic, and political matters; women on aesthetic, social, and religious matters.

The *Minnesota Multiphasic Personality Inventory*, known for short as MMPI, is a widely used test designed to measure many aspects of personality, from introversion and extroversion to tendencies toward schizophrenia or paranoia. The test is composed of 550 statements like those illustrated in FIGURE 14.25; the subject is asked to indicate whether the statement is true or false of his own overt behavior and thoughts or to mark "cannot say." The answers are scored on nine or ten different scales for various personality traits and four other scales that measure the subject's attitude toward the test, resulting in personality profiles like those in FIGURE 14.26. Numerous studies made with the MMPI have indicated that high scores on scales 1, 2, and 3 are often made by neurotics; high scores on scales 6, 7, 8, and 9 by psychotics. A high peak on scale 4 is characteristic of delinquents.

SITUATIONAL TESTS   In a *situational test*, the examiner observes the behavior of the subject in a situation deliberately created to test some aspect of his personality. A good example was a test used in World War II for selecting men to work as agents behind enemy lines. The subjects were put in charge of a difficult task like building a tower of heavy logs, with the assistance of "helpers" who were in fact stooges and who behaved in an uncooperative and insulting fashion. Some subjects remained calm, while others became enraged or broke down and wept (41).

It is difficult to devise situational tests that seem real to the subject and impossible to know whether his motivation is the same in the test situation

FIGURE 14.25   *MMPI Items*   The Minnesota Multiphasic Personality Inventory is made up of statements like these, which the subject is asked to score as true, false, or "cannot say." (39)

1. I have certainly had more than my share of things to worry about.
2. I think that I feel more intensely than other people do.
3. I have never done anything dangerous for the thrill of it.
4. I think nearly everyone would tell a lie to keep out of trouble.
5. I am happy most of the time.
6. I tend to be on my guard with people who are somewhat more friendly than I had expected.
7. My mother or father often made me obey even when I thought that it was unreasonable.
8. I feel uneasy indoors.
9. I refuse to play some games because I am not good at them.
10. I find it hard to keep my mind on a task or job.

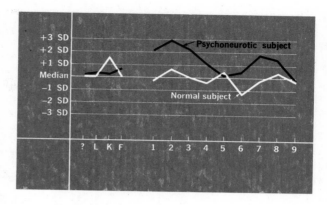

MMPI Profiles The curves show the profile of scores of two subjects on the Minnesota Multiphasic Personality Inventory (40). The key to the thirteen different scales is as follows:

?   Number of "cannot say" answers.
L   Indicates faking on test in attempt to look good.
K   High score shows attempt to defend self against possible criticism; low score an excessive tendency to reveal defects.
F   Shows carelessness in answering questions.
1   Indicates anxiety over health; hypochondria.
2   Shows feelings of depression, worthlessness, and pessimism.
3   Shows tendency toward psychosomatic ailments.
4   Shows lack of social and moral responsibility.
5   For men, high score shows a tendency to be feminine in interests and emotions; for women, high score indicates an aggressive and masculine attitude.
6   Indicates tendencies toward delusions of persecution.
7   Indicates phobias and compulsions.
8   Indicates bizarre patterns of thought and hallucinations, as in schizophrenia.
9   Indicates tendency to be manic in mood; emotional excitability.

as it might be in real-life circumstances. Moreover, two observers watching the subject's behavior may reach different conclusions about it. Thus situational tests, though an interesting approach to the study of personality, have problems and need improvement.

PROJECTIVE TESTS   The *projective test* can best be described in connection with FIGURE 14.27, which shows a picture similar to those presented to the subject in the *Thematic Apperception Test,* known for short as the TAT. The subject is asked to make up a story about the picture, telling what has led up to the scene, what is now happening, and how events will turn out. The theory is that he will project his own personality traits into the picture and will make up a story that reveals his own feelings, motives, and anxieties.

FIGURE **14.27**

What Is Happening Here? What kind of story does this picture tell? What led up to the situation? What is happening? How will events turn out? These are the questions asked about the pictures in the Thematic Apperception Test, to which this drawing is similar. The student may want to try making up his own story before reading the discussion and the story made up by one subject, which will be found in the text. (42)

For example, one subject told the following story about the picture in FIG-URE 14.27.

The older woman represents evil and she is trying to persuade the younger one to leave her husband and run off and lead a life of fun and gaiety. The younger one is afraid to do it—afraid of what others will think, afraid she will regret the action. But the older one knows that she wants to leave and so she insists over and over again. I am not sure how it ends. Perhaps the younger woman turns and walks away and ignores the older woman.

The TAT technique has been used with considerable success in measuring the strength of the achievement motive (43). A tendency to invent stories that contain frequent and intense elements of striving and ambition—or that on the contrary show little concern with achievement—appears to be a better criterion of this motive than the judgment of people who know the subject well (44) or even the subject's own assessment of his desire to achieve (45). Much of the research that has been done on the origin and operation of the achievement motive has been based on ratings made with the TAT technique.

Another well-known example of a projective technique is the *Rorschach Test,* in which the subject is asked to tell what he sees in a series of inkblots like the one illustrated in FIGURE 14.28. There are ten such blots, some in black and white and some in color, and ordinarily the subject sees twenty to forty different things in them. His answers are scored for a number of

FIGURE 14.28

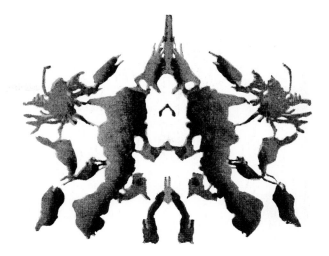

What Do You See Here?
This is an inkblot like those used in the Rorschach Test. Subjects are asked to examine it and report everything they see. (46)

different dimensions. For example, a tendency to respond to the blot as a whole is considered to indicate that the subject thinks in terms of abstractions and generalities; a tendency to pick out many minor details that most people ignore may indicate on overconcern for detail.

The *Holtzman Inkblot Test* uses forty-five inkblots, and the subject is asked to make a single response to each. Answers to this test have been standardized for a number of different groups. The scores of a college student, for example, can be compared with those of other students or with those of a group of known schizophrenics. The Holtzman test represents an approach toward a more objective method of scoring projective tests.

Most projective tests require a high degree of skill and experience on the part of the person who gives and interprets them; even trained examiners may reach different conclusions. Aside from the TAT research into the achievement motive, they have been used mostly by clinical psychologists, who find them a valuable and time-saving supplement to other methods of exploring the problems of patients.

SUMMARY

1. A psychological test is a device for measuring a sample of behavior, often in an attempt to predict future behavior.
2. The four requirements of a test are that it be:
   a. *Objective*—resulting in the same score regardless of who administers or scores it.
   b. *Standardized*—used on a large and representative sample so that the individual's score can be compared to the scores of the population as a whole.

  c. *Reliable*—yielding similar scores when the same person is tested on different occasions.

  d. *Valid*—found to measure the characteristic that it is supposed to measure.

3. A *group test* can be given to many people at the same time. An *individual test* is given by a trained examiner to one person at a time.

4. An *aptitude test* measures the subject's capacity to learn a new skill. An *achievement test* measures his present level of skill or knowledge.

5. Intelligence tests provide a measure of the subject's *intelligence quotient,* or *I.Q.* The I.Q. is obtained by comparing the individual's raw score on the test with the scores of a standardization group of people his age.

6. All modern intelligence tests have a high degree of reliability and a correlation of around .40 to .60 with school and college grades.

7. Since intelligence tests must rely to a certain extent upon the subject's present level of knowledge, they tend to result in lower than average I.Q. scores for people who have grown up in environments providing less than average language stimulation. City children tend to make higher average scores than farm children; children from upper- and middle-class homes make higher average scores than children from lower-class homes; and whites make higher average scores than Negroes.

8. Intelligence can be defined as *the ability to profit from experience, to learn new pieces of information, and to adjust to new situations.*

9. According to Thurstone, intelligence is composed of seven *primary mental abilities* (verbal comprehension, word fluency, number, space, associative memory, perceptual speed, and general reasoning) plus a "general factor."

10. Studies of identical twins and foster children have suggested that intelligence is determined partly by heredity and partly by environmental influences.

11. A study of children tested every year from the ages of two to twelve showed that the I.Q. remained relatively constant for about half the children but changed upward or downward for the others, sometimes by as many as fifty points.

12. Young people make the best scores on intelligence tests—at ages between the late teens and early thirties, depending upon the kind of test. People over thirty-five make lower scores on all items except those measuring vocabulary.

13. The 2.28 percent of the population with an I.Q. below 70 are described as *mentally retarded.* The 2.28 percent with an I.Q. above 130 are described as *mentally gifted.*

14. In addition to intelligence tests, other tests include a) *vocational aptitude tests,* measuring the ability to perform specialized skills required in various kinds of jobs; b) *tests of interests,* measuring the individual's

interests in and preferences for various kinds of activities; and c) *personality tests.*

15. There are three classes of personality tests:

   a. *Objective tests,* such as the Allport-Vernon-Lindzey Study of Values and the Minnesota Multiphasic Personality Inventory.

   b. *Situational tests,* in which the examiner observes the behavior of the subject in a situation deliberately created to reveal some aspect of his personality.

   c. *Projective tests,* such as the Thematic Apperception Test and the Rorschach Test, in which the subject is supposed to insert or to project aspects of his own personality into the stories he makes up to ambiguous pictures or into the kind of objects he sees in inkblots.

RECOMMENDED READING

Anastasi, A. *Psychological testing,* 2nd ed. New York: Macmillan, 1961.

Cronbach, L. J. *Essentials of psychological testing,* 2nd ed. New York: Harper & Row, 1960.

Cronbach, L. J. The interpretation and application of ability tests. In his *Educational psychology,* 2nd ed. New York: Harcourt, Brace & World, 1963, pp. 233–67.

Murstein, B. I. *Theory and research in projective techniques.* New York: Wiley, 1963.

Robinson, H. B. and Robinson, N. M. *The mentally retarded child: a psychological approach.* New York: McGraw-Hill, 1965.

Sontag, L. W., Baker, C. T., and Nelson, V. L. Mental growth and personality development: a longitudinal study. *Monogr. Soc. Res. Child Dev.,* 1958, 23 (No. 2).

Terman, L. M. and Oden, M. H. *The gifted child grows up.* Stanford, Calif.: Stanford University Press, 1947.

Terman, L. M. and Oden, M. H. *The gifted group at mid-life.* Stanford, Calif.: Stanford University Press, 1959.

Vernon, P. E. *Personality assessment: a critical survey.* New York: Wiley, 1964.

PART
8

THE CHILD, THE ADULT, AND SOCIETY

Previous chapters have been concerned mostly with the *individual*. Now, in the concluding section of this introduction to psychology, it is necessary to describe some of the ways in which the individual's behavior and mental processes are dependent upon other people.

As the poet John Donne wrote, "No man is an island"; he does not live in isolation. Even if we know a great deal about how the individual learns, interprets the world, acquires his motives and emotions, and is shaped into a unique personality, our knowledge of him is still incomplete unless we go on to view him as one man among many—a member of society, constantly interacting with the other members of society.

This final section of the book consists of two chapters. Chapter 15, on developmental psychology, describes the manner in which the newborn baby acquires the patterns of behavior and thinking and the motives, emotions, and conflicts that go to make up his adult personality. This process, it will be seen, involves many complex interactions with other people—at first his parents, later his teachers and his schoolmates. Chapter 16, on social psychology, explains how adult behavior is influenced by other individuals and by society as a whole.

INDIVIDUAL DIFFERENCES AT BIRTH

Activity
Sensory Thresholds and Adaptation
Physiological Reactions

Irritability
The Role of Inborn Differences

PHYSICAL DEVELOPMENT

How the Body Develops
Development of Motor Skills

The Role of Maturation
Practical Considerations

MENTAL DEVELOPMENT

The First Two Years
Language Skill
Language and Concepts

Perception
Conceptual Intelligence
The Course of Mental Development

THE DEVELOPMENT OF PERSONALITY

BIRTH TO EIGHTEEN MONTHS: THE "CARETAKER" PERIOD

The Mother's "Reward Value"
The Neglected Child
Two Experiments in Caretaking

The Beginnings of Anxiety
Separation Anxiety

AGES EIGHTEEN MONTHS TO THREE YEARS: THE FIRST SOCIAL DEMANDS

Punishment and Anxiety
Exploring and Destroying
Why Toilet Training Is Important
Harsh Training and Its Results
    Negative Perception of the Mother; Lowered Self-Esteem;
    Aggression and Other Behavioral Problems; Sexual Problems

AGES FOUR AND FIVE: THE PRESCHOOL YEARS

Identification   Conscience   Sex Typing

AGES SIX TO TEN: THE CHILD AND HIS PEERS

The Child in School
The Influence of Peers
The Peer Group's Verdict

Dominance and Submission
Motives and Standards
Anxieties and Defenses

15

DEVELOPMENTAL PSYCHOLOGY

More than 300 years ago the poet Milton wrote:

> The childhood shows the man,
> As morning shows the day.

Today we have ample evidence that Milton was right. Studies of children —especially studies in which the same individuals have been observed from the time they were babies until they were adults—have demonstrated that much of the behavior and many of the personality traits of the adult can be traced to events and influences in childhood, particularly during the first ten years. Note, for example, the following reports written by two different trained observers about the same person, the first when he was a child, the second when he was a young adult.

Peter X., Age 3½

Babyish in appearance . . . . He showed extreme caution and would back away from any situation that smacked of danger. When threatened he would shake his head, clasp his hands, and beg in a frantic tone, "No, no, no." His role with peers was a sedentary, passive, and shrinking one. He stayed out of the swirl of activities of the other children . . . . With the staff of the nursery school he was highly conforming and very dependent. He liked to clean up, liked to wash, liked to take a nap . . . . Whenever he dirtied something, wet himself, or committed what he regarded as a violation, he became very tense and apprehensive, as if he felt that he had been a bad boy.

Peter X., Age 21

He was frail of build and spoke in a soft and high-pitched voice. When interviewed he often meditated for several minutes before answering, and there was a prevailing air of caution and insecurity in his manner. He had decided to teach English at a high school. Although he was primarily interested in teaching at a college, he was afraid to begin there because he doubted his ability . . . . He admired all his high school and college teachers and retained a dependent tie to them. . . . He did not want to marry until he was financially secure, and he had serious doubts about his ability to support a family. He felt tense and uncomfortable when with girls and he preferred not to date. Sexual behavior was still a source of fear. . . . He had few friends and most of his leisure was spent alone. Because he felt tense with strange people, he avoided clubs and social groups. If someone irritated him, he walked away; and he rarely insulted or became sarcastic with anyone. With his parents he was close and conforming, and he enjoyed talking over his problems with them. Fearing a feeling of isolation from his family, he had decided to attend a college close to his home. (1)

The case of Peter X. is extreme, showing an unusually high degree of consistency between the behavior of the child and the behavior of the adult. But it demonstrates what has been established as a general principle. Behavior patterns formed in childhood often determine whether the adult will be dependent or independent, passive or aggressive, shy or friendly, cautious or daring, and also determine his goals, his philosophy of life, his feelings about marriage, and his role as a parent to his children. Moreover, clinical studies of disturbed people and criminals have shown that their problems almost always began in childhood.

Developmental psychology is the study of the processes by which the child gradually acquires patterns of overt behavior, thinking, problem solving, and, above all, the motives, emotions, conflicts, and ways of coping with conflicts that will go to make up his adult personality. For many reasons, developmental psychology is one of the most important and most rapidly growing branches of the science. For one thing, it is virtually impossible to understand adult behavior and the social problems that it often creates without knowing something about developmental psychology. Moreover, developmental psychology points the way to understanding individual children, suggesting methods of rearing them, and handling the difficulties inherent in child rearing. It also offers what is perhaps the best hope for relieving some of the psychological problems that now plague many people in our society— problems such as alcoholism, drug addiction, crime, suicidal depression, and schizophrenia. All these symptoms when found in established form among adults are difficult to treat and eliminate. The study of development, however, may eventually lead to methods of preventing or dealing with them more successfully in their early stages.

INDIVIDUAL DIFFERENCES AT BIRTH

To what extent does the baby represent the old idea of the *tabula rasa*, or "blank tablet," upon which anything can be written through learning and experience? Part of the answer has already been presented in various other chapters. The human baby is not imprisoned to any significant degree by inborn patterns of instinctive behavior. Learning will play a crucial role in shaping his behavior, and it will affect not only his thinking but also his motives, emotions, conflicts, and manner of dealing with conflicts. On the other hand, the genes he has inherited determine his basic body build, facial features, eye color, and many other characteristics, including his capacity to learn. To this knowledge, developmental psychology provides a number of important additions.

Most of the evidence provided by developmental psychology, you will discover, also leans toward the idea of the *tabula rasa*. The findings indicate strongly that a person's entire life is profoundly influenced by such factors as his earliest contacts with his mother, his first experiences with discipline, identification with his mother and father, and his relations with his teachers and other children in the first five or six years of school. But the study of development also has demonstrated that there are important individual differences at birth, indicating that the newborn child is by no means entirely a *tabula rasa*.

Activity

Observations of very young babies have disclosed that some of them are much more active than others. Some move their arms and legs with considerable force and tend to be restless when asleep. They suck vigorously when nursing or at the bottle and appear to have above-average appetites. As they get a little older they tend to make loud noises when they babble, to bang their toys together, and to kick at the sides of their cribs. Other babies are much more placid. Their movements are more gentle; they sleep more quietly and nurse less vigorously; later they babble in a softer voice and make less commotion with their toys (2). In general, boys seem to show a higher level of activity than girls (3).

Sensory Thresholds and Adaptation

Some babies respond with muscular reflexes to a very gentle stroking of the skin; others do not respond unless the stroking is fairly firm. Some display the startle reaction to sounds or light flashes of rather low intensity, others only when the intensity is quite high. The threshold for pain also seems to vary; for example, one study showed that newborn girls responded to mild electrical stimulation of the toe more readily than did boys (4).

When a sound loud enough to produce the startle pattern is repeated over a period of time, some babies quickly adapt and stop responding. Other babies have been found to react with the startle pattern even on the thirtieth presentation of the sound (5). Similarly, some babies appear to become "bored" with a stimulus rather quickly and to turn their attention elsewhere. A study of eight-month-old babies has shown that some of them will play with a rattle or other toy for no more than twenty seconds, then turn to some other object. Other babies continue to play with the same object for as much as ten minutes without any apparent loss of interest (6).

Physiological Reactions

Under stress, such as that caused by hunger or pain, babies show different kinds of reactions. Some respond with changes in heart or breathing rate, others with skin flushing or skin rash, still others with vomiting (7). All these changes presumably are triggered by the autonomic nervous system, and they point to inborn individual differences in the sensitivity and patterns of nervous impulses in the autonomic system.

Irritability

Closely related to the differences in physiological reactions and probably also to the differences in sensory thresholds is what for lack of a more precise word may be called irritability. Some babies begin to fret, whine, or cry at the slightest provocation, while others do not show this kind of behavior unless their discomfort or pain is quite intense. Moreover, some babies, once they have begun to fret, seem to work themselves up into what looks like a temper tantrum and soon are bellowing at the top of their lungs. Others may fret for a half minute or so, then stop, as if they possessed some kind of mechanism that inhibited the buildup of extreme upset (6).

The Role of Inborn Differences

In summary, babies appear to display rather wide individual differences in 1) level of activity, 2) sensory thresholds, 3) sensory adaptation and tendency to become "bored" by a stimulus, 4) quality and intensity of physiological reactions, and 5) irritability.

The active, easily bored baby tends to reach out—to "bang against" the world. He is more likely to explore his environment, find new stimuli, encounter new experiences, and come up against obstacles. He probably encounters considerable frustration early in life, but he may also learn to make a direct and vigorous attack on the obstacles. The less active, less easily bored, more contented and placid baby may encounter fewer new experiences and fewer frustrations and has less opportunity to learn about his environment and try to do something about the obstacles it contains.

The active, restless, irritable baby and the quiet, placid baby are also likely to produce quite different reactions on the part of their parents and therefore to be treated differently. The active, restless baby is likely to get into more mischief and meet with more discipline, while the placid baby stays out of trouble and meets with fewer restraints.

How the baby's inborn characteristics affect the parents depends to a considerable extent upon the atmosphere of the home and particularly upon the temperament of the mother. In a noisy home, where the parents are given to open display of affection, anger, and horseplay, the active and noisy baby may fit right in and be welcomed as a kindred spirit, while a placid baby may be viewed with disappointment and concern. In a quieter home the noisy baby may irritate the parents and be regarded with hostility rather than with affection, while the quiet baby is considered "good" and lovable.

Two mothers may react very differently to the fact that they have an irritable baby who cries often and loudly. One may regard the baby's constant fretting as a sign that he is "negative" and dislikes her, and she may come to consider him an enemy rather than an object of affection. Another mother may interpret the same kind of behavior as indicating that the baby is suffering from colic or some other physical problem, and she may wind up treating him more solicitously than if he were a quiet baby. In many ways the baby's inborn characteristics play a role in determining how the people around him will treat him and therefore affect the entire range of personal and social contacts that he will have.

There is another possible effect of inborn characteristics that has been the subject of some interesting speculation. This concerns the inborn patterns of physiological reactions—the tendency of one baby to react to stress with changes in heart rate, another with changes in breathing rate, another with skin responses, and still another with signs of digestive distress such as vomiting. It is not known whether these tendencies persist into later life. If they do, it may help account for the fact that psychosomatic diseases, caused by excessive stress, take such different forms as heart trouble, asthma, skin allergies, and stomach ulcers. A tendency toward one or another of these ailments may be present at birth or established in the early months of life.

Since physical measurements are the easiest of all to make, the baby's growth in size and in skill at motor **PHYSICAL DEVELOPMENT** performance has been the subject of many developmental studies. There is a considerable literature from which parents can learn the normal standards for height and weight at all ages from birth on and for the occurrence of such events as smiling, the appearance of the first tooth, crawling, the first step, the first recognizable word, and so on.

How the Body Develops

The newborn baby grows, as shown in FIGURE 15.1, from all head and tiny legs to an adult of quite different proportions. His skeleton, which at birth

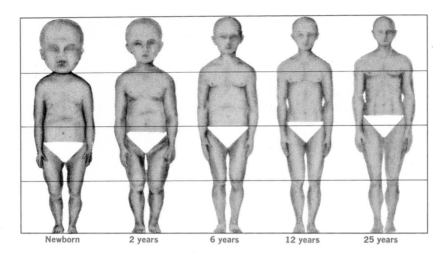

| Newborn | 2 years | 6 years | 12 years | 25 years |

Development of Body Proportions The newborn baby has a disproportionately large head and short legs; his head makes up a fourth of his total height, his legs only about a third. From birth to maturity the legs grow the most, to half the total height; and the head grows the least, becoming only about a tenth of the total height. (8)

FIGURE **15.1**

is largely composed of rather soft and pliable cartilage, hardens into bone. His baby teeth appear and later are replaced by permanent teeth. Although he has all the muscle fibers that he will ever have, these fibers grow until they eventually weigh about forty times as much as they weighed at birth. His nerve fibers grow and form additional connections to other fibers, and some of them develop protective sheaths that make them faster and more efficient conductors of nervous impulses. His brain, in particular, gains in size and weight very rapidly during the first two years, then more slowly until he is an adult.

Development of Motor Skills

Even in the womb the unborn baby begins to use his muscles; his kicking can be felt starting in about the seventh month of pregnancy. After birth his muscles of posture, crawling, and standing develop as shown in FIGURE 15.2, to the point where he is usually able to walk alone by the age of fifteen months. At first he cannot reach out and grab objects held in his visual field, but he gradually begins to reach for them as shown in FIGURE 15.3. His skill at using his hands and fingers increases rapidly as shown in FIGURE 15.4.

The ability to vocalize, which is also partly a motor skill, appears very early. In the first days of life the baby begins to utter some phonemes (the basic sounds of language). One study of babies from one to ten days old

540

Fetal posture (Newborn)

Chin up (1 month)

Chest up (2 months)

Reach (3 months)

Sit with help (4 months)

Sit on lap, grasp object (5 months)

Sit in high chair, grasp dangling object (6 months)

Sit alone (7 months)

Stand with help (8 months)

Stand holding furniture (9 months)

Crawl (10 months)

Walk with help (11 months)

Pull up (12 months)

Climb (13 months)

Stand alone (14 months)

Walk alone (15 months)

FIGURE **15.2**

From Birth to First Step
From birth to first step the child goes through a number of stages of gradually increasing motor ability. The ages indicate the average age at which each stage of development occurs. (9)

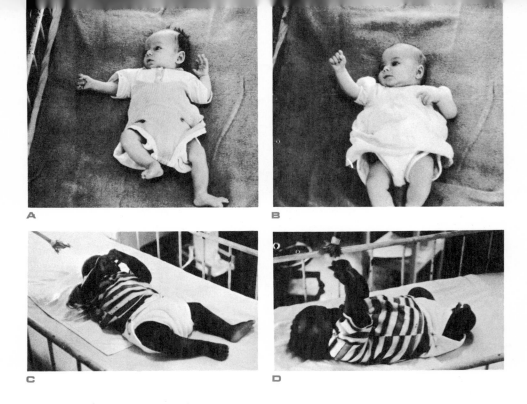

FIGURE 15.3   *First Attempts at Reaching*   How soon does the baby develop the desire and ability to grasp a brightly colored, toylike stimulus object held over his crib? The very young baby, typically lying with neck muscles holding his head to one side (A), pays only slight attention to an object (not visible in A and B). Later he occasionally watches his own hand, extended to the side toward which his head is turned (B); at this stage he will glance at an object when it is held on that side but focuses on it for only five to ten seconds at a time and makes no effort to reach it—though about two weeks later he often makes a quick, one-fisted swipe at it. By three to three and one-half months he no longer holds his head to one side and may move his hands in unison; when the object is held directly above him, he clasps his hands together beneath it (C). A little later he begins to raise his clasped hands toward the object (D). This is the final preliminary stage before he actually reaches toward the object with an open hand and attempts to grasp it. (10)

showed that all of them made the sound of *a* (as in *bat*) and that a number of them made the sound of *e* (as in *get*), *u* (as in *but*), *h* (as in *house*), and also of *w* and *k* (12). By the time the average baby is a year old he can utter eighteen different phonemes, or nearly half the number used by English-speaking adults (13).

Although the popular belief is that babies learn to make sounds by imitating their parents—much as a parrot might learn to imitate human speech

FIGURE 15.4

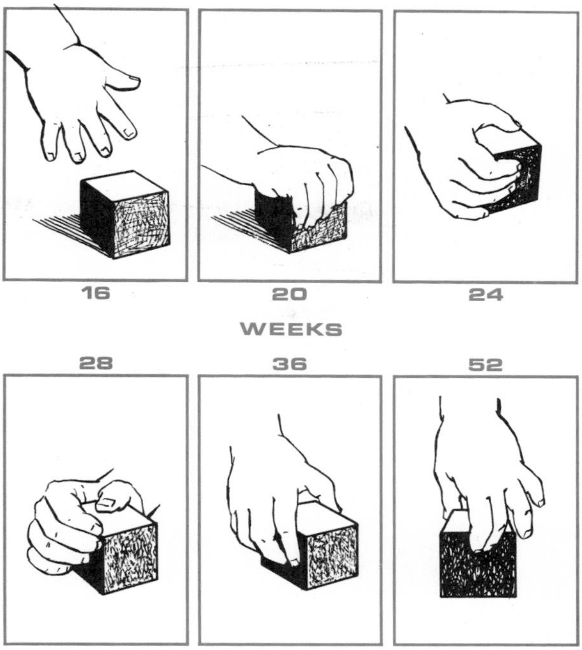

16   20   24

WEEKS

28   36   52

Development of Grasping Ability Studies made with a motion picture camera showed this sequence of development in the baby's ability at *prehension*—or grasping. The ages in weeks indicate the average age at which each stage is reached. (11)

—this is not true. The baby's first sounds appear to begin in connection with movements of the mouth, throat, and vocal cords associated with swallowing, breathing, and hiccoughing and to increase in number as the muscles and nervous system mature. The baby is not imitating sounds but originating them, as has been demonstrated by observations of a deaf baby both of whose parents were deaf and mute. During the first two months of life this baby who never heard a sound did substantially the same kind of babbling as any other (14). It also appears that children of all nationalities make the same sounds in their earliest babbling; American infants, for example, have been observed to utter phonemes that are not used by English-speaking adults but only by the French or Germans (15). It is only later that the baby, through learning from the people around him, begins to concentrate on the sounds appropriate to his own language and to eliminate the others. Rather strangely, many adult Americans who try to learn French or German are never able to pronounce some of the phonemes properly, even though they did so naturally when they were babies.

The Role of Maturation

The baby's growth and increasing skill at using his muscles are mostly the result of the process called *maturation*—physical changes, taking place after birth, that continue the biological development of the organism from fertilized egg cell to complete adult. To perform such feats as sitting alone and

543

walking, the baby must of course also do some learning, but the learning is impossible until maturation has provided the necessary muscular and nervous structures.

Babies brought up by Indian mothers who carry them about strapped to a board or by Russian mothers who keep them tightly bound in swaddling clothes appear to suffer no impairment of motor development, as can be seen in FIGURE 15.5. In an experiment with identical twins, one received intensive early training in climbing stairs, while the other did not. But a little later the twin who had not received this early training caught up with the other twin after a third as much practice (16).

Lack of opportunity to learn, however, does appear to delay and sometimes adversely affect development. The unfortunate effects of early sensory

FIGURE 15.5

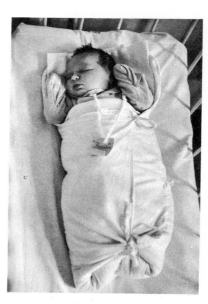

Does Swaddling Inhibit Motor Development? Russian babies are still bound tightly in swaddling clothes (*right*), a custom that was also popular at one time in the United States but has long since been abandoned in favor of greater freedom of movement. Yet Russian children appear to walk as soon and as well as any others and may grow up with the motor skills and physical grace of the girls in the Leningrad ballet class shown below.

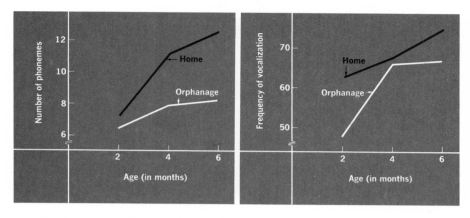

Language Development at Home and in Orphanages   Children aged
two to six months who have been reared in their own homes have
been found to utter a higher average number of phonemes than do
children of the same age in orphanages, as shown in the chart at left.
They also vocalize more frequently, as shown at right. (18)

FIGURE 15.6

deprivation have already been described (page 187). Moreover, a study of
babies brought up in institutions where they were confined to their cribs and
restricted in their opportunities to play or to sit up showed that they were
retarded in learning to walk (17). Development of language also appears to
be adversely affected among children brought up in orphanages, as shown in
FIGURE 15.6. Children brought up in middle-class homes, where presumably
their mothers talk to them frequently and thus encourage vocal responses,
appear to develop language skills considerably faster than children brought
up in working-class homes, as shown in FIGURE 15.7.

Language Development in Middle- and Working-Class Homes   Children of middle-class parents have been found to utter a somewhat
higher average number of phonemes than children of working-class
parents, as shown in the chart at left. The difference begins to appear
at about six months and becomes gradually larger. The middle-class
children also vocalize with considerably more frequency, as shown at
right. (19)

FIGURE 15.7

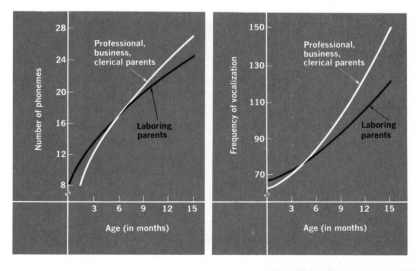

Practical Considerations

Study of physical growth and development of motor skills has established norms that are often very useful in dealing with individual babies. For example, the parents of an eight-month-old baby might have the vague feeling that he is not progressing as rapidly as he should, that he seems unresponsive to his environment. Examination by a trained observer might show that he is indeed retarded in sensory and motor development, and also in physical size, according to the standards for a baby that age. These findings might suggest the possibility of a mental defect called cretinism, which results from a deficiency of the thyroid gland. A medical examination might then verify this condition, in which case daily doses of thyroid substance, if begun early enough, can stimulate the child's physical and psychological development.

Mostly, however, the findings on physical development have their greatest practical value in relieving the fears of parents who might otherwise come to the false conclusion that their baby is retarded, simply on the basis of comparison with a previous child or a neighbor's child. Babies mature at different rates. It is not particularly unusual, for example, for a baby to sit as early as the age of four months and not alarming if sitting does not begin until he is eight months old or more. Studies also show that most babies go through stages in which development of various kinds seems to stop or even to go backward.

Another finding with practical value is that babies thrive on enriched environments—on the kind of stimulation provided by handling, fondling, and being talked to, and by ample opportunity to move about, see patterns and colors, and play with toys of various shapes and sizes. But "pushing" the baby to perform beyond his abilities is not likely to accomplish any good and may do harm. On this point, one of the most valuable lessons to parents comes from an experiment in which an attempt was made every day for seven months to teach a one-year-old baby to ride a tricycle. Not only was the experiment a failure, as might have been expected, but afterward, at the normal age for riding a tricycle, the child showed a pronounced lack of interest (20).

MENTAL DEVELOPMENT

As the baby develops physically, he also develops mentally. Even in the first months of life he makes giant strides in "operating" on and adapting to his environment—processes that are the core of intellectual ability. The very young baby presumably can deal in images, which are one of the elements of thinking. A little later he begins dealing with that even more important element, symbols—especially, beginning at about the age of two, with language. All through the preschool and early school years he uses language to acquire the third element of thinking, namely facts and premises. He also builds up an increasing ability to make the associations of thinking through the rules of logic and through that more freewheeling form of association called mediational clustering. By the time he is about eleven or twelve he perceives the world, labels it, and thinks about it much as does the adult.

The First Two Years

The Swiss psychologist Jean Piaget, whose studies have contributed greatly to the knowledge of development, calls the first two years of life the *sensorimotor period* (21). The child has not yet learned to use language to label the objects and events in his environment; he is dependent upon the raw evidence of his senses. He knows the world only in terms of his sensory impressions and his motor activities.

By the age of four to six months the child has started to operate on the environment; he will repeatedly kick at a toy that hangs over his crib, apparently to make it swing and thus produce a change of stimulus that he finds "interesting." By seven to ten months he acts to obtain a desired goal; he may knock down a pillow, for example, to get at a toy that has been hidden behind it.

Near the age of two years the child has developed to a level best described through the example of an infant girl studied by Piaget. The girl was playing with a chain and a box that had an opening too small for the chain. At any earlier age she would have tried to put the chain into the box—a tempting kind of game for a baby—before realizing that the task was impossible. In this stage of development she simply looked at the chain, then at the opening in the box, as if making a mental estimate of the possibilities, and appeared to "decide" that any attempt to put the chain into the box was futile. The incident suggests that at the end of the second year the child is capable of a kind of thinking akin to the problem solving through insight that is displayed by some animals.

Language Skill

The ability to deal with language is composed of two separate processes—*comprehension*, or understanding words, and *expression*, or speaking them. These are different processes and may be controlled by different areas of the brain (14). Comprehension is the first of the skills to develop. As is shown in FIGURE 15.8, there are indications that the child can recognize meaningful speech as early as eight months of age, and a few months later he shows signs of understanding simple requests and commands. Expression starts later but develops rapidly after the age of two.

Presumably infants learn how to use language to express themselves just as they learn anything else. Some of the sounds they make in their early

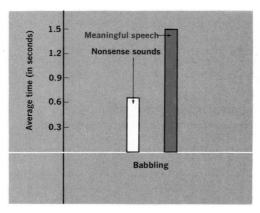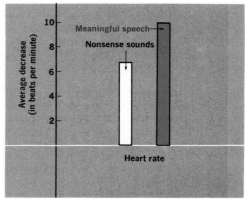

Reaction to Language by the Eight-Month-Old   As early as the age of eight months, children appear able to distinguish between speech and nonsense sounds. After a meaningful paragraph had been read to eight-month-olds, they responded with twice as much babbling of their own as when nonsense words were read to them. They also showed a greater decrease in rate of heartbeat, which is a measure of the interest an infant pays to a stimulus. (22)

FIGURE **15.8**

babbling are reinforced by the mother's smile or fondling or other behavior, and these sounds tend to be repeated. Others, not appropriate to the language spoken in the home, are not reinforced and tend to disappear. Later the child learns that he can operate on the environment by using language; just as the animal in the Skinner box can get food by pressing the bar, the baby can get food simply by saying such magic words as *milk, eat,* or *cookie.* The child is helped in his learning, of course, by examples that he can imitate. When he makes a sound that is anything like a real word, his parents usually say the real word for him and help him refine his language through a process akin to shaping, the kind of learning discussed on page 60.

The child's vocabulary increases rapidly. One study has shown that the average child can understand 3 words at the age of one year, 22 words at eighteen months, 272 words at the age of two, and 2000 words by the age of five (23). At the same time, the child's ability to express himself in sentences also shows steady and fast improvement, as is indicated by the differences in speech of a two-year-old and a three-year-old shown in FIGURE 15.9.

By the age of four the average child is constructing sentences that are quite accurate grammatically. By eight his pronunciation of words is virtually as good as an adult's. By age ten his grammar has also reached the adult level. It is interesting to note that the average American child's skill at using language apparently has increased in recent decades, as indicated by the studies summarized in FIGURE 15.10. The explanation seems to be that economic advances have resulted in enriched environments for many children and also that radio and television have provided increased stimulation.

Two-year-old girl	Three-year old girl
The rug	Hey, I found Captain Kangaroo
The pretty rug	Mummy?
Table	Can I have this?
Dish	What shall I fix with this?
Doggy tired	What did you found?
The book fall down	Won't it be fun to play with these?
Want hankie	I show you how to play animals
Other side	Hey, this is my dollie
Oh, other side	And then now I will line all mine up like this

In Language, What a Difference a Year Makes   These were the verbatim comments of two small girls, both of whom were playing with toys in the presence of their mothers and other adults. Note the much greater language skill of the three-year-old, including the ability to ask questions.

FIGURE **15.9**

FIGURE **15.10**   *Are Today's Children Better at Language?*   The average number of words used by children in a single remark or sentence was found to be higher in a 1957 study than in earlier studies reported in 1930 and in 1937. The 1957 study included children of ages three, three and one-half, four, four and one-half, five, six, seven, and eight. The 1930 study was of children aged three to four and one-half, and the 1937 study was of children aged five and one-half to nine and one-half. Note that the 1957 children seemed to show superior language ability at all ages covered by the studies. (Data for 1957, 24; for 1930, 25; for 1937, 26)

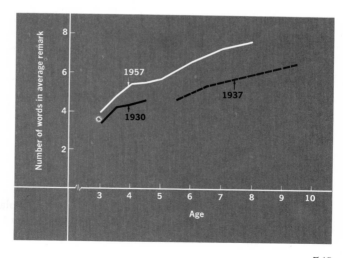

549

Language and Concepts

The use of language leads naturally to the formation of concepts, and in the early years of life the child takes at least four large steps toward developing the concepts he will use in his adult thinking and problem solving.

1. *More specific use of words.* To the three-year-old, the word *dog* may mean any four-legged animal, and the word *car* may mean any object with wheels. The word *eat* may mean the process of eating, the desire to eat, or even food. By the time he is five he has learned that words like these have a more specific meaning. He can use different words to distinguish a dog from a cat, a car from a wagon, and the process of eating from food.

2. *Acquisition of concepts.* The child learns such concepts as *animal,* to include both dogs and cats and other creatures as well, and *riding,* to include moving around in a car, a wagon, or even piggyback on his father's shoulders.

3. *Mediated generalization.* The manner in which language is used to generalize a response from one stimulus to another—the process called mediated generalization—was discussed on page 104. This process proceeds rapidly in the growing child. If the mother of an eight-month-old child hands him an object that he has never seen before and says, "Here is a piece of candy," the child is just as likely to try to play with the object or to throw it on the floor as to eat it. Once he has learned the concept of candy, however, he transfers the appropriate kind of behavior toward any new object that bears the name of candy; he pops it right into his mouth.

4. *The labels "good" and "bad."* The idea that some things are "good" and others "bad" develops quite early. An investigator who questioned preschool children found that they described a "bad" child as one who did such things as destroy objects or make a mess, disobey his mother or other adults, and cry or be cross. A "good" child was described as one who did such things as help his mother, do "nice things," play in an orderly way and dress himself, go to the toilet alone, and pick up his toys (27). Even before the school years the child appears to have acquired a solid foundation for the judgments of goodness and badness that will color much of his adult thinking and personality.

Perception

In the early weeks of life the baby clearly exhibits some inborn perceptual tendencies. He is strongly attracted to contrast; he tends to focus his eyes, as was mentioned earlier, on the apex of a black triangle seen against a white background. He is attracted to stimuli that move, such as a hand or bottle crossing his field of vision. He also seems to show a preference for visual

FIGURE 15.11

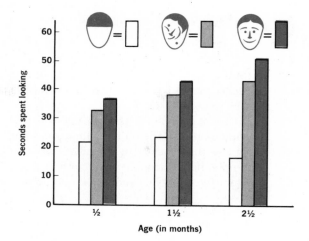

A Baby's Perceptual Preferences
The three ovals were shown to babies two at a time, in all possible pairings, for a period of two minutes. The bars show how many seconds babies of each age spent looking at each of the three. At all ages the real face and the scrambled face appeared to be considerably more "interesting" to the babies than the more simple oval with the black patch. (28)

stimuli that have a certain amount of pattern and complexity. An experiment that points to this conclusion is illustrated in FIGURE 15.11.

Learning begins to influence the baby's perception very quickly. By the age of eight to twelve months he has already started to devote his attention to stimuli that are slightly different from those with which he is most familiar—in other words, to what are called pacer stimuli (page 326). He will look for a longer time, for example, at a man who walks with an odd posture than at a man who walks normally.

Until the child is able to use language, he can only translate his sensory experiences into images. Suppose that a one-year-old sees this figure:

He can interpret it only as an image. But by the time he is six he is likely to perceive the same figure in a way that has been influenced by his language; he may say, "It looks like a finger" or "It looks like a pencil." If we show him the figure, then take it away and ask him to draw it—or ask him to find it in a group of figures that all look a little bit like it—he may make an error indicating that he perceived the figure as resembling a finger or pencil.

With increasing use of language and the increasing development of perceptual expectations based on past experience, the child's perception of the world changes rapidly. Let us say that the visual stimulus is a brown and white cow standing in a field of daisies next to a white wooden fence. To the child of one, it can be assumed, the scene is perceived merely as a pattern of figure and ground, with no one figure element outstanding. An older child perceives the scene quite differently. A child who has learned the words *daisy* and *fence* but not the word *cow* may concentrate on the objects that have a name and ignore the animal. An older child who has learned

551

the word *cow* may concentrate his attention on the animal but not notice any details such as its color. A boy who has learned to be afraid of being bitten may perceive the cow's mouth. A girl who once tore a dress on a sharp picket fence may notice at once whether the fence does or does not have pointed stakes.

Some general aspects of the development of perception are illustrated in FIGURE 15.12. The child of four tends to perceive objects as a whole and to ignore their parts. He is confused by the spatial position of objects; for example, he has trouble distinguishing the triangle shown with the base down from the triangle standing on one point. He needs considerable information

A Child's Perception To the child of about four, drawing A is likely to be perceived as "a box with lines" or "a design." The older child, at about seven or eight, notices the black dot and calls the drawing "lines and a black circle" or "a design with a black hole at the bottom." Drawing B is perceived by the four-year-old as "dirt" or "a rock"; the older child calls it "butterfly with wings and head" or "man with arms and no feet." The four-year-old has difficulty discriminating between the two triangles in drawing C and is unlikely to perceive the dashes in drawing D as a rabbit. The older child easily discriminates between the triangles and recognizes the rabbit. (1)

FIGURE **15.12**

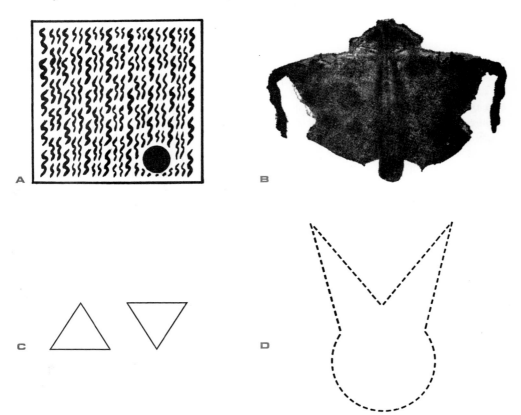

in order to recognize an object; he does not know that the dashed lines in FIGURE 15.12 represent a rabbit. Older children perceive such objects quite clearly; they can differentiate much better between stimuli that are similar but not exactly alike.

Three factors, all of which result from learning, appear to account for these various changes and refinements in perception. Two have already been mentioned: 1) the use of language labels and 2) the development of perceptual expectations. To these must be added 3) the development of motives and emotions, including anxiety—which is mediated by language. To a certain extent, the clarity of the child's perceptions is controlled by his goals and by the objects he fears. The child who is eagerly waiting for his mother to return is quicker to notice her voice or her step than the child who is less eager. The child who is afraid of lightning will be perceptually attentive at the first sign of a storm and will watch for the slightest sign of flashes in the sky.

Conceptual Intelligence

The child's varied forms of development after the age of two, when the sensorimotor period ends, have been said by Piaget to represent the stage of *conceptual intelligence*—a term that is derived from the child's increasing use of concepts to organize the evidence of his senses and to engage in ever more complex thinking and problem solving. The stage of conceptual intelligence represents a sharp break from the earlier sensorimotor period and continues into adulthood. Piaget has divided it into four substages.

1. *Preconceptual thought.* With increasing use of language the child of two or three begins to attach new meaning to the stimuli in his environment and to use one stimulus to stand as a symbol for another. At this age a girl may behave toward a doll as if it were a real child, and a boy may play with a stick as if it were a gun.

2. *Intuitive thought.* Around the age of four to six the child's concepts become more elaborate, but they are still based largely on the evidence of his senses. He can learn, for example, to select the middle-sized of three rubber balls. He attains what Piaget has called an *intuitive understanding* that the middle-sized ball is bigger than the small one but smaller than the big one. But, if three balls of very different size from the original three are then shown to him, he must learn to make the selection all over again (29). The child in the stage of intuitive thought is still fooled by the puzzle illustrated in FIGURE 15.13. Apparently the height of the jar is such an outstanding characteristic that he cannot help equating height with the number of beans the jar contains—a case in which his intuitive thought is incorrect.

FIGURE 15.13

A *Preschool Puzzle* The four-year-old child points to both of the squat jars to acknowledge that they contain an equal number of beans. But when the beans are poured from one of these jars into a tall, thin jar, he says that the tall jar then contains more beans. Not until he is six to seven years old will he state that the number of beans remains the same.

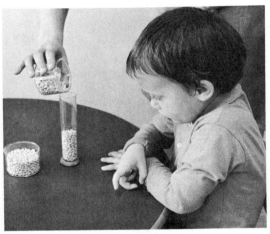

3. *Concrete operations.* The stage of *concrete operations* begins at six or seven after the child becomes aware that the number of beans does not change in the experiment illustrated in FIGURE 15.13—in other words, when he realizes that certain qualities remain constant regardless of appearances. If asked why the tall jar and the shorter jar contain an equal amount, he may say, "Well, this one is taller, but this one is fatter." A little later in the stage of concrete operations he may make the even more sophisticated statement, "If you poured the beans back from the tall jar into the other jar then it would be the same." Thus the child in the stage of concrete operations shows an ability to reason about objects, to manipulate facts, and to

apply rules. However, he still must have the objects in front of him. As Piaget's name for this stage implies, he can reason only about concrete objects; he has yet to learn to deal with abstractions.

4. *Formal operations*. Once the child has reached the age of about eleven he is released from dependence upon the actual presence of concrete objects. He can close his eyes and solve problems such as the one about the jar and the beans through the manipulation of symbols. In other words, he is now capable of thinking in the abstract like an adult. Piaget calls this stage of development *formal operations*, because the older child can apply the formal rules of logic—rules that of course are themselves abstractions.

The Course of Mental Development

At each stage of mental development the child understands only experiences and pieces of information that match the vocabulary, facts, and mediational clusters he has already acquired or that are just a bit in advance of his existing information. If a new experience or idea has no readily apparent connection to what he already knows, he is not likely to learn much if anything about it and may not even pay attention to it.

When we examine the mental ability of the adolescent and the adult, we find a complex and harmonious composite of many different mental processes, each of which began its most rapid growth and was integrated into the pattern of mental abilities at a different time. The vocabulary grew most dramatically during the period between two and five. The ability to stop and think about whether the solution to a problem is correct and to refrain from jumping to the wrong conclusion grew most rapidly between five and eight. The ability to sit with eyes closed and consider a number of hypothetical solutions to a problem increased most rapidly between nine and twelve.

There is an analogy between a description of adult intelligence and the appearance of a house. We cannot tell, by looking at the house, when or in what order the plumbing and wiring were installed. Similarly, we would not know how adult mental processes attained their rather elegant form were it not for the step-by-step observations of developmental psychology.

THE DEVELOPMENT OF PERSONALITY

As was noted on page 328, monkeys who are raised by "surrogate mothers"—even the preferred kind made of terrycloth—grow up exhibiting many symptoms of maladjustment; they are unfriendly, aggressive, and sexually incompetent. No human baby has ever been brought up by a terrycloth "surrogate," but many babies have been brought up in orphanages and other institutions where it was impossible to provide them with the constant stimulation, attention, and care that a baby ordinarily receives in the affectionate atmosphere of a good home. Studies of such children have shown that, like the monkeys in the surrogate experiment, they appear to suffer lasting damage to their personalities.

One investigator made a study of children who had spent the first three years of their lives in the impersonal atmosphere of an orphanage, then had gone to foster homes. He followed their subsequent development and compared them with a control group of children of the same age and sex who had been brought up from the start in foster homes, where presumably they had received considerably more personal care than was possible in an institution. Spending the first three years of life in an orphanage apparently left a permanent mark on the children. Compared to the control group, they were noticeably more aggressive; they showed strong tendencies to have temper tantrums, to kick and hit other children, and to lie, steal, and destroy property. They were more dependent upon adults than the control group and showed tendencies to demand attention and ask for unnecessary help. They were also more easily distracted and less self-controlled. They tended to be emotionally cold, isolated, and incapable of forming affectionate personal relationships (30).

This study is only one of many that demonstrate the importance of early experiences to the development of personality. To develop along normal lines, the child needs considerable close interaction in the early months of life with what is called a caretaker—that is to say, with his mother or another person who provides the same kind of intimate and continuing attention. Even after he has matured to the point where he is less dependent upon the caretaker, his development is greatly influenced by his contacts with other members of the family, with playmates, and later with schoolmates and teachers. The development of personality can best be understood by following it step by step through the years from birth to the age of about ten.

BIRTH TO EIGHTEEN MONTHS: THE "CARETAKER" PERIOD

Every baby, except in rare cases of abnormality, must in the nature of things suffer highly unpleasant sensations from time to time as a result of his biological drives. He suffers from the pangs of hunger, the discomfort of thirst, unpleasant sensations of heat and cold, and pain caused by pinpricks, bumps, and colic. Also in the nature of things he is unable to relieve any of these unpleasant sensations through his own efforts. He is helpless and utterly dependent upon a caretaker. Under favorable circumstances his frequent discomforts and his dependence upon the caretaker establish a firm foundation for the learning process and for the blossoming of personality. Under unfavorable circumstances they can thwart the whole course of normal development.

The Mother's "Reward Value"

At the beginning the baby's crying is a reflex response to pain or discomfort. But crying ordinarily brings the mother who relieves the discomfort—say, of the hunger pangs—and provides not only the pleasurable sensations of feeding but also the pleasures of handling, fondling, and tactual comfort. The normal baby soon learns that to cry is an effective way to obtain help. He also learns that the presence of the mother means pleasurable sensations and the relief of unpleasant sensations.

This early form of learning, representing the baby's first experience with another human being, has far-reaching results. The mother acquires "reward value"; she provides the first of the secondary reinforcements that will facilitate all the child's future learning. Moreover, through stimulus generalization her reward value becomes attached to other human beings. It is in the cradle that the child learns—if all goes well—that human beings are sources of comfort and gratification.

The Neglected Child

The importance of an affectionate and conscientious caretaker can best be demonstrated by examining what happens in other cases. Let us say that the mother did not want the baby, dislikes the idea of having him nurse, and resents the work involved in caring for him. Or perhaps she is merely anxious and tense about caring for him and therefore awkward and rather rough in handling him. Or perhaps she is ill or too busy with other duties to give him all the care he needs. Thus his cries often go unanswered. Feeding is too long delayed or becomes unpleasant because of rough handling or is broken off before the baby's hunger is fully satisfied.

In this case the mother may become a symbol of pain as well as of pleasure; besides reward value, she also acquires a negative value. The baby learns to hold mixed feelings toward her. Through the process of stimulus generalization the mother's negative value becomes attached to other people as well. It appears quite likely that—just as lasting attitudes of trust and affection for other people can be established in the first months of life by a caretaker who carefully nurtures the baby—so can attitudes of mistrust and hostility be created very early in life by a caretaker who neglects or rejects the child (31).

Neglect can have other serious effects as well. The child whose cries do not bring a caretaker to relieve his discomfort is forced to try other forms of behavior—none of which, because of his helplessness, can be constructive. He may try to get rid of the discomfort by withdrawing into sleep or by providing some kind of distracting stimulation such as pulling his hair, banging his head against the side of the crib, or monotonously rocking his body back and forth. All these are possible forerunners of types of behavior that indicate severe psychological disturbances in an older child.

Two Experiments in Caretaking

One experiment on the effects of early social experiences was performed with the equipment illustrated in FIGURE 15.14. Several groups of monkeys, raised under different conditions, were placed in the experimental chamber, which, being new and unfamiliar, presumably frightened them. Three of the groups are of particular interest to a discussion of the nurturing mother's reward value and of the neglected child. The monkeys in group 1 were raised by their own mothers, in cages where they also had contact with other baby monkeys. Those in group 2 were brought up alone in wire cages but had considerable contact with human beings who handled them, held them while feeding them from a bottle, and talked to them; these monkeys could climb the walls of the cage and see other monkeys in adjoining cages, but they had no physical contact with any other monkey. Group 3 was raised in total isolation; they did not see, hear, or touch another monkey or a human being.

The monkeys in group 1, raised by their own mothers, showed a pronounced tendency to prefer being near the other monkey in the experimental chamber. Those in group 2, brought up with human contacts but no

FIGURE **15.14**

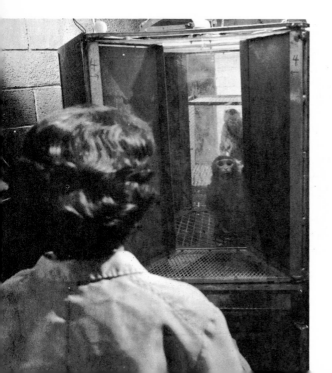

Effect of Early Social Contacts The monkey at center has just been placed in an unfamiliar and presumably frightening laboratory chamber. On one side it can see another monkey, on the other side a human being. To which of the two is it likely to run? For the answer, see the text.

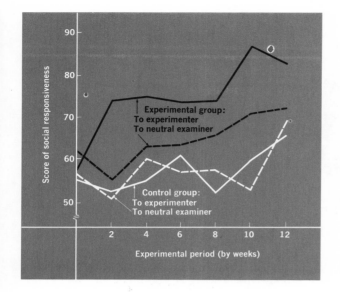

FIGURE 15.15

Social Effects of a Caretaker During a twelve-week experiment in which an experimental group of babies in an institution received specialized care by a substitute mother, these babies showed considerably higher degrees of socialization than did a control group that received no special care. Note that the social responsiveness was shown not only to the substitute mother (the experimenter) but also, though to a lesser extent, to a neutral observer. (33)

physical contacts with other monkeys, showed a strong tendency to prefer being near the human being. The group 3 monkeys, raised in isolation, spent most of the time in the middle of the chamber, as if withdrawing from any kind of social contact. When they did move to one side or the other, it was toward the monkey. For group 1 the monkey had acquired reward value, for group 2 the human being. For group 3 neither monkey nor human being had acquired much reward value (32).

An experimental study with human babies was made at an institution where the babies were living under the care of volunteer workers who served for one day a week or for several hours a day. In the course of a week, each baby might be fed or bathed by any number of women, none of whom had time to devote special attention to any one child. The investigator chose sixteen babies, all six months old, and divided them into a control group and an experimental group. The control babies continued to be cared for as before. For the other group the investigator undertook to act as a substitute mother, spending as much time with them as possible and giving them as much attention and affection as she could.

The experiment continued for twelve weeks, and each week the children were tested for signs of social response to the investigator and to another woman who served as a neutral examiner. As is illustrated in FIGURE 15.15, the children who received the benefit of the investigator's caretaking very quickly began to show more social responsiveness—not only to the investigator but also to the neutral examiner. The experiment seems to offer eloquent proof of the favorable effect of a caretaker upon the development of social behavior.

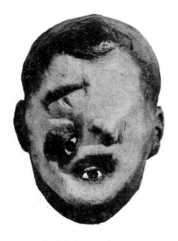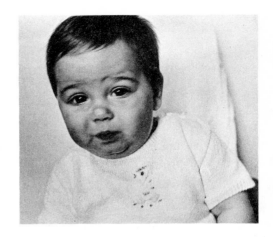

Perceptual Distortion and Anxiety Violation of perceptual expectancies makes the baby of about eight months express anxiety when he sees the distorted mask at left. At an earlier period, before he learned what the human face is supposed to look like, he might have smiled at the mask.

FIGURE **15.16**

The Beginnings of Anxiety

Another important phase of development in the first eighteen months involves the appearance of behavioral signs of anxiety. Usually this is first observed at about seven or eight months, in the form of what is called *stranger anxiety*. If the mother shows her face above the crib, the child of this age will often—though not always—smile. But, if the face is that of a stranger, the baby may show anxiety by turning away and perhaps crying.

Stranger anxiety appears at a time when the child has developed some perceptual expectations of what his mother's face looks like. When this perceptual expectation is violated, he experiences uncertainty and therefore anxiety. As illustrated in FIGURE 15.16, a similar kind of anxious behavior can be produced by presenting a distorted face to the seven- or eight-month-old child, although a younger baby usually does not cry in response to the same kind of stimulus (22).

Among babies reared in institutions, where many faces appear over the crib at various times and the baby does not learn to expect one special face, stranger anxiety is relatively uncommon. Thus stranger anxiety appears to be the inevitable result of close association with a caretaker and disproves the popular belief that any anxiety must, of necessity, indicate some kind of psychological disturbance.

Separation Anxiety

Another kind of anxiety appears around the age of ten or eleven months and can be observed in intense form at about fourteen months. This is *separation anxiety*, which is characterized by extreme upset and crying when the child sees the mother leave him or when she is away for long periods of time.

Separation anxiety has been observed under laboratory conditions by having a mother and baby enter a room containing toys. The mother sits in one corner while the child plays. Then, after a time, the mother leaves the room. Under these circumstances very few babies as young as eight months old show any sign of distress, but many thirteen-month-old babies immediately begin to cry vigorously (6).

Separation anxiety probably has its origin in the fact that the child's most intense sensations of discomfort take place in the absence of the mother. It is when she is away and cannot help him that he feels the greatest hunger or pain, and it is only when she is present that these discomforts are relieved. Thus separation anxiety, like stranger anxiety, is based upon a close relationship with the caretaker. Though anxieties are among the most unpleasant of emotions and the source of many behavioral problems, they appear to be an unavoidable result of growing up, even in the warmest and happiest kind of family.

AGES EIGHTEEN MONTHS TO THREE YEARS: THE FIRST SOCIAL DEMANDS

The second period of the child's life, roughly from eighteen months through three years, marks his first experience with the demands of society. Previously, though he was helpless and completely dependent upon the caretaker, he was nonetheless a king and a tyrant. He asked for food, water, warmth, and fondling—and received them. No one asked anything in return. Everything was given to him; nothing was demanded. Now the situation changes. He leaves the crib, which has been his own regal domain, and begins walking about the house, where he finds innumerable objects that look to him like toys provided for his own special benefit but that in fact are expensive and fragile pieces of household equipment or, like knives and electric light cords, are dangerous. For the first time, therefore, he encounters discipline; he discovers that he can no longer do whatever he pleases. The rules of the home say that he must not destroy valuable property and must not explore dangerous situations. At the same time he encounters a rule of society that says that the elimination drive must be relieved only in the bathroom; he undergoes that much-discussed process called toilet training.

His horizons widen; he leaves the self-centered environment of the crib and takes his place in the world of people, property, and property rights. Sometimes smoothly, sometimes with stormy difficulties that leave lasting blemishes on his personality, he begins to learn to become a disciplined member of society.

Punishment and Anxiety

In toilet training the child must learn *not* to do something—in this case, not to respond immediately to the sensations that call for relief of the elimination drive. Starting at about the same time, he must also learn *not* to respond to such external stimuli as the pantry full of dishes that he would like to explore or to the lamp that he would like to smash on the floor. In other words, he is learning in this period to *inhibit* forms of behavior that would ordinarily be the natural response to internal or external stimuli.

He learns partly through reinforcement in the form of reward. When he is successful in using the toilet, he is usually rewarded with praise and fondling. When he refrains from playing with a vase after being told "No," he sometimes receives the same kind of reward. But, since he is learning inhibition, he often learns mostly through punishment and anxiety. He is punished, physically or verbally, when he soils his pants, breaks something, or gets into a pantry where he does not belong. As a result of the punishment he acquires a twofold anxiety over committing the acts. He becomes anxious over the prospect of punishment and also, especially if his mother has high reward value, over losing her affection and regard. His separation anxiety (over loss of the caretaker) is now put to service in helping him become a social being. The same stimuli that urge him to an act of elimination or to explore or destroy come to arouse sufficient anxiety to inhibit what had previously been a natural kind of behavior. The closer his ties with the caretaker and the greater her reward value, the more readily does this kind of learning take place.

Exploring and Destroying

It is by exploring the world that the child comes into contact with new stimuli, develops new perceptual patterns, and learns the nature of his environment. It is by handling objects—and sometimes, unfortunately, destroying them—that he learns how to operate on the environment. He discovers that he can roam about in the world and in many cases rearrange it; he can reach for objects he wants; he can move them. He learns that he himself can satisfy many of his desires, without depending upon anyone else. By reaching into the cookie jar he can satisfy his hunger drive. By crawling under the coat that a visitor has thrown on the sofa he can find warmth.

By knocking down a tower of blocks (or by pulling down a tablecloth) he can satisfy his need for stimulus variability.

Parents who want to help their child develop along the most favorable lines face a problem at this period. The child must definitely learn to avoid danger; he must not carry his explorations to the point of risking electrical shocks, burns, or a fall from a window. He must also learn to curb his inclinations to let exploration turn into destruction. But there is a point at which the attempt to preserve the child's safety and make him a nondestructive member of society can begin to thwart his opportunities for normal development.

Some mothers are overprotective; they try to keep the child "tied to their apron strings" and object to any activity he attempts to undertake on his own. Others are too concerned with neatness and order; they scold or punish the child every time he makes the slightest amount of mess, gets the least bit dirty, or merely touches a newly waxed tabletop. When disciplined by an overprotective or overly neat mother, the child can acquire a crippling amount of anxiety. His fear of punishment or disapproval may generalize to any new object or new activity. He may therefore grow up with strong inhibitions against trying anything at all that is novel or challenging, including attempts to make adjustments to other people. Thus too strong an attempt to curb the child's inclination to explore and destroy may incline him to develop into a timid and fearful adult who lacks confidence in his own ability to cope with the world and with social relations.

The mother who is somewhat more permissive during this difficult period, on the other hand, sets the stage for spontaneous, self-reliant, and effective behavior. Though she must stop the child at times, she does not do so except when absolutely necessary. When he tries something new that is constructive, such as trying to draw pictures or ride a tricycle, she encourages and rewards him. Thus he learns that only some kinds of exploratory behavior are forbidden, not all, and that in fact many kinds are considered "good." He discovers that curiosity and new attempts to operate on the environment are approved, and he develops independence and self-confidence.

Why Toilet Training Is Important

The psychoanalysts believe that toilet training is a critical experience for the growing child because it concerns parts of the body that are "erogenous zones." Its importance can also be explained on much simpler grounds. Toilet training is often the child's first experience with discipline; most mothers begin it before the child is capable of moving around sufficiently to require restraint on the matter of exploration and destruction. Moreover, it is discipline with a sharp and unmistakable focus. The child is asked to inhibit two and only two very distinct kinds of behavior, defecation and urination, which are urgent responses to the stimuli of compelling biological drives. The child's desire to knock over an expensive vase can be made to disappear by putting the vase on a shelf out of his reach. But the desire to satisfy the biological drive for elimination whenever and wherever it occurs cannot be set aside in any such easy fashion.

Thus, in our society, toilet training usually represents the first major social demand to be put upon the child. If the situation were different and mothers were determined to teach their children to cut food with a knife and fork before they learned any other social grace, it is quite possible that "eating training" would be as prominent a topic of discussion as toilet training now is. (We might even have a society in which jokes about eating replaced today's frequent jokes about going to the toilet, which seem to be the self-conscious product of a continuing anxiety over the present childhood situation.)

Harsh Training and Its Results

Research findings are in general agreement that toilet training is best delayed until the child has matured to the point where he is "ready for it." His physical and neurological development does not appear to reach the level where he is capable of reliable bowel and bladder control until he is about eighteen months old, and training seems to be accomplished most easily and smoothly if delayed to the age of twenty months (34). Most mothers, however, begin training before eighteen months, at a time when the child has great difficulty learning to do what is expected of him. Because the learning process is therefore often slow, some mothers resort to rather harsh methods, using severe disapproval or physical punishment.

Harsh toilet training may be less important in its own right than as an indication of the mother's general attitude toward the child. As one investigator found, mothers who were harsh about toilet training also tended to display "a rather pervasive quality of strictness . . . . They had more tendency to drive rather than lead their children and they used a more punitive kind of discipline"(34). At any rate, harsh toilet training is believed to be correlated with at least four types of lasting damage to the child's personality.

NEGATIVE PERCEPTION OF THE MOTHER   If the mother's behavior during toilet training is harsh, and particularly if her previous reward value has been low, the child may acquire strong fears of her. He may begin to perceive her negatively, as a source of anxiety rather than of pleasure, and may reject the reinforcement that she could otherwise provide in helping him learn the skills he must acquire to become a mature person.

LOWERED SELF-ESTEEM   To the young child, parents are all-wise and all-knowing. He accepts their judgments on all matters, including his own value as a person. He also has difficulty discriminating between their general attitude toward him as an individual and their attitudes toward his specific behavior. Thus a child who is scolded for toilet training accidents and constantly told that he is "naughty" or "dirty" may come to think of himself as unworthy and unwanted.

AGGRESSION AND OTHER BEHAVIORAL PROBLEMS   Harsh toilet training can represent a form of frustration, and one of the frequent reactions to frustration is aggression. The harshly treated child may scream, bite, and kick. Or his aggression may take an indirect form; he may refuse to empty bowel or bladder while held on the toilet, then soil his pants immediately afterward. This aggression, and other forms of antisocial behavior associated with it, may persist into later life. Studies made in later childhood of children who underwent severe toilet training have shown not only aggression (35) but also such characteristics as negativism (36) and rigid and compulsive behavior (37). One study of problem children who were receiving treatment at a child guidance clinic for such symptoms as restlessness, tics, speech disturbances, and excessive fears of school showed that more than half of them had been toilet trained too early or quite harshly (38).

SEXUAL PROBLEMS   Because of the close connection between the organs of elimination and the organs of sexual function, anxiety over toilet training can become generalized into an anxiety over sex. Overly severe toilet training may be a forerunner of adult beliefs that sexual behavior is "dirty" or shameful and, therefore, contribute to such problems as frigidity and impotence.

AGES FOUR AND FIVE: THE PRE-SCHOOL YEARS

The preschool child is no longer a baby: he uses language and concepts; he is beginning to roam outside the home and play with other children; he may go to nursery school or kindergarten. The years of four and five witness some important changes. The child develops his first feelings of guilt, representing the workings of that rather strange mechanism called conscience. He learns that the world is divided into males and females, for whom society decrees quite different roles; the boy begins to take on characteristics that are appropriate to the male, and the girl takes on characteristics appropriate to the female.

One important reinforcement for the preschool child's learning continues to be provided by his parents in the form of praise and other rewards. He also molds his behavior in order to avoid disapproval or punishment and anxiety over these two unpleasant events. However, a new factor now enters. This is the period in which he begins to identify with his parents and to try to imitate them.

Identification

The nature of the process of *identification* is a matter of controversy. To the psychoanalysts it is a complex process that involves the Oedipus complex and the superego. To many psychologists it has a somewhat different meaning—mostly that the child thinks of himself as being like his parents and tries to imitate their behavior so that he can share vicariously in their strengths, virtues, skills, and triumphs. He notes that there are certain resemblances between him and his parents; for one thing, they bear the same family name, and, for another, he may be told that he looks like them. He generalizes these resemblances into the belief that he and his parents share a vital bond of similarity.

Children often tend to behave as their parents behave even more than as their parents wish. This becomes apparent during the school years, when pronounced differences in performance are found between children who grow up in middle-class homes where the parents show an active interest in study and knowledge and those from lower-class homes where this interest does not exist. Even though parents in lower-class homes may actively urge their children to study hard and punish them if they do not get good grades, nonetheless they do not provide the kind of model for identification that could best motivate their children to achievement in school.

Children with intelligent parents generally come to think of themselves as intelligent. A boy whose father holds a job requiring physical strength usually begins to think of himself as being strong, and a girl with an attractive mother thinks of herself as being attractive. Unfortunately, children identify with their parents' faults as well as with their virtues and it is not unusual for children to become aware of considerable criticism of their parents. They may be able to see for themselves that a father is unable to hold a job and is the object of ridicule in the community or that a mother drinks too much and is unwelcome in the houses of her neighbors. They may hear criticism of their parents from relatives or from a mother who, having divorced their father, tells them bitter stories about his conduct. Under these circumstances many children develop the belief that they too are unworthy, unlovable, hateful, stupid, lazy, or mean. Many children treated in guidance clinics for psychological problems have a background of identification with a "bad" parent.

As is shown in FIGURE 15.17 it has been found that a substantial number of delinquent boys come from homes in which a parent died. It has also been found that more delinquent than nondelinquent children come from

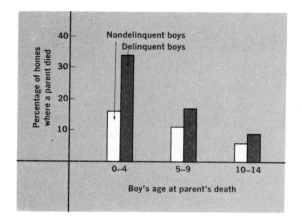

FIGURE 15.17

When a Parent Dies A study of the home backgrounds of delinquent boys, as compared to a matched control group of nondelinquent boys, found that considerably more of the delinquents had lost a parent through death—particularly when they were very young. (39)

homes where one parent was not present because of divorce. There are many ways in which the death of a parent or divorce can adversely affect the child's development, but certainly one possibility is that they interfere with the normal process of identification.

Conscience

One of the roles of parents is to provide discipline—to set standards, prohibit certain acts, and, when necessary, deal out punishment. Through reward and punishment and also through identification with the parents the child begins in the preschool years to develop what is generally called a conscience. The child of two who spills his milk experiences anxiety over the possibility of punishment or disapproval. The child of four experiences a different kind of anxiety; he feels *guilt*. His own conscience provides the disapproval.

Conscience and feelings of guilt develop in connection with the motive to live up to standards. Apparently the child first attempts to behave in accordance with what other people expect of him. Then he internalizes these expectations and turns them into his own standards. One of his first standards concerns toilet habits. At the start of toilet training he feels afraid when he has an accident, because he expects disapproval or punishment. Later he himself sets the standards and feels shame or guilt. Other early standards depend largely upon the family situation and the type of conduct that is approved or disapproved by the parents; they may concern aggression, displays of anger, dependent behavior, crying, or sexual play.

Sex Typing

Every society assigns different roles to men and women; they are expected to have different duties, attitudes, and standing in the community (40). The roles are not always the same as in our modern Western civilization. In some

567

societies, for example, men do most of the housework and women do most of the gainful labor. But, whatever the particular customs of the society, men are expected to act like men and women like women.

Children appear to become aware of this fact as early as the preschool years. When children are shown pictures of various objects and activities concerned with play—such as dolls, guns, kitchen utensils, cowboys, and Indians—and asked which they prefer, there are differences between boys and girls even at the age of three and quite pronounced differences at the ages of four and five (41).

The preschool boy seems to be asking, "How masculine am I?" and the girl to be asking, "How feminine am I?" Children of four and five are already developing the notions, which will come into full flower later, that women should be pretty and preferably small, while men should be tall and strong; that women should be passive, dependent, and submissive toward men, while men should be active, aggressive, and dominant. Their feelings of how well they measure up to these ideals are beginning to play an increasing part in their evaluation of themselves and their roles in society.

AGES SIX TO TEN: THE CHILD AND HIS PEERS   When the child starts first grade, an entirely new dimension enters his life. Up to this point his chief social contacts and sources of learning have been his parents and possibly his brothers and sisters. Now he comes into intimate contact with his own peer group—boys and girls of the same age, with whom he shares the experiences of school and of play. He also comes under the influence of his teachers. The home is still an important factor in his development, but other factors begin to play an increasing role. As the child takes his place in his own society, many developments take place in his self-evaluation, motives, standards, sources of anxiety, and defenses against anxiety.

The Child in School

Entering the first grade usually represents the child's first separation from the mother for a large part of the day. Now there is a new adult to whose discipline he must conform and whose acceptance he must court. Ordinarily the teacher is a woman, like the mother, and the child's behavior toward the mother is readily generalized toward her. Boys who are identifying with their fathers and rebelling against their mothers, however, often have trouble in the early grades. They may be less fearful of rejection by the teacher and therefore more reluctant to accept her influence. Boys typically get lower grades and cause more disciplinary problems in the lower grades than do girls.

The teacher usually plays a dual role in the child's development. In the first place she teaches the intellectual skills considered appropriate to our culture. In the second place, and perhaps even more important to personality development, she tries to encourage intellectual mastery. It is in the early years of school that the child acquires internal standards of intellectual mastery and begins to feel anxiety if he does not live up to these standards. By the age of ten, largely because of the school experience, many children have developed a pronounced fear of failure. The desire to avoid the anxiety attached to failure can become one of the strongest of motives.

The teacher also helps instill many of the social habits and attitudes of our particular culture. Usually she has a middle-class set of values; she rewards obedience, neatness, cooperation, and cleanliness and punishes disobedience and aggressiveness. This is one reason that children from the lower social classes and less educated homes generally have a more difficult time in school than do children from middle-class and well-educated homes.

The Influence of Peers

To the child of six through ten his peers take on a particular importance for three reasons.

1. *Evaluation.* It is by comparing himself with his classmates that the child judges his own value. By school age he has lost his original faith in the wisdom of adults; he seems to sense that his parents are either too full of praise for his virtues or too critical of his faults. He gets a more realistic reading, he seems to feel, from his relations with other children. For one thing, he can make a direct comparison; he can determine his rank among his classmates on such attributes as intelligence, strength, and skills of various kinds. For another thing, the opinion his classmates hold of him seems more objective, honest, and easily interpreted than his parents' opinion. He can see for himself whether other children his own age regard him as competent and likable or foolish and unpleasant.

2. *Assignment of role.* It appears to be a characteristic of human society, at least in our own kind of civilization, that every group has a leader, a "closest adviser" to the leader, and a scapegoat on whom the group takes out its aggressions. Often there are also an intellectual giant (or wise man), a court jester (or clown), and perhaps a rebel and a psychopath. These roles, into which individuals naturally gravitate or are pushed by the others, are found in groups of children as well as of adults. Once a child has achieved or been assigned a role in his group, he usually takes it seriously, receives some kind of satisfaction from it, and begins to take on more and more of the appropriate traits. The leader of the boys in the first grade, for example, is likely to develop many of the techniques of skilled leadership, while the class clown develops an increasingly buffoonlike personality.

3. *Rebellion.* Most school children, particularly boys, are to some degree in rebellion against the adult world—especially against its restrictions on the display of hostility and its demands for cleanliness, order, and quiet. In the society of his peers the growing child finds a place where he can express his hostilities, make a mess, be noisy, and do all the other things that the adult world forbids—and receive the admiration of his classmates rather than disapproval.

In a sense, children function for one another as psychotherapists. They help each other toward an objective evaluation of their own talents and position in society. They give each child a role to play and provide models that the child can identify with and imitate. They provide an outlet for feelings such as hostility on which the adult world frowns. Thus it is not at all surprising that the child begins in the years from six through ten to learn more from his peer group than from anyone else.

The Peer Group's Verdict

Since much of the child's personality development in the early school years depends upon the attitude his peers have toward him and the role they assign him, it is important to inquire into the factors that make a child more or less acceptable in children's society.

The factors have been found to differ by sex and to a certain extent by age. In the first grade, for example, the most popular boys are those who show physical strength and daring. The most popular girls are those who are gentle, kind, and not inclined to make trouble. In later grades boys appear to be judged mostly by their fairness at play and leadership ability. Fifth-grade girls are judged mostly on attractiveness and friendliness.

In general, two types of children are likely to be valued most highly by their peers. One type shows strong, positive characteristics such as leadership, enthusiasm, and active participation in the group. The other type is valued for a friendly attitude and cheerful disposition (42). Boys who appear frightened, passive, and too easily "pushed around" tend to be rejected, as do girls who are unfriendly or socially awkward.

One study of a number of groups of boys and girls in a summer camp showed that those who were highly regarded by their peers were well aware of their position, tended to feel more secure and accepted than did the others, and were able to influence the behavior of the others (43). The study was of children who were past the early school ages, but it seems to indicate that children in the six to ten age group are becoming increasingly aware of their standing in the community of their peers and that their standing strongly influences their self-evaluation, their personality development, and the part they play in the group.

Dominance and Submission

One personality characteristic that becomes partially set by the end of the early school years is the child's tendency to be dominant or submissive in his relations with other people. The child of ten who actively makes suggestions to the group, tries to influence and persuade others, and resists pressure to make him conform is likely to remain dominant in his social relations for the rest of his life. The child, especially the girl, who is quiet and readily follows the lead of others is likely to remain passive and submissive.

The tendency to be dominant or submissive is partly learned in the home, but it is also a function of group acceptance. The child who believes he has characteristics that are admired by the group is likely to develop self-confidence and to be dominant; the child who does not consider himself admired by the group is likely to develop feelings of inferiority and to be submissive. The child's physical attributes are important. The large, strong boy and the attractive girl are more likely to be dominant, the small boy and the unattractive girl to be submissive. Other factors are identification with a dominant or submissive parent and also the kind of control exercised by the parents. Permissive parents tend to influence their children in the direction of being dominant, while parents who restrict their children's activities tend to influence them in the direction of being submissive.

Motives and Standards

Another change that occurs in the early school years concerns the relative importance of motives and standards. The desire to live up to standards gradually begins to take top position in the hierarchy. For example, a four-year-old girl values her mother's kiss for its own sake; she has a motive to obtain signs of affection. By the time she is eight she is likely to have developed a standard that in effect says, "I should be valued by my parents." Her desire to live up to this standard of being valued is more general than her earlier motives for affection and more difficult to satisfy.

Four important standards that begin to take form in the early school years are as follows:

1. Being valued by parents and peers.
2. Mastery of physical and mental skills.
3. Behavior appropriate to sex typing—particularly strength, independence, and athletic skills among boys and conformity, dependence, and inhibition of aggression among girls.
4. Cognitive consonance between thoughts and behavior. (The child wants to behave rationally and sensibly and in a way that confirms his self-concept and his identification with his parents and other heroes.)

By the age of ten many of the child's standards are well-defined and have been patterned into hierarchies that are likely to persist into later life.

Anxieties and Defenses

Because of the rapid development of standards, children in the early grades of school tend to develop new anxieties connected with meeting these standards. They acquire anxieties and feelings of guilt about a wide variety of activities, especially those connected with achievement, sex typing, dependence, independence, aggression, submission, and sexual behavior. They also begin to show pronounced preferences for the various defenses against anxiety; some develop a tendency to withdraw, others to use rationalization, projection, denial, reaction formation, or the other defense mechanisms.

Children who are unsuccessful at coping with their anxieties in this period begin to display many of the symptoms of neurosis that are found in adults. These include abnormal phobias (often resulting in nightmares), stereotyped behavior such as ritualistic hand washing, obsessions, tics, and psychomatic ailments such as headaches, asthma, vomiting, skin disturbances, and even ulcers.

By the time the child is ten he is a vastly different organism from the helpless baby in the crib. He has grown physically and is capable of performing a wide variety of motor skills. He has mastered the language and acquired an almost staggering number of concepts, facts, and premises. His

Same Stimulus, Different Response Two New York City schoolboys exhibit very different reactions to a speech by their mayor—indicating personality differences that may still be apparent when they grow up.

FIGURE 15.18

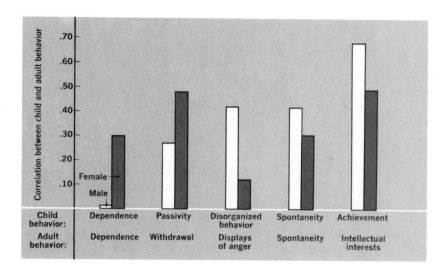

How Child Foreshadows Adult   The bars show the correlations between the behavior of boys and girls and their behavior later, as young adults. The children rated for dependence, passivity, and disorganized behavior were aged six to ten; those rated for spontaneity and achievement were ten to fourteen. (44)

FIGURE 15.19

personality has developed in a host of directions; and individual differences in personality among children of about that age are readily apparent to anyone who watches their behavior—even when caught in static moments like the postures of the two boys in FIGURE 15.18.

Many of the personality traits that the child has acquired will be carried through adolescence and into adult life, as indicated by the correlations illustrated in FIGURE 15.19. The trend of his physical development and the pattern of his mental processes have also been established. Thus the child's personality, physique, and thinking at ten offer a reasonably accurate preview of what he will be like as an adult and an indication of the kind of role he is likely to play in society.

SUMMARY

1. *Developmental psychology* studies the processes by which the child acquires his patterns of overt behavior, thinking, and problem solving and the motives, emotions, conflicts, and ways of coping with conflicts that will go to make up his adult personality.
2. Babies appear to differ at birth not only in capacity for physical devel-

573

opment but also in a) level of activity, b) sensory thresholds, c) sensory adaptation, d) physiological reactions, and e) irritability.

3. Inborn differences affect development chiefly in two ways: a) the active, easily bored baby is likely to encounter more stimulation and frustration than is the less active, less easily bored, and more placid baby, and b) the active and irritable baby may produce different reactions from his parents and thus be treated differently from the quiet and placid baby.

4. The ability to vocalize is a motor skill that appears in the first days of life and becomes more varied and differentiated as the child's muscular and nervous structures mature.

5. One important developmental process is *maturation*—physical changes, taking place after birth, that continue the biological development of the organism from fertilized egg cell to complete adult.

6. Physical maturation includes changes in proportions of the body, hardening and growth in length of the bones, increased size and weight of the muscle fibers, and changes in the nerve fibers, which include the formation of new connections to other fibers and, for some fibers, protective sheaths that make them faster conductors of nervous impulses.

7. Motor skills such as crawling and walking cannot be learned until maturation has made the child ready for them. Although lack of opportunity to learn and to exercise muscles appears to delay and sometimes adversely affect development, "pushing" the child into early performance may sometimes be harmful.

8. Mental development, like physical development, proceeds in an orderly and predictable fashion, partly through maturation and partly through learning. According to Piaget, the baby goes through a *sensorimotor period* from birth to the age of two, then a stage of *conceptual intelligence*, which is divided into four substages: a) *preconceptual thought*, ages two and three; b) *intuitive thought*, ages four through six; c) *concrete operations*, ages seven through ten; and d) *formal operations*, ages eleven through adulthood.

9. Skill in the use of language develops rapidly—from an average vocabulary of 3 words understood at the age of one to 22 words at eighteen months, 272 words at two, and 2000 words at five.

10. Concept formation in the early years of life includes a) increased specificity attached to words, b) acquisition of concepts, c) mediated generalization, and d) the use of connotations of "good" and "bad."

11. Perceptual development results in an improved ability to perceive parts as well as the whole, to distinguish spatial position, and to recognize an object from fewer clues.

12. Healthy personality development in the first eighteen months is usually characterized by a close relationship with the mother, who acquires

reward value and provides reinforcement for further learning, and by the appearance of *stranger anxiety* and *separation anxiety*.

13. The period from eighteen months through three years is characterized by the first experiences with the demands of society, in the form of toilet training and restraints on the urges to explore and destroy.

14. Among the types of lasting damage to the personality that may be associated with harsh toilet training are a) negative perception of the mother, b) lowered self-esteem, c) aggression and other behavioral problems, and d) sexual problems.

15. In the four- and five-year-old period the child identifies with his parents; develops standards, feelings of guilt, and a conscience; and acquires his first notions of sex typing and conduct appropriate to males and females.

16. In the early school years, at ages six through ten, the child is strongly influenced by his teachers, who not only help him acquire intellectual skills but also foster the motive for intellectual mastery. By the age of ten the child ordinarily has acquired strong anxieties attached to failure at mastery.

17. Another strong influence on the child of six through ten is his peers, who provide a) evaluation, b) role assignment, and c) an opportunity for rebellion against the restraints of the adult world.

18. The years six through ten are characterized by development of tendencies to be dominant or submissive, to establish sex role and mastery standards, and to adopt preferred defenses against anxiety.

RECOMMENDED READING

Flavell, J. H. *The developmental psychology of Jean Piaget.* Princeton, N.J.: Van Nostrand, 1963.

Hoffman, M. L. and Hoffman, L. W. *Review of child development research,* Vol. I. New York: Russell Sage Foundation, 1964.

Kagan, J. and Moss, H. A. *Birth to maturity: a study in psychological development.* New York: Wiley, 1962.

Kuhlen, R. and Thompson, G. G., eds. *Psychological studies of human development,* 2nd ed. New York: Appleton-Century-Crofts, 1963.

Mussen, P. H. *The psychological development of the child.* Englewood Cliffs, N.J.: Prentice-Hall, 1963.

Mussen, P. H., Conger, J. J., and Kagan, J. *Child development and personality,* 2nd ed. New York: Harper & Row, 1963.

Mussen, P. H., Conger, J. J., and Kagan, J. *Readings in child development and personality.* New York: Harper & Row, 1965.

Stendler, C. B., ed. *Readings in child behavior and development,* 2nd ed. New York: Harcourt, Brace & World, 1964.

MAN AND HIS SOCIETY

The Functions of Society
Social Versus Nonsocial Experience
Society's Norms
Why People "Obey" Norms
Culture and Social Structure
      Norms and Social Class; Differences in Norms; Barriers Between
      Classes; Upward Mobility

POSITION AND ROLE

The Categories of Position
The Nature of "Role"
Role and Personality

CONFORMITY

Conformity, Counterconformity, and Independence
Milgram's Experiment on Conformity
The Asch Experiment
The Crutchfield Experiments
Group Factors in Conformity
Individual Factors
Conformity Proneness

ATTITUDES

The Sources of Attitudes
Why Attitudes Persist
Attitudes and "Balance"
Applications of Balance Theory
Dissonance Theory
Dissonance and Attitude Change
Influencing Attitudes and Opinions

GROUPS AND LEADERS

The Qualities of Leadership
The Specialist and the "Great Man"
Group Dynamics

CHAPTER
16

SOCIAL PSYCHOLOGY

The scene is a street corner where a neon sign brightly spells out the command: WAIT. Several hundred pedestrians are observed to approach the corner. Almost all of them wait until the signal changes; only 1 percent violate the command. Now, while pedestrians are waiting at the corner, a rather untidy young man in denim shirt, patched trousers, and scuffed shoes proceeds to cross against the light. How many will be inclined to follow him? How many would follow a young man wearing a neat suit, white shirt, and hat?

This series of events took place in a well-known experiment on the effect of social influence. The young man in the denim shirt was a graduate student, and the well-dressed young man was the same student on a different occasion. As it turned out, 4 percent of pedestrians followed him through the "wait" signal when he wore the shabby clothes, 14 percent when he was dressed neatly (1).

This is only one of many experiments that have demonstrated the importance of social stimuli to human behavior. To a very considerable extent, all of us behave as we see the people around us behave or as we believe they expect us to behave. Our thinking is also molded in large part by the people around us. To a greater degree than most of us ever realize, we are the products of our social environments. Our development from child to adult, as was shown in the previous chapter, takes place not in a vacuum but in close interaction with our parents, families, teachers, and schoolmates. Our actions and mental life as adults are still shaped by others. Hence the importance of *social psychology*, which studies the behavior of the individual in his society and the influence that the actions and attitudes of the other members of his society have upon his overt behavior and his thinking.

Unlike some animals, man does not prowl the world
alone or with no company save that of a mate. Man
is a social animal. Ever since he appeared on the face of the earth he seems
to have lived in some kind of community, probably starting with the ancient
cave communities. When civilized man first came to America, he found the
Indians living in communities; the most primitive people still left in the
undeveloped parts of today's world are banded together in some kind of
mutual living arrangements. As was seen in the previous chapter, the human
baby cannot develop normally without close contacts with other human
beings. Similarly the human adult appears to need the company and cooperation of other human beings if he is to survive.

Society is the name applied to any organized group of people, large or
small. The people living in a group of jungle huts in Africa make up a society; so do the people living in a small Midwestern town or in New York
City. The United States itself is a society. Or one may speak of the entire
Western world as a society.

The Functions of Society

At first glance there seem to be such vast differences among societies that
one could hardly hope to generalize about the ways in which they function.
There seems to be no comparison, for example, between the African jungle
community and New York City. Yet studies have shown that the simplest of
societies and the most complex do in fact have a great deal in common. The
basic functions they perform are remarkably similar.

The essential function of every society—small or large, primitive or modern—is to do a better job than any individual man can do of providing the
necessities of life, such as food, shelter, and protection against enemies. To
accomplish this, all societies have adopted very similar methods. All of them
have set up some kind of division of labor by assigning different people in
the community to different kinds of jobs—such as hunter, fisherman, grower
of crops, builder of shelter, maker of clothing, cook, priest, and teacher. All
of them have set up some kind of system of communication, ranging from
primitive sign languages to modern communications satellites that bounce
radio, telephone, and television signals around the world. All of them have
established agreements about some of the essential concepts used in the society
—such as the agreement of the American Indians on the value of wampum
and the agreement in today's United States on the meaning of words such
as crime and justice.

Over and above the functions performed in the service of providing the
necessities of life, society develops a shared set of goals. In some societies
these are quite simple, consisting merely in the desire to live as comfortably

and peaceably as possible amid the bounties of nature. In the United States the goals are more complex and abstract; among them, as our Declaration of Independence states, are the preservation of life, liberty, and the pursuit of happiness. Society also sets rules that will help it attain its goals—such as laws against slavery, trespass, and murder. It attempts to hold down disruptive forms of behavior, through social disapproval and in more complex societies through the police and the courts of law. It also sets more informal rules for the expression of emotions, particularly of hostility and sexuality; it establishes standards for interaction with others—what we call courtesy and good taste.

Finally, every society functions in ways that attempt to guarantee that the society itself will survive. It provides for its own renewal, from one generation to the next, through customs and laws regarding courtship, marriage, and reproduction. It also provides for socialization—the training of the young in the ways of the society. In primitive societies this training may be done mostly by the family; in the United States it is accomplished not only in the family but through a school system on which the nation spends many billions of dollars a year.

These are the ways in which all societies seem to function (2). Listing them provides an eloquent statement of the wide-ranging and ever present influence that a society exerts on its members. As the list indicates, the child is born into a community that immediately begins to socialize him. He fills a position assigned by society; he finds a mate and reproduces according to the customs and laws of society; and, when he dies, the ceremonies and the display of emotions at his funeral are regulated by social custom.

Social Versus Nonsocial Experience

To this somewhat theoretical view of the importance of society's influence on human behavior, the evidence from an interesting study can be added. In this study, made in a small Midwestern community, the behavior of eight children was observed throughout the course of an entire day, and each separate one of their activities was listed. The mean number of behavioral acts that day was 969 for each child. Of this total, only 1 percent were "nonsocial"—that is to say, occuring when the child was alone. The great majority of acts, 85 percent, were "social"—that is, actions taken in relation to another person or persons. The others were termed "potentially social"—meaning that another person was present, although the child's action was not taken in relation to that person.

Significant here are the high proportion of "social" activities and the further finding that in 80 percent of these cases there was an interaction, in that the person to whom the child's behavior was directed responded in turn to the child. The figures may be somewhat inflated by the fact that an observer was present, but nonetheless they indicate the significant extent to which the waking hours of children are filled with social experiences (3). Even in childhood the individual is above all else an acting and interacting member of society.

Society's Norms

One of the ways society influences the individual is through what are known as *norms*, or mutually shared standards and expectations. Every society has a large number of norms regulating almost all kinds of behavior. The norms decree what kind of language will be spoken and what rules of grammar will be followed. They decree what kind of education the children will have, where and how people eat and go to the toilet, how they find and treat their mates, and how they bring up their children.

Norms frequently differ rather widely from society to society. In the United States, for example, all of us are expected to behave in accordance with such norms as driving on the right side of the road, eating with a knife and fork, having only one husband or wife at a time, dressing (usually) in men's suits and women's dresses, and being on time for business appointments. The norms in England call for driving on the left side of the road; in the Orient, for eating with chopsticks; in some Middle Eastern countries, for having many wives and dressing in robes and turbans; in many Latin countries, for disregarding clocks and appointment times.

Societies can even establish norms for perceptual processes, a fact that has been demonstrated in an experiment involving the autokinetic illusion that was described on page 157. In this illusion, you will recall, a stationary point of light seen in an otherwise totally dark room appears to move. In the experiment three persons viewed such a light together and were asked to call out, as soon as they were sure, how many inches the light had moved. The first time the light was shown, the three subjects tended to differ rather widely; one subject might say the light had moved 2 inches, another 8 inches, another 12 inches. On later trials the three judgments tended to shift closer together; the three subjects who had originally seen movement of anywhere from 2 to 12 inches now agreed that the light had moved around 6 to 8 inches.

Each group of three subjects developed its own consensus; the group might decide that the light had moved only a little or that it had moved a considerable distance. Within each group, however, there developed a general agreement—a "norm" that was accepted by all three members. When the subjects later were tested alone, they continued to perceive the motion as being within the agreed-upon range (4). Thus do social pressures, taking the form of mutually shared expectations called *norms*, influence even the way the world is perceived.

Why People "Obey" Norms

In civilized societies many norms are enforced by law and by the threat of formal punishment—such as the norms stating that a member of our society must not kill or rob, under penalty of going to prison. But we also obey norms for more informal reasons. One of them is to avoid punishment in the form of social disapproval. In many societies social ostracism has been the most feared of all punishments; in our own society the fear of disapproval by others remains a powerful force. For all of us, one reason we study in school, work at our jobs, mind our manners, are polite to strangers, wait our turn in line, and keep our tempers is our fear that to do otherwise would make us social outcasts.

Just as we seek to avoid punishment by social disapproval, we also seek rewards in the form of admiration and praise from other members of our society—which we are most likely to get if we obey the norms. A final reason for obeying the norms is identification with our parents and other prominent members of society; we tend to adopt the standards of these people as our own inner standards of behavior.

Culture and Social Structure

As has been noted, societies differ; they have different norms. Indeed the same society usually contains subsocieties that provide quite different social environments; the social environment of a college fraternity, for example, is quite different from that of a street corner gang. In discussing society's influence on the individual it is necessary to consider two aspects that are common to all societies: *culture* and *social structure.*

Culture can be defined as a pattern of norms—including customs, beliefs, values, and ideals—that a society develops and passes along to its new generations. These patterns vary more widely among societies than a person whose life has been lived in a single nation would be likely to imagine. In sharp contrast to the United States culture there are parts of the world in which women, not men, are expected to do the work, while the men devote themselves to ceremony and self-adornment (5). There are places where two friends would never dream of competing against each other, as at golf or in a card game (6). And of course styles of dress, eating preferences, social relations between men and women, and methods of bringing up children vary widely over the globe. One study of Jewish families who had recently settled in the new state of Israel showed some pronounced differences between those who went there from Europe and those from the Middle East. The husbands with a Middle Eastern background were found to shun household chores and frequently beat their wives, a form of behavior that the wives seemed to take for granted. In the families with a European background the husbands helped with the household work and even mild forms of aggression, let alone wife-beating, were considered shocking (7).

The United States, which has been settled over the years by people from many parts of the world, is a society of many cultures. For evidence, one need merely note the differences between the religious observances of the Jews, Episcopalians, and Amish, as in FIGURE 16.1, or go into neighborhoods where some of the customs shown in FIGURE 16.2 are observed. Even the "outdoor living" style of California is developing into a quite different culture from the more formal atmosphere of New England.

In addition to its culture, or its many cultures, each society also develops a *social structure* or organization of relationships among the people in the society. Social structure is of two kinds. One is *horizontal,* governing the relationships among people of equal standing in the society—such as brothers, the members of a social sorority, or the professors on a faculty. The other is *vertical* and constitutes what might be called society's status system. In ancient Rome the vertical social structure distinguished sharply among aristocrats, commoners, and slaves. The Middle Ages had lords and serfs. Modern India has a caste system. In the United States we have a rather informal but nonetheless important vertical division of society into *social classes*, the influence of which deserves examination in detail.

NORMS AND SOCIAL CLASS   Many people who have never studied the matter take for granted that social class is determined by money. But this is wrong. A school teacher is usually considered to be a member of the middle class despite a modest salary; a truck driver is usually considered working class even though he makes far more money than the teacher. An eccentric old junk dealer is considered to be a member of the lower class even though he may have $100,000 hidden in his mattress, while an elderly woman born into a prominent family may still be considered upper class even after all her money is gone and she is dependent upon the charity of relatives.

What really determines social class is shared standards; thus a social class can best be defined as *a subdivision of society made up of people who share the same norms.* Income and wealth play a part in determining social class, but only because people of similar incomes tend to have similar standards and expectations concerning dress, housing, social behavior, and recreation. Education plays a part, because people with similar amounts of education tend to have similar standards and expectations concerning many forms of overt and covert behavior, ranging from the grammar they use to attitudes on child rearing. Occupation plays a large part, for people in the same occupations share many norms concerning work standards, business practices, and goals in life.

Coexisting Cultures in the United States　Different religious groups in America include the Episcopalians (*above left*), Jewish (*above right*), and Pennsylvania Amish, each with different dress and ceremonies.

FIGURE 16.1

FIGURE **16.2**

Other Cultural Patterns Among the widely varying customs observed in the United States are the New Year's Day parade of the Chinese community in San Francisco, a boccie game in an Italian neighborhood of New York City, and a Mexican celebration of Charo Days in Brownsville, Texas.

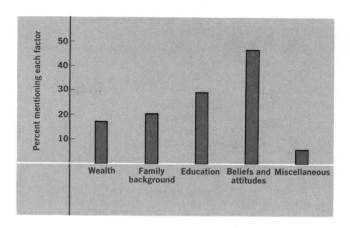

How People Judge Social Class A large group of American men were asked which of several matters, in addition to occupation, was most important to know in order to judge whether another person belonged to their own social class. The factors mentioned to them were "who his family is; how much money he has; what sort of education he has; or how he believes and feels about certain things." The chart shows the percentage of men who agreed on the importance of each of these factors. The total comes to more than 100 percent because some men mentioned more than one factor. (8)

FIGURE 16.3

FIGURE 16.3 shows the results of a study in which Americans were asked to think about the various factors that determine to which social class a person belongs. Note that they decided that wealth was an even less important factor than family background. The outstanding finding was that most Americans tend to regard themselves as being in the same social class as those who, in addition to doing work of a similar nature and prestige, think and feel as they do.

There are some American subcultures, of course, where the possession and spending of similar sums of money is considered the most important norm and where wealth is therefore the factor that determines social class. One example can be found in the sad and funny description of life in Hollywood given in FIGURE 16.4.

DIFFERENCES IN NORMS From the highest to the lowest social classes norms vary in many ways. One important difference concerns methods of rearing children, which often play a significant role in personality development. As is shown in FIGURE 16.5, mothers who may roughly be called middle class tend to be more permissive toward their children in many ways, including the highly sensitive matter of toilet training, than working-class mothers.

Presumably as a result of the different social environments in which they grow up, providing different kinds of models and incentives, children from

585

Money is Hollywood's life blood, its only standard, its status system, the only desideratum. Everyone talks of money. If a writer is out of work and broke, each of his friends knows it. When a writer is working, his acquaintances know about how much he is getting . . . . Friends are in approximately the same financial bracket. A poorly paid writer (except in the case of long years of friendship) would not be seen lunching with a well-known, successful producer, director, or top writer who gets perhaps $100,000 an assignment.

On one business trip to Hollywood, I was told by a top screen writer—a woman whose fee for writing a screenplay was in six figures—that she wanted to give a dinner party for me, and was there any particular person I wanted to have invited. I suggested a college classmate and close friend who was then writing TV westerns for the [lowest pay rate]. My hostess said she would be delighted to invite him. The next day she called me in great embarrassment. She told me that she had invited a certain motion picture star, the general manager of one of the studios, and various other well-known Hollywood characters, and that she hoped I would understand that my friend would be uncomfortable, and that she really should not invite him. My hostess had made inquiries and discovered what my friend was making.

In point of fact, I was also ineligible for the party on financial grounds, but as I came from New York no one knew. (9)

Money and Social Class in Hollywood   The above description of the social structure in Hollywood's movie and television community was written by a New York literary agent whose business often takes him to Los Angeles.

FIGURE **16.4**

FIGURE **16.5**   *Class Differences in Rearing Children*   Mothers in a New England metropolitan area were interviewed on the ways they had reared their children from birth to the age of five, and ratings were made. Note that a higher percentage of working-class mothers than middle-class mothers were rated "high" on the six items related to strictness and a lower percentage on the two items involving permissiveness. (10)

	Percentage of parents rated "high"	
	MIDDLE CLASS	WORKING CLASS
Severity of toilet training	15	26
Use of physical punishment	17	33
Use of ridicule	31	47
Stress on child's doing well at school	35	50
Pressure for neatness and order	43	57
Father's insistence on immediate obedience	53	67
Permissiveness for aggression toward parents	19	7
Sex permissiveness	53	22

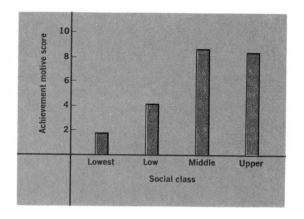

FIGURE 16.6

Social Class and Achievement Motive A study of high school sophomores in Connecticut found large differences in achievement motive between boys from the lowest and lower classes and boys from the middle and upper classes. Note that those from the middle class had the highest scores of all. (11)

the upper and middle classes show a greater amount of achievement motivation than do children from the lower classes. This fact, illustrated in FIGURE 16.6, may help account for the greater frequency with which middle-class children move up the social scale.

Members of the upper classes tend to be more conservative in their political and economic beliefs; typically a considerable majority of the upper classes has voted Republican, and the lower classes have produced strong Democratic majorities (12). Sexual behavior varies. The Kinsey studies showed, for example, that intercourse before marriage is relatively common but masturbation less common among young men of the lower classes, while the opposite is true among young men of the upper classes. Sexual foreplay was found to be more prolonged and varied among the upper classes, more simple and direct among the lower classes (13). Until recently, members of the various classes could be distinguished by their clothing; today the mass production of fashionable clothes and a growing tendency toward informality make this much less true. But the student will doubtless think of many ways in which the classes differ in customs, manners, beliefs, values, goals, and behaviors.

Studies have shown that members of the upper classes are generally considered more attractive than members of the lower classes; even children in elementary school appear to make this distinction (14). In any group situation members of the upper classes tend to be influential and are more likely to be chosen as leaders. A study of jurors who had been chosen by lot from all social classes, for example, showed that they tended to pick someone from a high occupational level as foreman (15).

BARRIERS BETWEEN CLASSES Although the standards by which a person is judged to belong to one class or another may be rather vague and flexible, the barriers between the classes tend to be quite well defined and rigid. The upper classes stay in their own sphere, forming friendships and social contacts within their own group, going to their own clubs and places of amusement. So do the middle classes; so do the lower classes.

Even children become quickly aware of the barriers between social classes and tend to confine their friendships and later their dating to members of their own class. FIGURE 16.7, showing the results of a study made in a small-town Illinois high school, demonstrates the strong tendency of students to date within their own social class and to venture only a small distance if at all outside that class.

UPWARD MOBILITY   The United States has always prided itself on being a nation where the barriers between classes could easily be surmounted by any worthy young person who wanted to advance his station in life or, to use a phrase coined by the sociologists, where anyone could demonstrate *upward mobility*. There is considerable evidence that the opportunities for upward mobility depend less upon our political ideals than upon a more pragmatic factor, the need that scientific and industrial development has created for ever increasing numbers of skilled people (17). At any rate, it is certainly true that many Americans in every recent generation have surpassed their parents in education, job level, income, and the other factors that help determine social class; it has not been unusual for a boy born into a lower-class

FIGURE 16.7   *Social Class and High School Dating*   In this study, high school students were divided into five social classes, the top two of which were lumped together for purposes of convenience. Note that boys of class I–II had 54 percent of their dates with girls of the same class, 38 percent with girls of class III, only 8 percent with class IV, and none with class V. Girls of class III had only 15 percent of their dates with boys of class I–II, 58 percent with boys of their own class, 27 percent with class IV, and none with class V. The study also showed that close friendships between members of the same sex were confined mostly to the same social class, and very rarely (in only 4 percent of cases) reached across two class lines. (16)

Members of social class shown below	had this percentage of their dates with members of the various classes:							
	I–II		III		IV		V	
I–II	54	50	38	35	8	15	0	0
III	18	15	53	58	27	27	2	0
IV	3	4	11	16	79	74	7	6
V	0	0	2	9	28	33	70	58
	BOYS	GIRLS						

home to become president of a large corporation and develop the behavior and attitudes of the upper class.

The idea of an open-end society where each person is free to find his own level, as dictated by his own abilities and motives, is an attractive one. It must be pointed out, however, that the differences among social classes that have just been discussed can pose some serious psychological problems for the person who moves up the social class ladder. At each step of the way his old norms no longer suffice, and he is likely to be highly self-conscious and uncomfortable until he has got rid of them and learned the standards of behavior appropriate to his new position. He may never feel entirely at ease in the company of people who have spent a lifetime developing the customs and attitudes of those in the classes above him.

One study, made in New Haven, Connecticut, compared men who had been born into the class of skilled workers and had remained there with other men who had moved up into the skilled worker group from the lower level of unskilled worker. Those born into the class tended to be satisfied with their way of life and to have a sense of dignity and self-esteem. Of those who had moved up into the class, a considerable majority (77 percent) were concerned about the sacrifices they had made to get where they were and tended to be less satisfied with their accomplishments and present position and more demanding of the future.

The same study also compared the "old rich" of the upper class in New Haven with those who had recently moved up from lower levels. The latter were found in many cases to show "conspicuous consumption," insecurity, and family instability, often leading to broken homes and divorce (18).

The same problem of conflicting norms that can plague the upwardly mobile member of society also operates to cause frequent difficulties in marriages that are made across class lines. Indeed "mixed marriages" of any kind, whether across social, religious, racial, or ethnic lines, tend to result in a higher divorce rate than marriages between people whose backgrounds and norms are similar (19). In marriages across social lines the difficulties seem to be most pronounced when it is the woman who marries down and the man who marries up (20).

POSITION AND ROLE

As an introduction to this section of the chapter, let us consider the following experiment.

A recording was made of what sounded like one end of a telephone conversation. From the conversation it appeared that the speaker was talking to a college instructor, whose words, at the other end, could not be heard. The speaker, it appeared, was about to visit the dean of the college department, to discuss the instructor's skill as a teacher. In the recorded conversation he told the instructor what he was going to say to the dean, beginning with the words, "I'm afraid your teaching hasn't been . . . ."

The recording was played to two groups of subjects, who were then asked to give their impressions of the speaker. One group was told that he was a college student; this group found his comments to the instructor quite critical and described him as "egotistical," "ambitious," "aggressive." The other group was told that the speaker was the chairman of the college department; this group found his comments to the instructor rather gentle, perhaps even wishy-washy, and described him as at best "compassionate" and at worst "hesitant" or "indecisive" (21).

In a very ingenious and direct way this experiment demonstrates the importance of what are called *position* and *role*. The subjects were saying, in effect, that a person in the position of student should not behave toward an instructor as the speaker on the record was behaving; to do so was arrogant and disrespectful. For a person in the position of department chairman to speak in such a manner, on the other hand, was quite the opposite; it was not sufficiently firm and decisive.

The word *position* means the particular place or niche that a person occupies in society. The word *role* means the kind of behavior that society expects from a person in a given position. The subjects in the experiment based their criticisms of the speaker on the telephone on their notions of the proper role for a person in the position of student or department chairman.

All of us occupy a certain position in society—indeed many positions held simultaneously. In each of them society expects us to play the role associated with that position. We are under pressure to play the role properly; we receive acceptance and praise if we do so, and we are punished in various ways if we do not. Thus each role has its own set of norms, to which any person holding the role is expected to conform.

The Categories of Position

Some of the positions we occupy are beyond our control; they depend upon our age or family background. Others depend upon our training and accomplishments. Five categories of positions have been suggested.

1. *Age and sex.* The baby occupies a different position in society from the school child, the school child from the college student, the college student from the middle-aged person, and the middle-aged person from the elderly. Boys are in a different position from girls, and men from women.

2. *Family.* Each of us is a member of a family. In our youth our position is that of son or daughter, grandson or granddaughter, nephew or niece. Later we create our own families and take the position of husband or wife, father or mother.

3. *Occupation.* Our position as the word is used in the job world is also an important kind of position as the word is used in social psychology. We are student, teacher, salesman, doctor, businessman, or housewife.

4. *Friendships and interests.* We also occupy a certain position in groups dictated by our friendships and interests. We are a member of a Friday night poker club or a Thursday afternoon bridge club; we are viewed in a certain definite way because of our special interest in classical music or stamp collecting.

5. *Social status.* Twin brothers, both lawyers, might occupy similar positions in all the preceding categories yet have a quite different position in the matter of status; one might be regarded by other people with considerably more respect and admiration than the other. It should be noted that the status position a person occupies can vary widely with circumstances. A woman may occupy a position of high status at meetings of the PTA, where she is known for her good common sense and organizing ability, but of low status at her golf club, where she is known as a poor player and as being temperamental.°

Everyone occupies a position in each of these five categories, and indeed often more than one position. In the family a woman may be wife to her husband at the breakfast table, then mother to her children until they go off to school, then, on a luncheon visit to her own mother, a daughter again. She may lead a troop of Girl Scouts, where she is the oldest person present, and be a member of a garden club where she is the youngest. She may be the member of a number of friendship groups and social clubs in some of which she is a leader and in some of which she is a follower and in each of which she has a different kind of status. The many positions that we occupy are often a source of conflict, particularly since, as will now be seen, each of them may involve rigid and demanding roles.

The Nature of "Role"

The word *role* is taken from the theater; it implies that, just as a role written by a playwright is supposed to be played much the same way regardless of who the actor is, so a role in society is supposed to be filled in much the same way regardless of the individual. Society says that a school teacher—*any* school teacher—should be neatly dressed, kind but firm to pupils, willing to help in community affairs, respectable in private life. It decrees that a college student —*any* college student—should take a certain number of courses, get a certain level of grades, refrain from cheating on examinations, and maintain a certain standard of personal conduct.

° The student who may take further courses in psychology or sociology should be warned that some social scientists use the word *status* as a synonym for what this book calls *position.*

Some of the conflicts that can be caused by roles have been summarized by Roger Brown, a social psychologist, in a description of the situation illustrated in FIGURE 16.8. The student in this case may be expected, in the role of son, to dress, behave, and hold opinions as dictated by the norms of his parents and to visit them on weekends. In the role of college freshman he may be expected to dress quite differently, behave in different fashion, hold other opinions, and spend his weekends studying (or attending football games or fraternity parties). Moreover, while the expectations of his parents are probably quite clear-cut, those of the people among whom he finds himself on the campus may be vague and contradictory. Some members of the faculty may expect him to study very hard, while others are less demanding. Some may give him good grades only if he memorizes their opinions, others only if he shows independence of thought. Some upperclassmen may reject him unless he plays the role of a studious intellectual, others unless he scorns good grades and spends most of his time socializing. He may find many contradictory expectations about cheating, style of dress, dating behavior, drinking, political orientation, religious views, and other matters. His discomfort may be further intensified by the fact that he went to a small high school, where he made good grades, was senior class president, and enjoyed a position of high status, while now, in the larger college, he makes only average grades, is not regarded as a leader, and feels that he has low status.

Role and Personality

The demands of a role may permit a considerable amount of leeway. The college student, for example, is free within limits to wear expensive clothes

FIGURE 16.8   *A Student's Role Conflict*   Charted here are some of the role conflicts that may beset a college student. This person occupies two important roles; he is a son, for whom his mother and father have set role expectations, and he is also a college freshman, who feels the pressure of expectations from both the faculty and the upperclassmen. His attempts to play the role of college freshman are further complicated, as indicated by the multiple arrows, by the fact that individual faculty members and upperclassmen do not seem to agree on what they expect from him. For a full explanation, see the text. (22)

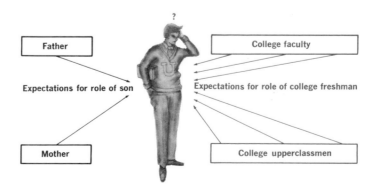

or cheap clothes, long hair or short, to join whatever political or social organizations he favors, to spend his spare time reading or shooting pool.

The same thing is true of most roles in life, although the rigidity of the norms varies from role to role. The college professor generally must live up to higher standards and expectations than the student. A physician usually faces more rigorous demands than a businessman, and a minister more inflexible demands than the physician. The role of mother generally involves more fixed expectations than the role of father.

To the extent that a role permits leeway, the manner in which an individual will fill it depends upon his own personality. Hence some physicians are quiet and detached, while others are blustering and sympathetic. Some mothers are strict, others permissive. On the other hand, the roles we take in life also affect our personalities. The college freshman arriving on the campus may at first consciously try to imitate the mannerisms of the upperclassmen and at the same time behave as the faculty seems to expect. After a time the conscious imitation is likely to become a way of life; the student actually becomes the kind of person he at first merely pretended to be. Thus every role leaves its mark on a person. Indeed it has been suggested that personality is in large part an integration of the various roles that the individual has played—an interesting and provocative sidelight to the social learning theory of personality.

CONFORMITY

Up to this point, the discussion has been mostly about norms—first the general standards for behavior and attitudes that are set by the particular society, culture, and social class, then the more specific expectations that are attached to different positions and roles in society. As has been mentioned briefly, society enforces its norms both through law and formal punishment and through the informal methods of social disapproval and praise. Let us enlarge upon this point now by considering some of the findings that have been made on the subject of *conformity* —which is defined as the yielding by an individual to pressures from another person or, more usually, a group.

Conformity, Counterconformity, and Independence

The word *conformity* has been a highly popular one in recent years. Many philosophers and social observers feel that we live in what might be called an "age of conformity"—in which all of us tend to dress alike, live in the same kind of houses, watch the same television shows, eat the same frozen TV dinners, hold the same kind of opinions, conduct the same kind of conversations, and in general behave meekly and imitatively like a flock of sheep. The leaders of the flock are not apparent; indeed there do not seem, according to this view of our present society, to be any leaders. We all seem to follow the lead of one another, trying to be alike and inconspicuous, taking up any new fad that appears, keeping up with the Joneses, staying in step.

There has also been a rebellion against this kind of conformity by some of the youth of America, expressed in such varied forms as beards, the wearing of sandals, campus protest meetings, picketing, new intellectual movements and new forms of music and literature, and sometimes experimentation with drugs.

It is difficult to make comparisons between different periods in history, and we have no scientific evidence to support or refute these views of our present society. People may or may not in truth conform more today than in previous times. The rebellion against conformity may be a real rebellion or, as some observers think, just a new way of conforming to some new norms. There is, however, considerable evidence about the tendency to conform and the factors that influence it.

Before going into the evidence, it is necessary to clarify some of the concepts that must be used in talking about this subject.

Conformity is a process that takes place only when there is a conflict between the individual's own desires, values, or opinions and the norms that society attempts to enforce. The individual who conforms abandons his own wishes and attitudes—or never dares develop any—and instead accepts the norms held by the people around him. There is a distinction between what have been called *true conformity* and *expedient conformity*. In true conformity the individual actually modifies both his behavior and his attitudes in accordance with the group pressure. For example, a working-class man who has been strongly in favor of labor unions may, after moving up into a conservative circle of upper-class businessmen, become actively and genuinely opposed to unions. In expedient conformity the individual only pays lip service to the norms, inwardly retaining his own attitudes. For example, a man who planned to vote for candidate A in a forthcoming election but found himself at a party where everyone else was strongly for candidate B might pretend to go along with the group simply to avoid argument.

Counterconformity is a sort of blind rebellion against society, engaged in by the kind of person who says, "If everybody else is for it, then I'm against it." Although the counterconformist may seem like the most rugged sort of individualist, actually he too is conforming—but in a negative direction. He disagrees with society automatically, no matter what position society takes.

Independence is the opposite of conformity; it describes a tendency to make up one's own mind and decide upon one's own behavior, taking society's norms into account but not giving them slavish devotion. One of the facts that make sweeping statements about conformity difficult is that the independent person may seem on the surface to be quite conventional. To preserve an orderly society every individual must observe a great many norms. Thus the independent person may dress, live, work, and play like everybody else but show a large amount of independence in making up his own mind, regardless of social pressures, on such issues as politics, religion, civil rights, and what kind of values to teach his children.

Milgram's Experiment on Conformity

One of the most dramatic experiments on conformity—in many ways a frightening experiment—was performed by Stanley Milgram at Yale. Like many persons interested in human nature, Milgram found himself haunted by the events in Hitler's Germany, where a great many ordinary sorts of people, presumably with ordinary social backgrounds and moral standards, took part directly or passively in a program that resulted in the mass execution of millions of European Jews. How, Milgram wondered, could such a thing happen? What in the human personality or in the structure of society could account for the willingness of so many people to take part in or at least go along with a slaughter of such magnitude?

In search of clues, Milgram devised the following experiment. Eighty men of various ages and occupational backgrounds were chosen as subjects and asked to take part in what they were told was an important experiment in learning. Each subject was assigned to a group of four people, the other three of whom, unknown to him, were Milgram's assistants. One of the assistants was the "learner" in the make-believe experiment; he was assigned to learn a laboratory task. The other two assistants and the subject were the "teachers," given the job of instructing the learner by punishing him with an electric shock when he made an error. The subject was put at controls that regulated the amount of shock, from mild to extremely intense and painful. Actually no electricity was hooked up to the controls and no learning took place; the learner deliberately made mistakes and only pretended to feel a shock when punished.

The purpose of the experiment was to learn to what levels the subjects would raise the amount of electric shock. Forty of the subjects were considered a control group and were not placed under group pressure. The other forty were urged by the other members of the team to raise the amount of electricity higher and higher, on the ground that this was essential to the experiment. The results were startling. The control subjects generally stopped at levels of shock intensity marked 3 or 4. But many of the other subjects, urged on by their fellow teachers, continued to raise the level even when the learner screamed and begged for mercy. Many of them showed signs of doubt and distress but went along anyway with the suggestions of their companions. On the average, they went all the way up to a shock level of 14 (23). Such can be the effect of social pressure and the tendency to conformity.

The Asch Experiment

Another well-known experiment on conformity was performed by Solomon Asch at Swarthmore College. It, too, involved subjects who were placed in groups of the experimenter's confederates, with the explanation that they were taking part in a study of perceptual discrimination. The experimenter showed pairs of white cards with black lines of varying length, such as the lines shown in their relative sizes in FIGURES 16.9 and 16.10. The group was asked which of the lines in FIGURE 16.10 matched the test line.

The group, consisting of seven to nine college students in all, was seated around a table, as shown in FIGURE 16.11. For what the experimenter claimed were reasons of convenience, they were asked to call out their judgments in order, beginning with the student at the experimenter's left. The subject was always placed near the other end, so that he would hear the judgments of several confederates before making his own. Sometimes the confederates gave the right answer, but on some trials they deliberately called out the wrong answer. On these trials 37 percent of the answers given by the subjects were also incorrect. In other words, the subjects conformed with the group's wrong judgment 37 percent of the time.

Some of the subjects conformed on all trials; others on some but not all; and some remained independent and did not conform at any time. Even the subjects who showed independence, however, experienced various kinds of conflict and anxiety, as is readily apparent from the photographs of the subject in FIGURE 16.12. Some of their comments later were: "Despite everything, there was a lurking fear that in some way I did not understand I might be wrong." "At times I had the feeling, to heck with it, I'll go along with the rest." "I felt disturbed, puzzled, separated, like an outcast from the rest."

FIGURE 16.9   *A Test Line*   This was the relative size of one of the lines shown to subjects in the Asch experiment. They were asked which of the lines in FIGURE 16.10, at right, matched it.

FIGURE 16.10

Which Line Matches?   Which of these three lines, the subjects in the Asch experiment were asked, matches the line shown in FIGURE 16.9? In one of the trials the experimenter's confederates insisted unanimously that it was line 1—the one which is in fact least like the test line. (24)

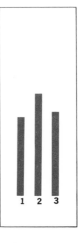

FIGURE 16.11   *A Group Studies the Lines*   One of Asch's groups begins its task in "perceptual discrimination." The subject is student 6. All the other students are in league with the experimenter.

The Crutchfield Experiments

An ingenious variation of the Asch experiment was devised by Richard Crutchfield at the University of California; the Crutchfield technique has permitted widespread testing of many aspects of conformity. The technique uses five individual booths; subjects sit in these booths and are asked to respond to problems or questions of opinion projected on the wall in front of them. Each booth is equipped with numbered switches that the subject uses to give his answers and with lights that are supposed to show the responses of the other four subjects. The subjects are told to respond in order, from booth A to booth E—but each subject believes he is in booth E and is supposed to wait until lights A through D go on before giving his own response. The lights are in fact controlled by the experimenter, who can thus persuade his subjects that the rest of the group has given any kind of answer he chooses. The technique does away with the need for "stooges" and permits the testing of five subjects at once.

As might be expected on a commonsensical basis, testing with the Crutchfield apparatus results in less conformity than does the Asch technique (25), presumably because a row of signal lights provides less social pressure than does the actual physical presence of other human beings. Nonetheless, some rather startling results have been obtained. When college students were questioned privately, only 19 percent agreed with the statement: "Free speech being a privilege rather than a right, it is proper for a society to suspend free speech whenever it feels itself threatened." In the experimental situation, led to believe that the rest of the group accepted the statement, 58 percent agreed. In a group of fifty military officers questioned privately, not one agreed with the statement: "I doubt whether I would make a good leader." Under the social pressure of the experimental situation, 37 percent agreed (26). One

FIGURE 16.12

An *"Independent" Subject—Shaken but Unyielding*   In the top photo, number 6 is making his first independent judgment at variance with the group's otherwise unanimous but incorrect verdict. In the other photos his puzzlement and concern seem to increase, until, preserving his independence despite the pressure, he announces (*bottom*), "I have to call them as I see them."

The United States is largely populated by old people, 60 to 70 percent being over 65 years of age. These oldsters must be almost all women, since male babies have a life expectancy of only 25 years. Though outlived by women, men tower over them in height, being eight or nine inches taller, on the average. The society is obviously preoccupied with eating, averaging six meals per day—this perhaps accounting for their agreement with the assertion, "I never seem to get hungry." Americans waste little time on sleep, averaging only four to five hours a night, a pattern perhaps not unrelated to the statement that the average family includes five or six children. Nevertheless, there is no overpopulation problem, since the USA stretches 6000 miles from San Francisco to New York . . . . The economy is booming with an average wage of $5.00 per hour. (27)

FIGURE 16.13

How Conformity Can Distort Fact   Would you believe the above statement? Under the pressure of the Crutchfield technique, some supposedly normal college students claimed to believe every bit of it.

experimenter using the Crutchfield technique found some of his college student subjects willing to accept the fantastic statements shown in FIGURE 16.13.

Group Factors in Conformity

Out of the many experiments a number of factors have emerged as important influences on the tendency of the individual to conform. Among them are the following characteristics of the group.

1. *Size.* Asch found that conformity generally increases with the size of the group in which the individual finds himself, but only up to a certain point. When the individual was in a group of two, with only one person opposing his judgments, there was very little conformity. The tendency to yield increased when the individual found himself in a group of three, with two opposed to him; and was still greater in a group of four or five. In fact groups of four or five produced just about as much conformity as did larger groups of fifteen or more.

2. *Unanimity.* Conformity has consistently been found greater in situations where the individual finds all the other members of the group unanimous in their opinion than if the group opinion is divided. Permitting the individual to have even a single "partner" who agrees with him has been found to greatly reduce the tendency to yield.

3. *Status.* If the individual perceives the other members of the group as having higher status than his own, he is more likely to conform. If he perceives them as having less status, he is less likely to conform.

4. *The individual's relation to the group.* In one experiment, before the

tests were made, some of the subjects were made to feel accepted by the group, others to feel rejected. Those who felt rejected and "on the verge of being outcasts" (in the words of the experimenter) showed a much higher degree of conformity than the others (28). In the Crutchfield experiments it has been found that, when the subject is a member of a racial or ethnic minority and the only such person in the group, there is generally a high degree of apparent conformity. The behavior of the person who perceives himself as rejected, however, is likely to represent expedient rather than true conformity; his private feelings may well remain the same. True conformity is likely to be greatest among those who feel they have a good chance of acceptance or whose status in the group is in the middle range (29).

Individual Factors

In tests of conformity, under many kinds of group situations, individual differences have been found in the tendency to conform. The various personality traits that go to make up what has been called a conformity-prone person or on the other hand a person who tends to perserve his independence are undoubtedly highly complex, and the same person may conform in one situation and behave independently in another. Several factors of especial importance, however, have been identified.

1. *Sex differences.* In the Crutchfield experiments women have consistently displayed a greater amount of conformity than men. Moreover, their tendency to conform appears to become greater as an experimental session goes on, while the tendency for men declines.

2. *Cultural background.* There appear to be substantial differences in the attitude of different cultures toward conformity. Among primitive societies, some have been found to demand a great deal of conformity, others very little (30). There is also some evidence of differences among modern civilized nations (31).

3. *The motive to be liked and accepted.* In general, people who conform are better liked and more readily accepted by other people (32). Thus a person with a strong motive to be liked and accepted may be more inclined to conform than a person in whom the motive is weaker. Teenagers are notoriously eager to conform in every possible detail to the customs of the peer group.

4. *Individual values.* A person is more likely to conform on matters that have little importance to him than on matters that he regards as highly important (33). A man who places little value on baseball but considerable value on history might be willing to change his mind and go along with a group judgment that Babe Ruth was a greater all-round player than Ty Cobb yet refuse to agree that Andrew Jackson was a greater president than Abraham Lincoln.

Conformity Proneness

When scores on conformity tests such as those designed by Asch or Crutch-field are correlated with various kinds of personality tests and ratings, it turns out that the person who can be described as strongly conformity-prone in a wide range of situations tends to have a characteristic kind of personality. In general he is less intelligent than the person who tends to be independent in many situations, and his mental processes tend to be more rigid. He is likely to have feelings of inferiority and anxiety, to be inhibited in the expression of emotions, and to have a low tolerance of stress. His attitudes and values are conventional and traditionally moralistic. On vocational interest tests he generally scores higher for conventional positions, such as real estate salesman, banker, and policeman, than for such positions as journalist, artist, physicist, and architect (17).

ATTITUDES

The word *attitude* has been used several times in this chapter, and the time has now come to define it and elaborate upon its importance as a concept in social psychology. It has already been stated that an attitude is a form of covert behavior and one of the many forms of behavior that are influenced by social pressures. By full definition, *an attitude is a consistent tendency to think and feel positively or negatively about a particular issue.*

Note the word *feel*. This means that attitudes contain an emotional factor, and it is the emotional factor that distinguishes attitudes from *beliefs* and *opinions*. A belief that the world is round has no emotional flavor. It is merely the cognitive acceptance of what is presumed to be a matter of fact; the person who holds this belief is neither for nor against roundness. Similarly, an opinion is also more purely cognitive, though usually based more on judg-ment than on factual information. Hence the term *public opinion polls* for studies that attempt to measure preferences among candidates or opinions on whether taxes should or should not be raised. By accepting this term the pollsters concede that they are measuring fairly superficial opinions—with-out getting at the deeper and more emotional attitudes from which the opinions probably spring.

To make the definition of attitude clearer, let us mention some specific attitudes. A man may have a positive attitude toward religion, inclining him to respond favorably to ministers and unfavorably toward profanity; a favorable attitude toward civil rights, making him respond favorably to attempts at integration and unfavorably to the statements of segregationists; a negative attitude toward working women, making him respond favorably to magazine articles that say a woman's place is in the home and highly unfavorably to his wife's desires for a job; a positive attitude toward permissiveness in child rearing, making him respond favorably to his son's steps toward independence and with disgust to scenes of harshness toward children.

The list could be expanded indefinitely, but these examples will suffice to indicate the nature of an attitude. It may concern a "big" topic like religion or world affairs or a "small" topic like working women. It is always, however, tinged with emotion. A person tends to perceive the world in accordance with his attitudes, to hold beliefs and opinions that are consistent with them, and to behave as his attitudes dictate. Earlier in the chapter, you will recall, it was mentioned that personality has been termed an integration of the various roles that the individual has played. It is perhaps equally true to say that personality is based in part on the individual's attitudes.

The Sources of Attitudes

Attitudes are of course learned—and learned in interaction with other people. We acquire many of them from our family backgrounds; consistent correlations have been found between the attitudes of parents and children toward political and economic affairs and religion (34). Other studies have shown that parents are often the first source of children's negative attitudes toward minority groups (35).

On the road from childhood to adulthood we also acquire many attitudes from our peer groups; the kind of companions we find in high school and college plays a crucial role in shaping the attitudes we will carry into adulthood. The culture of the society and social class in which we grow up also has an influence. Attitudes are among the norms that each culture, each society, and each part of the social structure attempt to foster and enforce.

Why Attitudes Persist

One of the outstanding characteristics of attitudes—and a fact that plays an important part in social behavior—is that they are durable. Although attitudes change as a person grows up, encounters new experiences, and enters new social groups, they do not change very rapidly or easily. They tend, on the contrary, to be remarkably persistent. The person who has a negative attitude toward Negroes or the Irish or South Americans when he is a schoolboy is likely to retain the attitude when he is an old man. The person who has a punitive attitude toward crime in his youth is likely to be arguing for the death penalty fifty or sixty years later. Among the reasons for the durability of attitudes are the following.

1. *The emotional element.* Emotions, as was seen in Chapter 10, are aroused by conditioned stimuli, and emotional responses are difficult to ex-

tinguish or countercondition. The emotion of anxiety, which is such an important factor in personality disturbances, often resists change even when a person undergoes a deliberate and planned course of psychotherapy. It is not surprising, therefore, that the emotional elements in attitudes should resist change under ordinary conditions of living.

2. *Selective perception.* The very existence of an attitude affects our perception of the world; we are most likely to perceive what is consistent with our attitudes. During World War II an experimenter selected two groups of college students, one favorable to the principles of Communism, the other opposed. Both groups listened to the reading of some political material, part of which was favorable to Communism and part of which was not favorable, and later were tested on what they had learned. The pro-Communist students, it turned out, had learned mostly the material favorable to Communism; the other students had learned mostly the material that was anti-Communist (36). Similarly, the person who has a strongly negative attitude toward a minority group is likely to notice every instance of undesirable behavior by a member of that group, to ignore good behavior, and in fact to condemn types of behavior as "bad" that he would accept in other people.

3. *Reinforcement by the group.* Our attitudes, as has been said, are one of the norms enforced by society; the groups with whom we associate expect us to hold the same attitudes that the rest of the members hold. Thus our attitudes are constantly rewarded and reinforced by the group, and any change in attitude is likely to be punished by rejection. All the factors that were discussed in the section on conformity operate to mold the individual's attitudes and preserve them.

Attitudes and "Balance"

Social psychologists have for many years been interested in the relationships among attitudes, beliefs, opinions, and behavior—which turn out to be more complicated than one might expect. One would suppose that all these factors would have some kind of mutual consistency. A person with a strongly positive attitude toward Christianity, for example, might be expected to believe in the Bible, to disbelieve in the theory of evolution, and, in his behavior, to be honest and charitable and to obey the Ten Commandments, including the prohibition of taking the name of the Lord in vain. Yet obviously many people with strong religious attitudes do not believe literally in all parts of the Bible, do accept the theory of evolution, are not particularly honest or charitable, and frequently use profanity. How can we explain this inconsistency?

One approach to this problem is known as the *balance theory*, which can best be explained by an example that has been suggested by two of the psychologists closely associated with the theory. The example is as follows.

A student at Yale must decide whether he favors having the school admit coeds for the first time. In this situation two elements are important. One is his attitude toward having coeds in his classes, which we will call C. Is his attitude positive $(C+)$ or is it negative $(C-)$? The other is his attitude toward getting good grades, which we will call G. Is his attitude toward good grades positive $(G+)$ or negative $(G-)$? With these symbols in mind, let us consider the case of two students who find themselves in very different situations. Both, as it happens, have favorable attitudes toward both elements; they can be described as $C+$ and $G+$. One of them believes that having coeds at the school will actually help him get good grades. Thus he is in balance; there is a plus sign between $C+$ and $G+$. The other, however, believes that coeds will interfere with his grades. Therefore he is in imbalance; there is a minus sign between $C+$ and $G+$.

In situations such as this, the balance theorists maintain, one of three things happens:

1. The person stops thinking about the problem.

2. He changes one of the two conflicting positive attitudes to a negative attitude. He restores balance by deciding that he does not want coeds on the campus (changing $C+$ to $C-$) or that he is not interested in good grades (changing $G+$ to $G-$).

3. He redefines the meaning of one of the attitudes. In this particular case the student might decide that what he meant by good grades was not all A's but merely B's, with which having coeds on the campus would not interfere at all. Thus he preserves his $C+$, along with a redefined $G+$, and is able to change the sign between the two from minus to plus (37).

Applications of Balance Theory

The balance theory provides an interesting framework within which to view human attitudes and behavior. Thinking in terms of the theory, let us take another look at the person whose beliefs and behavior sometimes seem at odds with his positive attitude toward Christianity. To avoid the discomfort of imbalance, he need not change any of these factors, regardless of how inconsistent they seem. He can avoid thinking about the imbalances, and this in fact seems to be what many such people do; they simply are not aware of any inconsistency between attitude and conduct. Or he can redefine some of the terms. He can decide that the casual use of profanity in conversation is not what the Third Commandment means. He can decide that the Bible is not necessarily the literal truth but can be revered for its spiritual and symbolic truths.

Dissonance Theory

A related theory, which has received much attention in recent years, is based on the motive for cognitive consonance, discussed on pages 335–38. According to this theory, proposed by Leon Festinger, a state of cognitive dissonance is created when a person does or says anything that is in violation of his attitudes and beliefs. Cognitive dissonance is uncomfortable and the person attempts to relieve the discomfort by returning, in any of several ways, to a state of cognitive consonance. Festinger has used the example of a person who has dissonance over the matter of smoking; he believes that smoking cigarettes is injurious to health but nonetheless he smokes. He can restore consonance either by quitting smoking or by changing his belief that smoking is dangerous. Or he can relieve the dissonance by controlling his flow of information (avoiding statistics on the danger of smoking, reading articles that claim there is no danger) or by seeking social support (in the form of other people who smoke) (38). In many cases—though not necessarily in this one—the method chosen is to change an attitude or belief.

In the discussion of cognitive consonance that began on page 335, a number of experimental studies were described. To these experiments, which the student may want to review, one more should now be added. In this case the subjects were college women who volunteered for what they were told was a study of the dynamics of group discussion. The subjects were told that, since the topic of discussion was to be the psychology of sex, they were required to take an "embarrassment test" to eliminate those who would find the discussions uncomfortable. The "embarrassment test," administered privately by a male experimenter, took two forms. For some subjects it was quite mild; they were asked to read aloud some material relating to sex that contained no words more shocking than *petting, virgin,* and *prostitute.* For other subjects the test was quite severe; they were asked to read, to the man administering the test, some of the raciest passages in current novels and also a list of obscene words.

After the "test" each subject listened to a recording of what she was told was an actual discussion by the group she would join. The experimenters had arranged for the recording to be as dull as possible—a stupid, unsophisticated, completely elementary discussion of some of the mating customs of lower animals. After listening to this, the subjects were asked to rate the discussion on a scale of dull to interesting and the people who took part in the discussion on a scale of unintelligent to intelligent.

For both groups, the experimenters theorized, there would be a certain amount of cognitive dissonance, caused by the two dissonant thoughts: 1) "I volunteered for these discussions" and 2) "These discussions are in fact dull and boring." The subjects who had gone through the more severe of

FIGURE 16.14

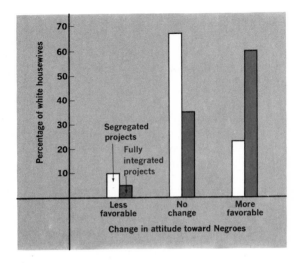

A Change in Racial Attitudes In segregated housing projects where white and Negro families lived in separate buildings or different parts of the project, there were rather small changes in the attitudes of the white housewives toward Negroes. In fully integrated projects where white and Negro families lived side by side, there were pronounced changes in a favorable direction. (40)

the two "embarrassment tests" would experience more cognitive dissonance than the others and would therefore have a stronger tendency to try to relieve the dissonance by claiming that the discussions were interesting and that the people who took part in them were intelligent. This is the way the ratings made by the two groups actually came out (39).

Dissonance and Attitude Change

Dissonance theory implies that ordinarily behavior precedes and brings about a change in attitude, rather than vice versa. This idea raises some important possibilities. It would indicate, for example, that the way to reduce racial discrimination and to promote integration is not through an attempt to change people's attitudes and thus hope to influence their behavior but to change their behavior and, as a result, to influence their attitudes.

One study that bears on this point is illustrated in FIGURE 16.14. In housing projects where whites and Negroes lived side by side, the attitudes of white housewives toward Negroes became more favorable in nearly 60 percent of cases, more unfavorable in only about 5 percent. In more segregated projects where there were fewer contacts, the attitude changes were less frequent, though still in a generally favorable direction. Dissonance theory would explain these results on the ground that the white housewives in the integrated project had met and taken favorable actions toward their Negro neighbors and that their attitudes changed as a result. (Another possible explanation, of course, is that the attitude changes resulted from the discovery that the Negro neighbors did not resemble the unfavorable picture dictated by prejudices.)

Influencing Attitudes and Opinions

Dissonance theory and the balance theory are important contributions to an area of social psychology that interests a great many people, for deliberate attempts to alter attitudes and opinions are common in our society. The politician wants to influence people in the direction of favorable attitudes and opinions toward him and his party. The advertising man and the salesman want to create favorable opinion toward the products they are selling. Many organizations are attempting to find support—that is, favorable attitudes—for kindness to animals, conservation, and various kinds of political programs. Even religious leaders and educators are in a sense attempting to influence attitudes and opinions, in the direction of the particular theology, philosophy, values, and moral code to which they adhere. On the world scene, democracy and Communism are often said to be in "a battle for men's minds."

Many studies have been made of *communication*, which is the transmission of information and opinions. Some kinds of communication, it has been found, are more effective than others in changing the attitudes and opinions of the people who receive them. As is shown in FIGURE 16.15, arguments

Credibility and Opinion Change All the subjects in this experiment read exactly the same messages arguing for a particular point of view on various current events. Subjects in the "high credibility" group were told that the messages came from sources such as *Fortune* magazine. Subjects in the "low credibility" group were told that the messages came from sources such as a Hollywood gossip columnist. Tests of the subjects' attitudes and opinions immediately afterward showed that the messages had a much greater influence when they were believed to come from respectable and reliable sources. The lasting effect of the messages, however, as determined by tests four weeks later, was about the same for both groups. The explanation seems to be that subjects in the low credibility group had forgotten the source of the messages but remembered and were influenced by their content. This is known as a *sleeper effect*. (41)

FIGURE 16.15

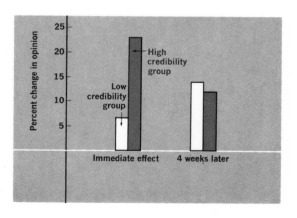

presented by a source of high credibility tend to have the greatest immediate effect, although arguments from a source of low credibility may influence the listener once he has forgotten where they came from. The speaker who presents only his own side of a controversial question is less likely to win over people from the opposite side than the speaker who presents a "fair" argument, admitting that the other side has its points (42). Arguments that appeal to a person's motives tend to be particularly successful—as do appeals to the listener's emotions (43). Appeals to the emotion of fear, however, may be less effective than one might imagine from their frequent use by politicians who play on the voters' fears of higher taxes and by advertisers who play on the fear of offending others through bad breath or perspiration odor. As is shown in FIGURE 16.16, the appeal to fear may backfire—presumably by causing the individual to stop thinking about the matter.

GROUPS AND LEADERS   Throughout literary history, authors have been fascinated by the conduct of people in groups, and countless novels have been written about people who find themselves thrown together by a long trip or a shipwreck or after some nuclear disaster of the

Failure of an Appeal to Fear   Three groups of high school students listened to lectures on dental hygiene. One lecture was designed to be "strong" in fear arousal; it dwelt on such unpleasant possibilities as decayed teeth, rotting gums, and cancer. Another lecture was "moderate" in statements that would produce fear, and the third was "weak." A week later a survey was made to determine how many students in each group had adopted improved habits in dental hygiene and how many had developed worse habits. As the bars show, the "strong" fear-arousing lecture proved to be the *least* effective in creating better habits; the "weak" lecture was the most effective. For the probable explanation, see the text. (44)

FIGURE 16.16

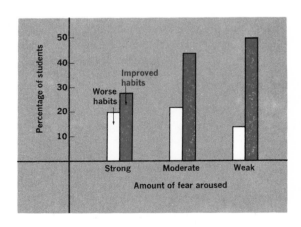

future. The novels are based on one of the central facts of social psychology —that in any group, some kind of social structure will be formed very quickly.

Human groups seem to form and organize themselves as naturally and spontaneously as crystals in a solution of chemicals or mold formations on a piece of bread. Almost automatically, someone in the group rises to top status and becomes the acknowledged leader. There will be coleaders and subleaders, perhaps, and followers of decreasing status, down to the lowliest. There may be a court jester who amuses the group and a scapegoat whom the others pick on.

The dynamics of social organization are fascinating not only to social psychologists but also, since so much of human behavior is social, to everyone who—like the novelist—is interested in psychology. The process has been the subject of many studies and much theorizing, from many different directions and points of view. Unfortunately, firm conclusions are difficult to reach, and these final pages of the book can only raise some of the questions involved and suggest a few of the factors that seem to be part of the answers.

The Qualities of Leadership

Even the personality characteristics that make for leadership are by no means easy to observe or define. One study has shown that, in general, leaders of groups tend to be people who are persistent and dependable, who are self-confident and popular, and who talk well and take a lively part in the group's activities (45). However, many people possess these qualities and yet do not become leaders.

Another study has shown that a person who becomes the leader in one group is likely to become a leader in other groups (46). This is true, however, only when the other groups are similar in the kind of people they comprise and their goals. There is no evidence for the old popular theory that some people are "born leaders" who would rise to the top in any kind of group under any circumstances. Quite on the contrary, the evidence shows that the selection of a leader depends not only upon the personality of the individual but also upon the particular nature and needs of the group.

One study that bears on this point was made with high school students who were assigned in pairs to plot some rather complicated data—an intellectual task—then were assigned with different partners to a clerical task, and finally with still different partners to a mechanical task. There was some tendency for the same student to take charge in all three situations, but not very much. The correlations between displays of leadership on the three tasks were .48 between intellectual and clerical, .32 between clerical and mechanical, and only .18 between intellectual and mechanical (47).

The Specialist and the "Great Man"

One study has indicated that three factors may be crucial in determining leaders: 1) amount of activity in the group, 2) ability to perform the task, and 3) personal likability. The three factors are not correlated, and the presence of all three in the same person is quite rare.

Many people rank low on all three characteristics; these people do not become leaders and indeed may be scorned and turned into scapegoats. Some are high in activity but low in ability and not well liked; these people may try to dominate the group, but they do not become true leaders and are often considered nuisances.

One type of leader is extremely well liked but ranks lower in activity and ability; this kind of person has been called a "social specialist." A more frequent type is high in activity and ability but less well liked; this kind of person has been called a "task specialist." Often a "task specialist" and a "social specialist" team up to operate a sort of dual leadership. Thus a hard-driving and able but not very popular administrator may have a righthand man who takes care of his problems in human relations, while an extremely popular but less dynamic and capable leader may have a righthand man who does most of the real work. In the rare cases where all three characteristics are combined in the same person, one finds the truly efficient, magnetic, inspiring leader—the "great man" (48).

Group Dynamics

The forces that operate in a group, not only to produce leaders but also to bring about other alignments, decisions, and activities, are called *group dynamics,* a term coined by social psychologist Kurt Lewin. Many studies of group dynamics have been made by Lewin and his followers, one of which will perhaps serve to illustrate some of the insights that have been obtained into group behavior.

In this study, made during wartime, an attempt was made to increase the consumption of three kinds of rather unpopular but plentiful meats—beef hearts, sweetbreads, and kidneys. Although the subject matter of the experiment may seem rather strange, nonetheless the experiment tells a great deal about group dynamics.

To increase consumption of the three unpopular meats, Lewin decided, it was essential to change the attitudes of housewives. But how best to do this? In the experiment two methods were tried. One group of housewives were persuaded to listen to lectures that presented an enthusiastic picture of the flavor of these meats, their value to health, and the benefit that would accrue to the war effort if they were more widely used. Another group took part in discussion groups at which the same points were made but where,

FIGURE **16.17**

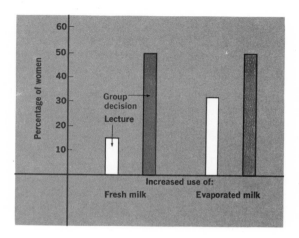

Effects of Group Decision As the bars show, housewives who took part in a group decision to use more milk actually did so in far greater numbers than did housewives who merely listened to a lecture on the advantages of using milk. The percentages were obtained in a survey made four weeks after the group decisions and lectures. (49)

in addition, the women were induced to come to a group decision to serve the three meats. The lecture was simply passive instruction. In the group discussions the housewives became involved with the problem, decided more or less of their own accord that the meats could be desirable, and took an active part in trying to think of ways to overcome any prejudice of their families against the meats. The results were striking. Of the women who listened to lectures, only 3 percent actually served one of the meats; of those who had reached a group decision, 32 percent did. As is shown in FIGURE 16.17, similar results were found in an experiment designed to persuade housewives to use more milk.

A somewhat similar experiment was made with mothers of newborn babies at an Iowa hospital. Before leaving the hospital some of the mothers received nearly a half hour of individual instruction from a nutritionist about the importance of giving their babies codliver oil and orange juice. Other mothers took part in group meetings of equal length at which they discussed nutrition and reached a group decision to use codliver oil and orange juice. As shown in FIGURE 16.18, the group decisions proved far more effective in influencing behavior.

FIGURE **16.18**

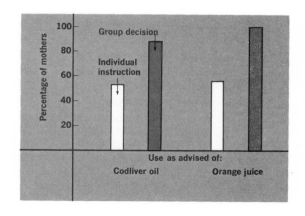

Group Decision Versus Individual Instruction As the bars show, group decision proved more effective than did individual instruction in persuading mothers to give their newborn babies codliver oil and orange juice. The percentages were obtained four weeks after the group decision or instruction. (49)

These experiments probably explain why a group approach such as that of Alcoholics Anonymous has been successful in inducing many people to stop drinking and why group treatment of juvenile delinquents appears to be more successful than individual attempts. Lewin concluded that it is usually easier to change the attitudes and behavior of people in groups than to change any one of the individuals separately (50). Such is the powerful influence of all the factors that operate in group dynamics—a field of study that will probably produce many of psychology's most exciting findings of the future.

SUMMARY

1. *Social psychology* is the study of the behavior of the individual in his society and the influence that the actions and attitudes of the other members of his society have upon his overt behavior and his thinking.

2. Society functions to provide the necessities of life, assign individuals to positions essential for providing the necessities and preserving the society, establish a system of communication, provide a shared set of goals, establish rules, control disruptive forms of behavior, regulate emotional expression, sexual customs, and reproduction, and socialize the young (that is, train them in the ways of the society).

3. Most behavior, even of young children, is social in the sense of being directed toward other people and usually involving interactions.

4. The mutually shared standards and expectations of society are called *norms*.

5. *Culture* is the customs, beliefs, values, and ideals—the pattern of norms —that a society develops and passes along to its new generations.

6. The *social structure* is the organization of relationships among the people in the society. Social structure takes two forms: a) *horizontal*, governing the relationships among people of equal standing, and b) *vertical*, taking the form of a *status system* which in the United States differentiates among the upper, middle, and lower *social classes*.

7. The particular place or niche that a person occupies in society is called his *position*.

8. The kind of behavior society expects from a person in a given position is called *role*. The individual is often placed in conflict because he simultaneously occupies several different positions in which he is expected to fill incompatible roles.

9. *Conformity* is the yielding by an individual to pressures from another person or, more usually, a group. In *true conformity* he actually modifies both his behavior and his attitudes. In *expedient conformity* he

merely pays lip service to the group pressures, while remaining inwardly unchanged.

10. *Counterconformity* is the tendency to be opposed to anything suggested by group pressure, regardless of its merits. *Independence* is the tendency to make up one's own mind and decide upon one's own behavior and thinking, taking into account but not giving slavish devotion to society's norms and pressures.

11. Factors that influence conformity are a) the size of the group, b) unanimity of the group, c) the status of the group, and d) the individual's relation to the group. Conformity is greatest when the group is as large as four or five, unanimous, and perceived by the individual as having high status and when the individual desires acceptance by the group and is somewhat doubtful of obtaining it.

12. Individual differences in the tendency to conform include: a) sex differences (women are more likely to conform than men), b) cultural background (some cultures foster more conformity than others), c) the strength of the individual's motive to be liked and accepted, and d) the individual's values (he is more likely to conform on matters he considers unimportant than on matters to which he attaches high value).

13. An *attitude* is *a consistent tendency to think and feel either positively or negatively about a particular issue.* As the definition indicates, an attitude contains both a cognitive and an emotional factor.

14. Attitudes tend to be durable and persistent.

15. The *balance theory* holds that when a person holds two conflicting attitudes he: a) stops thinking about the problem, b) changes one of the attitudes, or c) redefines the meaning of one of the attitudes.

16. *Dissonance theory* holds that doing or saying anything that is inconsistent with an attitude creates a state of cognitive dissonance, which a person then tries to relieve, often by changing his attitude. The theory implies that ordinarily behavior precedes and brings about a change in attitude rather than that a change in attitude precedes and brings about a change in behavior.

17. Some factors that influence the effectiveness of *communication* in changing attitudes are the following:
    a. Communication is more effective when it comes from a source believed to be expert and unbiased—that is, a source of high credibility.
    b. A "fair" argument presenting both sides of the question is generally more effective than a one-sided argument.
    c. Communication is often more effective when it promises to satisfy the listener's motives or provide an outlet for his emotions.
    d. Arousal of fear may backfire by making the person refuse to think about the subject.

18. Factors that appear to be crucial in determining leadership of a group are: a) amount of activity in the group, b) ability to perform the task, and c) likability. A leader who is well liked but ranks lower in activity and ability has been called a "social specialist." A leader who is high in activity and ability but lower in likability has been called a "task specialist." The rare person who possesses a high level of all three characteristics is the "great man" type of leader.

19. The forces that operate in a group, to produce leaders and other alignments and to create activities and decisions, are called *group dynamics*.

20. One important aspect of group dynamics is the finding that it is easier to change the attitudes and behavior of people in groups than to change any one of the individuals separately.

RECOMMENDED READING

Brown, R. W. *Social psychology*. New York: Free Press, 1965.

Cohen, A. R. *Attitude change and social influence*. New York: Basic Books, 1964.

Homans, G. C. *Social behavior: its elementary forms*. New York: Harcourt, Brace & World, 1961.

Jones, E. E. and Gerard, H. B. *Foundations of social psychology*. New York: Wiley, 1967.

Krech, D., Crutchfield, R. S., and Ballachey, E. L. *Individual in society: a textbook of social psychology*. New York: McGraw-Hill, 1962.

Proshansky, H. M. and Seidenberg, B., eds. *Basic studies in social psychology*. New York: Holt, Rinehart and Winston, 1965.

Secord, P. F. and Backman, C. W. *Social psychology*. New York: McGraw-Hill, 1964.

Steiner, I. D. and Fishbein, M., eds. *Current studies in social psychology*. New York: Holt, Rinehart and Winston, 1965.

GLOSSARY
REFERENCES AND ACKNOWLEDGMENTS
INDEX

GLOSSARY

A

abnormal behavior   Any behavior that seriously interferes with the individual's ability to work and to love.

abnormal psychology   The branch of psychology that studies mental and emotional disturbances and their treatment.

absolute threshold   The minimum amount of stimulus energy to which a receptor will respond 50 percent of the time.

acetylcholine   A chemical produced at a synapse when a nervous impulse reaches the end of the axon. Acetylcholine causes the dendrite of the second neuron to fire.

achievement test   A test that measures the individual's present level of skill or knowledge. (*Compare* **aptitude test.**)

adaptation   The tendency of the sensory apparatus to adjust to any steady and continued level of stimulation and to stop responding.

adrenal cortex   The outer part of an *adrenal gland.*

adrenal glands   A pair of endocrine glands, lying atop the kidneys. Each consists of two parts: an *adrenal medulla,* which produces the stimulants adrenalin and noradrenalin, and an *adrenal cortex,* which produces steroids essential to life.

adrenal medulla   The inner part of an *adrenal gland.*

adrenalin   A hormone, secreted by the adrenal medulla, which affects the rate of heartbeat, raises the blood pressure, and causes the liver to release increased quantities of sugar into the blood to provide additional energy. Adrenalin is associated with the bodily states in fear or "flight" situations.

aerial perspective   A clue to distance perception; refers to the fact that distant objects appear less distinct and less brilliant in color than nearby objects, because they are seen through air that is usually somewhat hazy.

affect   A term used to describe the feelings that accompany emotional states of the organism; it refers specifically to feelings rather than to patterns of nervous discharge, physiological changes, or the behavior that may result from emotion.

afferent neuron   A neuron that carries impulses from the sense organs toward the central nervous system.

afterimage   The visual phenomenon produced by withdrawal of a stimulus. Withdrawal is followed briefly by a positive afterimage, then by a negative afterimage.

617

aggression   A type of behavior arising from hostile motives; it takes such forms as argumentativeness, scorn, sarcasm, physical and mental cruelty, and fighting.

amnesia   Loss of memory. It may be caused by physical injury, or it may be a defense mechanism—an exaggerated form of repression.

amplitude   The characteristic of a sound wave that determines the loudness we hear.

anxiety   An emotion characterized by a vague fear or premonition that something bad is about to happen; a frequent result of conflicts among motives and a prominent factor in abnormal behavior.

anxiety reaction   A psychoneurosis in which the individual often describes himself as "chronically uneasy" for reasons he cannot explain; the anxiety is the outstanding symptom.

anxiety state   One rather large group of psychoneuroses, in all of which anxiety is a prominent symptom. The group includes *anxiety reaction, asthenic reaction, hypochondriacal reaction,* and *phobic reaction.*

apathy   A feeling of indifference in which the individual may seem to lose all interest in what happens to him; a result of frustration.

apparent motion   The perception of motion in stimuli that, though they change, do not actually move, as in *stroboscopic motion* or the *phi phenomenon. (Compare* **illusory motion.**)

applied psychology   The application of psychological knowledge and principles to practical situations in school, industry, social situations, and treatment of abnormal behavior.

approach-approach conflict   A conflict in which the aroused motives have two incompatible goals, both of which are desirable.

approach-avoidance conflict   A conflict in which the individual has a single goal with both desirable and undesirable aspects, causing mixed feelings.

aptitude   A capacity to learn or to perform, such as mechanical or musical aptitude; an inborn ability that exists and can be measured even though the individual has had no special training to develop his skills (such as at mechanical or musical tasks).

aptitude test   A test measuring the individual's *capacity* to perform, not his present level of skill or knowledge. (*Compare* **achievement test.**)

aroused motive   A motive the individual is actually thinking about at the moment; an active influence upon behavior.

asthenic reaction   An anxiety state in which the individual is chronically tired, listless, and unable to concentrate or work efficiently. At one time the condition was called neurasthenia.

astigmatism   A defect of vision caused by irregularities in the shape of the cornea or lens.

attachment unit   A unit of innate or previously learned behavior, overt or covert, to which a new stimulus can become attached.

attention   The process of focusing perception on a single stimulus or limited range of stimuli.

attitude   A consistent tendency to think and feel either positively or negatively about a particular issue. It contains both a cognitive factor and an emotional factor.

autokinetic illusion   The illusion of self-generated movement that a stationary object, such as a point of light seen in an otherwise dark room, sometimes creates.

autonomic nervous system   A complicated nerve network that connects the central nervous system with the glands and the smooth muscles of the body organs.

aversive conditioning   A type of behavior therapy that attempts to associate a behavioral symptom with pain and punishment rather than with pleasure and reward.

avoidance-avoidance conflict   A conflict in which there is simultaneous arousal of motives to avoid alternatives, both of which are undesirable.

axon   The fiber of the neuron that has end branches that transmit messages to other neurons or to muscles and glands; the "sending" portion of the neuron.

B

balance theory   A theory maintaining that, when a person holds two conflicting attitudes, he (1) stops thinking about the problem, (2) changes one of the attitudes, or (3) redefines the meaning of one of the attitudes.

basilar membrane   A piece of tissue dividing the cochlea more or less in half for its entire length; the organ of Corti, containing the hearing receptors, lies on this membrane.

behavior   The activities of an organism, both overt, or observable (such as motor behavior), and covert, or hidden (such as thinking).

behavior therapy   A type of psychotherapy that concentrates on eliminating the symptoms of personality conflict, which are regarded as conditioned responses, through counterconditioning.

behaviorism   A school of thought maintaining that psychologists should concentrate on the study of overt behavior rather than of "mental life" or consciousness.

binocular vision   A clue to distance perception; refers to the fact that the two eyes, being several inches apart, receive slightly different images of any seen object.

biological drive   A physiological pressure, usually influencing the organism toward certain types of behavior. The biological drives include hunger, thirst, sleep, sex, pain, breathing, elimination, and temperature.

blind spot   The point at which the optic nerve exits from the eyeball, creating a small and mostly insensitive gap in the retina.

brain stem   A group of brain structures, including the cerebellum, pons, and medulla, upon which the forebrain rests.

breathing drive   A biological drive aroused by physiological requirements for oxygen.

brightness   One dimension of the visual stimulus; dependent upon intensity.

brightness constancy   The tendency to perceive objects to be of consistent brightness regardless of the amount of light they actually reflect under different conditions of illumination.

C

Cannon-Bard theory of emotion   A neurological theory holding that stimuli in the environment set off patterns of activity in the hypothalamus and thalamus; these patterns are then relayed both to the autonomic nervous system, where they trigger the bodily changes of emotion, and to the cerebral cortex, where they result in the feelings of emotion.

cell body (of a neuron)   The portion of the neuron containing its genes, as opposed to the fiber portion of the neuron.

central nervous system   The spinal cord and the brain. (*Compare* **peripheral nervous system.**)

cerebellum   The portion of the brain stem that controls body balance and helps coordinate bodily movements.

cerebral cortex   The highest part of the brain, the surface of the cerebrum; a dense and highly interconnected mass of neurons and their cell bodies.

cerebrotonic temperament   A type of temperament ascribed by William Sheldon to the ectomorphic body type; characterized by mental overintensity, secretiveness, emotional restraint, fear of society, and love of privacy.

cerebrum   The large brain mass of which the cerebral cortex is the surface. It is divided into two separate halves called the left hemisphere and the right hemisphere.

character disorder (*also called* **personality disorder**)   A type of emotional disorder characterized by failure to acquire mature and efficient ways of coping with the problems of adult life.

chromosome   The mechanism of human heredity. There are twenty-three pairs of the tiny structures, forty-six in all, found in the fertilized egg cell and repeated through the process of division in every cell of the body that grows from this cell.

chunking   A term used to describe learning by logic rather than by rote; from the fact that materials related by logical principles "hang together" like a chunk of wood or stone.

ciliary muscles   The muscles that control the shape of the lens of the eye.

classical conditioning   The learning process through which a reflex becomes attached to a conditioned (or previously neutral) stimulus.

client-centered therapy   A type of psychotherapy, developed by Rogers, in which the therapist displays warmth and total acceptance toward the patient, thus providing a nonthreatening situation in which the patient is freed to explore all his thoughts and feelings.

clinical psychology   The branch of applied psychology concerned with the application of psychological knowledge to the treatment of personality problems and mental disorders.

cochlea   A bony structure of the inner ear shaped like a snail's shell; contains the receptors for hearing.

cognitive consonance   Consistency and agreement among one's thoughts, beliefs, and behavior.

cognitive dissonance   Lack of consistency and agreement among one's thoughts, beliefs, and behavior. The desire to relieve cognitive dissonance is believed to be an important human motive.

color blindness   A visual defect involving deficiency in color discrimination.

color constancy   The tendency to perceive a familiar object as of constant color, regardless of changes in illumination that alter its actual stimulus properties.

communication   As a term in social psychology, the transmission of information and opinions.

complementary hues   Two hues that, when added one to the other, yield gray.

complexity   The characteristic of a sound wave that determines the timbre we hear; caused by the number and strength of the overtones.

compulsion   An irresistible urge to perform some act over and over again.

concept   A symbol that stands for a common characteristic or relationship shared by objects or events that are otherwise different.

concept hierarchy   An arrangement of the associations that make up concepts; the very strong ones at the top are likely to be thought of immediately, and the weakest ones at the bottom are less likely to be used.

conceptual intelligence   The term used by Piaget to describe the developmental process after the age of two, in which the child increasingly uses concepts to organize the evidence of his senses and to engage in ever more complex thinking and problem solving.

conditioned operant   Behavior learned through operant conditioning; a type of behavior with which the organism "operates" on its environment to obtain a desired result.

conditioned reflex   A reflex that, through learning, has become attached to a conditioned (or previously neutral) stimulus; an example is the reflex salivation by Pavlov's dog to the sound of the metronome.

conditioned stimulus   In classical conditioning, a previously neutral stimulus (such as a sound) that, through pairing with an unconditioned stimulus (such as food), acquires the ability to set off reflex behavior (such as salivation).

conditioning   A learning process in which behavior becomes attached to new stimuli. (*See* **classical conditioning, operant conditioning.**)

cones   One of the two types of receptors for vision located in the retina. The cones are receptors for color and are also sensitive to differences in light intensity resulting in sensations of black, white, and gray.

conflict   The simultaneous arousal of two or more incompatible motives, resulting in unpleasant emotions.

conformity   The yielding by an individual to pressures from another person or, more usually, from a group.

connecting neuron   A neuron that is stimulated by another neuron and passes its message along to a third neuron.

connotation   The implied meaning of a word. Although *landlord* means only a person who rents property, to most people the word connotes stinginess.

control group   A group used for comparison with an experimental group. The two groups must be alike in composition and must be observed under the same circumstances except for the one variable that is manipulated in the case of the experimental group.

conversion reaction   A form of hysteria characterized by physical symptoms that have no organic basis.

cornea   The transparent bulge in the outer layer of the eyeball through which light waves enter.

corpus callosum   A large nerve tract that connects the left and right hemispheres of the cerebrum and enables the two hemispheres to cooperate and share in duties.

correlation   The degree of relationship between two different factors; measured statistically by the correlation coefficient.

correlation coefficient   A statistic that describes in numbers ranging from -1 to $+1$ the degree of relationship between two different factors.

cortisol   One of the steroids produced by the adrenal cortex.

counterconformity   The tendency to be opposed to anything suggested by group pressure, regardless of its merits.

covert behavior   Hidden processes (such as thoughts) that take place inside the organism and cannot be seen by an outside observer.

creative thinking   A highly imaginative and rather rare form of directed thinking in which the individual discovers new relationships and solutions to problems and may produce an invention or an artistic creation.

cretinism   A biological form of mental retardation caused by an abnormally low level of secretion by the thyroid gland.

critical ratio   A measure of the degree of difference between two groups.

culture   The pattern of norms of behavior that a society develops and passes along to new generations, including its customs, beliefs, values, and ideals.

curve of forgetting   A graph plotting the course of forgetting.

D

decibel   A measure of the amplitude of sound.

defense mechanism   A process, generally believed to be unconscious, in which the individual tries to convince himself that a frustration or conflict and the resulting anxiety do not exist or have no importance.

delusion   A false belief, such as imagining that one is already dead.

dendrite   The part of the neuron, usually branched, that has the special function of being sensitive to stimuli and firing off a nervous impulse; the "receiving" portion of the neuron.

denial   A defense mechanism, closely related to repression, in which the individual simply denies the existence of the events that have aroused his anxiety.

depression   The feeling of being in "a blue funk"; a result of frustration or loss of a valuable goal or love object. (*Compare* **neurotic depression.**)

descriptive statistics   A quick and convenient method of summarizing measurements. Important figures in descriptive statistics are the number of subjects (or *N*); measurements of the average, including the mean, median, and mode; and measurements of variability, including range and standard deviation.

developmental psychology   The study of the processes by which the newborn baby acquires his patterns of overt behavior, thinking, and problem solving and the motives, emotions, conflicts, and ways of coping with conflicts that will go to make up his adult personality.

didactic learning (*also called* **learning through exposition**)   A method of teaching in which the teacher explains a concept and then cites examples. (*Compare* **discovery learning.**)

difference threshold (*also called* **just noticeable difference**)   The smallest difference in intensity or quality of stimulation to which a sensory receptor will respond 50 percent of the time.

directed thinking   A process in which we try to forge a chain of associations that will reach a definite goal. The most important form of directed thinking is *problem solving.*

discovery learning   A method of teaching in which the teacher presents examples of a concept and lets the student discover the concept for himself. (*Compare* **didactic learning.**)

dissociative reaction   A form of hysteria in which the individual undergoes some form of loss of contact with reality; he dissociates himself in some manner from the conflicts that are troubling him. Three forms are amnesia, multiple personality, and sleep walking.

dissonance theory   A theory maintaining that doing or saying anything inconsistent with an attitude creates a state of cognitive dissonance that the individual then tries to relieve, often by changing his attitude.

distributed practice   A series of relatively short learning periods. (*Compare* **massed practice.**)

DNA (deoxyribonucleic acid)   The complex chemical of which genes are composed.

dominant gene   A gene, such as the one for brown eyes, that always prevails over a *recessive gene,* such as the one for blue eyes.

double approach-avoidance conflict   A conflict aroused by motives toward two goals that both have their good points and their bad.

drive   *See* **biological drive.**

ductless gland   *See* **endocrine gland.**

E

eardrum   A membrane between the outer part of the auditory canal and the middle ear.

ectomorph   One of three basic types of body build described by Sheldon; the ectomorph is characterized by a skin area and nervous system that are large in proportion to his size.

EEG   *See* **electroencephalograph.**

efferent neuron   A neuron that carries impulses from the central nervous system toward the muscles or glands.

ego   According to Freud's psychoanalytic theory of personality, the conscious, logical part of the mind that develops as a person grows up and that is his operational contact with reality.

ego ideal   The sum total of a person's standards; his notion of how, if he were as perfect as he would like to be, he would always think and behave.

eidetic imagery   The ability, possessed by a minority of people, to "see" an image that is an exact copy of the original sensory experience.

electroencephalograph (EEG)   A delicate instrument that measures the electrical activity of the brain.

electroshock therapy   A medical method of treatment of behavior disorders, in which an electric current roughly as strong as household electricity is passed through the patient's head for a fraction of a second.

elimination drive   A biological drive aroused by physiological requirements to get rid of the body's waste products.

emotion   A word used in four different ways: (1) by physiologists to describe various changes inside the body; (2) by neurologists to describe patterns of nervous activity; (3) by those interested in behavior to describe such actions as weeping or laughing, and (4) to describe the subjective feelings (also called affects) that bear such names as fear, anger, and so on.

emotional state   The condition of the organism during emotion, characterized by patterns of activity in the central nervous system and autonomic nervous system and by changes in glandular activity, heart rate, blood pressure, breathing, and activity of the visceral organs.

empirical   Based on controlled experiments and on observations made with the greatest possible precision and objectivity.

endocrine gland (*also called* **ductless gland**)   A gland that discharges chemical substances known as *hormones* directly into the blood stream, which then carries them to all parts of the body, resulting in many kinds of physiological changes.

endomorph   One of three basic types of body build described by Sheldon; the endomorph is characterized by a strong digestive system and tends to be round in build, with relatively weak bones and muscles.

energizing drugs   Drugs that relieve depression, presumably through action on the central nervous system.

engram   Some kind of lasting trace or impression formed in living protoplasm by a stimulus; a deliberately vague term often used to describe the learning connection or memory trace.

Eustachian tube   A passage between the middle ear and the air chambers of the mouth and nose, which keeps the pressure on both sides of the eardrum constant.

experiment   A scientific tool by which events are manipulated to study the effect of a given variable.

extinction   The disappearance of a conditioned reflex (or other learned behavior) when reinforcement is withdrawn.

extrinsic motivation   Motivation that comes from the outside, established artificially and created by rewards that have no real connection with the learning situation. (*Compare* **intrinsic motivation.**)

extrovert   An individual who dislikes solitude and prefers the company of other people.

F

fantasy   Images; daydreams.

feedback   In learning, knowledge obtained by the learner of how well he is progressing.

figure-ground   In perception, the tendency to see an object as a figure set off from a neutral ground.

forebrain   The top part of the brain mass, including the cerebrum, the thalamus, and the hypothalamus.

fovea   The most sensitive part of the retina, at the center; contains only cones, which are packed together more tightly than anywhere else in the retina.

free association   A tool of psychoanalysis in which the patient, lying as relaxed as possible on a couch, is encouraged to let his mind wander where it will and to speak out every thought that occurs to him.

free operant   Random, purposeless action, such as the movements of a baby in his crib.

frequency   The characteristic of a sound wave determining the tone or pitch that we hear; measured in number of cycles per second.

frustration   (1) the blocking of motive satisfaction by an obstacle; (2) the various unpleasant feelings that result from the blocking of motive satisfaction.

functional autonomy   A principle holding that an activity that is originally a means to an end frequently acquires an independent function of its own and becomes an end in itself.

functional fixedness   The tendency to think of an object in terms of its usual functions, not other possible functions; a common barrier to problem solving.

functional psychosis   A psychosis having no apparent connection with any organic disturbance.

G

galvanic skin reflex (GSR)   A change in the electrical conductivity of the skin caused by activity of the sweat glands.

gamma phenomenon   The apparent motion of a light when it gets brighter (and seems to draw closer) or dimmer (and seems to move away).

ganglion (*plural:* **ganglia**)   A mass of nerve cells and synapses forming complex and multiple connections.

genes   The tiny substances, composed of DNA, which make up the chromosomes. Each human cell contains an estimated 20,000 to 125,000 genes, which account for inherited individual differences. (*See* **chromosome, DNA.**)

general adaptation syndrome   A phrase coined by Selye for the sequence of events involved in prolonged stress; the initial shock or alarm, the recovery or resistance period, and at last exhaustion and death.

goal   An object or event toward which a biological drive, stimulus need, or motive is directed.

gradient of approach   The changing strength of the desire to approach a goal, dependent upon such factors as distance from the goal.

gradient of avoidance   The changing strength of the desire to avoid an unpleasant goal, dependent upon such factors as distance from the goal.

gradient of texture   A clue to distance perception; refers to the fact that nearby objects are seen more sharply and therefore appear "grainier" in texture than more distant objects.

group dynamics   The forces that operate in a group to produce leaders and other alignments and to create activities and decisions.

group test   A psychological test that can be given to many individuals at the same time.

group therapy   A type of psychotherapy in which several patients are treated simultaneously.

GSR   *See* **galvanic skin reflex.**

H

hallucination   An imaginary sensation, such as seeing nonexistent animals in the room or feeling bugs crawling under the skin.

Hering theory (of vision)   A theory holding that color vision is attributable to two types of cones with double action, one responsible for red and green, the other for blue and yellow. The Hering theory is now considered incorrect as to the nature of the cones but correct as to the type of nervous impulses sent from the eye.

higher order reinforcement   Reinforcement provided by stimuli that have acquired reward value through association with a secondary reinforcing stimulus or with another higher order reinforcing stimulus; that is, reinforcement even further removed from primary reinforcement than is secondary reinforcement.

homeostasis   An internal environment in which such bodily states as blood circulation, blood chemistry, breathing, digestion, temperature, and so on are kept at optimal levels for survival of the living organism.

hormones   Substances produced by the endocrine glands and poured into the blood stream, complicated chemicals that trigger and control many kinds of bodily activities and behavior.

hue   The proper scientific term for what is commonly called color; determined by the length of the light wave.

human engineering   A branch of applied psychology concerned with the design of equipment and machinery to fit the size, strength, and capabilities of the people who will use it.

hunger drive   A biological drive aroused by deprivation of food.

hypochondriacal reaction   An anxiety state in which the individual tends to excuse his failures on the ground of physical illness.

hypothalamus   The portion of the forebrain that serves as a sort of mediator between the brain and the body, helping control sleep, hunger, thirst, body temperature, and sexual behavior, and that is also concerned with emotions.

hysteria   A form of psychoneurosis; includes conversion reaction and dissociative reactions.

I

id   According to Freud's psychoanalytic theory of personality, the unconscious part of the human personality comprising the individual's primitive instinctive forces toward sexuality (the libido) and aggression.

identification   (1) A process in which the child tries to imitate the behavior of his parents or "heroes" so that he can share vicariously in their strengths and triumphs. (2) In psychoanalytic theory, the process through which the child resolves the Oedipus complex by absorbing his parents into himself. (3) As a defense mechanism, the process through which the individual identifies with another person, or more often with a group, in order to reduce his own conflicts and anxieties.

illusion   A perception that is a false interpretation of the actual stimuli.

illusory motion   The perception of motion in an unchanging stimulus, such as in the *autokinetic illusion*. (*Compare* **apparent motion**.)

image   The recollection of a sensory experience.

imitation   *See* **learning by imitation**.

incentive   A goal object that may serve as the stimulus to arouse a drive, need, or motive.

incidental learning (*also called* **latent learning**)   Learning that takes place casually, almost as if by accident, without incentive.

incremental learning   Learning that takes place in a series of steps, in which the amount of learning increases, sometimes quickly and sometimes slowly, until the learning is complete. (*Compare* **one-trial learning.**)

independence   As used in social psychology, the tendency to make up one's own mind and decide on one's own behavior and thinking regardless of society's norms and pressures.

individual difference   Any difference—as in physical size or strength, intelligence, sensory threshold, perceptions, emotions, personality, and so on—between the individual organism and other members of his species.

individual test   A psychological test that is given by a trained examiner to one person at a time.

industrial psychology   A branch of applied psychology, embracing the use of psychological knowledge in setting working hours, rest periods, relations between employer and employees, and so on.

inferential statistics   Statistics that are used to make generalizations from measurements.

inferiority complex   A concept introduced by Alfred Adler to describe the condition of a person who for some reason has been unable to develop feelings of adequacy, independence, courage, and wholesome ambition.

inhibit   To suppress behavior; for example, the child in toilet training must learn to inhibit his tendency to eliminate wherever and whenever the elimination drive occurs.

inhibition   The suppression of behavior; also frequently used to describe emotional and psychoneurotic barriers to action—such as an inhibition against competitive or sexual activity.

inner ear   The portion of the ear inward from the oval window; contains the cochlea, vertibular sacs, and semicircular canals.

insight   (1) In problem solving, the sudden "flash of inspiration" that results in a successful solution (*compare* **trial and error learning**). (2) In psychotherapy, the discovery by the patient of psychological processes that have caused his difficulties.

instinct   An elaborate and inborn pattern of activity, occurring automatically and without prior learning in response to certain stimuli in the environment.

insulin   A hormone, secreted by the pancreas, that burns up blood sugar to provide energy.

intellectualization   A defense mechanism in which the individual tries to explain away anxiety by intellectually analyzing the situations that produce the unpleasant feelings and making them a matter of theory rather than of action.

intelligence   The ability to profit from experience, to learn new pieces of information, and to adjust to new situations.

intelligence quotient (I.Q.)   A numerical value assigned to an individual as a result of intelligence testing. The average intelligence quotient is set at 100.

intelligence test   A test measuring the various factors that make up the capacity called intelligence. It measures chiefly the individual's ability to use his acquired knowledge in a novel way.

interest test   A test measuring the individual's interest or lack of interest in various kinds of amusements, literature, music, art, science, school subjects, social activities, kinds of people, and so on.

interference   The basis of a currently popular theory maintaining that interference among old and new mediational units accounts for forgetting. (*Compare* **memory trace.**)

intermittent reinforcement   *See* **partial reinforcement.**

interposition   A clue to distance perception; refers to the fact that nearby objects interpose themselves between our eyes and more distant objects.

interval scale   A scale (for example, a thermometer) on which the intervals are equal but no ratio between the intervals is implied.

interview   A scientific method in which the investigator obtains information through careful and objective questioning of the subject.

intrinsic motivation   Motivation that comes from inside the individual. It is an integral part of the learning situation; the individual seeks to learn not for any external reward, but for the joy of knowing. (*Compare* **extrinsic motivation.**)

introspection   Inward examination of a "mental life" or mental process that nobody but its possessor can see in operation.

introvert   A person who tends to be preoccupied with his own thoughts and activities and to avoid social contacts.

I.Q.   *See* **intelligence quotient.**

iris   A circular arrangement of muscles that contract and expand to make the pupil of the eye smaller in bright light and larger in dim light.

J

James-Lange theory of emotion   A physiological theory holding that stimuli in the environment set off physiological changes in the individual, that the changes in turn stimulate sensory nerves inside the body, and that the messages of these sensory nerves are then perceived as emotion.

just noticeable difference (j.n.d.)   *See* **difference threshold.**

L

latent learning (*also called* **incidental learning**)   Learning that takes place but lies latent, not being put into overt performance until reinforcement is provided.

learning   The process by which overt behavior and covert processes become altered or attached to new stimuli.

learning by imitation (*also called* **learning through modeling**)   A complex and characteristically human form of learning in which the behavior of another person (the model) is copied.

learning curve   A graph plotting the course of learning. In a learning curve of decreasing returns, progress is quite rapid at first; then the curve starts to level off. In a learning curve of equal returns, progress takes place at a steady rate, with each new trial producing an equal amount of improvement. In a learning curve of increasing returns, very slow progress in early trials is followed by rapid progress in later trials.

learning plateau   A period in which early progress in learning appears to have stopped and improvement is at a standstill; the plateau is followed by a new period of progress.

learning through exposition   *See* **didactic learning.**

learning through modeling   *See* **learning by imitation.**

lens   A transparent structure of the eye that changes shape to focus images sharply on the retina.

libido   According to Freud's psychoanalytic theory of personality, a basic instinctual force in the individual, embracing sexual urges and such related desires as to be kept warm, well-fed, and happy.

lie detector   A device designed to reveal whether a subject is telling the truth by measuring physiological changes, usually in heart rate, blood pressure, breathing, and galvanic skin reflex.

limbic system   A set of interconnected pathways in the brain related to the hypothalamus, some primitive parts of the cerebrum that have to do with the sense of smell, eating, and emotion, and other structures.

limen   *See* **threshold.**

linear perspective   A clue to distance perception; refers to the fact that parallel lines seem to draw closer together as they recede into the distance.

location constancy   The tendency to perceive objects as being in their rightful and accustomed place and remaining there even when we move and their images therefore move across our eyes.

logical thinking   An objective and disciplined form of thinking in which facts are carefully examined and conclusions consistent with the facts are reached.

loudness   The hearing sensation determined by the amplitude of the sound wave.

LSD (lysergic acid diethylamide)   A psychedelic drug.

M

management of learning   An attempt—often made by educators and by people desirous of learning—to arrange the most favorable possible conditions for learning to take place.

manic-depressive psychosis   A functional psychosis characterized by extremes of mood, often by wild swings from intense excitement to deep melancholy.

massed practice   A single, long learning session. (*Compare* **distributed practice.**)

maturation   The physical changes, taking place after birth, that continue the biological development of the organism from fertilized egg cell to complete adult.

mean   An average obtained by dividing the sum of all the measurements by the number of subjects measured.

measurement   The assignment of numbers to traits, events, or subjects according to some kind of orderly system.

median   A type of average; the point separating the lower half of measurements from the upper half.

mediated generalization   A process in which two stimuli are generalized through the use of language, although they do not possess any physical similarities. An example is the generalization of a small rubber ball and a giant stuffed animal because both are called toys.

mediated transfer   A special kind of transfer of learning in which language is the mediating factor.

mediational clustering   The association of words and concepts, not through formal rules of logic but through an informal clustering of ideas that are in some way related.

mediational unit   One term (the preferred term in this book) for the engram, association, bond, or memory trace formed in learning; a connection between a new stimulus and an innate or previously learned unit of overt or covert behavior.

medulla   The connection between the spinal cord and the brain; an important connecting link that is vital to life because it helps regulate heartbeat, blood pressure, and breathing.

memory trace   The basis of a theory of remembering, no longer popular, holding that learning left some kind of trace in the organism that was kept active through use but tended to fade away with lack of practice. (*Compare* **interference**.)

mental age   A person's age as measured by his performance on an intelligence test; a person who scores as well as the average ten-year-old has a mental age of ten regardless of his chronological age.

mentally gifted   Having an I.Q. over 130.

mentally retarded   Having an I.Q. below 70.

mesomorph   One of three basic types of body build described by Sheldon; the mesomorph is the athletic type, with strong bones and muscles.

metabolism   The chemical process in which the body converts food into protoplasm and energy.

middle ear   The portion of the ear between the eardrum and the oval window of the inner ear; contains three bones that aid transmission of sound waves.

mnemonic system   A form of memory aid in which a set of memorized symbols is used as the attachment units for new stimuli.

mode   A type of average; the measurement into which the greatest number of subjects fall.

modeling   *See* **learning through imitation**.

mongolism   A type of mental retardation apparently caused by the presence of an extra chromosome (making a total of forty-seven instead of the normal forty-six in each cell).

motion parallax   A term describing the fact that, when we move our heads, near objects move across our field of vision more rapidly than objects that are farther away.

motivation   A general term referring to the forces regulating behavior that is undertaken because of drives, needs, or desires and is directed toward goals.

motivational disposition   The possession of a motive; a potential influence on behavior that can at any time be aroused to become an active motive.

motive   A desire for a goal that, through learning, has acquired value for the individual.

motor skill   A coordinated series of movements, such as those required in walking or riding a bicycle.

muscle   Fibers capable of producing motion by contraction and expansion. Human muscles include *striped muscles* and *smooth muscles*.

myelin sheath   A fatty sheath, white in appearance, that covers many neuron fibers and speeds the transmission of nervous impulses.

N

naturalistic observation   A scientific method in which the investigator does not manipulate the situation and cannot control all the variables; he tries to remain unseen or as inconspicuous as possible.

negative transfer A process in which learning is made more difficult by interference from previous learning. (*Compare* **positive transfer.**)

nerve A group of neurons, small or very large in number, traveling together to or from the central nervous system; in appearance, a single large fiber that is in fact made up of many fibers.

nervous impulse A tiny charge of electricity passing from the dendrite end of the neuron to the end of the axon.

neuron The individual nerve cell, basic unit of the nervous system.

neurosis *See* **psychoneurosis.**

neurotic depression A form of psychoneurosis in which the individual appears to be particularly sensitive to unhappy events; his normal discouragement and grief are complicated and exaggerated by feelings of dejection, hopelessness, and guilt.

nomadism A form of withdrawal in which the frustrated individual wanders through life without ever putting down roots.

nominal scale A scale in which numbers are simply assigned to different categories (as when men are called group 1 and women are called group 2).

nonsense syllable A meaningless syllable, such as XYL or PLAM, used in the study of learning.

nonsocial behavior Actions that take place when a person is alone.

noradrenalin A hormone, secreted by the adrenal medulla, that produces bodily changes associated with anger or "fight" situations.

normal curve of distribution (*also called* **normal probability curve**) A bell-shaped curve that describes many events in nature; most events cluster around the average, and the number declines approaching either the lower or the upper extreme.

norms The shared standards and expectations of a social group.

O

object constancy The tendency to perceive objects as constant and unchanging, even under varying conditions of illumination, distance, and position.

objective personality test A paper-and-pencil test administered and scored according to a standard procedure, giving results that are not affected by the opinions or prejudices of the examiner.

obsession A thought that keeps cropping up in a persistent and disturbing fashion.

obsessive-compulsive reactions A group of psychoneuroses characterized by obsessions or compulsions.

Oedipus complex According to Freud, the conflict of mingled love and hate toward the parents that every child undergoes between the ages of two and a half and six.

olfactory epithelium The membrane, at the top of the nasal passages leading from the nostrils to the throat, that contains the receptors sensitive to smell.

one-trial learning Learning that takes place in a single step. (*Compare* **incremental learning.**)

operant avoidance Behavior, learned through operant conditioning, by which the organism attempts to avoid something unpleasant.

operant behavior Behavior that is not initially associated with or normally elicited by a specific stimulus. (*Compare* **respondent behavior.**)

operant conditioning The process by which, through learning, free operant behavior becomes attached to a specific stimulus.

operant escape Behavior, learned through operant conditioning, by which the organism seeks to escape something unpleasant.

ordinal scale A scale based on rank order.

organ of Corti The collection of hair cells, lying on the basilar membrane, that are the receptors for hearing.

organic psychosis A psychosis caused by actual damage to the brain by disease or injury.

organism An individual animal, either human or subhuman.

oval window The membrane through which sound waves are transmitted from the bones of the middle ear to the cochlea.

ovaries Glands that, in addition to producing the female egg cells, secrete hormones that bring about bodily changes known as secondary sex characteristics.

overlearning The process of continuing to practice at learning after bare mastery has been attained.

overlearning, law of The principle that overlearning increases the length of time the material will be remembered.

overt behavior Observable behavior, such as motor movements, speech, and signs of emotion such as laughing or weeping.

P

pacer stimuli A term, used in the theory of choice, that refers to stimuli of somewhat greater complexity than stimuli at the individual's ideal level of complexity.

pain drive A biological drive aroused by unpleasant or noxious stimulation, usually resulting in behavior designed to escape the stimulus.

pancreas The endocrine gland that secretes insulin, a chemical that burns up blood sugar to provide energy.

Papez-MacLean theory of emotion A neurological theory of emotion that emphasizes the role of the *limbic system.*

paradoxical cold A term for the fact that cold receptors in the skin respond to a stimulus of more than 110 degrees Fahrenheit as well as to stimuli that are actually cold.

paranoia A functional psychosis characterized by delusions, sometimes of grandeur, sometimes of persecution.

parasympathetic nervous system A division of the autonomic nervous system, composed of scattered ganglia that lie near the glands and muscles they affect. The parasympathetic system is most active in helping maintain heartbeat and digestion under normal circumstances. (*Compare* **sympathetic nervous system.**)

parathyroids A pair of endocrine glands, lying around the larger thyroid gland, that regulate the balance of calcium and phosphorus in the body, an important factor in maintaining a normal state of excitability of the nervous system.

partial reinforcement (*also called* **intermittent reinforcement**) Reinforcement provided on some but not all occasions.

peer group The group of psychological equals to which the individual belongs; among children, based largely on age.

peers For any individual, other people of about the same age and standing in the community; equals.

percentile A statistical term used to describe the position of an individual score in the total group.

perception   The process through which we become aware of our environment by organizing and interpreting the evidence of our senses.

perceptual constancy   The tendency to perceive a stable and consistent world even though the stimuli that reach the senses are inconsistent and potentially confusing.

perceptual expectation   The tendency to perceive what we expect to perceive; a special form of set.

performance   Overt behavior; used as a measure of learning.

performance test   An intelligence test or part of an intelligence test that measures the individual's ability to perform such tasks as completing pictures, making designs, and assembling objects. (*Compare* **verbal test.**)

peripheral nervous system   The outlying nerves of the body and the individual neurons that make up these nerves. (*Compare* **central nervous system.**)

persistence of set   In problem solving, the tendency to continue to apply a certain hypothesis because it has worked in other situations, often at the expense of trying different and much more efficient hypotheses.

personality   The total pattern of characteristic ways of behaving and thinking that constitute an individual's unique and distinctive method of adjusting to his environment.

personality disorder   *See* **character disorder.**

personality test   A test designed to measure the various characteristics that make up the individual's personality.

perspective   A clue to distance perception; refers to the fact that three-dimensional objects can be delineated on a flat surface, such as the retina of the eye. (*See* **aerial perspective, linear perspective.**)

phenomenal self   A concept proposed by Carl Rogers in his theory of personality; one's uniquely perceived self-image, based on the evidence of one's senses but not necessarily corresponding to reality.

phi phenomenon   Motion produced by a rapid succession of images that are actually stationary; the simplest form of stroboscopic motion.

phobic reaction   An anxiety state characterized by unreasonable fears.

phonemes   The building blocks of language; basic sounds that are combined into syllables and words.

pitch   The property of being high or low in tone, determined by the frequency (number of cycles per second) of the sound wave.

pituitary gland   The master endocrine gland that secretes hormones controlling growth, causing sexual development at puberty, and also regulating other endocrine glands.

place theory (of hearing)   The theory that special parts of the basilar membrane are "tuned" to various pitches and that the response of receptors in each particular place accounts for the sensations of pitch.

play therapy   A type of psychotherapy, usually used with children, in which patients express their feelings by drawing pictures, modeling, or handling puppets or other toys.

pleasure principle   According to Freud's psychoanalytic theory of personality, the demand of the unconscious id for immediate and total satisfaction of all its demands. (*Compare* **reality principle.**)

pons   A structure of neurons connecting the opposite sides of the cerebellum; it helps control breathing and is apparently the origin of the nervous impulses that cause rapid eye movements during dreaming.

position   The particular place or niche that an individual occupies in society.

positive transfer   A process in which learning is made easier by something learned previously. (*Compare* **negative transfer.**)

posthypnotic suggestion   A suggestion made during hypnosis, urging the subject to undertake some kind of activity after the hypnotic trance ends.

prehension   Grasping ability.

primacy   In learning, the fact of being near the beginning of a series of items to be learned. (*See* **primacy and recency, law of.**)

primacy and recency, law of   The principle that the learner tends to remember best the items that were first in a series (had primacy) or last (had recency).

primary mental abilities   According to Thurstone, the seven abilities that make up intelligence. They are verbal comprehension, word fluency, number, space, associative memory, perceptual speed, and general reasoning, plus some kind of "general factor" that is common to all individuals.

primary reinforcement   Reinforcement provided by a stimulus that the organism finds inherently rewarding—usually stimuli that satisfy biological drives such as hunger or thirst.

prior knowledge   The individual's storehouse of previously accumulated facts, which can serve as *attachment units* for new stimuli.

proactive inhibition   Interference by something learned in the past with the ability to remember new learning. (*Compare* **retroactive inhibition.**)

problem solving   Thinking that is directed toward the solution of a problem; the most common and important kind of *directed thinking.*

progressive part method (of learning)   A method of learning, frequently quite efficient, in which the first unit of the whole (such as the first stanza of a poem) is learned, then the second, then these two are combined; then the third unit is learned and combined with the first two; and so on.

projection   A defense mechanism in which the individual foists off or projects onto other people motives of his own that cause him anxiety.

projective personality test   A test in which the subject is expected to project aspects of his own personality into the stories he makes up about pictures or the objects he sees in inkblots.

protoplasm   The basic substance of living tissue, the "stuff of life."

psychedelic drugs   Drugs that often produce visual hallucinations and a sense of detachment from one's own body; used in psychotherapy to help patients talk more freely to the therapist.

psychoanalysis   A type of psychotherapy developed by Freud, in which the chief tools are free association, study of dreams and slips of the tongue, and transference. Psychoanalysis attempts to give the patient insight into his unconscious conflicts, which he can then control as they come into his awareness.

psychoanalytic theory of personality   A theory originally formulated by Sigmund Freud that emphasizes three parts of the personality: (1) the unconscious id, (2) the conscious ego, and (3) the largely unconscious superego.

psychodrama   A type of psychotherapy in which the patient is encouraged to act out his problems and fantasies in the company of other patients or therapeutic assistants who have been trained in the techniques of psychodrama.

psychology The science that systematically studies and attempts to explain observable behavior and its relationship to the unseen mental and physiological processes that go on inside the organism and to events outside the organism.

psychoneurosis (*also called* **neurosis**) A form of emotional disturbance characterized by high levels of stress and anxiety over a period of time.

psychopathic personality A character disorder in which the individual lacks a sense of social responsibility.

psychophysical methods Techniques of measuring how changes in the intensity or quality of a stimulus affect sensation.

psychosis The scientific name for the extreme forms of mental disturbances often known as insanity. The mental disturbance is so severe as to make the individual incapable of getting along in society.

psychosomatic illness An illness in which the physical symptoms seem to have mental and emotional causes.

psychotherapy A technique used by clinical psychologists, psychiatrists, and psychoanalysts in which a patient suffering from personality disorder or mental disturbance is treated by the application of psychological knowledge.

pupil The opening in the iris, admitting light waves into the eyeball.

Q

questionnaire A scientific method similar to the interview but in which information is obtained through written questions.

R

random sample A statistical sample that has been obtained by chance methods that avoid any bias.

range A measurement of variability obtained by subtracting the lowest measurement from the highest.

ratio scale A scale of measurement (such as height or weight) in which there is a true zero point and all the numbers on the scale fall into perfect ratios.

rationalization A defense mechanism in which the individual maintains that a goal he was unable to attain was not desirable or that he acted out of "good" motives rather than "bad."

reaction formation A defense mechanism in which the person behaves as if his motives were the opposite of his real motives; often characterized by excessive display of a "good" trait such as politeness.

reality principle According to Freud's psychoanalytic theory of personality, the principle on which the conscious ego operates as it tries to mediate between the demands of the unconscious id and the realities of the environment. (*Compare* **pleasure principle.**)

recall A way of measuring learning; the subject is asked to repeat as much of what he has learned as he can. (*Compare* **recognition, relearning.**)

recency In learning, the fact of being near the end of a series of items to be learned. (*See* **primacy and recency, law of.**)

receptor A specialized nerve ending of the senses.

recessive gene A gene, such as the one for blue eyes, whose effects are always inhibited if the other member of the pair is a *dominant gene,* such as the one for brown eyes.

reciprocal inhibition   A technique devised by Wolpe to reduce anxiety by associating its stimulus to some new and more benign response.

recognition   A way of measuring learning; the subject is asked to show that he recognizes what he has learned—for example, by picking out the right answer in a multiple choice test. (*Compare* **recall, relearning.**)

redintegration   A special kind of remembering in which the individual appears to reconstruct an entire incident from his past; for example, he remembers not only a poem but also events in the classroom and the appearance of his teacher on the day he learned the poem.

reflex   An automatic and unthinking reaction to a stimulus by the organism. A reflex is inborn, not learned, and depends upon inherited characteristics of the nervous system.

regression   A retreat toward types of activity appropriate to a lower level of maturity; a result of frustration.

reinforcement   In classical conditioning, the pairing of an unconditioned stimulus (such as food) with a conditioned stimulus (such as sound). In general, the process of assisting learning by pairing desired behavior with something that the organism finds rewarding.

reinforcing stimulus   The stimulus used in reinforcement; anything that strengthens and induces repetition of behavior in learning.

relearning   A method of measuring learning; the subject is asked to relearn to perfection something he had previously learned and partially forgotten, and the amount of time required for the original learning and for relearning are compared. (*Compare* **recall, recognition.**)

reliable test   A test that gives consistent scores when the same individual is tested on different occasions.

reminiscence   In psychology, the phenomenon responsible for the fact that performance of a learned task is sometimes better after a lapse of time than at the conclusion of learning.

representative sample   A statistical sample in which all parts of the population are represented.

repression   A defense mechanism in which an individual suffering anxiety over his motives seems to banish the motives from his conscious thoughts, pushing them into the unconscious.

respondent behavior   Behavior that is a response to a definite stimulus. (*Compare* **operant behavior.**)

response   A general term used to describe any kind of behavior produced by a stimulus.

reticular formation   A network of nerves in the brain stem and hypothalamus, serving as a way station for messages from the sense organs.

retina   A small patch of tissue at the back of the eyeball; contains the nerve endings called rods and cones that are the receptors for vision.

retroactive inhibition   Partial or complete blacking out of old memories by new learning. (*Compare* **proactive inhibition.**)

rods   One of the two types of receptors for vision located in the retina. The rods are receptors for light intensity, resulting in sensations of black, white, and gray.

role   The kind of behavior that society expects from a person in a given position.

S

sample A relatively small group whose measurements are used to infer facts about the population or universe. To permit valid generalization the sample must be representative and random.

saturation The amount of pure hue present in a color as compared to the amount of other light wave lengths mixed in; thus the complexity of the mixture of waves determines saturation.

schizophrenia A functional psychosis in which the patient appears to lose contact with reality and lives in a shell-like world of his own.

secondary reinforcement Reinforcement provided by a stimulus that has acquired reward value through association with a primary reinforcing stimulus.

selection In perception, the tendency to pay attention to only some of the stimuli that reach our senses.

self-actualization A term used by Maslow in his personality theory holding that men are innately virtuous and that normal and healthy development would enable each person to actualize his own true nature and fulfill his potentialities.

semantic differential A scale invented by Osgood to measure differences in the qualities and values that words connote, especially along dimensions of good-bad, strong-weak, and active-passive.

semicircular canals Three liquid-filled canals in the inner ear, containing receptors for the sense of equilibrium.

senile psychosis An organic psychosis caused by deterioration of the brain cells and other physiological changes due to aging.

sensorimotor period The term applied by Piaget to the first two years of life, when the child knows the world only in terms of his sensory impressions and his motor activities.

sensory adaptation The tendency of sensory receptors to adjust to a stimulus and stop responding after a time.

separation anxiety Fear of being separated from the caretaker; a form of anxiety that develops in the infant of about ten to eighteen months.

serial position The position that an individual item occupies in a series of items to be learned. (*See* **primacy, recency.**)

set A tendency to respond in a certain way; to be prepared or "set" so to respond.

sex drive A biological drive aroused by physiological requirements for sexual satisfaction.

shadowing The pattern of light and shadow on an object; often a clue to perception of three-dimensional quality.

shape constancy The tendency to perceive objects as retaining their shape regardless of the true nature of the image that reaches the eyes because of the viewing angle.

shaping The learning of complicated tasks through operant conditioning, in which complex actions are built up from simpler ones.

situational personality test A test in which the examiner observes the behavior of the subject in a situation deliberately created to reveal some aspects of his personality.

size constancy The tendency to perceive objects in their correct size regardless of the size of the actual image they cast on the eyes when near or far away.

skewed curve   A type of distribution curve that is irregular in that more scores fall on one side of the mode than on the other side.

sleep drive   A biological drive aroused by the physiological requirements for sleep.

smooth muscle   A muscle of the internal organs, such as the stomach and intestines, or of the pupil of the eye, over which the individual ordinarily has no conscious control.

social behavior   Actions taken in relation to another person or persons.

social class   A subdivision of society made up of people who share the same norms.

social learning theories of personality (*also called* **stimulus-response, or S-R, theories**)   Theories maintaining that personality is composed of habitual ways of responding to the environment that are learned responses to stimuli in the environment.

social psychology   The study of the behavior of the individual in his society and the influence that the actions and attitudes of the other members of his society have upon his overt behavior and his thinking.

social structure   The organization of relationships among members of a society. Horizontal social structure governs the relationships among people of equal standing in the society, such as brothers or the members of a social sorority. Vertical social structure takes the form of a status system that in the United States differentiates among the upper, middle and lower social classes.

socialization   The training of the young in the ways of the society.

society   Any organized group of people, large or small.

somatotonic temperament   A type of temperament ascribed by Sheldon to the mesomorphic body type; characterized by boldness of manner, physical courage, aggressiveness, and the love of physical adventure, risk, and chance.

spectrum   The range of hues created by breaking up a beam of sunlight with a prism, thus separating all the wavelengths of light from red to violet.

spontaneous recovery   The tendency of a conditioned response that has undergone extinction to occur again after a rest period.

S-shaped learning curve   A curve that shows very slow progress at the start, then faster progress for a time, and at last slower progress (or decreasing returns) as the ultimate limit of learning is approached.

standard   A rule that the individual sets for his own behavior. The desire to live up to standards is an important human motive.

standard deviation (SD)   A statistical device for describing the variability of measurements.

standardized test   A test that has been pretested on a large and representative sample so that one person's score can be compared with the scores of the population as a whole.

startle pattern   A complex human reflex that occurs in response to sudden and unexpected events, such as a loud noise. The muscles of the neck, arms, and legs tense; the head moves forward; and the mouth may open.

statistical method   The application of mathematical principles to a description and analysis of measurements.

stereotyped behavior   A tendency to repeat some action over and over again, almost as a ritual; a result of frustration.

steroids   Chemical substances produced by the adrenal cortex and essential for life.

stimulus   Any form of energy capable of exciting the nervous system.

stimulus complexity   The relative level of simplicity or complexity possessed by a sensory stimulus. The organism apparently has stimulus needs for stimuli of a particular level of complexity found the most "comfortable."

stimulus discrimination   The ability, acquired through learning, to make distinctions between stimuli that are similar but not exactly alike.

stimulus generalization   The tendency of an organism that has learned to associate a stimulus with a certain kind of behavior to display this behavior toward stimuli that are similar though not exactly identical to the original stimulus.

stimulus need   The tendency of an organism to seek certain kinds of stimulation. The tendency does not have the life-and-death urgency of a drive, nor is its goal as specific and clear-cut. Examples are the needs for stimulation, stimulus variability, and physical contact (or tactual comfort).

stimulus-response (S-R) theories   See **social learning theories of personality.**

stimulus variability   Change and variety in stimulation; believed to be one of the organism's inborn stimulus needs.

stranger anxiety   Fear of unfamiliar faces, one of the first forms of anxiety that develops in the child at about eight months.

stress   In psychological terms, a stimulus that threatens to damage the organism.

striped muscle   A muscle of motor behavior, over which the individual ordinarily has conscious control.

stroboscopic motion   Motion produced by a rapid succession of images that are actually stationary, as in motion pictures.

subliminal   A word used to describe a stimulus of lower intensity than required by the threshold, or limen.

substitution   A defense mechanism in which an unobtainable or forbidden goal is replaced by a different goal.

superego   According to Freud's psychoanalytic theory of personality, a largely unconscious part of the individual's personality that threatens punishment for transgressions.

supraliminal   A word used to describe a stimulus of intensity at or above the threshold, or limen.

syllogism   A three-step process of logical thinking, consisting of a major premise, a minor premise, and a conclusion that follows inescapably from the first two.

symbol   Anything that stands for something else. The word *water* is a symbol for the colorless fluid we drink; the skull and crossbones is a symbol for poison; mathematics is a collection of symbols.

sympathetic nervous system   A division of the autonomic nervous system, composed of long chains of ganglia lying along both sides of the spinal column. Its final axons secrete chemicals resembling adrenalin and noradrenalin, thus stimulating the glands and smooth muscles of the body and helping prepare the organism for "fight or flight." (*Compare* **parasympathetic nervous system.**)

synapse   The junction point between the axon of one neuron and the dendrite of another neuron.

syndrome   A medical term meaning the entire pattern of symptoms and events that characterize the course of a disease.

T

tabula rasa   A "blank tablet"; a phrase used to describe the theory that the mind of a human baby is a "blank tablet" on which anything can be written through learning and experience.

tactual comfort   Physical contact; one of the stimulus needs.

taste buds   The receptors for the sense of taste; found on the tongue, at the back of the mouth, and in the throat.

teaching machine   A device with which a student studies a subject in a series of brief steps. At the end of each step a question is presented to him; he writes in the answer, and the machine immediately tells him if he was right.

temperature drive   A biological drive aroused by physiological requirements that the body temperature be kept at a constant level (in human beings, around 98.6° Fahrenheit).

test   A measurement of a sample of individual behavior. Ideally, a scientific test should be (1) objective, (2) standardized, (3) reliable, and (4) valid.

testes   Glands that, in addition to producing the male sperm cells, secrete hormones that bring about secondary male sex characteristics, such as the growth of facial hair and change of voice.

thalamus   One of the brain's major relay stations, connecting the cerebrum with the lower structures of the brain and the spinal cord.

theory   A statement of general principles that explains events observed in the past and predicts what will happen under a given set of circumstances in the future.

theory of choice   A theory maintaining that every stimulus object has a certain complexity value (related to its information value), that every individual organism has its own ideal level of complexity, that the individual will seek out stimuli of this level, but that the individual will also explore objects of slightly greater complexity, called pacer stimuli.

thinking   The covert manipulation of images, symbols, and other mediational units, especially language, concepts, premises, and rules.

thirst drive   A biological drive aroused by deprivation of water.

threshold (*also called* **limen**)   The minimum amount of stimulation or difference in stimulation to which a sensory receptor will respond 50 percent of the time. (*See* **absolute threshold, difference threshold.**)

thyroid gland   An endocrine gland that regulates the rate of metabolism and affects the body's activity level.

tic   The involuntary twitching of a muscle.

timbre   The quality of a sound, determined by the number and strength of the overtones that contribute to the complexity of the sound wave.

tranquilizer   A drug that relieves tensions and anxieties, presumably by its effect on brain chemistry. Tranquilizers are used in mental hospitals to calm unmanageable patients and make them more amenable to psychotherapy.

transfer of learning   The effect of prior learning on new learning. (*See* **positive transfer, negative transfer.**)

transference   A psychoanalytic term for the tendency of the patient to transfer to other people (including the psychoanalyst) the emotional attitudes he felt as a child toward such much loved and hated persons as parents and siblings.

traveling wave theory (of hearing)   The theory that the basilar membrane responds as a whole to sound waves and that the sensation of pitch results from the fact that some parts of the membrane are activated more than others.

trial and error learning   A form of learning in which one response after another is tried and rejected as unsuitable, until at last a successful response is made. (*Compare* **insight.**)

truth serum (sodium amytal)   A narcotic used in medical therapy to induce a period of drowsiness in which the patient is able to recall and discuss experiences that he ordinarily represses.

U

unconditioned reflex   An automatic, unlearned reaction to a stimulus—such as the salivation of Pavlov's dog to food.

unconditioned stimulus   A stimulus that is innately capable of causing a reflex action—such as the food that originally caused Pavlov's dog to respond with reflex salivation.

unconscious motive   A motive that the individual is unaware of but that may influence his behavior nonetheless.

undirected thinking   A thinking process that takes place spontaneously and with no goal in view.

upward mobility   The tendency of an individual to surmount the barriers between social classes and advance his station in life.

V

vacillation   The tendency to be drawn first toward one resolution of a conflict, then toward the other; a type of behavior typical in conflict situations.

valid test   A test found to actually measure the characteristic that it attempts to measure.

variability   In statistics, the amount of variation found in a group of measurements; described by the range and standard deviation.

variable   A condition that is subject to change, especially one that is manipulated experimentally.

verbal test   An intelligence test or part of an intelligence test that measures the individual's ability to deal with verbal symbols; it may include items measuring vocabulary, general comprehension, arithmetical reasoning, ability to find similarities, and so on. (*Compare* **performance test.**)

vestibule   A chamber in the inner ear containing receptors for the sense of equilibrium.

visceral organs   The internal organs, such as the stomach, intestines, liver, kidneys, and so on.

viscerotonic temperament   A type of temperament ascribed by Sheldon to the endomorphic body type; characterized by relaxed posture, even emotions, love of physical comfort, tolerance, and complacency.

visual purple   A light-sensitive substance associated with the rods of the retina; chemical changes in the visual purple, caused by light, make the rods fire.

vocational aptitude test   A test that measures the ability to perform specialized skills required in various kinds of jobs.

vocational guidance   The technique of helping a person select the right lifetime occupation, often through tests of aptitudes and interests.

W

Weber's law   The rule that the difference threshold or just noticeable difference is a fixed percentage of the original stimulus.

withdrawal   A reaction in which the individual tries to relieve feelings of frustration by withdrawing from the attempt to attain his goals.

Y

Young-Helmholtz theory (of vision)   A theory stating that, since the entire range of hues can be produced by combining red, green, and blue, there must be three kinds of cones differentially sensitive to these wave lengths.

REFERENCES AND ACKNOWLEDGMENTS

CHAPTER 1 THE SCOPE AND GOALS OF PSYCHOLOGY

1. Penfield, W. The interpretive cortex. *Science*, 1959, **129**, 1719–25. Reprinted in Teevan, R. C., and Birney, R. C., eds. *Readings for introductory psychology.* New York: Harcourt, Brace & World, 1965.
2. Bexton, W. H., Heron, W., and Scott, T. H. Effects of decreased variation in the sensory environment. *Canad. J. Psychol.*, 1954, **8**, 70–76.
3. Lilly, J. C. Mental effects of reduction of ordinary levels of physical stimuli on intact, healthy persons. *Psychiatric res. Reports*, 1956, **5**, 1–9. Reprinted in Teevan and Birney, eds., *op. cit.*
4. Brady, J. V. Ulcers in "executive" mon-

keys. *Scient. Amer.*, 1958, **199**, 95–100.
5. James, W. *Principles of psychology.* New York: Dover, 1950.
6. Anastasi, A., and Foley, J. P., Jr. *Differential psychology*, rev. ed. New York: Macmillan, 1949.
7. Miles, G. H., and Angles, A. The influence of short time on speed of production. *J. Natl. Inst. Industr. Psychol.*, 1925, **2**, 300–02.
8. Harrell, T. W. *Industrial psychology.* New York: Holt, Rinehart and Winston, 1949.
9. Roethlisberger, F. J., and Dickson, W. J. *Management and the worker.* Cambridge, Mass.: Harvard University Press, 1939.

CHAPTER 2 THE PRINCIPLES OF LEARNING

1. From Jones, F. P. Method for changing stereotyped response patterns by the inhibition of certain postural sets. *Psychol. Rev.*, 1965, **72**, 196–214. Copyright © 1965 by the American Psychological Association, and reproduced by permission.
2. Landis, C., and Hunt, W. A. *The startle pattern.* New York: Holt, Rinehart and Winston, 1939.
3. Yerkes, R. M., and Morgulis, S. The methods of Pavlov in animal psychology. *Psychol. Bull.*, 1909, **6**, 257–73.
4. Pavlov, I. P. *Conditioned reflexes: an in-*

vestigation of the physiological activity of the cerebral cortex. London: Oxford University Press, 1927 [reprinted by Dover, New York, 1960].
5. Watson, J. B., and Rayner, R. Conditioned emotional reactions. *J. exp. Psychol.*, 1920, **3**, 1–14.
6. Sawry, W. C., Conger, J. J., and Turrell, R. B. An experimental investigation of the role of psychological factors in the production of gastric ulcers in rats. *J. comp. physiol. Psychol.*, 1956, **457**, 143.
7. Fel'berbaum, I. M. Interoceptive con-

ditioned reflexes from the uterus. *Trud. Inst. Fiziol. Pavlova*, 1952, **1**, 85–92.

8. Skinner, B. F. *The behavior of organisms.* New York: Appleton-Century-Crofts, 1938.

9. Grant, D. A. Classical and operant conditioning. In Melton, A. W., ed. *Categories of human learning.* New York: Academic Press, 1964.

10. Grice, G. R. The relation of secondary reinforcement to delayed reward in visual discrimination learning. *J. exp. Psychol.*, 1948, **38**, 1–16.

11. Perin, C. T. A quantitative investigation of the delay of reinforcement gradient. *J. exp. Psychol.*, 1943, **32**, 37–51.

12. Perkins, C. C., Jr. The relation of secondary reward to gradients of reinforcement. *J. exp. Psychol.*, 1947, **37**, 377–92.

13. Wolfe, G. B. The effect of delayed reward upon learning in the white rat. *J. comp. physiol. Psychol.*, 1934, **17**, 1–21.

14. Weinstock, S. Resistance to extinction following partial reinforcement under widely spaced trials. *J. exp. Psychol.*, 1954, **47**, 318–23.

15. Solomon, R. L., Kamin, L. J., and Wynne, L. C. Traumatic avoidance learning: the outcomes of several extinction procedures with dogs. *J. abn. soc. Psychol.*, 1953, **48**, 291–302.

16. Tolman, E. C., and Honzik, C. H. Introduction and removal of reward and maze performance in rats. *Univ. Calif. Publ. Psychol.*, 1930, **4**, 257–75.

17. Brogden, W. J. Sensory preconditioning. *J. exp. Psychol.*, 1939, **25**, 323–32.

18. Olds, J. Pleasure centers in the brain. *Scient. Amer.*, 1956, **195**, 105–16.

19. Solomon, R. L., and Turner, C. H. Discriminative classical conditioning in dogs paralyzed by curare can later control discriminative avoidance response in the normal state. *Psychol. Rev.*, 1962, **69**, 202–19.

20. Bandura, A., Ross, D., and Ross, S. A. Imitation of film-mediated aggressive models. *J. abn. soc. Psychol.*, 1963, **66**, 3–11.

21. Hunter, W. S. The delayed reaction in animals and children. *Behavior Monogr.*, 1913, **2**.

CHAPTER 3 LEARNING, REMEMBERING, AND FORGETTING

1. Bryan, W. L., and Harter, N. Studies in the physiology and psychology of telegraphic language. *Psychol. Rev.*, 1897, **4**, 27–53.

2. Ebbinghaus, H. *Memory.* New York: Columbia University, Teachers College, 1913 [reprinted by Dover, New York, 1964].

3. Leavitt, H. J., and Schlosberg, H. The retention of verbal and motor skills. *J. exp. Psychol.*, 1944, **34**, 404–17.

4. Luh, C. W. The conditions of retention. *Psychol. Monogr.*, 1922, **31** (No. 22).

5. Haber, R. N., and Haber, R. B. Eidetic imagery. *Perc. motor Skills*, 1964, **19**, 131–38.

6. James, W. *Principles of psychology.* New York: Dover, 1950.

CHAPTER 4 EFFICIENCY IN LEARNING

1. Gibson, E., and Walk, R. D. The effect of prolonged exposure to visually presented patterns on learning to discriminate them. *J. comp. physiol. Psychol.*, 1956, **49**, 239–42.

2. Glaze, J. A. The association value of nonsense syllables. *J. genet. Psychol.*, 1928, **35**(2), 255–69.

3. McGeoch, J. A. The influence of associative value upon the difficulty of nonsense-syllable lists. *J. genet. Psychol.*, 1930, **37**, 421–26.

4. Lyon, D. O. The relation of length of material to time taken for learning and the optimum distribution of time. *J. educ. Psychol.*, 1914, **5**, 1–9, 85–91, and 155–63.

5. Katona, G. *Organizing and memorizing.* New York: Columbia University Press, 1940.
6. Tyler, R. W. Permanence of learning. *J. higher Educ.,* IV (April 1933), Table I, p. 204.
7. Sarason, I. G., and Sarason, B. Effects of motivating instructions and reports of failure on verbal learning. *Amer. J. Psychol.,* 1957, **70,** 92–96.
8. Thorndike, E. L. *The fundamentals of learning.* New York: Columbia University, Teachers College, 1932.
9. Solomon, R. L., Punishment. *Amer. Psychologist,* 1964, **19,** 239–53.
10. Ward, L. B. Reminiscence and rote learning. *Psychol. Monogr.,* 1937, **49** (No. 220).
11. Pechstein, L. A. Whole vs. part methods in learning nonsensical syllables. *J. educ. Psychol.,* 1918, **9,** 379–87.
12. Krueger, W. C. F. The effect of overlearning on retention. *J. exp. Psychol.,* 1929, **12,** 71–78.
13. Gollin, E. Serial learning and perceptual recognition in children: training, delay, and order effects. *Perc. motor Skills,* 1966, **23,** 751–58.
14. Spence, K. W., and Norris, E. B. Eyelid conditioning as a function of the intertrial interval. *J. exp. Psychol.,* 1950, **40,** 716–20.
15. Starch, D. Periods of work in learning. *J. educ. Psychol.,* 1912, **3,** 209–13.
16. Gates, A. L. Recitation as a factor in memorizing. *Arch. Psychol.,* New York, 1917, No. 40. By permission of the Trustees of Columbia University in the City of New York.
17. Thorndike, E. L. Mental discipline in high school studies. *J. educ. Psychol.,* 1924, **15,** 83–98.
18. Bruce, R. W. Conditions of transfer of training. *J. exp. Psychol.,* 1933, **16,** 343–61. Published by the American Psychological Association.
19. Williams, A. C., Jr., and Flexman, R. E. An evaluation of the Link SNJ Operational Trainer as an aid in contact flight training. Tech. Rep. No. SDC 71-16-3. Port Washington, N.Y.: U.S. Navy Special Devices Center, 1949.
20. Hunter, W. S. Habit interference in the white rat and in human subjects. *J. comp. Psychol.,* 1922, **2,** 29–59.
21. Harlow, H. F. The formation of learning sets. *Psychol. Rev.,* 1949, **56,** 51–65.
22. McGeoch, J. A., and McDonald, W. T. Meaningful relation and retroactive inhibition. *Amer. J. Psychol.,* 1931, **43,** 579–88.
23. Jenkins, J. G., and Dallenbach, K. M. Oblivescence during sleep and waking. *Amer. J. Psychol.,* 1924, **35,** 605–12.
24. Newman, E. B. Forgetting of meaningful material during sleep and waking. *Amer. J. Psychol.,* 1939, **52,** 65–71.
25. Adapted from Underwood, B. J. Interference and forgetting. *Psychol. Rev.,* 1957, **64,** fig. 1, p. 51.

CHAPTER 5   PERCEPTION

1. Krech, D., and Crutchfield, R. S. *Elements of psychology.* New York: Knopf, 1958.
2. Salapatek, P., and Kessen, W. Visual scanning of triangles by the human newborn. *J. exp. Child Psychol.,* 1966, **3,** 155–67.
3. Boring, E. G. Apparatus notes: a new ambiguous figure. *Amer. J. Psychol.,* 1930, **42,** 444–45.
4. Street, R. F. *A gestalt completion test.* New York: Columbia University, Teachers College, 1931.
5. Ternus, J. Experimentelle Untersuchungen über phenomenale Identität. *Psychol. Forsch.* (Berlin, Springer), 1926, **7,** 81–136.
6. Allport, G. W., and Pettigrew, T. F. Cultural influence on the perception of movement: the trapezoidal illusion among Zulus. *J. abn. soc. Psychol.,* 1957, **55,** 104–13.
7. Segal, M. H., et al. Cultural differences in perception of geometric illusions. *Science,* 1963, **139**(22), 769–71. Copyright 1963 by the American Association for the Advancement of Science.
8. From *Psychology: the science of mental life* by George A. Miller. Copyright © 1962 by George A. Miller. Reprinted by

permission of Harper & Row, Publishers. FIGURE 5.19 is an adaptation of Fig. 12; FIGURE 5.22 is an adaptation of Fig. 11.

9. Bruner, J. S., Postman, L., and Rodrigues, J. Expectation and the perception of color. *Amer. J. Psychol.*, 1951, **64**, 216–27.

10. Stratton, G. M. Vision without inversion of the retinal image. *Psychol. Rev.*, 1897, **4**, 341–481.

11. Held, R., and Bosson, J. Neo-natal deprivation and adult rearrangement: complementary techniques for analyzing plastic sensory motor coordinations. *J. comp. physiol. Psychol.*, 1961, **54**, 33–37.

12. Gibson, J. J. *The perception of the visual world.* Boston: Houghton Mifflin, 1950.

13. Holway, A. H., and Boring, E. G. Determinants of apparent visual size with distance variant. *Amer. J. Psychol.*, 1941, **54**, 21–37.

14. *Experiments in optical illusion,* by Nelson F. Beeler and Franklin M. Branley. (Artist: Fred H. Lyon.) Copyright 1951 by Thomas Y. Crowell Company, New York, publishers.

15. Gibson, E. J., and Walk, R. D. The "visual cliff." *Scient. Amer.*, 1960, **202**, 64–71.

16. Rock, I., and Victor, J. Vision and touch: an experimentally created conflict between the two senses. *Science*, 1963, **143**, 594–96.

17. Riesen, A. H. Arrested vision. *Scient. Amer.*, 1950, **183**, 16–19.

18. Nissen, H. W., Chow, K. L., and Semmes, J. Effects of restricted opportunity for tactual, kinesthetic, and manipulative experience on the behavior of a chimpanzee. *Amer. J. Psychol.*, 1951, **64**, 485–507.

19. Senden, M. V. *Raun- und Gestaltauffassung bei operierten Blindgeborenen vor und nach der Operation.* Leipzig: Barth, 1932. Also Hebb, D. O. *The organization of behavior: a neurophysiological theory.* New York: Wiley, 1949.

20. Cool, S. J. Some effects of early visual environments on adult discrimination in the rat. Unpublished doctoral dissertation, University of Illinois, 1966.

21. White, B. *An experimental approach to the effects of experience on early human behavior.* Minnesota Symposium on Child Psychology. Vol. 1. Minneapolis: University of Minnesota Press, in press.

22. Siipola, E. M. A study of some effects of preparatory set. *Psychol. Monogr.*, 1935, **46** (No. 210).

23. Luchins, A. S. Forming impressions of personality: a critique. *J. abn. soc. Psychol.*, 1948, **43**, 318–25.

24. McClelland, D. C., and Atkinson, J. W. The projective expression of needs. I. The effect of different intensities of the hunger drive on perception. *J. Psychol.*, 1948, **25**, 205–22.

25. McClelland, D. C., and Liberman, A. M. The effect of need for achievement on recognition of need-related words. *J. Pers.*, 1949, **18**, 236–51.

26. Postman, L., Bruner, B., and McGinnies, E. Personal values as selective factors in perception. *J. abn. soc. Psychol.*, 1948, **43**, 142–54.

27. Lambert, W. W., Solomon, R. L., and Watson, P. D. Reinforcement and extinction as factors in size estimation. *J. exp. Psychol.*, 1949, **39**, 637–41.

28. Bruner, J. S., and Goodman, C. C. Value and need as organizing factors in perception. *J. abn. soc. Psychol.*, 1947, **42**, 33–44.

29. Ashley, W. R., Harper, R. S., and Runyon, D. L. The perceived size of coins in normal and hypnotically induced economic states. *Amer. J. Psychol.*, 1951, **64**, 564–72.

30. Maclay, H. An experimental study of language and non-linguistic behavior. *Southwest J. Anthrop.*, 1958, **14**, 220–29.

CHAPTER 6 LANGUAGE, THINKING, AND PROBLEM SOLVING

1. Kellogg, W. N., and Kellogg, L. A. *The ape and the child.* New York: McGraw-Hill, 1933. Also Hayes, K. *The ape in our house.* New York: Harper & Row, 1951.

2. Von Frisch, W. *Bees: their vision, chemi-*

cal senses, and language. Ithaca, N.Y.: Cornell University Press, 1950.

3. Davis, K. Extreme social isolation of a child. *Amer. J. Sociol.*, 1940, **45**, 554–65. Also Davis, K. Final note on a case of extreme social isolation. *Amer. J. Sociol.*, 1947, **54**, 432–37.

4. Heidbreder, E. The attainment of concepts: I. Terminology and methodology. *J. Gen. Psychol.*, 1946, **35**(2), 173–89.

5. Osgood, C. E., and Suci, G. J. Factor analysis of meaning. *J. exp. Psychol.*, 1955, **50**, 325–38.

6. Judson, A. J., and Cofer, C. N. Reasoning as an associative process. I. Direction in a simple verbal problem. *Psychol. Rep.*, 1956, **2**, 469–76.

7. Thorndike, E. L. *Animal intelligence.* New York: Macmillan, 1911.

8. Luchins, A. S. Mechanization in problem solving: the effect of einstelling. *Psychol. Monogr.*, 1954, **54** (No. 248). This material also appears in Luchins, A. S., and

Luchins, E. H., *Rigidity of behavior,* Eugene: University of Oregon Books, 1959; and in Seltzer, Samuel M., ed., *Einstelling tests of rigidity,* rev. ed., New York: Craig Colony School and Hospital.

9. Duncker, K. (trans. by Lees, L. S.). On problem-solving. *Psychol. Monogr.*, 1945, **58** (No. 270).

10. Birch, H. G., and Rabinowitz, H. S. The negative effect of previous experiences on productive thinking. *J. exp. Psychol.*, 1951, **41**, 121–25.

11. Mackinnon, D. W. The personality correlates of creativity: a study of American architects. In Nielsen, G. S., ed. *Proceedings of the XIV International Congress of Applied Psychology, Copenhagen, 1961.* Copenhagen: Munksgaard, 1962, pp. 11–39.

12. Wallach, M. A., and Kogan, N. *Modes of thinking in young children.* Copyright © 1965 by Holt, Rinehart and Winston, Inc. Reproduced by permission of Holt, Rinehart and Winston, Inc.

CHAPTER 7 THE GENES, GLANDS, AND NERVOUS SYSTEM

1. Tryon, R. C. Genetic differences in maze learning in rats. *Thirty-ninth Yearbk. natl. soc. stud. Educ.* Bloomington, Ill.: Public School Publishing Co., 1940, Part I, pp. 111–19.

2. Hall, C. S. The inheritance of emotionality. *Sigma Xi Quart.*, 1938, 26, 17–27.

3. Hirsh, J., and Boudreau, J. C. Studies in experimental behavior genetics. I. The heritability of phototaxis in a population of drosophila melanogaster. *J. comp. physiol. Psychol.*, 1958, **51**, 647–51.

4. Selye, H. *The stress of life.* New York: McGraw-Hill, 1956.

5. Evans, C. L. *Starling's principles of human physiology,* 9th ed. Philadelphia: Lea & Febiger, 1945.

6. Pfaffmann, C. Gustatory nerve impulses in rat, cat, and rabbit. *J. Neurophysiol.*, 1955, **18**, 429–40.

7. Eccles, J. C. *The physiology of synapses.* New York: Academic Press, 1964.

8. Eccles, J. C. The physiology of imagination. *Scient. Amer.*, 1958, **199**, 135–46.

Copyright © 1958 by Scientific American, Inc. All rights reserved.

9. Bennett, E. L., et al. Chemical and anatomical plasticity of the brain. *Science,* 1964, **146**, 610–19.

10. Hyden, H., and Egyhazi, E. Nuclear RNA changes of nerve cells during a learning experiment in rats. *Proc. Natl. Acad. Sci.*, 1962, **48**, 1366–73.

11. See, for example, Jacobson, A. L., et al. Differential-approach tendencies produced by injection of RNA from trained rats. *Science,* 1965, **150**, 636–37. Also Gross, C. G., and Carey, F. M. Transfer of learned response by RNA injection: failure of attempts to replicate. *Science,* 1965, **150**, 1749.

12. Wolf-Heidegger, G. *Atlas of systematic human anatomy.* New York: Hafner, 1962.

13. Nauta, W. J. H. Hypothalamic regulation of sleep in rats: an experimental study. *J. Neurophysiol.*, 1946, **9**, 285–316.

14. Levine, S., and Mullins, R. F. Hormonal

influences on brain organization in infant rats. *Science,* 1966, **152**, 1585–92.

15. Tang, P. C. Localization of the pneumotaxic center in the cat. *Amer. J. Physiol.,* 1953, **172**, 645–52. Also Wang, S. C., Ngai, S. H., and Frumin, M. J. Organization of central respiratory mechanisms in the brain stem of the cat: genesis of normal respiratory rhythmicity. *Amer. J. Physiol.,* 1957, **190**, 333–42.

16. Moruzzi, G., and Magoun, H. W. Brain stem reticular formation and activation of the EEG. *EEG clin. Neurophysiol.,* 1949, **1**, 455–73.

17. Kleitman, N. Patterns of dreaming. *Scient. Amer.,* 1960, **203**, 82–88.

18. Gibbs, F. A., and Gibbs, E. L. *Atlas of electroencephalography.* Reading, Mass.: Addison-Wesley, 1941.

19. Truex, R. C., and Carpenter, M. B. *Strong and Elwyn's human neuroanatomy,* 5th ed. Baltimore: Williams & Wilkins, 1964.

20. Crosby, E., Humphrey, T., and Lauer, E. W. *Comparative anatomy of the nervous system.* New York: Macmillan, 1962. Based on data in Figs. 337 and 339.

CHAPTER 8   THE SENSES

1. Amoore, J. E., Johnston, J. W., Jr., and Rubin, M. The stereochemical theory of odor. *Scient. Amer.,* 1964, **210**, 42–49.

2. Von Skramlik, E. Psychophysiologie der Tastsinne. *Arch. ges. Psychol.,* Suppl. Vol. 1937, **4** (Parts 1 and 2).

3. Chapanis, A. *Man-machine engineering.* Belmont, Calif.: Wadsworth, 1965.

4. Chapanis, A., Garner, W. R., and Morgan, C. T. *Applied experimental psychology—human factors in engineering design.* New York: Wiley, 1949.

5. Davis, H., and Silverman, S. R., eds. *Hearing and deafness.* Copyright 1947, © 1960 by Holt, Rinehart and Winston, Inc. Adapted and reproduced by permission of Holt, Rinehart and Winston, Inc.

6. Békésy, G. v. *Experiments in hearing.* New York: McGraw-Hill, 1960.

7. Wever, E. G. *Theory of hearing.* New York: Wiley, 1949.

8. Bloom, W., and Fawcett, D. W. *A textbook of histology,* 8th ed. Philadelphia: Saunders, 1962.

9. Wald, G. The photochemical basis of rod vision. *J. Opt. Soc. Amer.,* 1951, **41**, 949–56.

10. Liebman, P. Detection of color-vision pigments by single cell microphotometry—the method and its efficiency. Summarized in Riggs, L. A. Vertebrate color receptors. *Science,* 1965, **147**, 913.

11. Polyak, S. I. *The retina.* Chicago: University of Chicago Press, 1941.

12. Riggs, L. A., et al. The disappearance of steadily fixated visual test objects. *J. Opt. Soc. Amer.,* 1953, **43**, 495–501.

13. Pritchard, R. M. Stabilized images on the retina. *Scient. Amer.,* 1961, **204**, 72–78.

14. Reproduced by permission of the author of the Dvorine Pseudo-Isochromatic Plates, published by the Scientific Publishing Co., Baltimore, Md.

CHAPTER 9   MOTIVES

1. James, W. *Principles of psychology.* Vol. 2. New York: Dover, 1950.

2. Cannon, W. B. Hunger and thirst. In Murchison, C., ed. *Handbook of general experimental psychology.* Worcester, Mass.: Clark University Press, 1934, 247–63.

3. Morgan, C. T., and Morgan, J. D. Studies in hunger. II. The relation of gastric denervation and dietary sugar to the effect of insulin upon food-intake in the rat. *J. genet. Psychol.,* 1940, **57**, 153–63.

4. Tsang, Y. C. Hunger motivation in gastrectomized rats. *J. comp. Psychol.,* 1938, **26**, 1–17.

5. Wangensteen, O. H., and Carlson, A. J.

Hunger sensations in a patient after total gastrectomy. *Proc. Soc. Exp. Biol. Med.*, 1931, **28**, 545–47.

6. Davis, R. C. Hunger contractions and hunger pangs: are they normal? *Symposium on physiological psychology.* Washington, D.C.: U.S. Navy, Office of Naval Research, 1958, pp. 57–63.

7. Tschukitscheff, I. P. Über den Mechanismus der Hungerbewegungen des Magens. I. Einfluss des "satten" und "Hunger"-Blutes auf die periodische Tätigkeit des Magens. *Pflügers Arch. ges. Physiol.*, 1930, **223**, 251–64.

8. Anand, B. K., and Brobeck, J. R. Hypothalamic control of food intake in rat and cat. *Yale J. Biol. Med.*, 1951, **24**, 123–40.

9. Hetherington, A. W., and Ranson, W. W. Hypothalamic lesions and adiposity in the rat. *Anat. Rec.*, 1940, **78**, 149–72.

10. Miller, N. E., and Kessen, M. L. Reward effects of food via stomach fistula compared with those of food via mouth. *J. comp. physiol. Psychol.*, 1952, **45**, 555–64.

11. Chambers, R. M. Effects of intravenous glucose injections on learning, general activity, and hunger drive. *J. comp. physiol. Psychol.*, 1956, **49**, 558–64.

12. Epstein, A. N., and Teitelbaum, P. Regulation of food intake in the absence of taste, smell, and other oro-pharyngeal sensations. *J. comp. physiol. Psychol.*, 1962, **55**, 155.

13. Kleitman, N., and Kleitman, H. The sleep-wakefulness pattern in the Arctic. *Scient. monthly*, 1953, **76**, 349–56.

14. Clark, R. E., et al., The effects of sleep loss on performance of a complex task. Washington, D.C.: U.S. Dept. of Commerce, 1946.

15. Harlow, H. F., and Harlow, M. K. Social deprivation in monkeys. *Scient. Amer.*, 1962, **207**, 136–46.

16. Weiss, B., and Laties, V. G. Magnitude of reinforcement as a variable in thermoregulatory behavior. *J. comp. physiol. Psychol.*, 1960, **53**, 603–08.

17. Dember, W. N. The new look in motivation. *Amer. Scientist*, 1965, **53**, 409–27.

18. Dember, W. N., Earl, R. W., and Paradise, N. Response by rats to differential stimulus complexity. *J. comp. physiol. Psychol.*, 1957, **50**, 514–18.

19. Butler, R. A. Discrimination learning by Rhesus monkeys to visual-exploration motivation. *J. comp. physiol. Psychol.*, 1953, **46**, 95–98.

20. Spitz, R. A. Hospitalism: a follow-up report. In *Psychoanalytic study of the child.* Vol. II. New York: International Universities Press, 1946.

21. Jones, A., Bentler, P. M., and Petry, G. The reduction of uncertainty concerning future pain. *J. abn. Psychol.*, 1966, **71**, 87–94.

22. Winterbottom, M. R. The relation of childhood training in independence to achievement motivation. Unpublished doctoral dissertation, University of Michigan, 1953. Summarized in McClelland, D. C., et al. *The achievement motive.* New York: Appleton-Century-Crofts, 1953. Adapted by permission.

23. Lowell, E. L. The effect of need for achievement on learning and speed of performance. *J. Psychol.*, 1952, **33**, 31–40.

24. French, E. G., and Thomas, F. H. The relation of achievement to problem-solving effectiveness. *J. abn. soc. Psychol.*, 1958, **56**, 45–48.

25. Sadacca, R., Ricciuti, H. N., and Swanson, E. O. *Content analysis of achievement motivation protocols: a study of scorer agreement.* Princeton: Educational Testing Service, 1956.

26. Morgan, H. H. An analysis of certain structured and unstructured test results of achieving and non-achieving high ability college students. Unpublished doctoral dissertation, University of Michigan, 1951.

27. Crockett, H. J. The achievement motive and differential occupational mobility in the United States. *Amer. sociol. Rev.*, 1962, **27**, 191–204. By permission of the American Sociological Association.

28. Ehrlich, D., et al. Post-decision exposure to relevant information. *J. abn. soc. Psychol.*, 1957, **54**, 98–102.

29. Festinger, L., and Carlsmith, J. M. Cognitive consequences of forced compliance. *J. abn. soc. Psychol.*, 1959, **58**, 203–10.

30. Zimbardo, P. G., et al. Control of pain motivation by cognitive dissonance. *Science*, 1966, **151**(14), 217–19. Copyright 1966 by the American Association for the Advancement of Science.

31. Atkinson, J. W. *Motives in fantasy, action, and society.* Princeton: Van Nostrand, 1958.

32. Clark, R. A. The projective measurement of experimentally induced levels of sexual motivation. *J. exp. Psychol.*, 1952, **44**, 391–99.

33. Baldwin, A. Personal communication.

34. Allport, G. W. *Personality and social encounter.* Boston: Beacon Press, 1960.

CHAPTER 10 EMOTIONS

1. Young, P. T. *Motivation and emotion.* New York: Wiley, 1961. (After Darwin.)

2. Lindsley, D. B. Emotion. In Stevens, S. S., ed. *Handbook of experimental psychology.* New York: Wiley, 1951, pp. 473–516.

3. Kubis, J. F. In Smith, B. M. The polygraph. *Scient. Amer.*, 1967, **216**, 25–31.

4. Burger, O. K. The polygraph in crime investigation. *Annals west. Med. Surg.*, 1952, **6**, 300–01.

5. Hess, E. H. Attitude and pupil size. *Scient. Amer.*, 1965, **212**, 46–54.

6. James, W. *Principles of psychology.* Vol. II. New York: Dover, 1950.

7. Ax, A. F. The physiological differentiation between fear and anger in humans. *Psychosom. Med.*, 1953, **15**, 433–42.

8. Elmadjian, F. Excretion and metabolism of epinephrin. *Pharmacol. Rev.*, 1959, **11**, 409–15.

9. Funkenstein, D. H. The physiology of fear and anger. *Scient. Amer.*, 1955, **192**, 74–80.

10. Mandler, G. Emotion. In Brown, R., et al. *New directions in psychology.* New York: Holt, Rinehart and Winston, 1962, pp. 267–343.

11. Lacey, J. I., and Van Lehn, R. Differential emphasis in somatic response to stress. *Psychosom. Med.*, 1952, **14**, 73–81. Also Lacey, J. I., Bateman, D. E., and Van Lehn, R. Autonomic response specificity: an experimental study. *Psychosom. Med.*, 1953, **15**, 8–21.

12. Cannon, W. B. *Bodily changes in pain, hunger, fear, and rage,* 2nd ed. New York: Appleton-Century-Crofts, 1929.

13. Bard, P. A. A diencephalic mechanism for the expression of rage with special reference to the sympathetic nervous system. *Amer. J. Physiol.*, 1928, **84**, 490–515. Also Cannon, W. B., The James-Lange theory of emotions: a critical examination and an alternative theory. *Amer. J. Psychol.*, 1927, **39**, 106–24.

14. Schachter, S., and Singer, J. E. Cognitive, social, and physiological determinants of emotional state. *Psychol. Rev.*, 1962, **69**, 379–99.

15. Schachter, S., and Wheeler, L. Epinephrine, chlorpromazine, and amusement. *J. abn. soc. Psychol.*, 1962, **65**, 121–28.

16. Schachter, S., and Latané, B. Crime cognition and the autonomic nervous system. *Nebraska Symposium on Motivation.* Lincoln, Nebr.: University of Nebraska Press, 1964, pp. 221–75.

17. Richter, C. P. Rats, man, and the welfare state. *Amer. Psychologist*, 1959, **14**, 18–28.

18. Williams, R. J. *Biochemical individuality.* New York: Wiley, 1956.

19. Harlow, H. Personal communication.

20. Collins, R. L. Inheritance of avoidance conditioning in mice: a diallel study. *Science*, 1964, **143**, 1188–90.

21. Gellhorn, E., and Miller, A. D. Methacholine and noradrenaline tests. *Arch. gen. Psychiat.*, 1961, **4**, 371–80.

22. Lacey, J. I., and Lacey, B. C. Verification and extension of the principle of autonomic response-stereotypy. *Amer. J. Psychol.*, 1958, **71**, 50–73.

23. Maher, B. A. *Principles of psychopathology.* New York: McGraw-Hill, 1966.

24. Roberts, W. W. Fear-like behavior elicited from dorsomedial thalamus of cat. *J. comp. physiol. Psychol.*, 1962, **55**, 191–97.

25. Kagan, J., and Moss, H. A. *Birth to maturity.* New York: Wiley, 1962.
26. Taylor, J. A. The relationship of anxiety to the conditioned eyelid response. *J. exp. Psychol.,* 1951, **41,** 81–92.
27. Farber, I. E., and Spence, W. K. Complex learning and conditioning as a function of anxiety. *J. exp. Psychol.,* 1953, **45,** 120–25.
28. Spielberger, C. D. The effects of manifest anxiety on the academic achievement of college students. *Ment. Hyg.,* 1962, **46,** 420–26.
29. Spielberger, C. D., Denny, J. P., and

Weitz, H. The effects of group counseling on the academic performance of anxious college freshmen. *J. counsel. Psychol.,* 1962, **9,** 195–204.
30. Atkinson, J. W., et al. The achievement motive, goal setting, and probability preferences. *J. abn. soc. Psychol.,* 1960, **60,** 27–37.
31. Atkinson, J. W., and Litwin, G. H. Achievement motive and test anxiety conceived as motive to approach success and motive to avoid failure. *J. abn. soc. Psychol.,* 1960, **60,** 53–62.

CHAPTER 11   FRUSTRATION AND CONFLICT

1. Sanford, F. H. *Psychology, a scientific study of man,* 2nd ed. Belmont, Calif.: Wadsworth, 1965.
2. Sears, R. R., and Sears, P. S. Minor studies of aggression. V. Strength of frustration-reaction as a function of strength of drive. *J. Psychol.,* 1940, **9,** 297–300.
3. Lambert, W. W., and Solomon, R. L. Extinction of a running response as a function of block point from the goal. *J. comp. physiol. Psychol.,* 1952, **45,** 269–79.
4. Adelman, H. A., and Rosenbaum, G. Extinction of instrumental behavior as a function of frustration at various distances from the goal. *J. exp. Psychol.,* 1954, **47,** 429–32.
5. Haner, C. F., and Brown, P. A. Clarification of the instigation to action concept in the frustration-aggression hypothesis. *J. abn. soc. Psychol.,* 1955, **51,** 204–06.
6. Pastore, N. The role of arbitrariness in the frustration-aggression hypothesis. *J. abn. soc. Psychol.,* 1952, **47,** 728–31.
7. Barker, R. G., Dembo, T., and Lewin, K. Frustration and regression: an experiment with young children. *Univ. Iowa Stud. Child Welf.,* 1941, **18** (No. 386).
8. Hutt, M. L. "Consecutive" and "adaptive" testing with the revised Stanford-Binet. *J. consult. Psychol.,* 1947, **11,** 93–103, Table IV, p. 100.

9. Keister, M. E., and Updegraff, R. A study of children's reactions to failure and an experimental attempt to modify them. *Child Dev.,* 1937, **8,** 241–48. By permission of the Society for Research in Child Development, Inc.
10. Lewin, K. *A dynamic theory of personality.* New York: McGraw-Hill, 1935.
11. Brown, J. S. Gradients of approach and avoidance responses and their relation to motivation. *J. comp. physiol. Psychol.,* 1948, **41,** 450–65.
12. Brown, J. S. The generalization of approach responses as a function of stimulus intensity and strength of motivation. *J. comp. Psychol.,* 1942, **33,** 209–26. Also Miller, N. E., "Liberalization of basic S-R concepts: extensions to conflict behavior, motivation, and social learning. In Koch, S., ed. *Psychology: a study of a science.* Vol. II. New York: McGraw-Hill, 1959.
13. Lewin, K., Lippitt, R., and White, R. K. Patterns of aggressive behavior in experimentally created social climates. *J. soc. Psychol.,* 1939, **10,** 271–99.
14. Stressman, H. D., Thaler, M. B., and Schein, E. H. A prisoner-of-war syndrome: apathy as a reaction to severe stress. *Amer. J. Psychiat.,* 1956, **112,** 998–1003.
15. Masserman, J. H. *Principles of dynamic psychiatry,* 2nd ed. Philadelphia: Saunders, 1961.

16. Maier, N. R. F. *Frustration.* New York: McGraw-Hill, 1949.
17. Maher, B., Weinstein, N., and Sylva, K. The determinants of oscillation points in a temporal decision conflict. *Psychonometric Sci.*, 1964, **1**, 13–14.
18. Fenz, W. D., and Epstein, S. Gradients of physiological arousal in parachutists as a function of an approaching jump. *Psychosom. Med.*, 1967, **29**, 33–51.
19. Bluestone, H., and McGahee, C. L. Reaction to extreme stress: impending death by execution. *Amer. J. Psychiat.*, 1962, **119**, 393–96.
20. Sears, R. R. Experimental study of projection. I. Attribution of traits. *J. soc. Psychol.*, 1936, **7**, 151–63.
21. Bettelheim, B. Individual and mass behavior in extreme situations. *J. abn. soc. Psychol.*, 1943, **38**, 417–52.
22. Pavlov, I. P. *Conditioned reflexes: an investigation of the physiological activity of the cerebral cortex.* London: Oxford University Press, 1927 [reprinted by Dover, New York, 1960].
23. Masserman, J. H. *Behavior and neurosis.* Chicago: University of Chicago Press, 1943.
24. Hollingshead, A. B., and Redlich, F. C. *Social class and mental illness, a community study.* New York: Wiley, 1958.
25. Coleman, J. C. *Abnormal psychology and modern life,* 3rd ed. Chicago: Scott, Foresman, 1964.
26. Goldhamer, H., and Marshall, A. W. *Psychosis and civilization.* New York: Free Press, 1953.
27. Benedict, P. K., and Jacks, I. Mental illness in primitive societies. *Psychiatry,* 1954, **17**, 389.
28. Yerbury, E. C., and Newell, N. Genetic and environmental factors in psychoses of children. Reprinted from the *American Journal of Psychiatry,* Volume 100, pp. 599–605, 1943.

CHAPTER 12   PERSONALITY THEORY AND PSYCHOTHERAPY

1. Sheldon, W. H., and Stevens, S. S. *The varieties of temperament.* New York: Harper & Row, 1942.
2. Walker, R. N. Body build and behavior in young children. *Monogr. Soc. Res. Child Dev.*, 1962, **27** (No. 3, Serial No. 84).
3. Diamond, S. *Personality and temperament.* New York: Harper & Row, 1957.
4. Reprinted from *Self-analysis* by Karen Horney, M.D. By permission of W. W. Norton & Company, Inc. Copyright 1942 by W. W. Norton & Company, Inc.
5. Based on Chapter 3, The human situation —the key to humanistic psychoanalysis, from *The sane society* by Erich Fromm. Copyright © 1955 by Erich Fromm. Reprinted by permission of Holt, Rinehart and Winston, Inc.
6. Fromm, E. *The sane society.* New York: Holt, Rinehart and Winston, Inc., 1955.
7. Miller, N. E. Studies of fear as an acquirable drive. I. Fear as motivation and fear-reduction as reinforcement in the learning of new responses. *J. exp. Psychol.*, 1948, **38**, 89–101.
8. Miller, N. E., and Dollard, J. *Social learning and imitation.* New Haven, Conn.: Yale University Press, 1941.
9. Adapted from sub-headings on pp. 91, 90, 89, 84, 80 from *Motivation and personality* by A. H. Maslow. Copyright 1954 by Harper & Row, Publishers, Incorporated. Used by permission of the publishers.
10. Butler, J. M., and Haigh, G. V. Changes in the relation between self-concepts and ideal concepts consequent upon client-centered counseling. In Rogers, C. R., and Dymond, R. F., eds. *Psychotherapy and personality change: coordinated studies in the client-centered approach.* Chicago: University of Chicago Press, 1954, pp. 55–76.
11. Kubie, L. S. *Practical and theoretical aspects of psychoanalysis.* New York: International Universities Press, 1950.
12. Blakemore, C. B., et al. The application of faradic aversion conditioning in a

case of transvestism. *Behav. res. Ther.,* 1963, **1,** 29–34.

13. Wolpe, J. *Psychotherapy by reciprocal inhibition.* Stanford: Stanford University Press, 1958.

14. Strupp, H. An objective comparison of Rogerian and psychoanalytic techniques. *J. consult. Psychol.,* 1955, **19,** 1–7.

15. Blum, R., et al. *Utopiates: the use and users of LSD-25.* New York: Atherton Press, 1964.

CHAPTER 13 MEASUREMENT

1. Hebb, D. O. *A textbook of psychology.* Philadelphia: Saunders, 1958.

2. Harrison, G. A. *Human biology.* London: Oxford University Press, 1964.

3. Garrett, H. *Statistics in psychology and education,* 5th ed. New York: Longmans, Green, 1958. By permission David McKay Company, Inc.

4. Terman, L. M., and Merrill, M. A. *Stanford-Binet intelligence scale: manual for the third revision, form L-M.* Reprinted by permission of the Houghton Mifflin Company.

5. Tuddenham, R. D., and Snyder, M. M. Physical growth of California boys and girls from birth to eighteen years. *Child Dev.,* 1954, **1,** 183–364.

6. Ferguson, G. A. *Statistical analysis in psychology and education.* New York: McGraw-Hill, 1959. Copyright © 1959 by McGraw-Hill Book Company.

CHAPTER 14 MEASURING INTELLIGENCE AND PERSONALITY

1. Copyright (1967) by Harcourt, Brace & World, Inc. Reproduced by special permission of the publisher.

2. Cronbach, L. J. *Essentials of psychological testing.* New York: Harper, 1949.

3. Terman, M. L., and Merrill, M. A. *Stanford-Binet intelligence scale: manual for the third revision, form L-M.* Reprinted by permission of the Houghton Mifflin Company.

4. Copyright (1964, 1938) by Harcourt, Brace & World, Inc. Reproduced by special permission of the publisher.

5. Tyler, L. E. *The psychology of human differences,* 2nd ed. New York: Appleton-Century-Crofts, 1956.

6. Bond, E. A. *Tenth-grade abilities and achievements.* New York: Columbia University, Teachers College, 1940.

7. Wrenn, C. G. Potential research talent in the sciences based on intelligence quotients of Ph.D.'s. *Educ. Rec.,* 1949, **30,** 5–22.

8. McNemar, Q. *The revision of the Stanford-Binet scale.* Boston: Houghton Mifflin, 1942.

9. Janke, L. L., and Havighurst, R. J. Relation between ability and social-status in a midwestern community. II. Sixteen-year-old boys and girls. *J. educ. Psychol.,* 1945, **36,** 499–509.

10. Kennedy, W. A., Van de Riet, V., and White, J. C. A normative sample of intelligence and achievement of Negro elementary school children in the southeastern United States. *Monogr. Soc. Res. Child Dev.,* 1963, **28**(No. 6).

11. Thurstone, L. L., and Thurstone, T. G. Factorial studies of intelligence. *Psychometr. Monogr.,* Chicago: University of Chicago Press, 1941, No. 2.

12. Guilford, J. P., and Hoepfner, R. Structure-of-intellect factors and their tests. Report No. 36. Los Angeles: University of Southern California, 1966.

13. Newman, H. H., Freeman, F. N., and Holzinger, K. J. *Twins: a study of heredity and environment.* Chicago: University of Chicago Press, 1937.

14. Burt, C., and Howard, M. The multifactorial theory of inheritance. *Brit. J. statist. Psychol.,* 1956, **9**(Part II), 95–131.

15. Skodak, M., and Skeels, H. M. A final follow-up of one hundred adopted children. *J. genet. Psychol.,* 1949, **75**, 85–125.

16. Skodak, M. Mental growth of adopted children in the same family. *J. genet. Psychol.,* 1950, **77**, 3–9.

17. Speer, G. S. The mental development of children of feebleminded and normal mothers. *Thirty-ninth Yearbk. natl. soc. stud. Educ.,* Bloomington, Ill.: Public School Publishing Co., 1940, Part II, pp. 309–14.

18. Kephart, N. C. The effect of a highly specialized program upon the I.Q. in high-grade mentally deficient boys. *J. Psycho-asth.,* 1939, **44**, 216–21.

19. Sontag, L. W., Baker, C. T., and Nelson, V. L. Mental growth and personality development: a longitudinal study. *Monogr. Soc. Res. Child Dev.,* 1958, **23**(No. 2). By permission of the Society for Research in Child Development, Inc.

20. Wellman, B. L. I.Q. changes of preschool and non-school groups during the preschool years: a summary of the literature. *J. Psychol.,* 1945, **20**, 347–68.

21. Smith, S. Language and non-verbal test performance of racial groups in Honolulu before and after a fourteen-year interval. *J. gen. Psychol.,* 1942, **26**, 51–93.

22. Lee, E. S. Negro intelligence and selective migration: a Philadelphia test of the Klineberg Hypothesis. *Amer. soc. Rev.,* 1951, **16**, 227–33. By permission of the American Sociological Association.

23. Tuddenham, R. D. Soldier intelligence in world wars I and II. *Amer. Psychologist,* 1948, **3**, 54–56.

24. Jones, H. E., and Conrad, H. S. The growth and decline of intelligence. *Genet. Psychol. Monogr.,* 1933, **13**, 223–98.

25. Wechsler, D. *Wechsler adult intelligence scale, manual.* New York: Psychological Corp., 1955.

26. Owens, W. A., Jr. Age and mental abilities: a longitudinal study. *Genet. Psychol. Monogr.,* 1953, **48**, 3–54.

27. Harrell, T. W., and Harrell, M. S. Army general classification test scores for civilian occupations. *Educ. and psychol. Meas.,* 1945, **5**, 229–39.

28. Havemann, E., and West, P. S. *They went to college.* New York: Harcourt, Brace & World, 1952.

29. Wyatt, S., and Langdon, J. N. Fatigue and boredom in repetitive work. Industrial Health Research Board. London: Her Majesty's Stationery Office, 1937, No. 77.

30. Ryan, T. A. *Work and effort.* New York: Ronald Press, 1947.

31. U.S. President's Panel on Mental Retardation. *Mental retardation chart book: a national plan for a national problem.* Washington, D.C.: U.S. Dept. of Health, Education, and Welfare, 1963.

32. Wolfson, I. N. Adjustment of institutionalized mildly retarded patients twenty years after return to the community. Unpublished paper presented at the 1966 annual meeting of the American Psychiatric Association, Atlantic City, N.J.

33. Reproduced by permission. Copyright 1941 by Rensis Likert and William H. Quasha. Published by The Psychological Corporation, New York, N.Y. All rights reserved.

34. From *MacQuarrie Test for Mechanical Ability* by T. W. MacQuarrie. Copyright © 1925, 1953 by T. W. MacQuarrie. Used by permission of California Test Bureau, a Division of McGraw-Hill Book Company, Monterey, California.

35. Reproduced by permission. Copyright 1947, © 1961 for Verbal Reasoning, Numerical Ability, Abstract Reasoning, and Clerical Speed and Accuracy. Copyright 1947, © 1961, 1962 for Mechanical Reasoning, Space Relations, Language Usage —Spelling, Language Usage—Grammar. Published by The Psychological Corporation, New York, N.Y. All rights reserved.

36. Reprinted from *Kuder Preference Record —Vocational,* Form CM, by G. Frederic Kuder. Copyright 1948, by G. Frederic Kuder. Reprinted by permission of the publisher, Science Research Associates, Inc., Chicago.

37. Reprinted from *Profile Sheet for the Kuder Preference Record—Vocational* by G. Frederic Kuder. Copyright 1950, by G. Frederic Kuder. Reprinted by permis-

sion of the publisher, Science Research Associates, Inc., Chicago.

38. Reproduced by permission of Houghton Mifflin Company.

39. Reproduced by permission. Copyright 1943 by the University of Minnesota. Published by The Psychological Corporation, New York, N.Y. All rights reserved.

40. Gough, H. G. Tests of personality: questionnaires, A. Minnesota Multiphasic Personality Inventory. In Weider, A., ed. *Contributions toward medical psychology*, Vol. II. New York: Ronald Press, 1953. Copyright 1953, the Ronald Press Company.

41. U.S. Office of Strategic Services, Assessment Staff. *Assessment of men: selection of personnel for the office of strategic services*. New York: Holt, Rinehart and Winston, 1948.

42. Reprinted by permission of the publishers from Henry Alexander Murray, *Thematic Apperception Test*. Cambridge, Mass.: Harvard University Press; copyright, 1943, by the President and Fellows of Harvard College.

43. McClelland, D. C., Clark, R. A., and Lowell, E. L., *The achievement motive*. New York: Appleton-Century-Crofts, 1953.

44. French, E. G. Development of a measure of complex motivation. In Atkinson, J. W., ed. *Motives in fantasy, action, and society*. Princeton: Van Nostrand, 1958.

45. DeCharms, R. C., et al. Behavioral correlates of directly measured achievement motivation. In McClelland, D. C., ed. *Studies in motivation*. New York: Appleton-Century-Crofts, 1955.

46. From *The Rorschach technique: an introductory manual* by Bruno Klopfer and Helen H. Davidson, © 1962 by Harcourt, Brace & World, Inc., and reproduced with their permission.

CHAPTER 15 DEVELOPMENTAL PSYCHOLOGY

1. Mussen, P. H., Conger, J. J., and Kagan, J. *Child development and personality*, 2nd ed. New York: Harper & Row, 1963.

2. Irwin, O. C. The amount and nature of activities of newborn infants under constant external stimulating conditions during the first ten days of life. *Genet. Psychol. Monogr.*, 1930, **8**. Also Wolff, P. H. Observations on newborn infants. *Psychosom. Med.*, 1959, **21**, 110–18.

3. Knop, C. The dynamics of newly born babies. *J. Pediat.*, 1946, **29**, 721–28. Also Terman, L. M., and Tyler, L. E. Psychological sex differences. In Carmichael, L., ed. *Manual of child psychology*, 2nd ed. New York: Wiley, 1954.

4. Lipsitt, L. P., and Levy, N. Pain threshold in the human neonate. *Child Dev.*, 1959, **30**, 547–54.

5. Bridger, W. N. Sensory habituation and discrimination in the human neonate. *Amer. J. Psychiat.*, 1961, **117**, 991–96.

6. Kagan, J. Personality development. In Janis, I. L., ed. *Dynamics of personality*. New York: Harcourt, Brace & World, in press.

7. Grossman, H. J., and Greenberg, N. H. Psychosomatic differentiation in infancy. *Psychosom. Med.*, 1957, **19**, 293–306.

8. Adapted from *Morris' Human Anatomy*, 12th ed., edited by Barry J. Anson. Copyright © 1966 by McGraw-Hill, Inc. By permission of McGraw-Hill Book Co.

9. From *The first two years* by Mary M. Shirley. Institute of Child Welfare Monograph No. 7. University of Minnesota Press, Minneapolis, copyright 1933, renewed 1961 by University of Minnesota.

10. White, B. L., Castle, P., and Held, R. Observations on the development of visually directed reaching. *Child Dev.*, 1964, **35**, 349–64.

11. Halverson, H. M. An experimental study of prehension in infants by means of systematic cinema records. *Genet. Psychol. Monogr.*, 1931, **10**, 107–286.

12. Irwin, O. C. Vowel elements in the crying vocalization of infants under ten days of age. *Child Dev.*, 1941, **12**, 99–109.

13. McCarthy, D. Language development in children. In Carmichael, L., ed. *Manual of child psychology*. New York: Wiley, 1946, pp. 332–69.

14. Lenneberg, E. H. *Biological foundations of language*. New York: Wiley, 1967.

15. Miller, G. A. *Language and communication*. New York: McGraw-Hill, 1951.

16. Gesell, A., and Thompson, H. Twins T and C from infancy to adolescence: a biogenetic study of individual differences by the method of co-twin control. *Genet. Psychol. Monogr.*, 1941, 24, 3–122.

17. Dennis, W. Causes of retardation among institutional children: Iran. *J. genet. Psychol.*, 1960, 96, 47–59.

18. Brodbeck, A. J., and Irwin, O. C. The speech behavior of children without families. *Child Dev.*, 1946, 17, 145–56. By permission of the Society for Research in Child Development, Inc.

19. Irwin, O. C. Infant speech. *J. Speech and Hearing Disorders*, 1948, 13, 224–25 and 320–26.

20. McGraw, M. B. *The neuromuscular maturation of the human infant*. New York: Columbia University Press, 1943.

21. Piaget, J. *The origins of intelligence in children*. New York: International Universities Press, 1952.

22. Kagan, J. Unpublished data.

23. Smith, M. E. An investigation of the development of the sentence and the extent of vocabulary in young children. *Univ. Iowa Stud. Child Welf.*, 1926, 3(5).

24. Templin, M. C. Certain language skills in children: their development and interrelationships. *Child Welf. Monogr.*, Minneapolis: University of Minnesota Press, 1957 (Series No. 26). Copyright 1957 by the University of Minnesota.

25. McCarthy, D. The language development of the preschool child. *Child Welf. Monogr.*, Minneapolis: University of Minnesota Press, 1930 (Series No. 4). Copyright 1930 and renewed 1958 by the University of Minnesota.

26. Davis, E. A. Mean sentence length compared with long and short sentences as a reliable measure of language development. *Child Dev.*, 1937, 8, 69–79. By

permission of the Society for Research in Child Development, Inc.

27. Radke, M. J. The relation of parental authority to children's behavior and attitudes. *Child Welf. Monogr.*, Minneapolis: University of Minnesota Press, 1946 (Series No. 22).

28. Fantz, R. L. The origin of form perception. *Scient. Amer.*, 1961, 204, 66–72. Copyright © 1961 by Scientific American, Inc. All rights reserved.

29. Stevenson, H. W., and Bitterman, M. E. The distance effect in the transposition of intermediate size by children. *Amer. J. Psychol.*, 1955, 68, 274–79.

30. Goldfarb, W. Effects of early institutional care on adolescent personality: Rorschach data. *Amer. J. Orthopsychiat.*, 1944, 14, 441–47.

31. Erikson, E. *Childhood and society*. New York: Norton, 1950.

32. Sackett, G. P. Effects of rearing conditions upon the behavior of rhesus monkeys. *Child Dev.*, 1965, 36, 855–68.

33. Rheingold, H. L. The modification of social responsiveness in institutional babies. *Monogr. Soc. Res. Child Dev.*, 1956, 21(2). By permission of the Society for Research in Child Development, Inc.

34. Sears, R. R., Maccoby, E. E., and Levin, H. *Patterns of child-rearing*. Evanston, Ill.: Harper & Row, 1957.

35. Wittenborn, J. R. A study of adoptive children. *Psychol. Monogr.*, 1956, 70(Nos. 408–10), 1–115.

36. Macfarlane, J. W., Allen, L., and Honzik, M. P. A developmental study of the behavior problems of normal children between twenty-one months and fourteen years. *Univ. Calif. Publ. Child Dev.* Vol. II. Berkeley: University of California Press, 1954.

37. Despert, J. L. Urinary control and enuresis. *Psychosom. Med.*, 1944, 6, 294–307.

38. Huschka, M. The child's response to coercive bowel training. *Psychosom. Med.*, 1942, 4, 301–08.

39. Bowlby, J. Childhood mourning and its implications for psychiatry. Reprinted from the *American Journal of Psychiatry*, Volume 118, pp. 481–98, 1961.

40. D'Andrade, R. G. Sex differences and

cultural institutions. In Maccoby, E. E., ed. *The development of sex differences.* Stanford: Stanford University Press, 1966.

41. Brown, D. G. Sex-role preference in young children. *Psychol. Monogr.,* 1956, **70**(No. 421), 1–19. Also Fauls, L., and Smith, W. D. Sex-role learning of five-year-olds. *J. genet. Psychol.,* 1956, **89**, 105–117. Also Hartup, W. W., and Zook, E. Sex role preferences in three- and four-year-old children. *J. consult. Psychol.,* 1960, **24**, 420–26.

42. Bonney, M. E. The constancy of sociometric scores and their relationship to teacher judgments of social success and to personality self-ratings. *Sociometry,* 1943, **6**, 409–24.

43. Polansky, N., Lippitt, R., and Redl, F. An investigation of contagion in groups. *Human Relations,* 1950, **3**, 319–48.

44. Kagan, J., and Moss, H. S. *Birth to maturity.* New York: Wiley, 1962.

CHAPTER 16   SOCIAL PSYCHOLOGY

1. Lefkowitz, M., Blake, R. R., and Mouton, J. S. Status factors in pedestrian violation of traffic signals. *J. abn. soc. Psychol.,* 1955, **51**, 704–06.

2. Aberle, D. F., et al. The functional prerequisites of a society. *Ethics,* 1950, **60**, 100–11.

3. Barker, R. G., and Wright, H. F. *Midwest and its children.* Evanston, Ill.: Harper & Row, 1954.

4. Sherif, M. A study of some social factors in perception. *Arch. Psychol.,* **27**(187).

5. Mead, M. *Sex and temperament.* New York: Morrow, 1935.

6. McGrath, J. W. *Social psychology: a brief introduction.* New York: Holt, Rinehart and Winston, 1964.

7. Foa, V. G. Cross-cultural similarity and difference in interpersonal behavior. *J. abn. soc. Psychol.,* 1964, **68**, 517–22.

8. Centers, R. *The psychology of social classes.* Princeton, N.J.: Princeton University Press, 1949.

9. Reynolds, P. R. The Hollywood screen writers. *Sat. Rev.,* 1966, **49**, 52–53 and 60.

10. Adaptation of Table XII: 1, p. 426, *Patterns of child rearing* by Robert R. Sears, Eleanor E. Maccoby, Harry Levin. Copyright © 1957 by Harper & Row, Publishers, Incorporated. Used by permission of the publishers.

11. Rosen, B. C. The achievement syndrome: a psychocultural dimension of social stratification. *Amer. soc. Rev.,* 1956, **21**, 203–11. By permission of the American Sociological Association.

12. Lane, R. E. *Political life.* New York: Free Press, 1959.

13. Kinsey, A. C., Pomeroy, W. B., and Martin, C. E. *Sexual behavior in the human male.* Philadelphia: Saunders, 1948.

14. Bonney, M. E. Relationships between social success, family size, socio-economic home background, and intelligence among school children in grades III and IV. *Sociometry,* 1944, **7**, 26–39.

15. Strodtbeck, F., James, R., and Hawkins, C. Social status in jury deliberations. In Maccoby, E. E., Newcomb, T. M., and Hartley, E. L., eds. *Readings in social psychology,* 3rd ed. New York: Holt, Rinehart and Winston, 1958, pp. 379–87.

16. Hollingshead, A. B. *Elmtown's youth.* New York: Wiley, 1949.

17. Krech, D., Crutchfield, R. S., and Ballachey, E. L. *Individual in society: a textbook of social psychology.* New York: McGraw-Hill, 1962.

18. Hollingshead, A. B., and Redlich, F. C. *Social class and mental illness.* New York: Wiley, 1958.

19. Cavan, R. *American family,* 3rd ed. New York: Crowell, 1963.

20. Roth, J., and Peck, R. F. Social class and social mobility factors related to marital adjustment. *Amer. soc. Rev.,* 1951, **16**, 478–87.

21. Abravanel, E. A. A psychological analysis of the concept of role. Unpublished master's thesis, Swarthmore College, 1962.

22. Adapted with permission of the Macmillan Company from *Social Psychology* by

Roger Brown. Copyright © The Free Press, a Division of the Macmillan Company, 1965.

23. Milgram, S. Group pressure and action against a person. *J. abn. soc. Psychol.*, 1964, **69**, 137–43.

24. Asch, S. E. Studies of independence and submission to group pressure. I. A minority of one against a unanimous majority. *Psychol. Monogr.*, 1956, **70**(No. 416), Fig. 2, p. 7. Also Asch, S. E. Opinions and social pressure. *Scient. Amer.*, 1955, **193**, 31–35. Copyright © 1955 by Scientific American, Inc. All rights reserved.

25. Deutsch, M., and Gerard, H. A study of normative and informational social influences upon individual judgment. *J. abn. soc. Psychol.*, 1955, **51**, 629–36.

26. Crutchfield, R. S. Conformity and character. *Amer. Psychologist*, 1955, **10**, 191–98.

27. Tuddenham, R. D., and MacBride, P. D. The yielding experiment from the subject's point of view. *J. Pers.*, 1959, **27**, 259–71.

28. Dittes, J., and Kelley, H. Effects of different conditions of acceptance upon conformity to group norms. *J. abn. soc. Psychol.*, 1956, **53**, 100–07.

29. Homans, G. C. *Social behavior: its elementary forms.* New York: Harcourt, Brace & World, 1961.

30. Mead, M. *Cooperation and competition among primitive peoples.* New York: McGraw-Hill, 1937.

31. Milgram, S. Nationality and conformity. *Scient. Amer.*, 1961, **205**, 45–51.

32. Walker, E. L., and Heyns, R. W. *An anatomy for conformity.* Englewood Cliffs, N.J.: Prentice-Hall, 1962.

33. Vaughan, G. M., and Mangan, G. L. Conformity to group pressure in relation to the value of the task material. *J. abn. soc. Psychol.*, 1963, **66**, 179–83.

34. Hirschberg, G., and Gilliland, A. R. Parent-child relationships in attitudes. *J. abn. soc. Psychol.*, 1942, **37**, 125–30.

35. Horowitz, E. L., and Horowitz, R. E. Development of social attitudes in children. *Sociometry*, 1938, 1, 301–38.

36. Levine, J. M., and Murphy, G. The learning and forgetting of controversial material. *J. abn. soc. Psychol.*, 1943, **38**, 507–17.

37. Abelson, R. P., and Rosenberg, M. J. Symbolic psycho-logic: a model of attitudinal cognition. *Behav. Sci.*, 1958, **3**, 1–13. Also Rosenberg, M. J., et al. *Attitude organization and change.* New Haven, Conn.: Yale University Press, 1960.

38. Festinger, L. *A theory of cognitive dissonance.* Stanford: Stanford University Press, 1957.

39. Aronson, E., and Mills, J. The effects of severity of initiation on liking for a group. *J. abn. soc. Psychol.*, 1959, **59**, 177–81.

40. Deutsch, M., and Collins, M. E. *Interracial housing: a psychological evaluation of a social experiment.* Minneapolis: University of Minnesota Press, 1951. Copyright 1951 by the University of Minnesota.

41. Hovland, C. I., and Weiss, W. The influence of source credibility on communication effectiveness. *Public Opinion Quart.*, 1951, **15**, 635–50.

42. Hovland, C. I., Lumsdaine, A. A., and Sheffield, F. C. *Experiments on mass communication.* Princeton: Princeton University Press, 1949.

43. Weiss, W., and Fine, B. J. The effect of induced aggressiveness on opinion change. In Maccoby, E. E., Newcomb, T. M., and Hartley, E. L., eds. *Readings in social psychology*, 3rd ed. New York: Holt, Rinehart and Winston, 1958, pp. 149–55.

44. Janis, I. L., and Feshbach, S. Effects of fear-arousing communications. *J. abn. soc. Psychol.*, 1953, **48**, 78–92, Table 6, p. 84.

45. Stogdill, R. M. Personal factors associated with leadership: a survey of the literature. *J. Psychol.*, 1948, **25**, 37–71.

46. Bell, G., and French, R. Consistency of individual leadership position in small groups of varying membership. *J. abn. soc. Psychol.*, 1950, **45**, 764–67.

47. Carter, L. F., and Nixon, M. An investigation of the relationship between four

criteria of leadership ability for three different tasks. *J. Psychol.*, 1949, **27**, 245–61.

48. Bales, R. F. Task roles and social roles in problem-solving groups. In Maccoby, E. E., Newcomb, T. M., and Hartley, E. L., eds. *Readings in social psychology*, 3rd ed. New York: Holt, Rinehart and Winston, 1958, pp. 437–46.

49. Lewin, K. Group decision and social change. In Maccoby, E. E., Newcomb, T. M., and Hartley, E. L., eds. *Readings in social psychology*, 3rd ed. Copyright 1947, 1952, © 1958 by Holt, Rinehart and Winston, Inc. Reproduced by permission of Holt, Rinehart and Winston, Inc.

50. Lewin, K., and Grabbe, P., eds. Problems of re-education. *J. soc. Issues*, 1945, **1**(3).

PHOTO CREDITS

Photos by Edith Reichmann p. 2., 5.22, Plate VI

Brown Brothers 1.1a, 1.1b, 1.8 (*top right*), 1.9 (*right*), 12.3

Culver Pictures 1.1c, 1.10 (*left*), 12.7 (*bottom right*)

U.S. Office of War Information 1.1d

Library of Congress 1.1e, 5.6

Ford Motor Company News Bureau, Dearborn, Michigan 1.1f

French Cultural Services 1.1g

United Press International 1.1h, 2.1 (*bottom right*), 16.1 (*top left*)

New York *Daily News* 1.2 (*top left*), 1.2a (*bottom left*), 1.8 (*bottom right*), 13.2

The New York Times 1.2 (*top right, center left, bottom*), 1.2a (*top left*), 8.15, 15.18

Wide World Photos 1.2 (*center right*), 1.2a (*top right*) 1.8 (*bottom left*), 16.1 (*top right*), 16.2 (*center*)

William Vandivert. Prior publication in *Scientific American* 1.3, 5.28, 16.11, 16.12

Courtesy of Dr. José M. R. Delgado. Prior publication in "James Arthur Lecture on the Evolution of the Human Brain," 1965, The American Museum of Natural History 1.4

From Bell System Science Series film, *Gateways to the Mind* 1.5

Walter Reed Army Institute of Research 1.6

Harbrace 1.7 (*top*), 1.13 (*top*), 4.6, 5.21, 6.7, 6.8, 6.9, Plate III, 13.1, 13.3, 13.4

Astrology, Your Daily Horoscope 1.8 (*overlay*)

Bettmann Archive 1.9 (*left*)

Historical Pictures Service, Chicago 1.10 (*right*)

David Linton, courtesy New York University 1.11

Institute for Sex Research, Indiana University. Photo by Dellenback 1.12

Courtesy of Vocational Service Center, YMCA 1.13 (*bottom*), 14.17

AT&T 1.14

John A. Feher, FPG p. 42

Courtesy of the American Museum of Natural History 2.1 (*top left*), p. 228

U.S. Navy Photograph 2.1 (*top center*)

Leonard Lee Rue II from National Audubon Society 2.1 (*top right*)

Sabena Airlines 2.1 (*center left*)

National Film Board Photograph, Canada 2.1 (*bottom left*)

Courtesy of Dr. Franklin Jones. (The photograph of the startle pattern was first published in Jones, F. P., Hanson, J. A. and Gray, Florence E., Startle as a paradigm of malposture. *Perceptual and Motor Skills*, 1964, 19, pp. 21–22.) 2.2

Will Rapport, Harvard University 2.7

Courtesy of Dr. H. S. Terrace 2.8

Collection of the Ringling Museum of the Circus 2.9 (*top left*)

Marineland of the Pacific 2.9 (*top right*)

Reprinted from the April 29–May 5, 1967 issue of *TV Guide*® with permission. Copyright © 1967 by Triangle Publications 2.9 (*bottom*)

Photo by Hella Hamid, Grolier Educational Corporation 2.12

Yerkes Regional Primate Research Center of Emory University 2.13, 6.5

Courtesy of Dr. Albert Bandura 2.16

Western Union 3.1

Leonard McCombe, *Life Magazine* 3.8 (*left*)

Photos by Suzana Sak 3.8 (*right*), 15.13, 15.16 (*right*)

Courtesy of Dr. Nicholas Pastore, Queens College 3.9

Courtesy of Dr. Ralph N. Haber 3.10

Richard Hewett, Globe Photos 4.8

Courtesy of Aetna Life & Casualty 4.16 (*top*)

General Dynamics Corporation, Convair Division 4.16 (*bottom left*)

American Music Conference 4.16 (*bottom right*)

Courtesy of Dr. Harry F. Harlow 4.18

Marc Riboud, Magnum Photos, p. 150.

Photo by Jürgen Graaff 5.3

The Museum of Modern Art, New York, Philip C. Johnson Fund 5.4

Photo by Jim Theologus 5.16

Photos by Dr. James B. Maas, Cornell University 5.20, 8.2, 8.3

New York Central Railroad 5.25

United Nations Photo 5.27

Photo by Ted Polumbaum, Courtesy of *Life Magazine* 5.29

Three Lions 6.4

Gerry Cranham, Rapho Guillumette, p. 452

Courtesy of Dr. J. H. Tjio 7.1

Courtesy of Dr. M. H. F. Wilkins 7.2

Syndication International: Gilloon Photo Agency 7.6

Wolf-Heidegger, G. *Atlas of systematic human anatomy.* New York: Hafner, 1962 7.14

Photos by Arthur Leipzig 7.18

Hewlett-Packard 8.6

Courtesy of Munsell Color Company Plate II

Bruce Roberts, Rapho Guillumette, p. 312

Photos by Sponholz, University of Wisconsin Primate Lab 9.4, 9.7

University of Wisconsin Photo Lab 9.5

Courtesy of Lafayette Instrument Company 10.1

Courtesy of Dr. Eckhard H. Hess 10.3

Camera Clix, Inc. 10.4

Photo by Eric L. Brown p. 382

Courtesy of Dr. Michael Lewis, from Play behavior in the year-old infant: Early sex differences. Paper presented at the Biennial Meeting of the Society for Research in Child Development, New York, March, 1967 11.5

Courtesy of Dr. Jules H. Masserman, from *Principles of dynamic psychiatry,* 2nd ed. Philadelphia: W. B. Saunders, 1961; Plate I, p. 71 11.6

Prado Museum, Madrid, Spain 12.7 (*top*)

New York Library Picture Collection 12.7 (*bottom left*)

Copyright Bernie Cleff 12.8

International Business Machines Corporation 13.8

The Psychological Corporation 14.2

Courtesy of Houghton Mifflin Company 14.3

Monkmeyer Photos 14.16

Charles Harbutt, Magnum Photos p. 532.

Courtesy of Dr. Burton L. White. From White, Burton L., Castle, Peter, and Held, Richard, Observations of the development of visually directed reading. *Child Development,* 1964, **35,** 349–364 (figures 2,3,4, and 6 on tip-in between pp. 352–353) 15.3

Photos by Ernest Havemann 15.5

Courtesy of Gene P. Sackett, University of Wisconsin 15.14

Travel Development Bureau, Pennsylvania Department of Commerce 16.1 (*bottom*)

San Francisco Convention and Visitors Bureau 16.2 (*top*)

Photo Researchers 16.2 (*bottom*)

INDEX

(Page numbers in *italics* refer to illustrations.)